TENNESSEE HISTORY

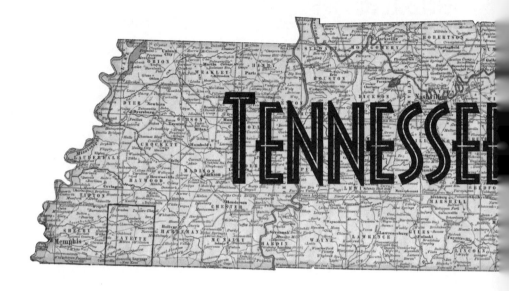

The University of ■

Tennessee Press ■

Knoxville ■

■

■

HISTORY

The LAND,

the PEOPLE,

and the CULTURE

Edited by CARROLL VAN WEST

Frontispiece: Map of Tennessee from *The Century Atlas of the World*, Benjamin E. Smith, ed. (New York: The Century Company), 1897, 98, 99. Courtesy of the U.T. Cartographic Services Lab.

All chapters previously published in the *Tennessee Historical Quarterly* and © 1998 by the Tennessee Historical Society.

The paper in this book meets the minimum requirements of ANSI/NISO Z39.48-1992 (R 1997) (Permanence of Paper). The binding materials have been chosen for strength and durability.

Library of Congress Cataloging-in-Publication Data

Tennessee history : the land, the people, and the culture / edited by Carroll Van West. —1st ed.

     p. cm.

Articles previously published by the Tennessee Historical Society in Tennessee Historical Quarterly, 1992–1996.

Includes bibliographical references and index.

ISBN 1-57233-003-1 (cl. : alk. paper)

ISBN 1-57233-000-7 (pbk. : alk. paper)

1. Tennessee—History. I. West, Carroll Van, 1955–

II. Tennessee Historical Society.

F436.T53 1998

976.8—dc21   97-21170

CONTENTS

■

■

■

Figures

■

■

■

TABLES

■

■

■

PREFACE

■

■

■

To celebrate the bicentennial of Tennessee statehood in 1996, the *Tennessee Historical Quarterly* published five special issues from the fall of 1995 to the fall of 1996. The authors and topics were selected from a nationwide competition of proposals submitted on a wide variety of topics, reflecting diverse research and methodological approaches. The special Bicentennial series created a scholarly forum in which the historians of Tennessee explored the significance of two hundred years of Tennessee history while, at the same time, they identified and discussed people, places, and events that had not received the attention they deserved. This edited collection, *Tennessee History: The Land, the People, and the Culture,* features fifteen articles from the bicentennial series. To complete its coverage of Tennessee history, the book contains five additional articles that appeared in the *Quarterly* from 1992 to 1995. These too represent specific initiatives by the editors of the *Tennessee Historical Quarterly* to present new scholarship about Tennessee's medical history, its agricultural past, and the history of its homefront during the Second World War.

In selecting these twenty essays, we strove to provide a balanced look at two hundred years of Tennessee history. We sought balance between the treatment of the nineteenth century and of the twentieth century. We sought balance among the broad categories of political, social, and cultural history. We also sought balance among the peoples who have shaped Tennessee's past, from Native Americans to Civil War generals, from the three presidents to rural reformers, and from women to African Americans. Finally, the different authors represent both the established scholars of the state's history and those of a newer generation, who will become the established scholars of the twenty-first century.

There were two goals for the publication of this collection. First, we wanted the scholarship of the bicentennial series to reach as many scholars and readers of southern history as possible. Second, we wanted to create a book that would be useful in teaching Tennessee history in classrooms and seminars across the region. To enhance student understanding of the individual essays, therefore, I have included a brief synopsis of the author's main themes at the beginning of each article.

Tennessee History would not have been possible without the dedication of the Tennessee Historical Society, an organization established in 1849 and dedicated to the collection, preservation, and interpretation of Tennessee history. It has been my distinct honor to serve as the Senior Editor of the Society's *Tennessee Historical Quarterly* since 1993. I gratefully acknowledge the support and leadership of Ann Toplovich, the Society's Executive Director, in making available the resources that make the *Quarterly* possible. Special thanks go to Susan Gordon, the Managing Editor of the *Tennessee Historical Quarterly,* for the work and dedication she puts into every issue of the *Quarterly*. She ably conducted the final copyediting and proofing of every article in the collection. Anne-Leslie Owens, the grant project coordinator at the Tennessee Historical Society, prepared the computer files for the individual essays in this collection. Final acknowledgments belong to the Editorial Advisory Board of the *Tennessee Historical Quarterly*. This group of distinguished scholars advised and reviewed every part of the bicentennial series. Their counsel and good judgment were, and are, invaluable. From 1993 to 1997, the members of the Editorial Board included Carole Stanford Bucy, Paul K. Conkin, Charles W. Crawford, Don H. Doyle, Cynthia G. Fleming, Kay Baker Gaston, Anita S. Goodstein, Robert L. Jones, James L. McDonough, James A. Ward, W. Bruce Wheeler, Thomas H. Winn, and Margaret Ripley Wolfe.

Finally, I thank each of the individual scholars represented in this collection for their initial submissions, their patience through the editorial process, and their willingness to include their fine work in this volume. They are collectively reshaping the contours of Tennessee history scholarship; I eagerly look forward to learning from their future research and insights.

Introduction: Two Hundred Years of Tennessee History

■

■

■

The word *Tennessee* evokes many different images of people, places, and events. Most of those images in the popular consciousness are associated with the years before the American Civil War. Scores of books, articles, dissertations, and even movies and novels, document the dynamic years from 1796 to 1861, when three Tennessee presidents strode across the national stage, when Fanny Wright attempted her bold social and cultural experiment at Nashoba, and when Tennesseans were transformed by a series of religious revivals that resulted in the creation of new, permanent churches and congregations. A troubling dark side existed in the early years as well: warfare and violence were commonplace; the Cherokees were forcibly ejected from the state; and the enslavement of African Americans increased as free blacks saw their own rights and freedoms diminish. It was an age of trial, triumph, and tragedy; a time for heroes. The official bicentennial portrait, "The Pride of Tennessee," conceived and executed by Mike Vaughn and Michael Sloan, includes eleven prominent Tennesseans. Six of these heroes—James K. Polk, Andrew Jackson, Davy Crockett, Sequoyah, John Sevier, and Andrew Johnson—belong to the era from 1796 to 1861.

For much of the twentieth century, historians of Tennessee presented and interpreted the state's initial seventy years as a golden age—when Tennessee truly cast an impressive shadow on the nation. The early-twentieth-century myth of a heroic Civil War demanded that the years prior to that titanic struggle be treated as a time of hope, prosperity, and promise in order to justify the bloody sacrifice made by so many Tennesseans on the battlefield and on the homefront. The romantic myth of the Old South, complete with its imagery of harmony between the races and classes, also justified the brutal policies of segregation.

The best scholarship of the first half of the century, ranging from Thomas P. Abernethy's *From Frontier to Plantation in Tennessee* (1932) to Frank

L. Owsley's *Plain Folk of the Old South* (1949), focused on the first half of the nineteenth century as the formative era of Tennessee politics and culture.[1] Because of the number and quality of his many graduate students, Owsley's influence on Tennessee history proved especially important. During his years at Vanderbilt, Owsley produced a prolific amount of work on the antebellum South, while Vanderbilt students crafted detailed studies of antebellum Tennesseans.[2] In more popular depictions of Tennessee history, like that by Owsley's friend and Vanderbilt colleague Donald Davidson, the past was a heroic one of stout, brave frontiersmen, who built a model society that modernism and industrialization later undermined.[3]

In the second half of the twentieth century, the primary state history textbook was Stanley J. Folmsbee, Robert E. Corlew, and Enoch L. Mitchell's *Tennessee: A Short History* (1969), which was a condensed version of an earlier multivolume history first published in 1960. It focused on the themes of settlement and politics in the pre–Civil War era. But in the next decade, new scholars and new research began to change and broaden the portrayal of Tennessee's past.[4] When Corlew prepared the textbook's second edition in 1981, he included more on the twentieth century and discussed African Americans and women to a greater degree than ever before.[5]

The new scholarship of the 1970s was only the beginning of a major reassessment of Tennessee history and culture. In the last two decades of the twentieth century, important case studies on rural life, material culture, Native Americans, politics, urban development, women, civil rights, and the twentieth century changed our way of identifying and interpreting the basic trends of Tennessee history.[6]

These new avenues of research and interpretation have clearly shaped the diverse contributions of this volume. The authors explore nineteenth- as well as twentieth-century people and events. They incorporate race, gender, and class into their analysis of past social, cultural, economic, and political development. They also demonstrate that Tennessee history was not created in a vacuum. Past experiences and traditions were shaped by regional and national personalities and events while, at the same time, the experiences peculiar to Tennesseans shed needed light on the complexity of people and events found in American history.

Four basic themes link the various articles of the collection. First, this is a "people's history"; in Tennessee, ethnic diversity is not a current buzzword but a historical fact. The state's past is a shared narrative, created by Native Americans, African Americans, women, Irish Americans, men, planters, common people, working-class Americans, and the political and economic elite. Each group made distinctive contributions.

Caneta Hankins's dissection of the material world of Irish immigrant Hugh Rogan, for instance, documents the complex road to acculturation in the Tennessee backcountry. Fred A. Bailey finds that clear differences existed between antebellum common folk and the political and economic elite; these differences underline the significant and lasting contributions of common people to state history and culture. John Finger's essay on Native Americans emphasizes their creative adaptations to changing political and economic realities during the backcountry era. The Tennessee Indians were often victimized, but they were not always victims; they had power, in several political and economic situations, to influence the state's early history. Margaret Ripley Wolfe takes a similar approach in her exploration of the significant contributions made by women to Tennessee history. Her themes of struggle, political commitment, reform, and perserverance are echoed in Connie L. Lester's study of Tennessee women and agrarian reform in the late nineteenth century, in Mary S. Hoffschwelle's discussion of country women and public health reform, and in Calvin Dickinson's and Patrick Reagan's story of the ill-fated textile mill strike by women workers in Harriman during the Great Depression.

African Americans too were more than victims in Tennessee history; they were active participants in the events that gave meaning to their lives. Kenneth W. Goings and Gerald L. Smith investigate how three different groups of African Americans created distinctive neighborhoods and traditions in post–Civil War Memphis. Paul Harvey uses Richard and Henry Boyd in Nashville to discuss how African Americans carved out cultural and economic niches during the oppressive years of Jim Crow segregation. Goings and Smith, as well as Harvey, explain how African American activism for civil rights has deep historical roots in Tennessee; Cynthia G. Fleming chronicles how these local traditions help to explain the state's unique history and national role in the civil rights movement of the 1950s and 1960s. These themes of African American power and activism, often in the face of apparently insurmountable odds, even have antebellum roots. Elizabeth F. Arroyo outlines the reciprocal relationships that sometimes bound poor whites, slaves, and free blacks, despite the issues of race and class that divided them.

A second basic theme is how issues about economic change shaped state political debates. Wayne Cutler argues that a defense of the moral economy of producer capitalism links the politics and policies of Tennessee presidents

Andrew Jackson, James K. Polk, and Andrew Johnson. When he views the ferocity of the local contests between Whigs and Democrats during those same years, Jonathan M. Atkins also finds questions of economic development dividing the parties.

Indeed, differences on the merits of market capitalism, the American System, and other mid-nineteenth-century economic issues help to explain, in part, the persistent allegiance to the Union held by antebellum planters, like Samuel Arnell of Maury County, as documented in the research of Kathleen R. Zebley. The careful statistical research of Robert Tracy McKenzie indicates that the Civil War and Reconstruction lessened the grip of agricultural elites on local communities, but it did not undermine their control. Connie L. Lester's study of agrarian reform movements, in fact, found rural Tennesseans of the late nineteenth century still striving for power and independence in a rapidly changing economic world. In both centuries, the small farm, providing the self-sufficient basis for many Tennessee lives, was the nurturing ground for the evolution and development of the state's significant religious and music traditions, which are discussed in Paul K. Conkin's overview of Tennessee's impact on national culture.

The interplay among reform, race, and class is a third shared theme in the collection. In the twentieth century, issues of economic modernization and improvement were tied to the agenda of progressive reform while they were limited by the brutal reality of racial politics and Jim Crow segregation. Racial and class politics shaped the very depiction of Tennessee society and history, as evident in the articles by Fred A. Bailey and Paul V. Murphy. Dewey Grantham explores the checkered, but still important, record for twentieth-century political reform by Tennesseans at the state and federal levels. Mary S. Hoffschwelle takes a detailed look at how northern public health reformers attempted to uplift rural life in Rutherford County. Progressives hoped to use this Tennessee county as a regional example of how the South could join the mainstream of American culture and economy without challenging segregation. The success was limited, and largely determined by the level of commitment and activism from the country people themselves. The articles by Goings and Smith, Harvey, Dickinson, and Reagan, and Fleming also document this pattern of twentieth-century Tennesseans taking the power they possessed, however little it might have been, and acting in their own interests.

A final major theme is that of war and its social impact. James L. McDonough examines why Tennessee served as a major Civil War battlefield and what happened when soldiers fought for control of the Volunteer State. The carnage and economic devastation influenced the state's development for decades, as shown in the essays of Goings and Smith, Zebley, and McKenzie. Traditional textbooks looked to the Civil War as the benchmark event in Tennessee history. In this collection, however, another struggle, the Second World War, looms as important, at least when its impact on the homefront in considered. Patricia Brake Howard outlines the war's tremendous influence on urban Tennessee and the push the war effort gave to industrialization, which has so affected Tennessee society, culture, and politics in the last half of the twentieth century.

War, economic transformation, race, class, gender, and reform are basic themes found in most modern studies of American history. Their importance in Tennessee history underscores how state history makes its greatest contribution to our understanding of the past—by showing us that we too have a direct, more personal connection to a shared national history and identity.

NOTES

1. Thomas P. Abernethy, *From Frontier to Plantation in Tennessee: A Study in Frontier Democracy* (Chapel Hill, N.C., 1932); Frank L. Owsley, *Plain Folk of the Old South* (Baton Rouge, 1949).

2. See, for example, Blanche Henry Clark, *The Tennessee Yeomen, 1840–1860* (Nashville, 1942); Thomas B. Alexander, "The Presidential Campaign of 1840 in Tennessee," *Tennessee Historical Quarterly* 1 (Mar. 1942): 21–43; Chase C. Mooney, "Some Institutional and Statistical Aspects of Slavery in Tennessee," *Tennessee Historical Quarterly* 1 (Sept. 1942): 195–228; Chase C. Mooney, *Slavery in Tennessee* (Bloomington, 1957); and Frank L. and Harriet C. Owsley, "The Economic Structure of Rural Tennessee, 1850–1860," *Journal of Southern History* 8 (1942): 161–82.

3. Donald Davidson, *The Tennessee,* 2 vols. (New York, 1946 and 1948; also see the article by Paul V. Murphy in this collection.

4. A sampling of this scholarship includes the following books: Paul E. Issacs, *Prohibition and Politics: Turbulent Decades in Tennessee, 1885–1920* (Knoxville, 1965); Roger L. Hart, *Redeemers, Bourbons & Populists: Tennessee, 1870–1896* (Baton Rouge, 1975); Joseph H. Cartwright, *The Triumph of Jim Crow: Tennessee Race Relations in the 1880s* (Knoxville, 1976); Robert B. Jones, *Tennessee at the Crossroads: the State Debt Controversy, 1870–1883* (Knoxville, 1977); Lester C. Lamon, *Black Tennesseans, 1900–1930* (Knoxville, 1977); David D. Lee, *Tennessee in Turmoil: Politics in the Volunteer State, 1920–1932* (Memphis, 1979).

   Also important was the University of Tennessee Press's Tennessee Three-Star Series, which was edited by Paul H. Bergeron. The series included brief interpretive monographs on state history, blacks, Indians, the three presidents, religion, geology, utopian communities, writers, music, and the Civil War.

5. Robert E. Corlew, *Tennessee: A Short History*, 2nd ed. (Knoxville, 1981).

6. Among the important book-length treatments that were published in these years are

Donald Winters, *Tennessee Farming, Tennessee Farmers: Antebellum Agriculture in the Upper South* (Knoxville, 1995); Robert Tracy McKenzie, *One South or Many?: Plantation Belt and Upcountry in Civil War–Era Tennessee* (Cambridge, 1994); Durwood Dunn, *Cades Cove: The Life and Death of a Southern Appalachian Community, 1818–1937* (Knoxville, 1988); Jeanette Keith, *Country People in the New South: Tennessee's Upper Cumberland* (Chapel Hill, N.C., 1995); James Patrick, *Architecture in Tennessee, 1768–1897* (Knoxville, 1981); John Morgan, *The Log House in East Tennessee* (Knoxville, 1991); Marion Moffett and Lawrence Wodehouse, *East Tennessee Cantilever Barns* (Knoxville, 1993); Carroll V. West, *Tennessee's Historic Landscapes* (Knoxville, 1995); Jefferson Chapman, *Tellico Archaeology: 12,000 Years of Native American History* (Knoxville, 1985); Paul H. Bergeron, *Antebellum Politics in Tennessee* (Lexington, 1984); Stephen V. Ash, *Middle Tennessee Transformed, 1860–1870* (Baton Rouge, 1988); Fred A. Bailey, *Class and Tennessee's Confederate Generation* (Chapel Hill, N.C., 1987); William F. Majors, *The End of Arcadia: Gordon Browning and Tennessee Politics* (Memphis, 1982); Michael J. McDonald and John Muldowny, *TVA and the Dispossessed: The Resettlement of Population in the Norris Dam Area* (Knoxville, 1982); W. Bruce Wheeler and Michael J. McDonald, *TVA and Tellico Dam, 1936–1979* (Knoxville, 1986); Charles W. Johnson and Charles O. Jackson, *City Behind a Fence: Oak Ridge, Tennessee, 1942–1946* (Knoxville, 1981); Michael J. McDonald and W. Bruce Wheeler, *Knoxville, Tennessee: Continuity and Change in an Appalachian City* (Knoxville, 1983); Don H. Doyle, *Nashville in the New South, 1880–1930* and *Nashville Since the 1920s* (Knoxville, 1985); Roger Biles, *Memphis in the Great Depression* (Knoxville, 1986); Margaret Ripley Wolfe, *Kingsport, Tennessee: A Planned American City* (Lexington, 1987); Anita Shafer Goodstein, *Nashville, 1780–1860: From Frontier to City* (Gainesville, 1989); Marsha Wedel, *Elite Women and the Reform Impulse in Memphis, 1875–1915* (Knoxville, 1991); Mary S. Hoffschwelle, *Rebuilding the Rural Southern Community: Reformers, Schools, and Homes in Tennessee, 1914–1929* (Knoxville, 1998); Richard A. Couto, *Lifting the Veil: A Political History of the Struggle for Emancipation* (Knoxville, 1993); Majorie S. Wheeler, ed., *Votes for Women: The Woman Suffrage Movement in Tennessee, the South, and the Nation* (Knoxville, 1995).

Tennessee Indian History: Creativity and Power

■ John R. Finger

■

■ *Editor's Note:* Finger argues that "the Indians were no mere obstacles or victims" in the early settlement era of Tennessee. "Both
■ before and after Europeans arrived they were active agents in the
historical process, creatively coping with changing circumstances."
■ For more than one hundred years prior to statehood, Native
Americans exerted considerable geopolitical power, shaping their
■ own lives as they influenced the early patterns of settlement and
development in the Tennessee backcountry. Too often, only In-
■ dian resistance and violence find a place in our history textbooks.
But many times during the 1700s, the assistance of native peoples
■ proved invaluable to the endeavors of those carving a new life on
the southwest frontier.

Tennessee's bicentennial is a convenient occasion to dispel the still
common misconception that our state's history began with the arrival of
Europeans. As we reflect on two hundred years of statehood, we should realize that our history actually extends back *sixty* times that far and encompasses
some five hundred generations of human experience. For almost all of those
millennia, Tennessee's native peoples—later misnamed "Indians"—were isolated from those of Europe and Africa. They and other Indians displayed an
astonishing vitality and creativity, continually reshaping themselves and their
cultures. Then, beginning with Columbus, they encountered white and black
peoples who were the vanguard of European colonialism. Not surprisingly,
white historical accounts of these contacts usually reflected that colonialism.
Indians were portrayed as exotic and sometimes savage people, who personi-
fied the dangers and moral uncertainties of the wilderness; they were mere
obstacles, resisting the expanding frontier of white settlement. Like other
exotic New World phenomena—the wolf, the bison, and untrammeled nature itself—they eventually disappeared or, perhaps, lurked as shadowy sym-

bols of the challenges and consequences of Manifest Destiny.[1] At best, sympathetic whites might write of Indian valor and the injustice of dispossession.

But the Indians were no mere obstacles or victims. Both before and after Europeans arrived they were active agents in the historical process, creatively coping with changing circumstances. As historian James Merrell has noted, the whites introduced Indians to a New World at least as challenging and intriguing as that faced by Europeans.[2] Amid these new dangers, uncertainties, and, yes, opportunities, Indians reacted rationally. Sometimes they resisted the newcomers, but more often their strategy was to understand, accommodate, and even control them. Within limits, they could shape white policies. They had power. Tennessee Indians, for example, were a major factor in southeastern geopolitics for nearly 150 years before being forced to accept the dictates of the United States government. Even then, they continued to demonstrate their creative adaptability. Indeed, creativity and the vicissitudes of power are two of the dominant themes of Tennessee Indian history from earliest times to the tragedy of removal in the 1830s. This essay will discuss certain aspects of those two themes as they apply to Indian relations with other Indians and with whites.

Over twelve thousand years ago, a small band of hunters became the first people to step foot in the state. These nomads, called Paleoindians by archaeologists, were descendants of people who crossed into North America during the last Ice Age, a time when gigantic glaciers formed, sea levels dropped, and a wide land bridge emerged linking Siberia and Alaska. Recent genetic and linguistic analyses point to three major prehistoric migrations from the Old World to the New.[3] We know that the first, and most important, of these occurred at least twelve to fifteen thousand years ago, but some scholars argue for much earlier arrivals.[4] Anthropologists categorize the Paleoindian Period as the first of four lengthy eras of human habitation in the Southeast; the others are the Archaic, Woodland, and Mississippian.

Paleoindian artifacts, including the distinctive projectile points of the Clovis Culture, are found in all parts of Tennessee. The otherwise scanty evidence suggests that small bands of nomadic hunters operated out of temporary base camps on river terraces, upland knolls, or in caves and rock shelters. In many parts of the United States, Paleoindians hunted large game animals like mammoths and mastodons, but no prehistoric habitation sites in Tennessee are indisputably associated with megafaunal remains; however, further research at the Coats-Hines Mastodon Site in Williamson County may provide such a link.[5] We should probably assume that Tennessee hunters, like other Paleoindians, pursued any large game animals they encountered but concentrated on smaller mammals and foraging for wild plant foods.[6] If so, their subsistence patterns differed from those of their successors in the early Archaic Period only in degree rather than in kind.

The Paleoindian Period had blended almost imperceptibly into the Archaic by about ten thousand years ago. The megafauna were now gone, and the climate in Tennessee was much as it is today, bringing the spread of extensive deciduous forests. During the next seven thousand years or so the hunter-gatherer economy shifted from seasonal base camps to denser populations in semipermanent camps or villages on favored riverine sites. Indians hunted game like deer, bear, and turkey, and the atlatl—or throwing stick—enabled them to propel their spears with great force. More dramatic dietary changes came with wide-scale gathering of nuts and wild fruits as well as consumption of fish, freshwater mussels, snails, and turtles.[7]

One of the most interesting Archaic sites in Tennessee is at Eva, in Benton County, occupied by many generations of settlers between about 6000 and 1000 B.C. The large middens (heaps of mussel shells, trash, and earth) tell us much about the residents' diet, technology, and burial patterns. Although deer bones represent some 90 percent of all mammalian remains, these people also consumed a variety of plant foods as well as birds, fish, and mussels. Eva reflects many of the increasingly complex cultural patterns of Archaic people: impressive stone technology, lithic workshop areas, and ceremonial burials of bodies arranged in flexed positions.[8] During the late phase of its occupation, the site was part of a trade network bringing a few residents prestige items like marine shells from the Gulf of Mexico and pieces of copper from the Great Lakes area; these items were apparently used mostly for ornamentation. This early trade affected only certain parts of the Southeast and was episodic.[9]

Cultural change accelerated with the advent of the Woodland Period about three thousand years ago. By now Tennessee Indians typically resided in communities on the floodplains and terraces of major streams. Subsistence still depended on hunting and gathering, but a major innovation was the advent of the bow and arrow sometime in the first millennium A.D. The origins of this technological advance—whether from Old World diffusion or New World reinvention—remain unknown. More important, Indian villagers embarked on the road to agriculture through increasingly systematic use of domesticated native plants like sunflowers, squash, and gourds. Indian corn (maize), though introduced from the Southwest at an early date, did not become important in Tennessee Indian diets until about A.D. 900. Beans appeared even later.[10]

Woodland cultural complexity was apparent in other ways as well. Ceramic pottery appeared and began an evolution that proceeded through distinct archaeological phases into the historic period. As the population increased, societies moved toward social stratification and loose unification, and burial mounds for important individuals became common. Palisades around towns indicate fear or wariness of neighbors, yet trading links with distant peoples brought Tennesseans new products, ideas, and cultural patterns. Ritualism became more prevalent and complex, though its many meanings are probably lost forever. One example is the misnamed Old Stone Fort near Manchester, apparently constructed over a period of several centuries and completed some sixteen hundred years ago; scholars now believe that this large, open area bounded by steep cliffs and stone and earthen embankments served as a ceremonial center.[11] Even more impressive are the systematically arranged Pinson Mounds near Jackson, dating mostly from about A.D. 100 to 300 and used for burials and ceremonies. One of these, Saul's Mound, is the second-highest Indian mound north of Mexico. Indians apparently traveled hundreds

Old Stone Fort, Coffee County, 1992. Native Americans centered a large ceremonial enclosure around these falls of the Duck River. Photograph by Carroll Van West.

Pinson Mounds, Madison County. Tennessee State Library and Archives.

of miles from other parts of the Southeast to participate in ceremonies there.[12] Neither Old Stone Fort nor the Pinson complex served as sites of permanent habitation.

About A.D. 900 the Woodland Culture gave way to the Mississippian Period, so-called because of startling new cultural developments that took their most dramatic form in the Middle Mississippi Valley but were found throughout the Southeast. The most famous example of these changes is the Cahokia site, across the river from present-day St. Louis, where a large palisaded community arose that dominated an extensive hinterland.[13] Trade and a growing reliance on corn enabled the population to grow to some thirty thousand people, bringing more social stratification and cultural accomplishments. Eventually, Cahokia and other incipient urban centers became chiefdoms ruled by hereditary leaders from distinguished clans or lineages; some centers emerged as paramount chiefdoms and exercised tributary authority over smaller chiefdoms.

The most striking feature of these towns was the large pyramidal mounds with flattened tops used as platforms for temples and the residences of chiefs or priests. The largest of these is at Cahokia. Often the mounds overlooked a large plaza around which there might be lesser mounds, homes of villagers, and public buildings. Chucalissa Village, on the south side of Memphis, is a reconstructed Mississippian village complete with mounds and Indian domiciles.[14] Hundreds of years later, long after the Mississippian culture had disappeared, white Americans would assume that no ancestors of contemporary Indians could possibly have produced such impressive structures; instead, they believed in an ancient race of "Mound Builders" who had emigrated from Europe, the Middle East, or even the Lost Continent of Atlantis.[15] Only in the late nineteenth century did archaeologists prove that the mounds were indeed Indian-built.

How and why this Mississippian culture appeared throughout the Southeast is a source of controversy, involving theories of diffusion, possible migrations, and on-site cultural adaptation.[16] What is clear is that in the several centuries before the Spanish arrived, a number of chiefdoms and paramount chiefdoms blanketed many of the larger river systems in the region. Moundville, Alabama, and Etowah and Macon, Georgia, are among the best-known Mississippian sites, each marked by impressive mounds. Among the many smaller mound sites in Tennessee is Toqua on the Little Tennessee River. By 1400, Toqua covered nearly five acres and had a population of 250 to 300 people. The surrounding palisade separating the town from outlying fields reflected another feature of Mississippian chiefdoms: frequent warfare, conducted more for revenge and status than territorial expansion.[17] By the mid-sixteenth century Toqua and other East Tennessee communities appear to have been tributary parts of a large confederation centered at Coosa, in northwestern Georgia.[18]

At many different Mississippian sites archaeologists have found a variety of strikingly similar artistic and symbolic objects that, because they suggest common politico-religious beliefs, comprise the Southeastern Ceremonial Complex, or the Southern Cult.[19] Many of these are ornaments like shell gorgets and other prestige items, and they are typically incised with intricate patterns. Popular motifs are the Greek cross, feathered serpent, swastika, circles with scalloped edges, and the human eye depicted in the palms of hands or with chevrons and other designs.[20]

Clearly, Tennessee's native inhabitants had a long and diverse history before they ever encountered whites. Their varied societies had succeeded in meeting their shifting needs, and during the Mississippian Period they enjoyed their greatest prosperity, complexity, and cultural achievement. The end of that period roughly coincided with—and perhaps began well before— arrival of the first Europeans. In May 1539, Hernando de Soto, a Spaniard who had helped destroy the Inca empire in Peru, landed at Tampa Bay with six hundred infantry and cavalry. His quest for precious booty led him on an erratic course through Florida, Georgia, the Carolinas, and westward into Tennessee.[21] The exact route is a source of great controversy. One of the most common assumptions, that de Soto followed the Hiwassee River into Tennessee and visited the chiefdom of Chiaha near today's Chattanooga, dates to an investigation of more than fifty years ago.[22] Recent studies, however, suggest that de Soto entered the state in June 1540 by way of the French Broad and Pigeon River valleys. According to this scenario, Chiaha was located on Zimmerman's Island near present-day Dandridge; unfortunately, the site is now submerged by Douglas Lake, a TVA reservoir. Whatever its location, most scholars agree that Chiaha was tributary to the paramount chiefdom of Coosa in Georgia. The Spaniards rested in Chiaha for more than three weeks, while two men were sent northward to investigate stories about the Chiscas, who, according to the scenario, resided near the upper Nolichucky River.[23]

There appears to have been no major trouble in this first encounter between Tennessee Indians and Europeans, but one may infer from de Soto's actions before and after his visit that he made demands for food, information, and probably women. No doubt the Chiahas were glad to see the Spaniards depart on June 28. The most recent argument is that de Soto headed down the French Broad, bivouacked for a night in present-day Knoxville, stopped at the Indian town of Coste on Bussell Island, and continued up the Little Tennessee River to the chiefdom of Tali, probably the site of Toqua or Tomotley. Continuing southward into Georgia, he proceeded to the main town of Coosa, where he remained a month and took the chief hostage.[24] The Spaniards then roamed westward for another two years, finding little wealth, making demands on their Indian hosts, and engaging in bloody battles. It is possible, though not likely, that they reached the Memphis area and visited Chucalissa. They wandered west of the Mississippi and then returned to that stream, where the dispirited de Soto died in 1542; the remnants of his army did not reach Spanish territory until September 1543.[25] In 1567, another Spaniard, Juan Pardo, retraced part of de Soto's route in East Tennessee before retreating under Indian threat back to the Carolinas.[26] After that, there is no evidence of Europeans visiting Tennessee until the late seventeenth century. Scholars call the 150 years bridging de Soto's expedition and the return of Europeans (and their written documentation) the Protohistoric Period, and only recently has it attracted serious study.

The dominant feature of this period was the widespread breakup of the Mississippian chiefdoms because of epidemic disease and perhaps internal stresses. The Spanish brought a host of diseases like smallpox, influenza, and measles, which killed thousands of Indians; indeed, it is possible these contagions originated with early coastal contacts and decimated some of the interior chiefdoms even before de Soto arrived.[27] Once again, necessity led to creativity. Amid the disruption and breakdown of Mississippian culture, surviving groups adapted rationally by moving out of afflicted areas and coalescing with other remnants. This partly explains the evolution of the Creek Confederacy, a sociopolitical bonding of diverse groups during the latter part of the Protohistoric Period; not until the early eighteenth century did it wield considerable power among both Indians and Europeans.[28] Likewise, the Choctaws of Mississippi created a new polity, a confederacy of sorts, out of the chaos.[29] The overall thrust of these changes was a remarkable adaptation (some call it a devolution) from the complexity and hierarchy of chiefdoms to the relative simplicity and autonomy of new tribal associations. The latter were also better suited to cope with the renewed and sustained pressures from Europeans.[30]

Among these emerging polities were the Overhill Cherokees of southeastern Tennessee, who figure so prominently in colonial records of the eighteenth century. One controversial question is whether their ancestors had occupied the Tennessee River Valley for hundreds of years and evolved (or devolved) from the Mississippian breakup in situ.[31] If so, they were the Tennessee Indians encountered by de Soto and Pardo. Other scholars believe the only conclusive Spanish-Cherokee contacts occurred near present-day Asheville and Marshall, North Carolina, where Cherokee chiefs traveled from towns that were probably in the Carolina mountains and foothills. A few Cherokee speakers might have resided barely within the borders of Tennessee, these scholars say, but linguistic analysis and other data suggest mid-sixteenth-century East Tennesseans were primarily non-Cherokees of Muskogean linguistic stock related to today's Creeks.[32]

If the latter argument is correct, most East Tennessee Indians migrated southward into Georgia and Alabama following the Spanish expeditions and eventually became Creeks. Such a move might be the result of disease-related exigencies or because of pressures exerted by an expanding population of Cherokee speakers. The Cherokees themselves may have been moving partly because of the attractive riverine sites in Tennessee and partly to escape increasing pressure from eastern and northern tribes who, supplied with fire-arms, were procuring Indian slaves for English traders in Virginia and South Carolina.[33] Whatever the reasons for migration, these Tennessee newcomers emerged as the Overhill Cherokees—so-called because they were across the mountains from the Lower and Middle Cherokees, whose villages were in the uplands of South and North Carolina, respectively.[34] By 1715, the Overhill Cherokees had evicted the few remaining proto-Creeks from East Tennessee. At this time the various divisions of Cherokees totaled perhaps ten to twelve thousand people, a sharp decline (no doubt disease-induced) from possibly thirty thousand or more in 1685.[35]

Tennessee's isolation from whites during the Protohistoric Period was not complete, for local Indians managed to obtain some European goods from tribes closer to the Atlantic and Gulf coasts—or even by making occasional visits to Spanish Florida. Whites did not return to the state until July 1673, when two Englishmen, James Needham and Gabriel Arthur, arrived in an Overhill Cherokee town after an arduous trek through the wilderness from tidewater Virginia.[36] They were in the employ of a frontier entrepreneur who hoped to open direct trade with the interior tribes. Needham was killed while returning to Virginia, but Arthur had many adventures with the Cherokees—narrowly avoiding execution by his hosts, accompanying them to Spanish territory, and helping them wage war against a rival tribe (probably the Shawnees). Within a year he was back in Virginia, but despite his reports significant English trade with the Overhill Cherokees did not develop until the early eighteenth century.[37] To the chagrin of Virginians, aggressive Carolina businessmen quickly dominated a far-flung exchange that radiated outward from Charleston and encompassed the Cherokees, Creeks, and other tribes all the way to the Mississippi.[38]

The Carolinians enjoyed a near-monopoly of the Cherokee trade, and despite their sometimes unscrupulous business tactics, they maintained a semblance of harmony with their clients through gifts and inviting disgruntled chiefs to Charleston for talks. But they encountered more serious problems in dealing with the distant and powerful Chickasaws, who claimed West Tennessee. Fierce warriors, the Chickasaws occupied villages in northern Mississippi and used their Tennessee lands primarily for hunting. They eagerly welcomed English goods, but this hospitality was threatening to the French, who were beginning to establish themselves in the lower Mississippi Valley. In 1673, the same year Needham and Arthur visited the Overhill Cherokees, Father Jacques Marquette and Louis Jolliet skirted the Chickasaw domain when they ventured partway down the Mississippi. More substantive contact came in 1682, when Robert Cavelier de La Salle's expedition paused at one of the Chickasaw Bluffs a short distance above Memphis. Pierre Prud-homme, a member of the expedition, disappeared while hunting, so La Salle constructed Fort Prudhomme on the bluff as a temporary base while search-ing for him. Upon encountering two Chickasaws, the French sent gifts and messages to their villages situated a few days away. Prudhomme finally ap-peared, and the expedition continued downstream to the Gulf, but the tem-porary garrison on Chickasaw Bluffs was a reminder that the Europeans were prepared for war as well as for trade and diplomacy.[39]

By the beginning of the eighteenth century, the French had established themselves at Biloxi and Mobile on the Gulf Coast, and in 1718, they founded New Orleans along the lower Mississippi River. They intended to promote settlement in the region, cement Indian loyalty by developing a mutually profitable trade, and maintain strong links with countrymen in the Illinois country and Canada via the Mississippi and its tributaries. Until the end of the colonial wars they encouraged their Indian allies, especially the Choctaws, to wage war against the Chickasaws and the Carolina traders. In fact, war was preferable to peace because the French lacked the goods to accommodate both their allies and the Chickasaws, and the constant intertribal bloodshed in-creased the dependence of their client tribes on French assistance.[40] On two occasions, in 1736 and 1739, French forces landed on the Chickasaw Bluffs to undertake major offensives against the Chickasaws. In the latter year, the governor of Louisiana, Jean Baptiste le Moyne d'Bienville, constructed Fort Assumption on the bluffs and assembled an army of some 3,600 soldiers and Indian allies (probably the largest military force in the interior to that time), but he was still unable to subdue his adversaries. Humiliated, he was forced to withdraw his forces from the bluffs and allow the recently constructed fort to return to wilderness.[41]

As the Protohistoric Period drew to a close, another group of Indians settled between the Cherokee and Chickasaw domains of East and West Tennes-see. These were the Shawnees, a fragmented people with bands scattered over much of the eastern United States. A number of them moved from Ohio into the Cumberland Valley during the mid-seventeenth century, and French maps of the period refer to the Cumberland as "Riviere des Chaouanons," or the Shawnee River. The fact that this area was claimed by both the Chero-kees and Chickasaws did not deter the newcomers. By the 1670s, many Shawnees lived in the Nashville basin, an area abounding with deer, bison, and other game animals. From there, they traded pelts as far south as Span-ish Florida and northward to French outposts in Illinois.[42] The Florida trade may have induced some to migrate to South Carolina, where they began dealing with the English and became embroiled in a series of local Indian wars and intrigues.[43] Those who remained in the Nashville area did business with Frenchmen such as Martin Chartier, who settled there in 1692, and Jean de Charleville, who operated a trading post at French Lick on the site of Nashville from about 1710 to 1714.[44]

Trade had been a fact of life for southern Indians for thousands of years, but its European phase had vastly more profound effects on native life. An array of abundant, relatively inexpensive items now became available not just to chiefs and other native leaders but ultimately to every Indian man, woman, and child. Trade items still conveyed status, but the market was democratic in the sense that all who contributed to its expansion would share in its benefits. Though Indians at first might employ items in traditional ways quite unrelated to their intended uses in Europe, they quickly realized how "rational" usage of these goods enhanced and made life easier. Firearms, the most dramatic and valued items, enabled their possessors to become more successful hunters and warriors; metal hoes, hatchets, and other utensils were superior to native counterparts of wood, stone, and pottery; and woolen strouds and other fabrics were easier to process, more colorful, and more comfortable than deerskins and other peltries.[45] Because Britain was in the early stages of the Industrial Revolution, English goods were generally more abundant, less expensive, and better made than those of the French.

To pay for their goods, many Indians first captured and sold other Indians as slaves to coastal merchants, often causing prospective victims to flee and coalesce with other groups. When this trade proved destructive to both races (and less economical than enslavement of blacks), Indians usually bought their goods with deerskins, which had a ready market abroad. Right up to the American Revolution, thousands of pounds of white-tailed deerskins were shipped annually from Charleston. This, of course, threatened to deplete the deer population through overhunting, but, for a while, there was an equilibrium in the exchange system whereby Indians could obtain goods by serving as diplomatic and military allies of their respective European suppliers. During such periods fewer deerskins were required, and it provided an opportunity for herds to rebuild in the buffer zones separating hostile tribes; hunting there on a regular basis posed too many dangers.[46]

On the other hand, these buffer zones and the hunting lands claimed by others were great temptations for aggressive tribes wishing to expand their trade. The Cumberland Basin, with an abundance of game, is a case in point. Tribes that claimed the area or hunted there included the Cherokees, Chickasaws, Creeks, and even the lordly Iroquois of New York, but only the Shawnees occupied it in the early eighteenth century. As the market expanded, however, their presence became intolerable to both the Chickasaws and Cherokees, who ventured increasingly afar from their villages to hunt deer. Thus, in 1715, those two nations combined to drive the Shawnees out of the region—and again in 1745, after a few small bands had returned.[47]

Trade served different purposes for Indians and whites. From the Indian point of view, it was usually the dominant consideration in relations with Britain, France, Spain, and later, the United States. Loyalty to any of these nations was conditional and dependent on a ready supply of inexpensive goods. Even the Chickasaws and Cherokees, both normally pro-English, sometimes threatened to switch their affections. Market demands, moreover, created divisiveness as tribal factions loyal to one European nation intrigued against factions loyal to others. In contrast to Indian priorities, European governments viewed trade mostly as a necessary tool for securing Indian political and military alliances in the escalating imperial rivalries. Such an objective caused those governments to vitiate somewhat the injustices of the trade but also inevitably involved Indians in wars far more sweeping and deadly than their traditional squabbles. Besides taking many lives, these conflicts disrupted normal subsistence patterns by preventing the surviving combatants from hunting on a regular basis and leaving women exposed to the enemy while tending their fields. And what would happen when the wars were over and only one imperial power remained? Indians would be at the mercy of profit-minded traders who would charge whatever the market would bear and further ensnare their victims through reliance on alcohol and credit.

Clearly, this trade inexorably led to a growing Indian dependency, though it did not always take identical forms or occur at the same time for all southern tribes. No single dependency theory—no model, for example, of cores and peripheries within an expanding capitalist system—can adequately describe the variations.[48] And yet the fact is that Indians became part of a market economy emanating from Europe, channeling through entrepreneurial or military middlemen along the Atlantic and Gulf coasts, and extending into the most distant reaches of the southern backcountry. Dependency was not so much a matter of ensnaring unsuspecting economic naifs, but rather of fully rational Indians apprising the risks and taking their chances. As anthropologist Bruce Trigger notes: "Native people appreciated the material benefits to be derived from many items of European technology and . . . sought to utilize this technology even at the cost of growing dependence upon their European trading partners. Native leaders also learned from observation to understand the motivations of the different European groups with whom they interacted and to devise strategies for coping with their demands."[49]

No strategy finally proved successful, but for most of the eighteenth century the Cherokees and other southern tribes creatively delayed the consequences of dependency. They did this on two levels: through realpolitik and cultural syncretism. On the first level, they simply mirrored European modes of statecraft. They resorted to balance-of-power diplomacy by playing off Britain, France, and Spain against one another and were successful enough to evoke grudging admiration from their temporary pawns. During the mid-1750s, for example, the Overhill Cherokees used the French presence in Alabama to demand the English garrisoning of a post on the Little Tennessee River; noncompliance would interrupt the thriving Carolina trade and perhaps, according to the Cherokees, force a rapprochement with France (a tribal faction was already intriguing with the French). Both Virginia and South Carolina agreed to take action, and the latter's Fort Loudoun, completed in 1757, was the first British fort of any significance west of the Appalachians. It became a flashpoint of violence when the Cherokees temporarily forsook their old allies and went to war against the British in 1759–61. The fort was besieged, and a number of its defenders were massacred after surrendering.[50]

Cultural syncretism, the second level of staving off dependency, entailed both creativity and a rough balance of power between the races. For most of the eighteenth century, Tennessee Indians greatly outnumbered whites and played a crucial role in the imperial machinations; whites still resided east of the Appalachians or, in the case of the French, in the lower Mississippi Valley. Those visiting Tennessee consisted of small detachments of military personnel or traders and their dependents. Though few in number, these whites controlled the flow of trade goods. Thus the power equation was roughly in balance, and because trade and alliances were seen as mutually beneficial, both Indians and whites consciously created what historian Richard White has called the middle ground, "the place in between: in between cultures, peoples, and in between empires and the non-state world of villages."[51] In Tennessee, the middle ground meant accommodating the peltry trade to the respective obligations of Indian-European alliances; the blending of traditional Indian practices of gift giving and European bribery; and the sexual and cultural mingling of traders and Indians that produced a class of mixed bloods. It also meant the presence of growing numbers of blacks who would become incorporated into Indian society in ways both familiar and novel.[52] This middle ground of mutual accommodation and benefit would help stave off

Indian dependency until the colonial wars ended and a rapidly growing white frontier population altered the balance of power.

In East Tennessee, the final phase of the middle ground began with the permanent settlement of white farmer-hunters about 1770. These individuals and their families were interested in Indian land rather than trade, and their arrival was in violation of the British Proclamation of 1763. If they even bothered to justify their actions, they did so with legal obfuscations and the pretext of "leasing" their lands from compliant Cherokees. Clearly, the Watauga Association of 1772 was an extralegal organization dedicated to protecting their illegal claims. By 1775, when Richard Henderson and his fellow speculators "purchased" millions of acres in middle Kentucky and Tennessee, some Cherokee leaders like Dragging Canoe realized that Indians would have to fight to protect their lands. As the American Revolution got under way, Tennessee leaders supported the patriot cause partly because of ideological principles and, perhaps even more, because they realized that loyalty to the Crown meant forfeiting claims to Indian lands acquired in blatant disregard of British law. The inevitable alliance of most southern Indians with Britain threatened not only the whole concept of frontier gain and improvement but life itself. Because a clear majority of whites from all social levels aspired to hold their lands—and indeed acquire more—local elites could employ force to ensure loyalty to the cause of independence and even to eliminate the middle ground.[53]

The most ambiguous frontier group during the Revolution consisted of white and mixed-blood traders who had helped create the middle ground by moving back and forth between Indian and white societies. Many of these were transplanted Scotsmen and their progeny—businessmen like John McDonald, Daniel Ross, Lachlan McGillivray, and the children of James Logan Colbert, who had settled among the Chickasaws in 1729. They usually cemented their positions through marriage or informal relationships with Indian women, sometimes while maintaining white families elsewhere. Such trader–Indian liaisons produced a number of prominent mixed bloods, or métis, who served as cultural brokers between Indians and whites.[54] To whatever extent these men were sometimes a fringe element in native society and "felt the tension of ethnic identity," there is no doubt that over a period of time their mixed status gave them a tremendous advantage in tribal societies.[55]

These trader-Indian alliances both modified traditional Indian society and created new grounds for common understanding with whites. In East Tennessee, for example, Joseph Martin acquired some of the prestige of his Indian wife's Wolf clan and of his mother-in-law, Nancy Ward, the famous Beloved Woman of the Cherokees. Clan-based relationships were persistent and powerful, "mediating frontier tensions through the kinship which flowed from marriage of Cherokee women . . . to white traders, settlers, and packhorse men."[56] The matrilineal and matrilocal clan system enabled Cherokee women to have a powerful—and usually ameliorative—role in interracial relations on the Tennessee frontier. During the siege of Fort Loudoun in 1761, Cherokee women moved freely between the fort and its native besiegers, selling the white garrison food and even providing military information; they simply laughed when rebuked by warriors.[57]

During the American Revolution, Nancy Ward, invoking her status as Beloved Woman, saved white captives from torture and strove to promote harmony between the races.[58] At a peace conference in 1781, she made an impassioned appeal to the white commissioners, invoking rhetoric typical of the common ground: "We are your mothers; you are our sons. Our cry is all for peace; let it continue. The peace must last forever. Let your women's sons be ours; our sons be yours." The commissioners were themselves aware of the protocol of the middle ground, and Colonel William Christian responded appropriately: "We are all descendants of the same woman. We will not quarrel with you, because you are our mothers. We will not meddle with your people if they will be still and quiet at home and let us live in peace."[59] The fact that Nancy Ward served as a mediator and even communicated military intelligence to whites did not make her a traitor in the eyes of most Cherokees. She was simply fulfilling the peaceful functions of a Beloved, similar to those of an alliance chief who was supposed to reconcile conflicting components of the middle ground.[60]

Indian heterogeneity during the Revolution was so pronounced that it is misleading even to speak of tribal affiliations in the sense of implying a formal social or political unity. Despite sharing broad cultural patterns—like residency in scattered, autonomous villages—Choctaws, Chickasaws, Cherokees, and Creeks engaged in periodic warfare and intrigues against one another and, indeed, among themselves. The fluidity and complexity of these relationships is best illustrated by Dragging Canoe and his so-called Chickamaugas. He had been the most prominent opponent of Richard Henderson's controversial land purchase and a leader of coordinated Cherokee attacks on settlers in 1776. When most Cherokee leaders sued for peace after savage retaliation by the colonists, he and his followers seceded and relocated to more secure villages farther down the Tennessee River, near Chickamauga Creek. Soon they would retreat even farther downstream—to five "Lower Towns" at readily defensible sites near the common boundaries of Tennessee, Alabama, and Georgia. These communities were at the hub of a network of trails, radiating throughout the Southeast, which offered war parties quick access to white settlements, especially on the Cumberland River. The Upper Creeks, who claimed this area, readily consented to the Chickamauga relocation.[61]

Although the Chickamaugas are generally considered "Cherokees," they were actually more complex in composition than such a label would suggest. Besides an undeniable core of Overhill Cherokees—as well as other Cherokee refugees—they incorporated an exotic mix of peoples whose common denominator was opposition to white settlement. These included Upper Creeks, northern Indians like Shawnees and Delawares who moved back and forth across the Ohio, a few blacks, and whites ranging from prominent traders and British (or Spanish) agents to French-speaking boatmen, "white Indians," and individuals described by settlers as banditti and the offscouring of humanity. Thus, the Chickamauga villages resemble in many respects the multiethnic village republics (small "r") arising in the middle ground of the Great Lakes region.[62] Whatever their composition, the Chickamaugas had at least five hundred warriors by 1780.[63] They were part of a pan-Indian—and even a panracial—resistance stretching from Tennessee to the Great Lakes. Besides their common aversion to Anglo-American expansion, many also shared a core of ritual and ceremony.[64]

The so-called peaceful Overhill Cherokees continued to live in the "Upper Towns" near the white settlements after being forced to make large land cessions following the abortive Cherokee War of 1776. For the rest of the Revolution, they represented a spectrum of sentiment, with some of the younger warriors periodically joining Dragging Canoe's forces. Chickamauga militancy reflected the widening fissures in Cherokee society as the middle ground disintegrated. Indeed, the Chickamaugas distinguished themselves from other Cherokees by referring to themselves alone as *Ani-Yunwiya,* "the real people."[65] They increasingly perceived the older civil chiefs and female Beloveds of the Upper Towns as accommodationists, and accommodation, of course, had been the cornerstone of the middle ground.

While East Tennesseans faced Chickamauga attacks or Shawnee forays through Cumberland Gap, their position was not as precarious as that of settlers in the Cumberland Basin, that most treasured of Indian hunting paradises. Shortly after its founding in 1780, Nashville was under constant threat of Chickasaw attack, as were other fortified stations ranging northward into central Kentucky. The Chickasaws, loyal British allies fresh from successes on the Mississippi, were joined by Chickamaugas, Creeks, Delawares, and Shawnees who raided from the south and north—making the region, as Dragging Canoe had warned, a "dark and bloody" ground. As the American Revolution wound down and the British lost their Gulf coastal possessions to Spain, a portion of the Chickasaws decided it was important to have friendly Americans as a counterweight to Spanish control of the lower Mississippi Valley. In November 1783, they signed a treaty of peace in Nashville. During the next dozen years, pro-Spanish and pro-American factions intrigued against one another and this, along with a costly war against the Creeks, left the Chickasaws little time or inclination to menace the Tennessee frontier. In 1795, the Spanish built Fort San Fernando de las Barrancas on the Chickasaw Bluffs as reassurance to their supporters, only to destroy it two years later following agreement with the United States on a series of boundary and trade-related issues.[66]

Meanwhile, the Chickamaugas, Upper Creeks, and Shawnees continued to fight against white expansion. For East Tennesseans, it was often easier dealing with the overt hostility of those groups than with the shifting currents of intrigue and self-interest affecting the Cherokees of the nearby Upper Towns. Frontiersmen realized that Cherokee peace after the treaty of 1777 was still conditional, dependent on whether frontiersmen continued to trespass and murder inoffensive Indians and whether the British or Americans were better able to provide necessities. Cherokee diplomacy was at its most devious and threatening when tribal leaders used British promises of trade goods, especially munitions, as leverage in negotiations with Americans. Whites on both sides saw this as duplicity, but it was simply a continuation of realpolitik. Little wonder frontier elites such as John Sevier and Arthur Campbell were skeptical about Cherokee professions of goodwill and quick to take preemptive military action against Chota and other nearby villages. These attacks, often indiscriminate in nature, continued through the Revolution and during the region's brief incarnations as the State of Franklin and the Southwest Territory. The end of the American Revolution meant that Indians could no longer play balance-of-power politics. The equation of power necessary for a middle ground had forever been altered in favor of white Americans. In 1788, their violence, trespassing, and demands for more land caused the Overhill Cherokees to abandon Chota and several other upper towns in Tennessee and remove their capital to Ustanali in Georgia; from these new towns, young warriors often joined Dragging Canoe's insurgents in campaigns against white Tennesseans.[67]

Tennessee's integration into a larger United States is reflected by the way the intensity of Indian warfare varied according to events elsewhere. The Ohio campaigns of William Crawford, Josiah Harmar, and Arthur St. Clair in the 1780s and early 1790s directly affected the scope of violence in Tennessee; indeed, Chickamaugas and Upper Creeks fought alongside their northern brethren in those engagements and gained incentive from their successes to resist even more fiercely in the South. Likewise, Anthony Wayne's 1794 triumph in Ohio had immediate consequences in reducing conflict in Tennessee and was an important factor in bringing about Chickamauga demoralization. Their final decision for peace came just a month after Wayne's victory when a militia force from Middle Tennessee surprised and burned two of their towns. Indian military resistance in Tennessee finally ended with Creek acquiescence in 1795.[68] There could no longer be even a pretense of a middle ground, of parity between whites and Indians. Indian creativity would now mean adjusting to the new realities and finding empowerment in forms other than military resistance.

The plight of Tennessee Indians can be measured against the twofold objectives of United States Indian policy: first, to acquire more tribal lands in order to accommodate an expanding white population; and second, to encourage—even coerce—tribes to become more "civilized," that is, to conform to white economic, cultural, social, and religious norms. The future of Native Americans was not as Indians but as red-skinned copies of whites. Trade acted as a lubricant for facilitating both objectives, providing Indians with the material aspects of civilization and fostering an indebtedness that could be used as leverage in winning new land cessions. At Fort Adams, and then, Fort Pickering on the Chickasaw Bluffs, the United States army supplied the Chickasaws with goods brought down the Ohio and Mississippi rivers; here, on the future site of Memphis, was a cosmopolitan gathering of military personnel, boatmen, traders, and Indians.[69] Chickasaws continued to hunt in West Tennessee, and as late as 1815, they sold $23,812 worth of skins at the Chickasaw Bluffs Trading House, operated by the federal government.[70] Trade, diplomacy, and other official relations with the Cherokees were conducted at Tellico Blockhouse on the Little Tennessee River, at Fort Southwest Point, and later, after additional land cessions, at the Calhoun agency on the Hiwassee River.

The first objective of federal policy, to acquire more Indian lands, had been manifest since British colonial days and then accelerated in the 1770s and 1780s with demands by ordinary settlers, powerful speculators, the state of North Carolina, and the presumptive State of Franklin. It continued under federal auspices in a series of treaties beginning in 1785 and took definitive form in the July 1791 Treaty of the Holston. Reacting to demands of William Blount, governor of the Southwest Territory and supervisor of Indian affairs for the Southern District, the Cherokees (excepting Dragging Canoe) ceded large chunks of their domain. This treaty became the model for additional land cessions, each supposedly the last.[71] By 1835, the remaining Cherokee lands in Tennessee consisted of only about four hundred square miles in the southeastern part of the state, encompassing some or all of five future counties. The rest of the tribal domain included portions of North Carolina, Georgia, and Alabama.[72] Federal treaties also nibbled away at the Chickasaw domain until finally, in October 1818, thanks to bribes paid by treaty commissioners Andrew Jackson and Isaac Shelby, tribal leaders ceded all their claims to West Tennessee—some 10,700 square miles.[73] This cession opened the area, precipitated a land and cotton boom, and prompted the phenomenal growth of the new town of Memphis.

The second federal objective, to civilize Indians, was also a prominent part of the 1791 Holston treaty and its successors. The federal government encouraged tribes to give up hunting and adopt white methods of agriculture, forsake tribalism, settle as nuclear families on individual plots of land, give up pagan beliefs and customs, learn English, and become Christians. Men would now become the farmers, while women, formerly the primary agriculturists, would content themselves with household duties like spinning, weaving, and tending their children. To further these objectives, the government paid for seed, implements, livestock, and resident white artisans and federal agents; a bit later, it even subsidized proselytizing by various Christian denominations. Reformers especially targeted the Cherokees because their sixteen thousand members in 1800 made them one of the largest tribes, and success among them might signal success for the entire civilization program.

By the early nineteenth century, the Cherokees were in fact becoming more "civilized," albeit in a qualified sense. Some of the more obvious features of this phenomenon are already well known: the spread of missionary schools (including four in Tennessee); adoption of white modes of agriculture; abandonment of traditional village life as nuclear farm families dispersed along rivers and creeks; abandonment of traditional sexual roles as men assumed primary responsibility for farming while women increasingly tended to household tasks; increasing emphasis on patrilineal descent rather than matrilineal clan-based descent; Sequoyah's invention of a written syllabary and the significant number of Cherokees who became literate in their own language; the rise of predominantly mixed-blood elites who controlled politics and owned large farms, black slaves, and a variety of other businesses; and the evolution of an increasingly centralized tribal government, culminating in 1827 with creation of the Cherokee Nation, complete with a constitutional system of government and a capitol at New Echota, Georgia. All of these changes are impressive indeed and, juxtaposed with the enforced removal of the 1830s, assume poignant and tragic dimensions, which popular writers and scholars alike have dramatized.[74]

But it is important to remember that civilization varied from place to place within the Cherokee Nation. It was more prevalent among the mixed bloods living in fertile, accessible parts of the tribal domain and much less so among fullbloods in the mountains. Even among the former, acculturation was often quite selective. For example, parents of pupils at the mission schools (a minority of tribal children) often supported the secular aspects of education but resisted missionary efforts to Christianize. Moreover, mixed-blood economic and political elites were careful to show proper deference to the fullerbloods, many of whom remained profoundly traditional in outlook. Indeed, when those same elites created the Cherokee Nation it was not so much an affirmation of white civilization as a pragmatic and creative adaptation to preserve tribal autonomy—a means of retaining Cherokee social and political identity even amid change.[75] Change and "progress" were also, paradoxically, a reflection of cultural conservatism.

The brittle and elusive nature of Cherokee civilization is apparent among the mountain Indians where outward change appeared in the form of new spinning wheels, farm implements, and other material goods recorded in various tribal censuses. But the traditional clan structures remained in effect and women continued to assert, in often subtle ways, their primacy as farm providers. Traditional stories, like that of Selu the corn mother, helped sustain the old ways. Traditional games were still played, traditional ceremonies still performed. Baskets, still woven by women, reflected familiar materials, patterns, and techniques (later they would cleverly incorporate white technologies and styles into what remained undeniably a native craft). In the mountains the look, the feel, the texture of tribal life reflected the old ways rather than the new.[76] It is not even clear to what extent the laws or other political processes of the Cherokee Nation had any impact in such areas.

This dichotomy of relatively unacculturated mountain Cherokees and more acculturated valley Indians is apparent in Tennessee. The 1835 tribal census lists 3,144 individuals on tribal lands within the state; these consisted of 2,528 Cherokees, 480 black slaves, 79 whites intermarried with Cherokees, and 57 others of mixed black or Catawba Indian heritage. More than four-fifths of the Cherokee families lived in the western part of the district near the Tennessee River, while those residing in the more mountainous area to the east, around Turtletown, had the highest percentage of fullbloods; they had less education, fewer slaves, fewer material goods, and smaller, less productive farms.[77]

Whatever its nature, Cherokee civilization did not prevent tribal dispossession and deportation. For federal policy makers, civilizing Indians was always secondary to acquiring Indian land.[78] In December 1835, a small minority of Cherokees signed the Treaty of New Echota, thereby renouncing ownership of their southeastern homelands and agreeing to move across the Mississippi. Principal Chief John Ross and the Cherokee majority attempted to prevent ratification and then resorted to passive resistance in an effort to avoid eviction. But to no avail. With the enforced removal of most Cherokees in 1838, the last tribal domain in Tennessee—and several other southern states—was opened to white occupation. The tragic story of the Trail of Tears and Cherokee relocation in present-day Oklahoma is well known.[79] There in the West the Cherokees and other emigrant tribes would continue to write new chapters in the old story of Indian adaptability, creativity, and empowerment through preservation of cultural boundaries.[80]

Today, Tennesseans are becoming increasingly aware that our Indian history did not end with the removal era; indeed, small isolates of Cherokees in places like Turtletown reflect the experiences of tribal remnants that managed to remain in every southeastern state.[81] Following removal, in a South dominated by white racial pride, these and other peoples of mixed Indian-black-white heritage generally remained inconspicuous and quiet about their origins. Today, fortunately, many are proudly proclaiming their Indianness and even seeking recognition from state and federal governments. To learn their histories since removal, it is often necessary to look beyond the tribal designations of the eighteenth and nineteenth centuries and instead unravel the interwoven fabric of small localized groups of mixed ethnicity interacting with one another. These stories, no less than those of their more famous ancestors, bespeak their creativity and striving for empowerment.

NOTES

The author thanks Jefferson Chapman and Gerald F. Schroedl for their comments and suggestions regarding this article.

1. Among the many studies assessing white America's views of Indians are Roy Harvey Pearce, *The Savages of America: A Study of the Indian and the Idea of Civilization,* rev. ed. (Baltimore, 1965); Robert F. Berkhofer, Jr., *The White Man's Indian: Images of*

the American Indian from Columbus to the Present (New York, 1978); Brian W. Dippie, *The Vanishing American: White Attitudes and U.S. Indian Policy* (Middletown, Conn., 1982); and Richard Slotkin's trilogy: *Regeneration Through Violence: The Mythology of the American Frontier, 1600–1860* (Middletown, Conn., 1973); *The Fatal Environment: The Myth of the Frontier in the Age of Industrialization, 1800–1890* (New York, 1985); and *Gunfighter Nation: The Myth of the Frontier in Twentieth-Century America* (New York, 1992). In addition, one should note Frederick Jackson Turner's famous 1893 essay, "The Significance of the Frontier in American History" (reprinted in many sources), which speaks volumes in its brief commentary on Indians.

2. James H. Merrell, *The Indians' New World: Catawbas and Their Neighbors from European Contact through the Era of Removal* (Chapel Hill, N.C., 1989).

3. Joseph H. Greenberg and Merritt Ruhlen, "Linguistic Origins of Native Americans," *Scientific American* 267 (Nov. 1992): 94–99, argue that the first arrivals comprised the Amerind linguistic family, from which most American Indians are descended, and that post–Ice Age arrivals were the Na-Dene (including today's Navajo and Apache), and the Eskimo-Aleut; see also Luigi Luca Cavalli-Sforza, "Genes, Peoples and Languages," *Scientific American* 265 (Nov. 1991): 104–10; Christy G. Turner II, "Teeth and Prehistory in Asia," *Scientific American* 260 (Feb. 1989): 88–96; Joseph H. Greenberg, Christy G. Turner II, and Stephen L. Zegura, "The Settlement of the Americas: A Comparison of Linguistic, Dental, and Genetic Evidence," *Current Anthropology* 27 (Dec. 1986): 477–97.

4. A lively and thorough account of the debates surrounding early man in the New World is Brian M. Fagan, *The Great Journey: The Peopling of Ancient America* (London, 1987). See also Jefferson Chapman, *Tellico Archaeology: 12,000 Years of Native American History,* rev. ed. (Knoxville, 1994), 29–30.

5. Chapman, *Tellico Archaeology,* 34; Emanuel Breitburg and John B. Broster, "A Hunt for Big Game," *The Tennessee Conservationist* 61 (July/Aug. 1995): 18–26, discuss the presence of stone tools and flakes at the Coats-Hines site and pose the fundamental question: do these tools actually prove the local people hunted big game or are they "simply an association of mastodon bones and tools produced by natural forces?" (20).

6. Charles Hudson, *The Southeastern Indians* (Knoxville, 1976), 42–43; Charles H. Faulkner, "The Quad Site Revisited: An Introduction," *Tennessee Anthropologist* 14 (Fall 1989): 97–101; Chapman, *Tellico Archaeology,* 33. As Vincas P. Steponaitis observes, "That Paleoindians in the Southeast occasionally hunted megafauna is now indisputable. There is no reason to conclude, however, that such animals formed the mainstay of the diet." Steponaitis, "Prehistoric Archaeology in the Southeastern United States, 1970–1985," *Annual Review of Anthropology* 15 (1986): 369.

7. Hudson, *Southeastern Indians,* 44–46; Chapman, *Tellico Archaeology,* 38–40.

8. Thomas M. N. Lewis and Madeline Kneberg Lewis, *Eva: An Archaic Site* (Knoxville, 1961); and Lewis and Kneberg, *Tribes That Slumber: Indians of the Tennessee Region* (Knoxville, 1958), 21–34.

9. Lewis and Kneberg, *Tribes That Slumber,* 30–31; Chapman, *Tellico Archaeology,* 51. Jay K. Johnson says the southeastern trade began about 3600 B.C. "Prehistoric Exchange in the Southeast," in Timothy G. Baugh and Jonathan E. Ericson, eds., *Prehistoric Exchange Systems in North America* (New York, 1994), 99–125. By the Late

Archaic, however, "long-distance exchange" was a major trend. Steponaitis, "Prehistoric Archaeology in the Southeastern United States," 374.

10. Chapman, *Tellico Archaeology,* 61, 63.

11. Charles H. Faulkner, *The Old Stone Fort: Exploring an Archaeological Mystery* (Knoxville, 1968), 10–15, suggests that Old Stone Fort reflects the influence of Ohio sites (notably Fort Ancient) associated with the dynamic Hopewell Culture.

12. Robert C. Mainfort, Jr., *Pinson Mounds: A Middle Woodland Ceremonial Center* (Nashville, 1986).

13. The "Mississippian" Period also reflects the assumption of many anthropologists that Cahokia—or other Mississippi Valley sites—represented a "heartland" from which the culture expanded to other areas through colonization, migration, and diffusion. For a critique of these assumptions, see Bruce D. Smith, "Mississippian Expansion: Tracing the Historical Development of an Explanatory Model," *Southeastern Archaeology* 3 (Summer 1984): 13–32.

14. Charles H. Nash and Rodney Gates, Jr., "Chucalissa Indian Town," *Tennessee Historical Quarterly* 21 (June 1962): 103–21. For a different interpretation of Chucalissa's social system and the variables defining it, see Ronald K. Robinson, "Social Status, Stature, and Pathology at Chucalissa (40SY1), Shelby County, Tennessee" (Master's thesis, Univ. of Tennessee, 1976).

15. Hudson, *Southeastern Indians,* 35.

16. Smith, "Mississippian Expansion," is a critical overview of varying interpretations. Gerald F. Schroedl and others suggest the transition to Mississippian culture in East Tennessee was more a process of an in situ cultural adaptation. Schroedl, C. Clifford Boyd, Jr., and R. P. Stephen Davis, Jr., "Explaining Mississippian Origins in East Tennessee," in Bruce D. Smith, ed., *Mississippian Emergence: The Evolution of Ranked Agricultural Societies in Eastern North America* (Washington, 1990), 189–92.

17. Chapman, *Tellico Archaeology,* 77, 80–81; detailed analysis of another nearby site is in Gerald F. Schroedl, ed., *Overhill Cherokee Archaeology at Chota-Tanasee* (Knoxville, 1986).

18. Chapman, *Tellico Archaeology,* 77.

19. Hudson, *Southeastern Indians,* 86; Patricia Galloway, ed., *The Southeastern Ceremonial Complex: Artifacts and Analysis* (Lincoln, Nebr., 1989).

20. Hudson, *Southeastern Indians,* 88–90.

21. The most recent and best edition of the four Spanish accounts of de Soto's expedition, including many ancillary materials, is Lawrence A. Clayton, Vernon James Knight, Jr., and Edward C. Moore, eds., *The De Soto Chronicles: The Expedition of Hernando De Soto to North America in 1539–1543* (Tuscaloosa, 1993). See also Paul E. Hoffman, "Hernando De Soto: A Brief Biography," in Clayton, Knight, and Moore, *The De Soto Chronicles,* 421–59.

22. This investigation was made by the eminent anthropologist John R. Swanton and others and appears as *Final Report of the United States de Soto Expedition Commission,* 76 Cong., 1st Sess., House Document 71 (Washington, 1939; reprint, Washington, 1985). For the conventional view that Chiaha was near Chattanooga, see Ronald N. Satz, *Tennessee's Indian Peoples: From White Contact to Removal, 1540–1850* (Knoxville, 1979), 10.

23. Charles Hudson, "The Hernando de Soto Expedition, 1539–1543," in Charles

Hudson and Carmen Chaves Tesser, eds., *The Forgotten Centuries: Indians and Europeans in the American South, 1521–1704* (Athens, Ga. 1994), 84. Additional information on de Soto's expedition is in Charles Hudson, *The Juan Pardo Expeditions: Exploration of the Carolinas and Tennessee, 1566–1568* (Washington, 1990). For a cautionary note on Hudson's methodology, see Gerald F. Schroedl's forthcoming review of *The Forgotten Centuries* in *Southeastern Archaeology* 14:2 (1995).

24. Hudson, "The Hernando de Soto Expedition," 84–86.

25. Ibid., 86–99.

26. The best discussion of the Pardo expedition is Hudson, *The Juan Pardo Expeditions.* See also Hudson, "Some Thoughts on the Early Social History of the Cherokees," in David G. Moore, comp., *The Conference on Cherokee Prehistory* (Swannanoa, N.C., 1986), 141–43.

27. Arguing for early pandemics are Henry F. Dobyns, *Their Number Became Thinned: Native American Population Dynamics in Eastern North America* (Knoxville, 1983); and Ann F. Ramenofsky, *Vectors of Death: The Archaeology of European Contact* (Albuquerque, 1987). More cautious about pre–de Soto disease but stressing the radical consequences of post–de Soto epidemics is Marvin T. Smith, *Archaeology of Aboriginal Culture Change in the Interior Southeast: Population during the Early Historic Period* (Gainesville, Fla., 1987), reiterated in Smith, "Aboriginal Depopulation in the Postcontact Southeast," in Hudson, *The Forgotten Centuries*, 257–75; see also Gerald T. Milanich, "Sixteenth Century Native Societies and Spanish Empire in the Southeast United States," *Archaeology of Eastern North America* 20 (Fall 1992): 1–18. Disputing the immediate impact of European diseases on one important chiefdom is Chester B. DePratter, "The Chiefdom of Cofitachequi," in Hudson, *The Forgotten Centuries*, 197–226; see also John H. Hahn, "The Apalachee of the Historic Era," in Hudson, *The Forgotten Centuries*, 330.

28. Vernon James Knight, Jr., "The Formation of the Creeks," in Hudson, *The Forgotten Centuries*, 373–92. Traditional scholarship dates the origin of the Creek Confederacy to before de Soto.

29. Patricia Galloway, "Confederacy as a Solution to Chiefdom Dissolution: Historical Evidence in the Choctaw Case," in Hudson, *The Forgotten Centuries*, 393–420.

30. One sophisticated version of this is discussed by Gerald F. Schroedl, "Toward an Explanation of Cherokee Origins in East Tennessee," in Moore, *The Conference on Cherokee Prehistory*, 122–38.

31. Ibid. Other views include Hudson, "Some Thoughts on the Early Social History of the Cherokees," in Moore, *The Conference on Cherokee Prehistory*, 139–50; and Roy S. Dickens, Jr., "An Evolutionary-Ecological Interpretation of Cherokee Cultural Development," in Moore, *The Conference on Cherokee Prehistory*, 81–90.

32. Hudson, "Some Thoughts on the Early Social History," 139–50; he says the "Chiscas" of the upper Nolichucky were likely Cherokee speakers and perhaps the residents of "Tenasqui" (near present Newport) were as well (ibid., 143); see also Hudson, *The Juan Pardo Expeditions*, 94–97. Lewis and Kneberg, *Tribes That Slumber*, chapter 8, argue that the Chiscas were Yuchis.

33. Hudson, "Some Thoughts on the Early Social History," 145; Smith, "Aboriginal Depopulation," 271; and J. Leitch Wright, Jr., *The Only Land They Knew: The Tragic Story of the American Indians in the Old South* (New York, 1981), 126–50.

34. Some scholars divide the Middle Towns into Middle, Out, and Valley towns. William G. McLoughlin, *Cherokee Renascence in the New Republic* (Princeton, 1986), 9.
35. Peter H. Wood, "The Changing Population of the Colonial South: An Overview by Race and Region, 1685–1790," in Peter H. Wood, Gregory A. Waselkov, and M. Thomas Hatley, eds., *Powhatan's Mantle: Indians in the Colonial Southeast* (Lincoln, Nebr., 1989), 38, Table I; Russell Thornton, *The Cherokees: A Population History* (Lincoln, Nebr., 1990), 16–17, 21. Thornton discusses the complex matter of Cherokee demography from the colonial period to present.
36. Historians have sometimes assumed that Needham and Arthur arrived in Chota, e.g., Grace Steele Woodward, *The Cherokees* (Norman, Okla., 1963), 27. Schroedl, in *Overhill Cherokee Archaeology*, 533, while admitting that "Cherokee occupation at Chota-Tanasee surely existed before 1700," says that there are not yet any ethnohistorical data or European-made artifacts confirming Cherokee occupation of that site before 1700–1710.
37. Details of the Needham-Arthur expedition were later recounted by Captain Abraham Wood. See Samuel Cole Williams, *Early Travels in the Tennessee Country, 1540–1800* (Johnson City, Tenn., 1928), 17–42.
38. A standard work on Cherokee trade is John P. Reid, *A Better Kind of Hatchet: Law, Trade, and Diplomacy in the Cherokee Nation During the Early Years of European Contact* (University Park, Pa., 1976); see also Tom Hatley, *The Dividing Paths: Cherokees and South Carolinians through the Era of Revolution* (New York, 1993), chaps. 3–4.
39. Arrell M. Gibson, *The Chickasaws* (Norman, Okla., 1971), 6, 31–33.
40. Good analyses of the French strategy and their use of Indian allies are in Richard White, *The Roots of Dependency: Subsistence, Environment, and Social Change among the Choctaws, Pawnees, and Navajos* (Lincoln, Nebr., 1983), chap. 3; and Daniel H. Usner, Jr., *Indians, Settlers, & Slaves in a Frontier Exchange Economy: The Lower Mississippi Valley before 1783* (Chapel Hill, N.C., 1992), part 1.
41. Gibson, *The Chickasaws*, chap. 2; James Troy Robinson, "Fort Assumption: The First Recorded History of White Man's Activity on the Site of Memphis," *West Tennessee Historical Society Papers*, 5 (1951): 62–78.
42. Jerry E. Clark, *The Shawnee*, rev. ed. (Lexington, Ky., 1993), 11–14.
43. Ibid., 18, 62–63.
44. Robert E. Corlew, *Tennessee: A Short History*, 2d ed. (Knoxville, 1990), 18, 28; Harriette Simpson Arnow, *Seedtime on the Cumberland* (New York, 1960), 73.
45. Anthropologist Bruce G. Trigger discusses this phenomenon in the context of opposing schools of cultural relativists and rationalists, the former arguing that traditional symbolic uses of trade goods was more important than utilitarian "rational" uses. He argues strongly for the latter. "Early Native North American Responses to European Contact: Romantic Versus Rationalistic Interpretations," *Journal of American History* 77 (Mar. 1991): 1195–1215.
46. White, *Roots of Dependency*, 65–67; Joel W. Martin, "Southeastern Indians and the English Trade in Skins and Slaves," in Hudson, *Forgotten Centuries*, 314, 319.
47. Satz, *Tennessee's Indian Peoples*, 34–35.
48. This model appears in its classic form in Immanuel Wallerstein, *The Modern World System: Capitalist Agriculture and the Origin of the European World Economy in the*

Sixteenth Century (New York, 1974), and *The Modern World System II: Mercantilism and the Consolidation of the European World Economy, 1600–1750* (New York, 1980). Richard White, in *Roots of Dependency,* applies this model to the Choctaws of the colonial and early national periods. See also Martin, "Southeastern Indians," 305.

49. Trigger, "Early Native Responses to European Contact," 1212–13.

50. David H. Corkran, *The Cherokee Frontier: Conflict and Survival, 1740–62* (Norman, Okla., 1962), chap. 16. It should be noted that British authorities and white settlers had committed similar atrocities against the Cherokees.

51. Richard White, *The Middle Ground: Indians, Empires, and Republics in the Great lakes Region, 1650–1815* (New York, 1991), x. White's analysis, while confined to events in the Upper Great Lakes region, is also useful in discussing Indian-white relations in other areas.

52. See, for example, Theda Perdue, *Slavery and the Evolution of Cherokee Society, 1540–1866* (Knoxville: Univ. of Tennessee Press, 1979); and, for a more general overview, Gary B. Nash, *Red, White & Black: The Peoples of Early North America,* 3d ed. (Englewood Cliffs, N.J., 1992), chap. 12.

53. For actions in the Tennessee backcountry during this period, see Samuel Cole Williams, *Tennessee During the Revolutionary War* (Nashville, 1944; reprint, Knoxville, 1974), especially chaps. 8–9. Interesting commentary on the ideological perspectives of frontier leaders is in Jack P. Greene, "Independence, Improvement and Authority: Toward a Framework for Understanding the Histories of the Southern Backcountry during the Era of the American Revolution," in Thad W. Tate and Peter Albert, eds., *An Uncivil War: The Southern Backcountry during the American Revolution* (Charlottesville, Va., 1985), 3–36. There is every reason to believe that Tennessee's settlers were similar to those in Kentucky in their quest for lands. See Stephen Aron, "Pioneers and Profiteers: Land Speculation and the Homestead Ethic in Frontier Kentucky," *Western Historical Quarterly* 23 (May 1992): 179–98. A fine account of Indian participation in events of the period is James H. O'Donnell III, *Southern Indians in the American Revolution* (Knoxville, 1973); see also Colin G. Calloway, *The American Revolution in Indian Country: Crisis and Diversity in Native American Communities* (New York, 1995), especially 182–212, for Cherokee participation and the central role of Chota.

54. For analysis of their counterparts on the northern middle ground, see White, *Middle Ground,* chaps. 5–6, 10. Recent discussion of *metis* in the South includes Hatley, *The Dividing Paths,* 59–63, 208–210; Kathryn Braund, *Deerskins & Duffels: Creek Indian Trade with Anglo-America, 1685–1815* (Lincoln, Nebr., 1993), 78–79 and chap. 9; and Gibson, *The Chickasaws,* 65, and chap. 4.

55. Hatley, *Dividing Paths,* 61.

56. Sara G. Parker, "The Transformation of Cherokee Appalachia" (Ph.D. diss., Univ. of California, Berkeley, 1991), abstract, 1. Parker's dissertation is not altogether convincing in evidence and argumentation, but many of her points regarding kinship and mediation are essentially correct.

57. Corkran, *The Cherokee Frontier,* 196; Hatley, *Dividing Paths,* 148.

58. Parker, "The Transformation of Cherokee Appalachia," chap. 4; see also Clara Sue Kidwell, "Indian Women as Cultural Mediators," *Ethnohistory* 39 (Spring 1992):

102–3; Norma Tucker, "Nancy Ward, Ghighau of the Cherokees," *Georgia Histori-cal Quarterly* 53 (June 1969): 192–99; and Ben Harris McClary, "Nancy Ward, Beloved Woman," *Tennessee Historical Quarterly* 21 (Dec. 1962): 352–64.

59. Quoted in Williams, *Tennessee During the Revolutionary War,* 201.

60. White, *Middle Ground,* 286; Parker, "Transformation of Cherokee Appalachia," 131.

61. Leonard Raulston and James W. Livingood, *Sequatchie: A Story of the Southern Cumberlands* (Knoxville, 1974), 23–24, 35–42; Williams, *Tennessee During the Revo-lutionary War,* 205–12; The best accounts of the Chickamaugas are John P. Brown, *Old Frontiers: The Story of the Cherokee Indians from Earliest Times to the Date of Their Removal to the West, 1838* (Kingsport, Tenn., 1938), and James P. Pate, "The Chicka-mauga: A Forgotten Segment of Indian Resistance on the Southern Frontier" (Ph.D. diss., Mississippi State Univ., 1969). See also Robert S. Cotterill, *The Southern Indi-ans: The Story of the Civilized Tribes Before Removal* (Norman, Okla., 1954), 54–55.

62. White, *Middle Ground,* chap. 5; Brown, *Old Frontiers,* 171; McLoughlin, *Cherokee Renascence in the New Republic,* 20.

63. Wood, "Changing Population of the Colonial South," 65.

64. Gregory Evans Dowd, *A Spirited Resistance: The North American Indian Struggle for Unity, 1745–1815* (Baltimore, 1992), chap. 3, and 109–110.

65. Dowd, in *A Spirited Resistance,* says the accommodationist chiefs at first saw the revo-lution as a means of retaining or regaining their earlier influence, but after their de-cisive defeats in 1776 "powerful Cherokee factions within the nation rejected any policy of militant resistance to the new republic" (49, 54 [quotes]). The key word here, perhaps, is *militant;* there is no doubt that even within those same factions less overt forms of resistance continued. See also Hatley, *Dividing Paths,* chap. 17. Parker, "Transformation of Cherokee Appalachia," discusses the Chickamauga impact on traditional Cherokee society.

66. Gibson, in *The Chickasaws,* chapter 4, discusses the intrigues of Spanish and Ameri-can factions among the Chickasaws; see also Joseph C. Clifft, "Pawns of the Game: The Role of the Chickasaws in United States–Spanish Relations, 1783–1803" (Master's thesis, Memphis State Univ., 1992); and Jack D. L. Holmes, "The Ebb-Tide of Spanish Military Power on the Mississippi: Fort San Fernando de las Bar-rancas, 1795–1798," *East Tennessee Historical Society's Publications* 36 (1964): 23–44. The Nashville treaty was actually with the state of Virginia, since in those confused times it was not clear whether the confederation government or the various states had jurisdiction in Indian affairs. The first federal treaty with the Chickasaws was at Hopewell, South Carolina, in January 1786.

67. Schroedl, *Overhill Cherokee Archaeology,* 14, 452; Cotterill, *The Southern Indians,* 79; McLoughlin, *Cherokee Renascence in the New Republic,* 23; Woodward, *The Chero-kees,* 109.

68. William Michael Toomey, "Prelude to Statehood: The Southwest Territory, 1790–1796" (Ph.D. diss., Univ. of Tennessee, 1991), 115–16, 189, 191–98.

69. James Roper, "Fort Adams and Fort Pickering," *West Tennessee Historical Society Papers* 24 (1970): 5–29.

70. Gibson, *The Chickasaws,* 95.

71. The various Cherokee treaties are conveniently consulted in Charles J. Kappler, ed., *Indian Affairs: Laws and Treaties* (5 vols., Washington, 1904–1941).

72. Extensive discussion of the various cessions, as well as detailed maps, are in Charles C. Royce, *The Cherokee Nation of Indians: A Narrative of their Official Relations with the Colonial and Federal Governments* (Washington, 1887; reprint, Chicago, 1975).

73. Gibson, *The Chickasaws,* 99–105; Satz, *Tennessee's Indian Peoples,* 53–54.

74. Many scholars have discussed Cherokee civilization, including William G. McLoughlin, *Cherokees and Missionaries, 1789–1839* (New Haven, 1984); McLoughlin, *Renascence in the New Republic*; Henry Thompson Malone, *Cherokees of the Old South: A People in Transition* (Athens, Ga., 1956); Grant Foreman, *The Five Civilized Tribes* (Norman, Okla., 1934); and Mary Young, "The Cherokee Nation: Mirror of the Republic," *American Quarterly* 33 (Winter 1981): 502–23.

75. William G. McLoughlin and Walter H. Conser, Jr., "The Cherokees in Transition: A Statistical Analysis of the Federal Cherokee Census of 1835," *Journal of American History* 44 (Dec. 1977): 702. An interesting analysis of this and related points is in Young, "The Cherokee Nation."

76. Sarah Hitch Hill, "Cherokee Patterns: Interweaving Women and Baskets in History" (Ph.D. diss., Emory Univ., 1991); see also Betty J. Duggan and Brett H. Riggs, "Cherokee Basketry: An Evolving Tradition," in Duggan and Riggs, *Cherokee Basketry* (Knoxville, 1991), 23–46. The Selu stories appear in James Mooney, *Myths of the Cherokee* (Washington, 1900), 242–49. See also Thomas Hatley, "Cherokee Women Farmers Hold Their Ground," in Robert D. Mitchell, ed., *Appalachian Frontiers: Settlement, Society, and Development in the Preindustrial Era* (Lexington, Ky., 1991), 49.

77. Extensive data on demography and property throughout the Cherokee Nation are in *Census Roll, 1835, of Cherokee Indians East of the Mississippi. With Index* (Microfilm T496, National Archives, Washington).

78. An excellent overview of Jacksonian Indian policy is Ronald N. Satz, *American Indian Policy in the Jacksonian Era* (Lincoln, Nebr., 1975).

79. A current listing of works related to this topic is William L. Anderson, "Bibliographical Essay," in William L. Anderson, ed., *Cherokee Removal: Before and After* (Athens, Ga., 1991), 139–47.

80. For insight on such matters, see Fredrik Barth, ed., *Ethnic Groups and Boundaries: The Social Organization of Culture Difference* (Boston, 1969), introduction.

81. Among those remnants are federally recognized tribes like the Eastern Band of Cherokee Indians in North Carolina. Two recent studies of this important group are John R. Finger, *Cherokee Americans: The Eastern Band of Cherokees in the Twentieth Century* (Lincoln, Nebr., 1991); and Sharlotte Neely, *Snowbird Cherokees: People of Persistence* (Athens, Ga., 1991). See also Walter L. Williams, ed., *Southeastern Indians Since the Removal Era* (Athens, Ga., 1979); and J. Anthony Paredes, ed., *Indians of the Southeastern United States in the Late 20th Century* (Tuscaloosa, 1992).

THE FEMININE DIMENSION IN THE VOLUNTEER STATE

■ MARGARET RIPLEY WOLFE

■

■ *Editor's Note:* In her chronicle of women's contributions to Ten-
    nessee history, from the prehistoric era to modern times, Wolfe
■   explores the interrelationship between women's status within soci-
    ety and the nature of gender relations between the sexes. The
■   shared work and dependence between men and women make the
    history of Tennessee women an integral part of the past. Events
■   such as the suffrage fight of 1919–20 transformed not only state
    politics, but also the national political culture. Famous women,
■   like Nancy Ward or Anne Dallas Dudley, as well as the not-so-
    famous, like Elizabeth Sexton, left Tennessee with "a rich heritage
■   and impressive record of strength and perseverance."

Much of the nation's and the state's written history has been characterized by sexism, ethnocentricity, and classism. Chroniclers, both professional and amateur, have tended to focus on "dead white men," to emphasize the European experience, and to reserve the past for the privileged.
Nonetheless, long before explorers ventured into the American South during the sixteenth and seventeenth centuries, rich, vibrant, self-sustaining
cultures had existed and even flourished. Indeed, the human experience in
the Tennessee country spans literally thousands of years, crosses racial boundaries, and cuts across class lines. The feminine dimension of that history is
surely no less varied. The female life cycle represents a common denominator regardless of race and class, and, to a greater or lesser degree, all of
Tennessee's women—red, white, and black—have known the subordination
of a patriarchal order. Beyond these two distinguishing and important factors, very little else lends unity to their collective lives. Nonetheless, after two
hundred years of statehood, women's status and gender relations remain in-
tertwined just as they were two centuries ago.

King's Mountain, the Alamo, Shiloh, Crockett, Boone, Houston, Jackson, Forrest, and York, symbols of the Volunteer State's martial spirit and the names of its mythic heroes, leap from the pages of the state's history. White males have most assuredly set the tone for the state's development and, for better or worse, have stamped their indelible influence upon it. Patriarchy has permeated both public and private life and has been reflected as much in the statute books as in family governance. Although male dominance has had a long-running heyday in the American South, historic forces have gradually undermined its overriding influence on female lives. Furthermore, Tennessee women, as well as those elsewhere in the United States, have been affected not only by local and regional but also by national and international forces.[1]

Describing and analyzing the history of Tennessee women is a report from the trenches in a field of research that is still relatively new. Feminist scholars have tried and failed to discover a golden age for their sisters and the sisterhood in the American past. Paradoxically, females in this state and the nation still constitute a *numerical majority* and a *political minority.* Achieving equality for the feminine gender in American society is a political objective, and expanding democracy is in keeping with American ideology. Women's studies and women's history have political overtones, but acknowledging the fact that the *personal* is *political* does not obviate the high quality and genuine significance of the research that has been done. Indeed, for the last twenty-five years or so, those cultivating the fertile field of women's history have amassed a considerable body of important and useful literature. Furthermore, a great deal of information about the circumstances of the feminine past can be gleaned from traditional social, political, and economic histories.

As a specialty, women's history is intricately linked to the so-called "new social history," which has contributed, above all else, to an awareness of the collective diversity of the national population. The "new social history" has legitimized the study of lower- and working-class elements, the full range of ethnic and racial groups, urban life, family structure, and gender and sex roles as well as other tantalizing topics. Indeed, the "new social history" has encouraged the study of history "from the bottom up" instead of "from the top down." Some Americans have lamented the passing of homogenized history, that is to say a unified concept of the past, but, in the long run, the gains have exceeded the losses. The result has been a more inclusive, less exclusive account of the past.[2]

Ironically, by their very devotion to traditional sources and methodology, historians have sometimes placed unnecessary constraints on their work. Where earlier generations once thought no evidence could be found to as-

sess "ordinary people and everyday lives," contemporary scholars have discovered a mother lode. Without forsaking the standard research techniques,
they have embraced more innovative methodology as well. Sometimes the
outcome has been to lift from obscurity the lives of those heretofore relatively
unknown. Historians in pursuit of the common people and inspired by the
"new social history" have also cast off the constraints of conventional written documents. They have looked to oral traditions, architecture, photographs, music, films, and material culture as well as more conventional
sources. Furthermore, they have sometimes forged successful alliances with
literary authorities, museum staffs, anthropologists, archaeologists, cultural
geographers, and folklorists.[3]

Historians, for example, are indebted to archaeologists for what is known
about Native Americans who occupied the Tennessee country before European explorers and travelers began to commit to writing their impressions of
the inhabitants. Between A.D. 1000 and 1500, Native Americans identified
as the Mississippian Culture built expansive towns that supported an ever-
increasing population. Flat-topped earthen mounds lifted the temples and
the dwellings of the elite above their more ordinary fellows. Such patterns of
existence placed a greater dependence on agriculture, which fell largely within
the purview of the females; corn became the principal crop. The prehistoric
version of the "Great Busk," or green-corn ceremony, marked the conclusion of the Mississippian ceremonial and agricultural year. This ritual, with
its dancing, gaming, and feasting, promoted unity among the clans, honored
outstanding warriors, and paid homage to the deities of fertility for a successful
crop. Along with concentrated populations and the reliance on agriculture,
organized chiefdoms also took shape. Political development of this nature,
albeit primitive, derived from the increased territoriality and more frequent
warfare that had come to characterize Native American society in the Tennessee country on the eve of European exploration and colonization.[4]

Reactions of Native American females to their initial encounters with the
Europeans went unrecorded. Relying on the accounts of soldiers, explorers,
and travelers, historians can only surmise what responses those contacts elicited. The de Soto expedition seems to have provided the first opportunity for
interaction of the two races in the Tennessee country. Although the accounts
are decidedly vague, the Spaniards may have been in or near present-day
Tennessee when they observed "a country covered with fields of maize of
luxuriant growth" and then later a village consisting of three hundred houses,
which "stood in a pleasant spot, bordered by small streams, that took their
rise in the adjacent mountains."[5]

As their travels continued, de Soto and his men found themselves lulled into a false sense of security by the seemingly peaceful nature of the natives. After what they claimed to be an unprovoked attack that reportedly lasted nine hours, the Europeans adopted a harsh approach. During 1541, in the vicinity of present-day Memphis, this same Spanish expedition came upon a village, "rushed into it in a disorderly manner, took many Indian prisoners, of both sexes and of all ages, and pillaged the houses." Although the native men had reportedly been "enraged" by how the Spanish had imprisoned their wives and children and abused their property, they finally decided to negotiate. Ultimately, "the prisoners and plunder were restored."[6] In 1673, more than 130 years later, the Frenchmen Jacques Marquette, a Catholic missionary, and Louis Jolliet, a fur trader, passed through the same vicinity. They recorded the presence of an Indian village at Chickasaw Bluff, noting that "the head-dress and clothing of their women were like those of the Huron squaws."[7] Yet more than another century later, in 1797, Francis Baily, a young Englishman, mentioned seeing on the bluff five or six white male settlers, who had allied themselves with the Indians by marriage.[8]

Whereas the Spanish, by their own accounts, tended to suggest that they wreaked violence upon Indian women, similar records of the English often claimed that Native American females besieged them with unwanted advances and overwhelmed them with uninvited attentions. In the warm summer climates of what became the southern United States, Native American women dispensed with unnecessary garments. European men in general associated nakedness with licentiousness and found the absence of clothing or scanty dress uncommonly arousing. They also scrutinized the relative sexual freedom and overall conduct of Indian women, condemning it on one hand but maximizing it to their advantage on the other. The bawdy sense of humor that some Indian women displayed, their directness in sexual matters, their seeming lack of modesty, as well as the occurrence of premarital relations, easy divorce, and the practice of sororal polygamy, contradicted European male notions of appropriate feminine conduct.[9]

Yet historians often find themselves at the mercy of limited and distorted written documents. It is reasonably safe to assume that the accounts of travelers in the American South reveal at least as much about European men as they do about Native American women. William Bartram, on a trip through the South during the 1770s, noted in his journal that Cherokee women were "tall, slender, erect and of a delicate frame, their features formed with perfect symmetry, their countenance cheerful and friendly, and they move with a becoming grace and dignity."[10] The eighteenth-century English trader-author James Adair, however, remarked with disgust that the Cherokee "have been a considerable while under petticoat-government, and allow their women full liberty to plant their brows with horns as oft as they please, without fear of punishment."[11]

What the European men found especially peculiar and grievous, given the fact that they regarded women as property, was the relative independence of Indian women and the seeming lack of concern or control on the part of their male counterparts. From the European perspective, an honorable man held the responsibility to protect the chastity of his wife and daughters. Native males sometimes not only tolerated but even encouraged sexual activity between visitors and women who "belonged" to the native men. Matrilocal residence patterns and matrilineal kinship proved equally baffling to the English as well as other Western Europeans. When marriage occurred among southern Indians, the male took up residence among his wife's relatives because all buildings, garden plots, and sections of the common fields belonged to her lineage. Children traced kinship through their female relatives, and when and if divorce occurred, children remained with their mothers. Men had no claim to either dwellings they occupied or the offspring they fathered.[12] By the early nineteenth century, southern Indians came to be known as the "Five Civilized Tribes" in recognition of the alacrity with which they had adapted to transplanted European culture. Among other things, this meant a redefinition of gender roles. As a consequence, "women began to fade from economic and political life in the early nineteenth century."[13]

In the meantime, however, white and red men found the Cherokee women to be a feisty lot. Indian men turned on Fort Loudoun, the westernmost English outpost in America located on the Little Tennessee River, during the French and Indian War and tried to starve the garrison into submission; Cherokee women, however, who had white "husbands" at the fort, smuggled food to their loved ones before the defenders ultimately surrendered. According to the commander, Raymond Demere, the native females also gathered much-needed intelligence, which was "amongst the Indians . . . always best." They likewise defied their own war chief who threatened to kill them if they did not stop their associations with the men at Fort Loudoun, laughed at him, and explained that their relatives would avenge their deaths. Cherokee females and the few of European descent at Fort Loudoun must have come in contact with each other.[14]

Of the Native American women who lent sustenance to the first white settlers, the name of Nancy Ward, "War Woman of the Cherokee," is in the forefront. Born around 1738, Nanye'hi of the Wolf clan at Chota in present-day Tennessee, the principal town of the Overhill Cherokee, she rose to the most exalted female position among her people when her Indian mate fell in battle around 1755. Taking up his gun, she assumed his place. With the prestigious political and ceremonial status of the "War Woman," there also reposed considerable authority. "By the wave of a swan's wing," wrote Lieutenant Henry Timberlake, she could "deliver a wretch condemned by the council, and already tied to the stake." Nanye'hi supposedly saved the captive, Lydia (Mrs. William) Bean, in 1776 but allowed a boy taken at the same time to be burned at the stake. Nanye'hi took as her second spouse a South Carolina trader, Bryant Ward, from which her English name, Nancy Ward, derived. He fathered Nancy's daughter, Elizabeth, before he returned to his South Carolina family after spending a few years in and around Chota. At the time of her death in 1822, Nancy Ward was keeping an inn along the federal road that ran from Georgia to Nashville; she died in the Ocoee River valley.[15]

Even as white influence undermined the political status of Cherokee women during the late eighteenth and early nineteenth centuries, the role of native females continued to transcend merely the ceremonial. In July 1781, white settlers in northeast Tennessee convened a peace conference with the Cherokee at Long Island on the Holston. Following what to the whites must have been considered a highly unusual occurrence—that is, a speech by a female, Nancy Ward—negotiations ceased; the Cherokee relinquished no additional land at that time.[16] In 1808–10, and again in 1817–19, the Cherokee Nation divided over the question of cession of lands and removal. During both 1817 and 1818, the women's councils, influenced by Nancy Ward, submitted petitions to their national council. Although their pleas seemed to be increasingly couched in what some historians have considered the deferential language of the "cult of true womanhood," the Cherokee women clearly opposed removal.[17] Nonetheless, by the 1830s, they, too, embarked on the "Trail of Tears" when the United States government coerced the Cherokee out of their homeland. The elderly, the sick, pregnant women, and the very young received no quarter. By around 1844, between one-quarter and one-third of southern Indians had died in the process, among them Quatie, the wife of Chief John Ross, who himself had opposed removal in principle and refused to sign the Treaty of New Echota.[18]

The interaction and intermingling of three races characterized early Tennessee history. Yet, the advancing frontier and the presence of males of European descent in the backcountry contributed to the declining status of Indian women within their native cultures, perpetuated and reinforced the

Women at the Thompson farm, Knox County, c. 1900. Susan Foust, Cleo Thompson, and Mary Miller show the tools of their trade as farm women. Century Farms Collection, MTSU Center for Historic Preservation.

subordination of white females, and introduced the enslavement of their black counterparts. The culture that was transplanted and adapted to the American environment not only permitted a patriarchal order but indeed perhaps an even more exaggerated version. Harriette Simpson Arnow, a native of Kentucky and the author of *Seedtime on the Cumberland* (1960) and *Flowering of the Cumberland* (1963), observed that "the old Southwest was not won by armies, but crept westward forted farm by forted farm," relying on females and families for the underpinnings of civilization.[19] In a 1958 newspaper interview, Arnow suggested that life was better for women in the eighteenth century because they "did not have to compete with men then." Instead, they were "yoke-mates, pulling together."[20] "That the frontier created a spirit of equality among the sexes could not be farther from the truth," counters historian David Hackett Fischer. Men expected women to perform the most grueling tasks associated with clearing forests, breaking ground, raising crops, and tending livestock, but that was about the extent of sharing and equality. "Travelers were startled to observe delicate females knock down beef cattle with a felling ax, and then roll down their sleeves, remove their bloody aprons, tidy their hair, and invite their visitors to tea."[21]

Calamities and tough choices occurred with regularity. Internecine frontier warfare interrupted the routine of settlers' lives and punctuated relations between the Indian inhabitants and the aggressive whites on the Tennessee frontier during the late eighteenth century. The Revolutionary experience also affected the daily existence of many American women.[22] More of them than not found themselves in passive roles, the acted upon rather than the actors, although this was not always the case. Backcountry females managed to stay out of the line of British fire, but King George III's Indian allies kept the frontier ablaze.[23] On Powder Branch in the Watauga settlement of what would become northeast Tennessee, Mary Patton made the gunpowder that sustained the Overmountain Men at the tide-turning Battle of King's Mountain in 1780. Her famous kettle reposes at Rocky Mount Historic Site.

As pioneers moved westward, the females among them experienced their share of hardships and dangers. The Donelson party, for example, came under attack as it traveled hundreds of miles by flatboats on backcountry rivers from northeast Tennessee to the vicinity of present-day Nashville. In one such instance, the boat of Jonathan Jennings "ran on a large rock." The leader of the expedition, Colonel John Donelson, recorded that "the boat was saved chiefly by the exertions of Mrs. Jennings, who got out of the boat and shoved her off." Mrs. Jennings and her daughter, Mrs. Peyton, "who was the night before delivered of an infant," also threw some articles overboard to lighten the load. Mary Purnell Donelson, the sixteen-year-old bride of John Donelson III, recalled that "accidentally with the blankets & bedding in the hurry, fear, & confusion, was thrown the young child of Mrs. Peyton, & did not discover the mistake until some time later."[24]

Violence against white women was hardly confined to Indian attacks; their own men sometimes tormented them. Although it remained for the twentieth century to provide a label, "battered wife syndrome," the practice itself is an ancient one. Early court records in Tennessee shed some light on the subject. The illiterate Elizabeth Crawley had lived with her new husband, William, for a few months around 1800 in North Carolina before moving to northeast Tennessee. She swore before a justice of the peace for Carter County, Tennessee, that her spouse "frequently beat and abused her in a cruel and outragious [sic] manner, that compelled her to leave him and seek shelter with a brother of hers without any cause or provocation; and kept her in great dread and alarm by threatening to blow up the house with gun powder and destroy her." According to her account, he abused her, burned all of her clothes except those on her back, and then abandoned her. In 1841, a male boarder at a residence in northeast Tennessee swore that he had been awakened during the night of March 31 "by a noyse [*sic*] between Said [Randolph] McAlister and his wife and . . . asked McAlister what was the matter[.] He McAlister made no reply but went out of the house and came in directly again and commenced beating her again and beat her three times and swore by his maker that he will kill her and send her to hell."[25]

Following wandering husbands often also meant separation from parents, siblings, relatives, and friends. For most frontier women, isolation and loneliness exacerbated an already difficult existence. "On the Southwestern frontier, the planter family underwent 'nuclearization.' . . . [M]en, women, and children found themselves alone, far from the many collateral relatives who populated the seaboard," according to historian Joan E. Cashin. Women "experienced all of the isolation of modernity with none of its easy geographic mobility. Freedom of movement was a privilege in the antebellum South, not a right, and most women's kinship networks deteriorated, just as they had feared. The final result of all these changes was that women became even more dependent on men than they had been at home." As for the men, they "expressed their independence . . . drinking, gambling, and fighting with a new sense of license," which may also have been reflected in relatively uninhibited sexual relations with slave women.[26]

A recent study of divorce and the legal status of women in Tennessee during the first six decades of the nineteenth century found that the divorce statute of 1799 was in keeping with "the Revolutionary ideals of personal freedom" to be found in the states west of the Appalachians and "the social flux of their own pioneer conditions." This law punished fallen females and protected virtuous women. Its "progressive quality," however, stemmed from a "conservative purpose." The 1799 legislation "set the standard for subsequent reforms of the divorce process that sought to ensure the spontaneous acceptance of patriarchal marriage by eliminating its worst abuses just as the southern master class would analogously eliminate gratuitous cruelties in the slave system during the ante-bellum period."[27]

The aggrieved parties were not always women, for early Tennessee had a fair number of lusty, aggressive females. Toward the end of the eighteenth century, Russell Bean, the son of the first acknowledged Tennessee settler and himself probably the first white child born in the Tennessee country, found himself confronted with prima facie evidence of his wife's infidelity. Returning home after an extended absence, which seemed to preclude his having fathered her new offspring, Russell discovered his wife possessed of an infant. He went off to Jonesborough and embarked upon a "roaring drunk." Making his way back to his residence, "he picked up the child from its cradle, pulled his hunting knife from its sheath and cut off both its ears, saying that he 'had marked it so that it would not get mixed up with his children.'"[28] During the early 1830s, Elizabeth Sexton of Blount County reportedly entertained two men at once in her husband's bed and had copulated with yet another somewhat publicly in broad daylight declaring him "much of a man." When a local deacon called attention to her unseemly conduct, she declared: "My ass is my own and I will do as I please with it."[29] The Beans divorced but were later reunited in holy matrimony. As for the cuckolded husband of Elizabeth Sexton, he failed to impress a divorce committee who regarded him as unmanly for having permitted such behavior without taking appropriate action.

On the Tennessee frontier, the prevailing view held that men should be men and women should be women. As fluid as pioneer society seems to have been, the trans-Allegheny folk had not divested themselves entirely of traditional cultural baggage and prescribed codes of conduct. Such antebellum ideals as those of "the southern lady" and "the true woman" grafted easily enough to the well-entrenched patriarchal order west of the mountains. The image of "the southern lady" derived from rules of conduct carried to America. That prescribed etiquette, in turn, drew on chivalric codes that lay deeply embedded in Western civilization.

The eminent historian Arthur M. Schlesinger, Sr., discovered that seventeenth-century English manuals of etiquette established the standards of modesty, chastity, godliness, and compassion for a gentlewoman. Obedience to her husband supplanted obedience to her parents. If her spouse proved unfaithful, she was expected to pretend ignorance of his infidelities; if he proved quick to anger, she was not to provoke him; and if he turned into a drunkard, she was to tolerate such behavior as a balance to her own weakness.[30] Immense tracts of land held by individual owners, the relative isolation of rural life in the South, evangelical Protestantism, and the practice of slavery also encouraged the patriarchal order and, in turn, the submission of women.[31]

The "southern lady" ideal reached its ascendancy during the antebellum era and coexisted with yet another American model for feminine conduct, the "true woman." Described by historian Barbara Welter, "true womanhood," which impinged particularly on the lives of women north of the Mason-Dixon line, required "four cardinal virtues—piety, purity, submissiveness and domesticity. Put them all together and they spelled mother, daughter, sister, wife—woman."[32] Although intended as codes of conduct for females of the upper classes, such ideals as the "southern lady" and the "true woman" may, in the long run, have had the greater consequences for the truly powerless—those poor unfortunates devoid of wealth and family prestige. Such women found themselves without political, economic, or social influence and therefore not only at the mercy of the male guardians of society but also would-be tormentors, who, in turn, had little to fear in the way of retaliation. Both class and race proved to be important variables.

Female behavior sometimes reaffirmed the ideals of the "southern lady" and the "true woman" but at other times abrogated them. Along with the thousands of nameless and faceless women who called Tennessee home during the first half of the nineteenth century, a cast of interesting and identifiable feminine characters paraded through the state during the antebellum era. They included the likes of Scotswoman Frances Wright of the doomed Nashoba emancipation experiment; Rachel Donelson Robards Jackson, who was first a bigamist and then a political liability; and Eliza Allen, whose failed marriage to Sam Houston contributed to his resignation from the governorship and catapulted him into the annals of the Lone Star State.[33]

Sarah Childress Polk served as James K. Polk's political advisor. She also dispatched political intelligence to him while he was on the campaign trail and sent announcements of his forthcoming visits to local newspapers. As his unofficial campaign manager, she helped win the governorship for her husband. Later, when he ascended to the presidency of the United States, Sarah continued to be his partner in politics as well as matrimony. Betty Boyd Caroli, in *First Ladies*, writes that Sarah Childress Polk was "the most outspoken and politically involved wife since Abigail Adams." When James K. Polk and Sarah Childress married in 1824, his relatives reportedly thought that she displayed "a great deal more spice and more independence of judgment than was fitting in one woman."[34]

During the antebellum era, a few Tennessee women managed to secure fine educations by the standards of the day while some others acquired the rudiments of learning; some participated in political rallies and religious revivals; and still others expressed themselves through charities and benevolence. Samuel Carrick, who headed Blount College in Knoxville, the forerunner of the University of Tennessee, admitted women as well as men. At least five females attended during the 1790s, among them Margaret Blount, the daughter of William Blount, governor of the Southwest Territory and Tennessee's first United States senator.[35] Church-sponsored schools probably offered young women the best hope for advanced instruction, among them the Columbia Female Institute, founded in Tennessee by Episcopal bishops Leonidas

Polk and James Hervey Otey.[36] The Nashville Female Academy garnered some recognition as one of the better educational institutions available to women of the antebellum South. Its graduates included the intelligent and beautiful Adelicia Hayes Franklin Acklen Cheatham who, during the Civil War, managed to move 2,800 bales of cotton through both Confederate and Union lines to New Orleans and ship it out to England.[37]

The rough-and-ready outdoor political rallies and religious revivals of the antebellum era may have served to loosen the constraints of traditional feminine roles. Historian Jayne Crumpler DeFiore observes in a recent article that women "engaged in the emotional antics evoked by itinerant preachers— falling, jerking, rolling, dancing, running, singing, laughing, and barking— and at political rallies in the emotional responses evoked by orators—singing, waving handkerchiefs, and quivering to the words of the speakers for hours on end."[38] Another historian, Joe L. Kincheloe, Jr., had earlier speculated that "an opportunity to assert themselves in a manner never before allowed in conventional society. . . may have aroused women's appetites for more important and autonomous roles in the society."[39] Such outlets seem not to have inspired much enthusiasm or sympathy among Tennessee women for abolitionism or feminism. Yet the anti-slavery movement commenced and intensified during this era, and the first women's rights convention in the United States convened at Seneca Falls, New York, in 1848.

Tennessee women, just as most of their southern and northern sisters, operated largely in a private realm with limited ventures into public life. Nonetheless, females of the antebellum South sometimes became involved in activities that took them beyond their proscribed sphere of home, farm, and plantation and the ordinary responsibilities of domesticity. The patriarchs usually deemed religious and charitable work appropriate to the female sex, and women remained relatively free of criticism from men, as well as others of their own sex, for what seemed to be such naturally feminine and pious outpourings. Autonomous women's organizations took shape during the decades before southern secession. Indeed, according to historian Marsha Wedell, "it was largely these religion-oriented societies that provided Memphis women with an established base from which support activities for the Confederacy would be quickly formed."[40]

Historian Carole Stanford Bucy has demonstrated that "community service through voluntary associations" represented "an important activity" for the distinguished Grundy family females. As early as 1816, Ann Rodgers Grundy and her daughter, Louisa Grundy McGavock, had formed a charitable society. Although the women had their own room at the First Presby-

terian Church's Society House, men managed by 1823 to usurp female authority for charitable work and to relegate their female counterparts to distributing Bibles. In 1820, Ann Rodgers Grundy had not only given birth to
her tenth child but had organized Nashville's first Sunday school to educate
poor children and provide them religious instruction. Grundy and her co-
hort in this endeavor, the Reverend Samuel P. Ament, a Methodist minister, drew criticism from the pulpits about town "for breaking the Sabbath
and disturbing the peace." To discourage prostitution and encourage virtue,
Nashville women founded the Women's Mission Home. The House of Industry for Females, organized in 1837 by a former mayor, Joseph Elliston,
trained women in needlework and other domestic skills in an effort to provide them with respectable and marketable skills.[41] On the eve of the Civil
War, the census takers counted 207 "professional prostitutes" in the state
capital, most of them native-born teenagers of Anglo-Saxon extraction. The
brothels of Tennessee reportedly ran the gamut from decadent opulence to
abject poverty.[42]

Among downtrodden females in Tennessee during the antebellum era, the
plight of poor white women, their about-to-be-dispossessed Native American sisters, and the enslavement of African American females suggested the
hypocrisy of southern chivalry, that much-touted and masculine-contrived
veneer of civility and decency. The "peculiar institution" of slavery, which
impinged more directly and forcefully on the lives of black women than any
other group associated with it, had been present in Tennessee since the earliest settlements. In 1800, just four years after statehood, East Tennessee
counted 5,510 black slaves; Middle Tennessee, 8,074; and West Tennessee,
at this point, none. Six decades later, in 1860, as the Civil War loomed, those
statistics stood respectively at 27,660; 146,105; and 101,954.[43] Not all of the
masters were white men, for the Cherokee at the time of removal owned slaves
themselves and had earlier been caught up in the traffic of Native American
captives with British slave traders during the eighteenth century.[44]

Historians know a tremendous amount about the practice of slavery
throughout the South and how it affected black men and women. Yet surprisingly little has been written about perpetual servitude and the lives of
African American females in the Volunteer State. Historian Lester C. Lamon,
for example, who himself laments historians' inattentiveness to the black
experience in Tennessee, offers noticeably little about African American females in his own books.[45] For the black woman, slavery meant that she faced
a life of perpetual servitude; that she could easily be sexually exploited by both
black and white males and mistreated and abused by white females; that her

children could be taken from her at the pleasure of her master; and that she herself was no more than property—to be bought, sold, mortgaged, swapped, or gambled away.[46]

The issue of miscegenation most certainly raised its head, and the slave trade, which operated side by side with the practice of slavery, flourished. By the late eighteenth century in Nashville, for example, according to historian Anita Shafer Goodstein, "Squire Molloy [had emancipated] his slave daughter and [made] her his heir."[47] Such individuals as future Confederate cavalry officer Nathan Bedford Forrest became heavily involved in the Memphis market during the 1840s and 1850s. Brian Steel Wills, one of Forrest's biographers, writes that "Forrest quickly established a widespread reputation as a good slave dealer. Contemporaries credited him with showing humanity, cleanliness, and care." Wills explains that "even if he did, it was due less to interest in the slaves than to self-interest. Whippings meant discipline. Discipline meant bad behavior. Bad behavior signaled trouble to potential customers. Self-interest demanded moderation." To be explicit, "it was in Forrest's best interests to treat his 'stock' [of both sexes] with some care."[48] Most Tennesseans owned no human chattel, but they sanctioned and supported the institution of slavery. On this issue, as well as the question of extending slavery into the territories, they found common cause with their southern brothers and sisters. This philosophical position placed them on a collision course with northern adversaries and positioned them for secession as the federal union began to disintegrate.

For the history of southern women in general and Tennessee women in particular, the Civil War stands as an important watershed. The bloody struggle itself and the ultimate Union victory eroded some of the underpinnings of the old patriarchal order. It would be a serious mistake, however, to suggest that male dominance in the region had come to a screeching halt because of Confederate defeat or that the outcome of the war foreshadowed the advent of a matriarchal society in Dixie. Indeed, historian Anne Firor Scott somewhat prematurely proclaimed in 1970 that the Civil War, in practical terms, had meant that "the patriarchy was dead, though many ideas associated with it lived on for years."[49] If that, in fact, had been the case—that patriarchy was dead from east to west and from north to south—then surely an Equal Rights Amendment would have been written into the United States Constitution before Scott's pronouncement. In those halcyon days of feminism, fondly remembered as "Women's Liberation," activists and scholars possessed a kind of youthful exuberance and optimism; time and defeat took care of most of that.

Scott, a pioneer in the field of southern women's history, produced path-breaking work and not only deserves respect but some latitude as well. Besides, other prominent historians, among them Mary Elizabeth Massey and Bell Irvin Wiley, had likewise tended to overestimate the war's subsequent influence on the lives of southern women.[50] Such sages as Wilbur J. Cash, however, had recognized that "sentimentality waxed fat on the theme of the Confederate soldier and the cause for which he had fought and died" and that fears of miscegenation between white females and black males produced "yet more florid notions about Southern womanhood and Southern Virtue" and fostered "yet more precious notions of modesty and decorous behavior for the southern female to live up to."[51] Northern victory and southern defeat did indeed bring emancipation of black men and women and may have undermined white masculine confidence for a spell below the Mason-Dixon line, but the outcome of the war did not mean an end to racial discrimination, class differences, or sexual subordination. Just as fervently as some daughters of Dixie anticipated the promise of the future, more of them either attempted to maintain the status quo or looked nostalgically to the past.[52]

For the southern women in question, the more immediate expedient was how they and their loved ones were to survive this bloody and chaotic era; for between 1861 and 1865, war literally came to their doorsteps. For Tennessee women it came especially quickly; by early 1862, Union troops had moved into the Confederate heartland of Middle Tennessee. In East Tennessee, Union sympathizers had to contend with martial law and the presence of Confederate soldiers. "Many women," historian Stephen V. Ash writes, "were especially unnerved by the prospect of confronting enemy soldiers while home alone. The thought of Yankee ruffians violating the sanctity of the home was disturbing enough; the thought of their violating a woman's body was terrifying." The fear of rape intensified as the occupation continued. The already relatively small number of women who dared to test and taunt the enemy diminished. Ash explains: "As Federal policy turned harsher and the soldiers grew less restrained and more vindictive, women became more anxious about their personal safety."[53]

During the mid-nineteenth century, even more than in the mid-twentieth, war remained a masculine arena. All of the leading roles went to men; women were merely supporting actresses. It fell to them to lend moral support, pray for divine intervention, nurse the sick, bury the dead, birth the babies, raise the children, and keep the home fires burning. A minuscule number dressed as men and took up arms, and a few of them spied on the enemy and passed information to Confederate officers. Most merely tried to keep a roof over their heads and to feed their children, helpless relatives, and themselves; some became homeless refugees, forced to rely on the kindnesses of acquaintances and strangers. Those with slaves sometimes faced off against surly and disobedient blacks, who expected any day to see freedom come riding up dressed in a blue uniform. When the last battle had been fought and the last army had surrendered, the public reconstruction of the South began; southern white women and men, who still had each other, began their own private one. Former slaves, newly emancipated by war, soon to be granted citizenship, and about to be enfranchised by constitutional amendment (the males among them supposedly acquired the right to vote), also commenced recreating their lives.[54]

Considering the devastation, destruction, and loss of life that had occurred, Tennesseans rallied remarkably well; and the state was spared the long, drawn-out Reconstruction experienced in some other sections of the South. The homegrown radicalism imposed on former Confederates by East Tennessee Republicans proved to be relatively brief, and that phase of the Volunteer State's history ended by 1870. Nonetheless, the highborn and the ordinary faced hard times and difficult readjustments during the latter part of the nineteenth century. Nationwide economic setbacks in the 1870s and 1890s affected Tennesseans, and perennial farm problems weighed heavily on a population that was still largely rural and agricultural. In this milieu, some rural women across the state participated enthusiastically, although often within carefully proscribed roles, in the agrarian protest movements. Historian Connie L. Lester remarks that "duty, harmony, and home were the words women used to characterize their sphere." Although "these were traditional values, phrased in old-fashioned language," they were "embraced by women looking forward, not backward." According to Lester, those particular rural women "demanded the same spirit of mutuality in the organization that defined their roles as working partners with their husbands."[55]

As rural life began to recede ever so gradually into American memory, the United States became a first-rate manufacturing power during the late nineteenth century. Urbanization and industrialization accompanied by dramatic changes in transportation and communication shaped this era in American history. Although Tennessee remained a rural state until the mid-twentieth century, its cities and towns, just as those elsewhere in the United States, grew rapidly during the late 1800s. Much of the reform impetus stemmed from urban problems, and reform crusades, in turn, often took shape in urban environments. Even those affecting rural populations usually emanated from, or revolved around, the state capitals or county seats. The impetus for women's involvement in public life, too, generally developed among females who resided in towns and cities or rural-based females who had the economic means and the wherewithal to establish contacts with like-minded women in other locations. The first generation of college-educated women in America made its way to institutions of higher learning, usually located in urban settings. Religious organizations and women's clubs proliferated in similar situations. Common experiences, however, did not always produce identical results. Both proactive and reactive women emerged from the same social, educational, and religious backgrounds. Furthermore, in the South, members of the United Daughters of the Confederacy and female reformers might be one and the same. Yet, the majority of women at the national, state, and local levels remained largely preoccupied with private matters and took no obvious interest in public life.[56]

Among the more civic-minded, religiosity shifted from personal piety to public concern and combined with other factors to catapult American women into "domestic politics."[57] The "true woman" gave way to the "new woman" during the late nineteenth century, and this era spawned the first generation of southern feminism. The range of interests included education, social welfare, settlement work, public health, temperance, race relations, labor conditions, and poverty, as well as the status of women. Modern-minded southern women embraced the club movement, which allowed them to dabble in respectable reform—meaning those efforts directed toward gradual, constructive change within acceptable parameters. *Southern lady* and all that it implied proved to be a blessing rather a bane as this generation of activists gingerly moved into the public arena. Caroline Meriwether Goodlett founded the United Daughters of the Confederacy in Nashville; Mary Clementia Currey Dorris helped to organize and charter the Ladies' Hermitage Association there; Silena Moore (Mrs. T. P.) Holman of Fayetteville became an outspoken advocate of temperance; and females in small towns and cities across the state enthusiastically embraced club work.[58]

Nor were such efforts lily-white. Black women, too, responded to the reform spirit of the day. In 1895, in Nashville, prominent African American females organized the Phyllis Wheatley Club, which devoted itself to social uplift in the black community; this group affiliated with the National Federation of Colored Women's Clubs. Similar clubs appeared in Knoxville, Chattanooga, Memphis, and Jackson.[59] During the same decade, however, Memphis-based Ida B. Wells, a black activist, educator, and newspaper editor, publicly denounced lynching, which placed her beyond the pale of proper conduct for females of either race and put her life in jeopardy.[60]

Prohibition preoccupied the Volunteer State's male politicians during much of the Progressive era, but woman suffrage brought national distinction to Tennessee as it became the pivotal state. During this era, the solons managed to give some time to such matters as working conditions for children and women and a married women's emancipation law. Just on the eve of the big ratification fight, they extended suffrage to females in national and municipal elections. The story of the battle to ratify the Nineteenth Amendment has been told and retold in the press and by professional historians.[61] Suffice it to say that after a long hot summer, a special session of the legislature, and an intense lobbying effort by both suffragists and anti-suffragists, the state's lawmakers did their duty in 1920. They approved the Susan B. Anthony Amendment, making Tennessee the thirty-sixth of forty-eight states to do so, and the Nineteenth Amendment became the law of the land. The heroines of the suffrage movement in the Volunteer State included such names as Elizabeth Avery Meriwether of Memphis, who seems to have been the state's pioneer suffragist; Lizzie Crozier French of Knoxville; Abby C. Milton of Chattanooga; Ann Keys Worley of Bluff City; and Anne Dallas Dudley of Nashville—to name but a few. Josephine A. Pearson, a native of Sumner County, led the opposition.

In the South, only Texas, Arkansas, Kentucky, and Tennessee counted themselves among the original thirty-six. A half-century later, the battle for ratification of the Equal Rights Amendment proved equally difficult in the southern states. Of the fifteen that refused to approve the ERA, which doomed it to failure, nine were former Confederate states. Tennessee also joined a few states where rescission efforts developed, voting in 1974 to reverse its original approval. Although rescission proved to be a moot issue when supporters found themselves three states shy of the number needed, it probably would not have survived a court fight.[62]

Despite its substantive and symbolic significance, ratification of the Nineteenth Amendment had hardly resolved the issue of sexual equity. Beset by serious schisms within the women's movement and major disagreements on such matters as protective legislation for women, Carrie Chapman Catt, in what seems to have been a serious strategic blunder, chose to convert the National American Woman Suffrage Association into the League of Women Voters. Not until the 1960s, which brought the formation of the National Organization for Women, did an umbrella organization exist in the United States that was devoted exclusively to the issue of sex equity.[63]

Implicit in Tennessee's ratification of the Susan B. Anthony Amendment was the promise of a better future for the state's females. Nonetheless, it hardly spelled an end to the continuing sexual discrimination, injustice, inequity, and outright degradation that, in one way or another, seriously impacted the lives of most women in the Volunteer State. Meanwhile, southern female activists of the interwar years and the civil rights era moved away from "respectable reform" and divested themselves of the more affected attributes of "ladyhood." As courageous as this may have been, it proved to be politically foolish in Dixie. Females who participated in strikes and militant marches found few friends in high places in southern state capitals. This more assertive posture virtually doomed their issues, which were already unpopular enough in the state legislative chambers of the South. Feminist gains since suffrage owe a profound debt to federal interventionism reflected in executive orders, congressional legislation, and Supreme Court decisions. As important as these developments have been to the status of Tennessee women, indeed all American women, it may not be too much of an exaggeration to suggest that ordinary garden-variety females have probably benefited more from effective birth control methods than from either federal or state actions.[64]

Factory women of the interwar years, as well as farm wives, often traveled in the company of hardship. Discontent over long hours, low pay, and work discipline that applied specifically to women, for example, produced several walkouts at the J. P. Bemberg Corporation, a German-owned rayon plant at Elizabethton, Tennessee, during the 1920s. Finally, on March 12, 1929, Margaret Bowen led a walkout at Glanzstoff, the sister plant, which set off a general strike. Described as a black-haired girl with high cheekbones suggesting Native American heritage, Bowen had previously been employed at a silk mill in Old Hickory, Tennessee, but company representatives had lured her to Elizabethton as a forewoman with the promise of high wages. Company officials, local entrepreneurs, and the political establishment at the county, city, and state levels arrayed themselves against the strikers, both male and female. Although work eventually resumed on company terms, this labor unrest, which began at Elizabethton, ignited a series of prolonged struggles across the Upper South and the Piedmont that put the lie to the conventional propaganda of docile, anti-union southern labor.[65]

With the onset of World War II, patriotic self-sacrifice tended to supplant social protest. Most Tennessee women, just as their counterparts across the country, kept the home fires burning, did their volunteer time with the Red Cross, the United Service Organizations, and similar associations, and mailed male-boosting letters and care packages. They lived with the constant fear of receiving telegrams from the War Department that their sons, husbands, friends, and sweethearts had been listed as missing in action or been killed or wounded in the service of their country. Furthermore, women entered the job market in unprecedented numbers. Females at the Y-12 plant in Oak Ridge, Tennessee, assisted in the development and production of the enriched uranium (U-235) contained in the bomb dropped on Hiroshima, Japan, August 6, 1945. Their counterparts at numerous war industries across the state valiantly helped to meet production quotas for the nation's mighty global effort. A few Tennessee women became flight instructors and pilots, and still others joined the various auxiliaries of the armed forces.[66]

During the fifty years since the end of World War II, two principal forces have dominated American history: the civil rights movement and its far-reaching consequences for the expansion of democracy and the challenges of the nation's role as the earth's preeminent superpower. Few Tennesseans of either sex could have entirely escaped being affected by related developments. In some respects, however, the crusade for human rights proved more immediate as the struggle of African Americans and their white supporters played itself out on the landscape of the Volunteer State, across Dixie, and, indeed, throughout the country. Highlander Folk School at Monteagle, Tennessee, a gathering place for activists, a base for workshops in nonviolence, and home to the development of citizenship schools, became a special target of segregationists. With the advent of the 1960s, black and white college students staged sit-ins in the state's principal cities. In the wake of *Brown v. Board of Education of Topeka, Kansas, et al.* (1954), Tennessee public schools and institutions of higher learning dealt with desegregation.[67] Women's Liberation, the most recent discernible phase of the women's rights movement in the United States, had strong connections to the civil rights efforts of the 1950s and 1960s.[68]

For all the progress that women have made and all the changes that have benefited them, they continue to face discrimination in the public arena. On the private front, sexual harassment, date rape, wife battering, and child abuse remain all too common. Poverty, disease, and infant mortality persist. Technological breakthroughs, global events, and ever-changing economic realities have also impinged on the lives of Tennessee women during the twentieth century. The likes of Elizabethton strike leader Margaret Bowen, Highlander Folk School's Zilphia Johnson Horton, country music star Kitty Wells, and aviatrix Cornelia Fort grace the pages of the state's recorded history. Rosa Parks, the mother of the civil rights movement, spent a brief interlude at Monteagle; astronaut-physician Rhea Seddon hails from Murfreesboro; entertainer Dolly Parton is a native of the Great Smoky Mountains. Poets, politicians, and professionals of almost every description have risen from native soil. Even contemporary Indian chiefs—Wilma Mankiller, who recently headed the Western Band of the Cherokee Nation in Oklahoma, and Joyce Dugan, elected to the highest position among the Eastern Band in North Carolina—have ancient tribal ties to the state and the region. In the chambers of the Tennessee General Assembly and the state supreme court, where the feet of no elected or appointed female trod for most of the state's history, there has developed a feminine presence.

Women have called the Tennessee country home for thousands of years. Their recorded history, however, spans not yet five centuries. What sights they must have seen and what changes they most assuredly have witnessed. Beset as they have been by all the usual human failings and foibles, they still bequeath to successive generations a rich heritage and an impressive record of strength and perseverance. With a new millennium at hand, there is no time for their heirs to rest on laurels or take feminist gains for granted. Even the cautiously optimistic must surely realize that the seemingly elusive quest for gender equality continues.

NOTES

1. For an interpretive history of southern women across four hundred years, see Margaret Ripley Wolfe, *Daughters of Canaan: A Saga of Southern Women* (Lexington, Ky., 1995).
2. Stephan Thernstrom introduced the phrasing "from the bottom up" in *Poverty and Progress: Social Mobility in a Nineteenth Century City* (Cambridge, 1964) For a discussion of the "new social history," see Peter N. Stearns, "The New Social History: An Overview," in James B. Gardner and George Rollie Adams, eds. *Ordinary People and Everyday Life: Perspectives on the New Social History* (Nashville, 1983), 3–21; see also Margaret Ripley Wolfe, "Beyond Provincialism: New Dimensions for Regional Studies," Tennessee Committee for the Humanities *Cross-Reference* 3 (Winter 1983): 4–5.
3. Gardner and Adams, *Ordinary People and Everyday Life,* passim; Alan Rogers, *Approaches to Local History,* 2d ed. (London, 1977); David E. Kyvig and Myron A. Marty, *Nearby History: Exploring the Past Around You* (Nashville, 1982); Thomas J. Schlereth, ed. and comp., *Material Culture Studies in America* (Nashville, 1982); Alf Lüdtke, ed., *The History of Everyday Life: Reconstructing Historical Experiences and Ways of Life,* trans. William Templer (Princeton, N.J., 1995).
4. This brief discussion of prehistoric Native American cultures in the Tennessee country draws on the exhibit files of the Tennessee State Museum, Nashville, Tennessee; and the author gratefully acknowledges the support and assistance of the museum staff. See also Stephen D. Cox, *Art and Artisans of Prehistoric Middle Tennessee* (Nashville,

1985), which deals with material from the Gates P. Thruston Collection of Vanderbilt University held in trust by the Tennessee State Museum; Jefferson Chapman, *The American Indian in Tennessee* (Knoxville, 1982); and T. M. N. Lewis and Madeline Kneberg, "The Prehistory of the Chickamauga Basin in Tennessee: A Preview," published by the Division of Anthropology, Univ. of Tennessee, Knoxville, Nov. 1941; typescript.

5. From quoted material in J. G. M. Ramsey, *The Annals of Tennessee to the End of the Eighteenth Century* (Kingsport, Tenn., 1967 [1853]), 24–25. It has long been assumed that the de Soto expedition made its way into the Tennessee country around present-day Chattanooga, but new research suggests that the Spaniards may have been as far north as the Nolichucky River.

6. Ibid., 25–31.

7. Quoted in Samuel Cole Williams, *Beginnings of West Tennessee: In the Land of the Chickasaws, 1541–1841* (Johnson City, Tenn., 1930), 7.

8. Ibid., 58.

9. Theda Perdue, "Columbus Meets Pocahontas in the American South," address before the Southern Association for Women Historians, Nov. 6, 1992, copy in the author's possession, graciously provided by Dr. Perdue. See also Perdue, "Southern Indians and the Cult of True Womanhood," in Walter J. Fraser, Jr., R. Frank Saunders, Jr., and Jon L. Wakelyn, eds., *The Web of Southern Social Relations: Women, Family, and Education* (Athens, 1985), 35–51.

10. William Bartram, "Travels Through North and South Carolina, Georgia, East and West Florida," in Alan Gallay, ed., *Voices of the Old South: Eyewitness Accounts, 1528–1861* (Athens, Ga., 1994), 62.

11. Quoted in Stephanie Coontz, *The Social Origins of Private Life: A History of American Families, 1600–1900* (London, 1988), 57–58.

12. Perdue, "Columbus Meets Pocahontas," 8–9, passim; Perdue, "Southern Indians and the Cult of True Womanhood," 36–37; Thomas Hatley, "Cherokee Women Farmers Hold Their Ground," in Robert D. Mitchell, ed., *Appalachian Frontiers: Settlement, Society, and Development in the Preindustrial Era* (Lexington, Ky., 1991), 37–51; and Jon A. Schlenker, "An Historical Analysis of the Family Life of the Choctaw Indians," *Southern Quarterly* 13 (July 1975): 323–34.

13. Perdue, "Southern Indians and the Cult of True Womanhood," 47–48.

14. Perdue, "Nancy Ward (1738?–1822)," in C. J. Barker-Benfield and Catherine Clinton, eds., *Portraits of American Women: From Settlement to the Civil War* (New York, 1991), 92–93.

15. Ibid., 85–90; Timberlake's quotation appears on 90.

16. Stanley J. Folmsbee, Robert E. Corlew, and Enoch L. Mitchell, *History of Tennessee* (New York, 1960), 1:135.

17. Theda Perdue and Michael D. Green, eds., *The Cherokee Removal: A Brief History with Documents* (Boston, 1995), 121–26. See also Barbara Welter, "The Cult of True Womanhood, 1820–1860," *American Quarterly* 18 (Summer 1966): 151–64.

18. Michael Paul Rogin, "Indian Removal," in Thomas R. Frazier, ed., *The Underside of American History,* 5th ed. (San Diego, 1987), 1:218–19; see also Grant Foreman, *Indian Removal: The Emigration of the Five Civilized Tribes of Indians* (Norman, Okla., 1953); Grace C. Woodward, *The Cherokees* (Norman, Okla., 1963); Arthur H.

DeRosier, Jr., *The Removal of the Choctaw Indians* (Knoxville, 1970); John R. Finger, "The Abortive Second Cherokee Removal, 1841–1844," *Journal of Southern History* 47 (May 1981): 107–26; and Ray G. Lillard, "Rattlesnake Springs," in Jim Stokely and Jeff D. Johnson, eds., *An Encyclopedia of East Tennessee* (Oak Ridge, Tenn., 1981), 408–9.

19. Harriette Simpson Arnow, *Flowering of the Cumberland,* with a foreword by Wilma Dykeman (Lexington, 1984 [1963]), 419.
20. Quoted in Wilton Eckley, *Harriette Arnow,* Twayne's United States Author Series (New York, 1974), 124–25.
21. David Hackett Fischer, *Albion's Seed: Four British Folkways in America* (New York, 1989), 676.
22. For overviews of women during the American Revolutionary era, see Linda Grant DePauw, *Founding Mothers: Women in America in the Revolutionary Era* (Boston, 1975); and Linda Grant DePauw and Conover Hunt with the assistance of Miriam Schneir, *Remember the Ladies: Women in America, 1750–1815* (New York, 1976); Mary Beth Norton, *Liberty's Daughters: The Revolutionary Experience of American Women, 1750–1800* (Boston, 1980); and Linda Kerber, *Women of the Republic: Intellect and Ideology in Revolutionary America* (Chapel Hill, N.C., 1980).
23. See Colin G. Calloway, *The American Revolution in Indian Country* (Cambridge, 1995).
24. Quoted in Pauline Wilcox Burke, *Emily Donelson of Tennessee* (Richmond, Va., 1941), 1:8–10. For a discussion of the dangers posed to women's health by pregnancy and childbearing, see Sally G. McMillen, *Motherhood in the Old South: Pregnancy, Childbirth, and Infant Mortality* (Baton Rouge, 1990).
25. Elizabeth Crawley's petition for divorce in the superior court, State of Tennessee, Washington district, Sept. 2, 1806, and statement of John Hokem [?] before William Gilleyland, justice of the peace, probably in Washington County, Tenn., Apr. 1, 1842, both documents from the private collection of Tony Marion, Blountville, Tenn.
26. Joan E. Cashin, *A Family Venture: Men and Women on the Southern Frontier* (New York, 1991), 4, 119, 120; Wolfe, *Daughters of Canaan,* 66–70.
27. Lawrence B. Goodheart, Neil Hanks, and Elizabeth Johnson, "'An Act for the Relief of Females . . .': Divorce and the Changing Legal Status of Women in Tennessee, 1796–1860, Part I," *Tennessee Historical Quarterly* 44 (Fall 1985): 321, 322; inclusive pages, 318–39; see also Goodheart, Hanks, and Johnson, "'An Act for the Relief of Females . . .': Divorce and the Changing Legal Status of Women in Tennessee, Part II," *Tennessee Historical Quarterly* 44 (Winter 1985): 402–16. Such historians as Suzanne Lebsock and Paul Goodman have also discovered that such protective legislation as homestead exemption and married women's property laws enacted during the nineteenth century derived from considerations having little to do with commitment to women's rights per se. See Suzanne Lebsock, "Radical Reconstruction and the Property Rights of Southern Women," *Journal of Southern History* 43 (May 1977): 195–216; and Paul Goodman, "The Emergence of Homestead Exemption in the United States: Accommodation and Resistance to the Market Revolution, 1840–1880," *Journal of American History* 80 (Sept. 1993): 470–98.
28. Paul M. Fink, "Russell Bean, Tennessee's First Native Son," *East Tennessee Historical Society's Publications* 37 (1965): 37–39.

29. Quoted in Bertram Wyatt-Brown, *Southern Honor: Ethics and Behavior in the Old South* (New York, 1982), 303.

30. Arthur M. Schlesinger, *Learning How to Behave: A Historical Study of American Etiquette Books* (New York, 1947), 6–10.

31. Wolfe, *Daughters of Canaan,* passim.

32. Welter, "The Cult of True Womanhood," 151.

33. Frances Wright's experiment is the subject of a novel, Edd Winfield Parks, *Nashoba* (New York, 1963); see Celia M. Eckhardt, *Fanny Wright: Rebel in America* (Cambridge, 1984); and Susan Kissel, *By Common Cause: The "Conservative" Frances Trollope and the "Radical" Frances Wright* (Bowling Green, Ohio, 1993); see also Nancy Woloch, *Women and the American Experience* (New York, 1984), 151–66. For a vignette of Rachel Donelson Robards Jackson and an assessment, see Betty Boyd Caroli, *First Ladies* (New York, 1987), 35–39. For a discussion of the ill-fated marriage of Eliza Allen and Sam Houston, see John Hoyt Williams, *Sam Houston: A Biography of the Father of Texas* (New York, 1993), 63–71.

34. Caroli, *First Ladies,* 65. The quotation about Sarah Childress Polk's "spice and independence" is from 59.

35. Robert E. Corlew, *Tennessee: A Short History,* 2d paperback ed. (Knoxville, 1987), 120.

36. Christie Anne Farnham, *The Education of the Southern Belle: Higher Education and Student Socialization in the Antebellum South* (New York, 1994), 57–58.

37. Ibid., 145, 170, passim; see also Carolyn Brackett, "Belmont Mistress makes Scarlett Look Meek," from *Tennessee Traveler,* reprinted in *Kingsport Times-News,* Sept. 24, 1989; and James A. Hoobler, "Adelicia Hayes Franklin Acklen Cheatham," *Distinctive Women of Tennessee* (Nashville, n.d.), 9.

38. Jayne Crumpler DeFiore, "'COME, and Bring the Ladies': Tennessee Women and the Politics of Opportunity during the Presidential Campaigns of 1840 and 1844," *Tennessee Historical Quarterly* 51 (Winter 1992): 201.

39. Joe L. Kincheloe, Jr., "Transcending Role Restrictions: Women at Camp Meetings and Political Rallies," *Tennessee Historical Quarterly* 40 (Summer 1981): 169.

40. Marsha Wedell, *Elite Women and the Reform Impulse in Memphis, 1875–1915* (Knoxville, 1991), 9–10.

41. Carole Stanford Bucy, "Quiet Revolutionaries: The Grundy Women and the Beginnings of Women's Volunteer Associations in Tennessee," *Tennessee Historical Quarterly* 54 (Spring 1995): 42–43. See also Mary S. Hoffschwelle, "Women's Sphere and the Creation of Female Community in the Antebellum South: Three Tennessee Slaveholding Women," *Tennessee Historical Quarterly* 50 (Summer 1991): 80–89; Anne M. Boylan, *Sunday School: The Formation of an American Institution, 1790–1880* (New Haven, 1988); and Lori D. Ginzberg, *Women and the Work of Benevolence: Morality, Politics, and Class in the Nineteenth-Century United States* (New Haven, 1990).

42. David Kaser, "Nashville's Women of Pleasure in 1860," *Tennessee Historical Quarterly* 23 (Dec. 1964): 379–82.

43. Lester C. Lamon, *Blacks in Tennessee, 1791–1970* (Knoxville, 1981), 116.

44. See Theda Perdue, *Slavery and the Evolution of Cherokee Society* (Knoxville, 1979);

and Perdue and Green, *The Cherokee Removal,* 5; see also Donald Davidson, *The Tennessee: The Old River—Frontier to Secession* (New York, 1946), 80.

45. In *Blacks in Tennessee,* 117, Lamon writes: "For the antebellum period in Tennessee's history only a few published works focus upon or include substantial information regarding black Tennesseans." See also Lamon, *Black Tennesseans, 1900–1930* (Knoxville, 1977).

46. The following are useful for an understanding of slavery and its impact on women's lives: Eugene D. Genovese, *Roll, Jordan, Roll: The World the Slaves Made* (New York, 1974); Herbert G. Gutman, *The Black Family in Slavery and Freedom, 1750–1925* (New York, 1976); Catherine Clinton, *The Plantation Mistress: Woman's World in the Old South* (New York, 1982); Jacqueline Jones, *Labor of Love, Labor of Sorrow: Black Women, Work, and the Family from Slavery to the Present* (New York, 1985); Deborah Gray White, *Ar'n't I a Woman? Female Slaves in the Antebellum South* (New York, 1985); and Elizabeth Fox-Genovese, *Within the Plantation Household: Black and White Women of the Old South* (Chapel Hill, N.C., 1988).

47. Anita Shafer Goodstein, *Nashville, 1780–1860: From Frontier to City* (Gainesville, 1989), 14.

48. Brian Steel Wills, *A Battle from the Start: The Life of Nathan Bedford Forrest* (New York, 1991), 30, passim.

49. Anne Firor Scott, *The Southern Lady: From Pedestal to Politics, 1830–1930* (Chicago, 1970), 81, 102.

50. See Mary Elizabeth Massey, *Bonnet Brigades: American Women and the Civil War* (New York, 1966); and Bell Irvin Wiley, *Confederate Women* (Westport, Conn., 1975).

51. W. J. Cash, *The Mind of the South* (New York, 1941), 130, 131. See also Wyatt-Brown, *Southern Honor,* 454.

52. See the following for an array of views on the outcome of the Civil War and women's roles: Catherine Clinton, *The Other Civil War: American Women in the Nineteenth Century* (New York, 1984), 89; George C. Rable, *Civil Wars: Women and the Crisis of Southern Nationalism* (Urbana, Ill., 1989), x, 288, passim; LeeAnn Whites, "The Civil War as a Crisis in Gender," in Catherine Clinton and Nina Silber, eds., *Divided Houses: Gender and the Civil War* (New York, 1992), 21; and Drew Gilpin Faust, "Altars of Sacrifice: Confederate Women and the Narratives of War," *Journal of American History* 76 (Mar. 1990): 1200–28.

53. Stephen V. Ash, *When the Yankees Came: Conflict & Chaos in the Occupied South, 1861–1865* (Chapel Hill, N.C., 1995), 197, passim.

54. The sources listed in notes 50, 52, and 53 are all useful in reaching an understanding of the female experience during the Civil War. An important addition to the historiography of southern women and the Civil War is Drew Gilpin Faust, *Mothers of Invention: Women of the Slaveholding South in the American Civil War* (Chapel Hill, N.C., 1996). See also Katharine M. Jones, *Heroines of Dixie: Confederate Women Tell Their Story of the War* (Indianapolis, 1955); Matthew Page Andrews, *The Women of the South in War Times* (Baltimore, 1920); Marilyn Mayer Culpepper, *Trials and Triumphs: The Women of the American Civil War* (East Lansing, Mich., 1991); Elizabeth Avery Meriwether, *Recollections of Ninety-two Years, 1824–1916* (Nashville,

1958); Sister Aloysium Mackin, ed., "Wartime Scenes from Convent Windows: St. Cecilia, 1860 through 1865," *Tennessee Historical Quarterly* 39 (Winter 1980): 401–22; William C. Harris, "East Tennessee's Civil War Refugees and the Impact of the War on Civilians," East Tennessee Historical Society's Publications 64 (1992): 3–19; Janet E. Kaufman, "'Under the Petticoat Flag': Women Soldiers in the Confederate Army," *Southern Studies* 23 (Winter 1984): 363–75; and Lee Middleton, comp. and ed., *Hearts of Fire . . . Soldier Women of the Civil War: With an Addendum on Female Reenactors* (Franklin, N.C., 1993). See also Stephen V. Ash, *Middle Tennessee Society Transformed, 1860–1870: War and Peace in the Upper South* (Baton Rouge, 1988).

55. Connie L. Lester, "'Let Us Be Up and Doing': Women in the Tennessee Movements for Agrarian Reform, 1870–1892," *Tennessee Historical Quarterly* 54 (Summer 1995): 91.

56. See Anne Firor Scott, "Women, Religion and Social Change in the South, 1830–1930," in Samuel S. Hill, Jr., et al., *Religion and the Solid South* (Nashville, 1972), 92–121; Anne Firor Scott, *Natural Allies: Women's Association in American History* (Champaign, Ill., 1992); Mary S. Sims, *The Natural History of a Social Institution—the Young Women's Christian Association* (New York, 1936); John Patrick McDowell III, *The Social Gospel in the South: The Woman's Home Mission Movement in the Methodist Episcopal Church, 1886–1939* (Baton Rouge, 1982); Mary Jean Houde, *Reaching Out: A Story of the General Federation of Women's Clubs* (Chicago, 1989); Allen F. Davis, *Spearheads for Reform: The Social Settlements and the Progressive Movement, 1890–1941* (New York, 1968); Martha H. Swain, "Clubs and Voluntary Organizations," in Charles Reagan Wilson and William Ferris, eds., *Encyclopedia of Southern Culture* (Chapel Hill, N.C., 1989), 1535–36; and Dorothy D. DeMoss, "A 'Fearless Stand': The Southern Association of College Women, 1903–1921," *Southern Studies* 26 (Winter 1987): 249–60.

57. Paula Baker, "The Domestication of Politics: Women and the American Political Society, 1780–1920," *American Historical Review* 89 (June 1984): 625.

58. Hoobler, *Distinctive Women of Tennessee,* 17, passim; exhibit files of the Tennessee State Museum; and Paul E. Isaac, *Prohibition and Politics: Turbulent Decades in Tennessee, 1885–1920* (Knoxville, 1965), 25–26, passim.

59. Lamon, *Black Tennesseans,* 213.

60. Alfreda M. Duster, ed., *Crusade for Justice: The Autobiography of Ida B. Wells* (Chicago, 1970).

61. A. Elizabeth Taylor, *The Suffrage Movement in Tennessee* (New York, 1957); Marjorie Spruill Wheeler, *New Women of the New South: The Leaders of the Woman Suffrage Movement in the Southern States* (New York, 1993); Marjorie Spruill Wheeler, ed., *Votes for Women: The Woman Suffrage Movement in Tennessee, the South, and the Nation* (Knoxville, 1995); Anastatia Sims, "'Powers That Pray and Powers That Prey': Tennessee and the Fight for Woman Suffrage," *Tennessee Historical Quarterly* 50 (Winter 1991): 203–25.

62. Wolfe, *Daughters of Canaan,* 197–98; Mary Frances Berry, *Why ERA Failed: Politics, Women's Rights, and the Amending Process of the Constitution* (Bloomington, Ind., 1986), 67, 75, 107.

63. Wolfe, *Daughters of Canaan,* 152–57.

64. Margaret Ripley Wolfe, "Feminizing Dixie: Toward a Public Role for Women in the American South," in John H Stanfield II, ed., *Research in Social Policy: Historical and Contemporary Perspectives* (Greenwich, Conn., 1987), 1:179–211; and Wolfe, "The View from Atlanta: Southern Women and the Future," in Joe P. Dunn and Howard L. Preston, eds., *The Future South: A Historical Perspective for the Twenty-first Century* (Urbana, Ill.: 1991), 123–57. For a treatment of birth control as a public issue in the state during the 1930s and 1940s, see William B. Turner, "Class, Controversy, and Contraceptives: Birth Control Advocacy in Nashville, 1932–1944," *Tennessee Historical Quarterly* 53 (Fall 1994): 166–79.

65. See James A Hodges, "Challenge to the New South: The Great Textile Strike in Elizabethton, Tennessee, 1929," *Tennessee Historical Quarterly* 23 (Dec. 1964): 343–57. Jacquelyn Dowd Hall, "Disorderly Women: Gender and Labor Militancy in the Appalachian South," *Journal of American History* 73 (Sept. 1986): 354–82, discusses women's part in the textile strike at Elizabethton.

66. For general treatments of American women during World War II, see Susan M. Hartmann, *The Home Front and Beyond: American Women in the 1940s* (Boston, 1982); and D'Ann Campbell, *Women at War with America: Private Lives in a Patriotic Era* (Cambridge, 1984). See also Doris Brinker Tanner, "Cornelia Fort: a WASP in World War II, Part I," *Tennessee Historical Quarterly* 40 (Winter 1981): 381–94; Tanner, "Cornelia Fort: Pioneer Woman Military Aviator, Part II," *Tennessee Historical Quarterly* 41 (Spring 1982): 67–80; and Janene Leonhirth, "Tennessee's Experiment: Women as Military Flight Instructors," *Tennessee Historical Quarterly* 51 (Fall 1992): 170–78.

67. For a history of Highlander, see John Glen, *Highlander: No Ordinary School, 1931–1962* (Lexington, Ky., 1988); see also Cynthia Griggs Fleming, "White Lunch Counters and Black Consciousness: The Story of the Knoxville Sit-Ins," *Tennessee Historical Quarterly* 49 (Spring 1990): 40–52; and Linda T. Wynn, "The Dawning of a New Day: The Nashville Sit-Ins, February 13–May 10, 1960," *Tennessee Historical Quarterly* 50 (Spring 1991): 42–54.

68. See Jo Freeman, *The Politics of Women's Liberation: A Case Study of an Emerging Social Movement and Its Relation to the Policy Process* (New York, 1975); and Sara Evans, *Personal Politics: The Roots of Women's Liberation in the Civil Rights Movement and the New Left* (New York, 1979).

Hugh Rogan of Counties Donegal and Sumner: Irish Acculturation in Frontier Tennessee

■ CANETA SKELLEY HANKINS

■

■ *Editor's Note:* Hankins draws upon material culture evidence in a creative, comparative interpretation of ethnic acculturation in Tennessee during the backcountry era. Before immigration, Rogan was a freedom fighter against the British occupation in his native Ireland. In his new country, however, Rogan aggressively fought against the original occupants—the Native Americans—to secure his place and property in his adopted Middle Tennessee homeland. When, at last, he established his permanent farmstead in 1798, Rogan had lived in the United States for over twenty years. Yet, he returned to his roots to construct a limestone rural cottage that was thoroughly Irish in its construction, appearance, and materials. The life of Rogan indicates that ethnic acculturation was complex, never immediate or automatic.

The landscape that for two centuries has been encompassed by the state boundaries of Tennessee is both an accumulation of the peoples who have lived on it and a reflection of the society that brought it into being. On it the past endures in the form of survey lines, land parcels, political jurisdictions, transportation routes, and, more familiarly, in architecture, cemeteries, abandoned rail lines, stone fences, nearly deserted small towns, and archaeological sites. Even as rapid and lasting changes are imposed on Tennessee's landscape, vestiges remain from other periods.[1] The role of individuals, not only key figures but lesser-known men and women, and groups of peoples who both altered the land and influenced the emerging culture of Tennessee can hardly be overestimated.[2]

For most of its two hundred years of settlement, the rural landscape of Tennessee has been defined by single-family farms and crossroads communities. This common pattern has significantly influenced, and continues to impact, though to a lesser degree as the twenty-first century approaches, the cultural, social, economic, religious, political, and educational traditions of Tennesseans. The predominant arrangement of the land into coexistent farms and villages is attributed, primarily, to the scores of Irish and Scotch-Irish settlers who entered the Cumberland Valley in the eighteenth and nineteenth centuries.[3]

Among the wave of Irish immigrants who crossed into the Cumberland Valley in the days before statehood was Hugh Rogan of Glentourne, County Donegal. Rogan was one of the "plain folk" who associated with principal pioneers, including James Robertson, John Donelson, Isaac and Anthony Bledsoe, James Winchester, Joseph Brown, and William Hall. Hugh Rogan provides an opportunity to move beyond what might be perceived as a topic of purely local interest to one that bridges state, national, and international boundaries during a critical forty-year period.

To partially define Irish acculturation in Tennessee through the representative figure of Hugh Rogan is possible through several avenues of inquiry. How do Rogan's land, his two-hundred-year-old stone house, and the nearby Sumner County village named for him contribute to the state's agrarian, architectural, and geographical history? How did Rogan's experience with cultural, racial, and religious discrimination manifest itself in pioneer society? How did he affect frontier society and, conversely, how did the frontier shape his life and fortune? To probe, even fractionally, the process of selection, transference, and adaptation of Irish culture to Tennessee requires, first, a basic familiarity with the reasons for the mass exodus from Ireland to the American colonies.

The departure of thousands of men and women from Ireland was the result of two major forces—economic instability and religious intolerance.[4] The defeat of the (Catholic) Stuart king, James II, by William III at the Battle of Boyne in 1690 permitted a century and a half of unparalleled change in the economy, society, and landscape of Ireland. A series of laws that, in effect, gave Irish lands and government to the Protestant minority that was loyal to England effectively accomplished this alteration. In the ensuing years, the confiscation of land and added legal pressures and prohibitions were enforced until, by 1778, when the so-called penal laws began to be relaxed, scarcely 5 percent of Ireland remained in the hands of the Roman Catholic majority.[5]

During the eighteenth century, the system of landlordism imposed by the English on the Irish effectively "condemned the mass of Roman Catholic peasantry to exist as serfs in a state of abject poverty, wretchedness and squalor, dependent on agriculture for a livelihood and potatoes for food."[6] The Roman Catholic population in the mid-1700s was disenfranchised and generally excluded from government protection and representation. Catholics were not allowed an education, could not live in a corporate town, and were barred from holding any government office, from entering the legal profession, and from holding commissions in the army and navy. Because of additional laws passed in 1704 and 1709, Catholics could not buy land nor lease property for longer than thirty-one years.[7]

The increasing peasant populace, which had never fared especially well under any landlords, now faced rising rents but ever-diminishing holdings. Rented property could not be worth more than thirty shillings a year, and the workers could not receive profits that exceeded one-third of the rent. Catholicism was forbidden. A particularly unsettling and demanding hardship was the collection of tithes for the Church of Ireland, the local embodiment of the Church of England, which now owned all the cathedrals, chapels, monasteries, and property formerly held by the Roman Catholic Church.[8]

Trade restrictions imposed by the English government on goods exported to England, Europe, and the American colonies were an even more devastating blow for the Irish farmer and manufacturer, especially the wool and linen producers and weavers. After a severe potato famine and crop failure in 1741, an entire generation was reduced by starvation, fevers, and malnutrition.[9]

Contemporary accounts of the wretched state of much of the population are plentiful. Jonathan Swift, dean of St. Patrick's in Dublin, wrote, "The people have already given their bread, their flesh, their butter, their shoes, their stockings, their house furniture and houses to pay their landlords and taxes."[10] Arthur Young, who kept a journal of his tour of Ireland in the 1770s, described the rented "cabbins" as "the most miserable looking hovels that can well be conceived," noting that the furnishings consisted of a pot for boiling potatoes, a table, a broken stool or two, and beds of straw.[11]

Conditions in County Donegal, where Hugh Rogan was born in 1747, were generally worse than in other parts of Ireland.[12] Estyn Evans, Ireland's eminent cultural geographer, describes eighteenth-century Donegal as "a model of a region of difficulty and survival."[13] In the first half of that century, stone houses and outbuildings were built in clusters and occupied by interrelated families who depended on each other for protection and help. Holdings, actually owned by usually absentee landlords, were a series of small narrow plots, usually about a "cow's grass" or three acres, held jointly by several relatives.

Cultivation of oats and potatoes, the staples for both people and animals, was entirely by spade. The subsistence farms had no hay meadows and no rotation grasses. The land was treeless and grazed to the dirt by free-ranging livestock. Transportation was generally by water, for roads were not fit for wheeled vehicles.[14] Though life in Donegal has traditionally been as hard as the plentiful stones used for building houses, barns, and fences, it is also a region renowned for its isolated but spectacular scenery, its megalithic monuments, and ancient lore. To this day, the people of Donegal, among whom are numbered some of the country's most treasured playwrights, poets, and musicians, are keepers of the Irish language, music, and legends, and they are survivors.[15]

As the eighteenth century progressed, the Irish viewed themselves as disgruntled colonists of England, subject to laws that were enacted to undermine, if not effectively destroy, their culture and commerce. As the penal laws squeezed them out of a livelihood, many farmers and weavers immigrated to the colonies.[16] The Irish, readily embracing the American cause as their own, joined the revolutionary forces to fight the British.[17]

Because of the religiously tolerant atmosphere created by the Pennsylvania charter of privileges in 1701, Philadelphia was one of the most common destinations for the Irish, particularly those from the six northern counties comprising Ulster. More than a quarter of a million people left northern Ireland before 1776, and another hundred thousand followed after 1783.[18]

By the 1770s, one-third of Pennsylvania's population of 350,000 inhabitants was Irish.[19] In that decade, Irish arrivals began looking beyond the crowded seaport, where they were often unwelcome and victims of racial discrimination, to the western lands. The deprivations and insecurity of frontier life seemed to be of little consequence to the Irish. They moved inland from Philadelphia and traveled south into the valleys of the Blue Ridge mountains of Virginia and the Carolinas in hopes of finding cheap and abundant farm land, free of rent and tithe.[20]

When Hugh Rogan left County Donegal in the spring of 1775, he followed precisely this common migration route, leaving from either Belfast or Londonderry (Derry) on a ship bound for Philadelphia.[21] From Pennsylvania, he traveled into North Carolina and, eventually, across the mountains into the western frontier. He was among the nearly three hundred thousand pioneers who came into the Cumberland Valley between 1775 and 1800, making the area the second "seed-bed" of Irish migration after Pennsylvania, especially for people from Ulster.[22]

Rogan not only followed the common migration route of so many Irish who came before and after him, but his reasons for emigrating were, like theirs, grounded in the overriding problems of economic instability and religious intolerance in Ireland. By the middle of the eighteenth century, unrest in the northern counties of Ireland was common. Here the minority Protestant rule over the Catholic majority was at it most exacting, and recurring instances of violence, rebellion, and retaliation were common from both factions.

Hugh Rogan was a member of a group of Catholic agrarian reformers who called themselves the "Irish Defenders." Their goal was to exact a change in laws that would allow at least ten acres of land for each family and some relief from tithes paid to the Church of Ireland. The Defenders were aggressive in raiding houses for arms (which were denied Catholics under the current laws) with which to protect their homes from Protestant "Peep o' Day Boys." Each of the opposing factions provoked incidents that continued the agitation and bloodshed and failed to improve the conditions of unrest and frustration in northern Ireland.[23]

Hugh Rogan's decision to emigrate in 1775 may have been the result of his role and activities in the Defenders. One source indicates Rogan feared arrest for his involvement with the group; another suggests that he feared conscription by the English army, which would likely have resulted in his being transported to the colonies to fight against American rebels, many of whom were Irish.[24]

Rogan and Daniel Carlen, who was married to Rogan's sister, "concluded that they would bring a few goods to America" to finance their trip and "by that means would see all the country and if they did like the country they would procure a place and then return to Ireland" and bring their families.[25] Rogan left his wife, Anne (called Nancy), and their infant son, Bernard, and sailed for the colonies. It would be twenty years before he saw either his family or his native country again.

Arriving in the Port of Philadelphia on one of the last ships to land before the War for American Independence began, he planned to join the Revolution and resume fighting the British. His temporary employer, a Quaker named Downey, gave him erroneous information that caused him to miss joining a marine fleet. Disgruntled by the deception of Downey, Rogan left Philadelphia and headed south. In his wanderings, he moved on to "The Hornet's Nest," an Irish settlement in North Carolina.[26] For the next three years, Rogan worked as a weaver, the trade he practiced in Ireland, and he may also have soldiered a part of that time. Rogan visited with Daniel Carlen, now living in North Carolina, and in 1778, he joined the guard for the survey team, led by Dr. Thomas Walker and General Daniel Smith, who were marking the state lines for North Carolina and Virginia. Rogan first came into the Cumberland Valley during this time, perhaps spending several months in the area.[27]

Contemporaries, including John Donelson, William Hall, John Carr, and Joseph Brown, provide most of the substantive information about Rogan. His name is among John Donelson's list of survivors who completed the harrowing river journey from Fort Patrick Henry to Fort Nashborough in 1780.[28] That year Rogan, along with 255 other men, signed the Cumberland Compact, the temporary instrument of government for the new settlements in the Cumberland Valley.[29] Rogan spent nearly two decades helping to establish and defend several of the eight forts, or stations, called for in the Cumberland Compact, which extended for thirty-six miles along the Cumberland River from the French Lick east to Bledsoe's Lick.[30] John Carr's *Early Times in Middle Tennessee* includes records of Rogan's adventures at two of these forts. "Col. Donelson, accompanied by Hugh Rogan and others, settled on Stones River, and built a fort at the point now known as Clover Bottom."[31] This fort had to be abandoned because of Indian raids and the settlers gathered at Mansker's Station. Some weeks later when they returned to Clover Bottom to harvest their corn crop, they arranged for a flatboat to be poled down the river, stopping at various intervals to load the crops. When it reached that part of the river where Rogan waited, those on board shouted to him that it was loaded to capacity. Rogan, left on shore, watched as the cargo continued on its river route. Before the boat was out of sight, however, Rogan witnessed an Indian attack on the vessel. Only one man survived, and Rogan, who made for the safety of the fort, told the story.[32]

In the fall of 1780, Mansker's Station and the other forts along the Cumberland were the target of numerous attacks led by the Cherokee Dragging Canoe and his Creek and Shawnee allies. Their plan was to isolate and destroy the settlements springing up in Middle Tennessee and then to mount a full-scale attack on intruders in East Tennessee, thus permanently expelling white settlers from their ancestral lands. The Native Americans were responding to trade abuses by the settlers and land speculators, deliberate and repeated violations of treaties, the destruction of Indian villages, and the rapid settlement of their hunting grounds. Many of the Native Americans believed that to protect their lands and their way of life, the white settlers must be obliterated.[33]

Following one attack, which left William Neely dead and his daughter captured, the settlers abandoned Mansker's Station to go north to a safer location. Carr writes, "All who could get horses went to Kentucky. That brave Irishman, Hugh Rogan, took charge of the widow Neely and her family and conducted them to safety in Kentucky."[34]

Historian W. W. Clayton provides an account of Rogan's participation in the Coldwater Expedition of 1787—a campaign led by James Robertson and Moses Shelby. Acting on information received from the Chickasaws, the band of settlers went by land and boat to Coldwater, near present-day Tuscumbia, Alabama, to confront a group of Creek and Cherokee renegades who were reportedly responsible for a number of murders and fires in the area. After destroying the camp, the men began their return journey to Nashville. Along the way Native Americans, seeking revenge for the destruction of the village, attacked the settlers. Several men, including Rogan, were injured.[35] Clayton describes Rogan as an "Irishman of superlative courage and strength of will, and though he was shot through one lung he not only marched home without assistance but carried his *gun and accoutrements.*"[36]

Joseph Brown, who was at Fort Bledsoe with Rogan, credits Rogan with saving that outpost in 1792. Isaac Bledsoe, Rogan, and other settlers left the fort one day, but soon spied an Indian party advancing in the direction of stockade. Realizing that there were no men left to defend the post, Rogan proceeded boldly to return to the fort in full sight of the Indians while the rest of the group went a circular route. All reached the fort safely, and Bledsoe was said to have remarked that Rogan, no doubt, had saved the fort, and would never want for a home.[37]

Rogan was one of the players in the drama surrounding the death of Colonel Anthony Bledsoe on July 20, 1788. A stockade surrounded the cabins at Bledsoe's Lick, at Castalian Springs, except for the one shared by brothers Anthony and Isaac Bledsoe. Around midnight, Anthony Bledsoe heard horses rushing by on the road in front of the fort and, calling to James Campbell, an Irish servant, to come with him, he stepped into the open passage to investigate. Immediately a volley of bullets was fired, instantly killing Campbell and mortally wounding Bledsoe.[38]

William Hall, Hugh Rogan, and others opened fire and the Indians retreated from the fort. When Bledsoe realized he was dying, he expressed a desire to leave a will so that his eight surviving daughters could inherit his considerable estate. He had no son and, according to the laws of North Carolina, under which the territory was governed at this time, without a will his brother would inherit his property and his daughters would receive nothing.[39]

In order to prepare the will, some light was needed, but no spark of fire could be found in the fireplaces of the fort's cabins. Understanding the gravity of the situation, Rogan volunteered to go to the nearby house of Katy Shaver, an old woman superstitiously feared and avoided by the Indians. The company opposed the plan because they knew the Indians were still close and would surely attack any person who ventured alone into the night. Rogan is said to have remarked that "a dying man should have his last request gratified" and slipped out the door.[40] Rogan returned safely some time later with embers for the fire, and the will was written, signed, and witnessed a few hours before Bledsoe's death. Clayton closes his account in period prose declaring the "self-sacrificing spirit of the brave Irishman has never been surpassed and rarely equaled. The act had in it all the elements of the 'heroic' in a superlative degree."[41]

Rogan was generally admired and respected, even considered somewhat of a legend. Cisco describes him as a "man without fear, with a big, kind heart," and one who was a general favorite among the pioneers.[42] This reputation was intact even in the latter part of the nineteenth century when Goodspeed characterized Rogan" as a brave soldier and an industrious farmer," and called him one of the "most intelligent, useful and daring pioneers of the State."[43] John Carr, who knew Rogan well, describes him as a "soldier and patriot."[44]

While it may be argued that the enmity between Ireland and England provided Rogan with circumstances that promoted, even invited and encouraged, armed conflict, it is also apparent that Rogan readily transferred his bravery, hostility, and considerable aptitude for nontraditional warfare toward the Native Americans who controlled what is now Middle Tennessee. Over a period of twenty years, Rogan participated in many skirmishes and most of the expeditions that were mounted against the Indians in the Cumberland region.[45] While it as a reality that the native tribes against whom he fought so long and hard were defenders, just as he was in Ireland, of their land, livelihood, and culture from invading forces, it is almost a certainty that Rogan and other settlers never viewed the conflict in this light.

Rogan, portrayed by his contemporaries and later historians as well liked and courageous, also abandoned his wife and child for more than twenty years. Why did Hugh leave Nancy and Bernard, presumably in poverty and dependent upon relatives, for so many years? Did he enjoy the freedom from family responsibilities or was he the victim of misinformation or a combination of both? Joseph Brown provides some clues about Rogan and his family.

Brown recalls that in 1787, as Rogan lay wounded during the Coldwater Expedition, he called to Moses Shelby, "Ah Captain, Captain, come and see if my wound is mortal and if it is that I may prepare for death; this is a judgement upon me for leaving my poor wife and child in Ireland."[46] Brown also indicates that this is the first his companions knew of Rogan's wife and child. Had his abandonment, then, been deliberate?

When Rogan and his brother-in-law Daniel Carlen left Ireland in 1775, they planned to travel in America, trade goods, see the land, and return with enough money to bring their families to America. But the American Revolution and the total restrictions on passenger travel to Ireland between 1776 and 1783 interrupted their return. Brown reveals that after a time, Carlen proposed to Rogan that they abandon the idea of returning to Ireland and bringing their families over to America. Carlen suggested that the better course would be to remarry and start anew. At this proposition, Brown writes, Rogan became very indignant and said that he [Carlen] could take his pleasure but as for himself "his marriage contract should stand [until it] was dissolved by his Maker."[47]

Brown describes Rogan as a man of "fine sense," one who was well informed, had a knowledge of history, and was " brave, honest, and strictly moral."[48] He recounts that Rogan, during the time he was living in North Carolina prior to 1779, was accused by the family of a young woman of being the father of her unborn child. When confronted by the woman's brother, Rogan answered adamantly that "it was a lie for he had not had intercourse with any woman in America."[49]

In Brown's version, the girl described the man as small and dark-skinned with black hair who told her his name was Rogan. The description fit Daniel Carlen. Because Hugh was "a stout chunky man with Sandy Hair Blue eyes and vearey fair skin," the brother of the woman was convinced that he had the wrong Irishman and returned home. Brown concludes this story saying, "Thus you see that Heaven will protect men that will be honest and it was seen in the maney Hairbredth escapes of Hugh Rogan for he was an Honest man in every way."[50]

Daniel Carlen was a recurring adverse influence on his kinsman's life and fortunes. William Hall, later governor of Tennessee, was well acquainted with Rogan and recalled that Rogan returned to Carlen's home in North Carolina in the spring of 1784 and remained there until the fall of 1785. Hall understood that Hugh had started back to Ireland to bring Nancy and his son to Sumner County. Passenger service had resumed between Ireland and the new United States, and Rogan was anxious to return to Ireland for his wife and ten-year-old son. But Carlen, not wanting his family (particularly the wife he left in Ireland) to know that he had truly abandoned them and remarried, lied to Hugh, saying he had received word that Nancy, having heard nothing from Hugh in his ten-year absence, believed him dead and had remarried.[51]

Rogan believed Carlen's story, or at least did nothing to corroborate it, and returned to his land to continue fighting and farming. Another ten years passed and a letter was delivered to Hugh by a nephew who had recently emigrated. The letter was from Nancy, and it told Hugh that she was not married and that she and Bernard, now a grown man, still waited for him to come for them.[52] With the Indian wars over and statehood about to be granted, Hugh Rogan signed a power of attorney on March 29, 1796, giving the care of his lands and business to his neighbor James Winchester and left for Ireland.[53] He returned in 1797 with Nancy and Bernard. Francis Rogan, a second son, was born in 1798.[54] As a new century approached, the Rogan family and other settlers had political and religious freedom, economic opportunities, and land.

In *Passing the Time in Ballymenone*, Henry Glassie observes the rural landscape of Ireland, its patterns, features, and the interdependence of people and their culture with the land. "Every gesture," writes Glassie, "has precedent and consequence. As the hand grips the spade, slaps brick, or grates spuds, historical time flows through the fingers and writes its narrative into the land."[55] The Irish who came into Tennessee brought their traditions, skills, and folkways; they applied and adapted their culture to shape a new state.

Irish and Scotch-Irish immigrants constituted the largest group of the first European farmers, and they adhered to the familiar plan of single-family farms and nearby unincorporated villages. As the wilderness was settled, especially in the South, that settlement pattern dominated the landscape. Rogan and many other Irish natives, though their acreage was now vast by comparison, continued to rely on the mutual cooperation of close groups for survival in a hostile environment. The Irish valued the land, for with its possession came status, independence, and freedom from rent. They believed strongly in the rights of the individual, participated in a representative but limited government, scorned class distinctions, and were intent on continuing their customs and practicing their religion.[56]

Hugh and Nancy, along with Bernard and Francis, developed the Sumner County land into a prosperous farm that was well known in the area for several generations. The original holding was 640 acres, half of which was granted to Rogan on April 27, 1793, for his services as a "soldier in the Commissioner's Guard for laying out the Military lands allotted the officers and soldiers" in the Continental army of North Carolina.[57] Rogan also received around 300 "corn" acres for planting that crop in the early days of settlement.

Rogan was first given land near the present location of Vanderbilt University, but traded that parcel for the combined tract in Sumner County.[58]

Rogan's property was near that of Isaac Bledsoe, on whose land the first permanent European family settlement in Sumner County was begun in 1779.[59] Nearby, Nathaniel Parker, who married Mary Ramsey, the widow of Anthony Bledsoe, built a log house and later a substantial brick dwelling.[60] Other settlers along Bledsoe's Creek included a number of Revolutionary War veterans, among them William Hall, John Morgan, David Shelby, John Carr, and James and George Winchester.[61]

The main source of water was Bledsoe's Creek, which bounded the Rogan farm on the east and was roughly one-quarter mile from the house. About the same distance from the house is a spring that may also have been used by the household.[62] Rogan's land included some level creek bottom acres and gently sloping hills, all covered with a variety of hardwood trees. Mentioned in the boundary description of Rogan's deed are sugar maples, a black oak, a Spanish oak elm, hickory, dogwood, and poplar trees.

Studies of Irish settlers in America indicate that land use was generally dominated by a corn and livestock economy.[63] As mentioned previously, Rogan was among the first to plant and harvest a corn crop after arriving at Clover Bottom in 1780. While no documentation exists for Rogan's other crops, four Sumner County Century Farms, all dating from the late eighteenth century, list grains (oats, corn, wheat) and cattle, sheep, and swine as crops common to the founders. Tobacco and maple syrup were also popular local commodities that Rogan may also have produced.[64]

The cultivation of fruit trees, except apple trees for cider making, was not a tradition among the early Irish settlers, and no remains of orchards are evident on the Rogan land. Crop rotation was not a usual practice among the Irish and Scotch-Irish who tended to plant the same crops each year in the same spot, resulting in soil depletion. Potatoes, the tragic staple of the Irish diet, were introduced into American frontier farms after only a few years. In America, they came to be known as "Irish" potatoes to avoid confusion with the native sweet potato.[65]

The common attribute of the crops raised on the farms of the earliest settlers is that all were easily cultivated by hand, requiring only the simplest of implements—hoe, spade, mattock—tools that had been used for generations in Ireland. Potatoes, squash, and corn were planted and harvested by "hilling." Thus, no fields had to be cleared and no plowing had to be done. These crops grew fast, choking out weeds, and harvesting was usually abundant and not difficult, only time-consuming.[66]

As farmers devoted less time to fighting Indians and more to clearing land and planting, row crops became more feasible. James Winchester, who operated a cotton gin at nearby Cragfont, logged in 1,726 pounds of cotton for Rogan's neighbor, Nathaniel Parker, in 1806.[67] As the years progressed, the Rogan family cleared more land and planted row crops. But in the 1790s, the wilderness would have been very close. The arrangement and use of space on Rogan's farm likely followed Irish tradition, now made even more practical on the frontier, of locating outbuildings near to and on a linear line with the main house.[68]

The oldest and most significant man-made element on the landscape is the dwelling.[69] Hugh Rogan built his house on a hillside above Bledsoe's Creek between 1795 and 1802. The house could have been built as early as 1795, but more likely the year was 1798 or shortly thereafter, when Nancy and Bernard returned with him from Ireland and Francis was born.[70] Because farmhouses often derive their design from the traditional role and work of women, it is probable that Nancy Rogan's wishes were incorporated into the house.[71]

"Rogana," the historic name of the house, is very modest in comparison to nearby Cragfont (1798–1802) and Rock Castle (1793–94). Cragfont was

Rogana complex, Sumner County, 1995. Photograph by Mike Gavin, Historic Sites Collection, MTSU Center for Historic Preservation.

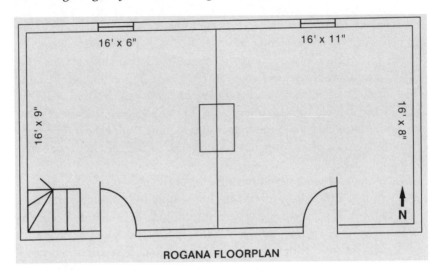

Rogana floorplan, 1995. Drawing by Jeri Hasselbring, Historic Sites Collection, MTSU Center for Historic Preservation.

built by Rogan's neighbor, the planter James Winchester; Rock Castle was home to Daniel Smith, Rogan's commander in the boundary surveys and some Indian conflicts. Though Rogana is devoid of architectural embellishment, the same careful attention is given to the cut stone in all three of these houses, which date within a decade or less of each other. All share the distinction of being among the earliest permanent masonry dwellings in the county and in Middle Tennessee.

More important, Rogana is a rare surviving example of American architecture that is clearly based on an Irish folk house in scale, materials, and plan. Unlike many of his countrymen, Rogan did not choose to build in the form of the Pennsylvania German log construction with central passage that is so commonly linked with the pioneer settlement of the Mid-Atlantic, Southeast, and Midwest.[72] Rather, Rogan built in the traditional two-room linear floor plan of Irish folk houses and used dressed limestone, a plentiful material in both his native County Donegal and his adopted Sumner County.

The entrances to the Rogan home, following Irish tradition, open directly into the room of the family. This arrangement effectively welcomed the visitor immediately to the hearth, as opposed to entering a central passage off of which rooms opened for privacy and formality.[73] Each room is entered by a central recessed doorway measuring 3 feet, 4 inches wide, with wooden lintels and stone sills. The existing modern wooden door appears to have had glass in the top half. If Rogan adhered to a very common Irish precedent, he would have installed half-doors, allowing the light and "good people" (the fairies of Irish legend) to come in the top while colder air and animals could be kept out by closing the bottom half.[74] Opposite each door is a window, also 3 feet, 4 inches wide. Practical for cross-ventilation, the feature of opposing openings is also grounded in Irish folklore. While interpretations vary, the openings were said to be situated to allow a direct path for the "good people" to come and go through the house, ensuring the continued luck of the occupants.[75]

The two rooms are almost the same size and roughly square. Internally, the west room measures 16 feet, 6 inches across, by 16 feet, 9 inches wide; the east room measures 16 feet, 11 inches across, by 16 feet, 8 inches. These rooms approximate the interior average of the traditional northern Irish farmhouse. They are also similar in space to the 16-foot-square dimensions of most log cabins built by English settlers (reproducing the English single-bay cottage) who came across the mountains from the tidewater area.[76] Rogan and whoever assisted him in constructing his house reproduced generally common dimensions for modest frontier dwellings.

The long rectangular shape of Irish folk housing and the linear linking of two or more rooms was customary and preserved by practice and superstition. A house, to be "lucky," must be only one-room wide. A folk saying from Rogan's County Donegal was "Widen the house and the family will get smaller."[77]

The hearth was the focal point of the room. Around the fire the cooking, eating, reading, singing, and storytelling took place. The wide hearth would have been fitted, as in Ireland, with crane, iron pots, flesh and pot-hooks, griddle, and frying pan. Practical and sturdy furniture such as shelves, presses, and tables would have lined the walls, leaving the center of the room free. Well into the nineteenth century, the center of the room, before and around the hearth, was the sleeping place for the entire family and any friends who stayed the night.[78]

In the Rogan house, each room was dominated by a fireplace that shared the central dressed-stone chimney. This chimney passes through the loft and straddles, in Irish fashion, the roof ridge. The east room fireplace has a massive stone lintel fully 5 feet across and 1 foot and 7 inches wide. In the west room, a radiating voussoir with keystone arch, now only partially intact, supports the chimney. Because of the more carefully constructed fireplace, and the fact that the loft is reached from a corner stairwell, this was probably considered the best room, and here family and friends would have congregated. Unlike most Irish houses of the period, which had dirt or flagged stone floors, Rogan laid poplar boards over red cedar sleepers. The lathed and plastered ceiling is 9 feet high.

The principal adaptation of Rogan's house, which departs from the Irish norm, is the separate loft running the full length of the house. While lofts were built in some parts of Ireland, their construction was haphazard, a structural afterthought, for the storage of food, more treasured possessions, and as the traditional sleeping place for children. Generally, the loft was but a raised platform at one end of the house, usually above the hearth and butted against the chimney breast for warmth and dryness. The massive central chimney in Rogan's house would have succeeded in keeping the loft reasonably warm, and wooden-shuttered windows at either of the gable ends provided light and ventilation. The steep, narrow wooden staircase to the loft was built at a right angle following the lines of the corner to save space. This method of building and siting stairs was a fairly common American modification contemporary to Rogan's.[79]

The roof of Rogan's house is also based on traditional Irish design. A-shaped couples support lighter timbers or purlins, which is typical for laying on a thatch roof.[80] Rogan may have first roofed his house with thatch, completing the effect of an Irish folk house.[81] This is indeed probable because Rogan likely knew how to thatch a roof, and locally grown oat straw would have been a suitable material. In eighteenth-century Ireland, roofing materials were almost always those that could be obtained locally, and roofs were usually built by the occupants. Only as society became more affluent and sophisticated did thatchers become a specialized group of laborers and craftsmen.[82] A thatched-roof house would have been economical, easy to install, and especially familiar for the Rogan family.

As Rogan brought Irish settlement patterns, farming methods, and folk architecture to the landscape, he also brought his religion to frontier society. At Rogana, his family is credited with establishing the Catholic Church in Sumner County.[83] The Rogans, devout Irish Catholics who had experienced the intolerance and persecution of eighteenth-century Ireland, were determined to practice their religion in America. In frontier Tennessee, however, Roman Catholicism was not a well-established nor a particularly welcome religion in a region dominated by Protestant congregations, including Methodists, Baptists, Scotch-Irish Presbyterians, and the locally founded Cumberland Presbyterians, of which Rogan's friend, Joseph Brown, was an early leader and minister.[84]

In spite of the lack of a priest and a formal church building, the Rogan family remained true to the Catholic faith. The homes of Hugh and Nancy and their son Francis, who did not see a priest until he was thirty years old, were the meeting places for area Catholics for over fifty years, until the denomination was formalized in Gallatin in 1837, and St. Peter's Church built in 1844.[85]

Around 1825, Francis built a brick house immediately adjacent and connected to the cottage.[86] This house is currently abandoned and in poor condition, but its design and features indicate that the American-born son of Irish emigrants was a prosperous farmer and well able to afford an impressive home. That he did not demolish the old stone dwelling, but rather connected the two buildings, may be interpreted in several ways.

After Hugh's death, Nancy may have preferred to continue living in the cottage that was reminiscent of her homeland. Or, it may have been convenient to have the solid stone building for storage or to house animals. As the years passed, the house served as a tangible reminder of the family's Irish roots and rather remarkable history. The stone house built and lived in by the Rogan family is a material culture resource surviving from the period of early statehood, and as a rare example of Irish folk housing adapted to the region, it has a significant place in Tennessee's vernacular architectural history.

From the farmhouse, the study of the landscape moves outward because the other features of the farm and community are related to it, both functionally and historically.[87] Francis, the second son of Hugh and Nancy, married Martha Read, the granddaughter of Isaac Bledsoe. Their son, William, inherited the property and houses, which remained in the family until well into the twentieth century.[88] A family cemetery, set apart from the surrounding farmland by a wrought-iron fence, is sited, typically, on a hillside overlooking the farm and house and away from crossroads and secular gathering spots.[89] One gravestone reads "Francis Rogan, born Sept. 14, 1798, died Sept. 26, 1885, Son of Hugh Rogan and Ann Duffy." A larger monument to "John Montgomery Rogan, Son of Martha Read and Francis Rogan, born Sept. 25, 1840, Died July 15, 1862" is also prominent. Several illegible stones and indentations indicate the presence of a number of other graves.

Mrs. Charles Rogan, the wife of one of Hugh's direct descendants, submitted an entry on the "Rogan Burying Ground" for a 1976 compilation of cemeteries. In it she stated that Hugh Rogan and his wife, Nancy Duffy

Rogan family cemetery, 1995. Photograph by Carroll Van West.

Rogan, were buried here. She also mentioned weathered stones for Richard Parkerville, who died in 1838, and Charles Duffy, born 1770, and died in 1826.[90] If these stones still exist in the cemetery, they are no longer legible.

Cultural geographers offer the analogy of the farmhouse as a parent surrounded by offspring that include not only the dependencies and features of the farm, including the family cemetery, but also buildings of the nearby community that existed because of the farm [or farms].[91] In Atlantic Europe, the communal, commercial, and religious needs of farms were met by small clusters of buildings at a convenient locale. Along with the single-family farm, the presence of the unincorporated hamlet or village at a crossroads is part of the lasting legacy of the Irish and Scotch-Irish culture on the Tennessee landscape.[92]

To a large extent, crossroads villages provide identity and vitality to the surrounding countryside and a sense of community for the people. They began to appear on the landscape when farmers had produced enough good harvests to erect satisfactory homes, barns, fences, and wanted goods and services beyond their capacity and that of their neighbors to produce. The owners of farmland along a frequently traveled trail, path, or road, often paralleling a water route, would survey or "plat" a village site where two or three roads crossed.[93]

The village that developed at the crossing of the trails or roads was usually named after one of the area's first settlers and a general store, tavern, and a few other buildings would be erected.[94] Near these villages, the social, commercial, educational, and religious aspects of the emerging society originated and were nurtured.[95]

The unincorporated community of Rogana followed this pattern of development emerging in the early nineteenth century at the point where trails following the routes of Bledsoe, Dry Fork, and East Fork Creeks crossed. Named for Hugh Rogan, the small town supplied the needs of nearby farm families for over a century. A flour mill, a general store, and a few other businesses were located at Rogana. When the railroad came to Sumner County, the tracks branched east off the north-south line at Rogana. A depot was erected by the Louisville and Nashville Railroad in the mid-1800s, and passenger service was available into the twentieth century. Rogana was also a shipping point for livestock.[96] Today, the paved Rogana and Dry Fork Roads follow the old trails, intersecting at the junction and giving credence to Estyn Evans's conclusion that the trails followed by the Scotch-Irish became roads, and their system of settlement and land use is stamped on the landscape.[97]

With the construction of U.S. Highway 31E and the easy accessibility to Gallatin, Lebanon, and Nashville that it brought, Rogana's reason for being ceased to exist; businesses closed and buildings were torn down. After the demolition of the depot in the 1960s, Rogana's identity was known only by its place name on maps, the road, and by longtime community residents.

Peirce F. Lewis explains that most major cultural change does not occur gradually but in "great sudden historic leaps, commonly provoked by such great events as wars, depressions, and major inventions."[98] After these leaps occur, the landscape is likely to look very different from before. Tennessee has experienced many such leaps in its two centuries, but, in a fortunate confirmation of Lewis's observations, many "pre-leap" landscape features inevitably remain, even though their reasons for being have disappeared.[99] The Rogana complex—the house, farm, cemetery, and community—is a prime example of this enduring landscape phenomenon. It is, like its Irish builder and namesake, a remarkable survivor and a telling and tangible document of Tennessee's early years.

Notes

The author gratefully acknowledges the courteous assistance, review, and comments of Tom Sweeney, architect (R.I.B.A.), inspector of schools, Department of Education, Dublin, Ireland.

1. D. W. Meinig, ed., *The Interpretation of Ordinary Landscapes, Geographical Essays* (New York, 1979), is one of the most practical and thoughtful publications on interpreting the rural landscape to date. Meinig, in his essay "The Beholding Eye," 33–48, and in his summation of the landscape analysis methods of geographer-author-editor-publisher J. B. Jackson in "Reading the Landscape," 228–29, discusses the basic concepts of analyzing the cultural landscape.
2. Marwyn S. Samuels, "The Biography of Landscape," in Meinig, *Ordinary Landscapes,* 67.
3. Here, "Irish" refers to the native majority population of the island who had maintained for centuries a distinctive culture and language and, in the eighteenth century, were predominantly Roman Catholic. Though "Scots-Irish" would be a more appropriate description, "Scotch-Irish" is a term of American origin used after 1850 to differentiate the earlier emigrants from the wave of "famine" immigrants who came in the 1840s and thereafter. The Scotch-Irish, generally Protestant and English-speaking, were descended from families first transplanted into Ireland during the reign of Elizabeth I to farm land confiscated from the Irish. In Blanche Bentley's essay on "Tennessee Scotch Irish Ancestry" in the *Tennessee Historical Magazine* 2 (Jan. 1920): 200–11, she lists a number of "first families" of Tennessee who were of Scottish origin but who had lived for several generations in the northeastern province of Ulster, particularly County Antrim. Among them were the Adairs, Campbells, Houstons, Blacks, Crawfords, Donelsons, Jacksons, and Alexanders (205).

    Emyr Estyn Evans, in "The Scotch-Irish: Their Cultural Adaptation and Heritage in the American Old West," presents a well-documented explanation of the contributions of the Irish and Scotch-Irish to frontier society and culture including landscape, architecture, agriculture, and religion. This work is included in E. R. R. Green, ed., *Essays in Scotch-Irish History* (London, 1969), 69–86.
4. In the 1600s, the land of Ireland changed hands. English armies under the Tudor monarchs slowly conquered Ireland in an effort to make Protestant England safe in the midst of European countries divided by religion. When Irish leaders, unwilling to accept the restrictions of English law, went into voluntary exile on the continent, British control over Ireland took place in the form of "plantation." Protestants from Scotland and England were transplanted to Ulster, the six northern counties of Armagh, Cavan, Coleraine, Donegal, Fermanagh, and Tyrone, and new communities were established with lands confiscated from the Irish. The embittered and degraded natives remained, however, as tenants and laborers in the Protestant areas,

always waiting for opportunities to avenge their enforced subjugation. The Irish took advantage of the conflict between Scotland and England to create confusion and disharmony. With the dissolution of the monarchy, Cromwell's army landed in Dublin with the sole purpose of finally bringing the Irish into total submission to the English government. The consequences of plantation and Cromwell's assault may be viewed as historical sources of the continuing "troubles" in Ireland today. Historian Aidan Clark of Trinity College, Dublin, provides a succinct discussion of "The Colonisation of Ulster and the Rebellion of 1641 (1603–60)" in T. W. Moody and F. X. Martin, eds., *The Course of Irish History* (Dublin, 1984), 189–203. See also A. R. Orme, *Ireland* (Chicago, 1970), 130–31.

5. A cogent interpretation of the circumstances resulting from the penal laws is provided by Maureen Wall in "The Age of Penal Laws (1691–1778)," in Moody and Martin, eds., *The Course of Irish History,* 217–31.

6. Orme, *Ireland,* 130.

7. Wall, "The Age of Penal Laws," 218–20. For a more complete description of the penal laws, see Seumas MacManus, *The Story of the Irish Race* (Old Greenwich, Conn., 1992), 454–69.

8. Wall, "The Age of Penal Laws," 221–24; Orme, *Ireland,* 131; and MacManus, *The Story of the Irish Race,* 458–59.

9. Wall, "The Age of Penal Laws," 221–24; R. B. McDowell, *Ireland in the Age of Imperialism and Revolution 1760–1801* (New York, 1979), 14–15.

10. William D. Griffin, comp. and ed., *The Irish in America, 1550–1972* (Dobbs Ferry, N.Y., 1973), 31. Swift's famous essay "A Modest Proposal" is a satire on the plight of the Irish peasantry.

11. Arthur Young, *A Tour of Ireland,* ed. Constantia Maxwell (Cambridge, 1925), 187.

12. E. Estyn Evans, *The Personality of Ireland* (Cambridge, 1973), 12. Jay Guy Cisco in *Historic Sumner County, Tennessee* (Nashville, 1909), 291, gives Hugh Rogan's date of birth as September 16, 1747, at Glentown or Glentourne (which means "home of outlaws"), County Donegal. Two villages by that name were located in County Donegal in the eighteenth century. One was in the northwestern part of Donegal in the Gweedore District; the other in the eastern section of the county twenty-five miles southwest of Londonderry (Derry) near Carrigans. Neither village exists today, though a few abandoned cottages mark the latter. It is probable that Rogan lived in the more eastern village, for his wife, Nancy Duffy, was from Lisduff, fifteen miles away in County Tyrone. This information was supplied by Tom Sweeney, Dublin, Ireland, in a letter to the author, Sept. 3, 1993.

13. Evans, *The Personality of Ireland,* 85.

14. Ibid., 88–91.

15. Elizabeth Healy, ed., "Northwards to Donegal," *Ireland of the Welcomes* 31 (Sept./Oct. 1982): 10–12.

16. R. B. McDowell, "The Protestant Nation (1775–1800)," Moody and Martin, *The Course of Irish History,* 217–18, 232–34; and Stephen Gwynn, *Henry Grattan and His Times* (Freeport, N.Y., 1971), 41.

17. In *The Irish in America,* 101, William Griffin notes that in 1778, General Sir Henry Clinton reported to the colonial secretary in London that among the American rebels, the Irish immigrants were to be looked on as the most serious antagonists. Griffin

points out that 1,492 American officers were of Irish birth or descent, and that 15 of the 26 generals of the Revolutionary forces were born in Ireland. See also Audrey Lockhart, "Some Aspects of Emigration from Ireland to the North American Colonies Between 1660 and 1775, " (M. Litt. thesis, Trinity College, Dublin, 1971), 163.

18. Dickson, *Ulster Emigration to Colonial America* 1718–1775 (London, 1966) 222–23; and David Noel Doyle, *Ireland, Irishmen, and Revolutionary America* (Dublin, 1981), 51.

19. Dickson, *Ulster Emigration,* 224–26; and Doyle, *Ireland, Irishmen, and Revolutionary America,* 74.

20. Dickson, *Ulster Emigration,* 224–26. See also Lockhart, *Some Aspects of Emigration,* 142; and Green, "Ulster Emigrants' Letters," in Green, *Essays in Scotch-Irish History,* 94.

21. David Hackett Fischer, *Albion's Seed* (New York, 1989), 608–12.

22. Ibid.; Evans, "The Scotch-Irish," Green, *Essays in Scotch-Irish History,* 75.

23. Cisco, *Historic Sumner County,* 291; Stephen Gwynn, *Henry Grattan and His Times* (Freeport, N.Y., 1971), 236, 250; and McDowell, *Ireland in the Age of Imperialism,* 462–63.

24. Cisco, *Historic Sumner County,* 291; Tom Stritch, *The Catholic Church in Tennessee: The Sesquicentennial Story* (Nashville, 1987), 39–40; and (Nashville) *Tennessean,* July 23, 1986, 1.

25. Draper Manuscripts, 31S189, the Collection of Lyman C. Draper, State Historical Society of Wisconsin, Madison, Microfilm, Tennessee State Library and Archives, Nashville. Included in this collection are several documents that mention Rogan. One of the most informative is a letter from Joseph Brown, a personal acquaintance of Hugh Rogan, to Lyman Draper, Sept. 4, 1845, from Cave Spring, Maury County, Tennessee (6XX11).

26. Weston A. Goodspeed, ed., *History of Tennessee* (Nashville, 1887), 916.

27. Ibid.; John Carr, *Early Times in Middle Tennessee* (Nashville, 1857, rpt. 1958), 12–13.

28. W. Woodford Clayton, *History of Davidson County, Tennessee, with Illustrations and Biographical Sketches of Its Prominent Men and Pioneers* (Philadelphia, 1880), 23.

29. Ibid., 35.

30. Robert E. Corlew, *Tennessee, A Short History,* 2d ed., (Knoxville, 1981), 53–54.

31. Carr, *Early Times,* 12.

32. Ibid., 12–13.

33. Ronald N. Satz, *Tennessee's Indian Peoples* (Knoxville, 1979), 68.

34. Carr, *Early Times,* 13.

35. Clayton, *History of Davidson County,* 61–63.

36. Ibid., 63.

37. Colonel Joseph Brown, interview by L. C. Draper, Sept. 20, 1844, Draper MSS, TSLA, 5XX52.

38. Clayton, *History of Davidson County,* 53–54; and Walter T. Durham, "Westward with Anthony Bledsoe: The Life of an Overmountain Frontier Leader," *Tennessee Historical Quarterly* 53 (Spring 1994): 16–17, provide accounts of the death of Bledsoe.

39. Clayton, *History of Davidson County,* 53–54; Durham, "Westward with Anthony Bledsoe, 16–17.

40. Clayton, *History of Davidson County,* 54.

41. Ibid.

42. Cisco, *Historic Sumner County,* 292.
43. Goodspeed, *History of Tennessee,* 917.
44. Carr, *Early Times,* 13.
45. Goodspeed, *History of Tennessee,* 916–917.
46. Brown interview.
47. Joseph Brown to L. C. Draper, Sept. 4, 1845, Draper MSS, TSLA, 6XX11.
48. Brown interview.
49. Joseph Brown to L. C. Draper, Sept. 4, 1845, Draper MSS, TSLA, 6XX11.
50. Ibid.
51. Hall, *Early History,* 33; (Nashville) *Tennessean,* July 23, 1986, 1–2.
52. Cisco, *Historic Sumner County,* 292; (Nashville) *Tennessean,* July 23, 1986, 1–2.
53. Walter T. Durham, *James Winchester, Tennessee Pioneer* (Gallatin, Tenn., 1979), 83.
54. Hall, *Early History,* 33.
55. Henry Glassie, *Passing the Time in Ballymenone: Culture and History of an Ulster Community* (Philadelphia, 1982), 603.
56. Desmond McCourt, "The Dynamic Quality of Irish Rural Settlement," in R. H. Buchanan, Emrys Jones, and Desmond McCourt, eds., *Man and His Habitat; Essays Presented to Emyr Estyn Evans,* (New York, 1971), 160. Henry Glassie provides a succinct discussion of Irish contributions to American architecture and the landscape in his essay "Irish" included in Dell Upton's *America's Architectural Roots* (Washington, 1986), 75–79. This essay summarizes the research and conclusions of Glassie's influential work on this topic over a period of years and in several publications, including *Passing the Time in Ballymenone.* Estyn Evans discusses the same topic in "The Scotch-Irish," in Green, ed., *Essays in Scotch-Irish History,* and draws on the work of both Glassie and Fred Kniffen. See also Kniffen's essay "Folk Housing: Key to Diffusion" in Dell Upton and John Michael Vlach, eds., *Common Places: Readings in American Vernacular Architecture* (Athens, Ga., 1986), 3–26.
57. Sumner County, Deed Book H-8, 74–75, Hugh Rogan, Grant No. 137, Apr. 27, 1793.
58. John Brown to Lyman Draper, Sept. 4, 1845, Draper MSS, TSLA, 6XX11; Tennessee Historical Commission, *Tennessee Historical Markers* (Nashville, 1972), 159–60, Marker 3 B 22.
59. Walter T. Durham, *The Great Leap Westward* (Gallatin, Tenn., 1969), 31.
60. William F. and Ruth Hagerty, "Parker-Bryson Historic District," National Register of Historic Places Registration Form, Jan. 1987, Tennessee Historical Commission, Nashville.
61. Cisco, *Historic Sumner County,* 33.
62. Corinne Alexander, telephone conversation with author, May 27, 1994. Robert and Corinne Alexander live adjacent to the property on which the Rogan house and cemetery are located. As longtime residents of the area, they are familiar with the landscape and the community's history.
63. Evans, "The Scotch-Irish," in Green, *Essays in Scotch-Irish History,* 74.
64. Tennessee Century Farms Nomination Forms consulted were the Bradley Farm (1795), Gillespie Farm (1785), Oak Haven Farm (1786), and Wallace Farm (1785), Sumner County, Century Farms Collection, MTSU Center for Historic Preservation, Murfreesboro, Tenn.

65. Evans, "The Scotch-Irish," 80–83; and Orme, *Ireland,* 135.
66. Evans, "The Scotch-Irish," 83.
67. Hagerty, "Parker-Bryson Historic District."
68. Glassie, "Irish," 77.
69. Meinig, *Ordinary Landscapes,* 228.
70. Cisco, *Historic Sumner County,* 29; *Tennessee Historical Markers,* 159–60.
71. John R. Stilgoe, *Common Landscapes of America, 1580–1845* (New Haven, 1982), 159.
72. The French naturalist F. A. Michaux, who traveled through Sumner County in 1802, commented on James Winchester's Cragfont and observed that most people in the area lived in "good log houses." His comments are found in Jessie Poesch, *The Art of the Old South: Painting, Sculpture, Architecture & the Products of Craftsmen, 1560–1860* (New York, 1983), 142. A number of publications deal with the ethnic origins, particularly the Scotch-Irish influence and development, of log buildings. The essays of by Fred Kniffen and Henry Glassie in Upton and Vlach, *Common Places,* are among the most widely accepted studies. See also Evans, "The Scotch-Irish," in Green, *Essays in Scotch-Irish History,* 76–81.
73. Glassie, "Irish," 76.
74. Evans, *Irish Folk Ways,* 48.
75. Ibid., 45; Timothy P. O'Neill, *Life and Traditions in Rural Ireland* (London, 1977), 17.
76. Evans, "The Scotch-Irish," 79.
77. Evans *Irish Folk Ways,* 41.
78. Ibid.; Evans, "The Scotch-Irish," 80.
79. Evans's discussion of the loft in *Irish Folk Ways,* 66–70, is helpful. See also Glassie's comments in Upton's *America's Architectural Roots,* 74.
80. O'Neill, *Life and Traditions,* 13.
81. Walter T. Durham and James W. Thomas, *A Pictorial History of Sumner County, Tennessee, 1786–1986* (Gallatin, Tenn., 1986), 16.
82. O'Neill, *Life and Traditions,* 14.
83. Durham and Thomas, *Pictorial History,* 117.
84. Herman A. Norton, *Religion in Tennessee, 1777–1945* (Knoxville, 1981), 47; William Bruce Turner, *History of Maury County, Tennessee* (Nashville, 1955), 18–24.
85. *Tennessee Historical Markers,* 159–60; Stritch, *The Catholic Church in Tennessee,* 39–40; Durham and Thomas, *Pictorial History,* 117.
86. Durham and Thomas, *Pictorial History,* 16.
87. Meinig, "Reading the Landscape," 228.
88. Goodspeed, *History of Tennessee,* 917.
89. Stilgoe, *Common Landscapes,* 221. A common belief in Ireland and Scotland was that Satan was most likely to frequent graveyards near meetinghouses and crossroads. This superstition was brought to America and explains, in part, the siting of so many older family cemeteries.
90. Jeanette Tillotson Acklen, comp., *Tombstones Inscriptions and Manuscripts* (Baltimore, 1976), 189. Charles Duffy may have been the nephew who delivered Nancy's letter to Hugh. His epitaph "A True Republican" proclaimed his political sentiments for an independent Irish nation. According to regional historian Walter T. Durham, Mrs.

Rogan was not wholly convinced that Hugh and Nancy Rogan were buried in the family cemetery, but her search of many years failed to reveal decisive information regarding their interment. To ensure that Hugh Rogan was remembered, she had a monument to him placed at Castalian Springs, appropriately near those of Isaac and Anthony Bledsoe.

91. Meinig, "Reading the Landscape," 228.
92. Evans, "The Scotch-Irish," 84–85.
93. Stilgoe, *Common Landscapes,* 256–57.
94. Ibid.
95. Lowry Nelson, *American Farm Life* (Cambridge, 1954), 8.
96. Robert Alexander, telephone conversation with author, Oct. 14, 1994.
97. Evans, "The Scotch-Irish," 74.
98. Peirce F. Lewis, "Axioms for Reading the Landscape," in Meinig, *Ordinary Landscapes,* 23.
99. Ibid.

Tennessee's Antebellum Common Folk

■ **Fred Arthur Bailey**

■

■ *Editor's Note:* Bailey turns to the words of the common folk themselves to reconsider the image of the "plain folk" in antebellum
■ Tennessee. Most common people lived as self-sufficient families on small farmsteads. Hard, "unrelenting toil" characterized a dis-
■ tinctive work culture that valued and respected labor while disdaining the planter class for its reliance on the labor of African
■ American slaves and tenant farmers. Common Tennesseans resented the educational opportunities of the plantation families;
■ even their understanding of recreation differed. Common people had no time, and little money, for gambling, dancing and horse-
■ back riding. The planter class and the common folk united in 1861 only because "Tennessee's common man responded to the
■ Civil War's crisis determined to defend family and friends."

Benjamin and Nancy Bailey lived out the humble saga of Tennessee's antebellum common folk, virtually anonymous individuals whose lives were memorialized in little more than scant census statistics. Far removed from the opulence of the South's slave-rich aristocracy in 1850, they scratched their sustenance from McNairy County's thin soil. Living on a tiny farmstead valued at only three hundred dollars, Benjamin and his wife struggled to provide for their six children, and Nancy was pregnant again. The decade proved unkind. By 1860, they had lost their land and, with it, their cherished independence. Illiterate and with few skills, Benjamin resettled near Mifflin in Henderson County, laboring as a tenant on another man's acres.[1]

Looming war threatened whatever felicity Benjamin Bailey enjoyed, and in common with many of his pineywoods neighbors, he saw little gain in a conflict dedicated to the preservation of the South's peculiar institution and the planters who profited from it. The Baileys committed to the Union, and in June 1863, William, their oldest son, journeyed to Corinth, Mississippi, to enlist in the Seventh Kansas Cavalry, a spirited regiment originally formed from abolitionist veterans of the state's bloody conflict over slavery.[2] The Baileys and thousands like them constituted the South's great inarticulate mass. Though their sojourns remain largely unchronicled, they contributed to Tennessee's rich heritage, and their values still impact its lively culture.

From the historian's perspective, the great majority of white southerners have remained silent, a people whose voices have been muted by the absence of letters, diaries, and personal memoirs. In the 1940s, Vanderbilt scholar Frank Lawrence Owsley pioneered common folk studies, becoming the first to promote the federal census as an instrument useful in providing statistics on landownership, personal wealth, and agricultural production.[3] But the ordered columns of government reports give no insight into a people's soul. How did they live before the Civil War? What were their aspirations and frustrations? What were the boundaries of their fellowship? Just what was it like to be a small farmer, a farmer's wife, or a farmer's child?

Acknowledging the essential limitations of the census, Owsley relied more heavily on sources apart from it. "Other important sources from which much can be learned . . . about the plain folk," he wrote, "are the old county and

Confederate veterans, 1923 reunion. Between 1915 and 1922, more than 1,600 Tennessee veterans of the Civil War completed questionnaires about their lives in the antebellum South. The three veterans in the center have been identified as Billy Nolen, Joe Couch, and Claudius Buchanan. Gift of Betty Ragsdale, Library Picture Collection, Tennessee State Library and Archives.

town histories, biographies, autobiographies, and recollections of men and women of only local importance—preachers, lawyers, doctors, county newspaper editors, and the like, who knew every family in the county and frequently in a much wider area."[4] Owsley failed, however, to appreciate the elitist perspective of these sources, that they were accounts in which the community's "best families" described the common folk rather than the common folk describing themselves. Faithful to his chosen sources, Owsley developed a patrician interpretation of the South's inarticulate masses, a portrait of the region's underclass as the upper class wished for them to have been.

Although Owsley's work, *Plain Folk of the Old South,* has reigned for almost a half century as the standard work on the common folk, in reality it was a polemic reflecting his career-long crusade against northern historians and his powerful aversion to the Marxist philosophy that, he believed, informed their scholarship.[5] Together with scores of other southern writers, he railed against Yankee-produced histories and textbooks that scored antebellum aristocrats as oppressors of African slaves and impoverished whites alike, and marked the South's leaders with the onus of war guilt.[6] To Owsley, suggestions of antebellum class conflict not only reeked of stale abolitionist propaganda, but also bore the whiff of Marxist ideology. "The Southern folk . . . were a closely knit people," he lectured. "They were not class conscious in a Marxian sense, for with rare exception they did not regard the planters and men of wealth as their oppressors."[7]

In Owsley's imagined South, small farmers and slave-rich planters lived together in absolute harmony. "There were," he explained, "important forces that diminished the feeling of class stratification and helped in the creation of a sense of unity between the plain folk and the aristocracy." From the wealthy to the impoverished, southerners resided in the same neighborhoods, worshipped at the same churches, and studied at the same schools. Through such associations the "rich and poor" developed "frequent ties of blood kinship," and any jealousy over differences in wealth was moderated by "the generally folkish and democratic bearing of the aristocracy." Given the decades-long critiques of northern historians, Owsley assured his readers that the "sense of unity between all social and economic groups cannot be stressed too much, in view of the strongly and widely held opinion to the contrary."[8]

If northern historians presented a misleading interpretation of the South's common folk, Owsley declared that older southern historians, those "born before 1890," had a "firsthand acquaintance with one and often two generations who had lived before 1860," and could from their own experiences testify to the reality of antebellum egalitarianism. Sadly, he reflected, these older scholars had neglected to record the recollections of those who best remembered life before the Civil War. "The truth of the matter is a lack of trained historians in the South until well after the opening of the present century" meant that the "testimony of these star witnesses, the survivors of the old regime, was not taken while they were numerous enough and young enough for their evidence to be both full and valid."[9]

Although Owsley did not specify what he meant when he spoke of the late-gathered "testimony of these star witnesses," such a collection existed a few city blocks from his own office on the Vanderbilt University campus. Housed in the Tennessee State Library and Archives was a rare and useful source giving voice to the impoverished and small farmers as well as the wealthy aristocrats—the Tennessee Civil War Veterans Questionnaires.[10]

Gustavus W. Dyer and John Trotwood Moore, the two Tennesseans responsible for developing and collecting the questionnaires, were also caught up in the southern reaction to northern historical criticisms of the South's class structure.[11] Believing the veterans' testimonies would serve as the foundation of a "true history of the Old South" that confirmed general social harmony, they requested from each individual a discussion of his background: how much land did his family own, did his family have slaves, what kind of house did his family occupy and how many rooms did it have, what kinds of activities were engaged in by his father and his mother, what type of work did he do as a boy, and how much education did he receive. This was followed by a series of questions soliciting the subject's opinions concerning social class relations: was there conflict or consensus between slave owners and non–slave owners, was slave ownership a factor in politics, and did economic opportunities exist for "a poor young man, honest and industrious, to save up enough to buy a small farm or go into business for himself?"[12]

Ironically, the approximately 1,650 individuals who returned their forms between 1915 and 1922 provided the source material for a "true history of the Old South" quite different from that envisioned by either Dyer or Moore or described by Frank L. Owsley. Given the opportunity to speak for themselves through the questionnaires, non-elite Tennesseans presented a picture of common folk life that varied dramatically from that remembered by their wealthy contemporaries.[13]

"My folks was working folks," boasted James Patton Walker, "not office Seekers nor preachers, lawers Doctors nor traders." Walker proudly counted himself a part of the common mass, subsistence farmers who considered themselves a people set apart from the planters and professionals with their emphasis upon commercial pursuits, party politics, and social prominence. A majority of these small farmers possessed some land and, with it, gained a degree of economic independence; a less contented minority had neither land nor slaves and struggled as tenants and laborers on property belonging to others; and all shaped their lives around the generational cycle of births, baptisms, marriages, and deaths, and the annual cycle of planting, cultivating, and harvesting. Conditioned to hard labor, they religiously quoted the injunction to follow "the plow as by the sweat of the Brow" and condemned as decadent any neighbor given to a leisure ethic. William Vardell recalled that almost everyone in his Rutherford County community worked, except "off course [for] a few worthless slaveholders that did not." George V. Payne concurred. "Labor was respected," he wrote, but "the men that owned Slaves did not work and did not have there children to do any work."[14]

Even though the common folk associated slave-rich aristocrats with an aversion to manual labor, many small farmers owned human property. Some of these lesser masters saw this as a judicious investment enabling them to shift from subsistence to commercial agriculture, thereby opening for themselves and their children the path to elite status. But for the vast majority the possession of an individual slave, or perhaps a family unit, simply meant extra hands in the fields, or a valued servant—a cook, a washwoman, a seamstress—for their careworn spouse. "We worked side by side with the slaves," F. S. Williams wrote of his Stewart County youth, an experience he shared with John H. O'Neal, Peter Donnell, and many others. "My father had 7 boys 6 older than myself," recalled O'Neal. "We all went to the field same as the Negroes." Raised in a similar environment, Donnell toiled on his father's land in Wilson County. "I worked . . . with the darkes[,] plowed howed mowed cut wheat oats split rales done anything the darkes don."[15]

Landownership, or the absence of it, determined the expectations of Tennessee's common folk. Those who farmed their own acres felt a sense of permanence that created in them a concern for neighborhood harmony and a desire to share with their relatives and friends the joys and sorrows of daily life. They anticipated that, in time, their children would marry within the community, would establish their own farmsteads, and would, in turn, rear the next generation according to traditions imparted by their parents and their grandparents before them. But landless Tennesseans held no such hopes. They remained in a neighborhood only so long as their landlord or their employer valued their services; when dismissed, they packed their meager belongings and trudged the country roads in search of other acres to sharecrop or other farmers needful of an extra hand. "My father farmed some at home on rented land," explained Robert R. Bayless. "He also worked away from home for the land lord upon whose property we lived and for others." Recalling his family's frequent moves, James B. West easily inventoried their few possessions: "one horse and cow and some hogs we was very poor."[16]

The common folks' housing reflected on the one hand the landless tenants' transitory lifestyle and, on the other hand, the landed farmers' commitment to family, community, and permanence. Although log cabins punctuated the Tennessee landscape, their quality varied according to each family's status, and the poorest, of course, dwelled in the least desirable of them. Living on another man's property, tenants and laborers felt little incentive to improve their miserable hovels, structures that generally contained one or two poorly furnished rooms, dirt floors, and walls improperly insulated against winter's chill. Looking back upon their deprived youths, impoverished veterans sadly remembered that "stick and dirt" chimneys advertised their destitute circumstance. Typically, William Beard's father was a "renter all his life and died so." The family lived in "several different houses all [with the] same description": "Log . . . two rooms with stick and dirt chimney."[17]

Landowners resided in comfortable, though often crowded, cabins. The son of a McNairy County farmer with one slave, J. P. Wilson described his

Log dwelling near Culleoka, Maury County, 1995. Single-pen cabins like this were once typical dwellings for Tennessee's antebellum common folk. Photograph by Carroll Van West.

house as a "room 16 feet square built of logs." Eventually, "an other room was added with a hall whear was born 12 children[.] 9 grew to be men and women." Such houses of two, three, four, and occasionally more rooms contained amenities not found in the poor's less desirable habitations. Small farmers' sons took care to detail "nicely hewn" logs of poplar or cedar wood, "cracks ... chinked and daubed with lime mortar," slab floors, and chimneys of brick or stone. Apart from the main house, a kitchen building allowed the farm wife to prepare her meals secure in the knowledge that an accidental fire would cause little damage to other buildings. Barns, smokehouses, and sheds protected the farmers' animals, tools, and supplies. Having grown up in a two-room log cabin with a separate kitchen, John W. Headrick explained that "the commun peopel live[d] in looge Houses in thos [days.] the best farmers had fram dwellings."[18]

In every neighborhood, a few of the more affluent farmers significantly improved their log cabins. Some weatherboarded the exterior facings, others plastered the interior walls, and still others added rooms of frame construction. Gilbert Marshall's Williamson County house illustrates the progression from a comfortable dwelling to a substantial habitation. "The original house was log," recorded his son, "consisting of a two-story part (one large room below and one above) and a large single story room. The two story part was connected with [the] one-story room by an open passage. Later the open passage was closed in, [the] house weatherboarded and other frame rooms added until there were eight rooms in all."[19]

Whether Tennessee's common man made his home in a wretched hovel or a weatherboarded cabin, he and his family spent most of their time in the open. The essential nature of subsistence farming required them to cultivate their own food, to grow the fibers necessary for their own clothing, to nurture animals valued for muscle power, meat, and hides, to make and repair tools, fences, and outbuildings, to saw firewood in prodigious amounts, and much more. Testifying in their questionnaires, veterans described a cultural work ethic in which unrelenting toil characterized each day from first light to last. In Monroe County, C. W. Hicks's family labored "from early morning until after sun down, plowing, hoeing, grubbing, chopping, hauling, mowing by hand, cradling etc., except one hour at noon and rarely a half holliday on Saturday to fish or hunt squirrels." He added: "Prior to the civil war the few farming tools in use were clumsy, slow and inefficient." Flavius Landers's father exemplified the pride of independence engendered by this lifestyle. He "was a man of all work," boasted the son. He "done his own carpenter work [made] his own plows made all the family shoes made the first pare of boots he ever owned made his own grain cradles and made the first Buggy he ever owned."[20]

While the common Tennessean was largely self-sufficient, skilled artisans played an important role in the community. Millers, blacksmiths, carpenters, masons, and tanners formed an integral part of an essentially cashless economy in which payment was more often in kind than in currency. W. F. Blevins, William D. Harkleroad, and George W. Samuel recorded that their fathers owned local gristmills and, by custom, received two sacks of corn or wheat in exchange for one of flour. Among the sons of blacksmiths, Phillip Copeland wrote that his father wielded a hammer "making nails, hoes, plows, and" horseshoes, and Joe Rich reported that his father owned his own shop, where he produced plows, wagons, and carts. Demarus Cunningham's father was a carpenter who "made all kinds of furniture, Tables, Cupboards, Bedsteads, Bureaus [and] coffins" using "cherry and walnut timbers," while Elijah Thompson's father was a mason who "built Chimneys . . . and stone walls, flues and smokestacks." Several veterans grew up in the homes of tanners, who were appreciated by farmers who needed leather to make shoes, straps, whips, harnesses, saddles, and bridles. Jacob Young described how his father "killed his [own] beefs [and] carried the hides to the tan yard where they were made into leather." For payment, he exchanged two green hides for every one that had been cured.[21]

The contributions of rural women to the family's well-being touched almost every part of the farm. While cooking, sewing, and child rearing devoured her time, a woman would also join her husband in the field when needed. With large families the rule, households with eleven, twelve, or thirteen children were common. Although the wife spent numerous hours feeding chickens, milking cows, tending the garden, and hauling water, the better part of her day was devoted to the manufacture of cloth and the sewing of it into shirts, pants, dresses, and bed linens.[22]

Reflecting on the duties of the farm wife, J. W. Askew wrote that his mother "had a loom and made all of her own clothes," William Hollingsworth testified that his mother "carded spun and wove all . . . the clothes for the family," and Benjamin Swafford remembered that his mother "worked by fire blase till late Bedtime every winter Knight to make close for the family."[23] These simple statements only suggest the tedious process by which the Tennessee woman laboriously manufactured her family's raiment.

In the fashion of subsistence farming, a family's wardrobe actually began with the farmer and his wife producing their own fibers. James McKnight's parents "raised sheep for wool . . . and flax for sheets and clothing." Other families grew small amounts of cotton and painfully hand-picked the seeds from its precious lint. The wife, assisted by her older daughters, then carded the fibers, twisted them onto a spinning wheel to create thread, and dyed the threads with pigments extracted from natural sources. William Cox recalled that his mother "colored [her threads] with herbs of all kinds," and Josiah House reminisced that he had "carried . . . many [a] basket of bark from the woods for Mother to dye the goods she was going to make [into] clothes for the family." Bent over her loom, the farm woman wove the threads into untold yards of fabric. Then ensued countless hours of cutting and stitching until at long last she had completed the desired garment. Such women prided themselves on their craftsmanship. Paralee Musgrove, one of the few women to complete a questionnaire, wrote that in youth she had made her own clothes. "In those days each girl tried to see which could make the prettier dress to wear to Church."[24]

Seeking relief from endless domestic chores, a few fortunate wives employed a slave or two as servants. This rarely freed them from all their responsibilities, but at least it exempted them from their more onerous tasks. While W. H. Barrow's mother "did work needed in the house [and] made clothes for the children," she saw to it that a "Negro woman did the cooking." Growing up in a similar household, Thomas Bryan described his family's somewhat rigid division of labor. "The negro woman did the cooking," he explained. "My sisters did the Spinning [and] my step mother helped with all the house work." For the owner of a few slaves, however, agricultural production generally took precedence over domestic needs. As Columbus London recalled, his family had "one negro woman [who] worked some in [the] house, when not at work in the field." While the possession of a slave or two contributed to the contentment of some wives, those among their peers without this luxury occasionally took umbrage. As one veteran confided in his questionnaire: "Sometimes I have heard the women folk say. . . . 'Oh she is stuck up because she has a negro.'"[25]

Tennessee's common man considered labor a precious commodity, and for that reason he introduced his children to the virtues of hard work at the earliest possible moment. Mothers expected their older daughters to watch after their younger siblings, and at the appropriate time every girl learned the mysteries of cooking, weaving, and midwifery. Fathers not only valued their sons as laborers, but also felt keenly the necessity to impart to them the vital skills of a subsistence farmer. In turn, the young boys developed a sense of familial responsibility and most looked forward to the day they graduated to the plow. William Beard testified that he "pulled weeds with older boys when

4 to 9 yrs old" and shortly after his ninth birthday "made a regular hand in the field." Looking back on their youths, veterans boasted of the tender age at which they struck their initial furrows. Among them William Frazier, James Giles, and Uriah Payne first turned earth at age eight; Burl Flemming, Pinkney Martin, and Linzey Thompson did so at age nine; and James K. Polk Andrews, J. V. Deck, and Robert Pafford commenced this manly responsibility when only ten years old. Given the veterans' numerous paeans to industry, A. M. Bruce's rare confession of indolence is somewhat refreshing. "I never liked [work] any to well," he admitted. "But I always had to do my part or take a limbing. . . . when it came to hoeing I generally had the cleanest row if it was not quite so long."[26]

Committed to a life of toil, the common man's children deeply resented the leisure ethic flaunted by the sons and daughters of Tennessee's slave-rich aristocrats. "Some times the Children of large Slave owners Showed a defiance," wrote William Needham of Hardeman County, and he shared this feeling with James Calvin Hodge, William Wilkins, Thomas Mason, and David Moss. The fact that "the Slave Holders [and] especially their sons" led idle lives angered Hodge. "They Hunted fished and went to school." To be sure, the rich and the poor often came together at community functions, but the wealthy always "showed a distinction especially in schools and to a great extent in church." Wilkins remembered that the largest slave owners "dident want a poor boy to go to see his girls," and Mason explained that "those who owned many slaves didnot associate Freely with non Slave holders[,] Especially the Children of the Slave holders." Moss also complained that "the most [of the] Slave Holders thought They was Better than men that Did not ow Slaves," and this was "Just so with the Boys and Girls." James Thompson recalled the hauteur of aristocratic women and their daughters. At public gatherings, he wrote, "females seemed to have a distant feeling toward each other," especially the "young girls who seemed at times to shun poor girls."[27]

Formal education also drove a wedge between Tennessee's upper classes and their less affluent neighbors. Even as wealthy veterans proclaimed absolute class harmony, they amended their testimonies with qualifiers based on intellectual attainment. "The slaveowner did not act with egotism," protested Joseph Cardwell of Smith County. "In fact his actions were less egotistical than the nonslaveowner due to his better education and knowledge." In Fayette County, declared Joshua Mewborn, total equality existed between slave owners and non–slave owners "where the latter had the culture and intelligence to merit it"; in Madison County, John Johnston had "no recollection of any instance where men who were slave owners affected any superiority over those who did not own Slaves," though "there was . . . a distinction between cultured refined people and uneducated, illiterate people." And in Roane County, John Osborne assured posterity that "if refinement and education were equal" little hostility existed; "they were not antagonistic if they were of equal intelligence."[28]

Those who lived on the lower rungs of the social ladder fully appreciated the significance of the wealthy's educational advantage. "Men who owned slaves did not mingle with those who did not own slaves," wrote Leander Baker of Hardeman County. "The Slave holder had private schools for his children." Looking back on their youth, William Barnes of Madison County explained that he "didnt attend no school as there wasnt no school to attend the rich class of people harred thair own teachers," and John Fergus of Rutherford County simply stated that "there was a school on Stewarts creek that Slave holders attended." This reality created among the impoverished a basic sense of fatalism. "Rich men Sent there boys to college," reflected William Eads in his questionnaire. "Slave holders had a better chance to Educate there boys rich men has the best chance now." James Clifton agreed. "True wealthy slaveholders were able to give their sons advantages in the way of education etc which the poor man could not."[29]

Even as the common man's sons labored in the fields and his daughters assisted in the household, the aristocrat's children pondered in the classroom. For ten months out of twelve, privileged youths advanced from elementary lessons in reading and writing to the more intense subjects of classical languages, geography, and mathematics, and often added polishes of rhetoric for the boys, and art and piano for the girls. Such an environment honed the skills of a young gentleman and made of the young women ideal wives to adorn a planter's mansion. Having attended the University of North Carolina, Thomas Webb boasted that his "Father was a strong advocate of education and told us wealth was precarious and education the safest fortune."[30]

Poorer Tennesseans received formal instruction decidedly inferior to that of their affluent contemporaries. When given the opportunity, they went to common schools that assembled from mid-July to early September, or, in colloquial terms, from when the corn was laid by until fodder-pulling and wood-hauling time; occasionally, they returned to class for a few weeks in January or February. In a few cases, the county provided free instruction, but more often parents paid tuitions of one dollar per month per child. Assembling in churches, poorly constructed cabins, and abandoned tobacco barns, the children sat on split log benches, had few books and little in the way of supplies, and learned their lessons by rote from teachers of the poorest quality. "The first school I went to," grumbled Samuel Matthews of Maury County, "was taught by a woman [who] couldnt spell toBaker." At best, wrote another veteran, these were schools "where you could learn to spell read write and figure a little."[31]

The sons of laborers and small farmers pointed out that agricultural responsibilities took precedence over formal education. All too often, remembered Thweatt McCartney, he "had to stay at home and work." School attendance was irregular, explained Carter Upchurch, because "the most of us had to work most of the time." William Miller agreed, noting that in his community "nearly all [were] poor and they had to work," and Thomas Booker stated simply that some children attended regularly, but "some did not the poor boys had to work." Typical of his generation, James Wiser sadly lamented that he "Did not go enough to learn the alphabet."[32]

Just as education separated the social classes, recreation also led to distinctions between patricians and plebeians. The wealthy turned toward leisure while the small farmers emphasized labor. Affluent Tennesseans enjoyed such pleasures as receptions, dances, gambling, and horseback riding—all activities with little utilitarian outcome. Uncomfortable with such frivolities, hardworking farmers engaged in pastimes that combined fun with function. Neighbors enjoyed fellowship at quiltings, hog killings, log rollings, corn shuckings, and barn raisings, and, in the process measurably contributed to the community's weal. Noting the stern moral code of her youth, Paralee Musgrove recalled the practical recreations that passed for pleasure in her Montgomery County neighborhood and then stressed that among her people there was "no dancing."[33]

Given the sharp contrasts in the lifestyles of Tennessee aristocrats and small farmers, expressions of class distinction naturally surfaced. Ensconced at society's top, the wealthy strictly defined the boundaries of their fellowship. "A large majority of [the planters] always recognized and spoke courteously to the class that did not own slaves," wrote the prosperous J. F. Osborne of life in antebellum Maury County. But these aristocrats "did not invite them to their social functions given by their families, or in any way encourage familiarity Socially." To be sure, he continued, at "public gatherings, there was far more familiarity shown and every one seem to act with less restriction and in a way that carried with it the thought [that] our rights and privileges were equal." Such pandering to the nonslaveholder was necessary, he explained, because the planters depended upon the nonslaveholders to serve in the "patrols," the citizen-constabulary responsible for tracking down runaway slaves and guarding the community against potential slave rebellions.

A more succinct observation came from W. M. Courtney, who stated that in Williamson County "all mixed freely in Church, Lodge, or in a business way, But of course . . . did not visit in a Social way." Marcus Toney acknowledged that in Davidson County, "Slave owners were a class unto themselves . . . while not antagonistic the slave owners were aloof"; and William Lillard proclaimed that in Rutherford County, while "the laboring man did not visit the aristocratic girls, [the planters] respected the laboring man if they thought he was honest."[34]

However fervent the wealthy's expressions of social harmony, they generally judged others according to their own elitist code. They would share fellowship with the common man, provided he was "honorable," or "a gentleman," or "of good character." Non–slave owners were respected, declared Hampton Cheney, "if they were well bred, honorable men, who conducted themselves properly, and were not offensive in their opposition to slavery." Jeremiah McKenzie made a similar affirmation. Acknowledging the existence of "separate and distinct classes," he emphasized that "the southern gentleman . . . always recognized worth and merit under all circumstances, and mingled freely with those who were respectable and honorable regardless of property." Of course, the aristocrats defined for themselves the standards of respectability and determined who met its criteria. "There was some distinction between the slaveholders and non-slaveholders," lectured Daniel Long, "as the more intelligent and cultured class owned slaves while the shiftless and ignorant had none."[35]

Such aristocratic arrogance highly offended Tennessee's laborers and small farmers. While William House resented the fact that "the laboring class was looked by a few of the Richest people as being a low class," James Hill scolded the "Large slaveholders [because they] felt themselves better than the poor white trash as they called" the common farmers. Growing up in Williamson County, Robert Mosley remembered that manual labor "was looked on as a low caling by most of the welthy peple" who "calde [working men] clod hopers." In turn, Tennessee's common folk condemned their slave-rich neighbors because they "felt their selves above the common people," because "tha didnt seem to be as friendly as tha aught to of bin," because they "regarded themselves as superior to the peasantry," because "some felt Self important and Puffed Up with Pride," and because "they felt biggety and above poor folk who did not have slaves." John M. Patrick of Benton County was disgusted by the actions of antebellum aristocrats. "Once an awhile one [would] turn up hise nos at a Pore man."[36]

The planters' conspicuous display of wealth, and the political and social power that accompanied it also offended Tennessee's common folk. Given the advantages of money, superior education, and family connections, aristocratic sons monopolized society's best positions, and, more often than not, treated their successes as their class's natural right. Among these, William Lillard, who grew up on a plantation cushioned by the labor of one hundred slaves, recalled that "when a young man became 21 years old his father would set him up . . . in some profession, merchant business, or on [a] Farm." His less well-heeled contemporaries could expect no such assistance, and, indeed, many believed that the planter class intentionally discouraged the poor. "The Slave holder generally would try to discourage the young people," declared James Trusty. "They wanted every thing for themselves." Having worked as a common laborer in his youth, Anderson Roach cursed that "when a slave holder hired a non slave holder he was principally looked on a being no better than a slave and was treated as one." J. P. Dillehay simply affirmed that the "slave holders thought more of their slaves than they did a poor honest Young white man." John L. Young of Davidson County well expressed the lifelong frustration felt by thousands of his peers: "As to employment for poor boys[,] the sons of rich men always got in first I know and have felt it."[37]

Tennessee's common man responded to the crisis of civil war determined to defend family and friends. Most sided with the Confederacy, a significant minority remained loyal to the Union, and all experienced the deprivations of camp life and the brutalities of battle. In time, however, thousands of those who marched in the ranks of gray questioned their role in a war fought so that rich men could prosper by the sweat of other men's brows. Looking to their own self-interest, they abandoned the Confederate cause.[38] Fissures born in the Old South became manifest during the Civil War and later erupted in the agrarian protests of the Grange movement of the 1870s and the Populist revolt of the 1890s.

A century and more has passed since Benjamin and Nancy Bailey anguished over their family's welfare. Had it not been for the Tennessee Civil War Veterans Questionnaires, their saga and the sagas of hundreds like them would have been long forgotten. These were not the "movers and shakers" of society counted alongside Andrew Jackson, James K. Polk, Andrew Johnson, and scores of lesser luminaries. They wrote no books, gave no passionate orations defending the "southern way of life," took no leading role in the secessionist crisis of 1861. But the Civil War impacted their lives, disrupted their domestic felicity, and dramatically altered their cultural aspirations. Whether saints or sinners, Tennessee's common folk adjusted to life's challenges as best they could, and in that context loved, hated, hoped, and died.

Today their children's children replicate their rituals in a human drama as old as civilization.

NOTES

1. Seventh Census of the United States, 1850: McNairy County, Tenn., 109; Eighth Census of the United States, 1860: Henderson County, Tenn., 205.
2. William C. Bailey, enlistment and service records, Seventh Kansas Cavalry Volunteers, 1863–1865, National Archives, Washington. The author of this essay is a linear descendant of Benjamin and William Bailey.
3. Frank Lawrence Owsley, *Plain Folk of the Old South* (Baton Rouge, 1949), 7–17.
4. Owsley, *Plain Folk,* 6 (quotation), 36–37, 144n.
5. Recognizing the polemical importance of Owsley's *Plain Folk,* several conservative scholars have praised it as a bulwark against liberal teachings. Melvin E. Bradford, "What We Can Know for Certain: Frank Lawrence Owsley and the Recovery of Southern History," *Sewanee Review* 78 (Oct. 1970): 665; Clyde Wilson, "Introduction," *Recovering Southern History,* a special issue of *Continuity: A Journal of History* 9 (Fall 1984): iv; Grady McWhiney, "Historians as Southerners," *Continuity: A Journal of History* 9 (Fall 1984): 22–23. Beginning their work in the early 1930s, Frank and Harriet Chappell Owsley, along with several of his graduate students, produced a number of works reflecting his investigation of the South's common people. See Frank Lawrence Owsley and Harriet Chappell Owsley, "The Economic Basis of Society in the Late Ante-Bellum South," *Journal of Southern History* 6 (Feb. 1940): 24–45; Frank Lawrence Owsley and Harriet Chappell Owsley, "The Economic Structure of Rural Tennessee, 1850–1860," *Journal of Southern History* 8 (May 1942): 161–82; Frank Lawrence Owsley, "The Pattern of Migration and Settlement on the Southern Frontier," *Journal of Southern History* 11 (May 1945): 147–76; Blanche H. Clark, *Tennessee Yeomen* (Nashville, 1942); Harry L. Coles, Jr., "Some Notes on Slaveownership and Landownership in Louisiana, 1850–1860," *Journal of Southern History* 9 (Aug. 1943): 381–94; Herbert Weaver, *Mississippi Farmers, 1850–1860* (Nashville, 1945). Two recently published volumes written by Vanderbilt historians expand the Owsley model: Robert Tracy McKenzie, *One South or Many? Plantation Belt and Upcountry in Civil War Era Tennessee* (Cambridge, 1994); and Donald L. Winters, *Tennessee Farming, Tennessee Farmers: Antebellum Agriculture in the Upper South* (Knoxville, 1994). Although McKenzie argues that measurable social mobility existed in antebellum Tennessee, his statistics demonstrate a notable inequity in the state's wealth distribution, which remained constant from the antebellum to the Reconstruction periods. Across the state, he discovered that in 1860 the richest 5 percent of the population possessed about 40 percent of the total wealth, while the bottom half of the population held between 4 and 6 percent. By 1870, little had changed, except that in the western cotton counties the elite 5 percent had increased its economic share to almost 50 percent and the bottom half had dropped to less than 4 percent. In the end, McKenzie admits that "absolute economic mobility deteriorated after the [Civil War]," but still concludes that "it would be a gross exaggera-

tion to speak of the proletarianization of white common folk during" the post war decades. McKenzie, *One South or Many?*, 98–99, 119, 194.

6. Harriet Chappell Owsley, *Frank Lawrence Owsley: Historian of the Old South* (Nashville, 1990), 134–35. "History textbooks have been written by Yankees," Owsley explained to his friend Allen Tate in 1932. "The purpose of my life will be to undermine by 'careful' and detached,' 'well documented,' 'objective' writing the entire Northern myth from 1820–1876. My books will not interest the general reader. Only the historians will read them, but it is the historian who teaches history classes and writes textbooks and they will gradually and without their own knowledge be forced into our position." Quoted in Harriet Owsley, *Frank Lawrence Owsley*, 78–79. For examples of Owsley's attacks upon the northern historiographic tradition, see Frank Lawrence Owsley, "The Irrepressible Conflict," in *I'll Take My Stand: The South and the Agrarian Tradition* (New York, 1930), 61–91; Frank Lawrence Owsley, "The Fundamental Cause of the Civil War: Egocentric Sectionalism," *Journal of Southern History* 7 (Feb. 1941): 3–18.

7. Owsley, *Plain Folk*, xxi, 133 (quotation). Owsley accused his critics of left-wing and Marxist proclivities. See Frank Lawrence Owsley, review of *Origins of Class Struggle in Louisiana: A Social History of White Farmers during Slavery and After, 1840–1875*, by Roger W. Shugg, *Journal of Southern History* 6 (Feb. 1940): 116–17; Frank Lawrence Owsley, "Reply to Fabian Linden's review of *Mississippi Farmers, 1850–1860*, by Herbert Weaver," *American Historical Review* 53 (July 1947): 845–49.

8. Owsley, *Plain Folk*, 134.

9. Ibid.

10. The questionnaires have been transcribed and published. Colleen M. Elliott and Louise A. Moley, comps., *Tennessee Civil War Veterans Questionnaires*, 5 vols. (Easley, S.C., 1985). Although Owsley never directly referred to the questionnaires, the evidence is strong that he knew of their existence. Blanche H. Clark wrote her doctoral dissertation under his direction and used a selected number of the questionnaire responses to support her and Owsley's image of antebellum class harmony. Later, when the dissertation was published, Owsley wrote the work's introduction. In addition, Frank and Harriet Owsley began research on their study of the South's plain folk in 1933 and did much of their work at the Tennessee State Library and Archives. They were assisted by Mary Daniel Moore, the head archivist and widow of John Trotwood Moore, who was largely responsible for the questionnaires' collection. Mary Brown Daniel Moore considered the questionnaire project one of her husband's more important contributions to Tennessee's heritage. Blanche Henry Clark, "The Agricultural Population in Tennessee, 1840–1860: With Special Reference to the Non-Slaveholders, 1840–1860" (Ph.D. diss., Vanderbilt Univ., 1939); Clark, *Tennessee Yeomen*, xvii–xxii, 11–20; Harriet Owsley, *Frank Lawrence Owsley*, 136; Mary Brown Daniel Moore, "The Tennessee State Library in the Capitol," *Tennessee Historical Quarterly* 12 (Mar. 1953): 15–18.

11. The son of a comfortable country merchant in Henry County, Virginia, Gustavus W. Dyer (1867–1948) taught sociology at Vanderbilt University and served briefly as director of the Tennessee Department of Archives and History (1913–1915). He developed the Tennessee Civil War Veterans Questionnaires from a shorter question-

naire that he had orally administered to twenty-five Virginia veterans while writing his doctoral dissertation at the University of Chicago. Throughout his career, Dyer "denied that the South was dominated by aristocracy and . . . insisted that historians were incorrect in their statements that 'slavery was holding back the progress of the South.'" Leaving office shortly after he mailed the first questionnaires, he collected relatively few of them. When John Trotwood Moore became the head of the newly established Tennessee State Library and Archives in 1919, he renewed Dyer's efforts and retrieved the vast majority of the responses. Eighth United States Census, 1860: Henry County, Virginia, 44; Gustavus W. Dyer, *Democracy in the South before the Civil War* (Nashville, 1905), 86–90; (Nashville) *Tennessean*, Feb. 29, 1948, 8; Mary Daniel Moore, "The Tennessee State Library," 15–18.

12. In his cover letter to the veterans, Dyer explained that he was "convinced after much critical study and much original research, that the leading history of the United States grossly misrepresents conditions in the old South. . . . The true history of the South has yet to be written." Gustavus W. Dyer to dear Sir, Mar. 15, 1915, in Robert Josephus Dew folder, Tennessee Civil War Veterans Questionnaires (hereafter cited as TCWVQ).

13. Fred Arthur Bailey, "Caste and the Classroom in Antebellum Tennessee," *Maryland Historian* 13 (Spring/Summer 1982): 39–54; Fred Arthur Bailey, "The Poor, Plain Folk, and Planters: A Social Analysis of Middle Tennessee Respondents to the Tennessee Civil War Veterans Questionnaires," *West Tennessee Historical Society Papers* 36 (1982): 39–54; Fred Arthur Bailey, "Tennessee's Antebellum Society from the Bottom Up," *Journal of Southern Studies* 22 (Fall 1983): 260–73; Fred Arthur Bailey, "Class and Tennessee's Confederate Generation," *Journal of Southern History* 51 (Feb. 1985): 31–60; Fred Arthur Bailey, "Class Contrasts in Old South Tennessee," *Tennessee Historical Quarterly* 45 (Winter 1986): 273–87; Fred Arthur Bailey, "Class Contrasts in the Antebellum Trans-Mississippi: An Analysis of Twenty-nine Confederate Autobiographical Questionnaires," *Louisiana History* 33 (Fall 1992): 363–80; Fred Arthur Bailey, *Class and Tennessee's Confederate Generation* (Chapel Hill, N.C., 1987).

14. James Patton Walker, William J. Mantlo, William Anderson Vardell, George V. Payne, TCWVQ. See also Andrew Jackson Alexander, T. B. Alexander, James Merdith Atkins, William Landon Babb, Thomas Booker, Isaac N. Broyles, James Jackson Carroll, A. J. Childers, Meriwether Donaldson, John Norris Epps, Arin W. Goans, Thomas Hodge Hightower, Baxter Ragsdale Hoover, T. J. Kersey, Timothy Walton Leigon, James Henry McClister, John L. McMurty, Newton Green Maddox, James Dallas Martin, Julius C. Martin, W. T. Martin, Constantine Perkins Nance, B. F. Neville, William E. Orr, William H. Roach, Matthew M. Smith, Benjamin Larkin Swafford, TCWVQ. Note: All quoted materials conform to the subjects' often unlettered grammatical and spelling styles.

15. F. S. Williams, John H. O'Neal, Peter Donnell, TCWVQ. See also J. W. Ashmore, William Henry Blackburn, Ridley Shadrick Brown, John Ephriam Gold, J. F. Littleton, John M. Prewitt, Powhetan Perkins Pullen, John F. Sehon, James C. Shofner, Thomas B. Utley, J. G. Williamson, TCWVQ.

16. Robert Bayless, James B. West, TCWVQ. For other examples of the poor's migratory lifestyle, see William W. Archer, Francis Marion Arnold, William David Beard,

Tom Childress, A. J. Ferrell, George W. Frank, John W. Garren, T. J. Kerey, Robert Lackey, William Thomas Mays, William Henry Patterson, William Straley Phillips, Ephriam Oliver Randle, William Anderson Vardell, James V. Walker, Daniel Webster, TCWVQ.

17. William David Beard, TCWVQ. See also James K. Polk Agnew, William Baugh, Richard Thomas Beech, George W. Benson, John Turner Clayton, Edward Silas Doe, Robert Lackey, J. R. Miles, William V. Mullins, William Straley Phillips, Francis Marion Tripp, TCWVQ.

18. J. P. Wilson, John Holland Bittick, Thomas Hodge Hightower, John W. Headrick, TCWVQ. See also George Lafayette Adkisson, Samuel Adkisson, Leander K. Baker, James Lemuel Bary, Jesse C. Brown, Russell L. Brown, Jesse Benton Caudle, John Franklin Clinton, Moses Garton, William Jesse Gregory, Andrew White Guffee, C. W. Hicks, Hugh L. Hope, William James Kirkham, Flavius S. Landers, William Smith McCollum, William Starbuck, George F. Wray, TCWVQ.

19. Joseph Kennedy Marshall, TCWVQ. See also James Howard Bandy, J. W. Barnes, Benjamin Blanks Batey, John Walter Bell, Ridley Shadrick Brown, John David Bryant, Samuel Bond Clemmons, Sumner Flemn Cocke, Thomas Hatchett, Thomas Higgason, Daniel Wesley Long, Andrew J. McNeill, George Washington Martin, Pinkney Tallmage Martin, James Alexander Moore, Reuben Thomas Moore, William Robinson Perkins, J. H. Peyton, George A. Rice, Henry Martin Slinger, John Henry Walthall, William Henry Yates, TCWVQ.

20. C. W. Hicks, Flavius S. Landers, TCWVQ. See also James Frederick Anthony, Ambrose Bennett, William James Bennett, Tom Childress, Robert Sanford Holman, Theodoric Ervin Lipscomb, Julius C. Martin, William Lowrey Morelock, Edwin Sanders Payne, Joe Sullivan, Carter Upchurch, George Washington Willing, TCWVQ.

21. W. F. Blevins, William D. Harkleroad, George W. Samuel, F. M. Copeland, Joe Rich, Demarus Perry Cunningham, Elijah Thompson Hassell, Jacob Young, TCWVQ. See also James Aiken, William P. Baker, George Washington Barrow, John M. Barron, J. W. Bradley, James E. Dickinson, Wiley Dotson, William Thomas Fields, John A. Forwalt, Gilbert Fox, H. C. Furry, Napolean Bonaparte Johnson, William Harrison Key, William Jasper McLarrin, James S. Pearce, James Carrel Prichard, Milton Neely Rowell, George William Sanford, John Scruggs, Samuel Shrader, A. J. Williams, TCWVQ.

22. J. Press Abernathy, Lemuel Jackson Beene, Harrison W. Farrell, Overton Gore, William Harrison Key, C. W. Hicks, B. P. Hooker, Pinkney Tallmage Martin, John H. O'Neal, D. T. Patton, William Polk Sims, J. P. Wilson, TCWVQ.

23. W. J. Askew, William Oziour Hollingsworth, Benjamin Larkin Swafford, TCWVQ. See also Andrew Jackson Allen, John B. Allen, William Gibbs Allen, James A. Anderson, James Berey Anderson, Isaac N. Broyles, James Polk Byrne, Harrison W. Farrell, Jeptha Marion Fuston, Pleasant Hunter, Sims Latta, William J. Mantlo, William Thomas Mays, William Frank Smith, Joseph Fredrick Wilson, TCWVQ.

24. James McKnight, J. W. Andes, Robert L. Jones, R. P. Lanius, William Anderson Vardell, William Kincheloe Cox, Josiah Stewart House, TCWVQ; Paralee Matilda Musgrove, Tennessee Biographical Questionnaires, Tennessee State Library and Archives, Nashville, Tennessee (hereafter cited as TBQ). This collection of 150 folders

was collected by John Trotwood Moore between 1920 and 1922. Only a few individuals were sent the veterans' questionnaires, most filled out a much less informative biographical form. These questionnaires have been transcribed in Colleen Morse Elliot, comp., *Biographical Questionnaires of 150 Prominent Tennesseans* (Easley, S.C., 1982).

25. W. H. Barrows, Thomas Ledbetter Bryan, Columbus C. London, James S. Tyner, TCWVQ. See also John Fain Anderson, Lemuel Jackson Beene, Alexander Green Felts, Thomas Gideon Harris, John M. Powell, Powhatan Perkins Pullen, John R. Reagan, Ephraim Perkins Riddle, Benjamin Carroll Seaborn, James C. Shofner, M. B. Tomlinson, Jacob Young, TCWVQ.

26. William David Beard, William Frazier, James Calvin Giles, Uriah McDaniel Payne, Burl White Flemming, Pinkney Tallmage Martin, Linzey Loson Thompson, James K. Polk Andrews, J. V. Deck, Robert Collins Pafford, A. M. Bruce, TCWVQ. See also Joel A. Acuff, George Washington Alexander, Mark LaFayette Anderson, Henry Clay Arrington, Thomas Alexander Barnett, C. L. Broyles, Samuel Bond Clemmons, Marion Finger, George W. Frank, Jeptha Marion Fuston, Gilbert H. Harrell, Julius C. Martin, John L. Moore, Robert Ewell Moss, George W. D. Porter, William Carroll Pullen, James Monroe Rogers, Lee Sadler, Levi James Satterfield, William Polk Sims, James LeRoy Singleton, William Starbuck, James Stiles, Thomas Harrison Whitfield, J. P. Wilson, TCWVQ.

27. William Cornelius Nedham, James Calvin Hodge, William A. Wilkins, Thomas Mason, David Moss, James Bouldin Thompson, TCWVQ.

28. Joseph Leonard Cardwell, Joshua Wilson Mewborn, John Johnston, John Wright Osborne, TCWVQ. See also M. B. Dinwiddie, Gentry Richard McGee, William Hays Halbert, Robert Ewell Moss, John A. Pickard, Isaac Nelson Rainey, Christopher Wood Robertson, Thomas Hamilton Williams, TCWVQ.

29. Leander K. Baker, William Thomas Barnes, James K. Clifton (second quotation), John Tyler Constant Fergus, William Winston Eads (first quotation), TCWVQ. See also William Landon Babb, Edward Norville Gannaway, James Asa Gross, Samuel D. Miles, George W. Norwood, D. T. Patton, Anderson Roach, James Taylor, Mart Wiks, Jefferson Wilson, TCWVQ.

30. George Booth Baskerville, Marcus Vines Crump, Henry Melvil Doak, William G. Lillard, Thomas Webb (quotation), TCWVQ; Rachel Jackson Lawrence, TBQ. See also Gideon Hicks Baskett, Richard Beard, Thomas Blackwell, William Francis Greaves, John Nettleton Johnson, William Alston Johnston, James Monroe Jones, Walter Thomas Lenoir, Charles Stephen Olin Rice, John Ambrose Reid, Charles Stephen Olin Rice, John Wiley Shaw, James Norborn Shivers, Zack Thompson, Marcus Breckenridge Toney, James Anderson Vincent, John W. Wade, TCWVQ.

31. Leander K. Baker, William T. Baldridge, William Davis Beard, James Jackson Carroll, Carroll Henderson Clark, John Turner Clayton, Arthur Davis, J. C. Davidson, William Ezekial Deason, Robert Joseph Dew, John Lewis Dismukes, James M. Frazer, Gilbert Harrell, William Sidney Hartsfield, James Anderson Holder, R. C. Holmes, William M. Hunter, J. W. Jones, Andrew Jackson Killebrew, J. F. Littleton, Julius C. Martin, Samuel E. Matthews, Reuben T. Moore, William Robinson Perkins, William Smith Rogers, John Smith, William Frank Smith, Joseph H. Stamper, John

Paton Stribling, Jasper Newton White, Halyard Wilhite, F. S. Williams, Elijah H. Wolfe, Thomas Walter Wood, George F. Wray, TCWVQ.

32. Thweatt Harrison McCartney, Jr., Carter Upchurch, William Henry Harison Miller, Thomas Booker, James Matheton Wiser, TCWVQ. See also Mark LaFayette Anderson, Elijah C. Barnes, James Monroe Cole, Jesse Collins, William Thomas Durrett, William T. Eskew, Burl White Flemming, John Westley Foster, William Jesse Gregory, Gilbert B. Harrell, John Green Herbert, James Calvin Hodge, R. C. Holmes, David Jennae, Asa Johnson, William J. Mantlo, David Wesley Martin, William Robinson Perkins, Gilbert Holland Petty, Milton Williamson Prewitt, Josia Martin Reams, Benjamin Carroll Seaborn, Matthew M. Smith, John Riley Spurlock, John H. Travis, William Manning Whitsom, TCWVQ.

33. Paralee Matilda Musgrove, TBQ. See also Isaac Griffith, William James Kirkham, George Washington Lewis, Edwin Sanders Payne, William Jeremiah Tucker, TCWVQ.

34. J. F. Osborne, Marcus Toney, William G. Lillard, TCWVQ. See also John Cavanaugh, Meriwether Donaldson, William Francis Greaves, Joshua Wilson Mewborn, Milton Neely Rowell, TCWVQ.

35. Hampton J. Cheney, Jeremiah M. McKenzie, Daniel Wesley Long, TCWVQ. See also Gideon Hicks Baskett, Robert Baxter Bates, Lee T. Billingsley, David Shires Myers Bodenhamer, William Carroll Boze, T. D. Coffey, Aratus T. Cornelius, James Wesley Chisom, M. B. Dinwiddie, Herman Melvil Doak, Charles Ambrose Driskell Faris, Alexander Green Felts, Pleasant E. Hunter, John Nettleton Johnson, William Alston Johnston, Amos Branch Jones, Samuel B. Kyle, John Lipscomb, Victor M. Locke, Andrew Kennedy Miller, George W. Nowlin, George W. D. Porter, Isaac Nelson Rainey, Harrison Randolph, John Ambrose Reid, Henry Jordan Rogers, John Wiley Shaw, James Glenn Sims, Robert Z. Taylor, William Timberlake, F. A. Turner, Lemuel Hiram Tyree, John W. Wade, TCWVQ.

36. William Duke House, James M. Hill, Robert Hartwell Mosley, George Washington Willing, James B. West, Robert Morrison, John L. Moore, William Dickson, John M. Patrick, TCWVQ. See also E. C. Alexander, J. K. P. Andrews, William W. Archer, Henry Clay Arrington, William Landon Babb, John Wilson Barnett, John Wesley Carter, Henry Sowell Cherry, A. J. Childers, John Turner Clayton, J. P. Dillehay, John Thomas Duke, John Norris Epps, Gilbert Fox, Overton Gore, Lewis F. Gulley, C. W. Hicks, Alfred M. Hocker, John S. Howell, Ezekiel Inman, William J. Jones, T. J. Kersey, James Anderson King, Robert P. Lankey, James Benjamin Liner, John S. Luna, Howell Davis McClanahan, Francis Marion McClure, James McKnight, James O. McMeen, William J. Mantlo, James Dallas Martin, William Thomas Mays, Albert A. Meador, George W. Norwood, L. B. Odeneal, David Fletcher Patterson, George V. Payne, Benjamin Franklin Pope, Isham Qualls, Samuel N. Reynolds, William Roberts, Jacob Elias Slinger, Matthew M. Smith, Jacob Spickard, John Riley Spurlock, Elijah Steele, James Taylor, M. B. Tomlinson, John H. Travis, William Anderson Vardell, Marcellus Lauderdale Vesly, James Patton Walker, John Shad Welch, James B. West, John Henry West, Timothy Witaker, Thomas Harrison Whitfield, Mart Wiks, Richard M. Winn, TCWVQ.

37. William G. Lillard, James William Trusty, Anderson J. Roach, J. P. Dillehay, John

L. Young, TCWVQ. See also Joel A. Acuff, James Davis Adair, John Benton Allen, William Wryley Archer, William David Beard, Ambrose Bennett, Samuel Bankenship, J. W. Bradley, A. T. Bransford, William Brewer, Samuel Arthur Brown, James Jackson Carroll, A. J. Childers, John Turner Clayton, Jesse Collins, James H. Coop, Thomas Jefferson Corn, J. M. Davis, William Dickson, William C. Dillihay, John W. Dinsmore, John Thomas Duke, William T. Eskew, J. H. Feathers, A. J. Ferrell, S. H. Freeze, Thomas S. Glenn, N. C. Godsey, Isaac W. Grimes, Isaac Grindstaff, Lewis Wesley Hayes, John Calvin Hodge, Ezekiel Inman, Henry C. Johnson, John Wesley Ketron, Robert P. Lackey, Robert Milton McAlister, John Henry McClister, Thomas Mason, John Richard Mullins, John Price Ewens Nicely, Ephriam Oliver Randle, Anderson J. Roach, Jonathan K. Rogers, John Riley Spurlock, A. W. Tripp, John Shad Welch, Wesley Welch, W. M. Willis, TCWVQ.

38. Frank L. Owsley, "Defeatism in the Confederacy," *North Carolina Historical Review* 3 (July 1926): 445–56; Georgia L. Tatum, *Disloyalty in the Confederacy* (Chapel Hill, N.C., 1934); Paul D. Escott, *After Secession: Jefferson Davis and the Failure of Confederate Nationalism* (Baton Rouge, 1978), 94–135; Stephen V. Ash, "Poor Whites in the Occupied South, 1861–1865," *Journal of Southern History* 57 (Feb. 1991): 30–62.

Poor Whites, Slaves, and Free Blacks in Tennessee, 1796–1861

■ Elizabeth Fortson Arroyo

■

■ *Editor's Note:* Differences in race and class separated poor whites from free and enslaved African Americans in antebellum Tennessee, but "numerous areas of social and economic alliance" also existed. These included labor shared by hired whites and slaves, their shared participation and membership in evangelical churches, and "their interracial gambling, drinking, and other socializing." Despite often intense hatred, mutual interests sometimes bound poor whites and blacks, an antebellum social reality often difficult to find in the records because it "existed in defiance of the closed ranks that white southerners liked to present to the world."

The antagonism between the antebellum South's poor whites and its slaves and free blacks has figured prominently in the region's history, literature, and mythology. Reasons for mutual suspicion abounded, and many whites of the middling and upper classes encouraged such antipathy.

Numerous areas of social and economic alliance existed, however, between poor whites and black people, slave and free. The history of these peoples in Tennessee provides several examples of coexistence, even codependency. Hired, landless white laborers worked with black people in fields, factories, and mines, dug ditches and constructed roads and public buildings. They shared membership in evangelical churches. And some participated in an illicit market of stolen goods and enjoyed interracial gambling, drinking, and other socializing. Most white southerners, of course, found any activity connoting equality between the races both distasteful and potentially subversive of the social order. Political leaders soon erected legal and social barriers to prevent overfamiliarity. Many black people, meanwhile, disdained the "lowest" classes of white people and also feared any heightening of racial tensions that could result from too familiar interactions between black and white. Still, on numerous occasions black people and poor whites defied the racial caste system of the antebellum South.

Why juxtapose these two groups and their experiences in Tennessee? First, the written record is slanted; their mutual hatreds have been made infamous. It is surprising and intriguing to learn when, where, and how they joined forces socially and economically. Second, the history of the two groups begs a basic question about the antebellum period: why were poor whites and blacks not natural allies against those, such as planters, employers, or monopolist merchants, who seemed to oppress them both? Examples of attempts at such interracial alliance exist, but they come after the Civil War—for example, the Populist movement, farmers' co-op organizations, and various unions. To understand why antebellum poor whites, free blacks, and slaves never fully exploited their mutual interests, one must examine where poor whites fit in the southern social order, as well as where black people did. One must also understand how these groups perceived their own self-interest, what improvements in their lives they hoped to effect, and which other members of southern society could help or hinder them.

Historian Stephen V. Ash has defined poor whites in the mid-nineteenth-century South as "any whites who owned no land, no slaves, no herds, and little or no property of any sort." They formed a group separate from the yeomen and herdsmen who "had peculiar interests, goals, and world views shaped by their role as property-owning petty producers." Historians such as J. Wayne Flynt have emphasized not only poor whites' economic marginality but aspects of their distinctive culture, such as music, dance, and foods. Furthermore, I. A. Newby has pointed out how southerners have defined them in terms of character, discriminating between the "respectable" poor and the "shiftless" poor.[1]

Poor white southerners, though nonslaveholders, nevertheless lived in a slaveholding society and could not avoid some relationship to the institution of slavery. Slaveholders knew that they had to cultivate poor whites' support for slavery and the various measures necessary for its maintenance. For example, poor whites were an important component of slave patrols, particularly in the black-belt areas where slaves outnumbered whites, and they also served in militias. They were furthermore a political force to be courted. And when the South made its bid for secession, in a war effort in which the needs and perquisites of slave owners became a sore point, poor whites had to accept stated war aims and help fill the armies.

Valuation of John Porter's slaves, 1836. McCutchen Collection, Tennessee State Library and Archives.

The black people of the South, similar to poor whites in certain material, occupational, and even cultural ways, nevertheless occupied a fundamentally different place in southern society. As slaves, they were a coerced source of cheap labor, a people whose abilities, loyalties, and relationships to their owners played a significant role in how whites viewed their society. As free men and women, they also provided cheap labor and lived with strict limits on their freedom prescribed by their race. Free black people constituted a troubling presence in this slave society, a living counterpoint to pro-slavery arguments because of their self-sufficiency and their very desire to live as free people. And last, black people, both slave and free, made up a social element that white people believed had to be controlled with eternal vigilance. The specter of slave rebellion haunted white southerners, masters and non-slaveholders alike, as did the supposed overweening desire held by black men for white women. For these reasons, black people were defined socially in ways that put them at odds with poor whites.

Scholars have attributed the antipathy that developed between poor whites and blacks to a number of causes. Pierre L. van den Berghe and George M. Fredrickson have argued that a caste system based on color elevated poor whites to inclusion in a "*herrenvolk* democracy," a perceived commonality of interests and identity among whites of all classes.[2] Also, white laborers some-times feared competition for jobs from both free blacks and slaves whose masters hired them out. Less directly, they competed with slaves in general, whose owners, without their chattel servants, might have hired white work-ers. Furthermore, some poor whites resented the advantages held by slaveholders, who did not have to produce a livelihood by the sweat of their own brows, and whose fortunes rested on the labor of a despised caste.

Some poor whites also may have felt uneasy when considering how close they were to the status of slavery. Slaves were landless in an agricultural soci-ety, had few material goods, and in nearly all cases could expect little or no advancement in life. Many poor whites found themselves in a very similar situation.

In the colonial period, in fact, the status of many poor whites had often been similar to that of black servants of the time. Indentured servants could be separated from their families, given insufficient necessities, whipped, and sexually coerced. They also endured the uncertainty of knowing that by com-mitting ill-defined "infractions," they could extend their servitude beyond the original agreement. Indentured white servants, like slaves, ran away from cruel masters. As would be the case with their descendants, some of them formed alliances with the black people with whom they lived or worked. They ran away from masters together; they had children together.

The antipathy between blacks and poor whites was not one-sided. Black people, as their later narratives would attest, tended to look down on the poorest whites, the "trash" and the "crackers." If poor whites believed that their whiteness elevated them above blacks, slaves and free blacks, in their turn, often disdained those whites, who in many ways seemed inferior to black people in material matters, work habits, and hygiene. (Indeed, slavery's apolo-gists liked to point out that slaves were materially better off than many whites in the South and North, or abroad.) Black southerners expressed disgust over the fact that poor whites had a degree of personal freedom and legal rights that almost all blacks, slave or free, could only dream about, yet many poor whites refused to match their opportunities with industry.

Blacks and poor whites also squared off for reasons less abstract than es-tablishing their respective rungs at the bottom of southern society's ladder. The slave patrols were one of their most common, and bitter, points of in-teraction. Poor white men formed the backbone of the patrols, whose pur-pose was to make sure that the black population was where it belonged at all times. In this capacity, many took the opportunity to prey on slaves and free blacks, with or without passes; the narratives of former slaves refer constantly to such attacks. Slaves could be caught in a crossfire: poor whites sometimes avenged themselves on particular slaveholders by attacking their slaves—in Bertram Wyatt-Brown's words, "preferably in the name of teaching both parties a lesson"—or by burning crops or outbuildings.[3] Poor whites also filled the ranks of overseers, professional slave catchers, and "nigger-breakers," who were hired to tame especially strong-willed slaves.

While poor whites and black people kept an eye on each other, other southerners kept an eye on them. As a general rule, whites of the middling and upper classes were not unhappy to see antipathy between the two groups—as long as it did not threaten slave property or the principles of slave ownership—and frequently stated concern about interactions between poor whites and blacks. On occasion, planters bought out the lands of their poorer neighbors in order to put boundaries between the neighbors' and the plantation's slaves.[4] They worried not only about the implications of socializing on an equal level, but also about prospects for illicit trade between the two. Slave owners, as well as employers of slaves, free blacks, and poor whites, complained a great deal that slaves and employees stole goods for such commerce. Of particular concern was the fact that this trade sometimes provided slaves with such prohibited goods as liquor, guns, and forged travel passes. The implications of such commerce for a slaveholding society were ominous.

Tennessee is an intriguing state to study because it was sharply divided internally, known as the "three states of Tennessee," East, Middle, and West, due to its economic and political sectionalism. Tennessee also represented much of the South's diverse topography and economy, encompassing cotton plantations in the west; large tobacco, livestock, and wheat farms in the middle section; and smaller mountaineers' farms in the east. Also, as the antebellum era waned, there was some question as to whether the state would form stronger ties to its neighbors to the south or to the north. In economic matters, Tennesseans were pressing as early as the 1830s for state and even federal funds for internal improvements in order to send goods to markets to the North, South, and East, as well as to Europe; it was not clear which trading partners would become most important. Politically, remnants of the Whig Party—the American Party, the Know-Nothings, even some Republicans—threatened to make inroads through patronage in the decade before the Civil War. The story of Tennessee in this period thus illustrates larger tensions in the United States at midcentury, as the slave and free-labor economies increased their competition. This time of social and economic change, of new possibilities and allegiances, forms an important backdrop to a consideration of alternative and unexpected racial alliances in a southern state.

Tennessee provides many examples illustrating the nature of contact between blacks and poor whites. For example, concern over illegal trade existed even in the preterritorial era. In 1741, when the area was still part of North Carolina, efforts were made to discourage trade with slaves by manipulating prices. At first, a person trading with a slave had to pay triple the ordinary cost for an item, as well as six pounds of "proclamation money." Even this did not provide sufficient disincentive; a territorial act in 1788, and then a state law in 1799, added further restrictions, requiring detailed written consent from masters and punishing with thirty-nine lashes any slaves caught with forged travel passes or certificates of freedom. The law of 1799 penalizing trade with slaves also punished anyone found enticing slaves from their masters' service or harboring any runaway servant.[5] By 1806, no white person or free black could be in the company of a slave for any reason, without the consent of the slave's owner.[6]

Much as slave owners wished to curtail illicit trade, law enforcement officials could never stamp it out. Slaves earned extra money and goods through working on their own time. Slave owners most typically blamed outsiders—traveling peddlers, foreigners, and/or Jews—for the problem, but historians Eugene Genovese and Stephanie McCurry have noted that local poor whites were usually the persons involved.[7]

In Tennessee, citizens poured out their concern to legislators throughout the antebellum period about the dangers of letting slaves trade with outsiders, white or black. Numerous petitioners decried the "evil + injurious effects" of allowing free blacks to peddle, or requested that the legislature stop or monitor the white peddlers who not only might "stir up" the blacks, but who also competed with local stores for customers, and did so without paying taxes.[8]

In addition to this economic threat, most white southerners also feared that relations of social equality between blacks and whites would undermine a caste society. A crucial underpinning of pro-slavery ideology was the belief that African Americans were inferior, and their inferiority—in taking care of themselves, in having a work ethic without coercion, in avoiding a criminal lifestyle, and in following Christian teachings—justified and even demanded their enslavement. If some blacks and whites operated as social equals, might blacks not soon demand general social and political equality? Also, positive relationships with black people might undermine poor whites' support for, or at least disinterest in, slavery.

But intimacy between blacks and whites also posed a more concrete and immediate threat. Most major slave revolts, whether actual, threatened, or imagined, involved white conspirators as well as blacks. Therefore, some whites obviously could not be trusted, and nonslaveholders—especially those who might resent the rich—were prime suspects.

Laws were passed to address this possible result of racial mingling. In antebellum Memphis, police were instructed to "disperse all mixed crowds of whites and persons of color assembled for any other purpose than that of worship; and in such cases to whip the slaves, whether with or without passes, and to arrest the white and free persons." Furthermore, the state decreed that any white person who held unlawful meetings with slaves, or harbored or entertained them without their masters' consent, must pay a fine of ten to twenty dollars. Free blacks caught harboring slaves were given fifteen lashes, as were the slaves. Militia captains were to appoint patrols as necessary to search African American houses. In 1803, three years after Gabriel Prosser's insurrection scare, a state law forbade "using words in the hearing of a slave or person of colour, either publicly or privately, that may have a tendency to inflame their minds, or induce them to insurrection." (This was a notable exception to the state constitution's protection of free speech.) In 1861, acting on the concern over security of the new Confederate nation, the General Assembly passed a law providing for the arrest of any free black, white, or slave engaged in any way with insurrection.[9]

The laws also sought to restrain both poor whites and black people concerning an act of aggression common to both—attacking property—that was relatively safe for the powerless to commit against the powerful. Allowed by law to come onto plantations with impunity, patrollers sometimes attacked slaves to revenge themselves against the slave owner. Less blatantly, whites and blacks attacked other forms of property. Arson was a popular tool because it was easily accomplished under cover of night, it could devastate a property owner, and yet it was all but impossible to prove. A law of 1803 punished with fines and imprisonment any "willful or malicious" burning of crops, fences, timber, or lumber, as well as any harming of animals.[10]

State law clearly indicated that nonslaveholders, lacking the necessary interest in and loyalty to slavery, could not be trusted to make certain legal decisions concerning the institution. A number of laws similar to one enacted in 1815, for instance, specified that in slave trials, freeholders or slaveholders must make up the jury. Slave owners evidently assumed that nonslaveholding jurors might be too quick to condemn an accused slave to death, without giving proper weight to the mitigating fact that a serious financial investment would be destroyed. Some poor whites, furthermore, might punish the accused slave out of a simple animus toward black people. And again, some might use the case as a pretext to harm the slave's owner, safely and with social sanction.[11]

Hatred due to race and social position was a common aspect of the relationship between whites and blacks. But a number of social and economic situations brought poor whites into contact with blacks, slave and free, with different results. Despite the mutual hatreds of the two groups, many individuals got along and even socialized together.

Liquor, for example, was responsible for bringing many people of both races together. Often considered an undesirable influence on the southern population at large, alcohol was seen as a particularly dangerous commodity for slaves. Slave owners were convinced that slaves stole property so they could buy liquor—which could then incapacitate a workforce or lead to altercations among slaves. And if *in vino veritas,* then alcohol's propensity to strip individuals of modified behavior could produce troublesome scenes between slave and enslaver. Across the state, prohibitions existed against selling alcohol to slaves.[12]

Although blacks and whites traded for liquor and by numerous accounts drank it together—Frederick Law Olmsted, among others, describes widespread concern over their "constantly associating licentiously" in this manner—the most explosively condemned social relationship between white and black southerners involved interracial sex.[13] Despite the white South's vehement condemnation, however, interracial sex and romances did occur, involving overseers, laborers, and probably fellow church members.[14]

The state had a number of legal mechanisms to combat miscegenation. In 1819, the General Assembly decreed that if a woman married while pregnant and the baby turned out to be a "child of colour," the couple could be granted a divorce. In 1822, it was enacted "That if any white man or woman shall intermarry with a negro, mustee, or mulatto man or woman, or any person of mixed blood, bond or free . . . every person . . . so offending shall be liable to a penalty of five hundred dollars." Any minister or justice of the peace marrying them faced the same penalty. Three years later, the legislature was moved to make it illegal for a child of color to inherit the estate of the mother's husband, unless the husband was himself a man of color. But legislation notwithstanding, interracial sex and romances continued.[15]

The number of these relationships between whites and blacks created a potential base of alliance. But in Tennessee, as elsewhere in the South, important differences in their status undermined potential solidarity. Poor whites' advantages over blacks made them unlikely to seek interracial alliances against the governmental or social institutions that treated them better than blacks.

One such difference in status concerned the fact that poor whites could to some extent look to the state for assistance. Poor white women in Tennessee, for example, could expect a certain level of county support for illegitimate children, not to exceed forty dollars the first year, thirty dollars the second, and twenty dollars the third. After that, the court might dispose of a child according to its best interests, "either by giving it to the reputed father, or binding it out to some suitable person in [the court's] discretion."[16] There is no evidence that this law applied to free blacks as well as indigent whites, though free blacks in Tennessee did retain some trappings of citizenship, such as the right to vote, until 1834. They also were considered citizens enough to have to work on the public roads, "under the same rules . . . as free white males."[17]

Free black people, however, were restrained economically in ways that poor whites were not. For example, the many attempts of free black men to be allowed to purchase and free their families, or to keep them in the state, entailed lengthy efforts and staggering expenses that no poor white man faced in order to live with his family. A partial economic consolation was that some lines of work, such as barbering or certain unskilled occupations, were considered fit only for blacks.

In addition, poor whites also had access to such state-sponsored benefits as hospitals, which free blacks, the overwhelming majority of whom lived in poverty, did not. In the ordinances of Memphis, for example, "Free white residents of Tennessee" were "to be admitted always as patients, with or without pay." (Slaves had access to hospital care, as well, if their owners could pay.)[18] Poor whites also had recourse to poorhouses.[19] Free blacks may have, as well, but since slaves seeking emancipation had to post a bond so that they did not become public charges, one can infer that the government did its best to keep blacks out of poorhouses.

As for public schooling, any examples of interracial schools are, as of yet, unknown. When aging Civil War veterans from Tennessee filled out questionnaires for a study begun in 1915, they mentioned attending only "free white schools." They also often noted, however, that poor farmers' sons could rarely afford much time away from the fields.[20]

In the working world outside the farm or plantation, free blacks and hired-out slaves were generally scrutinized more closely and kept on a tighter leash than whites. For example, in Memphis, white drivers of hired vehicles only had to get a license in order to ply their trade. A "free person of color" had to give the City Register a certificate, signed by "three respectable inhabitants," that he owned the dray, cart, or whatever conveyance he was going to use. This illustrates how free blacks often had to secure the backing of "respectable" whites to be allowed to go about their business.[21]

For all their differences, poor whites and blacks did share some similarities in their standing in Tennessee. One situation that poor Tennesseans of either race might face was having their children bound out to live with and work for others, when the parents could not provide for them. The legislation perhaps sounds disingenuous because it routinely granted courts the power to bind out free black children when it would be "to the advantage of" such children. But indigent white children were also bound out by a state that had little concept of social services as we know them today, and in an agricultural society in which children were expected to work. Poor whites did not, however, have to contend with the numerous attempts, legal and illegal, to reenslave free blacks.[22]

Studying these relationships on the margins of the slave economy reveals a good deal about slavery's indirect influences on the South as a whole. Historians have long been intrigued by the question of why (and whether) slavery was central to the society, economy, and politics of the South, when only a fraction of white people owned slaves and only a fraction of these were planters. Poor whites sometimes straddled the fence on the subject of slavery, encouraging unusual liberties for certain individual slaves or free blacks, yet being firmly in favor generally of maintaining slavery and limiting the autonomy of free blacks. Poor whites often endorsed the ways in which the institution of slavery controlled the black population, even when they simultaneously complained about how cheaper slave labor allowed planters to concentrate their wealth and monopolize farmland, or how slavery rendered white men unable to compete in labor markets.

The history of poor whites, free blacks, and slaves in Tennessee does not romanticize interracial relationships or imply that a shadowy, quasi-revolutionary underground came close to turning the planter-dominated Old South on its head. It is clear, however, that relationships between blacks and whites of the lower classes existed in defiance of the closed ranks that white southerners liked to present to the world. These relationships, both in actuality and in potential, were unsettling to the great majority of white southerners.

NOTES

This article is from a forthcoming dissertation being completed at Columbia University. The author would gratefully like to acknowledge Jose C. Arroyo and Charles and Elizabeth Fortson for their unflagging assistance.

1. Stephen V. Ash, "Poor Whites in the Occupied South, 1861–1865," *Journal of Southern History,* 57 (Feb. 1991): 41. See J. Wayne Flynt, *Dixie's Forgotten People: The South's Poor Whites* (Bloomington, Ind., 1979), 1–10; and I. A. Newby, *Plain Folk in the New South: Social Change and Cultural Persistence, 1880–1915* (Baton Rouge, 1989), 9–13.
2. See Pierre L. van den Berghe, *Race and Racism: A Comparative Perspective* (New York, 1967), chap. 1, and George M. Fredrickson, *The Black Image in the White Mind: The Debate on Afro-American Character and Destiny, 1817–1914* (New York, 1971), 58–70.
3. Bertram Wyatt-Brown, "Community, Class, and Snopesian Crime," in Orville Vernon Burton and Robert C. McMath, eds., *Class, Conflict, and Consensus: Antebellum Southern Community Studies* (Westport, Conn., 1982), 184.
4. Eugene D. Genovese, "'Rather Be a Nigger Than a Poor White Man': Slave Perceptions of Southern Yeomen and Poor Whites," in Hans L. Trefousse, ed., *Toward a New Perception of America: Essays in Honor of Arthur C. Cole* (New York, 1977), 81.
5. *Acts of the General Assembly of the State of Tennessee,* 1799, 63, Tennessee State Library and Archives, Nashville (hereafter cited as TSLA).
6. Caleb Perry Patterson, *The Negro in Tennessee, 1790–1865* (rpt. New York, 1968), 46.
7. Eugene D. Genovese, "'Rather Be a Nigger,'" 87–88; Stephanie McCurry, "Defense of Their World: Gender, Class, and the Yeomanry of the South Carolina Low Country, 1820–1860" (Ph.D. diss., State Univ. of New York at Binghamton, 1988), 157; 161–62n. 71; 166.
8. For example, Petitions to the State Legislature 200–1849–2 and 59–1853, 1849 and 1853, TSLA.
9. L. J. Dupree, *Digest of the Ordinances of Memphis, 1826–1857* (no dates given for individual laws passed, but all were enacted between 1826 and 1857), 125–26. TSLA; and *Acts of the General Assembly of the State of Tennessee,* 1806, 135–38; 1803, 49–50; and 1861, 38..
10. *Acts of the General Assembly of the State of Tennessee,* 1803, 44, TSLA.
11. See, for example, *Acts of the General Assembly of the State of Tennessee*: 1815, 175–76; and 1819, 59–60.
12. See, for example, *By-Laws of the Town of Nashville,* 1814, 17, TSLA; Dupree, *Digest of the Ordinances of Memphis,* 125, 153; and *Acts of the General Assembly of the State of Tennessee,* 1825, 12–13.
13. Frederick Law Olmsted, *A Journey in the Seaboard Slave States in the Years 1853–1854, with Remarks on Their Economy* (New York, 1856), 84–85, quoted in Eugene D. Genovese, *Roll, Jordan, Roll: The World the Slaves Made* (New York, 1974), 641.
14. Eugene D. Genovese contends in *Roll, Jordan, Roll* that "white laborers and local poor

whites . . . fathered an undetermined number of mulatto children, but in most cases the women had the option of refusal" (421–22).

15. *Acts of the General Assembly of the State of Tennessee,* 1819, 45; 1822, 22–23; 1825, 12–13.
16. *Acts of the General Assembly of the State of Tennessee,* 1822, 29–30.
17. *Acts of the General Assembly of the State of Tennessee,* 1821, 34.
18. Dupree, *Digest of the Ordinances of Memphis,* 130.
19. *Acts of the General Assembly of the State of Tennessee,* 1815, 179–81.
20. See Colleen Morse Elliott and Louise Armstrong Moxley, eds., *The Tennessee Civil War Veterans Questionnaires,* 5 vols. (Easley, S.C., 1985).
21. Dupree, *Digest of the Ordinances of Memphis,* 115.
22. On efforts to enslave or reenslave free blacks: An 1857 law provided for the voluntary enslavement of free black people (*Acts of the General Assembly of the State of Tennessee,* 1857–1858, 55–56), as did an 1860 law aimed at emancipated blacks whose former masters could not or would not pay their way to Africa (*Acts of the General Assembly of the State of Tennessee,* 1859–1860, TSLA, 117). Illegal efforts are indicated by legislation penalizing theft and reenslavement of free blacks. See *Acts of the General Assembly of the State of Tennessee,* 1826, 33; and 1829, 30.

Jackson, Polk, and Johnson: Defenders of the Moral Economy

■ Wayne Cutler

■

■ *Editor's Note:* More than mere partisan allegiance to the Democratic party bound the politics and policies of the three Tennessee
■ presidents. Cutler addresses how Jackson, Polk, and Johnson's interpretation of republicanism shaped the political dialogue and
■ institutions of nineteenth-century America, especially in their defense of the "producer capitalism" of farmers, tradesmen, and arti-
■ sans from the encroaching grasp of the "market capitalism," controlled by early American financiers and corporations. The
■ insistence by the three Tennessee presidents "upon a general government of limited powers," concludes Cutler, "assumed that the
■ consolidation of political power could only lead to an unwanted,
unjust, and undemocratic redistribution of wealth from the many
■ to the few."

Deeply devoted to the preservation of the Union and convinced of
its underlying fragility, Tennessee's three presidents of the United States
opposed the use of the general government in changing the young republic's
economic orientation from producer to market capitalism. Their vision of a
moral economy looked to an ever wider distribution of wealth predicated
upon the labor of independent farmers and artisans; and their insistence upon
a general government of limited powers assumed that the consolidation of
political power could only lead to an unwanted, unjust, and undemocratic
redistribution of wealth from the many to the few.[1]

Claiming the mantle of Thomas Jefferson and the more radical traditions
of the American Revolution, the Jacksonians favored the diffusion of political and economic power as the moral economy's first line of defense. Although
the term "moral economy" did not have currency in Jacksonian America, the

notion of a communitarian lifestyle did dominate farm and village life from colonial days forward, both as plantation and common green. Farmers and craftsmen controlled the means of production as well as the distribution of their products; they fitted their labors and prices to what they called a "competency" or "living"; they took incidental surpluses to local markets for sale or barter. The work ethic of their producer capitalism sanctioned the independent status of their labor and the virtue of their plain living. Speculating on commodity futures and sweated labor contracts did not comport with those moral sensitivities derived from their faith in republican simplicity.[2]

From a political point of view, the union of republican states would provide mutual protection against foreign domination and intrastate trade wars. Strong and weak states would form what Thomas Jefferson called an "empire of liberty" as opposed to the colonial empires of commercial privilege. On the other hand, leaders of the nineteenth-century market revolution, variously called National Republicans, Whigs, and Republicans, saw little purpose in having a union that did not create greater national wealth and power. Although Andrew Jackson, James K. Polk, and Andrew Johnson focused their political wars against market consolidation and did so with varying degrees of success, they have appeared in many accounts as agrarian conservatives devoted to the expansion of slavery, the obstruction of progressive reforms, and the preservation of states' rights.[3]

Yet this recurring Whig version of history has masked one of the most radical premises of Jacksonian Democracy—that the voluntary union of the states rested upon the ascendancy of producer capitalism. Stated negatively, the market interests of the North, South, and West stood in opposition one to another and could not be bridged more closely than the compromises struck in the Constitution itself. Whig efforts to bind the nation together commercially assumed a natural comity of sectional interests that had never existed; and when put to the test, national economic integration could not be effected apart from military coercion. Jacksonians expressed their opposition to the market revolution in many venues, but perhaps nowhere more clearly or more ably than in the veto messages of their presidents. In those arguments, the three Tennessee presidents took common ground in defense of the Old Democracy.[4]

On July 10, 1832, Andrew Jackson vetoed the bill rechartering the Bank of the United States. He did so for several reasons, not the least of which was the Bank's attempt to defeat his bid for reelection. Nicholas Biddle, president of the Bank, fully expected Jackson to veto its recharter no matter when Congress might take action; the question could not be put off, for the Bank's

Jackson, Webster, and Clay lithograph, mid-nineteenth century. Tennessee Historical Society Collection, Tennessee State Library and Archives.

twenty-year charter would expire before the end of a second Jackson term. Thus to assure the Bank's continuance, he had to defeat Jackson or any other Democrat likely to be nominated in his place. President Biddle calculated that his Bank's influence in Congress also extended down through the ranks of the American electorate and that the voters would retire Jackson to the Hermitage if he killed the Bank. With the help of Senators Henry Clay and Daniel Webster, President Biddle sent Jackson the recharter bill on July 3, just four months before the presidential election; and an ailing chief executive remarked upon receipt of the bill that the Bank was trying to kill him but that he would do the killing. And so with the help of Amos Kendall and Roger Taney, he wrote the most famous veto message in American history.[5]

Jackson took his case to the American people over the heads of both Congress and Court, not because he wanted to assert an imperial legislative power or diminish the sphere of judicial advice, but because he understood that the de facto basis for the union of states resided in the harmony of interests and political cohesion of an acquiescent majority. The foundations of all democratic rule rested on the consent of the governed, and on that score Jackson submitted the Bank question to the rulers for their judgment. In so doing, he risked both place and reputation, and the magnitude of his trust flattered his countrymen more than any prior compliment in their republican tradition. The Hero of New Orleans knew the American people and their wishes better than their legislators and judges.

The producing class of independent yeomen and journeymen filled the ranks of the acquiescent majority, and to that class prejudice Jackson addressed his veto message. He rejected the utopian notion that human institutions could produce an "equality of talents, of education, or of wealth." Problems of inequality in a just society did not arise in and of distinctions themselves but from their "artificial" sources:

> In the full enjoyment of the gifts of Heaven and the fruits of superior industry, economy, and virtue, every man is equally entitled to protection by law; but when the laws undertake to add to these natural and just advantages artificial distinctions, to grant titles, gratuities, and exclusive privileges, to make the rich richer and the potent more powerful, the humble members of society—the farmers, mechanics, and laborers—who have neither the time nor the means of securing like favors to themselves, have a right to complain of the injustice of their Government. There are no necessary evils in government. Its evils exist only in its abuses.[6]

The "humble members of society" category did not include those who were in various states of dependency such as children, women, Indians, and slaves. In the South, where dependents formed the numerical majority of residents, the "humble members" wrapped themselves in a libertarian creed with a knowing regard for their double standards. Yet, the most revolutionary aspect of the republican experiment lay precisely in the fact that the second generation of white males had lifted themselves from the dreaded state of dependency and earned their own competency on their own land and in their own trades. Moral sensibility, neither then nor now, can excuse their failure to widen the scope of civil and economic independence; nor with any greater ease can it ignore their very real struggles to retain their own independence. As the market revolution came to dominate the American economy, millions of native white males lost their economic independence and joined their immigrant counterparts in the dependency of waged labor. The myth of American social progress has justly celebrated the ending of the legal dependency of slaves and women, but those advances have come without viable economic independence. Indeed, the vast majority of American adults and youth now work for wages and possess neither land nor craft with which to sustain economic independence.

Jackson allowed that the general government could create a national bank for the necessary and proper purposes of collecting, keeping, and disbursing Treasury funds. He reminded Congress that in his second annual message he had so stated, but that he had also warned that the Bank charter of 1816 granted powers and privileges quite beyond the test of what was necessary and proper. Legislative precedent cut both ways, for various congresses of the past had approved and disapproved of national banking charters. Jackson noticed that the Supreme Court had given its favorable opinion of Congress's power to charter a bank and define what might be necessary and proper; he disagreed with the Court's conclusion that the states could not tax the profits on private, nonpublic funds apportioned to the Bank's branch offices. Jackson argued heatedly that Congress had no power to restrict the taxing power of the states, much less to create tax-free monopolies designed to transfer the wealth of one state to another. In any case, the Congress and president, acting in their legislative capacities of writing and approving laws, had no obligation to accept the Supreme Court's view of the Constitution beyond "such influence as the force of their reasoning may deserve."[7]

Equally odious to a free citizenry, foreign shareholders would be exempted altogether from paying state taxes on their stock holdings. A truly national bank would exclude foreign ownership of stock for a number of reasons: profits would remain at home, foreign influence on bank policy would diminish, and in case of war, government loans might be facilitated and protected. Although the latter point might appear to be no more than flag waving, Jackson no doubt knew how the first Bank of the United States influenced the government's credit prior to the War of 1812. The first Bank had never indicated any interest in financing a war with Great Britain. Indeed, the peace faction in James Madison's cabinet, led by Albert Gallatin, had promoted the recharter of the Bank in 1811 as the principal means of blocking the more hawkish members of Congress and their demands for military action against Great Britain. Subjects of Great Britain owned over half of the Bank's stock, and the Federalists who headed the Bank could hardly be counted on to finance a war against the interests of their foreign owners. Had the French owned the Bank in place of the British, Congress might have taken action well before 1812.[8]

Jackson pointed out that the recharter bill did not allow competition in the purchase of the Bank's stock. If Congress had to sell monopolies, why not open the Bank's books for a new subscription. The bill proposed to leave a fourth part of the stock in foreign hands and the remainder in the possession of a few hundred of the richest men in the country. Arguments for continuing the present monopoly rested on fears that dissolution would bring about great economic distress; but that argument, if valid, only suggested a perpetual monopoly to be passed down from generation to generation somewhat like hereditary privileges. Jackson found no difficulty in conceiving "that great evils to our country and its institutions might flow from such a concentration of power in the hands of a few men irresponsible to the people."[9]

Concluding his trenchant denunciation of the Bank bill, Jackson warned that invading the rights and powers of the states would destroy the Union. Attempts to strengthen the general government would only weaken it, for its true strength lay not in its power but in its charity, not in controlling its citizens but in protecting them, not in binding the states to the center but in leaving them in their separate orbits. He went further: "Many of our rich men have not been content with equal protection and equal benefits, but have besought us to make them richer by act of Congress. By attempting to gratify their desires we have in the results of our legislation arrayed section against section, interest against interest, and man against man, in a fearful commotion which threatens to shake the foundations of our Union."[10]

The notion that government power might be used to redistribute the wealth of the few to the many probably never occurred to Jackson and certainly did not frame his arguments against the consolidationists of his day. Political democracy in America rested squarely on the foundations of economic democracy; the proliferation of monopolies, however useful to the development of new markets and manufactures, would make Washington the object of competition and prize. A generation earlier, John Taylor of Caroline had proclaimed the kerygma of the republican faith when he wrote: "Wealth, like suffrage, must be considerably distributed, to sustain a democratick [*sic*] republic. . . . As power follows wealth, the majority must have wealth or lose power." He thought it highly unlikely that natural property, that wealth derived from land and labor, would fall victim to the sudden and violent plunder by the dispossessed poor; rather, the threat must come from the invention of artificial property, the kind "by which the rich plunder the poor, slow and legal."[11] The struggle between artificial and natural wealth did not die with the veto of the recharter bill and Jackson's election to a second term.

James K. Polk, chairman of the House Ways and Means Committee and Jackson's floor leader during the Bank and tariff controversies, inherited his Jeffersonian creed from his grandfather, Ezekiel Polk, and made it his own in combat during his seven terms in Congress, the last two of which he served as Speaker of the House, 1835–39. He won his party's presidential nomination in 1844 as the nation's first "dark horse" and Jackson's personal choice. A lawyer by training and a politician in practice, "Young Hickory" devoted most of his career to blocking the Whig program of corporate welfare. In his journey to the White House, Polk no doubt secretly rejoiced in having the opportunity to meet and defeat Henry Clay, principal architect of the American System of economic consolidation and the "Great Embodiment" of the Whig Party. The presidential election of 1844 ended in a very tight finish with Polk winning slightly more than 49 percent of the popular vote; although the eleventh president and his party would enjoy majorities in both houses of the Twenty-ninth Congress, legislative divisions often confirmed the almost even split in the body politic over government policy.

Near the end of its first session, Congress sent Polk two of the three bills that he would return. By Jacksonian standards, both pieces of legislation could be classified as fairly ripe pork: the first appropriated $1,378,450 for harbors and rivers improvements, and the second, $5 million for settling pre-1800 French spoliation claims. Preoccupied with management of the Mexican War, Polk wrote a rather cursory veto message of the harbors and rivers bill; he drew heavily on Jackson's Wabash River veto and extended the arguments so far as to exclude all similar maritime improvements, for such spending "must produce a disreputable scramble for the public money, by the conflict which is inseparable from such a system between local and individual interests and the general interest of the whole."[12] As for the indemnity claims long sought by New England insurance companies, Polk observed that prior congresses had declined to appropriate money for such purposes even when blessed with large treasury surpluses; in time of war and with its attendant debt creations, he thought that the spoliation issue should be put aside. The president returned the bill, he said, entirely for reasons of expediency and without regard to constitutional scruples.[13]

At the end of its short session, Congress revisited the corporate pork barrel and sent Polk a second, although smaller, harbors and rivers bill; unable to prepare a timely response, the president decided to pocket-veto the bill and to defer sending a message until the next congress assembled. Polk researched the constitutional and legislative history of maritime improvements in the early years of the Second Republic and prepared a more extended explanation of his views on internal improvements.

Lamenting the introduction of the American System some twenty years before, Polk expressed alarm that within just a few years, the proposals to

Congress for internal improvements had exceeded $200 million and would have continued without limit had Jackson not vetoed the Maysville Road and Wabash River bills. In some states, appropriations for publicly financed monopolies had plunged the governments so deeply into debt that the people amended their state constitutions so as to require statewide referenda on such expenditures. With respect to demands for harbors and rivers improvements alone, the general government could find no rational basis for choosing one work over another, for every community wanted to be enriched by developing its avenues of trade. Making America rich through internal improvements must create a "potent political engine" certain to corrupt Congress, heighten sectional discontent, increase taxes, and create a perpetual national debt.[14] Yet, there did exist a practical as well as constitutional means of identifying and providing for such maritime improvements as might truly justify public support.

Recalling the last provision of the ninth section of Article I of the Constitution, the president noted that no state could lay tonnage duties without the consent of Congress; he wryly added that the object of this reservation of power to the states was not hidden. He proceeded to list fourteen state laws levying tonnage duties on vessels arriving in the ports of Rhode Island, Massachusetts, Pennsylvania, Virginia, North Carolina, South Carolina, Georgia, and Maryland; in every instance, Congress had consented to state duties, which in every case provided for navigation and/or port facilities. This excellent system of improvements had been instituted without an enlargement of the general government's power or patronage:

> Its safeguards are, that both the State legislatures and Congress have to concur in the act of raising funds; that they are in every instance to be levied upon the commerce of those ports which are to profit by the proposed improvement; that no question of conflicting power or jurisdiction is involved; that the expenditure, being in the hands of those who are to pay the money and be immediately benefited, will be more carefully managed and more productive of good than if the funds were drawn from the National Treasury and disbursed by the officers of the General Government; that such a system will carry with it no enlargement of Federal power and patronage, and leave the States to be the sole judges of their own wants and interests, with only a conservative negative in Congress upon any abuse of the power which the States may attempt.[15]

By levying tonnage duties, the states could take care of the really important improvements and Congress could avoid those latitudinarian constructions of its powers that had set states and sections against one another in the scramble for wealth and power.

Polk reviewed James Madison's minutes of the Constitutional Convention and recounted the several instances in which members rejected proposals to give the general government a right of jurisdiction over state soil. The framers wrote into the document restrictions whereby the general government could not purchase land without state consent and then it could do so only "for the erection of forts, magazines, dockyards, and other needful buildings." The Convention rejected proposals to give the general government power to appoint a Secretary of Domestic Affairs, to cut canals, and to grant charters of incorporation. According to Polk, the Convention ruled out granting such powers because they were inexpedient, not because specificity was unnecessary.[16]

The president then took exception to the more current argument that Congress's power to regulate commerce could be stretched to include the improvement of harbors and rivers. First, he argued, commerce must subsist between foreign nations or among the states or with the Indian tribes, for the power to regulate "admits or affirms the preexistence of the thing to be regulated." The existence of the commerce presupposes "the means by which and the channels through which commerce is carried on." Polk incredulously observed the vast expanse of power that might follow a less strict construction of the commerce clause: "If the definition of the word "regulate" is to include the provision of means to carry on commerce, then have Congress not only power to deepen harbors, clear out rivers, dig canals, and make roads, but also to build ships, railroad cars, and other vehicles, all of which are necessary to commerce. There is no middle ground."[17]

He had set forth his arguments both practical and constitutional, but he worried that the internal improvements debate had not ended with any greater certainty than those respecting a national bank, protective tariffs, or territorial expansion. At the end of each session of the Thirtieth Congress, Polk went to the capitol armed with veto messages in hand to reject internal improvements, restrictions on slavery in the new territories, and congressional intrusion upon the executive's appointive powers.[18] Congress did not pass the bills that Polk had expected to veto, but the vital issues of his unused messages against consolidation would bring an end to America's Second Republic and its structures of diffused power.

Andrew Johnson's approach to reconstituting the Union at the end of the Civil War almost certainly would have resulted in a restoration of Jacksonian Democracy and a slowing of the market revolution. In his earlier congressional years, Johnson had opposed the Whig program of bank monopolies, tariff protections, internal improvements, and high land prices. A tailor by trade, he supported the independent yeomen and worked for passage of homestead legislation even though there were no federal lands in Tennessee. He resented bitterly those who spoke disparagingly of the working man and disliked passionately those who took pride in their purse. When his party and nation divided in 1860, Johnson chose to remain loyal to the Union, for he thought that the farmers and mechanics, North and South, must remain united or give way to the growing power of the commercial world. The Union must be preserved as Jackson had maintained, but by the end of the Civil War, producer capitalists would rule neither North nor South.

Both radical and conservative Republicans watched with increasing alarm the president's postwar measures for restoring the Union. Republicans had won the war and did not intend to lose the peace. And winning the peace meant retaining political and economic control of the North as well as the South. Political reconstruction of the South provided the means of controlling the federal government and giving free reign to those who had financed the military victory. Republicans must neutralize the Democrats in the White House, disfranchise Democrats in the South, and demonize Democrats in the North. Only then could the business of America move forward to greater wealth and power. With Peace Democrats scrambling to ride out the victory celebrations, Republican leaders in both houses of Congress could put together enough votes to block the seating of the southern delegations and to override the meddling of the last Jacksonian.[19]

Confronting opponents of his restoration plans, Johnson argued his case with impeccable logic and constitutional correctness. If the Southern states had seceded from the Union in law and as well as fact, then the war to restore the Union could not have been a just war, and he could not have been eligible for election to the vice presidency. On the other hand, if the Southern states had not left the Union, then they had retained their constitutional rights and could not be denied representation in the Congress or the electoral college. His arguments carried no more weight than his numerous vetoes, for he could do nothing to seat the Southern delegations, which were composed largely of former rebel officers and enemies of the Republican party. Congress would decide for itself whom to seat and for what purposes, and from that decision there could be no appeal other than to the people and their state legislatures. In the House and Senate elections of 1866, Republicans convinced large numbers of Northerners that radical measures must be undertaken to avoid a second Southern rebellion, and they pointed to Johnson's restoration governments as evidence of his attempt to steal the peace. Less demagogic issues such as tax relief, debt funding, currency contraction, and government corruption received little or no play in the elections. Johnson did not ignore those questions, but his attempts to settle pressing constitutional crises had blurred the electorate's vision of far-reaching changes in the economic structure of the Union.

In early 1866, Congress passed the New York and Montana Iron Mining and Manufacturing Company Bill, which would have overturned the underlying principle of the Homestead Act of 1862. Johnson vetoed the giveaway. Terms of the grant provided that the company might purchase in Montana Territory up to twenty sections of land, three of which might be chosen for their iron and coal minerals, and the remaining ones for their timber; that the government would sell the land at the minimum price of $1.25 per acre; and that the company would pay for the surveys and erect works capable of manufacturing 1,500 tons of iron annually. The grant would include no other mineral rights and convey no other privileges beyond those of ordinary preemption with respect to timber, except the company could cut so much as might be required for building construction and iron manufacturing.[20]

In his veto message, Johnson proposed to consider two basic questions: Should such privileges be granted to any person or persons? And, if so, should they be granted to a corporation? The president then asserted that the public lands were "a national trust, set apart and held for the general welfare upon principles of equal justice, and not to be bestowed as a special privilege upon a favored class." By means of public auction, followed by private purchase at minimum price, the government had sold the public lands to raise revenue; through grants of preemption rights, Congress had encouraged actual settlement and occupation of the land. "By progressive steps it has advanced to the homestead principle, securing to every head of a family, widow, and single man 21 years of age and to every soldier who has borne arms for his country a landed estate sufficient, with industry, for the purpose of independent support." Nowhere in their laws did the American people write more clearly their belief in the moral economy: "for the purpose of independent support" each family or veteran might receive an estate of 160 acres, provided they resided there and cultivated the land. The Homestead Act interdicted any other use of the land such as for mining or trading; individuals might purchase 160 acres of coal lands at a minimum price of twenty dollars per acre. For over twenty-five years the government had extended a one-time preemption right on "offered" land to individual settlers, who might purchase 160 acres of land, provided they did not own more than 320 acres elsewhere. Preemptors would pay the minimum price of $1.25 per acre with twelve months' credit. Indian lands would remain beyond the reach of the land office. On previously "unoffered" land, payment would be made the day of the public offering. Those rather basic and uncomplicated provisions would ensure that the public lands would be used "to encourage the expansion of population and the development of agricultural interests."[21]

Not without a remarkable sense of irony—or cynicism—the businessman's Congress proposed to co-opt the plain folks' land program and convert it to corporate expansion opposed to the interests of both farmers and mechanics. If the company received all the preemption rights of "natural" persons, the privileges so granted would be "in direct conflict with every principle heretofore observed in respect to the disposal of the public lands." The bill would grant land for purposes of mining and manufacturing as opposed to farming, overturn prohibitions on mineral extraction, expand the size limitation from 160 to 12,800 acres, remove timber protections, and sell the land at one-sixteenth the established minimum price with double the allowed time for payment. Considering the heavy war taxes burdening the American people, the president concluded that no such "gratuity" could be justified even if there were not yet two other fatal flaws.[22]

Not only would the bill give special privileges to corporate interests without obtaining a reciprocal public benefit, the grant would give the corporation first choice of lands in Montana, which to date had not been surveyed or even organized into a land district. This legislation would "be the precursor of a system of land distribution to a privileged class, unequal, unjust, and which ought not to receive the sanction of the General Government." To be certain, the railroads had received large land concessions, but the justification for those grants rested almost entirely on expediting the expansion of settlement and sale of the alternating sections of public lands. Putting corporate interests ahead of actual settlers for no purposes other than the private profits of the company's stockholders would constitute a complete revolution of the nation's land policy. And finally, the bill would allow the company to preempt Indian lands without the government first extinguishing the Indian titles thereon. The one restriction would be that they not encroach on reservation lands proper; that provision as much as any other would exemplify "the spirit in which special privileges are sought by incorporated companies." Radical Republicans could not pass the New York and

Montana bill over Johnson's veto; instead, they tacked essentially the same provisions onto a measure creating a surveying district in Montana. The president held his ground and vetoed the second bill, and Congress sustained his decision.[23]

Jackson, Polk, and Johnson spoke for plain Americans and their vision of a social order based on producer capitalism and its limits for sustaining a moral economy. Labor for the sake of a competence and an independence of person appealed to that half of the populace unwilling to gamble its future on national markets and the unseen, impersonal corporate hands controlling the means of production and distribution. Jacksonian political and economic democracy could retard but could not prevent the triumph of the market revolution. Whigs and then Republicans promised greater wealth for all. Given power, they would protect home industry with high tariffs, construct national market networks with cheap transportation, raise eastern land and labor values with closed frontiers, and protect the Protestant ascendancy with reduced Catholic immigration. The government would take care of the rich and let the rich take care of the poor. That the market revolution could not accommodate the diverse and conflicting economic interests of the Union strained the will of the American people to remain united on a voluntary basis. In the Third Republic, business accommodations would be challenged but, to date, never seriously threatened.

NOTES

1. For a balanced survey of the Jacksonian struggles to rebuild and sustain Jefferson's agrarian-artisanal democracy, see Harry L. Watson, *Liberty and Power: The Politics of Jacksonian America* (New York, 1990); for a more synthetic and somewhat provocative account of the same conflicts, see Charles G. Sellers, *The Market Revolution: Jacksonian America, 1815–1846* (New York, 1991); for a seminal study on the rise of the market economy and the deskilling of the American craftsman, see Sean Wilentz, *Chants Democratic: New York City & the Rise of the American Working Class, 1788–1850* (New York, 1984); and for two impact studies of market expansion into the hinterland, see Steven Hahn, *The Roots of Southern Populism: Yeomen Farmers and the Transformation of the Georgia Upcountry, 1850–1890* (New York, 1983) and Lacy K. Ford, *The Origins of Southern Radicalism: The South Carolina Upcountry, 1800–1860* (New York, 1988). For reviews of Jacksonian studies since 1945, see Sean Wilentz, "On Class and Politics in Jacksonian America," *Reviews in American History* 10 (Dec. 1982): 45–63; Harry L. Watson, "The Venturous Conservative Reconsidered: Social History and Political Culture in the Market Revolution," *Reviews in American History* 22 (Dec. 1994): 732–40.
2. For summary accounts of recent scholarship on early American capitalism and its

moral economy, see James A. Henretta, *The Origins of American Capitalism: Collected Essays* (Boston, 1991). For a pathbreaking essay on the concept of the moral economy, see E. P. Thompson, "The Moral Economy of the English Crowd in the Eighteenth Century," *Past and Present* 50 (Feb. 1971): 76–136.

3. After World War II, the new consensus, or neo-Whig school of American historiography, took the lead in explaining how the United States had achieved its supreme heights of economic, political, and military power. Divisive issues that had commanded the attention of the progressive historians found little play in the revised story of entrepreneurial America's search for wealth and power. Partisan battles became realpolitik games between the ins and the outs; economic and social conflicts between the haves and have-nots dissolved into a single middle class devoted to building the liberal capitalist state. Consensus historians reconstructed Andrew Jackson as a rugged individualist with a mean streak; generally, they ignored Polk and vilified Johnson. By the time the New American Nation Series had published through most of its prospectus, many professional historians had moved away from political and economic history in favor of the new social history and its interest in the quantifiable past. Historians of the ground-up approach brought statistically defined individuals into aggregate forms and hoped for more certain conclusions about collective behavior such as voting, owning, working, marrying, and so forth. The task of understanding the past in its own terms and in its own incompleteness still remains enough of a challenge to keep historical inquiry alive and well. To be sure, Jackson did not see himself as a crypto-Whig or as a rugged individualist winning the American dream.

4. Jackson vetoed twelve bills, Polk three, and Johnson twenty-one. The first seventeen presidents used the veto power eighty-eight times; subsequent presidents have returned to Congress over two thousand pieces of legislation. Robert J. Spitzer, *The Presidential Veto: Touchstone of the American Presidency* (Albany, N.Y., 1988), 52–53. For a comprehensive survey of key presidential vetoes, see Carlton Jackson, *Presidential Vetoes, 1792–1945* (Athens, Ga., 1967). For an analysis of Jackson's Maysville Road veto, see Carlton Jackson, "The Internal Improvement Vetoes of Andrew Jackson," *Tennessee Historical Quarterly* 25 (Fall 1966): 261–79.

5. For an excellent summary and judicious evaluation of the Bank veto, see Watson, *Liberty and Power*, 132–71.

6. James D. Richardson, ed., *A Compilation of the Messages and Papers of the Presidents, 1789–1897* (Washington, 1896–99), 2:590.

7. Ibid., 2:582.

8. For an informative debate on the influence of foreign investors in the first Bank of the United States, see the Senate recharter speeches by William H. Crawford, William Branch Giles, and Henry Clay, in *Annals of Congress*, 11th Cong., 3d Sess. (1810–1811), 142–50, 175–208, 218–19.

9. Richardson, *Messages*, 2:580–81.

10. Ibid., 2:590.

11. John Taylor, *An Inquiry into the Principles and Policy of the Government of the United States* (Fredericksburg, Va., 1814), 274–75. For a contextual analysis of Taylor's arguments against the aristocracy of fictitious wealth, see Arthur M. Schlesinger, Jr., *The Age of Jackson* (Boston, 1945), 18–26.

12. Richardson, *Messages*, 4:464. For an overview of Polk's three veto messages, see Paul

H. Bergeron, *The Presidency of James K. Polk* (Lawrence, Kans., 1987), 192–200. For analysis of the shifting congressional coalitions that facilitated passage of the improvements and spoliation bills, see Charles Sellers, *James K. Polk: Continentalist, 1843–1846* (Princeton, N.J., 1966), 468–76. For a close examination of public reactions to Polk's vetoes, see Jackson, *Presidential Vetoes,* 87–98.

13. Richardson, *Messages,* 4:466–69.
14. Ibid., 4:612–15.
15. Ibid., 4:616–17.
16. Ibid., 4:622–23.
17. Ibid., 4:625–26.
18. Library of Congress, *James K. Polk Papers* (Presidential Papers Microfilm), series 6, reel 61.
19. Reconstruction historiography has focused largely on the South rather than the North, for the continuing need to purge the stains of slavery and racism from our historical psyche overrides almost all other concerns about the postwar years. For an early attempt to focus on the advance of the market revolution and the empowerment of big business in America, see Howard K. Beale, *The Critical Year: A Study of Andrew Johnson and Reconstruction* (New York, 1930), 225–99.
20. Richardson, ed., *Messages,* 4:416–17.
21. Ibid., 4:417–18.
22. Ibid., 4:418–19.
23. Ibid., 4:420–22, 426–27.

Politicians, Parties, and Slavery: The Second Party System and the Decision for Disunion in Tennessee

■ Jonathan M. Atkins

■

■ *Editor's Note:* When white male Tennesseans voted to join the
Confederacy during the summer of 1861, they made the most
■ momentous political decision of the century, one that came after a
generation of intense political activity. Atkins finds that voters
■ were "profoundly influenced by the experience of politics they
had gained from the Second Party System." The bitter political
■ wars between Democrats and Whigs lasted from the mid-1830s to
the years immediately preceding secession. The debate was often
■ characterized by rollicking rallies, images of log cabins, and over-
heated rhetoric. Yet, real ideological differences on the nature of
■ republicanism and the nation's economic future divided Democrats and Whigs. "Party rhetoric in the antebellum era," Atkins
■ concludes, "thus presented much more than merely the puffery of
politicians."

No doubt the most critical moment in Tennessee history occurred
in 1861 when the state decided to cast its lot with the Confederate States of
America. So powerful has been the impact of Tennessee's association with
the Confederacy that it is easy to forget that the decision for disunion was
made neither immediately nor unanimously. While the Lower South states
seceded as soon as it became clear that Abraham Lincoln had been elected to
the presidency, Tennessee joined the other Upper South border states to seek
a settlement of the sectional controversy within the Union, a course approved
by the state's voters in a popular referendum. With the onset of war, however, public opinion in Middle and West Tennessee underwent a dramatic

conversion. Aside from a few pockets of Unionism, white inhabitants in these regions united in support of Tennessee's membership in the Confederacy and enthusiastically supported resistance to perceived Northern aggression. "Every person, almost, was eager for the war," recalled Maury County's Sam R. Watkins, "and we were all afraid it would be over and we would not be in the fight."[1] Only in East Tennessee did pro-Union sentiment remain dominant. Throughout the war, the Eastern grand division remained a source of inspiration for the North and a thorn in the side of the South.

Despite the importance of Tennessee's decision, the sources of the state's unionism and disunionism, along with its sudden shift during the secession crisis, have received the attention of surprisingly few historians.[2] In recent years, historians of nineteenth-century politics have emphasized the importance of the nation's two-party system toward understanding the politics of the antebellum era, the origins of the nation's sectional conflict, and the outcome of the crisis of Union of 1861.[3] In Tennessee, Whigs and Democrats engaged in one of the nation's most heatedly contested and closely divided party competitions. In contrast to states in the North and Lower South, Tennessee party competition continued through the 1850s even as the national party system collapsed over the issue of slavery's expansion and realigned into sectional organizations. The political experience of the antebellum years profoundly influenced Tennesseans' response to the sectional conflict and the secession crisis. Voters perceived the emergence of sectional issues in national politics according to the ideological appeals that party spokesmen formulated and presented to party adherents at elections during the prewar era. Their perception of sectional conflict, as shaped by the antebellum political parties, helps to explain why voters confidently believed that they could remain loyal to the Union despite Lincoln's accession to the presidency. It also helps to illuminate why, once conflict descended into war, Middle and West Tennessee voters saw disunion as the only alternative while so many East Tennesseans maintained their loyal stance long after their state had formally become part of the Confederacy.

The Second American Party system, in which a national Whig Party battled a national Democratic organization, developed during Andrew Jackson's presidency from the conflict over national economic policy and Old Hickory's presumed abuse of presidential power.[4] In Jackson's home state, party competition emerged later in the 1830s. Tennessee voters had solidly backed Jackson through most of his presidency, but when he attempted in 1836 to promote Vice President Martin Van Buren as his successor, Tennessee politicians who had been alienated by Jackson's fiscal and patronage policies condemned his "dictation" and led a majority to support a native-son candidate, Senator Hugh Lawson White. With the onset of economic hard times following the Panic of 1837, White's supporters attributed the depression to the policies of Jackson and Van Buren and openly identified with the Whig Party. They championed its "American System," including a national bank, a protective tariff, and federally funded internal improvements as the solution to the economic crisis. Loyalists to Jackson's Democratic Party, meanwhile, warned voters that the Whig agenda threatened states' rights, and they encouraged Tennesseans to remain faithful to the Democratic doctrines of limited government and a strict construction of the Constitution.[5]

The 1839 state elections solidified party identification among Tennessee's voters. That year Jackson lieutenant James K. Polk retired from his position as Speaker of the U.S. House of Representatives to challenge incumbent Whig Newton Cannon for the governor's office. Polk centered his campaign on convincing voters that the choice between Cannon and himself was equivalent to the choice between Henry Clay's Whigs and Jackson's Democrats. The challenger likewise oversaw the selection of congressional and legislative candidates who were devoted to the Democratic Party and who would present the same choice to voters in their own contests. Polk's offensive in the 1839 state elections presented Tennesseans, for the first time, with a clear choice between statewide Democratic and Whig parties. Both organizations' aggressive and energetic campaigning brought almost 90 percent of the voters to the polls—a far higher figure than that of any other previous election. Democrats gained control of the legislature while Polk won a narrow victory, but the significance of the 1839 elections lay in the pattern that it established in state politics. For the next two decades, Democrats and Whigs would compete in a series of hard-fought elections with high voter turnout and with the outcome of a contest usually in doubt.[6]

The messages that Whig and Democratic spokesmen presented to voters during the years of party competition drew heavily upon the rhetoric of republican ideology that Tennesseans, like the nation as a whole, had inherited from the generation of the American Revolution. According to republican precepts, the Revolutionary fathers had overthrown a corrupt, tyrannical British monarchy in order to establish the only truly free governments left in the world. While the exact meaning and implications of republicanism might have been vague, voters throughout the nation agreed that the American state and federal governments provided the most appropriate institutions for the protection of individual liberty; they presented, in Thomas Paine's words, an "asylum for mankind" through the preservation of freedom by governments based upon popular will. They were also, however, viewed as part of a "republican experiment," testing whether freedom and order could survive in governments without the stabilizing presence of an aristocracy or a monarchy. The greatest threat to republican freedom within the republic came from ambitious, power-hungry opportunists, who sought to establish themselves as an aristocracy in fact if not in name. Such demagogues would gain the favor of the people by assuring them of their respect for the popular will, but, once in office, they would gradually expand their power until citizens found themselves subjected to the will of despots. The only security against such tyranny, adherents of republicanism maintained, lay in the vigilance of "the people" themselves. Voters were expected to keep watch on their elected officials and to frustrate attempts to limit their freedom. As Bedford County's Joseph Kincaid declared in the state assembly in 1826, "The greatest safety of the people consists in the check they have on their public servants."[7]

The republican conception of politics intensified with the emergence of the party system. Whig and Democratic spokesmen both portrayed their parties as the defenders of liberty against the manipulations of demagogic politicians. Party politics were thus presented to voters as a constant struggle to perpetuate republican freedom by casting ballots for the party that would protect that freedom. In effect, "the second party system thereby institutionalized the enduring republican crisis," as one historian recently concluded, for "party conflict offered the electorate a symbolic struggle to save the republic and white liberty and equality from corruption and tyranny."[8] The era's persistently high voter turnout—nationally more than three-quarters of eligible voters usually cast ballots in the presidential elections between 1840 and 1860, and in Tennessee turnout averaged more than 80 percent in state and national contests in those years—suggests that republican appeals struck a responsive chord among voters. Whatever the specific issues of a contest, the issues would be interpreted as part of the larger conflict between "the people" and potential aristocrats. Voters perceived party competition as a portentous contest between their own party's loyal statesmen, who would utilize power in the proper republican manner, and the rival party's scheming demagogues, who would abuse power in their quest to subvert the republic.

Whigs portrayed the party conflict as a battle between the people and a "spoils party," the Democratic Party's collection of selfish politicians who had abandoned principle in their quest to obtain the perquisites of government office. The spoils party had coalesced during Jackson's second presidential term, Whigs explained, and led by the scheming Martin Van Buren, they had persuaded the Old Hero to abandon republican principles and exercise presidential power as a tyrant. Since then the spoilsmen had continued to encourage the consolidation of power in the executive branch; their ultimate goal, Whigs warned, was to establish a de facto monarchy, for then their hold on offices would depend upon the pleasure of one man rather than upon the popular will. Through promises to limit presidential patronage and reduce the expenditures of the federal government—by which abuses a corrupt executive could buy political support—Whigs claimed to stand as the true heirs of Andrew Jackson's legacy, prior to his apostasy, as the defenders of republican liberty. Specifically, Whigs advocated a constitutional amendment that would limit an individual's service in the presidency to one term; this restriction, they believed, would compel an incumbent to devote his energy to public service rather than to seeking the means to continue in office. Likewise, they called for the abrogation of the presidential veto, since the veto subjected the acts of the people's representatives to "the *arbitrary* will of one man."[9]

Democrats, meanwhile, rejected the "spoilsmen" label and denounced their opponents as descendants of the Federalist Party. Tracing the origins of party division to the era of the founding fathers, Democratic spokesmen maintained that the country's rich and powerful had always "feared the turbulence of popular violence, and apprehended anarchy[,] inefficiency, and weakness, if the people were invested with supreme power and governed themselves." This "money power" sought to undermine popular sovereignty through the consolidation of authority in a federal government under their own control; ultimately "they would endeavor to bring us to the footstool of an aristocracy of wealth, and subvert the very principles of our government." Tennesseans had once stood solidly behind Thomas Jefferson and Andrew Jackson to defeat the money power when it worked through the old Federalist and National Republican parties. Now, Democrats warned, "Federalism has changed its odious name to whig," and the rich and powerful had gained a following in Tennessee by deluding voters through Hugh L. White's presidential candidacy and through the seductions of the American System. To counter the Federalists' schemes, Democrats advocated the long-standing Jeffersonian-Jacksonian doctrine of a narrow and strict construction of the state and federal constitutions. Such limitations on power, along with necessary protections like the presidential veto, would prevent the Federalists from enhancing their power through using government authority to grant themselves special privileges that would eventually overthrow popular liberty.[10]

The economic crisis in which the party system emerged entrenched each party's explanation of politics more deeply in the electorate. The Panic of 1837 severely shook the Tennessee economy, and another panic in 1839 brought on a severe depression that persisted until the mid-1840s. Whigs promised to use available government power to promote economic recovery, and they strongly championed the American System as the means of restoring prosperity. Democrats pledged to remain faithful to strict construction while predicting the return of good times without government intervention; the Whig panacea of a national bank, Democrats warned, had "always been the hobby of Federalism," and they countered their opponents' plan with their own proposal for an Independent Treasury system—a "divorce of the government from the Banks" that would remove altogether any government fiscal affairs from the national economy.[11] The crisis allowed both parties to portray their leaders as statesmen who stood for policies that would most appropriately promote the public interest against the demagoguery of their opponents.

More important, the parties merged their explanations for the sources of hard times into their established ideological conflict. The crisis revealed the incompetence and selfishness of the spoilsmen, Whigs insisted. Not only had they convinced Jackson to destroy the Second Bank of the United States in 1832—and, with it, "the best circulating medium, the world ever enjoyed"—but Democrats refused to offer citizens any assistance during this time of need. Instead, Whigs insisted, the Democrats' Independent Treasury plan would "keep the public monies in the hands of an unprincipled set of office-holders, appointed by the President, and by him retained to do his dirty work." Democrats countered that the "money power" had used its influence over the country's credit system to cause the depression in order to further their political ends; the Federals sought in the crisis to "induce the people to cry out for a National Bank, as a panacea for existing evils."[12] By linking the source and solution of the depression to their appeals for the defense of republican liberty, party spokesmen took the Whig and Democratic competition from the level of ideological confrontation to one of concrete interest and, in so doing, further internalized the party's ideological appeals within voters. After the experience of hard times in the early 1840s, voters went to the polls still convinced that they could best perpetuate their freedom by upholding the pure republican principles of their chosen party, but they also recognized that the success or failure of their chosen party would determine their material prospects for years to come.

Party rhetoric in the antebellum era thus presented much more than merely the puffery of politicians for the manipulation of voters. No doubt some aspirants viewed rhetoric as a means for manipulation, while others no doubt truly believed in parties' creeds. Most probably acted upon some mixture of selfish interest and sincere devotion to public service. For most voters, however, the Democratic and Whig appeals provided ideological explanations of the course of Tennessee and American politics. The intensity of belief may have varied among individuals, but the average voter went to the polls with some degree of understanding of party competition as a crusade against demagogues and aristocrats to preserve the republican freedom bequeathed to him by the Revolutionary fathers. Whether debating the implications of state or national economic policy, or the value of territorial expansion, Democrats and Whigs emphasized that their stand for freedom against "Federalists" or "Spoilsmen" provided the core of their existence as parties. When faced with the sectional conflict resulting from the issue of slavery's expansion—and with the decision for disunion in 1861—voters' responses likewise proved to be profoundly influenced by the experience of politics they had gained from the Second Party system.

The emergence of the issue of slavery's expansion in national politics challenged a fundamental institution in Tennessee's society. North Carolina law permitted slavery in the western counties that would become Tennessee, and when those lands were transferred to the United States government in 1790, the act of cession stipulated that slaves could not be emancipated without their owners' consent. Upon attaining statehood in 1796, Tennessee's constitution recognized the legality of slavery. Anti-slavery advocates at an 1834 state convention, called to revise the constitution, encouraged the inclusion in the new document of a gradual emancipation plan. Instead, the convention's delegates refused to consider emancipation and inserted the original North Carolina restriction prohibiting emancipation without owner's consent. As the nineteenth century passed, slavery became more deeply entrenched in the state. By 1850, more than one in five white families in Tennessee owned slaves, and by 1860 slaves made up almost 25 percent of the state's population.[13]

Slavery's intensity varied across the state's "grand divisions." By 1860, in twelve of the eighteen counties in West Tennessee, where production of cotton and tobacco staple crops provided the chief economic activity, slaves composed from nearly a quarter to well over half of the population. Across the western district about one-third of the white families possessed slaves, while in some of the most heavily producing cotton counties, one-half to nearly three-quarters of the free population belonged to the slaveholding class. Middle Tennessee farmers devoted less attention to cotton cultivation and instead found a profitable market in the production of corn and livestock.

Still, slaves and slave ownership were fairly widespread in the Middle region, with slaves comprising nearly 30 percent of the population. One-third of Middle Tennessee's white families, and more than 40 percent of those residing in the fertile Cumberland Basin, held slave property. In East Tennessee's "mountain district," slavery was less prevalent. With the vast majority of farmers cut off from easy access to markets and practicing more traditional "safety-first" semisubsistence agriculture, few could afford or had a need for slave labor. In thirteen of East Tennessee's thirty counties the proportion of slaves in the population ranged between 10 and 15 percent. In the remainder of the district, fewer than 10 percent of the people were enslaved. Although in a few counties about one in five families owned slaves, in most, ownership was restricted to only the wealthiest decile of the white population.[14]

Despite this diversity, by the late 1830s white Tennesseans presented a united front in defense of slavery's necessity. Whites united in defense of slavery because it had become a crucial institution in Tennessee's economy, society, and culture. Nineteenth-century American racial assumptions convinced white Tennesseans that the descendants of Africans were an inferior, even savage race that possessed few of the attributes necessary for republican citizenship. The characteristics of the races were so different that they could never coexist peacefully in the same society, whites presumed, so slavery provided the necessary means of social control over the supposedly brutish blacks. Slavery's presence was also understood to provide a cornerstone for white freedom and equality. The presence of a black workforce outside of the white citizenry guaranteed that poorer whites would never become a laboring class for their wealthier neighbors, thus ensuring the political and social independence of all white citizens. The condition of the black slave, in fact, came to be seen as the opposite status to which all whites belonged, for racial identity gave whites membership in a "*herrenvolk* democracy" in which members of a master race presumed equality with each other at the expense of an assumed inferior race. Likewise, since cotton or tobacco planting offered the most promising route to material fortune, slave ownership appeared to aspiring farmers to be a crucial institution on the road of upward economic mobility. Even modest yeomen practicing the more common "safety-first" farming, emphasizing food production and subsistence rather than market crops, recognized that with hard work and luck they could enhance their production through ownership of a slave or two.[15]

Before the expansion of slavery emerged as an issue, however, the institution played only a minor role in Tennessee politics. Whigs and Democrats ritually accused each other of failing to defend Southern rights in the national arena, but these accusations occupied a subordinate place in party debate behind arguments over economic policy and the defense of freedom. The most frequent early use of the slavery issue, in fact, suggests that charges of infidelity to the institution were used mostly in desperation: Democrats harped on slavery most heavily during the 1840s, a period of Whig ascendancy and a time when economic issues worked against the Democrats' favor.[16] Congressional debate over the Wilmot Proviso, an 1846 proposal to prohibit slavery's existence in the territories acquired during the Mexican War, brought the slavery question to the forefront of political debate. The proviso's threat to exclude slavery in these lands angered Southern whites who believed slavery's existence to be necessary for the protection of social peace, republican freedom, and economic progress. More ominously, it appeared to represent the politicization of abolitionism. Northern politicians now appeared willing to sacrifice Southern interests for anti-slavery votes. The prohibition of slavery from the territories would ensure the eventual admission of these lands to the Union as free states. With the slave states in a minority, the nonslaveholding states could ratify a constitutional amendment—despite Southern protests—that would secure the Abolitionists' long-standing goal of abolishing slavery without owners' consent.[17]

Several traits in Tennessee's political culture, however, discouraged an extreme response to sectional conflict. For one, Andrew Jackson's denunciation in 1832 of South Carolina's attempt to "nullify" a federal tariff law had labeled anyone advocating extreme pro-Southern measures as a "disunionist." Jackson denounced nullification as "the wild theory and sophistry of a few ambitious demagogues," and his proclamation in response to South Carolina's defiance attributed the crisis to rival politicians who sought to dissolve the Union. Tennesseans, while sympathetic with Southern opposition to the protective tariff law that South Carolina challenged, nevertheless solidly stood behind Jackson. A public meeting in Elizabethton endorsed his belief that the Union of states "should not be dissolved by the wild and reckless ambitions of a few designing, selfish, and unprincipled politicians."[18] A decade and a half later, during debates over slavery's expansion, radical demands for the protection of Southern rights appeared to revive the schemes of the Nullifiers, and advocates of an extreme response to the Wilmot Proviso seemed as dangerous and demagogic as did the Abolitionists. As Governor Neill S. Brown declared in 1849, Southern extremists appeared to want to destroy, merely for selfish gain, "this glorious confederacy, built up, and cemented together by the blood of Patriots." Leaders of both parties in Tennessee found it necessary to justify their standing as defenders of the South and its institutions, without becoming associated with the dangers presented by the "Southern Burrs."[19]

The significant variation in the distribution of slaves across Tennessee also discouraged radical appeals. While supported in general by whites throughout the state, slavery played a different role in the society, economy, and culture of East Tennessee than it did in the western grand divisions: what appeared in West and Middle Tennessee to be a vital institution for economic progress and social peace must clearly have seemed in the mountains a luxury reserved only for the privileged few. No more than 3 percent of the vote decided the gubernatorial contests between Whigs and Democrats between 1839 and 1855, and in some statewide elections only a few hundred votes had determined the outcome. With the prospect of victory based on the standard ideological and economic appeals a possibility in each contest, few political leaders were willing to gamble with definite positions on new issues. Calls for the protection of slavery, even to the disruption of the Union, might win a few votes in the western grand divisions, but the possibility always existed that those same appeals would lose votes in those same sections; and, radicalism would most surely alienate East Tennessee voters, who would hesitate to break up the Union over what appeared to them an elitist privilege. Instead, party leaders balanced their declarations for a defense of slavery with assurances of their devotion to perpetuating the Union as the surest guarantee of the South's constitutional rights in the institution.

Finally, the existence of the party system itself mitigated sectional passion. Whigs and Democrats were part of national coalitions that had formed before the question of slavery's expansion had become the central national issue. The perpetuation of political support from both North and South appeared crucial if a party hoped to win the presidency or to gain control of the national Congress. With the appearance of political anti-slavery in the Wilmot Proviso debates, both parties in Tennessee maintained that abolitionist sentiment was not widespread in the North, but prevailed only in the Northern wing of a party's rival. Democrats echoed Whigs in insisting that their own allies in the free states remained committed to respecting Southern rights in slave property. Adherence to one's party would not only present the best means of protecting slavery, but it would also promote the continuation of a transsectional compact devoted to maintaining the rights of all members of the Union. As long as the parties continued to compete, enjoyed support in the North, and appeared to have a realistic chance of winning a national election, Tennessee voters could remain confident that the Union could be preserved and that the extremists of both sections—the Abolitionists of the North and the Nullifiers of the South—could be defeated.

Thus, the emergence of sectional conflict in national politics did not disrupt Tennessee's party competition. Instead, Tennessee's political leaders absorbed the sectional confrontation into their existing struggle. Whigs and Democrats both insisted that their chosen organization alone presented a national institution with the support of both Southerners and of patriotic Northerners. Both proclaimed that the success of their party provided the only hope for the preservation of the Union. The ideological appeals of both parties expanded from the republican rhetoric of safeguarding freedom from either "Federalists" or "Spoilsmen" to the preservation of the constitutional Union from the assaults of the Abolitionists and Nullifiers. Democrats tended to see the greater danger in an Abolitionist threat to slavery, while Whigs proclaimed a Nullifier attempt to dissolve the Union to be the greater peril. As a result, with Congress debating the Wilmot Proviso and no solution for the territorial question in sight, the Democratic gubernatorial candidate in 1849, William Trousdale, proclaimed the Democrats' intention to defend Southern rights "to the last extremity." In these uncertain conditions, Trousdale narrowly defeated the Whig incumbent, Neill S. Brown, who had pledged that he *was for the Union* AT ALL HAZARDS." The Compromise of 1850 appeared to provide a settlement for the sectional issue, however—and after the Southern convention held in Nashville that summer appeared to present the Fire Eaters' first steps toward making disunion a reality—Whigs won a resounding victory in 1851 by stressing their role as part of a "great conservative party of Union." Two years later, Democrats abandoned the "last extremity" pledge for a new strategy that emphasized their own support for the Compromise while reviving their traditional opposition to "Federalism" through the nomination of the "Mechanic Statesman," Andrew Johnson, for governor. Johnson's victory in 1853 combined with the Democrats' abandonment of the "last extremity" doctrine to enable the party in position to carry Tennessee for James Buchanan in the 1856 presidential election. With the demise of the national Whig organization after congressional passage of the Kansas-Nebraska Act in 1854, the Democrats were now able to declare that their party alone presented a "great conservative party of Union."[20]

The disruption of the national Whig Party forced an alteration of the state's political balance. In the North, a new Republican Party, committed to preventing slavery's expansion and appealing only for Northern votes, filled the void left by the Whigs' decline. White Tennesseans condemned the "Black

Republicans" as the newest political expression of abolitionism, but they were aware that the increase in Northern population meant that the free states, if united, could elect a Republican president and dominate Congress with no Southern support. Tennessee's Whigs tried to revive their image of nationality by attaching themselves to the nativist American Party, but the strength of the Republicans and sectional strife within the national American organization forced thousands of Tennesseans to abandon their Whig tradition and support the Democrats as the only national party that could defeat the sectional Republicans. Buchanan won Tennessee with the largest margin in a

The 1860 presidential campaign. The splintered nature of the 1860 Democratic Party is lampooned in this Currier & Ives lithograph issued the same year. Political divisions are illustrated using the party symbol, the rooster: Stephen Douglas crowing atop the body of lame duck president James Buchanan, while former Whig John Bell of Tennessee, the Constitutional Union candidates, holds John C. Breckinridge of Kentucky, who was nominated by the pro-slavery Democrats. Emil Hurja Papers, Tennessee Historical Society Collection, Tennessee State Library and Archives.

presidential election in the state since the days of Jackson. Democratic dominance in Tennessee appeared confirmed in 1857 when Isham G. Harris won the governor's office in a landslide.[21]

Sectional conflict during Buchanan's term finally destroyed the Democrats' claim to stand as the only national political organization. In 1860, the party's division manifested itself when two candidates—Stephen A. Douglas of Illinois and John C. Breckinridge of Kentucky—claimed to be the legitimate nominee of a Democratic Convention. Most Tennesseans joined other Southern Democrats to support Breckinridge; enough accepted Douglas as the party's actual candidate, however, to allow the Whigs—now aligned with a hastily formed Constitutional Union Party—to carry Tennessee for native-son candidate John Bell. Throughout the 1860 presidential campaign, advocates of all three aspirants claimed that their party alone had the national foundation necessary to protect slavery and Union through preventing the election of the Republican nominee, Abraham Lincoln. With so many aspirants in the field, few could have been surprised when the election resulted in Lincoln's triumph. The Republican candidate won an overwhelming victory in all of the free states and would become president without any Southern support. The extent of his majority in the electoral college—winning nearly 60 percent of the electoral vote while gaining less than 40 percent of the nation's popular vote—seemed to confirm the political power of Northern abolitionism.[22]

The success of the Republican ticket presented Tennessee's voters with an unprecedented choice. For more than a decade, they had worked to preserve the Union through support for a national party. With Lincoln's election, however, seven states in the Lower South seceded from the Union to avoid ever experiencing "Black Republican" rule. These states created the Confederate States of America at a convention in Montgomery, Alabama, in February 1861. The formation of the new country evoked the prospect of war: Republicans refused to acknowledge the right of secession while the Deep South states pledged their determination to defend their new union on the battlefield. Tennessee's voters thus had to decide whether their liberty would be better protected in a Union dominated by the Abolitionist Republicans, or in a Southern republic inaugurated by the disunionist Fire Eaters. They also knew that whatever course they took might determine whether the Union would be either saved or else permanently divided.

Yet there was no clear choice for Tennessee's voters, for the crisis put into direct conflict two cardinal values in the state's political culture. On the one hand, the election of a Republican president seemed to present a clear threat to state rights and slave property; the "eternal enemies to slavery and Southern rights" now had the power and, it seemed entirely plausible, the willingness to soon take some action against slavery. On the other hand, voters believed that their own freedom depended upon the perpetuation of the Union of states. The generation of the American Revolution, after all, had created the federal constitution as an experiment in the human capacity for self-government, and Andrew Jackson's firm denunciation of Nullification had sealed for Tennesseans the conviction that liberty and Union were inextricably linked. Despite the Republican threat to Southern rights, a dissolution of the Union would result in the destruction of "the wisest [government] ever yet devised by man." There was no guarantee that a newly constructed government in a Southern nation would preserve the same freedoms enjoyed under the federal constitution. "I wish we could form a southern confederacy, if such a thing could be affected," John F. Henry told his mother, "but when we cut the cord that now binds the Union together, no man can tell when the scattered Fragments can ever be gathered together again[;] each state will fly off with its own notions of Gov. Which it will not be willing to surrender to any others."[23]

White Tennesseans sympathized with the Lower South's fears of the incoming Lincoln presidency, but most hesitated to endorse secession. Throughout the winter of 1860–61, they took hope from the fact that the Republicans had not yet performed any overt or hostile action against the South. Lincoln's administration, in fact, had yet to take office before the organization of the Confederate states; the Republican platform had promised to respect slavery in the states where it already existed, and the president-elect had given few indications that direct action against slavery could be expected. After experiencing the sectional debate through the lens of the state's party battles, most Tennesseans believed that the country had been thrown into the crisis because of the demagoguery of both Northern and Southern sectional extremists. Tennessee's political leaders now united to proclaim the old party system obsolete as they called upon voters to unite in defense of the Union in a new "Union Party." This party, Unionists believed, would represent the true sentiment of the people of the state, frustrate the schemes of disunionist demagogues, and compel Tennessee to pursue a moderate course in the crisis. Moderation would allow Tennessee's Unionists to join with Unionists throughout the country to preserve the integrity of the Union from the assaults of the sectional radicals.

According to Union Party spokesmen, the present crisis had yet to produce a need for separation. Lincoln, they assured voters, was known to be a

moderate member of his party, and as chief executive he would be constrained
by the Constitution. The Republicans' opponents dominated Congress and
kept the new president's party in a minority. No Republican had yet been
named to the Supreme Court, and the fact that 45 percent of the voters in
the free states had voted against Lincoln in the election showed that the South
still had loyal allies in the North. Also, separation would undermine slavery
in Tennessee because Northerners would no longer be compelled to return
fugitives to seceded states. These facts all indicated that the current crisis was
due solely to the Fire Eaters' long-standing desire to create a government of
their own. With the creation of a Southern republic now an unpleasant reality, Unionists warned that secessionists would act upon their well-known
dissatisfaction with popular government by establishing a landed oligarchy—
perhaps even a monarchy—that would destroy republican freedom and transform Southern citizens into "hewers of wood and drawers of water for a set
of aristocrats and overbearing tyrants." "With all power concentrated in the
hands of a few," announced the once-Whig, now-Unionist *Nashville Republican Banner,* the Southern republic "would, from the beginning, be a centralized despotism, and within a very short period it would become a military one; and in no long period, a great Southern kingdom."[24]

The best security for Tennesseans, Unionists maintained, was to remain
in the Union. Since demagogic politicians created the crisis, the "real people"
of the country would rebuke both the Republicans and the Fire Eaters and
assert their devotion to the Constitution. Tennessee's loyalty would encourage Northern voters that the Union could be preserved. At the same time,
Tennesseans would join together with citizens in the other border states to
demand a compromise that would force Northerners to abandon forever attacks on slavery and to respect Southern rights. Such a compromise would
allow the people of the Lower South to repudiate secession with dignity.
Should politicians obstruct efforts at compromise, then Tennessee's Union
Party would become a crucial component of a national Union Party that
would, like the old Whig and Democratic parties, present a transsectional
alliance of those opposed to sectional extremism. The new party would then
keep the Republican administration in check until Lincoln and his party could
be defeated at the next election. "We have a million and a half good friends
in the northern states, and it is not only suicide but ingratitude combined,
to desert them when they would do us all the service in their power," one
Unionist told Andrew Johnson. Johnson's friend and former Democratic
congressman George W. Jones likewise counseled from Fayetteville that "in
1864 [Lincoln] and his party will be swept from the high places of trust in

the government. . . . Better, it seems to me, for us to hold on to our rights under the Constitution, and in the Union . . . with the certainty that at the end of four years the people themselves will vindicate our every right."[25]

Unionists acknowledged their loyalty to be conditional. An open assault on Southern rights, especially with the approval of the people of the North, would abrogate the spirit as well as the letter of the Constitution. Even though Tennessee's Unionists disagreed with the Lower South's decision to secede, they conceded that the people of that region had exercised their republican right of revolution—the right to cast off a presumed oppressive government. Should the Lincoln administration embark upon an attempt to coerce the Deep South back into the Union, Tennesseans would have no alternative but to defend the rights of their Southern comrades. "We would cease to value a Union maintained by force," a Memphis Unionist observed, "and our sympathies with the Cotton States would readily induce us to espouse their quarrel."[26] Nevertheless, Unionists remained confident that Tennessee would not need to invoke its own right of revolution. Northern newspapers, they believed, daily brought evidence of Lincoln's moderation and the North's desire for compromise. Compromise proposals before Congress, especially that of Kentucky senator John J. Crittenden, offered the promise of an impending settlement. And Unionists perceived that Tennessee's voters accepted their explanation of the crisis and endorsed the new party's plea for restraint. "Nearly everybody hopes & wishes that the controversy may be settled, in the Union, honorably & safely," another Memphis Unionist observed, while East Tennessee's Robert Johnson told his father that "if the Crittenden proposition will only pass, Tennessee will accept it by an overwhelming majority. Disunion will be burried [*sic*] so deep that it can never be resurrected."[27]

Not all political leaders in Tennessee accepted the Unionists' plea. A faction of Democrats, led most visibly by the incumbent governor, Isham G. Harris, had always favored Southern unity in response to the Abolitionist threat. They now called upon Tennesseans to join the other slave states to present an ultimatum to the Republicans, even if resistance resulted in disunion. At first, these Democrats encouraged Tennessee to meet in convention with all of the slave states to present an unyielding demand for constitutional guarantees for Southern rights in slavery. Republican ascendancy alone presented a dire threat to those rights, they maintained, and "there is no better time than the present to determine and ascertain whether the Union is to be used as a Black Republican engine to depreciate and degrade the South, or whether we are to have peace, equality, and respect in it." As the Lower South states seceded, Tennessee's Southern Righters concluded that the Union was irreparably destroyed, and they openly advocated secession. While remaining in the Union, Tennesseans could expect a Republican attack on slavery; it might come in the form of a direct military assault, or through more subtle political maneuvers, either through building an Abolitionist Party in the state or through admitting the remaining territories as free states and using them to ratify a constitutional amendment eliminating the institution. In either case, without an explicit renunciation of the Abolitionists' anti-slavery program, there could be no need to remain in the Union to await an inevitable assault.[28]

Wanting to distance themselves from too close of an association with the earlier Nullifiers and the Fire Eaters, Tennessee's Secessionists focused their appeal on the dangers of "coercion," an expected military attempt to force the departed states back into the Union. Lincoln, they insisted, planned to invade the Lower South states at the first opportunity, and in so doing, he would take advantage of the emergency to establish himself in power as a military dictator. Force thus threatened not only the South but also the free states; military action would transform them into "conquered provinces" under a despotic government. "The day, therefore, that Lincoln would attempt by military force to coerce a State would mark his administration with the usurpations of a tyrant," Jonesborough's Landon Carter Haynes concluded. "It would be a subversion of all written limitations of power and a conversion of the Federal Government into a military despotism." No citizen could submit to the authority of such a dictatorship, Secessionists claimed, and should Tennessee fail to act, it would soon find itself "the southern tail to a northern abolition Confederacy." Conflict could be avoided only if all of the slave states united to show the Republicans the futility of force. Tennesseans could contribute to preserving the peace by arming their state and providing for a quick alliance with the Southern republic. "The South must consolidate for safety," the *Memphis Appeal* admonished. "The prompt secession of some, if not all of the border slave States, alone can save us from the horrors of civil war."[29]

Secessionists also assured voters of the advantages of membership in a Southern republic. Obviously, the central government would sustain slavery, and there would be no abolition element in the Confederacy to endanger the institution. Nonslaveholders, as well as slaveholders, would benefit. Tennessee's railroad connections linked the state to the cotton South, while her trade in produce predominantly headed for those same states. In the Southern confederacy, Tennessee farmers would find these markets guaranteed without competition from the Northwest, and they would prosper with other border state yeomen as the republic's chief suppliers of food and livestock. Moreover, the South's need for finished products would provide the opportunity to expand Tennessee's mining operations and to establish profitable manufacturing ventures. "Place Tennessee in a Southern Confederacy with her manufacturing, mineral, and agricultural resources," Nashville's *Union and American* exhorted, "and what limit can there be to her material prosperity!"[30] Economic considerations aside, the Southern republic would provide the surest guarantee of republican liberty. Repudiating charges that Lower South planters favored an aristocracy, Secessionists insisted that the new confederation would be built upon the same constitutional principles that had provided the foundation for the Union before it had been subverted by the Northern abolitionists. "We will not secede from the principles, the spirit of the Union," they promised; "we will take the Union and the Constitution of our fathers and leave the enemies of both to enjoy alone their mad revel of Black Republican fanaticism."[31]

With the prospect of compromise, however, and with the Republican administration not yet in office, the Unionist argument proved more persuasive to Tennessee's voters. Sensing public support, Unionists in the legislature were able to thwart Secessionist efforts to spur the state into secession. Governor Harris called a special session of the General Assembly to meet in January 1861, and at this session the governor and his allies pushed a program that would authorize a state convention to secede without submitting the decision to the state's voters; provide for Tennessee's representation at the upcoming meeting of the seceded states in Montgomery; establish an effectual separation of Tennessee's economy from that of the Northern states; and create a state army, under Harris's command, "to repel invasion and suppress insurrection." Whig and Union Democratic legislators, however, formed a Unionist coalition to block the Secessionist program. Unionists did agree to authorize a state convention, but only if approved in a popular referendum and with the stipulation that any convention action "having for its object a change of the position or relation of this State" would likewise be submitted to the voters for their approval.[32] In the February 9, 1861, election for convention delegates, the Union Party scored its greatest triumph. No pro-secession candidate won election as a delegate, and Unionist candidates across the state captured more than two-thirds of the votes cast. Yet, the election for delegates proved a moot point, for on the same day voters in the referendum rejected a convention by more than 12,000 votes out of 127,000 cast.

The results of the February referendum exceeded the Unionists' expectations. Historian Daniel W. Crofts's analysis of the election returns confirms the importance of antebellum party affiliation and slaveholding in determining the outcome. Whigs provided the basis of Unionist strength as they voted virtually unanimously in favor of the new party. Among Democrats, slaveholders tended to support secession, but nonslaveholding Democrats broke with their old allies and joined with Whigs to give the Unionists their lopsided victory.[33] With such a solid popular mandate, Tennessee's Unionists began to prepare for the upcoming state elections in August, and they looked forward to an easy triumph over Governor Harris and the Secessionists. Party leaders scheduled a convention on May 2 to nominate a candidate to challenge Harris, and several aspirants began maneuvering to win the party's endorsement for what looked like a sure victory.[34] Had the uncertainty that prevailed in the winter of 1860–61 continued, or had Lincoln's administration made it clear that it would not pursue a policy of coercion against the seceded states, the Unionists' hopes probably would have been realized. Harris and all other politicians favoring separation would have been voted out of office, and a newly elected state government, more firmly committed to preserving the integrity of the Union, would have worked to avoid war by making Tennessee part of a new national anti-Lincoln, anti–"Black Republican" coalition.

Uncertainty and the prospect of conciliation, however, came to an abrupt end. Nine weeks after the February referendum, conflict between North and South broke into war when Confederate batteries fired upon Fort Sumter in Charleston harbor. Tennesseans anxiously followed the battle, but Lincoln's call for 75,000 volunteers to put down rebellion—particularly the request for Tennessee to supply two regiments—met widespread condemnation in Middle and West Tennessee. Governor Harris replied to the request for Tennessee troops with the stern declaration that "Tennessee will not furnish a single man for purposes of coercion but 50,000 if necessary for the defence of our rights and those of our Southern brothers." The governor then called the General Assembly back into session; within a week of its convening, the legislature approved the creation of a state Army of Tennessee, a state Declaration of Independence from the Union, the negotiation of a military alliance with the Confederacy, and preparations for Tennessee's admission to the Confederacy. West and Middle Tennessee voters overwhelmingly endorsed the legislature's actions in another referendum on June 8.[35] Less than 15 percent of the voters in these regions disapproved, as thousands of young men like Sam Watkins rushed to enlist. The Republicans, it seemed, had demonstrated their intention to create a military dictatorship and to coerce the seceded states back into the Union, thus transforming Tennessee's secession advocates from a faction of anti-Republican disunionists into a collection of prophetic statesmen. They alone had warned of the true dangers presented by a Republican administration, and their prediction of an inevitable assault on Southern rights appeared to be coming true.

Northern aggression undermined the basis for existence of the Unionist party. Unionist sentiment had justified itself upon the presumption that Lincoln would be compelled to observe the Constitution and the laws, that a sectional compromise could be achieved, and that the border states' loyalty would contribute to the Republicans' defeat at the next national election. These premises had been based upon the assumption that a conservative sentiment favoring a preservation of the Union prevailed in the North. Lincoln's call for volunteers indicated to Tennesseans that the new president would neither abide by the Constitution nor respect Southern rights, and Northern public approval of that call forced most Unionists to conclude that the Union no longer presented the surest guarantee of liberty. Tennessee's citizens now had no alternative but to resort to their own right of revolution to throw off an oppressive, despotic government. "I would have given all I have to preserve the union, and the rights and benefits of the South," wrote Felix K. Zollicoffer, who eight months later would lie dead on the battlefield at Mill Springs, Kentucky. "But our reasonable demands were refused—security and equality of our rights were denied us—we could obtain no safety to our institutions. They would sustain the Union by force . . . while they deny us terms of safety in the Union. They are now united in a purpose to overwhelm and humiliate us. . . . There is nothing left to us but to fight, or to be crushed and humiliated."[36]

Prominent Middle and West Tennessee Unionists initially persisted in their calls for moderation, but their pleas quickly gave way to public pressure for Tennessee's separation from the United States. Even John Bell, Tennessee's longtime champion of a conservative party of Union, acknowledged publicly that "the reports wafted to us on every breeze that comes from the North" brought news "of the intense and increasing excitement in that section and the united and determined purpose to wage a war for the subjugation of the South."[37] East Tennessee alone persisted in its loyalty to the Union. Voters in that section rejected separation in the June referendum by a more than two-to-one margin, and upon learning these results Unionist leaders organized a convention in Greeneville to petition the legislature to grant East Tennessee's independence as a separate state that would remain in the federal Union. When the Assembly rejected the convention's petition, Unionists planned another convention in Kingston to declare the mountain district's independence. Only the arrest of the leader of the independence movement, Congressman Thomas A. R. Nelson, and the military occupation of the region prevented the proposed convention and kept Tennessee united as the state began its experience in the Confederacy.[38]

There was little doubt that Tennesseans, once forced to choose between slavery and Union, would divide along geographic lines. With slavery and slave ownership relatively widespread across Middle and West Tennessee, whites in these regions saw themselves closely allied in interest, if not in politics, with those who had precipitated secession in the Lower South. Among East Tennessee's mountain dwellers, on the other hand, the slave population was so small that the prospect of emancipation presented no significant threat to the social order, while the limited extent of slave ownership made the institution appear as one whose benefits were reserved for the elite. While in two-thirds of the state, slavery's protection—even at the expense of the Union—appeared essential for the preservation of society and its future, in the East slavery could not have appeared as an institution important enough for which to destroy the Union.[39] The extent of slavery in Tennessee thus ultimately explains why the state as a whole sided with the Confederacy. Like Virginia, North Carolina, and Arkansas—the other Upper South "border states" that withdrew from the Union after the conflict at Fort Sumter—slavery was a strong enough presence that the majority of whites could see little choice but to resist, if the institution seemed threatened by a hostile party in control of the central government.

Slavery alone, however, fails to account for Tennessee's hesitation to side with the Confederacy until the outbreak of war, nor does it provide an appreciation of how Tennesseans understood their actions. The experience that Tennesseans had gained from the competition of their antebellum two-party system provided the framework through which voters perceived the crisis of Union. Built largely upon the precepts of revolutionary republicanism, Tennessee's Whigs and Democrats competed upon the charge that the manipulative demagogues leading their rivals sought to consolidate political power at the expense of popular liberty. With the emergence of the territorial issue, party adherents absorbed the sectional conflict into their established party appeals and insisted that ambitious politicians in both sections of the country agitated the slavery issue merely to serve their selfish ends. The need to keep the parties united across a state where the distribution of slavery varied significantly encouraged party leaders to preach moderation on sectional issues. Concurrently, the belief that the Northern wing of one's chosen party respected Southern rights in slave property sustained the hope that sectional confrontation could be resolved through the normal political process. Despite the election of a "Black Republican" president, the majority of Tennessee voters remained confident that they could defeat Abolitionist schemes and preserve the Union through the formation of a new national political party. Yet when North and South resorted to arms, whites in Middle and West Tennessee saw the greatest danger and the source for war in Abolitionist aggression, while in the slave-poor East it seemed equally clear that the most menacing threat and the responsibility for conflict lay at the feet of the aristocratic nullifying Fire Eaters.

It was not inevitable that Tennessee would become part of the Confederacy. A determination by President Lincoln to abandon Fort Sumter, or by Jefferson Davis's government to delay the attack on the fort, might have permitted Tennessee to remain in the Union indefinitely, notwithstanding the Lower South's secession. It is even conceivable that, under certain circumstances, Tennessee could have aided the Northern government—led by the Lincoln Administration—in a war to subjugate the Lower South states.[40] Of course, historians have long debated whether there really could have been another possible outcome to the secession crisis. What is clear, though, is that Tennessee's response to the crisis emerged from a state political culture shaped by the ideals of republicanism, the presence of slavery, and the competition of the antebellum political parties. The interrelationship of these forces, and the actions of the Federal and Confederate governments, resulted in Tennessee's decision for disunion, a decision that profoundly altered the course of the state's history.

NOTES

The author would like to thank David Elrod, Richard Goode, John Quist, and Carroll Van West for their comments on an earlier draft of this essay.

1. Sam R. Watkins, *"Co. Atych": A Side Show of the Big Show* (New York, 1962), 20.
2. The standard work on Tennessee in the secession crisis is Mary Emily Robertson Campbell, *The Attitude of Tennesseans Toward the Union, 1847–1861* (New York, 1961); other important works include James W. Fertig, *The Secession and Reconstruction of Tennessee* (Chicago, 1898); John E. Tricamo, "Tennessee Politics, 1845–1861" (Ph.D. diss., Columbia Univ., 1965); J. Milton Henry, "The Revolution in Tennessee, February, 1861, to June, 1861," *Tennessee Historical Quarterly* 18 (June 1959): 99–119; Charles L. Lufkin, "Secession and Coercion in Tennessee, the Spring of 1861," *Tennessee Historical Quarterly* 50 (Summer 1991):98–109. Daniel W. Crofts

presents an excellent comparative study of Unionism in Tennessee, North Carolina, and Virginia in *Reluctant Confederates: Upper South Unionists in the Secession Crisis* (Chapel Hill, N.C., 1989).

3. See especially Michael F. Holt, *The Political Crisis of the 1850s* (New York, 1978); William J. Cooper, *The South and the Politics of Slavery, 1828–1856* (Baton Rouge, 1978); William W. Freehling, *The Road to Disunion: Secessionists at Bay, 1776–1854* (New York, 1990); George C. Rable, *The Confederate Republic: A Revolution Against Politics* (Chapel Hill, N.C., 1994).

4. The best recent survey of the development of the national party system can be found in Harry L. Watson, *Liberty and Power: The Politics of Jacksonian America* (New York, 1990).

5. Jonathan M. Atkins, "'A Combat for Liberty': Politics and Parties in Jackson's Tennessee, 1832–1851" (Ph.D. diss., Univ. of Michigan, 1991), 56–187; Paul H. Bergeron, *Antebellum Politics in Tennessee* (Lexington, Ky., 1982), 35–63.

6. Atkins, "Combat for Liberty," 158–87.

7. Robert H. White and Stephen V. Ash, *Messages of the Governors of Tennessee* (Nashville, 1952–), 2:184. For an introduction into the voluminous literature on republicanism and its role in nineteenth-century politics, see Robert E. Shalhope, "Toward a Republican Synthesis: The Emergence of an Understanding of Republicanism in American Historiography," *William and Mary Quarterly* 29 (Jan. 1972): 49–80; Shalhope, "Republicanism and Early American Historiography," *William and Mary Quarterly* 39 (Apr. 1982): 334–56; Daniel T. Rodgers, "Republicanism: The Career of a Concept, " *Journal of American History* 79 (June 1992): 11–38; and Marc W. Kruman, "The Second Party System and the Transformation of Revolutionary Republicanism," *Journal of the Early Republic* 12 (Winter 1992): 509–37.

8. Kruman, "The Second Party System," 536.

9. *Address to the People of Tennessee, by the Whig Convention, which assembled at Knoxville, on Monday, the 10th of February, 1840* (Knoxville, 1840), 4–7; William G. Brownlow, *A Political Register, Setting Forth the Principles of the Whig and Locofoco Parties in the United States, with the Life and Public Services of Henry Clay* (Jonesborough, Tenn., 1844), 12, 15, 17–18, 22–24, 120, 132–37; *Nashville Republican Banner*, July 24 and Aug. 21, 1839; Jan. 6 and July 31, 1840; Nov. 29, 1843; *Elizabethton Tennessee Whig*, Nov. 21, 1839; Feb. 6 and May 14, 1840; *Jonesborough Whig*, May 6 and Oct. 7, 1840; Sept. 1 and Dec. 15, 1841.

10. *Address to the Republican People of Tennessee, by the Central Corresponding Committee of the State* [No. 1] (Nashville, 1840), 3–4; *Address to the Republican People of Tennessee, by the Central Corresponding Committee of the State* [No. 2] (Nashville, 1840), 3, 15; *Nashville Union*, Feb. 13, 1839; Apr. 16, June 1, and Sept. 17, 1840; Feb. 18, May 6, and Sept. 2, 1841; Dec. 2, 1843; *Clarksville Jeffersonian*, Mar. 25, 1843; July 13, 20, and Nov. 2, 1844; *Knoxville Argus*, June 23, 1840; Aug. 4, 1841; May 24, 1843.

11. *Address by the Whig Convention*, 3–4; Nashville *Republican Banner*, Mar. 5 and July 31, 1840; Mar. 24 and Aug. 2, 1841; Mar. 29 and June 21, 1843; *Nashville Whig*, Oct. 1, 1841; Feb. 9, 1843; *Nashville Union*, Feb. 8, May 17, and Aug. 23, 1839; Apr. 16, 20, 1840; May 24 and Aug. 16, 1842; *Memphis Appeal*, Dec. 20, 1844; *Clarksville Jeffersonian*, May 25, 1844.

12. *Address by the Whig Convention,* 7; *Nashville Republican Banner,* Nov. 2, 1839; Feb. 3, 1843; Feb. 5, 1845; *Nashville Whig,* Aug. 30, 1839; Feb. 26 and Mar. 18, 1840; Aug. 20, 1842; *Elizabethton Tennessee Whig,* Oct. 31, 1839; Mar. 5, 1840; *Jonesborough Whig,* July 8 and 15, 1840; *Nashville Union,* Aug. 30, Oct. 18, and Nov. 4, 1839; Apr. 20, 1840; Sept. 5, 1843; *Knoxville Argus,* Jan. 13, 1841.

13. *Journal of the Convention of the State of Tennessee. Convened for the purpose of revising and amending the constitution therof* (Nashville, 1834), 87–93, 125–30; Thomas Perkins Abernathy, *From Frontier to Plantation in Tennessee: A Study in Frontier Democracy* (Chapel Hill, N.C., 1932), 104, 112–13; Chase C. Mooney, *Slavery in Tennessee* (Bloomington, Ind., 1957), 101–26.

14. Blanche Henry Clark, *The Tennessee Yeoman, 1840–1860* (Nashville, 1942), 28; Robert Tracy McKenzie, *One South or Many? Plantation Belt and Upcountry in Civil War–Era Tennessee* (Cambridge, 1994), 14–16; Donald L. Winters, *Tennessee Farming, Tennessee Farmers: Antebellum Agriculture in the Upper South* (Knoxville, 1994), 30–75; Stephen V. Ash, *Middle Tennessee Society Transformed, 1860–1870: War and Peace in the Upper South* (Baton Rouge, 1988), 1–22; Mooney, *Slavery in Tennessee,* 104–5. The proportions of slave ownership have been calculated by dividing the number of slave owners reported in Schedule 2 of the 1860 manuscript census by the number of families recorded in *Statistics of the United States, (Including Mortality, Property, &c.,) in 1860; Compiled from the Original Returns and Being the Final Exhibit of the Eighth Census, Under the Direction of the Secretary of the Interior* (Washington, 1866). While this method produces high estimates, since in several families more than one person owned slaves, it nevertheless provides a useful index for the extent of ownership in each grand division.

15. On nineteenth-century Southern and American assumptions about race and slavery, and on the roots of these assumptions, see George M. Fredrickson, *The Black Image in the White Mind: The Debate on Afro-American Character and Destiny, 1817–1914* (Middletown, Conn., 1971); Winthrop D. Jordan, *White Over Black: American Attitudes Toward the Negro, 1550–1812* (Chapel Hill, N.C., 1968); Edmund S. Morgan, *American Slavery, American Freedom: The Ordeal of Colonial Virginia* (New York, 1975); J. Mills Thornton, III, "The Ethic of Subsistence and the Origins of Southern Secession," *Tennessee Historical Quarterly* 48 (Summer 1989): 80–82; James Oakes, *The Ruling Race: A History of American Slaveholders* (New York, 1982); and Larry E. Tise, *Proslavery: A History of the Defense of Slavery in America, 1701–1840* (Athens, Ga., 1987). On safety-first agriculture, see Gavin Wright, *The Political Economy of the Cotton South: Households, Markets, and Wealth in the Nineteenth Century* (New York, 1978), 62–74; and McKenzie, *One South or Many?,* 31–48.

16. See, for example, the appendix to the first *Address* issued by the Democratic Party's Central Committee during the presidential election of 1840. In the *Address* the Committee warned of dire consequences to slave property in the event of Whig candidate William Henry Harrison's election, but Democratic nominee Martin Van Buren still lost the state by a 56-to-44-percent margin.

17. David M. Potter, *The Impending Crisis, 1848–1861* (New York, 1976), 18–89; Holt, *Political Crisis of the 1850s,* 52–56; Freehling, *Road to Disunion,* 455–74.

18. Andrew Jackson to Joel R. Poinsett, Nov. 7, 1832, in John Spencer Bassett, ed., *Correspondence of Andrew Jackson,* (Washington, 1926–1935), 4:486; James D.

Richardson, *A Compilation of the Messages and Papers of the President* (New York, 1897–1911), 3:1173–95; "Preamble and Resolutions by the Citizens of Elizabethton, in response to hearing Jackson's Proclamation on Nullification, December 20, 1832," Thomas Amis Rogers Nelson Papers, Calvin M. McClung Collection, Knox County Public Library, East Tennessee Historical Center, Knoxville.

19. *Knoxville Whig,* Mar. 16, 1850; *Nashville Whig,* July 2, 9, 16, and Sept. 10, 1844; *Nashville True Whig,* May 12, 15, June 5, 19, 21, 30, and July 31, 1849; *Nashville Republican Banner,* June 26, and July 3, 1844; Feb. 7, Apr. 21, 25, May 12, and 22, 1849.

20. *Nashville Union,* Apr. 20, 1849; May 10 and 14, 1853; *Nashville Republican Banner,* Apr. 25 and May 22, 1849; May 29, June 14, 23, and Aug. 7, 1851; *Nashville True Whig,* Feb. 1, Mar. 8, and June 12, 1851; *Nashville Union and American,* June 25, July 1, 6, 13, 1853, and Nov. 12, 1856; *Memphis Appeal,* Nov. 6, 1856. On the Southern Convention of 1850, see Thelma Jennings, *The Nashville Convention: Southern Movement for Unity, 1848–1851* (Memphis, 1980).

21. *Athens Post,* June 27, 1856; *Nashville Union and American,* Feb. 23, June 10, 15, 21, Oct. 2, 8, and 16, 1856; *Memphis Appeal,* June 8, 20, July 8, 22, Aug. 16, and 21, 1856; John Bell, *Speech of the Hon. John Bell, Delivered at a Mass Meeting of the American Party, held at Knoxville, Tenn., September 22, 1855* (n.p., n.d.), 6, 14–18; [W. N. Bilbo], *The American's Text-Book, Being a Series of Letters, Addressed by "An American," To the Citizens of Tennessee, In Exposition and Vindication of the Principles and Policy of the American Party* (Nashville, 1852), 5–9, 21–22, 30–31, 35; [James Williams], *Reflections and Suggestions on the Present State of Parties. By An Old Clay Whig* (Nashville, 1856), 16–19, 74–88.

22. Potter, *Impending Crisis,* 405–47; *Nashville Union and American,* July 1, 18, 20, 25, Oct. 14, 17, and 20, 1860; *Memphis Appeal,* May 9, July 21, and 24, 1860; *Nashville Republican Banner,* July 26, Sept. 7, 18, 19, 29, Oct. 16, 18, 20, and 21, 1860.

23. *Nashville Republican Banner,* Sept. 17, 1857, and Jan. 22, 1861; John F. Henry to Marion Henry, Jan. 5, 1861, Gustavus A. Henry Papers, Southern Historical Collection, Univ. of North Carolina, Chapel Hill.

24. *Nashville Republican Banner,* Nov. 21, 28, Dec. 4, 6, 13, 14, 15, and 29, 1860; Jan. 4, 6, 31, Feb. 1, 3, 6, 23, 24, and Mar. 5, 1861; *Nashville Patriot,* Nov. 13, Dec. 13, 18, 20, and 25, 1860; Jan. 2, 12, 26, Mar. 6, and Apr. 3, 1861; Andrew Johnson, *The Constitutionality and Rightfulness of Secession. Speech of Hon. Andrew Johnson, of Tennessee, in the Senate of the United States. On Tuesday and Wednesday, December 18 and 19, 1860* (Washington, 1860), 17, 20; Emerson Ethridge, *Speech of the Hon. Emerson Ethridge, of Tennessee. Delivered in the House of Representatives, January 23, 1861* (Washington, 1861), 5, 6.

25. O. N. Chapin to Andrew Johnson, Dec. 20, 1860, in Leroy P. Graf, Ralph W. Haskins, and Paul H. Bergeron, eds., *Papers of Andrew Johnson,* 4:58; John Lellyett to Andrew Johnson, Dec. 20, 1860, in Graf, Haskins, and Bergeron, *Papers of Andrew Johnson,* 4:62; John C. McGaughey to Johnson, Feb. 21, 1861, in Graf, Haskins, and Bergeron, *Papers of Andrew Johnson,* 4:324–25; George W. Jones to [torn], Nov. 20, 1860, George W. Jones Papers, Southern Historical Collection, Univ. of North Carolina, Chapel Hill; *Nashville Republican Banner,* Nov. 25, 27, Dec. 8, 11, 13, and 28, 1860; *Clarksville Jeffersonian,* Dec. 19, 1860; Feb. 6, 1861; *Nash-*

ville Patriot, Nov. 8, 13, 29, Dec. 3, and 18, 1860; Jan. 11, 1861; Johnson, *Constitutionality and Rightfulness of Secession,* 22.

26. A. Waldo Putnam to Andrew Johnson, Feb. 18, 1861, in Graf, Haskins, and Bergeron, *Papers of Andrew Johnson,* 4:310–11; *Clarksville Jeffersonian,* Nov. 14, 1860; Jan. 16, 1861; *Nashville Republican Banner,* Dec. 13, 1860, Feb. 6 and 10, 1861.

27. Henry G. Smith to Andrew Johnson, Dec. 23, 1860, in Graf, Haskins, and Bergeron, *Papers of Andrew Johnson,* 4:79; Robert Johnson to Andrew Johnson, Jan. 17, [1861], in Graf, Haskins, and Bergeron, *Papers of Andrew Johnson,* 4:178; *Nashville Republican Banner,* Nov. 16, 1860, 6; Feb. 10, 1861. Crittenden's proposed compromise would have provided constitutional protection for slave property while restoring the Missouri Compromise principle of dividing the western territory into slave and nonslave regions.

28. *Nashville Union and American,* Nov. 8, 9, 17, 18, 20, 21, 25, 27, Dec. 1, 2, 7, 14, and 19, 1860; Jan. 8, 9, 13, 19, 22, 23, Feb. 5, 6, and 27, 1861; *Memphis Appeal,* Dec. 5, 8, 11, 13, 18, and 21, 1860; Jan. 12 and 13, 1861; C. R. Barteau, *A Brief Review: What Has Been Done in Tennessee* (Hartsville, Tenn., 1861), 5–8.

29. *Nashville Union and American,* Dec. 6, 7, 25, 28, and 29, 1860; Jan. 2, 3, 20, 22, Feb. 12, 13, and 26, 1861; *Memphis Appeal,* Dec. 14, 1860; Jan. 9, 11, 23, Feb. 3, 14, Mar. 8, 15, and 21, 1861.

30. *Nashville Union and American,* Jan. 8, 13, 24, Feb. 16, and Mar. 3, 1861; *Memphis Appeal,* Jan. 22, 1861.

31. *Nashville Union and American,* Dec. 28 and 29, 1860; Jan. 15, 1861.

32. The Southern Rights offensive can be followed in the *Journals* of the state House and Senate for the first extra session of the Thirty-third General Assembly; see also White and Ash, *Messages of the Governors,* 5:255–69; William H. Carroll to Andrew Johnson, Jan. 2, [1861], in Graf, Haskins, and Bergeron, *Papers of Andrew Johnson,* 4:117; Michael Burns to Johnson, Jan. 13, 1861, in Graf, Haskins, and Bergeron, *Papers of Andrew Johnson,* 4:156; Roderick R. Butler to Johnson, Jan. 15, 1861, in Graf, Haskins, and Bergeron, *Papers of Andrew Johnson,* 4:169; Return J. Meigs to Johnson, Feb. 7, 1861, in Graf, Haskins, and Bergeron, *Papers of Andrew Johnson,* 4:263–64; John W. Richardson to Johnson, Feb. 8, 1861, in Graf, Haskins, and Bergeron, *Papers of Andrew Johnson,* 4:265–66; Jackson B. White to Johnson, Feb. 22, 1861, in Graf, Haskins, and Bergeron, *Papers of Andrew Johnson,* 4:329–30; *Nashville Republican Banner,* Jan. 9, 15, and 31, 1861; *Nashville Union and American,* Jan. 10, 1861.

33. Crofts, *Reluctant Confederates,* 341–45, 371.

34. Campbell, *Attitude of Tennesseans Toward the Union,* 185–89.

35. *Journal of the House of Representatives* (second extra session), 1861, 32, 57, 79; *Journal of the Senate* (second extra session), 32–33, 55, 68–69; White and Ash, *Messages of the Governors,* 5:285; *Nashville Union and American,* Apr. 14, 18, 25, May 1, 18, 29, and June 8, 1861; *Memphis Appeal,* Apr. 16 and 18, 1861; *Nashville Republican Banner,* Apr. 19, 1861.

36. Felix K. Zollicoffer to William B. Campbell, May 15, 1861, David Campbell Papers, Duke Univ., Durham, N.C. See also William F. Cooper to Edmund Cooper and Henry Cooper, May 21, 1861, Cooper Family Papers, Tennessee State Library and Archives, Nashville; Andrew J. Donelson to Mary Donelson Wilcox, May 24, 1861, Andrew Jackson Donelson Papers, Library of Congress; *Nashville Republican*

Banner, Apr. 17, May 12, 25, and June 7, 1861; *Nashville Patriot,* Apr. 19, 20, 24, May 4, 5, and 12, 1861.

37. *Nashville Republican Banner,* Apr. 16, 18, 19, 21, 24, 27, May 7, 9, 10, 11, and June 2, 1861; *Nashville Patriot,* Apr. 14, 16, 17, 19, 24, May 7, and 16, 1861; Joseph Howard Parks, *John Bell of Tennessee* (Baton Rouge, 1950), 396–400.

38. Charles F. Bryan, Jr., "A Gathering of Tories: The East Tennessee Convention of 1861," *Tennessee Historical Quarterly* 39 (Spring 1980): 37, 39–44; Oliver P. Temple, *East Tennesseans and the Civil War* (Cincinnati, 1899), 343–65.

39. John C. Inscoe suggests that East Tennessee's Unionism, in contrast to western North Carolina's support for secession, despite the two regions' social and economic similarities, was attributable to East Tennessee's "long-nurtured inferiority complex" and western North Carolinians' belief that they lived in "a region on the rise"; see Inscoe, "Mountain Unionism, Secession, and Regional Self-Image: The Contrasting Cases of Western North Carolina and East Tennessee, "in Winifred B. Moore, Jr., and Joseph F. Tripp, eds., *Looking South: Chapters in the Story of an American Region* (New York, 1989), 115–29. See also Temple, *East Tennesseans and the Civil War,* 544–64; Eric Russell Lacy, *Vanquished Volunteers: East Tennessee Sectionalism from Statehood to Secession* (Johnson City, Tenn., 1965), 183–91; and Peter Wallenstein, "Which Side Are You On? The Social Origins of White Union Troops from Civil War Tennessee," *East Tennessee Historical Society's Publications* 63 (1991): 72–103.

40. On this possibility, see Daniel Crofts' speculations in *Reluctant Confederates,* 353–55.

Tennessee and the Civil War

■ James L. McDonough

■

■ *Editor's Note:* Tennessee and Tennesseans played a significant role
in the outcome of the American Civil War, second only to the
■ state of Virginia. The struggle between North and South came
early to the state's people and land, due to Tennessee's location,
■ river systems, economy, and railroads. Key Union victories at the
battles of Fort Donelson, Shiloh, and Stones River quickly sealed
■ the fate of the Confederacy in Tennessee. By 1863, most of the
state was occupied Federal territory, and for the last two years of
■ the war, incessant violence and marauding from both Federal and
Confederate armies wrecked cities, towns, and the countryside. In
■ many communities, a very uncivil war erupted between those in
favor of and those opposed to the union. The end result was "a
■ tragedy without parallel for the state of Tennessee."

"Tennessee will not furnish a single man for purposes of coercion,
but 50,000 if necessary for the defense of our rights and those of our southern brothers." Thus wrote an angry Isham Greene Harris, governor of Tennessee, in reaction to the April 15, 1861, call of President Abraham Lincoln
for 75,000 volunteers to put down the rebellious states of the Deep South.
In his initial draft of the response, Harris started to write the figure 75,000
(perhaps mocking Lincoln's 75,000?), but then reconsidered, scratching
through the "75," and settling on 50,000 instead.[1]

Actually, the war would be far more demanding on Tennessee's manpower
than Governor Harris, or probably anyone else, ever imagined. Already known
as the "Volunteer State," because of a readiness to enlist in earlier conflicts
like the Mexican War—where 2,800 soldiers were requested and 30,000
offered their services—Tennessee once again lived up to its sobriquet. When
the Civil War ended, the Volunteer State probably had sent more men to fight
for the Confederacy than had any other state, some 186,000, according to

one source. More conservative estimates range from 115,000 to 135,000. But that was not the whole story. Contrary to what Harris's message conveyed— that Tennesseans would "not furnish a single man for purposes of coercion"— about 31,000 Tennesseans are officially credited as having joined the Federal forces during the war, according to a report by the U.S. Provost Marshal General. This 31,000 number was more than those from all the other Confederate states put together and does not include Andrew Johnson's pro-Union state militia of more than 15,000 whites and 4,000 blacks, nor the perhaps as many as 7,000 Tennesseans who enlisted in out-of-state regiments and were credited to other states. Without question, more men from Tennessee fought in the Civil War than from any other Confederate state.[2]

Clearly, Tennesseans were divided about their role as the great crisis of the Union unfolded. In fact, Tennessee was the last of the eleven Confederate states to secede, with the vote for a "declaration of Independence," the equivalent to secession, not taking place until June 8, 1861. The count, in round numbers, was 105,000 to 47,000. Four months earlier, when several of the Cotton Belt states were seceding, Tennesseans had voted in a special election on whether or not to call a convention to consider secession. At that time, a clear majority—by a margin of 69,000 to 57,000—were against even meeting to talk about secession.[3]

Between the two votes, however, came the fighting at Fort Sumter, and many Tennesseans changed their minds. Of course, some Tennesseans had been "fire-eating" secessionists from the start, like people in Franklin County on the Alabama border, who were ready to secede from Tennessee and join Alabama if Tennessee did not itself secede and join the Confederacy. Governor Isham Harris, incidentally, was a native of Franklin County, although a resident of Memphis when elected governor.[4] Many more Tennesseans became secessionists only after Lincoln's call to arms following the crisis at Fort Sumter. There were also citizens, especially in East Tennessee, who never wavered in their staunch loyalty to the Union, a loyalty reinforced, in some cases, by a resentful feeling toward West and Middle Tennessee, especially the latter, for having come to control the state's political affairs. (East Tennessee had elected the governors and dominated the state legislature in earlier times, but for the last forty years, only Governor Andrew Johnson hailed from East Tennessee.) In fact, while West and Middle Tennessee strongly voted for disunion in the June referendum, East Tennessee just as strongly rejected secession by a margin of 33,000 to 14,000.[5]

The pro-Union vote in East Tennessee would be of no consequence in determining the state's official action, however, because the majority of Tennesseans had come to favor secession. Already the state legislature in Nashville, correctly anticipating approval of its actions in the June vote, had not only declared Tennessee independent; it had entered the state into a military league with the Confederacy. It also approved the Confederate constitution and sanctioned the recruitment of a volunteer army of some 55,000 men.[6] Soon, young men were rushing to join as war fever swept across the state, and some Tennesseans were quickly off to Virginia, where they fought at Bull Run (Manassas). Those who went to fight in Virginia were exceptions to the rule. The majority of Tennessee Confederates fought in what became known as the Western Theater, the great region from the Appalachian Mountains to the Mississippi River. In July 1861, the Tennessee state army was released to the Confederacy and became the core of the main Rebel army on the western front, eventually to be known, appropriately enough and for the last two and a half years of the conflict, as the Army of Tennessee.

In East Tennessee, however, many flocked to the Union colors. Some slipped across the border into Kentucky to join Federal units, while others openly rebelled against the Confederates. The Reverend William G. "Parson" Brownlow, circuit-riding Methodist preacher, bombastic editor of the *Knoxville Whig,* and confirmed Unionist—even if he did strongly support slavery— was perhaps the foremost of several staunch Union leaders in East Tennessee. Other important Unionists were Horace Maynard, Thomas A. R. Nelson, and Connelly F. Trigg. Andrew Johnson of Greeneville refused to resign from the U.S. Senate, the only senator from a seceded state to remain in his seat. Several East Tennessee counties continued to send representatives to Washington, and a convention assembled in Greeneville, hoping to foster the separation of East Tennessee from the rest of the state. Before long, East Tennessee guerrillas were actively harassing Confederates, burning railroad bridges and supply depots, and hoping for the early appearance of a Union army in the region.[7]

Abraham Lincoln certainly wanted to send an army into East Tennessee, since the region was his main source of Union strength in the South. Writing to General Don Carlos Buell that he would prefer a point on the railroad south of Cumberland Gap than to take Nashville, which was not on a major east-west railroad, Lincoln also argued for an East Tennessee campaign: "It is in the midst of loyal people, who would rally around it, while Nashville is not. . . . My distress is that our friends in East Tennessee are being hanged and driven to despair, and even now I fear, are thinking of taking rebel arms for the sake of personal protection. In this we lose the most valuable stake we have in the South."[8]

As the war developed, unfortunately from Lincoln's point of view, he and the Federals would not be able to place an army in East Tennessee until well into 1863. But Lincoln's fear that the loyalists would turn rebel proved groundless, at least in most cases. When Confederate General Edmund Kirby Smith took the new Rebel "Army of East Tennessee" into the region in early 1862 to keep order in the divided land, he soon observed that East Tennessee was "an enemy's country."[9]

Kirby Smith was right; his pronouncement dramatically pointed to a basic division within the state. In popular concept today, Tennessee is generally perceived, pure and simple, as a Confederate state. But truly, East Tennessee was different from the rest of Tennessee and, for that matter, from the rest of the South.

Many important factors are involved in explaining this difference. One of the most obvious is that fewer slaves were in East Tennessee than in the rest of the state. Only 9.2 percent of East Tennessee's population was slave, compared to one-third in West Tennessee and 29 percent in Middle Tennessee.[10] Charles F. Bryan's excellent study of East Tennessee in the Civil War brings attention to other important reasons. There was a sense of isolation, caused in part by the Cumberland Plateau that separated East and Middle Tennessee and in part by a railroad system than stretched from Virginia through East Tennessee to the lower South, rather than running east-west and linking the three grand divisions of Tennessee. The population of East Tennessee was diminishing in size relative to the other two sections, and this demographic trend coupled with declining political power and divergent political loyalties. The Whigs held sway in East Tennessee from the time of their stand against Andrew Jackson, while Democrats were stronger in Middle and West Tennessee. In neither agricultural production nor manufacturing did East Tennessee equal Middle Tennessee.[11]

But it would be a mistake to think that all Tennessee Unionists were residents of East Tennessee, for many were in the western counties along the Tennessee River, as well as scattered in various parts of Middle and West Tennessee.[12] Equally, it would be wrong to assume that East Tennesseans were solid, unwavering Unionists. Many Confederate sympathizers lived in the southern portion of East Tennessee, and even in the northern portion lived some pockets of Confederates.[13] Tennessee was indeed a complex maze of divided loyalties throughout the Civil War.

Nevertheless, Tennessee was destined to play a major role in the conflict, a role more important than any other Confederate state, with the possible exception of Virginia. One of the many reasons for this prominence was the size of Tennessee's population. Of the secessionist states, only Virginia had a larger white population than Tennessee: 1,047,299 to 826,722. The third-largest was North Carolina, with nearly 200,000 fewer whites than Tennessee, while Florida and Texas, today easily the largest of the former Confederate states, then had only 77,747 and 420,891, respectively. The population figures, although not the only answer, help explain why Tennessee sent more men to fight than did any other Confederate state. (It was not simply that Tennesseans were spoiling for a fight or more militant than their southern neighbors.)[14]

Tennessee's vital role goes far beyond the large number of men sent to war. Nonhuman resources were important too, especially those that were indispensable for war. Middle Tennessee was the most significant of the "Three Grand Divisions" in this regard. The region possessed prime farming and grazing lands that were devoted to general agriculture rather than concentrating solely on cotton. It produced large amounts of wheat, corn, hogs, cattle, horses, and mules, as well as tobacco and some cotton. Nashville, the regional trade center, was the western Confederacy's main war production center and storehouse for its armies, while northwest of Nashville, along the Cumberland River, were important Confederate gunpowder mills. Between the Cumberland and Tennessee rivers, stretching from the Kentucky line to the Alabama border, was the Confederacy's greatest iron production center, where huge quantities of raw iron were smelted, to be fashioned into swords, rifles, revolvers, artillery pieces, and other weapons of war.[15]

East Tennessee also boasted important resources; more wheat, for example, than Middle Tennessee, and far more than West Tennessee. From East Tennessee came large quantities of livestock, some corn, rich resources of saltpeter for manufacturing gunpowder, as well as lead, copper, iron ore, and bituminous coal. West Tennessee, in addition to its cotton, possessed an important river port in Memphis, which was, next to Nashville, the most significant center of war production and supply in the western Confederacy.[16]

The state's shape and location were also factors of great importance. Tennessee had less land area (42,244 square miles) than any of the Confederate states except South Carolina, but its long, narrow, east-west configuration and its geographic location assigned to Tennessee a role far out of proportion to its size.[17] Tennessee's northern boundary is noticeably longer than the northern boundaries of Mississippi, Alabama, and Georgia put together, while its shorter southern boundary, which, of course, adjoins those states, still stretches all the way across Mississippi and Alabama and halfway across Georgia. As one historian observed: "A Union army could scarcely reach the lower South without marching through [Tennessee]."[18]

Rather than marching, however, the Federals wanted to use the Iron Horse as much as possible to overrun and conquer the Confederacy. Besides moving men, the railroads were equally important for transporting all types of material with which an army must be equipped. From the strategic river port of Louisville on the Ohio, the Louisville & Nashville Railroad provided an obvious line of advance straight into the Confederacy at Nashville, with rail connections from Nashville into Alabama at both Decatur and Stevenson on the Memphis & Charleston line—in other words, directly into the central South. From Stevenson, Alabama, it was only a short distance into Chattanooga, which was the Tennessee terminus of the Western & Atlantic Railroad, which ran through the heart of Georgia and on to Savannah. From Chattanooga, too, ran the East Tennessee and Georgia Railroad (and from Knoxville northeast the East Tennessee and Virginia Railroad), which combined to form the most important and direct rail link joining Confederate armies in the Western theater with those in Virginia.

Also, from Columbus, Kentucky, on the great Mississippi River, the Mobile & Ohio Railroad extended directly south through Union City and Humboldt to Jackson, Tennessee. From Jackson, two rail lines extended south: the Mobile & Ohio continued to its junction with the Memphis & Charleston at Corinth, Mississippi, and thence on through most of Mississippi to Mobile; a second rail line ran to the Mississippi state capital at Jackson and eventually ended in New Orleans. Another West Tennessee line was the Memphis, Clarksville & Louisville Railroad, which ran from Bowling Green, Kentucky, to Memphis. Clearly, key invasion routes to the Confederacy ran along the Tennessee railroad system, a strategic reality grounded in the geography of the South.

It was as if nature had conspired with earlier mankind to ensure that control of Tennessee would be strategic for both sides. Boundary lines and railroads were the doings of humans, but nature was responsible for the river systems. The very best avenues of Union invasion were the waterways into the South. The Cumberland River, in Yankee hands, was a route into the heart of Middle Tennessee at Nashville. The Tennessee River penetrated to northern Alabama, where the Confederacy's most important east-west railroad, the Memphis & Charleston, would be vulnerable. The Mississippi River, meandering along the western border of Tennessee, pierced the Confederacy all the way to the Gulf of Mexico.

These are the major reasons why Tennessee was destined to be the prime battleground in the western theater. If Kentucky—which, like Tennessee, extends east-west for a long distance, possesses the same important rivers flowing through it and by it, and has the same railroads stretching southward over it—had seceded and joined the Confederacy, then the Bluegrass State would have been in the strategic location to bear the brunt of much of the fighting in the West, or, at least, to share it with the Volunteer State. Kentucky, of course, did not secede, leaving Tennessee in the keystone position for the crucial campaigns to control southern rivers and railroads.

General Albert Sidney Johnston bore the responsibility of defending Tennessee, and, in fact, the Confederacy's entire line in the Western Theater. A native Kentuckian who attended Transylvania College and graduated from West Point, Johnston was a close friend of Jefferson Davis's and possessed a reputation as one of the top military men in the nation. When Johnston arrived in Nashville in September 1861 to take command of the Confederate Department of the West, the general made an impressive appearance. A large crowd cheered his brief speech, and doubtless many Tennesseans felt a sense of relief to know that the defense of their state was in the hands of General Johnston.

But Johnston faced an awesome, perhaps impossible, task. His command stretched from the Appalachian Mountains westward to the Indian Territory, embracing the states of Tennessee, Arkansas, and part of Mississippi. Prior to Johnston's arrival, Rebel defensive preparations, with Leonidas Polk and Gideon Pillow playing key roles, had centered upon the Mississippi River, resulting in other vulnerable points being relatively neglected. Johnston lacked adequate manpower. His command totaled 72,000, and most regiments were inadequately armed, with more than a fourth located west of the Mississippi River. Federal commanders Henry W. Halleck and Don Carlos Buell had well over twice as many troops. Johnston tried to raise more men, but the early run to volunteer had dwindled to a trickle by the fall of 1861. The citizens of the threatened states were "not up to the revolutionary point," reported Johnston.[19] But even with more men and earlier preparation, Johnston's task still would have been extremely difficult. Tennessee had too many vulnerable points—the places where it was pierced by navigable rivers and railroads.

Unionists in East Tennessee were a major threat to the operations of the East Tennessee and Virginia Railroad, the only Confederate rail link west of the Appalachian Mountains that led directly to Virginia. At least it did not seem likely that the Federals could invade Tennessee by this route—not anytime soon anyway—which certainly was not the case with the rails and rivers in Middle and West Tennessee. To defend the Louisville & Nashville Railroad, the Cumberland River, the Tennessee River, the Mobile & Ohio Railroad, and the Mississippi River, the Rebels were deployed in a line defense. This defense proved very weak because the Yankees could easily and quickly concentrate superior numbers against a point of their choosing. The Confederates would require time to respond with reinforcements, even if they had the numbers to do so, which, of course, they did not.

Kentucky's neutrality was broken in September 1861, when Leonidas Polk, acting without orders, moved into Columbus. Johnston then transferred his headquarters from Nashville to Bowling Green. Probably he expected the Federals to advance by the Louisville & Nashville Railroad or on the Mississippi River—or both—rather than an invasion that would use other rivers or the Mobile & Ohio Railroad. And Johnston probably assumed that a Federal invasion would not happen before the spring of 1862. But fundamentally, Johnston and the Confederates never planned to "cover all the bases," so to speak, and Johnston accordingly wanted a reserve force positioned at Nashville.[20] However, even if the reserve army had been created, Johnston always would have lacked a railroad to move it quickly to the forts defending the Tennessee and Cumberland rivers. The closest connection still would have left reinforcements some seventeen to twenty miles from the forts, compelling them to march the remaining distance and consuming still more precious time once the invasion and fighting began.

One historian took Johnston to task for attempting "to defend everything at once," and contended that Johnston should have placed "strong garrisons" at the river forts, and then concentrated the army "at some point in the rear, such as Chattanooga, from which it could have been moved to any part of Tennessee."[21] Time, of course, would have been the critical factor with such a strategy. Another historian concluded: "Laterally there were no rail lines except the Memphis & Charleston, which lay so far south as to be discounted in planning operations along the northern border of the state." Without rail connections "between the center and either wing," he contended, "there was no possibility of rapid concentration." The fatal flaw in Confederate strategy was an "inability to concentrate," which left the Rebels, whatever else they did, with "a serious handicap," unless there had been more men and materials.[22] This historical analysis seems like a realistic assessment.

The war was ten months in duration before it came to Tennessee in full force. Suddenly and dramatically the Federals struck during the winter of 1862, and the results were disastrous for the Confederate cause. In early February, a combined land and water invasion force under U. S. Grant and

Andrew H. Foote breached the Confederate defensive perimeter across southern Kentucky. Driving south up the Tennessee River and the Cumberland River, the Yankees quickly captured Fort Henry and Fort Donelson, upon which the defense of those strategic waterways depended. The heart of Tennessee was thereby laid open to Union invasion and occupation.

Fort Henry fell to the Federals first. Lying on the east bank of the Tennessee River, a short distance south of the Kentucky state line, Fort Henry was "miserably located" on low ground, "poorly armed,"[23] and threatened "almost as much by the rising river as by the . . . Yankees."[24] The Confederates dueled Andrew Foote's gunboats for about two hours on February 6. With one-third of their fortifications under water, and their two big guns out of commission, the Rebel defenders, commanded by Lloyd Tilghman, chose to surrender. Most of the garrison already had made its escape across the twelve-mile neck of land from Fort Henry to Fort Donelson.

With the fall of Fort Henry, the Tennessee River was opened as an avenue of penetration all the way to Alabama and Mississippi. Advancing on the Tennessee River, which parallels the Mississippi River, proved just as helpful for Yankee strategic goals as moving down the Mississippi itself. In fact, control of the Tennessee was strategically preferred in some ways. The Federals were able to flank the Confederate stronghold on the Mississippi at Columbus, Kentucky, as well as quickly sever the east-west transportation corridor of the Memphis, Clarksville, & Louisville Railroad, which crossed the Tennessee only seventeen miles south of Fort Henry. Three Union gunboats quickly destroyed the railroad bridge. The potential for even greater Yankee gain loomed ominously: Federal troops traveling the Tennessee River could soon threaten the Memphis & Charleston Railroad, which would then mean that Confederate positions at Memphis were outflanked. The Rebels' entire Kentucky-Tennessee defensive position could collapse under such multiple threats to their lines of communication.

That, in fact, was precisely what did happen, and probably sooner than even the Federals might have expected. With the fall of Fort Henry, General Albert Sidney Johnston abandoned Bowling Green, retreating through Nashville to northern Alabama, where he intended to concentrate his forces for a counteroffensive. However, he ordered half of his troops to Fort Donelson in the vain hope of maintaining control of the Cumberland River and protecting Nashville from Federal occupation. This decision, according to Johnston biographer Charles Roland, was a "grave mistake."[25] Ten days after the loss of Fort Henry, Fort Donelson also collapsed, following some hard fighting as well as considerable Confederate blundering, in a battle transpiring amidst cold winter scenes of snow and sleet. The Union captured between fourteen and fifteen thousand Confederate prisoners, opened a second avenue of invasion via the Cumberland River to Nashville (which would become the first Confederate state capital to fall to the Federals), and ensured, if there remained any doubt, the collapse of the entire Rebel defensive line in the region. The surrender of Fort Donelson also provided General Ulysses S. Grant with an enduring and famous nickname, "Unconditional Surrender," taken from his reply to Confederate General Simon B. Buckner when the latter asked for Grant's terms of capitulation. About the only saving grace for the Confederacy was the refusal of a then-unknown colonel of cavalry to surrender. Nathan Bedford Forrest led several hundred men out of the fort to safety to live and fight another day.

The fall of Forts Henry and Donelson was the turning point of the war in the Western theater. A series of Union triumphs would follow, several directly or indirectly stemming from the victories at the forts, which, taken together, left the western Confederacy struggling to survive, and from which it would never be able to recover.[26] But certainly the Rebels, shocked and angered by the Federal successes, attempted to recover. Indeed, that spring witnessed a major attempt.

Smarting from widespread criticism of his generalship since the fall of the forts, Albert Sidney Johnston led the effort to reverse the tide of the war. Assisted by General P. G. T. Beauregard, who had recently come from Virginia where he enjoyed hero status as a result of his contributions at the Battle of Bull Run, Johnston concentrated in force around Corinth, Mississippi, the strategic junction of the Memphis & Charleston and Mobile & Ohio railroads. From all over the South came Rebel troops determined to roll back the Federal army. The result was another clash on Tennessee soil, a monumental battle, much larger than the fights for either of the river forts. The Battle of Shiloh, as the Confederates named it, was the first truly great battle of the Civil War. It took place near Pittsburg Landing (the Federal name for the struggle), on the west bank of the Tennessee River, about twenty miles north of the Mississippi state line.

More than 100,000 men were involved in the two-day struggle. The Confederates struck at dawn on Sunday, April 6, surprising the Union Army under the command of U. S. Grant, and driving back many disorganized Federal troops before their advance. The initial Rebel success was aided by the fact that the Yankee encampments lacked any tactical formation, had no field fortifications, and green troops were in advance positions. But the Federals rallied, many of them making a determined stand in a strong position known

ever after as the "Hornets' Nest," a Confederate name for this place of prolonged and bloody fighting. In attempting to reduce the "Hornets' Nest,"
Albert Sidney Johnston lost his life. (While many generals would be killed
during the Civil War, Johnston was the only Confederate army commander
to be killed in action.) Beauregard then took command.

The determined defense of the "Hornets' Nest" gave the Union valuable
time to organize a strong defensive line covering Pittsburg Landing, to which
the entire Union army could fall back. This new line, on higher ground,
supported by a massive battery of artillery, with reinforcements from General Buell's army coming by river to the landing, placed the Yankees in position not only to hold out on April 6, but to take the offensive early the next
morning and sweep the Confederates from the field. Shiloh was, up to that
time, the biggest battle of American history, an engagement that resulted in
nearly twenty-four thousand casualties,[27] and was an ominous harbinger of
what was to come before the great bloodletting between the Blue and the Gray
would grind to its final conclusion.

The Confederates had almost won. For a few hours on April 6, victory had
seemed clearly within reach—but the Federals had held. Their narrow tactical triumph was a strategic victory of major proportions. Shiloh left a large
Federal army, with reinforcements soon swelling it to one hundred thousand
strong, deep in the western Confederacy. The Confederates had lost a possible opportunity to undo what the Union had accomplished in the winter
and spring. From this time on, the pressure of the Federal invasion would be
unrelenting. By early June, the Yankees would have possession of the Memphis & Charleston Railroad at Corinth, Mississippi; Memphis would be in
their hands after the fall of Island Number 10 in the Mississippi River; and
they would be moving on the Confederate fortress at Vicksburg, Mississippi.
Tennessee would experience more major battles, and many minor ones (454
battles and skirmishes have been attributed to the state)[28] but perhaps none
has quite the combination of casualties, significance, drama, and aura as
Shiloh.[29]

Despite the blow that the defeat at Shiloh represented to Confederate
morale, Rebel leadership soon conceived another attempt to counter the
Union victories, although this offensive came only after still more damage—
most notably the Federal capture of the great port of New Orleans—had been
inflicted on the western Confederacy. In the late summer and fall of 1862,
General Braxton Bragg, who was Jefferson Davis's choice to replace the fallen
Johnston, devised and inaugurated this second bid to turn the war around
after the disasters of the previous winter and spring. Effectively deceiving the

enemy in his front and using the railroads to best advantage, Bragg shifted to a new line of operations, successfully leading a turning movement, on a grand scale, to the east at Chattanooga and thence northwest into Tennessee.

Bragg had placed his forces in position to threaten the rear of General Buell, whose Federals had been moving across north Alabama in an attempt to take Chattanooga. Those Yankees were compelled to retreat in order to prevent their supply line from being severed. The Confederate offensive then took the form of an invasion of Kentucky, in conjunction with the forces of General Edmund Kirby Smith, which moved from East Tennessee northward across the mountains into the Bluegrass, while Bragg's army, after marching into Middle Tennessee, crossed into Kentucky a little to the east of Bowling Green. The movement finally came to a climax on October 8, 1862, southeast of Louisville, at the little town of Perryville. An intriguing, confused, and bloody encounter unfolded, in which the Confederates drove back the Yankee's left wing corps, only to retreat and soon withdraw into East Tennessee. Bragg had concluded that the Kentuckians would not rise to support the Confederacy and thus the campaign could not achieve anything of lasting significance. But in the perceptions of many officers and soldiers, whether deservedly or not, Bragg's ability to lead was seriously damaged when the Kentucky campaign was over.

Nevertheless, Bragg was soon moving the army forward again, concentrating in Middle Tennessee around the town of Murfreesboro, thirty miles southeast of Nashville, along the banks of a stream known as Stones River, which meandered its way northward to the Cumberland, and along the route of the Nashville & Chattanooga Railroad. The Federals returned to Nashville in force, albeit with a new commander, as General William S. Rosecrans replaced Buell. The day after Christmas, Rosecrans moved out, proceeding southeast along the railroad line and seeking the Rebels. His strength was about forty thousand, while the Grayclads numbered three or four thousand less. The two armies came together just west of Murfreesboro.

On December 31, 1862, thousands of Confederate soldiers streamed out of the dim light of the cold early morning to stun the Federals, many of whom were still breakfasting in their camps. With surprise on their side, the Confederates mauled and drove most of the right side of the Union line for two and a half miles; the center of the Union line also fell back. Nine months earlier, the Rebels had charged the Yankees in a similarly devastating surprise attack at dawn during the Battle of Shiloh. By the time the fighting was over at Stones River, this battle resembled Shiloh in other ways. The casualty toll rivaled the twenty-four thousand of Shiloh, and, although the early advan-

Nashville and Chattanooga Railroad yards, 1864. Nashville became a key supply depot for later Federal invasions into the Deep South in 1864 and 1865. Nashville Tennessee Historical Society Collection, Tennessee State Library and Archives.

tage lay with the Confederates, the outcome was another defeat for the South. The surprise attack failed to gain possession of either the Nashville Pike or the Nashville & Chattanooga Railroad, and Bragg was unable to cut off the Federals from their Nashville base. The fighting ended in a tactical draw at nightfall on January 2, 1863. Fearing that his position would be enfiladed by Yankees occupying higher ground on his right flank, Bragg withdrew his army to the Shelbyville-Wartrace-Tullahoma area of Middle Tennessee. His retreat allowed the Federals to claim victory in the first major battle in the Union campaign to seize the Nashville-Chattanooga-Atlanta corridor.

Not until midsummer 1863 did the Federals move again. General Rosecrans then mounted a brilliant campaign, advancing from Murfreesboro to flank a puzzled Bragg out of position and forcing the Confederates to retreat to Chattanooga. Rosecrans had gained the lower half of Middle Tennessee with only a relative handful of casualties. He next moved to threaten the Western & Atlantic Railroad, the Rebels' communication line south of Chattanooga, and again forced Bragg to retreat and give up Chattanooga for a new position in north Georgia. This series of maneuvers made Rosecrans look like the best general in the Union army. But bad luck and disaster overtook him at the Battle of Chickamauga, fought a few miles over the line in Georgia. The Confederate Army of Tennessee finally won a major battle—one of the bloodiest of the war—which probably would have become a total rout of the Yankee army if not for the outstanding leadership of General George H. Thomas, known ever afterwards as the "Rock of Chickamauga."

Driven into Chattanooga, the shaken Rosecrans seemingly could not recover from the defeat at Chickamauga. General U. S. Grant, recently victorious at Vicksburg, was given command of the Union forces. His troops still held the prize, the railroad center of Chattanooga, setting the stage for more major fighting. The Rebel forces occupied the ridges and mountains east and south of town, hoping to lay siege and starve the Federals into surrender.

It was not to be. The Confederates did not use their forces effectively, failing to adequately invest the town, as well as sending General James Longstreet's corps, recently arrived from Virginia, to reinforce the Army of Tennessee before the Chickamauga battle, to a new campaign at Knoxville, where it was hoped they would drive out the occupation troops of Union General Ambrose Burnside. Grant soon succeeded in opening a supply line for his army in Chattanooga. He brought in thousands of reinforcements and in late November 1863, he attacked. In dramatic, spectacular fighting on Lookout Mountain and Missionary Ridge, Bragg's forces were defeated decisively when their center was broken on Missionary Ridge. The Confederates withdrew to Dalton, Georgia. The fighting for Chattanooga, incidentally, constituted the only time in the war when the four generals who are usually considered to be the best the Union produced saw action: Grant, Thomas, William T. Sherman, and Phil Sheridan.

After the defeat at Chattanooga, Bragg resigned from command and was replaced by Joseph E. Johnston. The Army of Tennessee passed for a time from the Tennessee theater of action as it participated in the Atlanta campaign during the spring and summer of 1864. General Longstreet, upon learning of Bragg's defeat at Chattanooga, lifted the siege of Knoxville, withdrew to the east and made winter quarters near Morristown. No more major action would take place in Tennessee until the fall of 1864.

By early September, Atlanta had fallen to General Sherman's Union troops. The Confederate Army of Tennessee moved to the north of the city, hoping to threaten Sherman's railroad connections. The new Rebel commander was General John Bell Hood, who relieved General Johnston after the latter retreated to the outskirts of Atlanta without ever launching a major attack to stop the Federal advance against Atlanta. Although the Confederates under Hood's command had suffered heavy casualties in unsuccessful attacks around Atlanta, the general soon determined to pursue a more ambitious objective than wrecking Sherman's railroad. Hood planned to invade Tennessee and to grab Nashville. If that proved successful, Hood would then be poised to carry the fight all the way to the Ohio River.

In late November, as freezing weather descended upon the region, Hood led the Confederates north from Florence, Alabama, into Middle Tennessee. Twenty miles south of Nashville, at the little town of Franklin, Hood ordered the Army of Tennessee into an ill-advised frontal assault against a strong Union position. On the afternoon of November 30, an unseasonably warm and sunny day, the Confederate army valiantly charged the Federal position, but met devastating fire and destruction. Some 1,750 Confederates died, including six generals killed or dying and another half dozen wounded or captured, while 5,500 more men were wounded or taken pris-

U.S. warehouses and steamboats on the Tennessee River at Chattanooga, 1864. Chattanooga was an important river and rail point in the Union supply line. Tennessee Historical Society Collection, Tennessee State Library and Archives.

oner. The Federals, commanded by John M. Schofield, had less than 200 killed in the battle. The Yankees withdrew to Nashville, where they joined forces with troops being assembled under the overall command of General George Thomas.

Despite the irreplaceable losses suffered at Franklin, Hood continued on to Nashville, where, on December 15 and 16, the Rebel army was driven from its positions, badly beaten and forced into a pell-mell rush to escape an overwhelming Union force. What remained of the army managed to recross the Tennessee River to safety on December 27. This was the last major action to take place in Tennessee, the war ending within a few months.[30]

In addition to its major battles and campaigns, Tennessee also experienced a vast amount of small-scale actions, especially cavalry operations. The latter produced one of the all-time great cavalry commanders, General Nathan Bedford Forrest. His exploits at Fort Donelson, Murfreesboro, Parker's Crossroads, Brice's Crossroads (in northern Mississippi), and along the Tennessee River near New Johnsonville were only some of the episodes that stamped the untutored native of Chapel Hill, Marshall County, as a military genius. Noted for leading from the front and credited with personally dispatching some thirty enemy soldiers, Forrest was a figure of legend well before the war ended. Despite the controversial Fort Pillow affair in April 1864, in which some of his command killed black soldiers who were trying to surrender, Forrest's stature as a military leader is firmly established.

Admiral David Glasgow Farragut was another native Tennessean who achieved great fame during the Civil War. He fought on the Union side—fittingly, perhaps, since his early years were spent in East Tennessee—and gained renown by engineering the conquest of New Orleans, as well as winning the battle of Mobile Bay, where he uttered the famous words: "Damn the torpedoes! Full speed ahead!" While no other Tennesseans of the Civil War era matched the military records of Farragut and Forrest, a number of others made significant military or political contributions. Among these people would be John C. Brown, William G. Brownlow, Benjamin F. Cheatham, Sam Davis, Isham Harris, Andrew Johnson, Gideon J. Pillow, Leonidas Polk, and Alexander P. Stewart.[31]

Tennessee's vital role in the Civil War was not something to be envied. While the war's transforming fury surely was an experience without parallel for the few who craved some kind of an ultimate adventure, for many Tennesseans the conflict was the most traumatic psychological and economic event of their lives. No doubt it left some mentally disturbed. Losses in property were immense and virtually incalculable, while physical pain and suffering (not counting the soldiers wounded in battle) were widespread. None of the state's three grand divisions was hit harder than Middle Tennessee, a region that, ironically, had recently achieved an unprecedented level of economic prosperity and cultural progress.

The Federals came early to Middle Tennessee and occupied the important towns as long as the war continued, except for Rebel challenges in reclaiming some eastern and southern portions of the area, first from late fall through the spring of 1862–63, and again, for a much shorter time, in the fall of 1864. As Stephen V. Ash has pertinently observed: "No other major Southern region, except northern Virginia, endured enemy occupation during the Civil War for as long as Middle Tennessee."[32] The result, after four years of war, with more than three of those years under Yankee occupation, was physical devastation.

Armed conflict obviously was one destructive factor, with Middle Tennessee being one of the most fought-over battlegrounds. But the passage of both Confederate and Union armies, together with the long Yankee occupation, account for most of the region's destruction. When the Confederates retreated following the fall of Fort Donelson, for example, they demolished industries, tore up railroads, burned stored supplies and bridges, and foraged off the countryside. Advancing Union troops destroyed even more. Because of Nashville's strategic location and the rich resources of Middle Tennessee, the Yankees developed the state capital as the center of their western war endeavors. The region became the army's breadbasket, not only while the troops were in Middle Tennessee, but also after the fighting resumed around Chattanooga and then moved into Georgia. Both to ensure that the region's resources would continue to flow to its armies, and deny their use by the Rebels, large Union garrisons occupied the large towns (about ten thousand soldiers in Nashville, for instance) and important points on the railroads and turnpikes.

Thus the Federals appropriated everything from horses, pigs, and cows to corn, hay, cotton, fence rails, firearms, and tools. Sometimes these appropriations resulted from formal requisitions, and sometimes they resulted from pillaging by poorly disciplined troops. Often there was an element of willful "just-for-the-hell-of-it" destruction. "It does us good to distroy the greesey belleys property," said a Yankee soldier. "When some of the boys get holt of any property of any kind belonging to the rebels they distroy it as fast as they can and then say dam him he was the coss of bringing us here."[33]

As if the Federal and Confederate troops were not doing enough damage, Middle Tennessee also was preyed upon by gangs of bandits and, to some degree after 1862, by newly freed blacks, some of whom were of a mind to help themselves to the possessions of their former masters. Conditions seemed to become steadily worse, with the entire fabric of society ripped, or at the least, severely strained, as hardly anyone, whatever their socioeconomic standing, political persuasion, gender, or race, was immune to the hardships and vicissitudes of the struggle.

The ravages of war were legion. Want and famine stalked various parts of Middle Tennessee as the war progressed. Many schools closed down. Churches in the towns sometimes were taken over as hospitals, or harassed because of known or suspected Rebel sympathies on the part of pastors or prominent members. Churches in the rural areas found it difficult to continue with regularly scheduled services. In fact, rural people increasingly stayed at home, afraid to go anywhere, when they considered the possibilities of abuse by the Federals, conscription by the Rebels, and violence from guerrillas and bandits. One bright spot (if such a description is appropriate for any aspect of war) was government in the towns. The Union army used the towns as bases of operation and was determined to have law and order. To that end, the Federals rendered assistance to local authorities, but in the countryside, little law, justice, or government existed by 1863. Many instances of harassment and recrimination occurred throughout the war, as Confederates sometimes seized an opportunity to strike at Union sympathizers, and vice versa. Middle Tennessee's national political stature was also a victim of the war. By 1865, it was almost as if James K. Polk and even Andrew Jackson had never lived.[34]

In West Tennessee, Federal troops appeared within weeks of their occupation of Middle Tennessee. Memphis fell on June 6, 1862, to a Union flotilla under Charles Davis, whose ironclad and rams defeated an inferior Rebel river fleet. Seven of the eight Confederate boats were either sunk or captured. Dismayed Memphis watched from the bluffs of the Mississippi while their only hope of salvation from the Yankees met its demise. In response to Davis's demand for surrender, the mayor of Memphis replied: "by the force of circumstances, it is in your hands." The sole consolation for the Confederates was that they had time to destroy stores and supplies before the Yankees took control of the city.[35]

A few days earlier, the Yankees had gained control of the Memphis & Charleston Railroad at Corinth, Mississippi. From this time on, the Union presence in West Tennessee was felt primarily in Memphis and its environs, and secondarily, along the one hundred or so miles of railroad from Corinth to Memphis as well as along the Mobile & Ohio through Jackson, Humboldt, and Union City, and the rail line from Humboldt to Memphis.

Colonel G. N. Fitch took military possession of Memphis. He requested all citizens, many of whom had fled, to return home, and he urged business-men to reopen stores, promising that the city's civil government would con-tinue to function and that the military would cooperate fully to support it. Nevertheless, the problems of occupied Memphis mounted and seemed to defy solution.[36]

Many of the propertied and more able people left the city, while those who remained sometimes withdrew from their business affairs. Some merchants and traders declined to take an oath of allegiance to the Union and were not permitted to conduct business. Taking their place were many northern trad-ers who descended upon the city. Also, a host of camp followers of all de-scriptions arrived in Memphis. Within a few days after the Federal takeover, the provost marshal banned lewd women from the streets after sunset and prohibited them from talking to soldiers on duty. Blacks who abandoned surrounding plantations to seek asylum with the Federal authorities also flooded the city. And while the military authorities naturally focused upon the large disloyal population, the city's internal conditions grew steadily worse as drunkenness, disorder, theft, and robbery abounded.[37] Besides facing a largely hostile population in Memphis, the Federals soon found that guer-rilla bands were widespread throughout West Tennessee, boldly attacking communication lines, ambushing small troop units, firing on Union naval and merchant vessels from the banks of the river, and, in general, constantly harassing the Federals. Beginning in July and continuing through Novem-ber 1862, Major General William T. Sherman was the Federal commander in Memphis who tried to deal with the Rebel challenges to Union occupa-tion. His views on how to conduct the war, which originally were rather mild, became increasingly harsh.

Most notably, Sherman announced a policy of collective responsibility, which held civilians responsible for guerrilla attacks in their neighborhoods and liable for Federal reprisals. When a Union forage train was ambushed near the Wolf River, Sherman arrested twenty-five locally prominent Con-federates and sent them to a Federal prison in Kentucky.[38] On other occa-sions when attacks occurred, Sherman burned the homes of local Confeder-ates. After Rebel guerrillas fired at Union vessels from the banks of the Mississippi River, Sherman destroyed all houses, farms, and cornfields along the river's east bank for a stretch of fifteen miles. Another time, in response to guerrilla fire on a passing boat, Sherman had the town of Randolph in Tipton County burned, leaving only one standing house to remind people of the price for not stopping the guerrilla activity. How effective such measures were in stopping guerrillas is a debatable question.[39]

Even after Sherman left for a new posting at Vicksburg, conditions in West Tennessee, especially in Memphis, did not improve but grew worse.[40] The winter of 1862–63 was very difficult, especially for families whose grown men were away at war. They sometimes lacked the necessities of life, and in Memphis, overcrowding compounded every problem. The population of Memphis in February 1863 was estimated at "11,000 original whites, 5,000 slaves, and 19,000 newcomers of all kinds, including traders, fugitives, hangers-on, and negroes."[41]

The Federals achieved little in developing Union sentiment in West Tennessee. During the last year of the war, according to historian Joseph Parks, "many left Memphis to avoid the draft, and the majority of those who remained merely submitted to military domination." Social life, Parks concluded, was "almost nonexistent" in a city where "no ball, dance or entertainment" could be held without military consent. Only a few men took interest in politics, as "the masses refused to be stirred." Parks wrote that Confederate sympathizers "still held aloof from Union politics," even when it was generally recognized that the end of the war was at hand.[42] West Tennesseans, though beaten, obviously were unrepentant and nonapologetic for their support of the Confederacy.[43]

In East Tennessee, the Federals did not arrive as soon as they had in the other two regions. Nevertheless, largely Unionist East Tennessee experienced a spectrum of war-related problems from the earliest days of the conflict. Most residents sympathized with the Union and refused to recognize Confederate authority. At the same time, a significant minority supported the Rebel cause. Both sides took the issue in deadly earnest and neighbors, politicians, business partners, fellow church members, and sometimes even family members became bitter enemies. It was a civil war within a civil war, with which neither Rebel nor Yankee authorities were able to deal successfully.[44]

The Confederates first confronted the problem. Unionists had already "organized regional and local political structures, established military companies known as home guards, and seized control of most counties." Some went to Kentucky to join Union regiments forming there, and others began to harass and kill Confederate supporters in hopes of driving the survivors from the state.[45]

The Confederacy sent in two regiments and initially began a policy of conciliation, which, it was assumed, would gradually win converts to the Southern cause. The first Rebel commander was Felix K. Zollicoffer, who soon died at the battle of Fishing Creek (Logan's Crossroads), just across the state line in Kentucky. Zollicoffer's tenure exhibited remarkable restraint in dealing with the aggressive Unionists. He promised that rights, property, and privileges would be undisturbed and allowed business to continue as usual as long as they did not give aid to the Federal cause. He even allowed Parson Brownlow to continue publishing his pro-Union newspaper.[46]

Zollicoffer's approach proved futile as Federal guerrillas engaged in widespread sabotage. The Confederates turned to tougher measures, arresting many alleged "Unionists," sometimes on flimsy evidence, and charging them with treason. Hundreds of men were jailed or sent to an Alabama military prison. After five bridges were destroyed in November 1861, a few Unionists were hanged.[47] Still, Confederate officers maintained some hope for a successful conciliatory policy and sought an acceptable balance between suppression and persuasion.

Then came the announcement of Confederate conscription of men into military service in the spring of 1862. Many East Tennesseans fled to Kentucky to escape the draft, while their friends and families resented the presence of Confederate authority more than ever. Witnessing firsthand the ill effects of the draft, Confederate commander Edmund Kirby Smith persuaded Richmond to suspend the East Tennessee draft and urged East Tennesseans to return home. But soon the Confederate government again reversed policy and reinstituted the draft, disregarding the hostile opinion prevalent in East Tennessee. The result was more distrust, bitterness, and violence. The rather rapid turnover of Confederate department commanders (eight men in a little over two years) undermined consistent policies and effective implementation of government policy, whatever its nature. Confederate rule, by 1863, was more harsh than it had been in 1861. Nevertheless, one historian has recently concluded that the Confederates, given the problems they faced, displayed "a remarkable restraint in East Tennessee." He particularly pointed to Zollicoffer, Kirby Smith, and Major General Sam Jones, maintaining that "all drew a line between dissenting actions and dissenting beliefs, punishing the one but tolerating the other." All of this was "a marked contrast to Federal policies in East Tennessee."[48]

The Federals occupied East Tennessee in September 1863. Already the devastation of the region was pronounced, and it only became worse upon their arrival. As in Middle Tennessee, the Yankees foraged liberally, ravaging still more of the countryside. They also quickly arrested people for disloyal statements "or even supposed sentiments, and they detained a far greater percentage of the enemy population than their Confederate counterparts."[49]

By the last year and a half of the war, East Tennessee was at the mercy of regularly constituted Federal troops, both Yank and Reb guerrilla bands, and bushwhackers who roamed the region. Much of the region's social and economic fabric was devastated, with want and suffering rampant throughout the area.[50]

When the Civil War finally ended in the spring of 1865, the conflict had been a tragedy without parallel for the state of Tennessee. The loss of life and the destruction of property had been appalling. The stigma of rebellion would long endure and part of that cost was the loss of power in national politics. Slaves were emancipated, but the status and security of the newly freed people were uncertain. Many would suffer in the years to come as they made the transition from slavery to freedom. Many whites, of course, were determined to treat the freed people as inferiors, just as some blacks sought vengeance for past and present injustices. Thus, to all the other difficulties were added racial divisions, different from those before the Civil War but perhaps even more intense. Tennessee was destined to be a long time in recovering from the Civil War.

NOTES

1. Robert H. White, *Tennessee: Its Growth and Progress* (Nashville, 1944), 587.
2. Robert E. Corlew, *Tennessee: A Short History* (Knoxville, 1981), 139, 269; Wilma Dykeman, *Tennessee: A History* (Newport, Tenn., 1993), 16, 78; James A. Crutchfield, *Tennesseans at War: Volunteers and Patriots in Defense of Liberty* (Nashville, 1987), 86; Civil War Centennial Commission, "Guide to the Civil War in Tennessee," (Nashville, 1961), 4; Richard Nelson Current, *Lincoln's Loyalists: Union Soldiers from the Confederacy* (Boston, 1992), 59, 60. Dykeman says that as many as twenty thousand black Tennesseans were soldiers in the war and that Tennessee "could claim the highest percentage of Union casualties of any state." See also Thomas L. Livermore, *Numbers and Losses in the Civil War in America, 1861–1865* (New York, 1969), 19–26; Frederick H. Dyer, *A Compendium of the War of the Rebellion* (Des Moines, 1908), 11; Clarence C. Buell and Robert U. Johnson, eds., *Battles and Leaders of the Civil War,* (New York, 1887–88), 4:767; Randolph H. McKim, *The Numerical Strength of the Confederate Army: An Examination of the Argument of the Honorable Charles Francis Adams and Others* (New York, 1912), 52–61.
3. Stanley F. Horn, ed., *Tennessee's War, 1861–1865, Described by Participants* (Nashville, 1965), 15.
4. Stanley J. Folmsbee, Robert E. Corlew, and Enoch L. Mitchell, *History of Tennessee* (New York, 1960), 2:31; Corlew, *Tennessee,* 282.

5. Charles F. Bryan, Jr., "East Tennessee in the Civil War" (Ph.D. diss., Univ. of Tennessee, 1978), 12, 53.

6. Charles Roland, *An American Iliad: The Story of the Civil War* (Lexington, Ky., 1992), 36; Thomas L. Connelly, *Civil War Tennessee: Battles and Leaders* (Knoxville, 1979), 4.

7. "Guide to the Civil War in Tennessee," 4; James C. Kelly, "William Gannaway Brownlow, Part 1," *Tennessee Historical Quarterly* 43 (Spring 1984): 26, 30–31; and "Part 2," *Tennessee Historical Quarterly* 43 (Summer 1984): 1; Digby G. Seymour, *Divided Loyalties: Fort Sanders and the Civil War in East Tennessee* (Knoxville, 1982), 4, 10–38; Connelly, *Civil War Tennessee,* 8.

8. Roy P. Basler, ed., *The Collected Works of Abraham Lincoln* (New Brunswick, N.J., 1953), 5:91.

9. Connelly, *Civil War Tennessee,* 8.

10. Bryan, "East Tennessee in the Civil War," 19.

11. Ibid., 8, 12, 13, 17. See also Jesse Burt, "East Tennessee, Lincoln and Sherman, Part 1," *East Tennessee Historical Society's Publications* 34 (1962): 4, 5.

12. "Guide to the Civil War in Tennessee," 4. The June 8 vote for separation from the Union saw nearly thirty-three thousand vote against it in East Tennessee, more than eight thousand against it in Middle Tennessee, and some six thousand opposed it in West Tennessee. Folmsbee et al., *History of Tennessee,* 2:34.

13. Bryan, "East Tennessee in the Civil War," 23.

14. These figures are from the 1860 census returns, as reported in James G. Randall and David Donald, *The Civil War and Reconstruction* (Lexington, Mass., 1969), 68.

15. Stephen V. Ash, *Middle Tennessee Society Transformed, 1860–1870: War and Peace in the Upper South* (Baton Rouge, 1988), 12, 16–19; Connelly, *Civil War Tennessee,* 14, 15, 17.

16. Bryan, "East Tennessee in the Civil War," 8, 13, 16–17; Connelly, *Civil War Tennessee,* 11, 17.

17. Corlew, *Tennessee,* 3; Mary French Caldwell, *Tennessee: The Volunteer State* (Chicago, 1968), 1. When West Virginia separated from Virginia in 1863, Virginia became slightly smaller than Tennessee.

18. Connelly, *Civil War Tennessee,* 7.

19. Roland, *An American Iliad,* 58.

20. Ibid.

21. Connelly, *Civil War Tennessee,* 21.

22. Peter Franklin Walker, "Building a Tennessee Army: Autumn, 1861," *Tennessee Historical Quarterly* 16 (June 1957): 104.

23. Robert S. Henry, *The Story of the Confederacy* (New York, 1931; rpt., 1957), 79 (page reference is to reprint edition).

24. James M. McPherson, *Ordeal By Fire: The Civil War and Reconstruction,* 2d edition (New York, 1992), 223.

25. Roland, *An American Iliad,* 59.

26. For the fullest and best account, see Benjamin Franklin Cooling, *Forts Henry and Donelson: The Key to the Confederate Heartland* (Knoxville, 1987).

27. Livermore, *Numbers and Losses,* 77–80.

28. Dykeman, *Tennessee*, 78; Dyer, *Compendium*, 837–45. The latter work lists more than 1,500 battles, campaigns, actions, raids, expeditions, etc.

29. For a full treatment of Shiloh, see James L. McDonough, *Shiloh–in Hell Before Night* (Knoxville, 1977).

30. For more detail about the campaigning in Tennessee, the reader may consult Stanley Horn, *The Army of Tennessee* (Norman, Okla., 1952), as well as the author's books, which form the basis of the preceding account: *Shiloh—in Hell Before Night*; *Stones River–Bloody Winter in Tennessee* (Knoxville, 1980); *Chattanooga—A Death Grip on the Confederacy* (Knoxville, 1984); *Five Tragic Hours: The Battle of Franklin*, with Thomas L. Connelly (Knoxville, 1983); and *War in Kentucky: From Shiloh to Perryville* (Knoxville, 1994).

31. If not born in Tennessee (though most were), they were sufficiently associated with the state to be recognized as Tennesseans.

32. Ash, *Middle Tennessee Society Transformed*, 87.

33. Ibid. The original spelling and grammar have been retained.

34. In preparing this section on Middle Tennessee, the author is very much indebted to Ash, *Middle Tennessee Society Transformed*, especially chapter 5, pp. 84–105. Anyone who is seriously interested in Tennessee during and after the war should read this excellent book. On Nashville, Walter T. Durham has contributed two important studies: *Nashville: The Occupied City. The First Seventeen Months, February 16, 1862, to June 30, 1863* (Nashville, 1985), and *Reluctant Partners: Nashville and the Union, July 1, 1863, to June 30, 1865* (Nashville, 1987). Also helpful on Tennessee as a whole is Fred A. Bailey, *Class and Tennessee's Confederate Generation* (Chapel Hill, N.C., 1987).

35. McPherson, *Ordeal By Fire*, 232; Joseph H. Parks, "Memphis Under Military Rule, 1862–1865," *ETHS Publications* 14 (1942): 31, 32.

36. Parks, "Memphis Under Military Rule," 32.

37. Ibid., 34–38

38. *War of the Rebellion: A Compilation of the Official Records of the Union and Confederate Armies*, vol. 17 (Washington, 1880–1901), ser. 1, pt. 1, 23 (hereafter cited as *OR*).

39. *OR,* 17, pt. 2, 280–81; *OR,* 17, pt. 1, 144–45; *OR,* 17, pt. 2, 235–36; Noel Fisher, "'Prepare Them For My Coming': General William T. Sherman, Total War, and Pacification in West Tennessee," *Tennessee Historical Quarterly* 51 (Summer 1992): 84–85.

40. Parks, "Memphis Under Military Rule," 53.

41. Ibid., 54.

42. Ibid., 57, 58.

43. See the following articles for additional interesting information on West Tennessee during the Civil War: George Sisler, "The Arrest of a Memphis *Daily Appeal* War Correspondent on Charges of Treason," *West Tennessee Historical Society Papers* 11 (1957): 76–92; Bobby L. Lovett, "The West Tennessee Colored Troops in Civil War Combat," *WTHS Papers* 34 (1980): 53–70; Nathan K. Morgan, "'No Alternative Left': State and County Government in Northwest Tennessee During the Union Invasion, January–June 1862," *WTHS Papers* 46 (1992): 13–33.

44. Bryan, "East Tennessee in the Civil War," 344–54.

45. Noel Fisher, "'The Leniency Shown Them Has Been Unavailing': The Confederate Occupation of East Tennessee," *Civil War History* (Dec. 1994): 275–76.
46. Ibid., 277.
47. Ibid., 281.
48. Ibid., 290.
49. Ibid.
50. Bryan, "East Tennessee in the Civil War," 344–54. See also Burt's article cited in note 11.

Unconditional Unionist: Samuel Mayes Arnell and Reconstruction in Tennessee

■ Kathleen R. Zebley

■

■ *Editor's Note:* Zebley finds that Unionist sentiment was not confined solely to East Tennessee during the Civil War and Recon-
■ struction. Samuel Mayes Arnell, a Maury County planter, served
as one of the Republican party's most stalwart and effective voices
during the attempted reconstruction of Tennessee politics after
■ the end of the Civil War. From 1865 to 1870, Arnell championed
a different future for Tennessee, placing political power in the
■ hands of Unionists, taking the vote away from Confederates, protecting Unionists and African Americans from intimidation and
■ terrorism, and establishing a public education system for all Tennesseans. Unlike many Tennesseans then and since, Arnell considered the years of war and Reconstruction as "when a great nation
■ was not lost, but saved—rebuilt on better foundations."

After the death of President Abraham Lincoln in April 1865, Radical Republicans in Congress and President Andrew Johnson began to wrangle
over the details of reconstructing the former Confederate states. Tennessee
did not experience Congressional Reconstruction but did encounter four years
of Radical Republican policies emanating from Nashville. Samuel Mayes
Arnell of Columbia served as a key figure during these stormy years, playing
an active role in Tennessee's General Assembly and later in the United States
House of Representatives. Arnell hitched his political career to the success of
the Radical Republican Party of Tennessee. While the party remained in
power from 1865 to 1869, Arnell commanded the authority to propose
measures guaranteeing and extending Radical control of the state by Unionists. His primary contribution as a legislator concerned the franchise acts of
1865 and 1866, which enhanced the power of his party by assuring an elec-

torate more sympathetic to Unionists. Like other Unionists in the Upper South and border states, Arnell channeled his wartime loyalism into the Republican Party.[1] The issues he championed in Tennessee—disfranchisement of Confederates, protection of Unionists and black citizens, and promotion of public school education—remained his principal concerns after his election to Congress.

Arnell's life and political career afford a glimpse into the turbulent times of Tennessee during the Civil War and during the governorship of William G. Brownlow. For loyalists like Arnell, the years of Radical control placed power in the hands of Unionists who had suffered in the war. For the majority of Tennesseans, however, Radical Republicanism was a painful experience that was soothed once the Conservatives reclaimed the state government in 1869.

At first glance, Arnell fits the stereotype of a scalawag, a native white southerner who entered the realm of politics for the first time during the Reconstruction years. Indeed, Arnell had no prior political experience when he entered Tennessee's House of Representatives in 1865. Like other scalawags, he owned extensive tracts of land, was well educated, had been a member of the antebellum Whig Party, and labored to improve the South and restore it to the Union. Love of country, respect for his ancestors, and concern for the future welfare of his family motivated Arnell to risk his life and prosperity by supporting the Union. He did not manipulate his political power for pecuniary gain, but maintained his objectives of returning Tennessee to the Union, granting equality to blacks, and bolstering education in the South.

Born on May 3, 1833, and the son of a Presbyterian minister, Arnell was a slaveholder, owned two thousand acres of land valued at $35,000, and was a prominent citizen and lawyer in Columbia. He lived on his plantation, Oakland, two miles outside of Columbia, with his wife, Cornelia Orton Arnell, and their five children. Originally educated for the church, Arnell chose not to enter the ministry, but instead attended Amherst College, where he studied law and later gained admittance to the bar in Tennessee. He also spent time teaching at a classical school in Columbia. Two years before the Civil War, he and other partners established a leather manufacturing company in Lewis County, Tennessee.[2]

Though the Volunteer State failed to support Abraham Lincoln for president in 1860, most of the populace accepted the election results. Tennessee had endorsed its native son, John Bell, as candidate of the Constitutional Union Party for president, because voters suspected the Democratic Party could not safeguard the Union.[3] Former members of Tennessee's Whig Party adopted a Unionist stance and also supported John Bell. These men neither demanded emancipation nor lauded slavery. In fact, a good number owned slaves and trusted that the continuation of the Union would protect their chattel.

Arnell understood Tennesseans' concerns about the future of their land and investments. His family had resided in Middle Tennessee for more than fifty years. His father, the Reverend James M. Arnell, had served the Zion Community as pastor of the Presbyterian Church from 1832 to 1850, and the Arnells belonged to its first group of settlers.[4] Widespread ownership of slaves characterized Zion Community, as it did the whole of Middle Tennessee. Maury County's location in the fertile soils of the Central Basin and its numerous planters contributed to a slave population of over ten thousand by 1860.[5]

Arnell felt a strong attachment to the Union. His grandfather, Dr. Samuel Mayes, fought at King's Mountain and was taken prisoner by the British in 1780. Cornelia Arnell's grandfather, Major Orton, served seven years in the Continental Army and received land in Tennessee for his military service. To the Arnells, secession seemed like dividing up the family.[6]

Arnell admitted: "So this red corpuscle of patriotism, naturally was in my blood and it seemed like giving up a part of my inheritance to talk of giving up "the Union." Therefore, it occurred to me that it was a duty—possibly I owed to my family to go out and take part in the general movement against secession and to make some public addresses for the Union and I did so."[7]

In January and February 1861, Arnell worked arduously to keep Tennessee in the Union. After his first speaking engagement at Hampshire, Union men of Mount Pleasant and Newburg contacted Arnell to speak to their communities. In his various speeches, Arnell stressed Abraham Lincoln's constitutional election and the benefits of remaining in the Union. He reasoned that his slave owner status could calm local fears and persuade voters to oppose secession. He advised the people not to worry about the issue of slavery in the territories, because cotton could not grow in that climate.[8]

The night before the February 1861 referendum, Arnell spoke in Columbia, reiterating the benefits of remaining in the Union. He was relieved when the state voted against holding a convention to decide whether to join the Confederacy. The attack on Fort Sumter, however, suddenly changed the pro-Union atmosphere. In June, Tennessee voted for secession, a shift in attitude Arnell attributed to Major Robert Anderson's surrender at Fort Sumter and John Bell's endorsement of secession.[9]

Arnell's Unionist position made him an enemy to local Confederate supporters. As a member of an old, established family, his unpopular stance cost
him friends and, later, personal property. Social ostracism proved to be the
method Middle Tennesseans chose to employ against Unionists when
Federals remained in the community. If the Federals did not station troops
in the area, then local folks terrorized the loyalists, threatening and physically
abusing them.[10]

Unionists could not even find solace in their churches. Ministers added
to war sentiments by praying that the waters of southern rivers would cover
"dead Yankees" as the Red Sea covered the pursuing Egyptians. Parishioners
noticed those who did not join in the prayers for the Confederacy, and the
loyalists soon found themselves without a congregation in Middle or West
Tennessee. The Arnells quit attending Presbyterian services because their
minister harangued the North and offered prayers and sermons for the victory of the South. Arnell blamed the preachers for helping to turn "Middle
Tennessee away from the national government."[11]

Andrew Johnson. R. H.
Howell Photo Album,
Library Photograph Col-
lection, Tennessee State
Library and Archives,
Copy by Karina
McDaniel.

Tennessee's membership in the Confederacy proved short-lived. The Confederate reign of Tennessee expired on February 16, 1862, when Fort Donelson fell to Union troops. Governor Isham G. Harris, a Confederate sympathizer, and the state legislature abandoned Nashville, making way for martial rule. After Union troops occupied West and Middle Tennessee, President Lincoln appointed Andrew Johnson as military governor on March 3, 1862.[12]

Initially, Johnson's policy was one of moderation and conciliation toward the residents of Tennessee. Once the ringleaders of the rebellion had been stripped of power, he maintained, Tennesseans would divest themselves of Confederate sympathies and return to the United States. By the fall of 1862, Johnson recognized that leniency accomplished nothing. His efforts of quieting secessionists in Nashville, his embrace of Tennessee prisoners of war, and his overtures to restore civil political operations in Tennessee did not break the Confederate spirit.[13]

Outside of Nashville, popular sympathies in West and Middle Tennessee also remained with the Confederates. People who dared to endorse the Union risked life and property. Middle Tennessee experienced destruction and incessant warfare throughout the duration of the Civil War. Residents not only had to worry about Confederate and Union troops but also agonized over the guerrillas who annoyed the Federal occupiers and roamed the countryside terrifying those who dared to aid the Union cause. The bandits found refuge in the homes of friends and Confederate sympathizers. With their contacts in various other communities throughout the region, the brigands knew who cooperated with the Federals.[14]

Arnell and his family escaped personal injury from guerrilla bands but suffered property losses. On at least two separate occasions, one in July and another in August 1864, guerrillas robbed Arnell of goods totaling $756.50. The raiders absconded with a bay mare valued at $150, a double-barreled gun, a hat, one lot of leather, and $210 in cash. A month later, bandits returned to confiscate more leather, coats, hats, boots, clothes, a watch, and jewelry. These losses preceded the greater destruction and loss of wealth for Arnell that occurred in the latter part of 1864.[15]

On a cool November morning in 1864, while the Arnell family ate breakfast, Federal soldiers approached their home and began to occupy the property in preparation for a battle with the Confederates. The Arnells had to evacuate to avoid being shelled or burned out during the skirmish. Because of Arnell's prominent position as a Unionist, the commanding Union officer volunteered to take the family within the lines. In addition, the officer positioned eight soldiers around the home to guard it as long as the Union forces remained. The family retreated to Columbia, where they lodged with Arnell's Aunt Salina; and the next day Arnell journeyed to Nashville. People scurried into Columbia from the surrounding countryside, bringing harrowing tales of burning homes and the theft of household items.[16]

After the Federals retreated from Arnell's home, Cornelia and a gentleman friend left Columbia to go to Oakland. The house was in disarray since the raiders had either stolen or scattered the Arnells' most valuable possessions throughout the house. While Mrs. Arnell assessed the damage, Confederate soldiers sauntered in and out of the home.[17] As she was straightening up the house, a Confederate colonel entered and curtly inquired as to the whereabouts of her husband. Cornelia refused to disclose her husband's location. The officer then retorted that it was Mr. Arnell's business to be at home with his wife and children. Next, the officer asked if Cornelia knew who had destroyed her home. After she answered "no," he remarked that he and his soldiers came to the property as soon as the "damned Yankees" left. He and his men took an ax, beat down the door, and spent the night. He told her: "[I]f I could have caught your husband I'd have hung him to the tree out there. The neighbors told me all about him, what a traitor he is to the South, how from the beginning he plotted, informed and helped the Yankees."[18] Flabbergasted at the audacity of the Rebel officer, Mrs. Arnell breathed a sigh of relief that Samuel had fled to Nashville with other Unionists to stay at the home of Colonel John T. Wilder. Cornelia never forgot the suffering her family experienced when the Confederates controlled their area and ransacked their home. It was one price Arnell paid for sympathizing with the Union.[19]

After the Battle of Nashville, December 15–16, 1864, Governor Andrew Johnson commissioned Arnell to raise a regiment of mounted infantry for a term of one year. Arnell began the task in Columbia, but became ill and remained in bed for three months. The death of his young daughter added to his woes. He attributed her death to the exposure she received when the family had to flee from their home and could not return because of its destruction by Rebels.[20] Even though illness thwarted Arnell's scheme to assist the Union cause, he soon had another opportunity to serve his state.

Even before the Civil War ended, President Lincoln and Governor Johnson discussed the status of Tennessee. As early as 1863, Lincoln and Johnson planned for Tennessee's return to the Union. Both leaders agreed that political power in the state must rest in the hands of unconditional Union men. President Lincoln recognized the power that southern Unionists would possess in rebuilding state governments. He also regarded former Whigs as the natural leaders of the Republican Party in the South, since the majority had allied with the Union and were hostile toward Democrats.[21] Lincoln and Johnson realized that loyalists desired to return their state to the good graces of the Union and would prevent former Rebels from seizing power and throwing the state into chaos. Both men concurred that emancipation and the writing of a new constitution had to be a component of the reconstruction of the state.

A convention of Tennessee Unionists met in Nashville on January 9, 1865. Some of their resolutions included a constitutional amendment abolishing slavery and a schedule to declare all acts of the Confederate government as null and void. The Unionist convention also nominated William G. Brownlow for governor and composed a general ticket of candidates for the General Assembly. Because of his public advocacy of the Union, his fidelity to the United States during the rebellion, and his earnest desire to restore Tennessee to the Union, Arnell's Union friends nominated him to be a candidate for the General Assembly in 1865.

Brownlow, the fiery editor of the *Knoxville Whig* and future governor, deemed immediate emancipation of slaves necessary to the reconstruction of Tennessee, since the rebellion had started and continued with slaveholders. For Brownlow, gradual emancipation translated into gradual suppression of the rebellion. On February 22, more than twenty-five thousand voters cast ballots in favor of the amendment abolishing slavery and the schedule voiding Confederate government acts. Less than two weeks later, on March 4, voters elected Brownlow governor and also elected members of the state legislature.[22] Arnell won his seat in the March election and recalled years later that "Maury County gave me then, as she always did afterwards a fair and honorable support at the poles [sic]."[23]

Arnell, a former Whig turned Republican, represented Williamson, Maury, and Lewis Counties in the General Assembly, while also serving on the Claims, Education and Common Schools, and Judiciary committees.[24] His first interest was education. When approached as to his preference of committee chair assignments, Arnell replied: "I prefer the chairmanship of the 'Committee on Education' above all others. To help shape the future school system of my native state and make it the best possible was my earnest desire."[25] His interest in education, however, soon took second fiddle to his determined efforts to keep Republicans in power.[26]

Brownlow established the tone of the new Unionist legislature in his message to the Senate and General Assembly on April 6, 1865. He denounced secession, spoke of the casualties of war, and recalled the sacrifices of Tennesseans who sided with the Union. He laid special emphasis on the qualifications of voters and reminded the legislature that the people of the state had entrusted these bodies to limit the elective franchise. He advised the legislators not to determine the franchise with emotions of vengeance, sympathy, or pity but to guard the ballot box against treason.[27]

Brownlow had no stronger supporter than Samuel Arnell, who remembered the sacrifices and hardships he, his family, and other Unionists had endured at the hands of the Confederates. Arnell resolved to reward only loyal men and to punish the ex-Confederates. In his haste to protect the ballot box from former Rebels and secure state government in the hands of unconditional Unionists, he and other Radicals twisted the law to their own benefit to preserve their grasp over the state by ensuring a devout, loyalist electorate.

Arnell's franchise bill of 1865 proved to be one of the most important laws approved during Brownlow's administration. Arnell and Brownlow realized that Tennessee had to elect Unionists to congressional seats if the state hoped to be readmitted to the Union. In order to do so, the elective franchise needed restrictions to prevent ex-Confederates from voting.[28]

Arnell's bill stipulated that persons of legal age and residence who had been unconditional Unionists from the start of the war, loyal citizens of another state, or persons who had become twenty-one since March 4, 1865, could vote. In addition, those honorably discharged from the Union Army or Union men conscripted into the Confederate Army qualified to vote, as did voters in the elections of November 1864, February 22, 1865, or March 4, 1865. Others had to prove their loyalty and have two witnesses vouch for them. Confederate government officials, military officers, and individuals who had assisted the Confederacy were disfranchised for fifteen years. Confederate soldiers were forbidden to vote for five years. The bill also stipulated that county court clerks register voters and issue certificates permitting the bearer to vote. Furthermore, election judges and candidates had to recite an oath declaring loyalty to the constitutions of the United States and the state of Tennessee.[29]

This bill passed the Senate without a hitch, but fierce debate erupted in the House and discussion lasted several days. Arnell's bill triumphed and became law on June 5, 1865. According to Brownlow's newspaper, "The vote is decisive in favor of disfranchising rebels, and is, all in all, the best bill that has been presented to the Legislature."[30]

Tennessee Unionists soon realized that the new franchise law did not absolutely prevent the disfranchised from attempting to vote. Its first test came in August 1865 during the state's initial postwar congressional election. State leaders believed this election would gauge the qualified voters' approval or disapproval of the Radicals' leadership and policies.[31]

Interestingly enough, Horace Maynard (Second District), William B. Stokes (Third District), and Isaac R. Hawkins (Seventh District) were the only Radicals elected to Congress. Conservative candidates Nathaniel G. Taylor (First District), Edmund Cooper (Fourth District), William B. Campbell (Fifth District), Dorsey B. Thomas (Sixth District), and John W. Leftwich (Eighth District) defeated their Radical opponents. Ironically, Arnell originally lost in the Sixth Congressional District to the Conservative Dorsey B. Thomas, who differed with Brownlow and the Radicals as to the methods of reconstruction in the state and allied with President Andrew Johnson. The vote of the people disappointed Brownlow and clearly expressed popular condemnation of the Radicals in Tennessee.[32]

The strategy of Radicals included convincing voters that the actions of extreme Conservatives might plunge the country back into war or place Tennessee under military rule. Brownlow dismissed the votes of Humphreys, Lawrence, Maury, Montgomery, and Stewart Counties because of illegal registration and/or improper voting. He accepted the votes of Decatur, Perry, and Lewis Counties as correct. The governor followed no particular method when accepting or barring returns of counties. He recognized Wayne County's totals as correct, for instance, even though some voters had registered without proper proof. Brownlow accepted the returns from Hickman County even though questions on forms had not been answered. Dickson County failed to follow the governor's directives, yet he accepted the total. In the end, Brownlow awarded the certificate of election to Arnell. Brownlow felt a sense of duty to rescue the author of the franchise act and seat him in Congress. To ensure present and future Radical control, the methods of registration had to be revamped.[33]

In February 1866, before he assumed his congressional seat, Arnell submitted a tougher resolution. He urged his fellow legislators to pass the measure before the Radical Party in Washington took disciplinary action. The new law excluded persons who fought for the Confederacy, held an office in the Confederate States of America, donated money and property to the disunion effort, and everyone else who had endorsed secession and the Confederacy. Every man except Union soldiers had to present two legal voters who vouched for the person's loyalty, and the individual also had to take the ironclad oath. Now, special commissioners appointed by the governor disbursed voting certificates, replacing the county court clerks who had performed the task under the first franchise law. Brownlow now had a tighter grasp over the electorate, since he could hire and fire commissioners at will.[34]

During the first months of 1866, the Radicals worked feverishly to pass this stricter disfranchisement bill. Some Conservative legislators did not attend the sessions when a vote on the bill was scheduled, and other Conservatives refused to vote. Only after the manipulation of numbers needed for a quorum and the exclusion of several Conservative members, did the franchise law of 1866 finally pass the House on April 12, and become law on May 3.[35] In this way, the Radicals bent the laws to their own purposes. Their self-righteous attitude and conviction that only strict Unionists had Tennessee's best interests at heart caused them to disregard the wishes of the people who had elected Conservative representatives to the General Assembly.

John T. Trezevant, Gustavus A. Hanson, and William K. Poston, members of the Memphis Citizens' Committee, complained to President Johnson about the Radical Republican leadership in Tennessee. They noted that the legislature had disqualified nine out of ten voters in the state by claiming that the disfranchised had rebelled against the United States. They concluded that "an accidental majority of a Legislature representing a small minority of the people of the State, has usurped despotic power & set aside, as of no value, the representative feature of our Government."[36]

Another unpopular measure followed the franchise bill of 1866. Congress denied seats to Arnell and the rest of the Tennessee delegation because the congressional Radicals stipulated that ratification of the Fourteenth Amendment must precede the readmission of a state to the Union. The Fourteenth Amendment extended equality to blacks and prohibited persons who had aided the Confederacy from holding any state or federal office until Congress removed the provision. Brownlow summoned the General Assembly on July 4, 1866, to ratify the Fourteenth Amendment. Again, Conservatives left the General Assembly to block passage of the amendment. Arnell offered a resolution requiring the Speaker of the House to issue warrants for the arrest of delinquent members. The General Assembly ordered the arrest of two absent members, regarded the prisoners as present for the vote, and ratified the amendment on July 19, 1866. The amendment's passage allowed Tennessee's congressmen to take their seats and enabled the Volunteer State to rejoin the Union. But the process of approving the new franchise law disgusted many people. William S. Cheatham, a former Nashville councilman and alderman, wrote President Johnson declaring that the state legislature oppressed Tennesseans by passing laws without a quorum.[37] Arnell's hometown paper, the

Columbia Herald, always maintained that the people had fairly elected Dorsey Thomas over Arnell and described the actions of Governor Brownlow and the Congress as unjust.[38]

The controversy followed Arnell to Washington. Congress had the final decision as to whether Arnell had been elected fairly and, after some discussion, chose to uphold Brownlow's decision. The former slaveholder of Maury County and other members of the Tennessee delegation took their seats at the start of the second session of the Thirty-ninth Congress in December 1866.

Arnell's resolutions, speeches, and votes in Congress paralleled his actions in Tennessee's legislature. He fought to exclude former Confederates in other states from the franchise and served on the Committee of Education and Labor. As a Union supporter who had suffered because of his loyalty, he desired to protect other Union men from losing power to former Confederates.

Arnell reserved some of his most emphatic remarks to oppose a new bill concerning the government of insurrectionary states. The Senate had sent the House of Representatives an amended bill that would permit loyal men (Unionists) and disloyal men (ex-Confederates) to jointly reorganize the government in the former states of the Confederacy. Disloyal men could vote, elect delegates to the state's constitutional convention, and even be elected delegates to those conventions. A prolonged debate ensued in the House of Representatives on February 18, 1867, lasting until almost midnight. Arnell expressed his horror and outrage that the House of Representatives would even consider a bill that would allow Rebels to assist in the process of Reconstruction. He spoke of the experience of Tennessee in establishing a new state government, reminding the congressmen that it required Union men to return the state to the nation. Objecting to any bill that gave power and leadership to the Rebels, Arnell recalled the loss of life that accompanied the Northern victory in the Civil War. He exclaimed: "Gentleman tell us that we must not disfranchise the masses of the South or the "intelligence and honor" of the South. Was it not this "intelligence and honor" that opened your three hundred thousand Union graves, whose occupants today are not safe from sneers in their very coffins. And have these martyrs not died in vain if our reconstruction is rebel reconstruction?"[39]

Arnell reminded his fellow legislators of the groups of Unionists in the nonreconstructed states that needed congressional support. If the House passed this measure, he contended, it would be abandoning the loyal men who had already suffered for their efforts. Passage of this bill meant the abolition of the current governments organized in Tennessee, Missouri, and West Virginia. "In Tennessee we have planted ourselves upon the broad platform of the 'rights of man.' All this had been effected by loyal suffrage. A new civilization is beginning at the South. Do not turn it backward," begged Arnell.[40] The House followed the wishes of Arnell and other congressmen and refused, by a vote of 98 to 73, to pass the bill as amended by the Senate.

To retain their grip on political power, the Tennessee Radicals decided to enfranchise blacks. This law further irritated many Tennesseans because they saw whites denied the vote and blacks given the privilege of suffrage. Arnell had long supported black suffrage. While in the General Assembly, he had encouraged enfranchisement of Tennessee's blacks as well as supported their right to testify in state courts. Arnell and state legislators W. J. Smith of Hardeman and Thomas A. Kercheval of Lincoln, for example, submitted a minority report from the Judiciary Committee urging the Tennessee General Assembly to permit blacks to testify in state courts. The report concluded: "We believe that the interests of both races, justice and humanity, alike demand such a law, and that it is in accordance with the enlightened spirit of the age, and the example of our sister Free States."[41] In 1866, James Rapier expressed to Arnell the gratitude blacks had for the legislator. In fact, some Columbia blacks regularly followed Arnell home to ward off possible assassins. Rapier assured Congressman Arnell that 90 percent of the African Americans in Columbia would vote with the party that had emancipated them. Blacks realized the benefits of their alliance with the Radicals, and would not be deceived by the artificial concern of the ex-Rebels.[42]

Tennessee's bill granting freedmen the right to vote passed on February 25, 1867, and subsequently produced a Radical victory in the general elections of 1867. To buttress their party at the state level, Arnell, William B. Stokes, and Horace Maynard had campaigned for Radical candidates, especially the ailing Brownlow, in the months before the August election. Radical whites and blacks reelected Brownlow governor over his Conservative challenger Emerson Etheridge and sent all but three Radical candidates to the state legislature.[43]

Arnell's role in the key political changes of 1866–67 (such as the enfranchisement of blacks and the disfranchisement of whites) made him a marked man. Threats from the Ku Klux Klan and other violent groups worried Arnell considerably. His political best interests and hopes for reelection dictated that he act to deter and to punish the Klan members, especially once the violence escalated in 1868. Klan members rode around Maury County with hoods over their heads terrorizing black residents. Their tactics worked, and African

Americans hesitated to notify the chief of the Freedmen's Bureau for fear of reprisals. Since the bureau received no news of this intimidation, officials assumed peace and quiet. C. H. Douglas wrote Arnell in Washington and warned that if the blacks did not receive any help, they would vote with the Rebels in the next election because the government was not doing anything to protect them.[44]

On June 13, 1868, Klansmen boarded a train with "pistols and rope in hand" searching for Arnell, who was traveling home from Washington. Fortunately for Arnell, he was not aboard that particular train. Upon returning to Columbia, he immediately telegraphed Brownlow about the threat against his life.[45]

Arnell's report convinced Brownlow to ask General George H. Thomas, commander of the Department of the Cumberland, to gather Federal troops to enforce law and order in the troubled counties of Lincoln, Marshall, Obion, Dyer, and Gibson. Thomas delayed, however, citing regulations that prevented him from deploying troops and claiming to lack enough men.[46] The

A Klansman, 1892. Tennessee State Museum Collection, Tennessee State Library and Archives, June Dorman, photographer.

governor had hoped to station troops in counties in Middle and West Tennessee where the Klan thrived and smash its terrorism before the upcoming election, since voters would not support the Radicals if the party could not protect citizens from thugs. Brownlow had to settle for a regiment scattered among several counties in Middle and West Tennessee.

Less than a month after the attempt on Arnell's life, a Fourth of July celebration in Columbia quickly turned into tragedy. During the day, African Americans had celebrated the holiday with a picnic and the reading of the Declaration of Independence. When night came, approximately five hundred Klansmen accompanying some of the most influential men of Columbia arrived at the scene brandishing weapons. The Klan started whipping the blacks, especially women and children. Black men retaliated by firing into the group of attackers and wounding several of them. Some African Americans fled to Nashville for safety, but the Klan tracked them and killed those they found.[47] The 1868 legislature responded by designating Klan membership a felony and granting Brownlow permission to declare martial law. He did this on February 20, 1869, in nine Middle and West Tennessee counties where the KKK flourished.[48]

While Brownlow suppressed the Ku Klux Klan on a state and local level, Arnell took the fight to Washington. He proposed a resolution demanding that the government extend full protection to its loyal citizens in the South. In addition, he requested the creation of a special committee to investigate the alleged KKK outrages.[49] Arnell further demanded a House investigation of the murder of two United States soldiers: one in Nashville and the other in Somerville. Already a House committee was investigating the murder of Union soldiers in South Carolina.[50] Arnell also asked the Committee on the Treatment of Union Prisoners to report the facts surrounding two additional killings of ex-Federal soldiers in Maury County.[51] He even took on cases outside of Tennessee, presenting to the Congress a petition from black farmers in Alabama who desired a repeal of the 3 percent tax on cotton.[52]

The protection and welfare of Unionists and black citizens consumed Arnell's thoughts and actions in Washington in 1868. Citing newspaper reports of barbarities inflicted on loyalists and blacks, Arnell urged his fellow congressmen to sustain the Freedmen's Bureau: "In Middle Tennessee the only guardian for these colored people that is capable of ferreting out these outrages and bringing them to public notice," he emphasized, "is the much abused bureau."[53]

Arnell realized the Freedmen's Bureau provided safety for blacks and simultaneously checked the actions of former Rebels anticipating a return to power. Representative Halbert E. Paine of Wisconsin suggested the federal government issue arms to the militias of southern states to combat the Ku Klux Klan and other ruffians. The Wisconsin legislator marveled at the inability of the government of Tennessee and its loyal people to fight off attackers and insisted that the state should be capable of defending blacks. As Paine noted, the congressmen from Tennessee never provided any clues as to why the state or local governments could not guarantee the rights and lives of its citizens. If the lack of weapons presented a challenge, then the United States government could remedy the situation.[54] That solution did not satisfy Arnell and the other Tennessee legislators. Perpetuation of the Freedmen's Bureau meant continuation of Radical control. Once the government dissolved the Freedmen's Bureau, ex-Confederates would step up the intimidation techniques, frighten blacks and loyalists from the polls, and convince voters that the state would be safer in Conservative hands. On the opposite side, critics of the Radicals pointed to the chaos and violence in the state evident since Brownlow and his cronies had assumed power.

In 1869, Arnell and the Tennessee Republicans lost the fight for political control in Tennessee. Declaring that peace and order had been restored, on February 25, 1869, Governor Brownlow relinquished the helm of government in order to become a U.S. senator. DeWitt Clinton Senter became governor, and Tennessee soon returned to Conservative control.

A native of East Tennessee, DeWitt Senter had supported the Union in the Civil War, and had voted for Rebel disfranchisement and martial law. Once in office, however, Senter relaxed Radical policies and reformed Arnell's franchise law. He also restored civil authority, dismissed the militia, and appointed new registrars. These new policies, Senter thought, would please Democrats and create a broad base of white support for his candidacy for a full term in office.[55]

In the gubernatorial election of 1869, Arnell supported his fellow congressman William Stokes over the Conservative, Senter.[56] In August 1869, Tennesseans elected Senter over the Radical Stokes, and Conservatives gained a majority in the legislature. One of the first acts of the new government was to organize a constitutional convention.

The 1870 Constitutional Convention removed the restrictions Arnell had placed on white male voters but retained black suffrage. In addition to addressing financial matters, the convention also specified the number of days that constituted regular and special sessions of the General Assembly. The delegates wanted to prevent a repeat of the long, expensive sessions that had become standard fare during the Brownlow administration. The draft constitution also increased the difficulty of declaring martial law and stipulated that only the legislature could suspend the writ of habeas corpus.[57]

Arnell and other Radicals failed to stop the adoption of a Conservative constitution when the state went to the polls in the spring of 1870. Citing numerous examples of atrocities, the Radicals asked Washington to restore military reconstruction and to dismantle the recently elected Conservative government. State newspapers reacted harshly. The *Nashville Union and American* demanded that the Radicals offer proof of crimes. The *Knoxville Weekly Whig* accused Brownlow, Horace Maynard, Arnell, and other Tennessee congressmen of selling out Tennessee to advance their own political positions. The Radical leaders lamented that ruffians murdered loyal men and pleaded for protection or else they would be killed.[58] Skeptical members in Congress and the *Knoxville Weekly Whig* demanded proof and details of atrocities committed against blacks and Unionists, but the accusers had no evidence. Unsubstantiated charges proved detrimental to the credibility of the Tennessee delegation. The *Whig* also predicted that after the November 1870 election Brownlow, Arnell, and other Radicals would resume private lives since voters would not reelect them.[59] The newspaper noted that the vote in favor of the constitution should convince the Radicals that reconstruction was unnecessary because the new constitution guaranteed the ballot to blacks without being coerced to do so by the federal government.[60]

The return of Conservatives to power in Tennessee convinced Arnell not to run for reelection to Congress. No doubt he sensed his unpopularity, particularly in the former Confederate stronghold of Middle Tennessee, which he represented. Especially damaging had been his attempt to convince the federal government to send troops to the state in hopes of securing a Radical victory. Arnell spent his last days in Congress focusing on his duties as chairman of the Committee on Education and Labor. Although he once called the committee "ornamental," the influence of George F. Hoar of Massachusetts fashioned the committee into an important one that presented a plan for national education, prevented the termination of the Bureau of Education from the Interior Department, and tried General Oliver O. Howard on malfeasance charges presented by Fernando Wood in relation to Howard University.[61] Arnell and the committee also conducted a hearing to investigate allegations of Howard's misappropriation of funds as head of the Freedmen's Bureau. In the end, Arnell and the majority of the committee found Howard innocent of all the charges.[62]

The Arnells remained in Washington for a few years, while Samuel practiced law. He returned to Columbia, resumed his law practice, and served as postmaster from 1879 to 1885. By the time Arnell and his family returned to Columbia, the Democrats were firmly ensconced in the state government of Tennessee; therefore, he no longer posed a threat to the political or social order. As a native of Maury County, he returned to his roots in hopes of assisting the community. He tried to improve local education, pleading with the county court for a superior system of public schools. After his appointment as one of the three school directors of Maury County, he organized a grade school. The success of the school encouraged people to place more importance on public education.[63]

His indefatigable work for the improvement of education convinced a Democratic county school board to elect him superintendent of public schools, 1885–88. During Arnell's tenure as superintendent, the schools gained in popularity and improved the curriculum.[64] After his term expired, he and his family moved again to Washington, where they lived until 1894. In that year, the Arnells moved to Johnson City because of his failing health. He died on July 20, 1903, at the age of seventy, survived by his wife and three of his six children.[65]

Arnell's love of country, his loyalty to the memory of his ancestors, and his belief that secession was unconstitutional encouraged him to support the Union. These considerations, in addition to memories of a home destroyed by guerrillas and Rebels, the lives of family members disrupted, and most important, the death of his own daughter due in his mind to the family's evacuation of their dwelling, spurred Arnell to author legislative measures punishing former Confederates. While his bills prohibiting former Rebels from voting and his endorsement of increased rights for black citizens resembled typical platforms espoused by scalawags in other southern states, his resolutions for an improved system of education for all people in the southern states exemplified his desire to boost the region's welfare, not just Tennessee's. This committed Radical continued to lobby for better schools in his area years after he retired from state and national politics. When he saw his political ship sinking in 1869, furthermore, he refused to abandon the concept of black suffrage.

The dynamics of the Civil War and Reconstruction period served as a catalyst for Arnell's involvement in public life. In the heyday of Radical Republican politics, Arnell had been a key leader in the General Assembly by sponsoring bills that extended and guaranteed Radical control of the state and punished former Rebels. His participation in the attempt to have the state militarily reconstructed after his party lost the state elections of 1869 tarnished his public image. Arnell's determination to follow his conscience whether it cost him friends, family, or money, made him an unpopular figure during the Civil War and Reconstruction, but he never regretted his decisions. Rather, Arnell thanked God that He "permitted me to live between the years 1861–'71; permitted me to be an eyewitness of that most magnificent period of human advancement, when a great nation was not lost, but saved—rebuilt on better foundations; and that He allowed me too, to witness reconciliation of North and South."[66]

NOTES

I would like to thank Dr. Paul H. Bergeron, Dr. James C. Cobb, and Andrew S. Moore for reading earlier drafts of the manuscript, and William Eigelsbach and Curtis Lyons of the University of Tennessee Special Collections Library for directing me to the Samuel Mayes Arnell Manuscript Collection.

1. Eric Foner, *Reconstruction: America's Unfinished Revolution, 1863–1877* (New York, 1988), 300.
2. S. M. Arnell to Charles Lanman, Dec. 8, 1866, MS-790. The Samuel Mayes Arnell Manuscript Collection, Univ. of Tennessee, Knoxville, Special Collections Library, is cataloged under five different manuscript numbers: MS-163, MS-164, MS-790, MS-823, and MS-1297. Eighth Census of the United States, 1860, Tennessee Agricultural Schedule, Maury County, District 9.
3. David L. Porter, "Attitude of the Tennessee Press Toward the Presidential Election of 1860, *Tennessee Historical Quarterly* 29 (Winter 1970–1971): 390–91.
4. Mary Wagner Highsaw, "A History of Zion Community in Maury County, 1806–1860," *Tennessee Historical Quarterly* 5 (Mar. 1946): 22. James M. Arnell's salary as pastor ranged from $400 to $800 per year.
5. Mary Wagner Highsaw, "A History of Zion Community in Maury County, 1806–1860 (continued)," *Tennessee Historical Quarterly* 5 (June 1946): 123; Carroll Van West, "The Democratic and Whig Political Activists of Middle Tennessee," *Tennessee Historical Quarterly* 42 (Spring 1983): 5, 11–12.
6. Samuel M. Arnell, "Reminiscences: Ten Years of War and Reconstruction," MS-823, 4. Arnell never finished this book.
7. Samuel M. Arnell, "The February Election Auto-Biographical," MS-823.
8. Samuel M. Arnell, "Reminiscences: Ten Years of War and Reconstruction," MS-823, 10–11, 14; S. M. Arnell to Charles Lanman, Dec. 8, 1866, MS-790.
9. James Walter Fertig, *The Secession and Reconstruction of Tennessee* (Chicago, 1898; rpt., New York, 1972), 11, 15, 21; Arnell, "Reminiscences," MS-823, 18–19, 22–23, 25.
10. Stephen V. Ash, *Middle Tennessee Society Transformed, 1860–1870: War and Peace in the Upper South* (Baton Rouge, 1988), 15.
11. Samuel M. Arnell, History of Tennessee Notes 7; Cornelia Arnell, "A Union Woman's Remembrance of Hood's Raid," MS-823, 7.

12. James W. Patton, *Unionism and Reconstruction in Tennessee, 1860–1869* (Chapel Hill, N.C., 1934), 26, 29–30.
13. Peter Maslowski, *Treason Must Be Made Odious: Military Occupation and Wartime Reconstruction in Nashville, Tennessee, 1862–65* (Millwood, N.Y., 1978), 74, 80.
14. Ash, *Middle Tennessee Society Transformed,* 147; Stephen V. Ash, "Sharks in an Angry Sea: Civilian Resistance and Guerrilla Warfare in Occupied Middle Tennessee, 1862–1865," *Tennessee Historical Quarterly* 45 (Fall 1986): 217, 223–24.
15. Samuel M. Arnell, "Property Taken at my House by Guerrillas in July 1864 and August 5, 1864"; itemized list, Apr. 26, 1865, MS-1297.
16. Cornelia Arnell, "A Union Woman's Remembrance," MS-823, 3, 7. Confederate and Union troops converged on the area surrounding Columbia in late November 1864. Confederate General John Bell Hood and his troops reached Mount Pleasant, eleven miles southwest of Columbia on November 25, 1864, and eventually moved closer to the town. Hood was trying to reach Nashville before Union commander John M. Schofield beat him to the city; in Richard McMurry, *John Bell Hood and the War for Southern Independence* (Lexington, Ky., 1982) 169–74.
17. Cornelia Arnell, "A Union Woman's Remembrance," MS-823, 10–13.
18. Ibid., 14.
19. S. M. Arnell to Charles Lanman, Dec. 8, 1866, MS-790; Cornelia Arnell "A Union Woman's Remembrance," MS-823, 32–33.
20. S. M. Arnell to Charles Lanman, Dec. 8, 1866, MS-790.
21. Richard H. Abbott, *The Republican Party and the South, 1855–1877: The First Southern Strategy* (Chapel Hill, N.C., 1986), 44–45; Maslowski, *Treason Must Be Made Odious,* 85.
22. Peter Maslowski, "From Reconciliation to Reconstruction: Lincoln, Johnson, and Tennessee, Part II," *Tennessee Historical Quarterly* 42 (Winter 1983): 348, 360; Maslowski, *Treason Must Be Made Odious,* 93; *Brownlow's Knoxville Whig and Rebel Ventilator,* Jan. 11, 1865; Patton, *Unionism and Reconstruction,* 49–50, 88; Philip Hamer, *Tennessee: A History, 1673–1932* (New York, 1933), 2:596.
23. Samuel M. Arnell, "My School Work," MS-823.
24. Fertig, *Secession and Reconstruction,* 63; "House Journal of the First Session of the General Assembly of the State of Tennessee, 1865, Convened at Nashville, April 3," 36.
25. Samuel M. Arnell, "My School Work," MS-823.
26. Although overshadowed by the continuing fight to maintain Republican power in Tennessee, Arnell's interest in education never waned. During his first term in Congress, he initiated a bill to extend the Morrill Act of July 1862 to Tennessee. This act donated public lands to states and territories for the creation of an endowment for colleges. His energies and ideas for improving education also extended beyond the borders of Tennessee. In 1871, in his last term, he introduced a bill to appropriate funds earned from the sale of public lands during the following five years to common schools of the South. He also proved instrumental in securing the passage of a bill that donated the marine hospital at Natchez, Mississippi, to the state for educational uses. His resolutions can be found in Congress, House 39th Cong, 2d Sess. *Congressional Globe,* Jan. 24, 1867, 710–14, (1-752), and Congress, House 41st Cong. 2d Sess. *Congressional Globe,* Mar. 30, 1870, 2294, (1889–2832).

27. "House Journal of the First Session of the General Assembly of the State of Tennessee, 1865, Convened at Nashville, April 3," 31.

28. Fertig, *Secession and Reconstruction,* 64; Abbot, *Republican Party and the South,* 51.

29. Fertig, *Secession and Reconstruction,* 66; Thomas B. Alexander, *Political Reconstruction in Tennessee* (Nashville, 1950), 75; Hamer, *Tennessee,* 605–6.

30. *Brownlow's Knoxville Whig and Rebel Ventilator,* June 7, 1865; Fertig, 66; Alexander, *Political Reconstruction,* 73; Hamer, *Tennessee,* 605.

31. Alexander, *Political Reconstruction,* 77–78.

32. Patton, *Unionism and Reconstruction,* 110; Robert E. Corlew, *Tennessee: A Short History,* 2d ed. (Knoxville, 1981), 331. The twelve counties of the Sixth District were Decatur, Dickson, Hardin, Hickman, Humphreys, Lawrence, Lewis, Maury, Montgomery, Perry, Stewart, and Wayne.

33. Alexander, *Political Reconstruction,* 96–97. Alexander noted that Brownlow did not mention Hardin County in his report.

34. Patton, *Unionism and Reconstruction,* 115, 118; Hamer, *Tennessee,* 110–11.

35. Patton, *Unionism and Reconstruction,* 106–9; Hamer, *Tennessee,* 610.

36. John T. Trezevant, Gustavus A. Hanson, and William K. Poston, to President Andrew Johnson, May 28, 1866, in Paul H. Bergeron, ed., *The Papers of Andrew Johnson, vol. 10, February–July 1866,* (Knoxville, 1992), 544–45.

37. William S. Cheatham to President Andrew Johnson, July 29, 1866, in *Papers of Andrew Johnson,* 10:752–53.

38. Alexander, *Political Reconstruction,* 110–11; 113; House Journal of the Extra Session of the 34th General Assembly for the State of Tennessee, Convened July 4, 1866, 19–20, 22, *Columbia Herald,* May 20, 1870.

39. Congress, House, 39th Cong. 2d Sess. *Congressional Globe* Feb., 18, 1867, 1338 (753–1504).

40. Ibid.

41. "House Journal of the Adjourned Session of the General Assembly of the State of Tennessee, 1865–6," Convened on Monday, Oct. 2, 1862. The bill allowing blacks to testify in state courts was passed on January 25, 1866, in a slightly amended form.

42. S. M. Arnell to Charles Lanman, Dec. 8, 1866, MS-790; James Rapier to Arnell, Mar. 3, 1867, MS-1297.

43. Thomas Alexander, "Kukluxism in Tennessee, 1865–1869," *Tennessee Historical Quarterly* 8 (Sept. 1949): 195; Corlew, *Tennessee,* 335.

44. C. H. Douglas to S. M. Arnell, June 8, 1868, MS-1297.

45. Alexander, "Kukluxism in Tennessee," 205–7; Alexander, *Political Reconstruction,* 187; "Senate Journal of the Extra Session of the 35th General Assembly of the State of Tennessee, Convened 27 July 1868," 5.

46. "Senate Journal of the Extra Session of the 35th General Assembly of the State of Tennessee, Convened 27 July 1868," 6.

47. Douglas to S. M. Arnell, July 7, 1868, MS-1297; Alexander, "Kukluxism in Tennessee," 205.

48. Alexander, "Kukluxism in Tennessee," 207; J. A. Sharp, "The Downfall of the Radicals in Tennessee," *East Tennessee Historical Society's Publications* 5 (Jan. 1933): 106.

49. Congress, House, 40th Cong., 2d Sess. *Congressional Globe,* July 13, 1868, 4003, (3073–4096).

50. Congress, House, 39th Cong., 2d Sess., *Congressional Globe,* Jan. 8, 1867, 341, (1–752).
51. Congress, House, 40th Cong., 2d Sess. *Congressional Globe,* June 1, 1868, 2752, (2049–3072).
52. Congress, House, 39th Cong., 2d Sess., *Congressional Globe,* Jan. 17, 1867, 537, (1–752).
53. Congress, House, 40th Cong., 2d Sess. *Congressional Globe,* July 13, 1868, 4006 (3073–4096).
54. Ibid., 4007.
55. Foner, *Reconstruction,* 413, 440; Abbott, *Republican Party and the South,* 207–9; Hamer, *Tennessee,* 650.
56. *Knoxville Whig,* June 16, 1869.
57. Alexander, *Political Reconstruction,* 233; Hamer, *Tennessee,* 656.
58. *Nashville Union and American,* Mar. 16, 1870, *Knoxville Weekly Whig,* Mar. 16, l870. At this time, the *Knoxville Weekly Whig* was edited by Joseph Mabry, Jr., an ex-Confederate officer.
59. *Knoxville Weekly Whig,* Mar. 23, 1870.
60. Ibid., Apr. 6, 1870.
61. Samuel M. Arnell, "My School Work," MS-823.
62. Congress, House of Representatives, Committee on Education and Labor, *Charges Against General Howard,* 41st Congress, 2d Sess., July 13, 1870.
63. Samuel M. Arnell, "My School Work," MS-823.
64. E. H. Hatcher to S. M. Arnell, Mar. 24, 1889, MS-1297.
65. *Jonesborough Herald and Tribune,* July 29, 1903.
66. Samuel M. Arnell, "Reminiscences: Ten Years of War and Reconstruction in Tennessee, 1861–1871," MS-823.

Civil War and Socioeconomic Change in the Upper South: The Survival of Local Agricultural Elites in Tennessee, 1850-1870

■   Robert Tracy McKenzie

■

■   *Editor's Note:* The Civil War left in its wake thousands of dead,
    devastated farms, and, temporarily at least, a new political order,
■   but it did little to overturn the economic hegemony of the
    wealthy agricultural class in rural Tennessee. McKenzie under-
■   takes a painstaking quantitative analysis of federal census records
    to trace the impact of war and Reconstruction on local agricul-
■   tural elites. These white, middle-aged men suffered great losses
    during the war: they were far less wealthy in 1870 than they had
■   been twenty years earlier. Yet, the economic inequality between
    the richest and poorest Tennesseans remained "an incredibly du-
■   rable phenomenon, surviving the cataclysm of war and emancipa-
    tion without substantial diminution." Their grip on wealth and
■   high social status was, perhaps, more tenuous after the war, but
    local agricultural elites still wielded considerable economic power
■   and prestige in their communities.

"Times are getting hot with the war," West Tennessee slaveholder
John Alexander Taylor observed in his diary as Union and Confederate soldiers converged on Manassas Junction in July 1861. "God in mercy defend
the right." Although initially a hesitant supporter of secession, the "right,"
Taylor now firmly believed, wore gray in the fields of Virginia, not blue. His
fervent prayer reflected his prescient recognition of all that was personally at
stake as the two armies moved inexorably toward battle. A member of one
of the oldest and wealthiest families in Haywood County, owner of fifty-six

slaves and twelve hundred acres of prime cotton land, secession and war would either safeguard his way of life or hasten its destruction.[1]

His anxiety notwithstanding, nearly a year passed before the war interfered directly with the daily routine of life on Taylor's plantation. Despite "rain[,] War, and complaining negroes," the land yielded 110 bales of cotton in the fall of 1861, a quantity far above that of the previous year and a lucrative source of encouragement. During the following February, however, a Union army under Ulysses Grant secured control of the Tennessee River and opened up West Tennessee to Federal invasion. By early June Union troops were in Brownsville, the county seat a few miles from Taylor's home. "It is generally thought the South is about to be subjugated," Taylor remarked in his diary, doubtless stunned by the rapidity with which the security of his world had collapsed. "God only knows what will result from this war."[2]

For generations historians have sought to answer Taylor's question, an anguished cry in the face of the unknown that echoed in countless variations across the war-torn Confederacy. Although their efforts have resulted in numerous evaluations of the fate of the antebellum elite during the Civil War era, collectively their labors suffer from a deficiency that characterizes the literature on so many issues of importance in southern history. The most prominent investigations have focused disproportionately—indeed, almost exclusively—on the major cotton-producing regions of the deep South. In contrast, our knowledge of the war's impact upon local elites in the upper South, home to two-thirds of southern whites during the postbellum era, is almost nonexistent.

This essay seeks partially to correct this deficiency by exploring the fate of local agricultural elites in eight Tennessee counties between 1850 and 1870. It first examines the 1850s, comparing local antebellum elites in plantation and nonplantation areas across the state. It then assesses and compares the impact of war and emancipation upon local elites, placing greatest emphasis upon changes in their relative economic condition.

Although popular belief in a fundamentally different postwar South appears to have emerged almost immediately after the Confederate surrender at Appomattox, the theme was given its most eloquent scholarly expression by historian C. Vann Woodward a century later. The Civil War, according to Woodward, constituted the "death struggle of a society which went down in ruins." Central to this collapse of the old order was the demise of the prewar elite. In his 1951 classic, *Origins of the New South,* Woodward argued that war and emancipation had destroyed the power of the antebellum planters; those who had retained title to their lands were "rather the exception than the rule." They were replaced in status and influence by "new men" of "middle-class, industrial capitalist outlook, with little but a nominal connection to the old planter regime."[3]

For more than two decades historians largely accepted Woodward's thesis and frequently repeated his requiem for the antebellum elite.[4] During the mid-1970s, however, a number of scholars began to challenge Woodward's basic assumption that southern landholding patterns had been substantially reconfigured during and immediately after the Civil War. For all the brilliance of his analysis, Woodward's contention of a "revolution in land titles" was based upon minimal empirical evidence; when historians began to test his thesis through the painstaking analysis of tax and census records they consistently found it wanting. In 1976 Jonathan Wiener analyzed the extent of "planter persistence" during the Civil War era in the Alabama Black Belt and found that, of the wealthiest landholding families in five western Alabama counties, 43 percent maintained their elite status throughout the 1860s. Although a seemingly low rate of survival, Wiener noted that elite persistence during the war decade compared favorably with that for the 1850s, and he credited death and geographic mobility, not the extensive loss of property, as the prime causes of nonpersistence.[5] Subsequent studies repeatedly reinforced Weiner's conclusions and buttressed Henry Grady's century-old claim: the typical antebellum planter had remained "lord of acres if not of slaves."[6] Most historians now accept that, in the Black Belt at least, southern landholding patterns survived the disruption of war and emancipation with impressive continuity.

This extended, lively debate, however, has largely excluded the upper South. Scholars have always been fascinated with the plantation and the plantation owner. Traditionally preoccupied with regional rather than local issues, and concluding that large slaveholders exercised inordinate economic, social, and political influence in the region *as a whole,* historians have understandably focused intensively upon the plantation belt of the deep South. Recently, however, students of southern history have demonstrated a growing appreciation of the region's pronounced internal diversity and have turned their attention to issues of social and economic development outside of the Black Belt.[7] In doing so, however, they have continued to ignore the postwar fate of local elites.

This has happened because of historians' common penchant for absolute rather than relative definitions of economic status. The unstated presumption seems to be that, having agreed upon standard definitions of "planter" and "yeoman," the classification and comparison of local social structures

Cartwright-Russell farm, Smith County, late 1800s. Century Farms Collection, MTSU Center for Historic Preservation.

becomes straightforward and simple, indeed, may be reduced to a mathematical formula.[8] All too often, as a consequence, areas that contained few "planters"—usually defined as owners of twenty or more slaves—are automatically designated as "yeoman enclaves," socially and economically undifferentiated regions for which the power and influence of local elites may be safely ignored. It is not a coincidence that, as scholars have shifted their focus away from the Black Belt during recent years, they have simultaneously turned their attention from the "planter" to the "yeoman," leaving our knowledge of the fate of local elites in small-farming regions still woefully inadequate. Consequently, this essay fills an important gap in our understanding of what happened to local southern elites during and after the Civil War.

The eight Tennessee counties selected for this study were chosen specifically to reflect the remarkable agricultural diversity that characterized both the Volunteer State and the South as a whole.[9] (See table 10.1.) Three of the sample counties, Grainger, Greene, and Johnson, lie in East Tennessee, a region that local boosters were fond of describing as "the Switzerland of America."[10] In this section of the state, thin rocky soil and mountainous terrain discouraged the development of large-scale commercial agriculture and inhibited the growth of a large slave population. Whites owned and cultivated the many small farms of the region; only one-tenth of farm households owned slaves. Three other sample counties, Lincoln, Robertson, and Wilson, are situated in the Central Basin of Middle Tennessee, the garden of Tennessee. Benefiting from rich, fertile soil and a well-developed network of railroads and navigable rivers, on the eve of the Civil War the section's farmers employed slave labor significantly—more than one-third of farm households owned slaves—while concentrating heavily upon the commercial production of corn, wheat, tobacco, and livestock. Unusual in the Old South, the area was one of a handful below the Mason-Dixon line in which farmers were simultaneously committed both to slavery and to the extensive commercial production of foodstuffs. The final two sample counties, Fayette and Haywood, lie adjacent to each other in the southwestern corner of the state, not far from Memphis. This section of the state closely resembled the major cotton-producing regions of the Deep South; it was an area of plantations and cotton fields, numerically dominated by slaveholding farmers (approximately two-thirds of all household heads) wholeheartedly committed to the cotton economy.

To identify and analyze the economic elites of such disparate regions, I have followed two basic propositions. The first, borrowed from Edward Pessen, is that in the nineteenth century "wealth appears to have been the

TABLE 10.1

STATISTICAL PROFILE OF FREE AGRICULTURAL HOUSEHOLDS, SAMPLE TENNESSEE COUNTIES, 1860

	EAST	MIDDLE	WEST
Mean Total Wealth ($)	2,907	8,065	19,822
Mean Farm Size[a]	79.8	108.2	206.1
Percentage Owning Slaves[b]	10.4	36.3	62.4
% of Farm Operators Planting Cotton	0.5	4.4	89.9

SOURCE: Eight-county sample. For discussion of the sample, see Robert Tracy McKenzie, *One South or Many? Plantation Belt and Upcountry in Civil War-Era Tennessee,* appendix A.

[a]In improved acres.
[b]Figures apply to slaves owned or rented within the county of enumeration only.

surest sign of social, as well as of economic, position."[11] Although wealth-holding data are clearly an imperfect barometer of individual status, they constitute the most reliable information systematically available to the modern historian. The second, taken from Fabian Linden, is that "the status, prestige, and influence of the farmer depended not so much on the absolute size of his acreage, but more on his rank within his *immediate universe,* on his place in the 'pecking order' within the circumference of his own barnyard."[12] Relative definitions that reflect local contexts of status and influence, in other words, are more valuable than absolute, statewide definitions. The local distribution of wealth, consequently, becomes a key to comprehending the social structure of a nineteenth-century community.

In keeping with these propositions, I have defined the "local agricultural elite" of each sample county as the heads of the top 5 percent of local white agricultural households in value of real estate owned, as enumerated on the federal manuscript censuses of population for 1850, 1860, and 1870.[13] The number of household heads so designated for these years equaled 628, 610, and 723, respectively. All three years have been examined to enable comparison of antebellum and postbellum patterns.[14]

The comparison of local agricultural elites in Tennessee during the late antebellum era reveals unexpected similarities among the three groups of elite farmers that are every bit as striking as the substantial differences. (See table 10.2.) On the one hand, the average wealth of the local elite varied greatly from region to region. The wealthiest farmers in East Tennessee, for example, commonly owned a mere handful of slaves (five) and several hundred acres of land. At the other end of the state, in contrast, the agricultural elite of Fayette and Haywood counties owned an average of sixty-one bondsmen and more than twenty-one hundred acres. While the typical eastern elite would have been considered of middling wealth had he relocated in West Tennessee,[15] numerous West Tennessee planters were rich enough to have purchased literally hundreds of East Tennessee farms. To cite the most drastic example, on the eve of the Civil War the real and personal property of Haywood County's James Bond—including 220 slaves and five plantations—exceeded in value the combined worth of all 399 farms in Appalachian Johnson County.[16] Bond's wealth was extreme, even for a major plantation county such as Haywood. Yet the fact remains that West Tennessee elites on average owned real and personal property two and one half times more valuable than the elite of Middle Tennessee and nearly seven times more valuable than that of the East Tennessee elite.

Tennessee's antebellum elite also shared a surprising number of common

Table 10.2

Wealth Profile of Agricultural Elite, Sample Tennessee
Counties, 1860 (mean values)

	East	Middle	West
Value of Real Estate[a]	$12,401	$29,884	$57,207
Acres Owned in County	710	805	2,114
Value of Personal Estate[a]	$9,214	$28,030	$87,068
Slaves Owned in County	5	20	61
Total Wealth[a]	$21,616	$57,995	$144,511
Combined Share of Local Total Wealth (%)	40.7	39.6	38.9

Source: See text.

[a]May include property owned outside of the county of enumeration.

characteristics. On average, in 1860 they were nearly identical in age—approximately fifty-two years old in East Tennessee and fifty-one in the central and western regions. They were residents of long standing in their counties, at least seven-eighths having lived in the same community for at least a decade.[17] Regardless of region, they commonly followed diverse economic pursuits in addition to farming, investing most frequently in mercantile concerns or grist and lumber mills, but also in hotels, iron forges, and even stagecoach lines. Typically they were aggressive boosters, championing the economic development of their regions, particularly along paths that would facilitate commercial agriculture and enhance the profitability of their own farms. The elite of Haywood and Greene counties, for example, were almost identical in their financial support of local railroad construction during the mid-1850s, the former promoting the construction of the Memphis and Ohio Railroad, which would connect them to the largest internal cotton market in the South, the latter encouraging the completion of the East Tennessee and Virginia Railroad in order to facilitate the shipment of foodstuffs into Georgia and the Carolinas.[18]

Even more important, although the amount of wealth among the local elites differed dramatically from region to region, little difference existed in the proportion of local wealth that they collectively controlled. As the last line of table 10.2 indicates, the top 5 percent of households controlled almost precisely two-fifths of the total agricultural wealth of their counties. In relative terms, then, the richest farmers of East and Middle Tennessee towered above their local communities just as impressively as the wealthiest planters in West Tennessee. Admittedly, none could match James Bond's seventeen thousand acres. Still, neighbors in East Tennessee must have maintained a healthy respect for the $100,000 fortune of Greene County farmer and merchant Peter Earnest, just as the mountaineers of nearby Johnson County must have been quite conscious of the wealth of Taylorville's M. M. Wagner, who owned property in land and slaves worth nearly $90,000. Within their local contexts, both possessed fortunes proportionally about as large as that of James Bond. Bond's household wealth was roughly thirty-seven times the mean for all agricultural households in his county, Earnest's thirty-two times, and Wagner's forty-five times.

This same similarity is found in Middle Tennessee. Major A. Price, one of the largest land- and slaveholders in Wilson County, owned property worth about thirty-five times the county average. Robertson County tobacco planter George Augustus Washington, whose $519,000 worth of real and personal estate established him as one of the wealthiest men in the entire Central Basin, owned property valued at seventy-eight times the average for his county. In rural Tennessee, at least, a disproportionately powerful local elite was a characteristic found consistently across the countryside from the Appalachians to the Mississippi.[19]

Tennessee's local elites also tended to stay in the same place. In his study of the antebellum Black Belt, Jonathan Wiener was taken aback that 61 percent had remained ("persisted") in the same location throughout the 1850s, proclaiming them "the most persistent rural group known . . . to social science."[20] Clearly, the Alabama elite were not as extraordinary as Wiener then believed. As table 10.3 shows, about six of every ten of Tennessee's agricultural elite continued to reside in the same county ten years later, almost precisely the pattern that Wiener calculated for western Alabama.[21] Significantly, the inordinately wealthy plantation owners of West Tennessee were neither considerably more nor less likely to stay put than the local elite of small-farm regions elsewhere in the state, effectively discrediting Wiener's implication that the largest slaveholders of the Black Belt were peculiarly stable. As Wiener's boast would suggest, however, rates of nearly 60 percent or more were exceptionally high, at least when compared with rates among typical rural whites in other parts of the South and Midwest during the same period.[22]

When *socioeconomic* persistence is considered, the similarity among local elites throughout Tennessee remains striking, although the impression of great social stability across the state is weakened. Socioeconomic persistence, as

TABLE **10.3**

GEOGRAPHIC AND SOCIOECONOMIC PERSISTENCE AMONG THE
AGRICULTURAL ELITE, SAMPLE TENNESSEE COUNTIES, 1850–1860
(PERCENTAGES)

	EAST	MIDDLE	WEST
Geographic Persistence within County	62.6	57.6	61.0
Socioeconomic Persistence within County	41.2	37.4	36.6

SOURCE: See text.

defined here, involved both geographic persistence within the county as well
as an ability to stay within the ranks of the local elite, that is, among the top
5 percent of all agricultural households as measured by the value of real estate owned. The antebellum elite seldom fell very far, but in all three regions
approximately one-third of the geographically persistent dropped out of the
top 5 percent of farm households.[23] Consequently, only 37 to 41 percent of
the top landholders in 1850 could have been found among the local elite just
ten years later. Given such extensive turnover, one may rightfully question
whether truly stable local elites existed anywhere in the Volunteer State. This
much seems patently clear: in Tennessee the extent of turnover among local
elites varied insignificantly across a broad variety of socioeconomic regions.

In sum then, local agricultural elites in late antebellum Tennessee varied
markedly between plantation and small-farming areas in their amount of
wealth and, presumably, in their potential to wield economic and political
influence in the broader arena of state or regional affairs. When evaluated
within the context of their own communities, conversely, their relative economic status was virtually identical.

The unprecedented social and economic disruption engendered by the
American Civil War, however, had the potential of changing the position of
the wealthy elite in each grand division. With the exception of Virginia, no
other southern state was the site of more major battles, sent more of its young
men into military service, or suffered more physical damage.[24] A congressional
committee calculated the state's losses—including the value of its 280,000
former slaves—at over $185 million, an astounding two and a half times the
gross agricultural product of the state during the banner year of 1859.[25]
Through the extensive physical destruction that it inflicted, as well as through

the emancipation of slaves that it made inevitable, the war weakened the agricultural foundation of the state and threatened to topple the social system that was built upon it.

The costs of the war were not distributed uniformly across the state, and as a result, neither were the forces promoting social upheaval. Just over one-half of the total financial loss, $96.5 million, represented the direct cost of emancipation to Tennessee slaveholders.[26] Though substantial, that figure cannot begin to reflect the enormity of the slaveholders' loss. Emancipation did far more than effect the simple redistribution of wealth from one social group (the former masters) to another (the former slaves). Rather, reflecting the peculiar properties of a form of wealth that was essentially capitalized labor, the end of slavery severely undermined masters' privileged control of a reliable agricultural workforce, an advantage of priceless value in an overwhelmingly rural, technologically underdeveloped society. Undoubtedly, the burden of such a loss would have been comparatively light in the sample counties of East Tennessee, where only one-tenth of farm households had owned slaves, far heavier in those of Middle Tennessee, where approximately one-third of farmers had owned slaves, and positively crushing in the sample West Tennessee counties, where two out of three farmers had been masters.

The extent of physical destruction sustained during the war was also dreadful. Congress estimated the total value of nonslave property losses in Tennessee at approximately $89 million, or just under one-third of the value of all nonslave property in the state on the eve of the war. Such damage was more evenly distributed than the losses resulting from emancipation, but differences existed across the state, less in the extent of devastation than in the circumstances under which it was inflicted.

Perhaps the greatest irony of Tennessee's Civil War was that those areas most forcefully opposed to secession were made to endure Confederate rule the longest, while sections where secessionist fervor had been strong fell quickly to Union occupation. The bulk of both Middle and West Tennessee—where support for secession had been overwhelming—came under federal military rule early in 1862. Mercifully, many counties in these regions escaped extreme physical destruction. Indeed, one historian of Haywood County has argued that her loss "in the way of property was perhaps as light as that of any other county in the state."[27] The "inconvenience" accompanying three years of military occupation was not slight, however. In both regions it mattered little whether the color of the uniforms was blue or gray—the proximity of soldiers invariably resulted in widespread destruction of livestock and crops. With a tone of bitter frustration that must have been common among property holders, a West Tennessee slaveholder lamented that soldiers of both armies took turns stealing his property, "each pretending to fear it may fall into the hands of the other and be turned against them."[28]

The experience of East Tennesseans was much different. Confederate and Union armies struggled for control of the Valley of East Tennessee intermittently for three years, waging major campaigns in 1863 and 1864. Indeed, it was early 1865 before Union forces established dominance in remote counties such as Johnson. In the meantime, both armies supplied themselves by living off the land. In this regard, Union occupation was no more desirable for the predominantly Unionist population than was the presence of Confederate troops. Prominent East Tennessee Unionist T. A. R. Nelson observed as much at the end of 1863: "The Union Army is more destructive to Union men than the rebel army ever was. Our fences are burned, our horses are taken, our people are stripped in many instances of the last vestiges of subsistence, our means to make a crop next year are being rapidly destroyed, and when the best Union men in the country make appeals to the soldiers, they are heartlessly cursed as rebels."[29]

In purely economic terms, the combined effects of war and emancipation were devastating to local agricultural elites all across the Volunteer State. On average, the value of real wealth owned by those who stayed in place declined by between one-third and one-half between 1860 and 1870. (See table 10.4.) Part of this decline reflected the actual loss of land, part the tangible physical destruction inflicted by contending armies, part the depreciation resulting from the deterioration of buildings and soils, and part—perhaps a large part—resulted from declining expectations of future profitability. This last consideration likely varied in significance across the state in accordance with the antebellum importance of slavery. In West Tennessee, for example, where the decline was greatest, the plummeting value of real wealth among the 1860 elite undoubtedly stemmed not only from physical damage but also from the confusion and foreboding that gripped large landowners with little confidence in the viability of free black labor. In terms of personal wealth, the effect of emancipation upon the local elite was even more catastrophic; the decline in value of personal property among those who remained in the same county ranged from a low of approximately 59 percent in East Tennessee to a high in West Tennessee of nearly 92 percent. With regard to the latter section it is but the slightest exaggeration to say that the personal wealth holdings of the elite were wholly obliterated.

Yet, nowhere in the state did these severe losses foreshadow the emergence of a fundamentally more egalitarian local wealth- holding structure. As table

TABLE 10.4

DECLINE IN WEALTH AMONG GEOGRAPHICALLY PERSISTENT MEMBERS
OF THE 1860 AGRICULTURAL ELITE, SAMPLE TENNESSEE COUNTIES
(MEDIAN PERCENTAGE-POINT CHANGE)

VALUE IN 1870 OF:	EAST	MIDDLE	WEST
Real Estate	-33.3	-45.6	-51.2
Personal Estate	-58.5	-84.1	-91.6
Total Estate	-42.1	-62.7	-70.8

SOURCE: See text.

10.5 shows, the effect of emancipation in particular lessened somewhat the inordinate disparity across the state in the amount of wealth; on average in 1870 the West Tennessee elite owned property "only" four times—rather than seven times—more valuable than the typical elite farmer of East Tennessee. At the local level, however, in all three regions of the state the top 5 percent of white agricultural households in 1870 continued to control disproportionately large shares of local real and personal wealth. A comparison with table 10.2 reveals that the percentage of total wealth commanded by the local elite declined slightly in both East and Middle Tennessee, yet in both regions the top 5 percent of white farm households still owned between 36 and 38 percent of local wealth. In West Tennessee, on the other hand, the share belonging to the top 5 percent actually increased markedly during the 1860s, so that by 1870 the agricultural elite owned just under one-half of all locally owned agricultural property. Evidently, the largest land- and slaveholders in the western sample counties had been seriously weakened during the decade of war and emancipation, but the less wealthy had lost proportionally even more.[30]

Without question, the still powerful economic position of the Tennessee agricultural elite in 1870 demonstrates that economic inequality was an incredibly durable phenomenon, surviving the cataclysm of war and emancipation without substantial diminution. It does not necessarily follow, however, that numerous members of the antebellum elite were not individually deposed and replaced among the local ranks of rich farmers. To address that possibility, table 10.6 presents rates of geographic and socioeconomic persistence among local elites during the Civil War decade. When compared with

TABLE 10.5

WEALTH PROFILE OF AGRICULTURAL ELITE, SAMPLE TENNESSEE
COUNTIES, 1870 (MEAN VALUES)

	EAST	MIDDLE	WEST
Value of Real Estate	$10,168	$16,628	$38,876
Value of Personal Estate[a]	$3,055	$6,788	$13,064
Total Wealth[a]	$13,223	$23,416	$51,940
Combined Share of Local Total Wealth	(%)36.3	38.1	47.8

SOURCE: See text.
[a]May include property owned outside of the county of enumeration.

TABLE 10.6

GEOGRAPHIC AND SOCIOECONOMIC PERSISTENCE AMONG THE
AGRICULTURAL ELITE, SAMPLE TENNESSEE COUNTIES, 1860–1870
(PERCENTAGES)

	EAST	MIDDLE	WEST
Geographic Persistence within County	57.8	60.3	60.2
Socioeconomic Persistence within County	36.0	43.1	40.9

SOURCE: See text.

similar figures for the 1850s (see table 10.3), one finds that an impressive continuity with prewar patterns obtained in each region.

During the 1860s elite farmers in every region of Tennessee remained highly stable geographically, exhibiting rates of geographic persistence closely analogous to those for the 1850s. Only in East Tennessee did this measurement decline, and even there the change was not large, the rate falling by fewer than 5 percentage points. In West Tennessee the rate of persistence was essentially unchanged from the previous decade, while in Middle Tennessee geographic stability among the elite actually increased slightly. Overall, the momentous events of the 1860s appear to have affected minimally the migration patterns of Tennessee's prewar agricultural elite.

The proportion of the antebellum elite who stayed in place geographically while also maintaining their rank among the wealthiest landholders (socioeconomic persistence) also closely resembled antebellum patterns, although the extent of continuity across time and among regions was marginally less pronounced. At first glance, the fact that on average approximately three-fifths of the local 1860 elite were missing from among the top 5 percent of farm households in 1870 looks like persuasive evidence of the incredible social upheaval engendered by war and emancipation. When compared to the corresponding figures for the 1850s, however, this change should be interpreted instead as compelling testimony to the stubborn continuity of local socioeconomic patterns in the face of unprecedented social and economic disruption. Indeed, socioeconomic persistence declined slightly in East Tennessee—by approximately 5 percentage points—but elsewhere in the state the local elite was actually more likely to retain its relative economic position during the 1860s than during the wildly prosperous 1850s, as the rate of socioeconomic persistence increased by more than 4 percentage points in West Tennessee and by nearly 6 percentage points in Middle Tennessee. The changes during the 1860s within the ranks of the local agricultural elite were not signs of social disarray, but reflected rather the continuation of patterns of economic predominance already common in the late antebellum period.

During and immediately after the Civil War members of the Tennessee elite maintained their positions of local economic predominance about as successfully as during the preceding decade of peace and prosperity. Even so, cases of extreme hardship and decline certainly occurred. Consider, for instance, the experience of Middle Tennessee's Hiram Drennon. Drennon, an Englishman, came to Wilson County during the 1840s, and quickly became involved in livestock production and the cedar lumber business. By 1860 Drennon had acquired real and personal property worth nearly $250,000, and was the third-richest man in the county. Before the war's end, however, Drennon was forced to mortgage all of his land in both Wilson and Rutherford counties, plus a sawmill and other machinery to cover debts of over $11,000. Between May 1865 and January 1866, creditors filed twenty-six separate lawsuits against Drennon for delinquent debts. Drennon died in mid-1867, beleaguered and embittered.[31]

Greene County's Joseph Henderson experienced a similar downfall. In 1860, this East Tennessean owned over seven hundred acres of land and seventeen slaves, making him one of the wealthiest and most influential men in his community. An agent for R. G. Dun & Co. described the sixty year old farmer as "a man of family[,] good moral char[acter] and high respectability." The war years were bad ones, however, for Henderson was a prominent Southern sympathizer in a strongly Unionist county. His fate during the war is captured by the terse entry of the Dun agent in the fall of 1865: "Bad rebel[,] entirely broken up and hopelessly insolvent." Henderson's farm was eventually attached by nearly two dozen creditors and finally sold at a sheriff's sale in the fall of 1867. In an ironic and ignominious ending, his farm was bought by an ardent local unionist, U.S. Senator David T. Patterson, who ultimately sold it to perhaps the only Greene Countian who hated the slaveholding elite more than himself—President Andrew Johnson. Long before that time Henderson had fled to nearby Washington County, a haven for Confederate refugees; there he lived out his life in the household of his daughter, devoid of property and influence.[32]

The wartime experiences of Drennon and Henderson were not typical of the agricultural elite, but they did occur with considerable frequency. Altogether, a total of 118 members of the 1860 elite persisted geographically but did not remain among the top 5 percent of local farmers. Of these "skidders," 20, or approximately 17 percent, lost all of their real wealth. During the 1850s only 9 percent of skidders had experienced such extreme loss, an indication of the far greater stability of the last antebellum decade.

In spite of such instances of extreme decline, most skidders fell only marginally from their antebellum positions. In all three regions, between three- and four-fifths remained among the top 20 percent of farm households in 1870.[33] If no longer atop the wealth pyramid at decade's end, most of those who had fallen in economic position were still wealthy men compared with the great majority of their neighbors. For such individuals, war and emancipation had brought decline, not destruction. In the same way, most farmers who were new members of the elite in 1870 had not risen significantly from their antebellum positions. Most new members of the elite had been wealthy, long-standing residents of their county. Between 86 and 90 percent had been present in the same county for at least ten years, and, of these, approximately nine-tenths had been among the top quarter of farm households in 1860.[34]

Ostensibly, then, members of the antebellum elite held tenaciously to their positions of local predominance. Beneath the surface, however, for many the combination of declining wealth and increasing debt—pervasive by-products of the war—had introduced an element of uncertainty that rendered their positions precarious. In 1870, for example, Haywood County's Thomas Shapard retained enough real wealth to be numbered among that county's wealthiest citizens. What the real estate figures fail to show is that only the year before, Shapard had mortgaged "all his lands, tenements, and hereditaments" to cover debts in excess of $28,000.[35] Thomas Bond, younger brother of James Bond and, like his older sibling, one of the wealthiest land- and slaveholders in West Tennessee before the Civil War, ultimately held on to the bulk of his real estate, but only after forfeiting a portion of his lands in order to pay taxes upon the rest. Similarly, Bond's nephew, James Bond, Jr., lost much of his inheritance speculating in cotton futures and eventu- ally transferred nearly two thousand acres to his wife in order to frustrate his creditors.[36]

Similar problems plagued members of the elite in Middle and East Ten- nessee. For example, in Wilson County Colonel M. A. Price maintained his position as the wealthiest farmer in the county, but was forced to mortgage most of his lands in 1867 to cover debts of nearly $12,000. His neighbor Paulding Anderson also remained among the elite but found it necessary to mortgage his home and three business houses in Lebanon, two plantations, and all his household and kitchen furniture to cover debts of almost $15,000.[37]

Likewise, William D. Williams, son of one of East Tennessee's richest antebellum slaveholders (Alexander Williams, the "Grand Duke of Lick Creek"), and a wealthy postbellum farmer in his own right, successfully sat- isfied numerous debts and retained control of more than $100,000 in real and personal estate, but only after mortgaging literally everything he owned, not excluding his carriage, his "piano forte," and his copy of *Reese's Encyclo- pedia.* James Allen, one of Greene County's richest farmers before the Civil War, persisted among the elite but was forced to mortgage 1,071 acres in order to repay debts of over $4,000.[38] The county's wealthiest antebellum farmer, Dr. James F. Broyles, managed to survive the war decade without mortgag- ing his lands, but did transfer all of his property to his wife in late 1865. By his own account, Broyles did so in consideration of "the love and affection" that he bore toward "his beloved wife." More likely, the transfer was made with an eye toward the $25,000 civil suit against him pending in a Knox- ville court.[39]

This brief analysis of Tennessee's local agricultural elite between 1850 and 1870 has been limited in focus and modest in intent. Concentrating narrowly upon patterns of local wealth distribution and the economic fate of large land- holders in particular, I have sought both to compare the relative positions of local elites across the state at the end of the antebellum era and to assess the impact of war and emancipation upon their economic status within local hierarchies of wealth ownership. Although scholars must undertake similar investigations of areas outside Tennessee before firm judgments can be made, two primary conclusions seem inescapable, at least with regard to the Volunteer State.

First, despite great variation across the state in the amount of wealth that they controlled, Tennessee's local agricultural elites shared several important characteristics from section to section. It evidently mattered little where they were situated—whether in the Appalachian regions of upper East Tennessee, the state's prosperous Central Basin, or the Black Belt plantation areas near Memphis—Tennessee's antebellum communities were economically dominated by landholding elites exhibiting numerous common traits. Regardless of region, members of the elite tended to be men in their early fifties with long-standing roots in their locale who manifested diverse economic interests and controlled disproportionate (nearly identical) shares of local economic resources. They were about equally likely to remain in their communities during the 1850s and to retain their positions of elite economic status. While their potential to influence southern regional politics or economic development was undoubtedly unequal, on average each possessed an economic stature within his immediate universe—"the 'pecking order' within the circumference of his own barnyard"—that varied but slightly between the mountain elite of the Smokies and the cotton nabobs on the banks of the Mississippi.

Second, minor variations aside, in both plantation and nonplantation regions local elites demonstrated impressive resilience in the wake of military invasion and the demise of slavery. They had typically suffered substantial financial losses during and immediately after the war, but in every area members of the 1860 elite maintained their positions of economic prominence during the subsequent decade at rates closely resembling those for the 1850s. While considerable turnover in the ranks of the elite took place, new members in 1870 were, with few exceptions, long-standing residents of the community who were already quite wealthy when the war began. Their rise to predominance was less a reflection of social upheaval than of the essential stability of local socioeconomic patterns throughout the period. By 1870 the proportion of total wealth commanded by the postbellum elite—the top 5 percent of white farm households in that year—had declined but slightly from 1860 levels in East and Middle Tennessee and had actually risen sharply in West Tennessee, the area most affected by emancipation. Despite this divergence of trends, in each section the top 5 percent of agricultural households in 1870 continued to command inordinately large proportions of local wealth, evidence of the stubborn tenacity of inequality in both plantation and small-farming areas. In contrast to the halcyon days of the 1850s, however, Tennessee's postbellum elite, regardless of location, clung precariously to their positions of economic predominance. Their absolute wealth vastly reduced, many of the elite were haunted by debts to a degree unknown in antebellum years. Noticeably diminished in strength, their grip upon elite status was clearly more tenuous.

NOTES

1. Taylor's diary is reprinted in Taylor Kinfolk Association, *The Taylors of Tabernacle: The History of a Family* (Brownsville, 1957), quotations from p. 177. John Alexander Taylor's father, Richard, was among the first settlers in Haywood County, settling near Brownsville in 1825. By 1860, the Taylor family had accumulated collectively nearly five hundred slaves and twenty thousand acres of land.

2. Ibid., quotations from pp. 178, 182.

3. Vann Woodward, *American Counterpoint: Slavery and Racism in the North-South Dialogue* (Boston and Toronto, 1964), 281; *Origins of the New South, 1877–1913* (Baton Rouge, 1951), 179, 20.

4. For examples, see J. G. Randall and David Donald, *The Civil War and Reconstruction*, 2d ed. (Boston, 1961), 543–47; Clement Eaton, *The Waning of the Old South Civilization* (Athens, Ga., 1968), 139–40; Harold D. Woodman, *King Cotton and His Retainers: Financing and Marketing the Cotton Crop of the South, 1800–1925* (Lexington, Ky., 1968), 312–13; and Lee Soltow, *Men and Wealth in the United States, 1850–1870* (New Haven, 1975), 100–101.

5. Jonathan M. Wiener, "Planter Persistence and Social Change: Alabama, 1850–1870," *Journal of Interdisciplinary History* 7 (1976): 235–60; Wiener, *Social Origins of the New South: Alabama, 1860–1886* (Baton Rouge, 1978), chap. 1

6. Henry W. Grady, "Cotton and Its Kingdom," *Harper's New Monthly Magazine* 63 (1881), 719–34. Other studies that have discovered general stability in landholding patterns among the agricultural elite include Randolph Campbell, *A Southern Community in Crisis: Harrison County, Texas, 1850–1880* (Austin, 1983), 302–3; Lee M. Formwalt, "Antebellum Planter Persistence: Southwest Georgia—A Case Study," *Plantation Society* 1 (1981): 410–29; Kenneth Greenberg, "The Civil War and the Redistribution of Land: Adams County, Mississippi, 1860–1870," *Agricultural History* 52 (1978): 292–307; C. A. Haulman, "Changes in the Economic Power Structure in Duval County, Florida, During the Civil War and Reconstruction," *Florida Historical Quarterly* 52 (1973): 175–84; Crandall A. Shifflett, *Patronage and Poverty in the Tobacco South: Louisa County, Virginia, 1860–1900* (Knoxville, 1982), 16–23; A. J. Townes, "The Effect of Emancipation on Large Landholdings, Nelson and Goochland Counties, Virginia," *Journal of Southern History* 45 (1979): 403–12; Michael Wayne, *The Reshaping of Plantation Society: The Natchez District, 1860–1880* (Baton Rouge, 1983), 86–91.

7. Examples of such work include Ronald Eller, *Miners, Millhands, and Mountaineers: Industrialization of the Appalachian South* (Knoxville, 1982); Steven Hahn, *The Roots of Southern Populism: Yeomen Framers and the Transformation of the Georgia Upcountry, 1850–1890* (New York, 1983); David F. Weiman, "Petty Commodity Production

in the Cotton South: Upcountry Farmers in the Georgia Cotton Economy, 1840–1880" (Ph.D. diss., Stanford Univ., 1984); Lacy K. Ford, *The Origins of Southern Radicalism: The South Carolina Upcountry, 1800–1860* (New York, 1988); John Inscoe, *Mountain Masters, Slavery, and the Sectional Crisis in Western North Carolina* (Knoxville, 1989); Mary Beth Pudup, "The Boundaries of Class in Preindustrial Appalachia," *Journal of Historical Geography* 15 (1989): 139–62; Pudup, "The Limits of Subsistence: Agriculture and Industry in Central Appalachia," *Agricultural History* 64 (1990): 61–89.

8. For examples of studies pertinent to Tennessee that impose absolute definitions of economic status upon highly disparate areas, see Chase C. Mooney, "Some Institutional and Statistical Aspects of Slavery in Tennessee," *Tennessee Historical Quarterly* 1 (1942): 195–228; and Arthur Fred Bailey, *Class and Tennessee's Confederate Generation* (Chapel Hill, N.C., 1987).

9. To simplify the presentation of findings, I have consistently aggregated the elite by region—East, Middle, and West—and present appropriately weighted statistics for each. It is not my intention to suggest, however, that the counties are "representative" of their regions in a statistically rigorous sense. For the agricultural characteristics of the state's major regions, see Eugene W. Hilgard [Special Agent], *Report on Cotton Production in the United States* (Washington, 1884), 291, 409–11; Joseph Buckner Killebrew, *Introduction to the Resources of Tennessee* (Nashville, 1874; rpt., Spartanburg, S.C., 1974), 350–69; and James M. Safford, *Geology of Tennessee* (Nashville, 1869), 49ff.

10. Hermann Bokum, *The Tennessee Handbook and Immigrants' Guide* (Philadelphia, 1868), 8.

11. Edward Pessen, "How Different from Each Other Were the Antebellum North and South," *American Historical Review* 85 (1980): 1130. Although controversial, Pessen's view is widely shared among scholars of the nineteenth-century South. Gavin Wright, for example, maintains that "the social divisions of antebellum America were essentially wealth-holding categories. . . . In a word, wealth was a basic defining characteristic of social class." Gail O'Brien also points out that the close association between wealth and local influence or power in her study of Mecklenburg County, North Carolina, where "a superior economic position appeared almost a prerequisite for attaining powerful positions in the community." Similarly, Paul Escott contends that "the network of influence in a county worked through wealth." See Gavin Wright, *The Political Economy of the Cotton South* (New York, 1978), 37; Gail O'Brien, "Power and Influence in Mecklenburg County, 1850–1880," *North Carolina Historical Review* 54 (1977): 134; Paul D. Escott, *Many Excellent People: Power and Privilege in North Carolina, 1850–1900* (Chapel Hill, N.C., 1985), 19.

12. Fabian Linden, "Economic Democracy in the Slave South: An Appraisal of Some Recent Views," *Journal of Negro History* 31 (1946): 164, emphasis added. For similar opinions, see Frank Jackson Huffman, Jr., "Old South, New South: Continuity and Change in a Georgia County, 1850–1880" (Ph.D. diss., Yale Univ., 1974), 3; Bailey, *Class and Tennessee's Confederate Generation*, 26; and Robert H. Wiebe, *The Search for Order, 1877–1920* (New York, 1967), in particular Wiebe's assertion that "America during the nineteenth Century was a society of island communities" (xiii).

13. I define "agricultural household" as any in which one or more members reported a

farming occupation to the census enumerator, whether "farmer," "tenant," "farm laborer," or "farm hand." In sample counties in 1860, the ratio of agricultural to total households averaged 0.77 in East Tennessee, 0.78 in Middle Tennessee, and 0.81 in West Tennessee. The proportion of total local wealth (real and personal) held by farm households ranged from a low of 83 percent in the eastern sample counties to a high of 86 percent in the westernmost counties.

14. To preserve strict comparability it is necessary to define all three elite groups in terms of their command of real wealth alone. Although it would have been preferable to define these individuals based upon their holdings of both real and personal wealth (the latter of which included slaves), the federal population schedules did not request information regarding personal wealth until 1860. (Local tax records for 1850 typically recorded data on real estate holdings only and thus are an unacceptable alternative.) The disadvantages of this limitation appear not to be severe, however. Statistical analysis of wealth-holding patterns in 1860 reveals an extremely high bivariate correlation between real and total wealth in all three regions (0.92 or higher), indicating that little is lost by relying upon real wealth as a proxy for total wealth position.

15. Note that the mean total wealth among East Tennessee *elite* was $21,616 (see table 10.2), while the mean total wealth among *all* agricultural households in West Tennessee was but slightly lower, $19,822 (see table 10.1).

16. Bond estimated the mean total value of his real and personal property in 1860 at $796,755; in the same year the aggregate value of Johnson County farms, including the value of buildings and other improvements, was $786,806. Concerning Bond, see the manuscript population census for Haywood County; for the total value of Johnson County farms, see U.S. Census Office, Eighth Census [1860], *Agriculture of the United States in 1860* (Washington, 1864), 132.

17. This conclusion is based on an additional backward linkage of elites in three sample counties. The proportion of the 1860 elite living in the same county in 1850 was 98 percent in Haywood County (West Tennessee), 87 percent in Wilson County (Middle Tennessee), and 91 percent in Johnson County (East Tennessee).

18. The nonagricultural pursuits of nineteenth-century farmers are difficult to identify. Of greatest help with regard to the Tennessee elite are the credit ledgers of the Mercantile Agency of R. G. Dun & Co. The ledgers, organized by county, are contained in the R. G. Dun & Co. Collection, Baker Library, Harvard University Graduate School of Business Administration. Stock lists for both railroads may be found in series 1, subseries 1 of Record Group 5 (Records of Internal Improvements), Tennessee State Library and Archives (hereinafter cited as TSLA). Two members of the Haywood County elite were on the board of directors of the Memphis and Ohio (Nathan Adams and Thomas Shapard); six of the Greene County elite held similar positions with the East Tennessee and Virginia (Joseph Henderson, Daniel Kennedy, Reuben H. Davis, Joseph H. Earnest, John McGaughey, and John Shields). In both counties, approximately one-half of the elite subscribed stock in their region's railroad.

19. The average ratio of mean total wealth among the agricultural elite to mean total wealth among local non-elite farm households was 11.5:1 in East Tennessee, 11.5:1 in Middle Tennessee, and 11.2:1 in West Tennessee.

20. James Oakes, *The Ruling Race: A History of American Slaveholders* (New York, 1983), 76; Wiener, *Social Origins of the New South,* 239.

21. When searching for the elite household heads in subsequent census years, I confined my examination to the county of origin and made no further attempt to locate members of the elite who emigrated. Enumerators' chronic inconsistencies in spelling and inaccuracies in estimating ages often made verification of matches problematic. In order to confirm instances of persistence with greater confidence, I checked not only the name and age of the household head but also the names and ages of spouses and all dependent children residing in the parents' household in both census years. Although I did not rigidly follow any mechanical rule for verification, in general I rejected potential matches whenever the difference between the reported and "predicted" age of a possible persister equaled or exceeded ten years. If the difference was five to nine years I also rejected the potential match in the absence of significant corroborating evidence to the contrary, that is, matches for other household members. (If the difference was less than five years but other household data were inconsistent, I also rejected the match.) In order to lessen the possibility of oversight, I rechecked the manuscript rolls for all members of the elite not found upon first examination.

22. Compare with the rates historians have found for other rural counties in the Deep South during the 1850s: for Clarke County, Georgia—41.2 percent (based on all adult males); Dallas County, Alabama—38.7 percent (all household heads); Harrison County, Texas—35.6 percent (all household heads); Crawford Township, Iowa—31.8 percent (farm operators); Wapello County, Iowa—41.4 percent (farm household heads); Bureau County, Illinois—37.7 percent (farm household heads). See Huffman, "Old South, New South," 35; William L. Barney, "Towards the Civil War: The Dynamics of Change in a Black Belt County," in Orville Vernon Burton and Robert C. McMath, eds., *Class, Conflict, and Consensus: Antebellum Southern Community Studies* (Westport, Conn., 1982), 146–72; Randolph B. Campbell, *A Southern Community in Crisis: Harrison County, Texas, 1850–1880* (Austin, 1983), 382; Mildred Throne, "A Population Study of an Iowa County in 1850," *Iowa Journal of History* 57 (1959): 311; and Allan Bogue, *From Prairie to Corn Belt: Farming on the Illinois and Iowa Prairies* in the Nineteenth Centuries (Chicago, 1963), 26.

23. The proportion of persistent "skidders" remaining in the top 20 percent of local households was 0.73 in East Tennessee, 0.78 in Middle Tennessee, and 0.70 in West Tennessee.

24. Constantine G. Belissary, "The Rise of Industry and the Industrial Spirit in Tennessee," *Journal of Southern History* 19 (1953): 196.

25. For figures on estimated property losses, see "Affairs in the Late Insurrectionary States," H.R. 22, 42d Cong., 2d Sess., 1872, Pt. 1, 110. Based on wholesale commodity prices, I estimate the value of gross agricultural output for the state in 1859 at approximately $73.1 million.

26. "Affairs in the Late Insurrectionary States," 110.

27. *Goodspeed History of Tennessee* (Nashville, 1887), Pt. 2, 825. The proportion of voters supporting secession was 88 percent in Middle Tennessee and 83 percent in West Tennessee, but only 31 percent in East Tennessee. See Mary E. R. Campbell, *The*

Attitude of Tennesseans Toward the Union, 1847–1861 (New York, 1961), 291–94. On the Union occupation of Middle and West Tennessee, see Stephen V. Ash, *Middle Tennessee Society Transformed, 1860–1870: War and Peace in the Upper South* (Baton Rouge, 1988), 85; and Joseph H. Parks, "A Confederate Trade Center under Federal Occupation: Memphis, 1862–1865," *Journal of Southern History* 7 (1941): 291.

28. John Houston Bills, Diary, Southern Historical Collection (microfilm copy in TSLA), Oct. 19, 1863.

29. Thomas A. R. Nelson to Brigadier General S. P. Carter, 26 Dec. 1863, in *War of the Rebellion: A Compilation of the Official Records of the Union and Confederate Armies* (73 vols., Washington, 1880–1901), vol. 31, pt. 3, 508 (hereinafter cited as *OR*). See also General U. S. Grant to General W. T. Sherman, Dec. 1, 1863, *OR*, vol. 31, pt. 3, 297; and Sherman to Grant, Dec. 11, 1863, *OR*, vol. 31, pt. 3, 382. Charles Faulkner Bryan, Jr., provides the best scholarly discussion of military destruction in East Tennessee in "The Civil War in East Tennessee: A Social Political, and Economic Study," (Ph.D. diss., Univ. of Tennessee, 1978); but see also Harold S. Fink, "The East Tennessee Campaign and the Battle of Knoxville in 1863," *East Tennessee Historical Society's Publications* 29 (1957): 79–117.

30. Thus confirming the speculation of James L. Roark in *Masters Without Slaves: Southern Planters in the Civil War and Reconstruction* (New York, 1977), 173.

31. History Associates of Wilson County, *The History of Wilson County: Its Land and Its Life* (Lebanon, Tenn., 1961), 73; Office of the Registrar: Trust Deeds, Vol. NN, 195, 293, 311–12, 425; Circuit Court Minute Books, 1861–1868, 241–461, Wilson County Records, TSLA.

32. Tennessee Vol. 12, 217, R. G. Dun & Co. Collection; Circuit Court Minute Books, mf. no. 41, 410–795; Office of the Registrar, Deeds, Vol. 35, 573, Greene County Records, TSLA.

33. The proportion was 65 percent in West Tennessee, 79 percent in Middle Tennessee, and 59 percent in East Tennessee.

34. This is based upon a backward linkage analysis of three sample counties: West Tennessee's Haywood, Middle Tennessee's Wilson, and East Tennessee's Johnson. The proportion of new elite members present in the county for at least ten years was 88 percent in Haywood, 90 percent in Wilson, and 86 percent in Johnson. The proportion of those who had been in the top 25 percent of agricultural households in 1860 was 88 percent in Haywood, 89 percent in Wilson, and 88 percent in Johnson.

35. According to their official instructions, census enumerators were to record the "full market value" of property owned by each household regardless of "any lien or encumbrance." See Carroll D. Wright and William C. Hunt, *The History and Growth of the United States Census* (Washington, 1900). It is interesting to note that two-thirds of Shapard's debt was held by two other members of the Haywood 1860 elite, James Bond ($8,422) and Wiley Mann ($10,764). See Trust Deeds, vol. I, 63–64, Haywood County Records, TSLA.

36. Circuit Court Minutes, Civil and Criminal, Vol. 4, 292, Haywood County Records, TSLA; Tennessee Vol. 16, 480, R. G. Dun & Co. Collection.

37. Trust Deeds, Vol. NN, 393–95, 558–60, Wilson County Records, TSLA.

38. Trust Deeds, Vol. I, 367; Deeds, Vol. 35, 3–5; Vol. 36, 273–74, Greene County

Records, TSLA. For the nickname of Williams's father, Alexander, see David Warren Bowen, *Andrew Johnson and the Negro* (Knoxville, 1989), 19.

39. Broyles to Col. Temple, Apr. 19, 1865, Oliver P. Temple Papers, Special Collections, Univ. of Tennessee Library, Knoxville. Broyles won his case but struggled for the next two years to pay his legal fees, maintaining that he could have paid one thousand dollars before the war more easily than he could now pay "2 or 300." As compensation for services rendered, Broyles offered his attorney, among other things, land in Arkansas, an "excellent young horse," his pocket watch, and "40 or 50 fine" sheep. See J. F. Broyles to "My dear friend Oliver," June 29, 1867.

"Duty of the Hour": African American Communities in Memphis, 1862–1923

■ KENNETH W. GOINGS AND GERALD L. SMITH

■

■ *Editor's Note: Perseverance* is a key word to understanding the struggle of newly freed African Americans in the decades after the Civil War. The social and cultural Reconstruction of 1863 to 1877 changed lives, even if it failed to change the basic attitudes of whites toward free people of color. Goings and Smith uncover three distinct African American groups shaping Memphis from 1862 to 1923: the "talented tenth" of the black elite; racial accommodationists, again largely from the professional elite; and the largest of all, and the least studied and appreciated, African American migrants from rural places throughout the South. It would be the migrants who "planted the seeds of protest against racial injustice in the city."

On Friday evening, September 21, 1894, African American women of Memphis held a mass meeting at the Beale Street Baptist Church, the oldest African American church in the city. The purpose of this gathering was to organize a local Phyllis Wheatley Union and seek improvements in the conditions of African American women. Among those attending were six widows whose husbands had been recently lynched less than twenty miles from Memphis in what was one of the worst mass killings in the history of Tennessee. The lynchings had shaken the entire Memphis African American community; mass meetings were held in several churches for the victims' families in order to raise money on their behalf. The gathering of African American women at the Beale Street Baptist Church served as another occasion in which funds were collected for the widows of the lynchings.[1]

Julia A. Hooks, a prominent African American schoolteacher in Memphis, delivered the meeting's main address, titled "Duty of the Hour." In her presentation to the audience, Hooks solicited support for the public education of African American schoolchildren. "We women must unite on plans and means by which we may be able to deal directly with wickedness and crime rather than their causes. We must show to the tax payers this necessity, and they will agree with us. Strength and nobility of character can be secured by well-directed efforts in the schoolrooms."[2]

Hooks was praised by the *Memphis Commercial Appeal.* "She is a thoroughly educated woman," it observed, "and has done much for the uplifting of the colored race." In 1896, Hooks's essay "Duty of the Hour" was published in the *Afro-American Encyclopedia,* where she emphasized more clearly her argument. According to Hooks, "character building is to be considered the 'Duty of the Hour'. Some people argue that this belongs to the home, but in how many homes do we find it neglected on account of ignorance[?] Every child," continued Hooks, "has the possibilities of becoming a blessing or a curse to the State. . . . It is the duty of the State to see that her subjects grow up with noble characters. It is her fault, and she alone must bear the blame for every vicious act, for every diabolical crime done and perpetrated within her borders if she [neglects] this duty."[3]

Apparently Hooks believed, as did other African American elites, that "character building" and moral teachings would socially and economically uplift African Americans and prevent them from becoming the victims of violent crimes committed by whites. To be sure, this was a warped interpre-

African American children in West Tennessee, late 1800s. Manuscripts Photograph Collection, Tennessee State Library and Archives.

tation of the status of African Americans and the conditions they faced during the late nineteenth and early twentieth centuries. Although Hooks's suggestions received wide attention from local and national publications, they did not reflect the concerns and solutions of Memphis's entire African American population.

Hooks represented the ideals of the "talented tenth," and her beliefs were centered on assimilation as a means of gaining the equality and respect of white Memphians. But Memphis's African American population was diverse. African American leaders and their foot soldiers were not always in unison with one another on matters involving racial progress and race relations. This division was, in part, a consequence of the city's ever-increasing black population. That different African Americans from different places were migrating to Memphis at different times created a complex and diverse black community. While the African American community became more diversified in its class, education, and residential tenor, black survival skills used to challenge racial violence and discrimination in Memphis became more elastic.

Due to the economic and political influence of the talented tenth on the development of African American communities in the North and South, scholars have overly concentrated on the role they played in community development. Writing in 1944, Gunnar Myrdal argued that "though the upper class is relatively small in numbers, it provides the standards and values,

African American workers, Memphis vicinity, late 1800s. Manuscripts Photograph Collection, Tennessee State Library and Archives.

African American mother
and daughter, Memphis
vicinity, late 1800s. Gift
of Joe Kent, Library Pic-
ture Collection, Tennes-
see State Library and Ar-
chives.

and symbolizes the aspirations of the Negro community; being the most articulate element in the community, its outlook and interests are often regarded
as those of the community at large."[4] Basing his conclusions about African
Americans in Memphis on the activities of the city's talented tenth, Lester
Lamon, in *Black Tennesseans, 1900–1930,* claims "fear and a dulling environment held resistance in check in West Tennessee." Although Lamon acknowledges that "the firm dedication to accommodation that had characterized Tennessee's various black communities in 1900 deteriorated noticeably
during the next fifteen years," his study neglects to identify the black communities on a statewide or local basis.[5] Had Lamon completely pulled back
the veil to examine black Memphis, he would have found at least three communities bound by racial discrimination but differing in ideologies. The
accommodationist position he writes about was simply a stand taken by one
segment of the African American community.

At least three African American communities existed in Memphis between
1890 and 1920. Each represented the activities and ideologies of a particular
African American group. First, there were those who composed the talented

tenth. Most had secured an education, made economic investments in the city, and achieved an elite status in the community. They utilized the political and judicial systems whenever they could, but believed their *duty of the hour* was "character building" so that whites would have a more positive perception of all African Americans. Second, there were the accommodationists, including black professionals who refused to challenge segregation and racial discrimination in the city. For them, the *duty of the hour* was to promote "harmony" between the races by accepting second-class citizenship for African Americans. The third community consisted of migrants who ignored attempts by the Memphis white community to keep blacks in their "place." Many of the migrants participated in individual acts of resistance to racial indignities. As their numbers increased, they established an insulated African American community surrounded by schools, churches, business neighborhoods, and social organizations that met the needs of all black Memphians. This was important, considering the city's racial climate.[6]

Similar to other southern communities, Memphis restricted the social and political rights of African Americans after the Civil War. Whereas in 1867 the Tennessee General Assembly extended to African Americans the right to vote, it subsequently enacted legislation that systematically weakened the citizenship rights of African Americans. In 1870, the state's constitution mandated segregated public schools and outlawed interracial marriages. In 1881, the General Assembly required separate railroad coaches for black and white passengers. Eight years later, lawmakers passed several bills ostensibly for the purpose of electoral reform, yet these bills were also designed to minimize the influence of the black vote in the state.[7] Still, Memphis had a thriving African American population long before its northern counterparts in Chicago, New York, and Detroit. After the Federal occupation of Memphis in 1862, African Americans began working assiduously to advance the condition and status of their communities. Following the race riot of 1866, black Baptists and Methodists formed societies such as the Avery Chapel Building Fund and the Daughters of Zion No. 1 Building Fund to rebuild their churches. Black fraternal orders of Masons and Odd Fellows had established chapters in Memphis by the end of the 1860s. There were also several black schools, churches, and mutual aid societies in the city by the end of Reconstruction. Additionally, in 1870, the American Missionary Association established Lemoyne Normal Institute. Within three years, 280 students were receiving instruction from the school's black and white faculty members. According to Armistead L. Robinson, in his study of black leadership in Memphis, the "evidence suggests that in Memphis the recently freed managed to survive the emancipation experience without relying either upon crime or upon agencies of public welfare."[8]

While each black fraternal organization had its own handshakes, secret passwords, and rituals, all of them assured their members that they would receive financial assistance in paying medical expenses. Yet, following the race riot of 1866, divisions in the African American community became more apparent in Memphis. Elite African Americans petitioned the Freedmen's Bureau with a solution to resolve the problems that led to the riot. In their view, the newly arrived black migrants should be sent back to the countryside. According to Armistead Robinson, "The interest in reducing racial tensions within Memphis loomed larger in the calculations of these prosperous blacks than the safety and well-being of their poorer fellow blacks. Clearly, social class conflicts existed within the black community of Reconstruction Memphis."[9]

Meanwhile, elite African Americans, whose groups comprised both the talented tenth and accommodationist communities, appeared to be making significant racial progress. Between 1865 and 1890, black fraternal orders even played an important role in local politics. More than ten blacks served on the city council while several others were appointed assistant attorneys general, wharfmasters, and coal inspectors during the 1870s. Thomas Cassells and Isaac F. Norris were elected to the state legislature in 1881. Yet the influence of black fraternal orders declined as black confidence in the Republican Party withered and as whites adopted the black clergy to represent the black community.[10]

During the 1880s, the Reverend R. N. Countee, pastor of Tabernacle Missionary Baptist Church, the Reverend B. A. Imes from Second Congregational Church, and the Reverend W. A. Brinkley from the Washington Street Baptist Church led the criticism of black secret societies. Countee believed members of his congregation affiliated with these organizations should contribute to the church's treasury instead of their fraternities. Brinkley decided to oust the members of his church who refused to renounce their membership in these kinds of organizations.[11]

In 1880, Countee and Brinkley founded the Memphis Baptist and Normal Institute for West Tennessee Baptists. Members of black fraternal orders were not allowed to teach at the school, thus exacerbating the conflict that already existed between the two groups. Meanwhile, the school won considerable approval from the white community. According to historian David Tucker, "The Institute founders had shrewdly designed a curriculum which combined academic, religious, and industrial training, and therefore had a wide appeal. . . . Cooperation between the local white power elite and black ministers, for the support of Howe, as the Institute came to be called after its largest donor, would continue over the years accruing to the ministers important white contacts and greater prestige in the community."[12]

Black Memphians were divided over choosing their leaders and determining their relationship with whites. The evidence suggests they were not monolithic in their behavior and attitude toward the white community. Memphis had an ever-changing black population since it was centrally located in the mid-South. Consequently, most newcomers to the city were rural migrants who believed that Memphis offered an abundance of opportunities in employment, education, and housing. More than half of the persons migrating to the city were born in Mississippi, while at least one-fourth came from Arkansas, Alabama, and Louisiana.[13]

Memphis was attractive to African Americans because it offered an urban community with strong ties to a rural economy. In 1873, the Cotton Exchange was founded in the city. Factors loaned money to nearby planters and purchased their crop on the spot. The factors, in turn, sold the crop and received a commission and payment for whatever supplies or loan they had originally given to the planter. Because the Cotton Exchange was also engaged in the wholesale and retail grocery business it became the "center of trade in the Mid-South."[14]

Besides witnessing an increasing number of black migrants, Memphis experienced the arrival of white farmers from Mississippi and Tennessee who moved to the city during the 1880s and 1890s. They were, according to Gerald Capers, "a simple and virtuous country folk, but stubborn and often unlettered." In 1900, writes Capers, "Memphis presented a strange paradox— a city modern in physical aspect but rural in background, rural in prejudice, and rural in habit." Actually, noted one local historian, "Memphis was a small town with a lot of people in it."[15]

The presence of rural white migrants in Memphis created significant differences in the white community just as the presence of black migrants led to greater stratifications in the African American community. Elite whites who could utilize cheap black labor and who sought the political support of African Americans made friendly overtures to the black community, while working-class whites were threatened by their presence. Yet black migrants were inspired by the opportunities urban life offered. Three black newspapers were being published in the city by the end of the 1880s: the *Memphis Watchman,* the *Living Way,* and the *Free Speech and Headlight.* Socially, Memphis remained an exciting place for African Americans. Beale Street, in particular, was described as the "Main Street of Negro America." Both whites and blacks owned businesses on Beale Street; however, except for the Pee Wee Saloon, blacks owned enterprises from Hernando to Fourth Street. They included Charlie Carner's Movie House, Jackson's Drug Store, Smith's Cafe, and Gillis Brothers Hotel among others. Beale Street was where W. C. Handy popularized the blues. It was where African Americans met on the weekends to mix socially in the restaurants, saloons, and gambling dens. Because the atmosphere was clouded with crime and vice, one minister observed: "It seems that the devil left hell on a vacation, stopped over at Memphis, sat down on Beale Street and rewrote the Ten Commandments leaving the NOT out of each Commandment."[16]

Black migrants to Memphis took advantage of various employment opportunities not related to plantation labor. They worked on the levee, the steamship lines, and in the lumber industry.[17] Denied opportunities in skilled labor, some African American migrants were hired as cooks and maids and in other service occupations reserved specifically for them. By 1920, however, African Americans comprised only 39 percent of the Memphis workforce. This figure was a reflection of the continued migration into the city not only of African Americans, but of whites from the fields and small towns of the region. These white migrants were moving into traditional "negro" jobs and displacing African American workers.[18]

But the economic situation was not all bleak. African American migrants continued to provide a clientele for African American professionals and businesspeople. Besides the growth of African American businesses, there were increases in the number of doctors, lawyers, and teachers. African Americans also owned and operated grocery stores, barber and beauty shops, saloons, funeral homes, and other businesses that served the African American community.[19]

Although there were enough economic opportunities in Memphis to continue to attract African American migrants, the problem of the color line remained an important issue during the years immediately following emancipation. For instance, Robert Church, Sr., and Samuel J. Ireland, two African Americans, boarded a streetcar on Poplar Street on December 16, 1867. The conductor ordered them to stand on the platform, but they refused, since a recent state law did not require separate seating for the races. After being ejected from the car by the conductor, Church and Ireland filed a complaint against him, claiming he had violated the "Common Carriers Law." It is not known how this case was resolved but apparently Church and Ireland naively expected their newfound rights would be protected.[20]

As the late nineteenth and early twentieth centuries progressed, the reality of racial discrimination and racial violence created serious problems facing all segments of the African American community. Class, education, and generational differences influenced the shaping of Memphis's three African American communities. But the real passion and protest for justice was more clearly defined by the attitudes and actions of Africans Americans as they were subjected to racial inequality. The responses of the talented tenth were much different from those of the accommodationists and migrants.

In 1881, Julia Hooks was charged with disorderly conduct in a Memphis court when she complained about the segregation of theater seats. She was fined five dollars for the incident. Yet, in spite of this incident, Hooks maintained her philosophy devoted to "character building," which assumed that if all African Americans adopted a better character, the racial discrimination she faced would dissipate. Hooks's act of protest was not uncommon. According to historian Dorthy Sterling, "Black women with education and social standing rankled at the discriminate, legally enforced system of segregation in transportation." They believed they deserved first-class treatment when they paid first-class prices.[21]

Another incident, which received more publicity than the Hooks case, involved Ida B. Wells, a migrant to the city of Memphis who managed to achieve a notable standing in the African American community. In 1884, Wells, a young schoolteacher, challenged customary segregation on railroad cars in Tennessee. Wells had purchased a first-class train ticket in Memphis to ride to the school (at Woodstock, Shelby County) where she taught. The conductor refused to take Wells's ticket as she sat in the ladies' car, which was reserved for whites. He insisted that she sit in the smoking car (front car) and even tried to wrestle her out of her seat. But Wells fought for the seat and "fastened her teeth in the back of his hand." Determined to get Wells off the car, the conductor solicited assistance from a baggageman and finally removed her from the train.

Wells filed a lawsuit against the Chesapeake, Ohio & Southwestern Railroad Company. Her first attorney, T. F. Cassells, was black, but he was bought off by the railroad company. A white attorney, Judge Greer, took over the case and won it in circuit court. According to presiding Judge J. O. Pierce, the railroad company had violated Tennessee's 1881 statute that prohibited railroads from seating blacks in second-class cars while charging first-class fare. An 1882 statute mandating equal first-class accommodations for the races had also been violated. Therefore, the court awarded Wells five hundred dollars in damages.[22]

Three years later, the Supreme Court of Tennessee reached a different conclusion. After listening to the testimony of a witness, the court was convinced there was no one smoking on the front car as Wells had claimed and that the conductor had stopped her before she entered the rear. Consequently, the lower court's decision was reversed.[23]

Although Wells lost her case, her reputation as a race leader and anti-lynching crusader was enhanced following the mob execution of three African American males in Memphis in 1892. As the coeditor of *Free Speech and Headlight*, Wells used her position to convey to the public her anger over the lynching of black men. Not only did she write about lynchings, she spoke throughout the Northeast and even traveled to England to speak out against the brutal crime.[24]

Wells's articles stirred up the black and white communities of Memphis. On June 7, 1892, the city's black and white leaders met at the Cotton Exchange Building to discuss the apparent differences in the community. The meeting had been requested by black leaders who included several attorneys, ministers, and politicians. According to the *Memphis Appeal-Avalanche*, the highlight of the evening was a paper read by the Reverend B. A. Imes, who had served as pastor of the Second Congregational Church for more than a decade. In his message before the interracial meeting, Imes wanted whites to differentiate between "law-abiding" African Americans and the "individual negro criminal" in order that the rights of the former would be protected. He did not question the dubious reasons whites chose to lynch blacks. A few weeks after the interracial meeting, Imes and about a dozen of the "most prominent & respected" African Americans in Memphis prepared a statement for the press further distancing themselves from the writings of Ida Wells: "We desire to put on record a most positive disapproval of the course pursued by Miss Ida Wells through the medium of the *New York Age*, in stirring up, from week to week, this community and wherever that paper goes, the spirit of strife over the unhappy question at issue. We see no good to come from this method of journalism on either side. . . ."[25]

Clearly, African Americans differed on issues involving race. Julia Hooks, Ida B. Wells, and B. A. Imes represented the behavior of merely one community in Memphis—the "talented tenth." They wanted blacks to have equal rights but within the constraints and approval of the white community. Hooks, Wells, and Imes were not the only members of Memphis's talented tenth community. Josiah Settles and Benjamin F. Booth were noted attorneys in Memphis during the same period. In 1905, Settles and Booth argued the case of Mary Morrison, who refused to accept a seat on the newly established Jim Crow streetcars of Memphis. Although they lost the case in the state supreme court, their participation in the trial indicated, once again, that the talented tenth community was not rigid in its response to racial discrimination. Some were simply more outspoken than others on the race issue.[26]

One of the most successful members of the talented tenth community was Robert R. Church, Jr. In 1912, at the age of twenty-six, he returned to Memphis upon the death of his wealthy father, Robert R. Church, Sr. The younger Church became an active businessman and politician in the community. In 1916, he was the logical choice to replace the late Josiah T. Settles on the Republican State Executive Committee but was passed over. Working from within the party had not brought due recognition and power. Church needed an organization base; thus, in 1916 he founded the Lincoln Republican League. Challenging the party's lily-white policy, the Lincoln League ran its own slate of candidates in the 1916 local elections. Although Democrats won every office, Lincoln League candidates outpolled lily-white Republicans four to one. Church proclaimed that after the elections the League had become the "regular Republican Party."[27]

Throughout his political life in Memphis, Robert Church, Jr., would have to contend with Edward Hull Crump, a southern business "progressive" originally from Mississippi. Crump was elected mayor of Memphis in 1909. He quickly pushed to change the city council–mayor system of government to a commission system in which each commissioner would be elected at large. This ensured an all-white commission. One commissioner would be mayor and have veto power over any commission action. Serving as mayor from 1910 to 1916, Crump developed a political machine that would ensure his statewide political influence until the mid-1950s.[28]

The relation between Robert Church, Jr., and "Boss" Crump, at least until 1932, was a symbiotic one. In 1911, Church, along with two other local African American business leaders, Bert Roddy and Harry Pace, cashiers at the Solvent Savings Bank, formed the Colored Citizens Association of Memphis. It is through this organization that they endorsed Crump and his candidates for political office. As long as African Americans voted for him and his Democratic machine locally, Crump had no objection to Church's urging his supporters to vote Republican on the state and national levels. In exchange for these votes, Crump dispensed limited patronage to the African American community. He supported the request for a black park, paved some neighborhood streets, and did not attempt to disfranchise African American voters.[29]

The African American community, through some of its leaders, remained very active in politics even under the adverse conditions of the first two decades of the twentieth century. But racial violence was a constant problem in Memphis, and the white press tended to portray African Americans in a negative light. African Americans most often appeared in the white Memphis press when they were charged with some criminal offense. The *Commercial Appeal* claimed that racial integration was a "gross absurdity" and that the United States retained black troops in order to punish white students from West Point who established a poor record.[30]

Concerned about the increased racial violence, Bert Roddy tried unsuccessfully to create a local chapter of the National Association for the Advancement of Colored People (NAACP) in 1914. It was not until three years later, following the vigilante murder of an African American male named Ell Persons, that Memphis finally established a chapter. But not all African Americans in Memphis were pleased by the political and civil rights measures pushed by the talented tenth. Some chose to promote racial harmony in spite of resistance. As Willard Gatewood has noted in his book *Aristocrats of Color*: "At one extreme, were those who shunned involvement in racial affairs altogether and withdrew into the safe oasis of their own making in an effort to isolate themselves from the conflict and tensions of race."[31] These persons were accommodationists who had adopted the public philosophy of Booker T. Washington.

Four very important and prominent individuals who represented the accommodationist position were Robert Church, Sr.; G. P. Hamilton, principal of Kortrecht High School; the Reverend Sutton E. Griggs; and the Reverend Thomas O. Fuller. Born in Holly Springs, Mississippi, in 1839, Church was the mulatto son of Captain Charles B. Church, owner of several steamboats that traveled the Mississippi River from New Orleans to Memphis. As a young man, Robert Church worked as a steward on steamboats. After the Civil War, he invested in real estate, saloons, and hotel businesses. When Memphis was in debt and lost its charter following the yellow fever epidemics of 1878 and 1879, Church purchased the first taxing district bond. In 1890, the *Indianapolis Freeman* reported Church's wealth to be a quarter of a million dollars.[32]

The greatest manifestation of Church's wealth was the park and auditorium he built in Memphis in 1900. Located on Beale Street near Fourth and Turley, the site offered blacks a place to hold carnivals, graduations, and conventions. The *Planters Journal* described the facilities as "one of the largest and most profitable investments in the city. . . . It is beautifully landscaped with walks and handsomely kept grounds with flowers which show unusual taste in their arrangements."[33] Church was quite influential in developing the prestigious image of the black community. In 1906, he founded the Solvent Savings Bank and Trust Company, the city's first black bank since Reconstruction. Within four years, it was the most successful black bank in Tennessee with $86,568 in deposits. In 1910, two black funeral home directors, H. Wayman and J. Jay Scott, opened the Fraternal Savings Bank, giving the African American community at large another symbol of growth and development.[34]

In spite of Church's wealth, the *Memphis Commercial Appeal* observed that he had "not obtruded his affairs or his personality upon others. He has been unostentatious and unpretending. . . . [H]e has minded his own business."[35] The elder Church had endeared himself to the white community in 1901, when he contributed one thousand dollars toward a fund established to defray the entertainment expenses for a reunion of the United Confederate Veterans. In making his contribution to the event, Church stated: "I have tried to be liberal at all times and to help along this city whenever I could but I can say that I never gave a cent in my life so cheerfully or gladly as I gave that check to the veterans' entertainment fund." Unlike his son, the older Church was more accommodating of the racial climate. He had obviously put the 1867 streetcar incident behind him, ultimately capitulating to the racial etiquette of the era.

G. P. Hamilton was another accommodationist. In 1908, Hamilton published *The Bright Side of Memphis,* highlighting the various African American institutions, professionals, and business leaders in the city. Hamilton made a point of noting in the book: "The relationship between the two races in Memphis is as friendly and cordial as can be reasonably expected. Occasionally there may be rash and intemperate men of both races who, if not restrained by the conservative element, would possibly try to jeopardize this friendly relationship and cause unnecessary friction and strife; but the great majority of both races are sincerely desirous of peace."[36]

Similar to Church and Hamilton, Sutton Griggs, pastor of the Tabernacle Baptist Church, saw positive race relations in Memphis. Griggs worked to create an "institutional church" that would effectively work as a social welfare agency within the African American community. The church provided recreational activities, moral training, and employment services. The latter two activities brought Griggs to the attention of the Memphis Chamber of Commerce, which, through its Industrial Welfare Committee, funded a large part of his activities. All were concerned about labor leaving the mid-South area. A tireless worker who preached accommodation, Griggs urged African

Americans to stay in the South with their "true" friends during the great migration.[37]

The Reverend Thomas Oscar Fuller was pastor of the First Baptist Church and became principal of Howe Institute in 1902. Three years later, Fuller opposed staging a boycott of Memphis streetcars in response to the legal establishment of segregation on this form of transportation. In a letter to the *Commercial Appeal,* Fuller stressed the need for "perfect harmony and cooperation between the races."[38] It was a message assured to receive white support as well as wide publicity throughout the city. Yet, despite this kind of rhetoric, it was the third and largest African American community, comprised of migrants, that would actually have the most significant influence on building black Memphis.

African American migrants came to Memphis in search of economic opportunities that would allow them to escape the rigid racial structures of the agricultural South. And, upon arriving in the city, many refused to follow the racial etiquette accepted by older African Americans and others who had become acculturated to urban life. The migrants planted the seeds of protest

Memphis Sanitation worker, late 1800s. Gift of Joe Kent, Library Picture Collection, Tennessee State Library and Archives.

against racial injustice in the city. Yet, unlike the talented tenth and accommodationists, the migrants held the least prestige in Memphis. They were the least educated and had little contact with the white community. They worked in low-paying unskilled jobs, lived in shotgun-style houses, and were despised by the talented tenth and accommodationists for their uninhibited behavior. Additionally, being migrants, they experienced daily harassment from the local police, who were concerned with maintaining control over the growing African American population.

By 1900, Memphis had become the third-largest city in the South. African Americans comprised 49 percent of the more than 102,000 residents living in the city and 55 percent of the 153,000 total population for Shelby County. For the next twenty years, the African American population did not drop below 37 percent in either Memphis or Shelby County.[39]

African American migration provided a constant boost to black institutional growth in Memphis. Whites complained, however, of farm or labor shortages and streetcar congestion. Because of the large number of rural migrants coming into Memphis, police officers had "orders to stop all suspicious-looking negroes and search them." The police department even hired "Negro spotters," local African Americans who could identify the city's new black residents and point them out to officers.[40]

But the extent of how far race relations had really deteriorated was evident in the newspapers. There were numerous examples of police attacks against African Americans during the second decade of the twentieth century. It was, in part, an effort to harass migrants into leaving the city. Yet the African American migrant community did not passively accept these attacks. Instead, they engaged in an interracial struggle with white Memphians. When they were insulted or physically attacked by whites, black migrants often responded with an aggression uncharacteristic of the talented tenth and the accommodationists. On a number of occasions, migrants even resorted to physical force to defend themselves.[41]

Racial contestation in Memphis was most apparent on the city's streetcars. Even though "officially" segregated, they were one of the few places where African American and whites came into direct and regular contact with each other. Several newspaper accounts reveal African Americans arguing with streetcar conductors and refusing to surrender their seats to whites.[42] Clearly, these people were not accommodationists or members of the talented tenth. They were part of a community whose members often engaged in individualized acts of resistance. For them, the *duty of the hour* was confrontation.

However, "fighting back" did not stop the attacks. On May 22, 1917, Ell

Persons, a woodcutter, was burned to death just outside the city limits for allegedly raping and murdering a young white girl.[43] Neither the talented tenth, nor accommodationists, nor the migrants armed themselves to defend him. Perhaps the "communities" felt overwhelmed by the number of armed whites descending on Memphis, or perhaps they felt Persons was guilty and deserved what he got. While it is not possible to definitely know why no "community" came to his defense, it is entirely possible that the explanation lies in the fact that Persons had no clear ties to any "community." Ell Persons was not a member of the talented tenth. He was an itinerant woodchopper, a migrant to the area who lived a relatively isolated existence in a woods outside of Memphis. While assertive in defending themselves and members of "their" group, the talented tenth had not shown any inclination to make a strong defense of the migrants or the poor during the late nineteenth and early twentieth centuries. Their *duty of the hour* was still to work for racial uplift and to seek racial redress through legal channels. The accommodationists could not, in keeping with their *duty of the hour*, come to his defense. To interfere with the mob would only put their lives in jeopardy and would do nothing to "foster harmonious race relations." For those migrating to Memphis, one would have thought, their *duty of the hour* would have included the defense of another migrant. But one must remember that in pursuing racial justice migrants had often sought individualized strategies that were not necessarily inclusive of other African Americans. Although Ell Persons was a migrant, he was clearly not one of them. And so, tragically, he was left alone as each group continued to pursue its own *duty of the hour*, even though no strategy was inclusive enough to guarantee racial justice in Memphis.

Notes

1. *Memphis Commercial Appeal,* Sept. 2, 1894; Sept. 6, 1894; Sept. 22, 1894.
2. Ibid., Sept. 22, 1894.
3. Ibid., Julia A. Hooks, "Duty Of The Hour," *Afro-American Encyclopedia* (Nashville, 1896), 333, 335.
4. Gunnar Myrdal, *An American Dilemma: The Negro Problem and American Democracy* (New York, 1944), 2:689–708.
5. Lester Lamon, *Black Tennesseans, 1900–1930* (Knoxville, 1977), 3, 19.
6. As of 1920, thirty-five thousand of the city's sixty-one thousand African American population lived in the southeastern section of the city, according to T. J. Woofter: "All kinds of homes from cottages to shacks were mixed together." See T. J. Woofter, *Negro Problems In Cities* (New York, 1928), 104; Charles Williams, Jr., "Two Black

Communities In Memphis, Tennessee: A Study In Urban Socio-Political Structure," (Ph.D. diss., Univ. of Illinois at Urbana-Champaign, 1982), 109, 114, 139–40.

7. Joseph H. Cartwright, *The Triumph of Jim Crow: Tennessee Race Relations in the 1880s.* (Knoxville, 1976), 18, 104.

8. David M. Tucker, *Black Pastors & Leaders: Memphis, 1819–1972* (Memphis, 1975), passim. Three very important studies of Memphis's African American community include Kathleen Christine Berkeley, "'Like A Plague of Locust': Immigration and Social Change In Memphis, Tennessee, 1850–1880" (Ph.D. diss., Univ. of California at Los Angeles, 1980), passim; Armistead L. Robinson, "Plans Dat Comed from God: Institution Building and the Emergence of Black Leadership in Reconstruction Memphis, 1865–1880," in Orvil Vernon Burton and Robert C. MacMath, Jr., eds., *Toward A New South? Studies in Post Civil War Southern Communities.* (Westport, Conn., 1982), 82; Gloria Brown Melton, "Blacks In Memphis, Tennessee, 1920–1955: A Historical Study" (Ph.D. diss., Washington State Univ., 1982), 18.

9. See Robinson, "Plans Dat Comed from God," 95. Robinson writes: "This group of entrepreneurs and artisans insisted that it was 'for the welfare of a large portion of the present colored population of this city that they should be made to go into the country where their labor is needed by the farming community.'"

10. Melton, "Blacks In Memphis," 6–7, 14–15.

11. Tucker, *Black Pastors and Leaders,* 35–37.

12. Ibid., 39.

13. David M. Tucker, *Memphis Since Crump: Bossism, Blacks and Civic Reformers, 1948–1968* (Knoxville, 1980), 14.

14. Robert Sigafoos, *Cotton Row to Beale Street: A Business History of Memphis* (Memphis, 1979), 67.

15. Gerald M. Capers, *The Biography of a Rivertown: Memphis, Its Heroic Age,* 2d. ed. (Privately published, 1966), 207; Historian Charles Crawford as quoted in Ann Trotter, "The Memphis Business Community and Integration," Elizabeth Jacoway and David Colburn, eds., *Southern Businessmen and Desegregation* (Baton Rouge, 1982), 285.

16. Fred L. Hutchins, *What Happened in Memphis* (Memphis, 1965), 44.

17. See Melton, "Blacks in Memphis"; Berkeley, "'Like A Plague of Locust'"; Joel Roitman, "Race Relations In Memphis, Tennessee, 1880–1905 (Master's thesis, Memphis State Univ., 1964), 71, 74, 75; David M. Tucker, "Miss Ida B. Wells and Memphis Lynching," *Phylon* 32 (Summer 1971): 113, 116.

18. Denoral Davis, "Against the Odds: Postbellum Growth and Development in a Southern Urban Black Community, 1865–1900," (Ph.D. diss., State Univ. of New York at Binghampton, 1987), 50–55.

19. Melton, "Blacks In Memphis," passim.

20. *Memphis Daily Post,* Dec. 17, 1867.

21. Hooks, "Duty Of The Hour," 332–39; *Commercial Appeal,* Mar. 13, 1881.

22. Alfreda M. Duster, ed., *Crusade for Justice: The Autobiography of Ida B. Wells* (Chicago, 1970), 18–19; Mildred Thompson, "Ida B. Wells-Barnett: An Exploratory Study of An American Black Woman, 1893–1930" (Ph.D. diss., George Washington Univ., 1979), 24–26.

23. *Chesapeake, Ohio* & *Southwestern Railroad Company* v. *Wells,* Tenn. 4 SW, 85 Tenn 613, 627; Mildred Thompson, "Ida B. Wells-Barnett: An Exploratory Study of An American Black Woman, 1893–1930," 24–26.

24. Duster, *Crusader for Justice: The Autobiography of Ida B. Wells,* 58, 61–63, 66–67; Thomas C. Holt, "The Lonely Warrior: Ida B. Wells–Barnett and the Struggle for Black Leadership," John Hope Franklin and August Meier, eds., *Black Leaders of the Twentieth Century* (Urbana, Ill., 1982), 43; Tucker, "Miss Ida B. Wells and Memphis Lynching," 118–22.

25. For biographical information on Imes and his work in Memphis, see Tucker, *Black Pastors* & *Leaders,* 41–54, and Memphis *Appeal-Avalanche,* June 8 and 30, 1892.

26. Lamon, *Black Tennesseans, 1900–1930,* 32.

27. Ibid., 56–58.

28. Ibid., 45–46.

29. William D. Miller, *Mr. Crump of Memphis* (Baton Rouge, 1964), 103; Lamon, *Black Tennesseans, 1900–1930,* 56–58.

30. Thomas Harrison Baker, *The Memphis Commercial Appeal* (Baton Rouge, 1971), 206.

31. Willard B. Gatewood, *Aristocrats of Color: The Black Elite, 1880–1920* (Bloomington, 1990), 300.

32. Annette E. Church and Roberta Church, *The Robert R. Churches of Memphis: A Father And Son Who Achieved In Spite of Race* (Ann Arbor, Mich., 1974), 5–13; Fred Hutchins, *What Happened In Memphis* (Memphis, 1965), 101.

33. Church and Church, *The Robert R. Churches of Memphis,* 13–15; Hutchins, *What Happened in Memphis,* 101.

34. Lamon, *Black Tennesseans, 1900–1930,* 188–90; David M. Tucker, *Lieutenant Lee of Beale Street* (Nashville, 1971), 17.

35. *Commercial Appeal,* Jan. 30, 1901, 1.

36. G. P. Hamilton, *The Bright Side of Memphis* (Memphis, 1908), 9.

37. Randolph M. Walker, *The Metamorphosis of Sutton E. Griggs: The Transition from Black Radical to Conservative, 1913–1933* (Memphis, 1991), 26–28, 46.

38. Lamon, *Black Tennesseans,* 32.

39. Melton, "Blacks In Memphis, Tennessee, 1920–1955," 21; Capers, *The Biography of a Rivertown: Memphis, Its Heroic Age,* 207.

40. *Commercial Appeal,* Aug. 10 and Nov. 11, 1916.

41. Memphis *Commercial Appeal,* Aug. 6, 1916; *Commercial Appeal,* Aug. 14, 1916; *Commercial Appeal,* Nov. 11, 1916; *Commercial Appeal,* Dec. 4, 1916; *Commercial Appeal,* Oct. 29, 1916; *Chicago Defender,* Apr. 24, 1915; *Commercial Appeal,* Aug. 6, 1916; Melton, *Blacks of Memphis,* 21; U.S. Dept. of Interior, Bureau of Education, *The Public School System of Memphis, Tennessee,* Bulletin 50, 1919 (Washington, 1920), 13; U.S. Dept. of Commerce, Bureau of the Census, *Negroes in the United States, 1920–1932* (Washington, 1935), 3. We believe that migrants were well represented in the incidents cited above. In 1918, for example, the National Bureau of Education surveyed the parents of white and African American students in the public school system. They found that less than 2 percent of the 11,871 white parents and less than 5 percent of the 3,801 African American parents had been born in Memphis. In addition, the census shows that 53.6 percent of the African American population in Memphis was born outside Tennessee. In the state's next largest city,

Nashville, only 8.4 percent were born outside Tennessee. It is very likely that migrants were heavily involved in these incidents.

We have been unable up this point to trace many of the individuals involved in these altercations through the census and or police records for several reasons. The great mobility of the population during the years of this study and the rapid development of neighborhoods on the fringe of the city where migrants, at least initially, lived were not as closely tallied by census takers as the more established neighborhoods. We also have not been able to identify their birthplaces from police records because, for this time period, most have been destroyed, lost, or "misplaced." We are still searching through city and county records.

Our evidence about the identity of these individuals, migrant/working class, is thus circumstantial. However, we base our assessment on several factors. Perhaps the most important factor is the description of the individuals' dress and language in the newspapers. Even given the racist news reporting of the white press in Memphis, this coverage does give some indication of class background. It should be noted that during the time of this study when African American elites went out in public they were almost universally well dressed because they wanted to make sure that they would not be mistaken for "ordinary" African Americans. Also, the location of these incidents gives some indication of who was involved. While police harassment could and did affect African Americans all over the city, most of the incidents took place in the southern and southeastern parts of the city. These neighborhoods were the reception areas for the migrants. Also, increasingly over the time period of this study, the talented tenth and accommodationists were coming to an "understanding" with "Boss" Crump, while poorer African Americans were still clearly targets for police harassment and attacks. Increasingly, they were spared these assaults.

42. As for the incidents on the streetcars, we have additional but still circumstantial evidence that the individuals involved were migrants or working-class African Americans. Throughout this period, the talented tenth were removing themselves from streetcars to avoid the kinds of behavior we have described. In addition, the incidents on the streetcars generally took place on lines that ran to or through migrant and working-class neighborhoods. *Commercial Appeal*, Aug. 14, 1916, Oct. 22, 1916, and Nov. 10, 1916.

43. *Commercial Appeal*, May 22, 1917.

"Let Us Be Up and Doing": Women in the Tennessee Movements for Agrarian Reform, 1870-1892

■ Connie L. Lester

■

■ *Editor's Note:* Although accepting the confines of traditional gender roles, Tennessee women contributed socially and politically to the agrarian reform movement of the late nineteenth century. By studying women's activism in the Agricultural Wheel and Farmers Alliance, Lester found that rural women, even without the right to vote, "bravely asserted their rights to act within the Alliance, demanding admission, accepting local offices and speaking or writing on behalf of the organization." They shared an interest in the economic vitality of the farm and family with their husbands; this "spirit of mutuality" moved women to promote harmony, unity, and stability within the greater populist movement.

■ Let us then be up and doing,
with a heart for any fate
■ Still achieving, still pursuing,
learn to labor and to wait.
■   —Lillian Lee Hayes, 1889

In May 1890, Lizzie J. Dodd put aside her concerns regarding her perceived lack of literary skills and composed her only letter to the "Ladies Column" of *The Weekly Toiler,* the Tennessee Farmers' Alliance newspaper. She drew upon the words of a popular poem and urged women to "be up and doing" in the work of "the grand and noble order." As petty producers and working partners in the family farms across the state, women had a stake in the agricultural and economic reforms championed by the Alliance, and

Dodd encouraged them to act in their own interests by coming "modestly yet boldly to the front in this good work." Dodd's advice to act "modestly yet boldly" illustrated the paradox confronting women in the Tennessee agrarian movements of the late nineteenth century. On the one hand, the writer drew upon traditional perceptions of the proper sphere for women's activities when she urged her readers to "lend a helping hand, proving ourselves worthy helpmeets . . . by encouraging and aiding our brethren in every possible way in our sphere." Yet, at the same time, she clearly recognized the expansion of her sphere of activities and "boldly" addressed her letter to "all the brothers and sisters from Maine to California." She understood the obstacles that stood in the way of public roles for women, thanking the "true, honest, active male members" of her own union, who "give us the privilege of writing and reading essays," and she encouraged other women to grasp every opportunity afforded them to aid the work of reform. "We know our power and influence," she wrote. "Let's use it for good." Thus, while Lizzie Dodd exhibited the modesty she believed appropriate to female behavior, she also realized that the expanded sphere of which she wrote demanded bold action by Alliance women.[1]

As they presented themselves for membership in the Farmers' Alliance, women confronted a variety of personal, social, and organizational ambiguities. The Patrons of Husbandry, an early agrarian reform group, insisted upon the admission of women to its ranks and arranged a separate and complementary role for them. However, later organizations, including the Agricultural Wheel and the Farmers' Alliance, encouraged female participation without clearly defining the status or activities of women members. In a study of women in the North Carolina Farmers' Alliance, Julie Roy Jeffrey concluded that even without organizational guidelines women met few obstacles in gaining admittance or providing active public service since Alliance leaders in that state "stressed it [female membership] forcefully."[2]

Such was not the case in Tennessee. The persistent efforts of women to gain acceptance generated a spirited public debate over the proper sphere for their activities. This debate offers us a window onto the complexity of women's emerging public roles and illustrates the internal conflicts that afflicted the Alliance. Justification for admission of women rested on economic interests that mirrored those of their husbands. Within the organization, women expected to use their talents to achieve the goals set forth in the Alliance program. They entered the public arena to make speeches, write essays, pen letters, assume the responsibilities of minor offices in the Alliance hierarchy, or simply talk about reform. One woman encouraged her Alliance sisters to seize every opportunity and advocate reform "when you are standing on the corners, in your parlors, and anywhere you can find good material to listen to you." Despite the vigor with which women defended their rights to join the Alliance and participate in activities of the organization, Tennessee Alliance women never moved beyond the opportunities afforded by the programs of the larger agricultural reform movement. Where women found acceptance in the local unions, their interests coincided with those of male members. They demanded no political rights for themselves. Indeed, both women and men expected female members to maintain the modesty and moral superiority traditionally associated with their sphere. In this capacity, they were expected to unify the organization by providing a common purpose that focused on home and family. Popular perceptions of female morality presented the Alliance with the symbols of respectability it desperately needed to command respect and acceptance in the larger community of competing political and economic alternatives. While this complexity of demands forced Alliance women to recognize their own interests, act on their own behalf, and move into the public sphere, it also required that they uphold the values commonly attributed to them. Women encouraged one another as they maintained this balancing act by promising, as Dodd did, that there was "a better day coming."[3]

The "better day" farmers and their wives anticipated was the goal of various agrarian organizations that emerged during the period 1865–90. Tennessee's agricultural community began organizing shortly after the Civil War under the national banner of the Patrons of Husbandry, or the Grange, as it was popularly known. In addition to the opportunities afforded by participation in this national organization, local and state agricultural leaders encouraged farmers to rebuild county fair associations or take part in regional Farmers' Institutes sponsored by the Tennessee agricultural commissioners.[4]

Self-sufficiency through the reduction of expenses and increased production through the use of "scientific" farming methods were common goals of the local and state agricultural organizations. The annual Farmers' Institutes brought together leading farmers in each of the state's three grand divisions to discuss the use of chemical fertilizers, improvements in livestock breeding, and the latest technological advances of modern agriculture. County fair associations encouraged crop diversity and the use of improved farming techniques by offering premiums and prizes to local farmers. Endorsing the same objectives toward improvement of agricultural methods, the Grange went a step further to propose the reorganization of business relations "to bring producers and consumers, farmers and manufacturers into the most direct and friendly relations possible." The Grange disavowed political action in the pursuit of its aims and included in its Declaration of Principles the unequivocal statement that "no grange, if true to its obligations, can discuss political or religious questions, nor call political conventions, nor nominate candidates, nor discuss their merits in its meetings."[5]

One way to protect the farmers' interests while maintaining traditional hierarchies of power was to tie agricultural organizations to the existing network of religious and social groups common to every county. From its inception, the Grange built upon familiar organizational programs to create a sense of community among farmers and their neighbors. Indeed, historian Donald B. Marti has characterized the Grange as a "family organization," where men and women regularly crossed the boundary separating their spheres to share work and social enjoyments." The Patrons of Husbandry insisted upon the inclusion of women in the organization, and women played a prominent role in the Tennessee granges, though the evidence would indicate that their activities remained traditional and supportive. In the Wilson Grange No. 148 at Clarksville, in Montgomery County, six men and six women enrolled as charter members when the organization was established in 1873. By the end of the year, membership stood at twenty males and twelve females. Grange women advanced through a separate ritual within the organization, held offices within their ritual sphere, presented essays before county meetings, and wrote letters to the agricultural newspapers.[6]

An essay by Mrs. Fanny Montague, which was read before the Wayne County Grange, outlined the proper sphere for women. "I am not one of those who believe in any arbitrary limitation of woman's sphere," Montague began. "God created her to be the companion of man [and] in whatever form of labor he may honorably engage, she may honorably be his associate." Despite her bold beginning, as she continued her counsel to women, Montague confined her remarks to the creation of a pleasant home atmosphere and the need for a fuller social life for farming families.[7]

Letters from other farm wives and articles published in the *Rural Sun,* the Tennessee Grange newspaper, echoed Montague's view of the proper role for women. Articles aimed at women focused on efficiency in the performance of housekeeping tasks, recipes, and child rearing and revealed the upper-class origins of the authors in the prevalence of advice on the management of servants. Letters from women displayed a particular concern for the education of their daughters in a world at odds with tradition. Noting the movement for woman suffrage, Hester Holcombe observed that while there existed "a great need for some redress for 'woman's wrongs'" the cause of those difficulties began with "giddy and fashionable mothers who demand an ornamental smattering [of training and education] for their daughters." To avoid producing daughters who failed in life, she advised: "Give your daughters a good plain education, if you can do no more, and then to that add a thorough and complete knowledge of house-keeping; instead of encouraging them in the making of countless ruffles on countless dresses." Such a plan of action would ensure that "we would hear no more clamoring for woman's rights except by a few fanatics." Woman's sphere in the Tennessee Grange apparently included a complex mixture of domestic duties, social responsibilities, and educational supervision. Women clearly participated in an organization of farm families where their roles, if somewhat more public, diverged little from tradition.[8]

Membership in the Tennessee Grange reached a high point of 19,780 families in 1875. Thereafter, it began a steep and steady decline that ended in complete dissolution by 1880. Membership in 1876 was a reported 10,216 families. By 1877, it had dropped to 1,474. Perhaps the cause of the organization's demise rested in its view of agriculture. Whatever else may be said for the value of scientific agriculture, the cost of improved breeding stock, technically advanced farm machinery, and chemical fertilizers probably lay outside the reach of most Tennessee farmers. Although Grange leaders viewed farmers who continued to use antiquated tools and methods to plant cotton, corn, and tobacco on overworked fields as lazy and uneducated, they failed to take adequate notice of credit problems and debt, generally limiting their counsel on these subjects to calls for self-sufficiency.[9]

The gap between farmers such as those featured in articles on the pages of the *Rural Sun* and many of the farmers across the state becomes apparent in the diary of one West Tennessee Granger, Archelaus M. Hughes. A former schoolteacher and farmer, Hughes recorded a depressing litany of struggle and failure in his efforts to hold on to his farm during the period 1874–77. Education and effort proved to be feeble weapons against debt and bad weather, and Hughes was eventually forced to sell his farm. Self-sufficiency provided no relief for him, as he plaintively recorded: "I have lived closer, and the whole family have worn old clothes and shoes longer than we ever did before. For myself I have bought one pair of pants and 3 yards of domestic in the last six months, and not much more for Hattie and the children." Six months later, he could record no improvement in the family fortunes and took the occasion of the death of a prominent, though impoverished, acquaintance to comment on the problem of debt. "Debt is a grim monster," he wrote, "that drags down a man from his high position." Grange activities apparently brought little relief, and his final cursory reference to the organization included a telling observation. "Was at the grange yesterday," he wrote, "for the first time in five months. Nothing of importance was done."[10]

The demise of the Grange did not end the attempts by farmers to organize. In the 1880s, farmers again gathered to complain and seek solutions to the problems of depressed farm prices and mounting debt. Two separate groups, the Agricultural Wheel and the Farmers' Alliance, influenced the actions of Tennessee farmers. In February 1882, seven men gathered in Des Arc, Arkansas, and established the Agricultural Wheel. Their organization took its name from the belief that "agriculture is the great wheel or power that controls the machinery of the world's industries." Arguing from the Jacksonian belief that true wealth was produced by the laboring masses, the Wheelers saw bankers, stockbrokers, and financiers as "amassing fortunes" at the expense of the working class. The Agricultural Wheel grew from its unimpressive origins to a reported membership of 500,000 by 1887. In Tennessee, the State Wheel, headed by J. R. Miles, was organized in 1885, just a little over one year after the Wheel made its first appearance in the state in Weakley County. By the time the Agricultural Wheel merged with the Farmers' Alliance in 1889, Tennessee had 1,600 subordinate wheels scattered across the state.[11]

The Farmers' Alliance traced its origins to Lampasas, Texas, where disgruntled farmers organized under activists such as William Lamb. In 1887, the Farmers' Alliance established a national organization under the leadership of a self-taught lawyer and physician, Charles W. Macune, and began a series of mergers with various agricultural and labor organizations, including the Knights of Labor and the Agricultural Wheel. After the Tennessee Alliance merged with the Agricultural Wheel, the expanded organization claimed 99,440 white members in 2,436 subordinate unions, covering 93 of the 96 counties in the state. The Colored Farmers' Alliance in Tennessee added another 421 unions.[12]

Both the Wheel and the Alliance advocated currency reform, control of the nation's communication and transportation systems, and empowerment of the nation's farmers. Their demands included a graduated income tax, free coinage of silver, and the direct election of U.S. senators. The Alliance added a subtreasury system of crop storage and low-interest loans for farmers. Lecturers encouraged the formation of farmer cooperatives to control costs and raise agricultural prices and urged farmers to institute the latest methods of scientific farming as their predecessors in the Grange had done. The by-laws of both organizations disavowed partisan politics, but Wheel and Alliance publications declared agricultural problems a function of the laws that had been passed by state legislatures and Congress. Both groups called upon farmers to vote their own interests and use the laws to achieve their own ends, as the business community had done. The *Weekly Toiler*, the Wheel and Alliance newspaper, brimmed with political and organizational news. Lest anyone miss the difference, the editor noted that the Grange "sprang into existence on the sole idea of knocking out the middle man," adding that "the situation is quite different now," and "the ballot box is the only resort and the only hope for reform."[13]

Political elites of the period generally found the movement of farmers into politics a source of amusement, ridiculing them as "hayseeds," "clodhoppers," and "wool hat boys." Their appearances at county political conventions often elicited editorial head-shaking over the rowdiness of the proceedings and the overall lack of parliamentary decorum. In the summer of 1890, as county conventions met to appoint delegates to the state gubernatorial nominating convention in Nashville, newspapers reported farmers "rushing to and fro in the wildest confusion" as they bullied their way to control of the nominat-

Political rally for Peter Turney and Grover Cleveland. This Democratic rally took place in Chapel Hill, Marshall County, Tennessee. Looking Back at Tennessee Collection, Tennessee State Library and Archives.

ing process. Editors vied with one another for adjectives to describe the chaotic nature of the political activities, though the characterization of the Obion
County Convention as "wild and woolly and full of fleas" left no doubt as to
the rustic and presumably undesirable outcome of the nominations.[14]

In view of the apparent political agendas of the Alliance and Wheel, the
activities of women become even more interesting, especially since neither
organization defined the status of women. Nor was their position clarified
when one high-ranking official in the Tennessee Alliance ruled that they were
"both members and honorary members since they did not pay assessments
and dues." Many Wheels and sub-Alliances accepted women without question, but since they were not required to admit women, other local groups
stubbornly refused to accept them as members. Some prospective female
members even complained of "blackballing." If contemporary perceptions of
the extent of female membership were at all accurate, women were largely
excluded from the Wheel and Alliance in Tennessee. When the first State
Alliance meeting convened in Nashville in 1887, women accounted for approximately one-eighth of the membership of twenty thousand. In 1891,
political opponents, whose self-serving analysis perhaps overestimated the
number of unenfranchised members, asserted that women and boys too young
to vote made up one-fifth of the membership.[15]

The difficulty of determining the number of women members becomes
apparent from even a casual survey of membership reports. Some letters and
official correspondence made no mention of women, while others sporadi-
cally reported their presence. Within local unions that admitted women, the
degree of participation varied greatly. M. J. Manuel, a member of Wheel No.
127 from Maple Creek, Tennessee, wrote to the *Toiler* in 1888 to thank the
editor for establishing a "Ladies Column" and to encourage her sisters to fill
the space with "choice reading." In her letter, she divulged that the Maple
Creek Wheel was composed of "about sixty male and three female members,
[who] are all true wheelers and will never give up the struggle until victory
perches on our banners." Despite the low turnout of female members, Manuel
wrote enthusiastically: "I love to attend our meetings and think all our sisters ought to do so and encourage our husbands, brothers, fathers, and sweethearts all we can in the grand work." Women made up a much larger percentage of the membership in other local wheels and alliances. Wolf Creek
Alliance No. 404 in Cocke County reported twenty-seven male and ten female members, and Elridge Union No. 484 in Obion County included "30
'heroes' and 20 women members," while Lizzie Dodd claimed forty men and
an equal number of women in her union.[16]

Despite its commitment to "equal rights to all, special privileges to none," not all women found admission to the Wheel and Alliance an easy process, and the pages of the *Toiler* frequently carried letters voicing their complaints and concerns. Some women expressed their desires for membership, though a lifetime of inequality made them reluctant to be the first to step forward. Mrs. C. A. Mitchell of Cheatham County supported the idea of women in the Wheel and Alliance, yet she was not a member because "we have no lady members in Oak Lawn, and I am only waiting for others to join." Others decided to wait to apply for membership until the most prominent woman (often the wife of the local or county president) joined. Even that strategy did not always work, as a Weakley County woman complained: "Some of the best ladies of our community petitioned for membership, but were black-balled." A number of women thought they knew who stymied their entry into the order and pointed accusing fingers at the "old bachelors" and widowers in the local organizations. Women in Sullivan County named the culprit, the first president of the Stony Branch Alliance, "Uncle Jimmie," who openly stated that "he had been both a widower and a bachelor and he thought it best to have no lady members." While some women cried, "How Cruel Uncle Jimmie!" others supported a ban on female membership and wrote to the "Ladies Column" to present their arguments. One Sullivan County woman boasted she was "not a member of the Farmers and Laborers' Union—for this reason: I am a lady and argue in the order is not woman's proper place." On the opposite side of the state, a Lauderdale County "Wheeler's Wife" wrote that "the wheel is a good organization for men but [I] do not think it is for the ladies." She encouraged women to "stay at home and help their husband, father, or brother get ready to go to their meeting." She feared that Wheel activities drew men and women from more important religious du-ties, and that they would "turn out to their wheeler meetings at any time, rain or shine, [but] when it was prayer meeting at their church they would say it is too cold or too rainy or dark." Clearly, although Wheel and Alliance lead-ers welcomed women and encouraged their membership, many women found it difficult to gain admittance to the local unions. Perceptions of propriety, along with the public and political nature of the organizations, operated against their active participation. If women wanted a place, they would have to justify their inclusion in the order; soon a two-pronged argument presented by men and women emerged. First, they argued that women had a stake in the economic programs of the order both as farm wives and as petty produc-ers. Second, they entered into a wide-ranging debate on the proper sphere for women's activities.[17]

Women joined the Wheel and the Alliance because they agreed with the objectives of the two orders. "I shall ever be ready to perform any duty assigned me that is calculated to promote the cause of the laborer," promised Cora McLean in a welcoming address to the Carroll County Wheel. Her friend, Maggie Gwin, followed her to the podium and read an essay praising the faithfulness of women to the Wheel, describing woman as always "ready to help in a cause when there is so much at stake—the prosperity of her people and the liberty and freedom of her citizens." Individual letter writers displayed the same commitment to Wheel and Alliance principles. Describing herself as "a sister who loves the principles of our great and grand organization," Nancy Tarpley of Warren County urged women to join the Alliance "for we should all work together in love and harmony and help to down old monopoly [and] combined trusts." As a former Granger, Tarpley's dedication to Alliance programs displayed a zeal common to many *Toiler* correspondents. "Let us throw off our yoke of oppression," urged a Jefferson County woman, "and fight like men and women and work while 'tis called to-day." It was an enthusiasm born of experience, for women, no less than men, had a stake in the success of the Wheel and Alliance. As working partners they shared the toil, and as petty producers they encountered the risks associated with agricultural production.[18]

Traditionally, women's work was an extension of their domestic duties. The production of poultry, eggs, butter, jams, and jellies offered them the opportunity to make their own crucial cash contribution to the family farm without upsetting the gender roles dictated by tradition and society. Farm journals routinely offered advice from women for increasing the production of eggs, poultry stock, and dairy products. These commodities were invaluable items for barter exchange and cash transactions. Scarcely a single rural diary failed to mention the exchange of such items for soap, coffee, meat, and matches obtained at the local store. Women, in this way, made a critical contribution to the economic stability and profitability of the farm, especially in years of depressed farm prices. Robert Freeman, a Bedford County farmer, recounted a Saturday trip to Farmington, where he "had plow sharpened and one new shoe removed on Mule" for which he paid forty cents. He also purchased two yards of gingham, two backbands, tumblers, four collars, and a pair of boots for a total of $4.75. To pay for his purchases, he sold twelve dozen eggs, for which he received nine cents per dozen, and he charged the remaining $3.67. For many farm families the sale of cotton or tobacco paid the taxes and reduced the mortgage; the sale of butter and eggs bought family necessities without adding to the debt accumulating on the merchant's ledger books.[19]

To be productive, women required modest capital outlays, which returned equally modest profits. Mary Kirkpatrick Tinsley, who lived in Clay County, routinely purchased chicks for ten cents and later sold them to a local merchant for twenty-five cents each. But, as she never purchased more than four or five chicks at any one time, her poultry business remained small and tied to a local market. While Tinsley's diary is indicative of a person of limited means, an improved economic position did not appreciably change the productivity of women. The diary of a young West Tennessee woman portrayed a family with enough extra money to afford a "Busy Bee Washer" and a trip to a photographer. Nevertheless, her mother's poultry production seemed no more extensive than that of Mary Tinsley. In January and February, her father killed hogs and took the meat to Jackson to sell. On those two occasions, she and her mother dressed three and four turkeys for market.[20]

In such exchanges, women or their husband-agents appeared to be at the mercy of the local merchants. According to J. M. Cummings, a sub-Alliance lecturer from Robertson County, these store owners often acted as "middlemen" between producers and consumers, setting prices that were "unjust to the producer and perhaps extortionate to the consumer." To address this injustice he urged women "to organize with us to get the benefits of organization," and sell their products to consumers in the larger towns and cities of the state. To demonstrate the potential benefits of his proposal, he purchased butter and eggs from his neighbors at the local rate and sold their products in Nashville for a much higher price. On the basis of his experiment, he estimated that a producer cooperative established among the women in his area would generate an additional $5,450 per year through the sale of butter, eggs, and chickens. As he observed: "That much extra cash scattered around amoungst [*sic*] those sixty families in the course of a year, would make a mighty difference in their worldly condition." Cooperativism and economic reform were as vital to women as they were to men, according to Cummings. But, to gain those benefits, he concluded, "the ladies must join the Union."[21]

By the 1890s, poultry production had attracted the attention of men of greater financial means, with market visions extending far beyond the country store. As early as 1873, the *Rural Sun* championed poultry as an unappreciated moneymaker in the rural economy. Noting that poultry was "universally neglected and despised" by the farmer, who considered it "beneath the dignity of a grown man to look after such trash," the journal nevertheless encouraged men to provide wives and children "with all reasonable accommodations for taking care of the poultry." A modest investment of $40 in houses, feed, and stock of twenty hens and two cocks would produce an income of $84, with a clear profit of $44. The Agricultural Census of 1880 enumerated poultry and egg production for the first time. Although careful to recognize the statistical limitations of the reporting technique, the census bureau conservatively estimated the national annual value of egg production at $55 million, with an additional sale of 150 to 180 million pounds of meat. The growth of cities and the availability of rail transportation encouraged poultry production and initiated investments in improvements that eventually removed production from the domestic sphere to the realm of big business.[22]

In her recent study of rural women in Iowa, Deborah Fink found that midwestern men expressed no interest in poultry production until well into the twentieth century; the same cannot be said for Tennessee farmers. On May 2, 1890, the *Memphis Avalanche* noted, with approval, a meeting of "prominent poultry men" at the Farmers' Exchange. The purpose of the meeting was the organization of regional producers and the improvement of poultry stock. The election of Robert Gates, a prominent railroad advocate and Alliance opponent, as president of the organization served as a harbinger of market changes that increasingly impinged on female enterprise. This movement of men into an area traditionally reserved for women further threatened the domestic production of these petty producers and paralleled the situation faced by a large segment of Tennessee farmers.[23]

Tennessee farmers produced a variety of commodities, including wheat, corn, cotton, tobacco, peanuts, and livestock. While this diversity modestly cushioned the state against the worst problems of agricultural depression, it also placed farmers in the position of marginal, or petty producers, with regard to national markets, possibly making it more difficult for them to exert influence over market changes. Robert Cartmell of Madison County, an astute observer of agricultural problems and no friend of the Alliance, worried about Tennessee's decreasing share of cotton production. "Texas will soon make it all," he declared. "It is an empire of itself." Interestingly, Cartmell planned to diversify his own farming interests through poultry production. By 1890, he was busily engaged in the construction of poultry houses and the purchase of breeding stock.[24]

When women spoke of their contributions to farm life, they did not limit their activities to butter and eggs. Wherever they met resistance to their participation in local alliances, they asserted that their right to join the organization and their demands to participate as full voting members rested on recognition of their labors as agricultural partners with their husbands. Letters from women to the editor of the *Toiler* routinely recorded their work in the fields, as they claimed a share in the work of reform. As one woman wrote: "It would be better, methinks if the men would say, 'come join us in the fight against your enemy' with as bold a front as he says, 'come Betsy, help me hang the meat and drop the corn and potatoes. Or, while you are driving home the cows, just step over to the next meadow and salt the horses and let down the gap and drive the sheep through.'" The demands of farm life reduced the barriers that separated the work of men from that of women and roused the interest of agrarian women to the work of reform. Fannie Davis, a frequent contributor to the "Ladies Column," defiantly asserted the rights of Alliance women, reminding her readers that "we help to produce as well as to consume." Pressing her point further, she asked: "How many bales of cotton do you suppose the fair daughters of your honest farmers help to prepare for the manufacturers and speculators? Then allow us room among you." Boldly, women demanded the right to participate in a fight that affected their interests as fully as those of men.[25]

Some women claimed recognition as farmers, as they shouldered the responsibilities of farm management in the absence of husbands as the result of death or attention to other interests. On May 29, 1889, a woman from the Neely's Bend Wheel wrote to the editor of the *Toiler* to complain about the treatment of three women who applied for membership in the organization. Two of the women were "blackballed," while the third, a widow, was admitted. According to the complaint, at least one man revealed that the other two were denied admission solely because of their gender. Apparently, even where sub-Alliances proved reluctant to accept women into membership, they honored the claims of widows who farmed independently. Other women indicated a special interest in the problems of farming and demonstrated their knowledge of agriculture by offering advice on crops. Addie Grimes described the soil of Lawrence County as "heavy," noting that "it packs after each rain." She advised the incorporation of "an extended system of under drainage," and expressed hope that the local organization would "take steps to demonstrate the usefulness of an intelligent and industrious use of green crops as fertilizers and under drains to carry off the surplus water." Whether as producers of agricultural products, partners in the success of the family farm, or farmers themselves, women demonstrated their knowledge and interests in farming and asserted their rights to active membership in the organization.[26]

Women understood the problems of producing and marketing farm products from their long hours in the fields and barns, and the meager returns of their labors. And women, no less than men, felt the burdens of debt. Nannie Williams worried endlessly about the cost of maintaining her large family of ten children and stepchildren. The family's mounting debt, which she so aptly described as a "pursuing phantom," intruded on everyday life and special occasions, forcing frugality even at Christmas, when a degree of extravagance seemed more appropriate. No doubt some of Williams's concern arose from her own part in arranging for the credit that accounted for the largest portion of the family indebtedness. She negotiated the $1,300 note with her brother-in-law that her husband, Henry, signed. In an age when farmers seldom obtained credit through banking institutions, the social contacts and family ties of women were perhaps as important to the financial security of the farm as those of men. Therefore, the burdens of debt weighed heavily on women despite the fact that they had no legal standing as debtors. After years of living with her "white ghost," Williams described herself as "pinched and sour" and noted the aged and careworn disposition of her husband.[27]

To men and women of the nineteenth century mounting debt represented failure, and the efforts by families to maintain appearances while coping with the hopelessness of their situations raised insurmountable barriers to the development of community feelings. As one farmer poignantly observed: "In vain you preach reformation. I must needs do as my neighbors do, or it will be whispered round 'He is tight. He is broke. He can't pay his debts' and whenever such opinions as these are entertained in any neighborhood about any one of the neighbors that poor suspicioned neighbor begins to lose confidence in himself. His neighbors at first look coldly at him, then neglect and finally slight him. . . . Every man that he owes is ready to pounce upon him and seize and sell everything he has liable to seizure and sale." Under the circumstances men and women "made do" with what they had, hid behind assurance of future prosperity, and prayed desperately for one good year in which to pay the merchants, the taxes, and the mortgage.[28]

The desperation that accompanied years of falling farm prices became increasingly difficult to hide. Some families abandoned all hope of repaying debts and fled in the night to promises farther west. Others saw their lands sold to pay taxes and mortgages, while the majority just hung on from year to year. Part of the appeal of the Farmers' Alliance lay in its recognition of the loss of pride and dignity that years of economic hardship extracted from the farming community. Assurances of the dignity and necessity of their labors fell on the grateful ears of men and women long acquainted with the snubs of the more prosperous society of the nearby towns. The visits of farmers and their families on Saturdays and court days excited the curiosity of the young and the concerns of the adults in the towns that dotted the country-side. As Evelyn Scott reported in her reflections on Tennessee life, well-bred town children were forbidden to stray from the protection of the front yard when country people came to town. Scott risked parental displeasure to sat-isfy her curiosity about the farming families that crowded into Clarksville, and in doing so she left a moving description of the women who struggled to maintain a semblance of respectability in the face of poverty. The young girls wore muslin dresses "of the diluted raspberry color known in the south as 'nigger pink,'" according to Scott, while their mothers "wore the heart-breaking, cheap finery affected by country women visiting a town, costumes as shapeless as ruffled sofa cushions." Those infrequent visits to town must have filled women with excitement and pain as they "herded the children before them for bouts of window-shopping in which stoical hearts and va-cant imaginations were replenished (in the way of the poor!) with the mar-vel it was to see how prolifically objects were manufactured—how things existed to be bought by somebody!"[29]

Alliance leaders were acutely aware that the burdens of poverty and sub-sistence agriculture fell disproportionately on women. Bettie Gay, writing on women's activities in N. A. Dunning's *Farmers' Alliance History* (1891), as-serted that women were "the chief sufferers whenever poverty or misfortune overtakes the family." Twenty years later, the federal government's Commis-sion on Country Life reached similar conclusions, noting that "whatever general hardships, such as poverty, isolation, lack of labor-saving devices, may exist on any given farm, the burden of these hardships falls more heavily on the farmer's wife than on the farmer himself." In general, the report of the commission continued, "her life is more monotonous and the more isolated, no matter what the wealth or the poverty of the family may be."[30]

Farm families believed that they deserved a place among the respected and respectable producers of the national wealth, but they also realized the gap that separated them from the material benefits of industrial America. In her address before the Wilson County Alliance meeting in April 1890, Melia Wilburn called upon farmers to organize by asking, "Why is it that in the great middle class to which we belong as compared with twenty years ago we find ourselves so much lower down in the scale of real possessions?" Women boldly demanded admission to the Wheel and the Alliance because they, too, were producers, farmers, debtors, and sufferers of the injustices felt by the agricultural community.[31]

It was one thing to argue that women had a stake in the agricultural economy, but it proved to be quite another to grant them a voice in the public debate. Within a week after John H. McDowell, editor of *The Weekly Toiler*, established a "Ladies Column," protests began. In April 1889, Charles Thomas, who characterized himself as "an old bachelor," was one of those who wrote to protest the new column. "If all the Wheelers were like you," he complained, "the wheel would be crowded [with] women, and God knows what that will do." His criticism elicited a flurry of support, as well as letters from those who defended women's activities in the Wheel and Alliance.[32]

In the strongest language, women defended their right to full participation in Wheel and Alliance activities. Minnie Herrell of Anderson County sarcastically asserted that "if the union is such a disgraceful organization that ladies can't join they should disband and let monopoly rule." Biblical references to women as helpmeets and reminders that the value of a good woman exceeded that of rubies filled the column for weeks. A man from McLemoresville contended that a woman's "place is anywhere in God's universe that she can be instrumental in elevating and reforming any of God's creation." Furthermore, he argued that "her interest is our interest, and no one has more at stake in the upbuilding of the home than the wife and mother." Since, he added, "the Wheel in the beginning only aimed to elevate the conditions of home and to strengthen the moral atmosphere of society, it is woman's friend and women will stick with it with all the ardor of their nature." Women seemed to agree with this assessment of their role. Fannie Davis observed that "not only are the girls calculated to help do up the [farm] work, but they can cheer and assist society by their presence, for if love and peace does not dwell where ladies are, it's not to be found anywhere." Clearly, men and women envisioned a role for women that embraced the use of attributes traditionally ascribed to them.[33]

Yet the defense of home and the use of such traditional language did not obscure the recognition by rural women of the changes in their status. Hard economic times forced women into new situations, and changes in social attitudes afforded them new opportunities. No amount of isolation cushioned agrarian women against these changes. The daughters of Nannie Williams left home for employment in Nashville after receiving a modest education in local schools. Williams expressed concern for their futures, but she recognized the limited opportunities for marriage and advancement in the farming community, and accepted the fact that she lived in an "industrious age [where] no one is expected to sit and fold their hands." As she outlined a role for women that emphasized the traditional values of home and church, Lottie Love also recognized the changes that intruded on traditional views. "Public sentiment has changed wonderfully in the past twenty years and today you will find women in all the positions and avocations of life," she cheered. "Experience has taught woman that she must learn to be more independent and build the ladder by which she climbs. Give her a chance, don't curtail the circle of her influence and I venture she will be a 'helpmeet' indeed for the 'Lord's Creation.'" She concluded with a poem that aptly summarized the role accepted by women of the Tennessee Farmers' Alliance:

> For her sphere is bounded only
> By the talents God has given
> And her duty calls wherever
> Earth can be made more like heaven.[34]

Duty, harmony, and home were the words women used to characterize their sphere. These were traditional values, phrased in old-fashioned language, but embraced by women looking forward, not backward. These women were not at odds with change, but they were women who viewed their role as vital within the context of the Alliance aims. They demanded the same spirit of mutuality in the organization that defined their roles as working partners with their husbands.

In accordance with their perception of woman's sphere, women in the Wheel and Alliance accepted more public roles in which to exert their moral influence, but they did not attempt to supplant the dominant role of men. When a Kansas woman suggested that "if we women were running the government, as 'ignorant and weak and frivolous' as we are, we could manage to start things around a little faster than they are at the present," a Tennessee woman replied, "Let the men manage their affairs and we ours." Upheld as the moral center of the community and the family, women provided encouragement to overcome the fears attendant with Alliance membership, fostered commitment to the organization, and demanded fulfillment of duty. Both men and women believed their presence promoted harmony and unity among farmers of disparate needs and partisan loyalties. Women fulfilled their roles by attending rallies and meetings, accepting minor offices, and presenting essays to local and county unions.[35]

As Jean E. Friedman observed in her study of women and community, "complex ties of kinship" bound southern women to each other and to men, making "community less a village of proximate neighbors than an understanding of the heart among distant kinfolk and neighbors." Robert McMath drew a similar conclusion about the importance of community as the basis for Alliance organization. Both the Wheel and Alliance relied on the ties of church and family to build membership, with men and women referring to one another as brother and sister. Nor were these titles artificial constructs, since most members would have been able to say with Mattie Mahaffy: "I have a good portion of friends and relations who are members of the union." Awareness of the changes imposed by the influence of markets, growing towns, and more rapid transportation and communication tugged at the ragged edges of the southern sense of community, but the power of traditional ties should not be underestimated in an analysis of agrarian reform.[36]

Churches provided convenient and familiar meeting places, reinforced communal ties, and confirmed an ideology of cooperativism and agrarian life. Men and women called upon God to bless their efforts in speeches that allied agricultural reform with the will of the Almighty. Meetings opened with prayer, which, on occasion, was offered by a woman, as was the case at Little Doe Church in Johnson County, when Sister Sarah Lowe prayed for divine guidance. In essays and speeches women reminded farmers that "man's first duty is to God," while encouraging their listeners to "grasp each other by the hand and resolve by the help of God that our condition shall be bettered and the right of farmers and laborers shall be respected."[37]

The churches of the late nineteenth century also provided women with the skills and opportunities to serve in public roles. Historian Joe L. Kincheloe, Jr., argues that revivals and camp meetings in Tennessee in the earlier part of the century tacitly sanctioned more public roles for women. Praising and testifying were acceptable activities that provided opportunities for women to speak. Building on this observation, Jayne C. DeFiore explains the public activities of Tennessee women in the presidential elections of the 1840s by drawing parallels between the style and fervor of camp meetings and political rallies. Seizing a "window of opportunity," women moved into public and politically defined areas because they were temporarily sanctioned by their resemblance to religious activities. Within the churches of the 1890s, the roles of women further expanded as the Sunday school movement spread, and women flocked to support missionary efforts around the world. Tied to the existing religious supports of community, the activities of women in the Alliance were easily defined and more readily acceptable.[38]

Church-based communities in the rural South were not geographically compact, and most observers, then and now, recognized that the isolation of farm families presented a serious threat to the success of the Wheel and Alliance. Distance proved to be a debilitating factor in newly settled areas, while poor roads limited opportunities in every region. And, as already noted, the psychological isolation induced by debt often limited social contacts. To overcome this problem, the Wheel and Alliance encouraged picnics and excursions. These so-called jollifications brought together the best parts of camp meetings, political rallies, and dinners-on-the-ground to create a day of fun, camaraderie, and edification.

The Tullahoma Rally in the summer of 1889 brought together an estimated seven thousand people who arrived by horseback, wagon, and on foot, from Moore, Bedford, Franklin, and Coffee Counties. A special train, so packed with people "there wasn't hardly standing room," brought farmers and their families from Murfreesboro in neighboring Rutherford County. With banners snapping, the Alliance members marched from the train station in Tullahoma to the rally site in a mile-long parade, spirited along by the music of the Unionville Band, which rode in a forty-foot "carry-all" drawn by four mules. John McDowell reported that "the woods seemed to be literally swarming with men, women, and children," who spent the day playing, gossiping, discussing crops, and listening to speeches.[39]

Such was the enthusiasm for the Wheel and Alliance that attendance remained good at local meetings even in the winter. In February 1890, McDowell attended several county meetings and rallies in East Tennessee, where despite adverse weather conditions, farmers jammed the meeting rooms until "every foot of seating and standing room was densely packed." The editor of the *Toiler* was especially gratified to see "a host of beautiful women who had honored the occasion with their presence." When the speeches ended, McDowell reported that the Alliance women performed a familiar task and "spread out before us a bountiful supply of life's substantials and the inner man was truly refreshed." J. R. Miles, president of the State Wheel, was also excited by the turnout for the Weakley County meeting. Men and women from forty-six sub-Alliances braved swollen streams and muddy roads to attend the January assembly of farmers. Though not as poetic as McDowell, Miles was no less appreciative of the skills of women as he complimented their "baskets and boxes 'chuck full' of as good 'grub' as ever went into a union man's mouth." Women expressed a great deal of pride in their abilities to prepare the dinners that accompanied large meetings and rallies, and occasionally complimented one another for their efforts. A Marion County woman reported the activities of Sweden's Cove Union, which included a dinner under a grove of trees. Judging it "one of the best dinners I ever saw," she continued approvingly, "everyone ate until they were perfectly satisfied, and there was much of it left to be taken back home." The occasion made such an impression on the writer that she declared it "will be a bright spot in my memory for the rest of my life." Allowing for the overblown rhetoric of the age, the impression remained that these communal meals offered something more than filled stomachs. Sharing food with men and women of distant communities bound them together in a joint effort. The frequent references to abundance and excess must not have been ignored by people familiar with the biblical story of the loaves and fishes. These living examples of the benefits of cooperation sustained the Alliance efforts as readily as long-winded speeches.[40]

However, many rural and small town Tennesseans resisted the lure of the Wheel and Alliance, or actively opposed their efforts for reform. For example, the minutes of the Cocke County Alliance in East Tennessee outlined the efforts to establish a cooperative store—efforts that met strong resistance and eventually ended in failure. At their second county meeting in January 1889, the membership formed a committee to "make contact with some merchant or merchants to sell goods to the Farmers' Alliance." The merchants who were approached refused to make such arrangements, and in April, the Alliance resolved to "organize a capital stock for the purpose of establishing a store and warehouse at Newport." The organization finally negotiated an agreement with two merchants identified only as Boyd and Clevenger, who agreed to open an Alliance store. Enthusiastic reports followed until July 1890, when a committee was formed to negotiate with Valley Home and Fire Insurance Company to determine "why they had failed to pay the insurance to the Clevenger firm of Newport, Tenn." Thereafter, no mention was made of the store. It seems reasonable to assume that the firm met the fate of Alliance stores in other states and was burned by men who felt threatened by the organization of farmers.[41]

Women addressed this climate of concern and fear in their letters. Encouraging men to act in their own interests, they characterized reluctant farmers as "weak-kneed cotton-string backbone" fellows. In the same vein, they chided men who seemed to be waiting to join the Alliance until all danger had passed, comparing these men to the farmer in a current tall tale, who "ran upstairs while his wife killed the bear [and] after she had accomplished her work, came down with great love and sympathy, saying 'ain't we brave Betsy?'" These not-so-gentle jibes were accompanied by exhortations to duty. Maria Huffman thought it was "a duty obligatory upon us" to "help and encourage all we can." Cora McLean evoked the hallowed image of Robert E. Lee when she quoted from a letter in which Lee counseled his son that "duty is the most sublime word in our language." Duty called men to overcome their fears and accept the work of confronting their oppressors. Just as they had supported their husbands, brothers, and sons with encouragement and admonitions to duty during other difficult times, women shouldered the responsibility of strengthening the resolve of the unions.[42]

It was not enough to rouse men to action, they must also lay aside their personal and political differences in the name of harmony in order to achieve their objectives, and in the pursuit of this higher goal women believed they played a vital role. In Tennessee, the necessity for harmony and unity was especially acute in light of the strong partisan, cultural, and geographic divisions that separated the state into three distinct regions. Most Alliance men viewed partisan politics as the most serious threat to the organization. D. A. Vaughan of Bedford County warned against "the demon of party spirit," observing that "old party prejudices and ties are so strong that reason and even the general good are really lost sight of and trampled under foot." Wheel and Alliance leaders tried to entice the collaboration of partisans and promised that "the party that will purge itself of corruption and go before the country with [Wheel] principles and with the assurance of good faith, will receive the co-operation of every tiller of the soil." Wheel State president J. R. Miles bluntly repudiated his commitment to the Democratic Party, declaring: "I think the most difference between the Democrats and Republicans is a hustle to get there with both feet." Denunciations of partisan politics alone would not bring harmony to an organization that included the faithful of both parties. Agrarian leaders and "nonpolitical" women drew attention away from partisan differences and focused on "the cause of the oppressed against the money oligarchy." In 1890, as the Alliance fought for the election of men who supported the farmers' interests, letters emphasized the "grievous burdens" borne by farmers and directed the attack against the so-called courthouse rings that controlled the political life of the state. A Sullivan County woman's report on that county's convention to elect delegates to the Democratic gubernatorial convention hailed the farmers for their united stand against the "bosses and politicians." She believed it had been "a sad day for 'the bosses,' their sheep had strayed off into the alliance, gone through a training school and come out with their eyes wide open, as free men capable to think and act for themselves." In political matters, women encouraged farmers to act as a community in defense of their interests.[43]

Local disputes could be equally divisive. Obion County became embroiled in a bitter and quarrelsome dispute over the location of the county seat. When, after years of hostility between the opposing factions, the voters elected to designate Union City as the county seat, their adversaries claimed that the victors had voted "all of the living and most of those who had been in their graves since the close of the Civil War." Alliance leaders moved to limit the damage to the organization. After a "private discussion" with the State Lecturer, R. W. Tucker, the Obion County Alliance resolved not to "allow local matters to swerve us in questions of general importance."[44]

Sub-Alliances also faced problems of strife in the ranks. One man wrote to complain that "there are too many Solomans [sic] in the order, who if they can't work in the lead, they kick out of traces." The Cocke County Alliance hoped to nip just such dissension in the bud and received quarterly reports from a committee to evaluate the harmony of the sub-Alliances. Reports to the *Toiler* from local and county unions routinely reassured the readers that "harmony prevails in the union," while simultaneously reminding them that "brotherly love, charity, and a determination to stand together in defense of our rights is our only hope."[45]

Alliance members agreed that one way to reduce the tensions within local unions was to encourage the presence of women, who promoted harmony and unity, and facilitated the growth of the organization. Lillian Lee Hayes captured the general sentiment when she observed in a speech before her county Alliance that "woman has the tendency to elevate and refine. Man is made more moral, social, and refined by the influence of the true and noble woman." Lottie Love put these same lofty ideals into practical use when she suggested that a woman's attendance added to the harmony of the meetings, since "her presence, her smiles and counsel purifies the surroundings and helps on the good in which she is just as deeply interested as are the men." A man from Giles County agreed, noting that "their presence [has] a tendency to keep order and their counsel of wisdom certainly [can] be felt and realized." In view of the perils of internal divisions, the inclusion of women generated a spirit of harmony and demanded decorum in the presentation of conflicting opinions. Indeed, Bettie Gay went so far as to claim that the soothing and refining presence of women had the effect of controlling strong tempers and placed "a premium upon politeness and gentility." Without the presence of women in the organization, she declared, "it would be a failure."[46]

For women, the demand for their skills as peacemakers once again opened a window of opportunity to act within the public sphere, and, as Lizzie Dodd urged, the women of the Tennessee Farmers' Alliance "modestly yet boldly" entered the work of the order. Fully aware of the economic changes that affected their lives, they insisted on joining their husbands in the struggle against the trusts and monopolies that they believed offered the greatest threat to the future of middle class family farms. Equally aware of the social changes that provided new opportunities for women, they bravely asserted their rights to act within the Alliance, demanding admission, accepting local offices and speaking or writing on behalf of the organization. Finally, women recognized that internal divisions and external community perceptions threatened the unity and harmony of the Alliance. In their fulfillment of traditional gender roles, women served a vital function and acted as a symbol of Alliance ideals. Alliance women reconciled the old and the new: while accepting traditional roles assigned to the woman's sphere, they worked with their husbands in a spirit of mutuality, both on the farm and in the organization, and asserted their right to participate in the reforms that affected their interests. In short, they were up and doing in their modest, yet bold, way.

NOTES

1. The poem is quoted without citation to the author in a welcome address given by Lillian Lee Hayes and reprinted in *The Weekly Toiler,* July 31, 1889. Lizzie J. Dodd to *The Weekly Toiler,* May 28, 1890.
2. Julie Roy Jeffrey, "Women in the Southern Farmers' Alliance: A Reconsideration of the Role and Status of Women in the Late Nineteenth-Century South," *Feminist Studies* 3 (Fall 1975): 75. The activities of rural women in agricultural reform organizations has become the focus of recent scholarly investigation. The extent to which women were drawn into political activism and their subsequent demands for equality and suffrage are special areas of interest. In their studies of the Southern Alliance, Jeffrey and Robert C. McMath, Jr. (*Populist Vanguard: A History of the Southern Farmers' Alliance* [Chapel Hill, N.C., 1975], chap. 5), depict southern Alliance women as conservative in their views and hesitant to enter the public sphere. While southern women apparently did not play as broad a role in Alliance affairs as women from other regions, they did expand their activities beyond the traditional roles that southern womanhood allowed. Women from prairie states produced the most vocal and notorious Alliance women. While women in these states played a more expansive role in public and political affairs, historian MaryJo Wagner concludes that "joining the Alliance and supporting the Populist Party did not involve a change in ideology concerning women's roles" in defense of farm and family. See MaryJo Wagner, "Farms, Families, and Reform: Women in the Farmers' Alliance and Populist Party" (Ph.D. diss., Univ. of Oregon, 1986). Studies of the far western states reveal a similar pattern of utilizing gender-specific roles to further political ends. Marilyn P. Watkins suggests that the maintenance of community ties, a traditional female role, was vital to agrarian reform movements while it furthered women's political awareness and demands. See Marilyn P. Watkins, "Political Activism and Community-Building Among Alliance and Grange Women in Western Washington, 1892–1925," *Agriculture History* 67 (Spring 1993): 197–213. Alliance activities broadened the political outlook of rural women, but the degree to which they could, or did, avail themselves of the opportunity for expanded roles and further demands for equality and suffrage appears to have been dependent upon local and regional expectations and definitions of the proper sphere for women.
3. "A Wheeler's Wife," to *The Weekly Toiler,* Dec. 26, 1888.

4. Recent publications focusing on the Grange include Donald B. Marti, *Women of the Grange: Mutuality and Sisterhood in Rural America, 1866–1920* (New York, 1991) and Thomas A. Woods, *Knights of the Plow: Oliver H. Kelley and the Origins of the Grange in Republican Ideology* (Ames, Iowa, 1991). An older, but still useful, work is Solon Buck, *The Granger Movement* (Cambridge, Mass., 1913). Several contemporary studies of Tennessee agriculture and development provide information about the organization of farmers into clubs, fair associations, farmers' conventions and granges. See J. B. Killebrew, *Introduction to the Resources of Tennessee: First and Second Reports of the Bureau of Agriculture for the State of Tennessee* (Spartanburg, S.C., 1974, originally published Nashville, 1874); and T. F. P. Allison, Commissioner, *Biennial Report of the Bureau of Agriculture, 1893–1894* (Nashville, 1895), 55–64.

5. "Declaration of Principles as Set Forth by the National Grange at Its Seventh Annual Meeting," a pamphlet found in "Minutes of the Wilson Grange, Clarksville, Tennessee, 1873–1876," Manuscripts Division, Tennessee State Library and Archives, Nashville. Hereafter cited as TSLA.

6. Marti, 1; "Minutes of the Wilson Grange," Manuscripts Division, TSLA.

7. Essay, "Woman's Sphere," presented by Fanny Montague to the Wayne County Grange at Shady Grove Grange, Jan. 25, 1877, and printed in *Rural Sun,* Feb. 15, 1877, Special Collections, Univ. of Tennessee Libraries, Knoxville.

8. Hester Holcombe to *Rural Sun,* June 12, 1873.

9. Roger L. Hart, *Redeemers, Bourbons & Populists: Tennessee 1870–1896* (Baton Rouge, 1975), 111.

10. Archelaus M. Hughes, Diary, Jan. 27, Aug. 27, and Sept. 5, 1875, Manuscripts Division, TSLA.

11. W. Scott Morgan, *History of the Wheel and Alliance, and the Impending Revolution* (Hardy, Ark., 1889), 65–69; *Weekly Toiler,* Dec. 4, 1889.

12. Morgan, *History of the Wheel and Alliance,* 284–95; *Weekly Toiler,* Dec. 4, 1889; Dec. 23, 1891.

13. Morgan, *History of the Wheel and Alliance,* 92–94; *Weekly Toiler,* July 25, 1888.

14. *Memphis Appeal,* July 8, 1890; (Nashville) *Daily American,* July 2, 1890.

15. *Weekly Toiler,* Apr. 2, 1890. The editor explained that women could "get all the secret work and are initiated like male members. They can hold office, but do not vote unless the subordinate lodge, in making its by-laws, grants them that privilege. Ladies [cannot] be fined for non-attendance unless they accept an office, if the by-laws made by the sub union impose a fine for non-attendance." Statistics for the first State Alliance Meeting come from Hart, *Redeemers,* 122; M. V. Ingram to Edward Carmack, May 11, 1891, Edward Ward Carmack Papers, Box 5, Folder 12, Manuscripts Division, TSLA.

16. M. J. Manuel to *The Weekly Toiler,* Oct. 31, 1888; "Cocke County Farmers' Alliance Proceedings, 1889–1891," Apr. 20, 1889, McClung Collection, Lawson-McGee Library, Knoxville; *Weekly Toiler,* Jan. 8 and May 28, 1890.

17. Mrs. C. A. Mitchell to *The Weekly Toiler,* Oct. 17, 1888; "L.E.R." to *The Weekly Toiler,* Apr. 16, 1890; "Phoeba" to *The Weekly Toiler,* Mar. 19, 1890; anonymous to *The Weekly Toiler,* July 23, 1890; "Wheeler's Wife" to *The Weekly Toiler,* Jan. 23, 1889.

18. "Welcoming Address" presented to the Carroll County Wheel by Miss Cora McLean, Oct. 1889, printed in *The Weekly Toiler,* Dec. 4, 1889; essay read to the Carroll County Wheel by Miss Maggie Gwin, Oct. 1889, printed in *The Weekly Toiler,* Dec. 4, 1889; Nancy Tarpley to *The Weekly Toiler,* May 14, 1890.

19. Robert Freeman, Diary, 1885–1886, Apr. 18, 1885, Manuscripts Division, TSLA.

20. Mary Kirkpatrick Tinsley, Diary, 1891–1894, Manuscripts Division, TSLA; Mrs. Frank Robbins, Diary, 1897–1898, Manuscripts Division, TSLA.

21. J. M. Cummings to *The Weekly Toiler,* Apr. 30, 1890. The "extra cash" Cummings promised amounted to approximately $91 per year per family, or a weekly family income of $1.75. Although it appears to be a trifling increase, its value becomes apparent with the realization that the average value of farm production in Tennessee in 1890 was a mere $316. Lawrence Goodwyn argues in *Democratic Promise: The Populist Movement in America* (New York, 1976) that cooperativism was the driving force in the Alliance and Populist organizations. Where it flourished, the Alliance was strong.

22. "Poultry Yard," *Rural Sun,* Aug. 28, 1873; *Tenth Census of the United States,* 1880, Part 5, *Agriculture,* xxi.

23. Deborah Fink, *Open Country, Iowa: Rural Women, Tradition and Change* (Albany, N.Y., 1986), 57–62; *Memphis Avalanche,* May 2, 1890.

24. Robert Cartmell, Diary, Mar. 8, 1891, Manuscripts Division, TSLA. Under the leadership of the Wheel and Alliance, farmers organized associations among peanut and tobacco farmers to sell their agricultural products as a group. Plans were being discussed to sell the state's wheat crop directly to cotton farmers in Georgia and Alabama. The Farmers' Alliance in Meigs County petitioned Governor Robert L. Taylor to prohibit "the importation of dressed beef," since the "cattle growers of our state cannot compete with the cattle kings of the West." *Weekly Toiler,* Jan. 8, 1890. During the 1890s, two reports dealing with the agricultural depression were issued by Congress: *"Agricultural Depression: Causes and Remedies" a Report by Mr. Peffer Submitted to the Senate Committee on Agriculture and Forestry,* Feb. 15, 1894, Senate 3d Session, 53d Congress, 1894–95, Serial 3288. *"Report of the Committee on Agriculture and Forestry on Condition of Cotton Growers in the United States, The Present Prices of Cotton and the Remedy: and on Cotton Consumption and Production,"* Feb. 23, 1895, vol. 1, Senate, 53d Congress, 3d Session 1895, Serial 3290, Part 1. Recent scholarship into the problem of agricultural depression and the farmers' response to market changes include Anne Mayhew, "A Reappraisal of the Causes of Farm Protest in the United States 1870–1900," *Journal of Economic History* 61 (June 1972): 464–75; Steven Hahn, *The Roots of Southern Populism: Yeoman Farmers and the Transformation of the Georgia Upcountry, 1850–1890* (New York, 1983); and Gavin Wright, *Old South, New South: Revolutions in the Southern Economy Since the Civil War* (New York, 1986).

25. *Weekly Toiler,* Mar. 27, 1889; Fanny Davis to *The Weekly Toiler,* July 24, 1889. Nancy Grey Osterud observes in her study of rural women that "socially and culturally, women were defined in direct relation to men rather than in terms of their differences from men." This created the problem of a lack of female autonomy, but it also gave women the opportunity "to redefine the terms of those interactions." See

Osterud, "She Helped Me Hay It as Good as a Man," in Carol Groneman and Mary Beth Norton, eds., *"To Toil the Livelong Day": America's Women at Work, 1780–1980* (Ithaca, N.Y., 1987): 92.

26. Addie Grimes to *The Weekly Toiler,* Mar. 19, 1890; anonymous to *The Weekly Toiler,* May 29, 1889. Considerable attention has been given to women who shouldered the burdens of farm management in the absence of husbands as the result of death or attention to other interests. Women earned the respect of southern men for their devotion to duty during the Civil War. For more complete treatment of these aspects of women in agriculture, see Anne Firor Scott, *The Southern Lady: From Pedestal to Politics, 1830–1930* (Chicago, 1970). Of particular interest is chapter 5, "Door after Door Is Being Flung Open." Also of interest is George C. Rable, *Civil Wars: Women and the Crisis of Southern Nationalism* (Chicago, 1989). The Papers of Mary Elizabeth Stay Buckner contain an interesting account from the Civil War, in which Union officers blame southern women and their efforts on the home front for prolonging the war. See Mary Elizabeth Stay Buckner Papers, Microfilm, Reel 2, Box 7, folder 6, TSLA.

27. Nannie Haskins Williams, Diary, Nov. 8, 1888; Jan. 14 and Mar. 1, 1889, in the Southern Historical Collection, Univ. of North Carolina, Chapel Hill.

28. Archelaus M. Hughes, Diary, 27 Aug. 1875. Years after Hughes's observation, the editor of the *Toiler* came to a similar conclusion when he noted: "People strive to keep up appearances or what is termed respectability and maintain position in society, and for lack of money will mortgage property for extravagant living and speculations. Farmers do this on wild calculations of the next crop to bring them out, and realize at the end of the year that the crop must go at the creditor's own price, and not enough left to pay the ruinous interest account." *Weekly Toiler,* June 25, 1888.

29. Evelyn Scott, *Background in Tennessee* (Knoxville, facsimile of 1937 edition, 1980), 216–17.

30. N. A. Dunning, *The Farmers' Alliance History and Agricultural Digest* (Washington, 1891), 309. *Report of the Commission on Country Life* (New York, rpt. of 1911 edition, 1975), 104. The commission held hearings in Knoxville in November 1910, and presumably, some of its insights are a reflection of the lives of Tennessee women. Certainly, men and women of the late nineteenth century were aware of the burdens shouldered by rural women. Archelaus M. Hughes wrote movingly of the sacrifices made by his family in the face of mounting debt and poverty. Nannie Williams complained of the burdens associated with providing for such a large family of children and stepchildren. Even entertaining friends and neighbors exacted a toll on her time and means until she confided to her diary, "my soul rebels."

31. Alliance Meeting, Apr. 3, 1890, at Barton's Creek, Wilson County, reported in *The Weekly Toiler.* Recent scholarly work on the economic status of the members of the Farmers' Alliance has focused on the role of middle-class farmers in the organization, concluding that they played a significant role in providing leadership and shaping the political and economic demands. For examples of this scholarship, see Hart, *Redeemers,* 126–28. Edward L. Ayers, *The Promise of the New South: Life After Reconstruction* (New York, 1992), chap. 9, "Alliances." Jeffrey Ostler, *Prairie Populism: The Fate of Agrarian Radicalism in Kansas, Nebraska, and Iowa, 1880–1892* (Lawrence, Kans., 1993).

32. Charles Thomas to *The Weekly Toiler,* Apr. 24, 1889.
33. Minnie Herrell to *The Weekly Toiler,* Apr. 9, 1890; "Mama's Boy" to *The Weekly Toiler,* July 10, 1889; Fannie Davis to *The Weekly Toiler,* July 24, 1889.
34. Nannie Haskins Williams, Diary, Sept. 15, 1888; Lottie Love to *The Weekly Toiler,* Oct. 24, 1888.
35. Mrs. Florence Olmstead, Douglas, Kansas, to *The Weekly Toiler,* Feb. 5, 1890; "A.E.E.," Montgomery County, to *The Weekly Toiler,* Apr. 23, 1890.
36. Jean E. Friedman, *The Enclosed Garden: Women and Community in the Evangelical South, 1830–1900* (Chapel Hill, N.C., 1985), 3; McMath, *Populist Vanguard,* chap. 5; Hart, *Redeemers,* 113–23; Mattie Mahaffy to *The Weekly Toiler,* Apr. 30, 1890.
37. *Weekly Toiler,* Dec. 4, 1889; Feb. 5, 1890.
38. Joe L. Kincheloe, Jr., "Transcending Role Restrictions: Women at Camp Meetings and Political Rallies," *Tennessee Historical Quarterly* 40 (Summer 1981): 158–69; Jayne Crumpler DeFiore, "'Come, and Bring the Ladies': Tennessee Women and the Politics of Opportunity During the Presidential Campaigns of 1840 and 1844," *Tennessee Historical Quarterly* 51 (Winter 1992): 197–212; (Nashville) *Baptist and Reflector,* Oct. 30, 1890.
39. *Weekly Toiler,* Aug. 28, 1889.
40. *Weekly Toiler,* Feb. 5 and Mar. 19, 1890; "L" to *The Weekly Toiler,* Apr. 23, 1890.
41. Cocke County Farmers' Alliance Proceedings, 1889–1891," Jan. 1889, Apr. 1890, July 1890.
42. *Weekly Toiler,* Mar. 19, 1890; Nancy Tarpley to *The Weekly Toiler,* May 4, 1890; Cora McLean to *The Weekly Toiler,* Mar. 5, 1890; "Welcoming Address," *Weekly Toiler,* Dec. 4, 1889.
43. D. A. Vaughan to *The Weekly Toiler,* June 27, 1890; quote from *Tennessee State Wheel,* cited in Morgan, *History of the Wheel and Alliance,* 225, 254; M. J. Manuel to *The Weekly Toiler,* Oct. 31, 1888; anonymous to *The Weekly Toiler,* June 23, 1890.
44. Betty B. Wood and Rebel C. Forrester, eds. *"I Had a Real Good Time," The Making of a Country Editor: The Recollections of James M. Brice of the News-Banner* (Union City, Tenn., 1984), 151; *Weekly Toiler,* Apr. 23, 1890.
45. *Weekly Toiler,* Feb. 26, 1890; "Reports of the Committee on the Good of the Order," Apr. 30, 1889, July 12, 1889, Apr. 2, 1890, Oct. 9, 1891, in "Cocke County Farmers' Alliance Proceedings."
46. *Weekly Toiler,* July 31, 1889; Lottie Love to *The Weekly Toiler,* Oct. 24, 1888; "Wheeler" to *The Weekly Toiler,* June 26, 1889; N. A. Dunning, *Farmers' Alliance History,* 310.

"The Holy Spirit Come to Us and Forbid the Negro Taking a Second Place": Richard H. Boyd and Black Religious Activism in Nashville

■ Paul Harvey

■

■ *Editor's Note:* Harvey chronicles Richard H. Boyd and Henry
Allen Boyd of Nashville, a remarkable father and son combination
■ that influenced the course of African American religion, publishing, commerce, and protest in the capital city from the late 1890s
■ to the 1950s. The Boyds believed that "this long night" of segregation "would turn into a new morning of freedom, if one kept
■ the faith." They used various strategies to "keep the faith," from
organizing streetcar strikes in the early 1900s, opening the Na-
■ tional Negro Doll Company as well as a black-owned and -oper-
ated bank, and establishing the National Baptist Publishing
■ Board, which became the nation's largest black-owned publishing
house.

■
The Holy Spirit come to us and forbid the Negro taking a second
■ place.
—Richard H. Boyd, 1894

■
There is not so bright or glorious a future before a Negro in a
■ white institution as there is for him in his own. . . . A people who
man no enterprises show that they can have no spirit of progress
■ . . . and a people without this cannot command the recognition
of nations and the respect of the world.
■ —Emmanuel K. Love, 1953

Richard Henry Boyd was an unsung hero of Tennessee's urban black
middle class during the difficult years from 1890 to 1920. Born a slave in Mis-

sissippi and educated at Bishop College in Marshall, Texas, Boyd moved to Nashville around 1895. This was the year of Booker T. Washington's Atlanta Exposition Address, which advised blacks to "cast down their buckets" where they were, and also a year that witnessed over two hundred lynchings of black men and women. He died just after the close of World War I and the violence of the "Red Summer" of 1919. Boyd turned a Nashville-based venture in distributing Sunday school literature to black churches into an enterprise that became the largest black-owned publishing house in the nation. Boyd's National Baptist Publishing Board (founded in 1896) well fit the model exemplified by Booker T. Washington for using the resources of the insular black community, as well as outside white assistance, to build up a thriving business. At the same time, Boyd openly and publicly fought the imposition of Jim Crow, helping to organize a black boycott of streetcars and publishing (together with his son) a newspaper that took an outspoken position on public issues.

Late in his life, a rancorous dispute within his religious body, the National Baptist Convention (NBC), set the stage for how he is remembered today— as one party in a dispute that split the chronically divided black Baptist churches. But Boyd's entire career, not just this one episode, demands close attention. The complicated position of members of the African American middle class made their choices a fine balancing act between acknowledging the realities of white supremacy while also testing its limits and puncturing holes in the racial mythologies that undergirded the order. As a black Tennessean who performed this balancing act adeptly, Richard H. Boyd merits more consideration than he has received by historians of black life in the Jim Crow South.

During Reconstruction, prominent black ministers in the South fostered the creation of a whole new set of African American religious institutions and channeled electoral excitement into real political gains. Organizers of the Consolidated American Baptist Missionary Convention (CABMC), formed in 1866 as an early attempt to provide a central forum for black Baptist churches, expressed the possibility and necessity of black independence in the religious realm: "Brethren, we are watched. We are not accepted as a body or denomination qualified to manage our own missionary and educational work, and many of those who most discredit our capacity . . . have set themselves up as our benefactors, and call upon our friends to aid us through them. But our very organization is our proclamation to the world that we are able to do this work, and that we *ought* to do it."[1]

Black Baptists sought financial aid from whites, as their organizations could expect only small offerings from their impoverished congregations. But denominational leaders soon learned that this assistance came with many strings attached and usually with few African Americans involved in the actual distribution and control of the funds. The American Baptist Home Mission Society, the largest Baptist agency involved in work among freedpeople, increasingly fell under this accusation in the 1870s and 1880s.[2] Contacts between Home Mission Society leaders and officials of the white Southern Baptist Convention heightened the suspicions many black Baptists held toward their northern benefactors. "By thus co-operating with good men in this work," a white southern Baptist suggested about northern missionaries deemed to be "safe," white southerners could "neutralize the effect of ultraists who may come from the North to preach to the colored people."[3]

Increasingly suspicious black Baptists moved in the direction of separatism. In Tennessee, controversies over the actions of white administrators at Roger Williams College in Nashville alienated the black students of the northern-supported college from their benefactors.[4] Attacks on black Baptists traveling on trains to national meetings graphically demonstrated the reality of racism even to members of the respectable middle class.[5] By the 1890s, with the adoption of segregation and disfranchisement laws, African American Christians understood more clearly than ever that a strong national religious organization was necessary if black Baptists were to be heard. But the loose connection of independently established and administered Baptist congregations made such a dream difficult to achieve.[6]

Richard Henry Boyd emerged from this particular black social and denominational context. Coming of age as a lawyer in the 1880s, just at the time when political options for ambitious black men were being shut down, Boyd participated in the internal denominational debates between groups that historians have labeled (somewhat misleadingly) the "separationists" and the "cooperationists." The black Texans of the 1880s and early 1890s (including Richard H. Boyd) debated the issues of integrationism and separatism, as well as the proper response of African American religious leaders to racial oppression. In Texas and many other states, this debate eventually swung to the side of the separatists. In Texas in 1893, a group of black Baptists led by Sutton Griggs (soon to be a well-known minister and novelist in Memphis) and Richard Boyd founded a separate state convention avowedly in support of race enterprises. They justified their move with language that even the cooperationists could appreciate: "The Holy Spirit come to us and forbid the Negro taking a second place," they explained. Boyd and Griggs emphasized the ways in which white money and power, channeled through the American Baptist Home Mission Society, worked to hinder the development of black institutions and "black manhood": "We believe in letting all our Baptist schools live. . . . [Whites] simply say let your field grow up in weeds and work my land for fifty years. Let your wife and children do without the home for fifty years, and work for me; but they forget when the fifty years are out the Negro is just where he was when he started. Not one whit higher, cornered and unprotected."[7]

Their experience with the controversies in Texas convinced Boyd and his allies of the need for a viable national organization of black Baptists. They knew also that the ideological stance of black independence and separatism faltered at local levels, where poorly paid ministers and impoverished congregants of small churches lived in the shadow of white dominance. Somehow, separatism as an ideology had to be combined with cooperation as a practice. Neither would work without the other. Richard Boyd searched for a practical strategy to utilize white resources in building up a black enterprise.

In the early 1890s, the gathering currents of black separatism came to a head, resulting in the formation of the National Baptist Convention in 1895.[8] By 1906, the Baptist faith was more firmly entrenched then ever among African Americans. Baptists now numbered 60 percent of black churchgoers, or about 2.25 million communicants (most in churches affiliated with the National Baptist Convention). By 1916, nearly 3 million were in the fold. In fact, the National Baptist Convention claimed more communicants than the white Southern Baptist Convention (which itself totaled some 2.7 million members by 1916 and was the largest white denomination in the South). The black denomination was the third-largest religious organization in the country.[9]

After its formation, organizers of the National Baptist Convention debated the wisdom of setting up an independent publishing agency. The proposal had met much opposition since its first airing in the early 1890s. Opponents stressed the historic attachment of black Baptists to the American Baptist Publication Society, which was based in Philadelphia. Since the Civil War, the Society had placed inexpensively produced materials in the hands of black churches (often giving them away) and hired black agents to sell its publications. The society had been instrumental in aiding literacy efforts during Reconstruction. If the new black agency collapsed, opponents warned, this would prove to whites the inability of blacks to conduct their own affairs.[10] Opponents of the board (who were concentrated in the southeastern states, especially Virginia and North Carolina, where cooperation with the American Baptist Publication Society was historically the strongest) defeated a proposal to establish a publishing board within the constitution of the new National Baptist Convention itself. "It was hoped by the more learned," a black Baptist historian later explained of the opposition, "that the idea of printing was stamped out. The reason for this was said to be that all, or nearly all, who fought the idea were employees of the Northern Societies which were then furnishing literature for the Sunday schools of our churches and these workers felt that such steps would be construed as enmity against our white brethren and friends who had given so much, and endured so much for us."[11]

Proponents of a separate publishing firm for black Baptists often hailed from such southern states as Texas, Tennessee, and Arkansas, states that were hotbeds of denominational separatism among both white and black Baptists. Backers of the black publishing house pointed out that such an agency would symbolize black resistance to the growing tide of white supremacist rhetoric. The sentiments of "racial development" popular in the era also played a major role in the debate. As one advocate pointed out, "All races have a literature." He suggested that separate black publishing efforts could help Negro Americans resist "absorption" into the white mainstream, and also provide the practical benefits of employment, literacy, and a forum for black scholars and theologians who could not find publishing opportunities elsewhere.[12]

Sensing the ideological shift to separatism and the estrangement of many southern black Baptists even from their northern white friends, Boyd pushed hard for the publishing firm. The way was cleared, in part, by a controversy in the early 1890s. The American Baptist Publication Society in 1890 offended black religious leaders by withdrawing its offer to publish a series of articles by black Baptist authors. The offer was withdrawn because of objections from white southern Baptists, who feared that their children would be exposed to "incendiary" essays authored by blacks. Benjamin Griffith, head of the northern publishing society, tried to appease the situation by offering the black authors an alternative outlet, but the damage was done.[13]

Capitalizing on this affront to Negro Baptists, Richard Boyd used the force of his own personality and his oratorical skills as a "witty and resourceful debater." He impressed his fellow Baptists by foreseeing "possibilities which even the most far-visioned of his brethren failed to see at first."[14] His budding interest in the publishing business was contingent on black patronage, which in turn depended on wooing black urban congregations away from dependence on material from white northern presses. He persuaded many of the most prominent ministers (such as Emmanuel K. Love, pastor of Savannah's huge First African Baptist Church congregation) to join him in supporting a black Baptist publishing house.

In 1896, after the formation of the National Baptist Convention, a committee of the convention formed a publishing board that was to be under the auspices of the Home Mission Board of the National Baptist Convention. Richard Boyd was named the secretary-treasurer of both, ensuring his dominance in running the boards. Boyd secured a charter for his publishing agency, placing it under the control of the self-perpetuating board of nine men (effectively shielding it from denominational dictates). He placed his enterprise in Nashville, which had historically proven itself a prime location for publishing endeavors.[15] Located at 523 Second Avenue North at Locust Street, the main building of the publishing board was purchased for $10,000. After paying the debt down to $2,400, Boyd was later ordered by the convention to finish paying the debt. Three years later, however, it had increased to $5,000. It was discovered that Boyd's family had taken out personal mortgages on property that, so believed officials of the National Baptist Convention, belonged collectively to the convention. From its creation, Boyd viewed the publishing board as a personal enterprise, while other leaders of the National Baptist Convention conceived of the firm as a convention-controlled publishing house.[16]

The publishing houses for both the Southern Baptist Convention (white) and the National Baptist Convention (black) operated from Nashville. The railroads leading out of Nashville made it an ideal location to reach a wide and diverse market, and into regions (such as Mississippi and Texas) that were rapidly growing and expanding. The region itself was a stronghold of the Baptist faith among both whites and blacks. Boyd's tact and obvious personal skills secured the aid of James M. Frost, secretary of the Sunday School Board of the Southern Baptist Convention (established in 1891). Together the two men introduced successful business enterprises into their respective denominations, meeting the opposition to their efforts with rhetoric that stressed the necessity of the "development" and "uplifting" of their people. With buildings just a few blocks apart in the bustling downtown area of Nashville, and with a successful working relationship between the two religious entrepreneurs, the city dubbed the "Athens of the South" served Richard Boyd's purposes ideally.[17]

The alliance between the heads of the two agencies exemplified to many Baptist leaders of both races the way in which white and black southern Baptists could cooperate on specific projects even while following the rules of segregation. Frost offered funds, technical advice, printing presses, and literature to Boyd's publishing firm. At the beginning of this relationship, according to Boyd's account, some of his black Baptist associates assumed that the white board would subsume the black publishing agency. But Frost never dictated "what to preach or where to preach," and helpfully aided black Baptist endeavors. Boyd found a way to pursue his own sense of an attractive business venture, provide an example of a successful "race enterprise," supply pious material that aided the "uplift" of his people, and employ the resources of conservative southern whites in getting the venture off the ground.[18] As Boyd suggested in 1899, while other white Baptist bodies thought that "Negro Baptists have no rights that should be respected by them," white southern Baptists, dealt "on principles of equality and manhood" with independent black brethren.[19] He suggested that white northern Baptists should learn this lesson as well:

> The National Baptist Convention has a right to own and control its own business enterprises, to maintain, on a larger scale, distinctive educational institutions, and in the exercise of this priestly prerogative, no band of white brethren anywhere should undertake to embarrass or molest them. With the recognition of these rights and corresponding brotherly treatment, our white brethren will find in the constituency of the National Baptist Convention *ardent friends* and *loyal supporters.*[20]

For its part, the Southern Baptist Convention expressed itself "gratified" that black Baptists were producing publications "which do credit to their religious enterprise, intelligence, and their literary taste."[21]

The appeal to "race pride" prevalent among black Baptist spokesmen such as Richard Boyd, while rooted in decades of black nationalism, assumed new shades of meaning from the conceptions of "racial development" characteristic of Progressive-era thought.[22] Black Baptists joined with white cultural elites in envisioning the "mission" of races in the development of American culture. W. E. B. Du Bois, who attended Fisk University and wrote memorable essays about educating poor black youngsters in the Tennessee countryside, may have described the "problem of the twentieth century" as the "problem of the color-line," yet he also rhapsodized about the special "gifts" of the darker races. Negro music, dance, and humor, he suggested, could enliven an American culture obsessed with "dollars and smartness."[23] Black Baptists more often emphasized the way in which African Americans could achieve success in America as defined by whites—success through individual competition. Collective racial self-help would come through individual successes, while racial solidarity would enhance the black individual's success— or so ran the logic common among black Victorians.[24]

Boyd promoted the National Baptist Publishing Board as a thriving race enterprise, and at the same time as an important instrument of black cultural expression. White religious literature, he pointed out, often reinforced racist stereotypes, even when racial "moderates" sponsored it. When portrayals of heaven in white northern Baptist publications, for example, depicted angelic white figures, while black figures representing demons guarded the gates to hell, children would naturally assume "that the latter belong to an inferior creation." Only a black publishing house, Boyd insisted, could prevent such pandering to (or unintentional reinforcement of) racism in the nation's denominational publishing houses. White publishing houses controlled their own large markets, Boyd added, making their "invasion" of the Negro churches unjustified.[25]

Boyd advocated black Baptist independence both as an ideological stance and as a business opportunity. In January 1897, he released his first series of Sunday school lessons, authored by others but set in type by Boyd's presses. Again with assistance from James Frost, Boyd sold his publications to churches throughout the country and soon established a sizable market. By 1910, the board's presses pumped out over eleven million pieces of literature each year, and employed over 150 black workers. By 1915, the board could report that $158,298.33 had passed through the secretary's hands during the fiscal year, while over $2.5 million was handled during his incumbency. Boyd plowed back into the enterprise the agency's growing yearly profits. It soon supplied numerous churches with pews, benches, hymnbooks, pulpits, choir robes, and children's dolls.[26] Boyd's agency served as a base from which Boyd built other business ventures. More than any other factor, his enterprise held together the diffuse and loosely organized National Baptist Convention. His position of financial power and influence induced jealousy of Boyd among other convention leaders.[27]

With his personal track record of success, Boyd was loath to cede any personal control over his multifaceted enterprise. Richard H. Boyd possessed an acute business mind. In the publishing board's early days, he ensured its legal independence (by separately incorporating it in Tennessee in 1898) from the National Baptist Convention.[28] But facts that dribbled out about Boyd's management of his properties disturbed many in the NBC. Boyd took out mortgages and borrowed money against the publishing board's property, and used the funds to help finance several of his other ventures. Copyrights on Sunday school commentaries were in Boyd's own name and good for twenty-eight years, meaning Boyd himself would profit personally by selling religious literature to churches while the congregations themselves would think that their contributions to pay for the literature would go into the collective fund of the convention. Convention leaders asked Boyd to transfer his copyrights to the National Baptist Publishing Board. Boyd declared that the NBC did not create the publishing house but that he and eight other persons spawned it as a private enterprise affiliated with the convention but not controlled by it.[29]

Wrangling for control of the publishing board began in earnest in 1905 and continued over the next ten years. The ensuing series of skirmishes stalled the functioning of black Baptist national bodies. In 1915, the controversy exploded. In that year's National Baptist Convention meeting in Chicago, attended by over fifteen thousand delegates, denominational leaders allied with convention president E. C. Morris sought to establish the legal authority of the denomination over Boyd's firm (and over the Home Mission Board of the convention that Boyd headed and ran more or less as a publicity agency for the publishing board). After Boyd's attempt to stop the regular convention meeting failed, he bolted from the meeting hall and reconvened his supporters at a different church.[30] The Boyd forces took from the convention all the records of the publishing board and along with them the "members who declared that the secretary's argument in defense of his claim that the publishing house was his own private property was a perfectly just and reasonable one." Boyd also took along ten thousand dollars that had been contributed by white southern Baptists to the black Home Mission Board, setting off another legal battle as to who should control that set of funds. The original convention, led by E. C. Morris, immediately set about to incorporate itself. Though Boyd's own business was itself a corporation, he led his followers into the National Baptist Convention, Unincorporated, now known as the National Baptist Convention of America.[31]

The battle for control of black Baptist national politics raged for the next five years. The basic issue involved who would retain ultimate authority over the publishing house. Elias C. Morris, longtime president and former Boyd ally, posed this question as the fundamental issue at stake: "Shall the Baptists of this country own and control that which they, through their principal organization, have founded and built up, or shall its control be left to a few to be used for personal gain?" An arbiter hired to untangle the legal knot held that the various boards of the convention held property "in trust, for the uses and benefit" of the central convention. The legal counsel suggested that the convention create an executive board to transact business for the benefit of the denomination when the actual yearly business meeting was not in session.[32]

The Boyd faction in this dispute (those who supported the independence of the publishing firm) argued that the fiction of incorporation would hide what would be the personal control of the convention's agencies by E. C. Morris and his minions. Since the publishing board showed financial stability, whereas other denominational agencies never established a secure funding base, Morris allegedly wanted to exploit Boyd's own efforts for his own personal gain. Boyd contended that he stood for the "ancient doctrine" that Baptist conventions were merely voluntary associations from which individuals and groups could withdraw whenever they wished. He accused the Morris faction of pursuing a "strong centralization form of government, a permanent organization with the property rights vested in a central body." Boyd, in essence, objected to turning the denomination into a modern nonprofit corporation, a move that would subsume his personal success story—the growth of his publishing firm—and (in his view) wrest from him the crown jewel of his business empire.[33]

At the request of some of the black disputants, white Baptists in 1918 attempted to referee the fray. O. L. Hailey, a white Baptist later instrumental in the opening of the American Baptist Theological Seminary in Nashville, headed the committee of white arbiters. Hailey was warned that some white southern Baptists held "no sympathy with the effort to help the Negro. To picture this friction in its true colors would tend to confirm these brethren in their prejudice against the negroes." Hailey viewed his work as crucial not just for adjudicating this specific legal battle, but also for bringing together Negroes and whites in the missionary work that God had laid at the door of America: "The present World situation is calling for us to take care of the Negro, and strengthen ourselves for the coming aftermath. We are going to need the help of the Negro in the next period. And while we have them with us, we ought to help them that they may be ready to stand with us when the testing time comes, as it is destined to come soon."[34]

Hailey and the other white southern convention representatives favored the Morris side's philosophy of denominational control of all agencies. The committee failed to bring together the factions, and the schism grew permanent as each separate convention developed constituent churches and agencies. Some black ministers, moreover, questioned why whites should be trusted to resolve this dispute when "Negroes are lynched and burned right under some of these white commissioners nose and not one word spoken or protest uttered against it." Such evils, this ally of Boyd's suggested, were "more dangerous and damnable than all the dissension the race can create among themselves."[35]

Richard H. Boyd and Elias C. Morris both died in the early 1920s, leaving behind them the unfortunate legacy of this bitter legal split. The dispute over the legal control of the publishing board could hardly have come at a worse time. At a time when racial unity was most necessary, it was most lacking among black Baptist organizations. In this sense, the two sides of Boyd—his black entrepreneurial spirit, and his political activism—were at last separated and even in conflict with one another. Yet, within Nashville, Boyd's legacy involved political activism and lasting business institutions that well served African Americans through the early decades of the twentieth century.

As early as 1900, Boyd was warning black ministers that if African Americans did not "carefully guard [their] . . . interests," white politicians would "turn the hand backward on the political dial [by] a quarter of a century."[36] Like most of the black leadership of that era, Boyd could accept separate and equal, and could have probably reconciled himself to separate and incidentally unequal, but could not abide separate and deliberately, systematically, egregiously unequal.

When Nashville began enforcing laws requiring segregated streetcars, which provided inferior accommodations for blacks, Boyd responded first by organizing a streetcar boycott. "Those of the race who are able, [should] buy buggies and start to trim their corns, darn their socks, wear solid shoes, and walk," he advised. Boyd and his son, Henry Allen Boyd, also started the *Nashville Globe*, a paper that publicized and organized the boycott. Boyd's fellow Nashville Baptist ministers Sutton Griggs and Edward W. D. Isaac were active in raising money and urging black Nashvillians who had "express wagons" to make them available to transport blacks around the city.[37] Boyd also participated in the formation of the Union Transportation Company, a black-owned streetcar venture. In this way Boyd resisted segregation's pernicious underpinnings but at the same time sought to make bricks without straw by capitalizing on the realities of segregation to encourage black business enterprise. He also pursued this latter strategy as vice president of the National Negro Business League, an organization dominated by Booker T. Washington and his allies. Boyd joined the two sides to his work—the religious and the secular—by using the basement of the National Baptist Publishing House to install his own dynamo and generator that would run electric trains owned by the company.

The streetcar boycott and black-owned Union Transportation Company eventually failed, as the company's steam-driven vehicles were not powerful enough to negotiate Nashville's hills. A tax on streetcars imposed by the city finished off the undercapitalized endeavor. The boycott and the company both collapsed in 1906, but through his work, Boyd proved his central role in the community. The continued success of the *Nashville Globe* also demonstrated Boyd's connection to deeply felt impulses in Nashville's black community, including especially its small but active middle class.[38] The *Globe* regularly pronounced Boyd's political philosophy while also providing a publicity outlet for other business and financial concerns.

Through a separate enterprise known as the National Negro Doll Company, Boyd manufactured black dolls. Although Marcus Garvey and the United Negro Improvement Association are often credited with popularizing black dolls, Richard H. Boyd was in fact the first to market mass-produced dolls to black consumers. Boyd pushed the dolls as a way that black "personality and individuality" would not be "submerged" in the white world. For Boyd, this feeling was reinforced when shopping for appropriate dolls for his children. He could find none that were not gross Negro caricatures.[39] An advertisement for the dolls (which ran in the *Nashville Globe,* in other black newspapers, and in Boyd's Sunday school publications) conveys Boyd's sense of the importance of such tokens of cultural self-respect: "These toys are not made of that disgraceful and humiliating type that we have been accustomed to seeing black dolls made of. They represent the intelligent and refined Negro of today, rather than that type of toy that is usually given to the children, and as a rule used as a scarecrow. These toys are placed in the city and at the disposal of the people that they may teach their children how to look upon their people."[40] The dignified black doll would be a small token in the consumer world that the black man wished to be "a Negro, and an American," as Du Bois expressed it.

Another of Boyd's important Nashville-based ventures was the One-Cent Savings Bank and Trust Company, a conservatively run black banking enterprise that invested deposits solely in "gilt-edged" securities and assumed a slow-growth posture. Reasoning that the failure of the Freedmen's Bank during Reconstruction still lingered on as a painful spot in black folk memory, Boyd insisted that his bank would practice fiscal conservatism over a period of years to protect depositors. The bank, he wrote, "came upon the scene not for the purpose of investing and accumulating money for the stockholders, neither for the purpose of paying salaries to the officers, but for the purpose, first, of restoring confidence in the already industrious colored citizens and training young men in financial dealings."[41] Some of Boyd's initial partners, dissenting from his conservative policies, began their own bank with looser restraints on money investing and lending. But Boyd's investment strategy paid off. His bank persevered through difficult years while other Nashville banks, white and black, went insolvent.[42]

Boyd's two roles, as black religious entrepreneur and race spokesmen, also showed themselves in the positions he took in public discussions. On the one hand, Boyd consistently believed the notion that the "best chance" for the Negro could be found in the South. "The Southern white man has many peculiarities," he admitted, and "frightens too easily at the 'social equality' ghost, of which most Negroes never dream." But he insisted that the southern white man nevertheless gave "the industrious Negro the very best opportunity to make money with which to buy property, and to speculate in legal business ventures."[43] Boyd advocated this view even during the era of black migration northward during and after World War I. On the other hand, in both the *Nashville Globe* and the *National Baptist Union-Review* (a denominational newspaper that Boyd edited), Boyd launched forthright attacks on southern racism, much as he had in his days in Texas in the 1890s. Responding to an article in the Georgia *Christian Index* (a white denominational newspaper) in 1917 which suggested that Negroes had been "well managed" in the South, Boyd bristled, "we do not like the idea of being 'managed.'" He proclaimed that "the migration of colored people to the North is a great religious movement. God's hand in it is visible." The so-called Negro problem was in fact a dilemma created by whites who enforced "mob violence, starvation wages, peonage, shameful educational neglect, Jim Crow laws, enforced segregation, miscarriage of justice in the courts, brutal police relations, inadequate housing, . . . disfranchisement, mistreatment of our women and girls by a vicious element."[44] Nor did Boyd spare white northerners in his critique of American racism.

Boyd's son, Henry Allen Boyd, worked with his father and eventually became his successor in many of the enterprises. In 1906, Henry Allen Boyd, together with three other local businessmen, founded the *Nashville Globe* and later, the Globe Publishing Company. Henry Boyd took daily editorial charge of the paper, while his father's money (and frequent advertisements for National Baptist Publishing Board literature) helped to bankroll the paper. The *Globe* provides an invaluable record of Nashville's black world-within-a world, one largely unnoticed (and unreported) by whites of the era.[45] By the late 1920s, some 20 percent of Nashville's black families subscribed. Through the 1910s and 1920s, Henry Boyd continued the relatively aggressive editorial tone the paper originally had assumed during the streetcar boycott of 1905–6. The *Globe* advertised itself primarily as a paper for the promotion of the black entrepreneurial spirit, and indeed the paper tirelessly promoted black businesses of all kinds, from tiny barber shops to successful undertakers. But the *Globe* reached out beyond this Washingtonian emphasis on self-help. It publicized police abuses and provided a forum for local black protest thought. It demanded that more black faculty be added to the rolls at Fisk University and protested the change in 1913 from ward-based elections to at-large city elections, a move that diluted the black vote. A stalwart in Republican Party politics locally, Henry Boyd was instrumental in obtaining land grant money for what later became Tennessee State University. He called attention in his paper to the pittance blacks received for teacher education through the Peabody Fund and directed a campaign to build a black YMCA.[46] Henry Allen Boyd successfully managed the paper for decades while also participating in the One-Cent Savings Bank and other business enterprises.

Henry Allen Boyd also pursued his father's work in religious publishing. After the death of the elder Boyd in 1921, he produced the *National Jubilee Melody Song Book*, one of the first black religious hymnals that set to notation the nineteenth-century slave spirituals.[47] It helped to reintroduce black congregations to their own vital heritage of spiritual music. It also smoothed the path for the father of gospel music, Thomas Andrew Dorsey, who used the National Baptist Publishing Board to distribute many of his compositions.[48] After a long and productive career, Henry Allen Boyd died in 1958, leaving a considerable sum to his daughter in the form of stock in the Citizens Bank (the new name for the One-Cent Savings Bank). The Boyd legacy in Nashville was thus a long-lived one.

But this should not be the last word. In a time that represented, in the words of historian Rayford Logan, the "nadir of race relations" in the post–Civil War South, men such as Richard H. Boyd challenged white supremacy while forging strategic alliances with whites to foster black enterprises. Though little-known figures now in black history, Richard H. Boyd and his son fought in pragmatic and businesslike ways the battle that W. E. B. Du Bois fought in the pages of his essays—the struggle to define how to be a Negro and an American, maintaining that "double consciousness" in constant and fruitful tension. Boyd's work helped to sustain the small, struggling black middle class in Nashville and other cities through the long night of Jim Crow. He always implicitly trusted in the promise that this long night would turn into a new morning of freedom, if one kept the faith.

NOTES

The author wishes to thank the Southern Baptist Historical Library and Archives in Nashville for its invaluable assistance, and Carroll Van West and Susan Nishida Harvey for their editorial suggestions and encouragement.

1. Consolidated American Baptist Missionary Convention *Report,* 1869, 9, copy in microfilm at the Southern Baptist Historical Library and Archives, Nashville, Tennessee (hereafter cited as SBHLA).
2. William E. Montgomery, *Under Their Own Vine and Fig Tree: The African-American Church in the South, 1865–1900* (Baton Rouge, 1993), 189; Ed Crowther, "Interracial Relations Among White and Black Baptists in Alabama, 1865–1890," paper delivered at Southern Historical Association, Nov. 1994 (copy in author's possession); James M. McPherson, *The Abolitionist Legacy from Reconstruction to the NAACP* (Princeton, 1975).
3. *Religious Herald,* May 27, 1880.
4. Consolidated American Baptist Missionary Convention *Report,* 1869, 16, copy in SBHLA.
5. See Edward L. Ayers, *Southern Crossing: A History of the American South, 1877–1906* (New York, 1994), 94–95.
6. The material in this and the next few paragraphs comes from James Melvin Washington, *Frustrated Fellowship: The Black Baptist Quest for Social Power* (Macon, Ga., 1986), the seminal work on the formation of black Baptist denominational organizations in the late nineteenth century.
7. General Baptist State Convention of Texas *Minutes,* 1894, 20–32.
8. See Washington, *Frustrated Fellowship,* 160–70.
9. Bureau of the Census, *Religious Bodies, 1906* (Washington, 1910), 1:137–39; Bureau of the Census, *Religious Bodies, 1916,* Part 1 (Washington, 1919), 1:121–28; Montgomery, *Under Their Own Vine and Fig Tree,* 105–8; Evelyn Brooks-Higginbotham, *Righteous Discontent: The Women's Movement in the Black Baptist Church, 1880–1920* (Cambridge, Mass., 1993), 6.
10. M. Brawley, "The Duty of Negro Baptists, In View of the Past, the Present, and the Future," in Brawley, ed., *The Negro Baptist Pulpit* (Philadelphia, 1890), 297–98.
11. Lewis G. Jordan, *The National Baptist Convention, U.S.A., Inc.* (Nashville, 1930), 250.
12. Garland, "Why We Should Use the Sunday School Literature Published at Nashville, Tennessee," *National Baptist Magazine* (Sept. 1901): 352–57. The *National Baptist Magazine* was a forum for black Baptist church leaders that, while short-lived, proved crucial in articulating the emerging separatist consciousness of that era.
13. For a fuller account of this incident, see Washington, *Frustrated Fellowship,* 159–70.
14. Jordan, *The National Baptist Convention,* 250.
15. See Don H. Doyle, *Nashville in the New South, 1880–1930* (Knoxville, 1985), 114–16, for a discussion of the variety of black publishing enterprises centered in Nashville.
16. Jordan, *The National Baptist Convention,* 247–50.
17. See Lewis G. Jordan, *Negro Baptist History, U.S.A., Inc.,* (Nashville, 1930), 250. For an account of the Sunday School Board of the Southern Baptist Convention, see Robert Baker, *The Southern Baptist Convention and Its People, 1607–1972* (Nashville, 1974). Ironically, the same brouhaha with the American Baptist Publication Society that had angered black Baptists also persuaded many white southern Baptists to support their own publishing endeavor, the Sunday School Board, which began its work in 1891. The white southerners also felt "affronted" by the actions of Benjamin

Griffith, and objections raised to the publishing effort among whites were overcome
by a rhetoric very similar to that employed by the black Baptists five years later.

18. [National Baptist Publishing Board], *Twelfth Annual Report of the Home Mission Board, Together With Eleventh Annual Report of the National Baptist Publishing Board for the Fiscal Year Ending August 31, 1907* (Nashville, 1907); *National Baptist Union,* Sept. 27 and Oct. 4, 1902.
19. National Baptist Convention *Journal,* 1899, 42–43.
20. *National Baptist Union,* July 19, 1902.
21. Southern Baptist Convention *Annual,* 1897, Appendix B, LXXIV.
22. See George M. Frederickson, *The Black Image in the White Mind: The Debate on Afro-American Character and Destiny, 1817–1914* (New York, 1971).
23. See W. E. B. Du Bois, *The Souls of Black Folk* (rpt. New York, 1989), 8, 10, 187. See also the magnificent new biography of Du Bois by David Levering Lewis, *W. E. B. Du Bois, Biography of a Race, 1869–1919* (New York, 1993), esp. 277–96.
24. See August Meier's classic study, *Negro Thought in America: Racial Ideologies in the Age of Booker T. Washington* (Ann Arbor, Mich., 1963).
25. National Baptist Convention *Journal,* 1900, Report of the Publishing Board and the Home Mission Board.
26. Leroy Fitts, *A History of Black Baptists* (Nashville, 1985), 83.
27. For more information on Boyd, see Henry Lewis Suggs, ed., *The Black Press in the South, 1865–1979* (Westport, Conn., 1983), 313–55. Boyd's own description of the origins and growth of the publishing board, though biased because of a legal dispute over ownership of the board which racked the National Baptist Convention in the 1910s, is useful: Richard Henry Boyd, *A Story of the National Baptist Publishing Board. The Why, How, When, Where, and By Whom It Was Established* (Nashville, n.d.), copy in SBHLA.
28. See Boyd, *A Story of the National Baptist Publishing Board.*
29. The confusing facts of the publishing board's relationship to the NBC are set out in Jordan, *Negro Baptist History, U.S.A,* 252–55, though Jordan was hardly an impartial observer to the controversy (he was in the anti-Boyd faction).
30. See Fitts, *A History of Black Baptists,* 89–98, for a readily available detailed account of the dispute. Morris's speech was interrupted by a court injunction, which halted the convention's proceedings and caused chaos on the floor of the convention. Morris's speech was later continued, after the court allowed the convention to continue its business, and after Boyd had staged a walkout. *Lawyers Opinion Defining the Relation of the National Baptist Convention to the National Baptist Publishing Board and Its Other Boards,* 1915, copy in SBHLA.
31. Jordan, *Negro Baptist History, U.S.A., Inc.,* 127, 135.
32. "Statement of the Causes of Confusion," National Baptist Convention *Journal,* 1915, 33–34. An executive committee of this sort solved a recurring problem of Baptist conventions, namely that "conventions" legally existed only during the period of their annual meeting. Outside of those few days, they had no legal existence. But an executive committee appointed by the convention to transact business could maintain the legal life of the convention through the remainder of the year, thus avoiding legal difficulties such as the publishing house controversy.
33. National Baptist Convention of America *Journal,* 1916, 61–135, gives Boyd's side

of the controversy. The National Baptist Convention of America was commonly referred to as the "unincorporated convention," though it was, in fact, incorporated.

34. Edgar Young Mullins to O. L. Hailey, Jan. 8, 1919, in E. Y. Mullins's letterpress books, Boyce Library, Southern Baptist Theological Seminary, Louisville, Kentucky; O. L. Hailey to Edgar Young Mullins, Feb. 8, 1918, in Mullins letter files, Southern Baptist Theological Seminary; Southern Baptist Convention *Annual*, 1918, 67–69.

35. Chapman, "The Baptist Difference as Seen by a Texan," *National Baptist Union Review,* Apr. 5, 1919.

36. Quoted in Lester C. Lamon, *Black Tennesseans, 1900–1930* (Knoxville, 1977), 1.

37. Quoted in Faye Wellborn Robbins, "A World-Within-A-World: Black Nashville, 1880–1915" (Ph.D. diss., Univ. of Arkansas, 1980), 212–13.

38. See Lamon, *Black Tennesseans,* 12–14; Doyle, *Nashville in the New South,* 116–20; and Robbins, "A World-Within-A-World," 126–27, 212–13, 249–50.

39. *National Baptist Union,* Oct. 24 and Dec. 19, 1908.

40. Quoted in Samuel Shannon, "Tennessee," in Lewis Suggs, *The Black Press in the South, 1865–1979* (Westport, Conn., 1983), 332.

41. *Nashville Globe,* Jan. 12, 1912, 8, quoted in Christopher M. Scribner, "Nashville Offers Opportunity: *The Nashville Globe* and Business as a Means of Uplift, 1907–1913," *Tennessee Historical Quarterly* 54 (Spring 1995): 58.

42. See Lamon, *Black Tennesseans, 1900–1930,* 12–14, 184–85, and Robbins, "A World-Within-a-World," 249–50.

43. *National Baptist Union,* June 20, 1908.

44. *National Baptist Union Review,* July 28, 1917.

45. See Scribner, "Nashville Offers Opportunity: *The Nashville Globe,*" 54–67, for a lucid analysis of the paper and its relationship to the major themes of black accommodation and resistance in the early twentieth century.

46. See Samuel Shannon, "Tennessee," in Lewis Suggs, *The Black Press in the South, 1865–1979* (Westport, Conn., 1983), 313–55; and Scribner, "Nashville Offers Opportunity: *The Nashville Globe.*"

47. See Robbins, "A World-Within-a-World," 249–50.

48. See Michael W. Harris, *The Rise of Gospel Blues: The Music of Thomas Andrew Dorsey in the Urban Church* (New York, 1992), 175–78, for information on Dorsey's connections with A. M. Townsend and other figures in the black Baptist music publishing world.

Evangelicals, Fugitives, and Hillbillies: Tennessee's Impact on American National Culture

■ Paul K. Conkin

■

■ *Editor's Note:* Conkin's insightful interpretation of cultural patterns associated with Tennessee assesses literature, country music,
and religion, finding in the latter the most important contributions made by Tennesseans to the national culture. Religious beliefs and behaviors come closest of all of the cultural patterns "to
uniting Tennesseans of all races and from all parts of the state."
Ten denominations—representing some thirty-two million
Americans—have special institutional ties to the state. Although
these religious traditions of the state are not unique to Tennessee,
"it is because of their generality that Tennesseans have been able
to play a major role in shaping both a southern and national religious culture."

Rarely does anyone look at a state from a cultural perspective. Political boundaries need not be culturally significant. Thus, books and essays
that survey the culture of a given state are very few. No one has yet written a
comprehensive cultural history of Tennessee, even as hundreds of books and
articles explore every small detail of its role in the Civil War. The lack of such
a cultural history reflects not a scandal, not a failure of imagination on the
part of local historians, but rather documents the problem of adapting a cultural perspective for something as arbitrary as the boundaries of an American state.

The ambiguous word *culture* can have many meanings, but three are most
prevalent and will provide the framework for this essay. At the more general
level, culture refers to the beliefs and values of a people, which in turn are
tied to language and tradition. In this sense, everyone who learns to talk and
think shares in a culture. If Tennesseans were in any sense distinctive cultur-

ally, one would expect them to share some unique beliefs and values, some peculiarities in language, in myths, in folkways, in religion, in moral principles, that set them apart, even if only marginally, from other closely related populations, such as those that make up the American South or the United States as a whole. It is doubtful that Tennesseans, or the people of any state, meet this test. But Tennesseans do participate in various distinguishable regional cultures. In only one area—religious beliefs and behaviors—do cultural patterns come closest to uniting Tennesseans of all races and from all parts of the state. These religious beliefs are not at all distinctive to Tennessee. If they were, they would have small national significance. It is because of their generality that Tennesseans have been able to play a major role in shaping both a southern and a national religious culture. Thus, religion provides the major theme for the most general part of this essay.

Other meanings of culture are more restrictive. For many, the word *culture* attaches not to the total population, but only to a creative elite—those people who contribute to what are conventionally defined as the fine arts (music, literature, painting and sculpture, architecture), scholarship, and the sciences—and to the institutions that support such creative activity (educational institutions, laboratories, museums, galleries, and theaters). This is "high culture." For most of its history, Tennessee has not had the wealth, the resources, the educational institutions, the great urban centers, or the private patronage that normally supports such a "high" culture, but it has, for reasons that may be largely accidental, had at least a distinguished and broadly influential role in literature, which will provide a theme for the second part of this essay.

A final use of the word *culture* involves not elites but popular taste and the people who cater to it. This is "popular culture." It includes the less pretentious or purportedly more vulgar forms of literature, journalism, music, folk arts, and radio and television programming. In this area, Tennesseans have usually blended into the larger national population, but in one genre—popular forms of music—they have had a distinctive role, most of all in the development and marketing of what most call country music. This story will therefore dominate the final part of this essay.

Some very general characteristics of Tennessee are needed to offset the special problems that beset any cultural analysis. Despite all the problems of definition, and of boundaries, it is possible to distinguish regional cultures within the United States. These are tied to such variables as ethnic origin, religious belief, work patterns, kinship or family structures, and historic memories. The problem is that Tennessee shares in several regional cultures, making its state boundaries all but meaningless in any cultural sense. No one planned a state like Tennessee, a narrow strip of land that cuts across eight distinct geographical zones. It includes several strands of a mountain or Appalachian culture (the Unaka strip of the Blue Ridge along the North Carolina border, the sharp mountains and valleys north of Clinch Mountain, and the Cumberland Plateau); the special culture of the great eastern valley (a critical transportation corridor, and rich farming area, that stretches from the mouth of the Shenandoah to northern Alabama); the semi-mountain, small-farming culture of both the eastern and western highland rims and parts of northern West Tennessee; the smug and self-assured patrician culture of the geographically favored central basin; and the plantation and cotton based culture of the southwest. Few states are as varied; few have as many significant geographical barriers; few have as sharply delineated historic traditions.

To further complicate this variety, the state has always been distinguished by its three divisions. Citizens are self-consciously from East, Middle, or West Tennessee. These divisions, unfortunately, do not rest upon very clear geographical or cultural boundaries.

Given such geographical and cultural diversity, are there any commonalities that link the regions of the state? Yes, but these are commonalities that, however important, reflect the participation of Tennesseans in larger wholes. For example, Tennessee, even though originally identified with the West or the Southwest, eventually became a part of an identifiable and self-conscious South, one defined by commodity agriculture and the slave system, as well as by the climates and soils that supported such an economy. This southern identity and the role of slavery helped shape a state that was ethnically homogeneous, but with regionally varied racial mixes.

Few original Americans remained in Tennessee after 1838. Treaties, chicanery, warfare, and then removal under Andrew Jackson left only a tiny Indian population in the state (today, one-fifth of 1 percent). Thus, the population of Tennessee would largely be made up of immigrants from Britain and Africa. The early white settlements set an enduring pattern—the largest proportion with English roots, the second-largest with a Scottish heritage, but Scots who usually came to America by way of Ulster (the Scotch-Irish). In time, more and more blacks leavened this British population, particularly in West and parts of Middle Tennessee, or where a labor-intensive agriculture made slaves profitable. By the Civil War, the percentage of blacks had increased to around 25 percent; since 1900, this percentage has dropped at an accelerating rate to only 16 percent, or just above the near 13 percent national average.

Two races meant two cultural heritages. But by the time most slaves arrived in Tennessee, they had lost African languages and much of their memories of African religions, and by necessity had blended varied African cultural influences and then mixed this blend with the dominant white, European, Christian culture of their masters. Yet, in ways that defy measurement, African Americans remained culturally distinct, in nuances of their borrowed English language, in the subtleties of religious worship, in music and dance. What remains unresolved, a matter of scholarly conflict, is the breadth of the cultural differences, the extent of African survivals, and the degree to which cultural blending affected whites as well as blacks.

The most important cultural commonality, one that has helped shape most Tennesseans, has been an evangelical form of Protestant Christianity. By 1800, the label "evangelical" identified Christians who placed ever greater emphasis upon a crisislike conversion or rebirth, on a warm, free, and affectionate or spiritual style of worship and devotion, on a commitment to proselytizing or soul winning through various revival techniques, and on a nonworldly and near ascetic standard of personal holiness and moral purity. Such a religion has provided the most basic cultural bridge between whites and blacks and between the varied geographic regions of the state. Such an evangelical orientation has not been unique to Tennessee, for in fact it has been a characteristic of much of the South. But Tennessee has been distinctive in its originative and leadership role within evangelical Christianity, both white and black. No other southern state, and no other states in the North, save possibly Massachusetts and Pennsylvania, have had as important a national role in religion as has Tennessee.[1]

Beginning with the first white settlements in upper East Tennessee, three of the four largest evangelical denominations (Presbyterians, loosely organized Calvinist Baptists, and Methodists) almost monopolized church membership in Tennessee. This simply documented the English and Scottish background of the migrants, most from either the Piedmont of North Carolina or the great valley of Virginia. The only significant exception was a scattering of Germans (they established Lutheran, Church of the Brethren or Dunkard, and United Brethren congregations, particularly in upper East Tennessee). The first ministers and earliest congregations were Presbyterian, reflecting the high percentage of Scotch-Irish migrants (at least one-fourth). In the early history of Tennessee, such Presbyterians all but dominated secondary and college-level education, with their academies often the only early source of formal schooling. All early colleges were Presbyterian, including the present Maryville and Tusculum, plus the earliest incarnations of what later became the University of Tennessee (Blount College) and George Peabody College for Teachers (Davidson Academy). Competitive with Presbyterians almost from the first settlement were Baptist preachers who formed small congregations, often without formal denominational organization or the means to build academies and colleges. This led very early to some class differences, with Presbyterians more often in leadership positions, more prosperous, and more highly educated. Finally, the newly organized Methodists, the low-church or evangelical offspring of colonial Anglicanism, became the most successful proselytizers after the 1784 creation of the Methodist Episcopal Church. Its itinerant circuit riders and leading early bishop, Francis Asbury, launched a very successful mission effort in the South, meaning that soon after 1800 the Methodists became the largest denomination in Tennessee.

These three denominations, plus the New England Congregationalists (never strong in Tennessee), made up the evangelical mainstream of American Christianity. They were dominant in all parts of the United States, but most monopolistic in such new states as Kentucky and Tennessee. The shared evangelical style of Presbyterians, Baptists, and Methodists helped bridge wide and at times rancorous doctrinal differences. In the nineteenth century, immigrants considerably increased the religious heterogeneity of the North (Irish and German Roman Catholics, German and Scandinavian Lutherans, and central European Jews), but not in most of the South, which attracted only a few migrating Irish workers, who established the first Roman Catholic congregations in Tennessee.

Such evangelical denominations entered a period of rapid growth at the beginning of the nineteenth century. This religious boom had one of its key beginnings in the Cumberland area of Middle Tennessee and southern Kentucky. Between 1796 and 1800, six ministers (five Presbyterian and one Methodist) moved to Sumner County in Tennessee and Logan County in Kentucky. There they ministered to new congregations that had moved from their home congregations in the piedmont of North Carolina. One of the ministers, James McGready, was a particularly effective preacher, and he and his colleagues were able, in this newly settled but land-rich western country, to revive the old Scottish type of four- and five-day intercongregational communion services. These, held at individual churches in the summer, and in each case attended by all nearby congregations, had long been the occasion for conviction or conversion, including several waves of revival in North Carolina and southern Virginia in the period after 1787.

In 1800, a building religious fervor peaked in at least eight planned communions in the two counties and in Nashville. Many in attendance at the outdoor preaching, from a platform or tent, or in church buildings, fell in a near coma. This falling and other dramatic physical exercises created great excitement, led McGready to publish a long and enormously influential letter about the revival, and at Gasper River, in Logan County, stimulated the first extensive camping on the church grounds. Well publicized by the host minister at Gasper River, John Rankin, and recounted with great effects to congregations in East Tennessee and back in North Carolina, this precedent led, within two or three years, to the widespread development of campgrounds and annual camp meetings all around the country. This revival in the west climaxed at Cane Ridge in central Kentucky in 1801, and only gradually abated after 1805. But its precedents—camping, falling and other physical exercises, intense conviction, lay exhorting—remained new but soon accepted patterns in evangelical revivals, whether held at outdoor retreats or camps (soon a Methodist preference) or in extended and special proselytizing services in churches. The story is complex, but the point is that many of the innovations began in the Cumberland, and these innovations would have a tremendous impact upon American Protestantism. In this sense, Tennesseans were there at the creation.[2]

The fervor of the revivals and the disturbing physical exercises created doubts and divisions among the Presbyterians, who had hosted all the most explosive early revivals. The conversions and new ministerial candidates that sprang from the Cumberland revivals almost forced the Kentucky Synod to create a new presbytery in the Cumberland. This Cumberland Presbytery compromised the normal classical education required for licensing and ordaining new ministers, and allowed candidates to finesse the Westminster doctrine of double predestination (God elects both to salvation and to damnation). When the senior Presbyterian minister in the Cumberland, Thomas Craighead of Nashville, indicted the presbytery for its educational compromises, the synod investigated, found the greatest problem to be doctrinal, and insisted upon a doctrinal examination of all the young men. Supported by their seniors—McGready and the other architects of the 1800 revival—the young men refused, and as a result the synod expelled them. The battle raged for over five years, but eventually the Presbyterian General Assembly upheld the synodical expulsion. Some of the young men, led by socially prominent Finis Ewing, refused to capitulate, and in 1810 Ewing and a colleague, Samuel King, met at the cabin of Samuel McAdow (one of the original migrants from North Carolina) in Dickson County to form an independent Cumberland Presbytery. This grew into a denomination, only the first of several to originate in Tennessee. By 1860, the Cumberland Presbyterians, with doctrines midway between Presbyterian Calvinism and Wesleyan Arminianism, had surpassed in Tennessee the membership of the parent Presbyterian church. In 1906, a majority of Cumberland Presbyterians voted to merge with the northern Presbyterian church. Several individual Cumberland presbyteries rejected this merger and, alone in Tennessee, won a court battle to keep the existing property. This meant that the small surviving Cumberland Presbyterian denomination would have a unique Tennessee focus, with its only remaining college (Bethel) at McKenzie, and its boards and publishing house in Memphis.[3]

The Cumberland schism, a lack of qualified ministers, a more ordered and sedate religious style, and the rigorous demands of orthodox Calvinism retarded Presbyterian expansion. Thus, the two confessions that gained most from the explosive revivals were the Methodists and Baptists, who remained in first and second place in Tennessee church membership throughout the nineteenth century, only to reverse the order in the twentieth.

These two largest Protestant confessions in America have both retained a special tie to Tennessee. After both the main Baptist and Methodist denominations split over the issue of slavery, the southern branches created their own denominational agencies. The Methodists led the way. Because of the generosity of a former Methodist circuit preacher who had gained considerable wealth, Alexander L. P. Green, the Methodist Episcopal Church, South, located its publishing house in Nashville. Soon, its bishops met there, and other boards and agencies located in Nashville, making it the capital of southern Methodism. With the 1968 merger of northern and southern Methodists, the merged church distributed its boards and commissions, but as a gesture to the former southern wing established several of its most important agencies in Nashville, including those involved with discipleship, communications, and higher education. Perhaps most important of all, both economically and in terms of widespread religious influence, it kept its publishing house in Nashville.[4]

As the Southern Baptist Convention matured a quasi-denominational structure after its break from the Baptist General Convention in 1845, it eventually chose Nashville as home. Its central headquarters (its Executive Committee) and many of its major commissions and boards are in Nashville, including its huge publishing house.[5]

By the end of the nineteenth century, one could identify deep tensions within these older, evangelical denominations. To an extent, a majority of even southern Methodists and Presbyterians, and a minority of Baptists, relaxed some of the earlier moral rigor, became more inclusive in membership requirements, transformed the rebirth experience into something closer to confirmation, changed the former revivals and camps into milder forms of education, and variously reinterpreted central doctrines or relaxed an inflexible biblicalism. In the sense of the early nineteenth century, these mainline evangelicals were no longer very evangelical. Such shifts, and the resulting intramural controversies, led to major doctrinal counterattacks, often loosely labeled as fundamentalist, and tied to a few key doctrines (biblical inerrancy, the initiatory role of Jesus in launching a millennium, and the key doctrines tied to rebirth). At the same time, others who resisted the modernizing trends downplayed doctrines, and instead tried to retain, or recover, the emotional warmth or spirituality of the old-time evangelicalism, and along with that the moral purity or holiness. From this wing of reaction came the late-nineteenth-century holiness movement and, early in the twentieth century, a rapidly growing Pentecostal movement, one that added to the older evangelicalism a new emphasis upon charismatic gifts (prophecy, healing), with speaking in tongues elevated to a key position as a necessary witness to spiritual baptism. In all these changes, Tennessee once again occupied a central position, one much more important in the history of Christianity than its anti-evolution legislation or the famous Scopes trial at Dayton in 1925.

The Nashville-based Southern Baptist Convention was not unaffected by liberal and more inclusive trends in the mainline denominations. But it was much more resistant than the reunited Methodist and Presbyterian denominations, and never moved close to any union with the northern American Baptist churches. Since the early 1980s, the Convention (technically a fellowship and not a denomination) has moved, at the central level and in elected leadership, to a clear and emphatic defense of both the doctrines and the devotional style of nineteenth-century evangelicalism, and is now the largest voice for this tradition. Today, as the largest Protestant denomination in the United States, it both reflects and fosters a religious style that is quite pervasive in Tennessee, perhaps as pervasive as in any other American state.[6]

Even as the Baptists have held firm, or moved back toward an older evangelicalism, the United Methodist Church and the Presbyterian Church (U.S.A.) have more fully embraced a broad, latitudinarian approach. They tolerate a wide spectrum of beliefs and practices in their churches, but have a national profile that is decidedly liberal, in the sense of inclusiveness in tests of membership, flexibility in biblical interpretation, openness to biblical scholarship or to the implications of scientific knowledge, and a commitment to social outreach as well as to individual salvation. Thus, in Nashville, a few blocks apart, one can observe the polarities in the formerly mainstream evangelical denominations, with a growing and ever more monolithic and exclusive Southern Baptist denomination challenging the shrinking and tolerant United Methodists.

Other conservative or evangelical denominations have their home in Tennessee. From the eighteenth century on, a small Free Will Baptist movement, with salvation doctrines close to Methodism, challenged majority Calvinist Baptists. Many of these Free Will Baptists remain independent or associate in loose local fellowships. Membership statistics do not exist, but impressionistic evidence suggests that independent Free Will Baptists have been growing very rapidly in the last two decades, particularly in the mountains of East Tennessee. Some, but far from all, southern Free Will Baptists joined in a conference in 1921, and united with a smaller northern counterpart in 1935 to form the present National Association of Free Will Baptists. Its headquarters, Bible college, and several boards are all in Nashville.

To further establish the priority of Nashville in world Baptism, one must chart its centrality in the black, National Baptist movement. Black Baptists first organized independent boards or commissions under the guidance of American Baptists (northern), but formed their own loose National Baptist Convention in 1886. The organizational history is complex and contested. In any case, in 1915 the original National Convention split over publishing (the occasion was a publishing enterprise in Nashville); today, the National Baptist family includes four related but separate denominations. The largest wing of this movement, the National Baptist Convention of the U.S.A., Inc., has its national headquarters, a new and impressive world center, a college and seminary (American Baptist), and a publishing house in Nashville. This largest black Baptist denomination (over five million), when added to fifteen million Southern Baptists, means that well over twenty million American Baptists have their headquarters and publishing houses in Tennessee.[7]

Black Methodists eventually formed three major denominations. The smallest of these, the Colored Methodist Episcopal Church (today, the Christian Methodist Episcopal Church), reflected a friendly separation of blacks from the Methodist Episcopal Church, South. This white patronage may have hurt its growth. In any case, its headquarters and main boards, including one on publications, are now in Memphis, further documenting the centrality of Tennessee in black Christianity.[8]

In the Upper South, the first effective competition with the three main evangelical denominations came from the restoration churches (variously denominated Christians, Disciples of Christ, and Churches of Christ). One branch of this movement, led by Barton Stone, originated out of the Kentucky revivals of 1801. By 1832, Stone's western churches, usually called Christian, effected a partial and unofficial merger with a movement founded by Thomas and Alexander Campbell, and by then called Disciples of Christ. Both the Stoneites and Campbellites won early converts in Tennessee, and by 1850 Nashville was one of the leading centers of this movement.

The Restoration churches were not evangelical. They did not emphasize an explosive conversion or rebirth, but instead a reasoned, step-by-step response to the Gospels, climaxing in a remitting baptism. They also repudiated the extreme emotionalism associated with most revivals. Much more than most Baptists, they eschewed any denominational organization, although a major Baptist reform movement, Landmarkism, which originated in Nashville, came close. Even by the Civil War, tensions had developed between rural, most often southern, rigidly anti-mission or anti-organization and restorationist Disciples, and many of their northern, less rigidly congregational and separatist, ecumenically oriented brethren. One leader of the restorationist and separatist congregations was Tolbert Fanning of Nashville, who edited the most influential journal of this very conservative faction of the movement, one that rejected any form of intercongregational organization or any instrumental music. These cleavages led, by 1900, to distinct fellowships (no denomination existed), and the choice by these conservative congregations to distinguish themselves from the main body of Disciples of Christ. Because of the influence of Fanning and his successor in Nashville, David Lipscomb, the conservative faction outgrew the more liberal in the Nashville area and in the state as a whole. These Churches of Christ make up a vague and deeply splintered national fellowship today without any headquarters. Yet, in a loose way, one could argue that Nashville is at the center of the fellowship, for the Churches of Christ are stronger (have a larger share of church membership) in Middle Tennessee than in any comparable area of the United States. David Lipscomb is one of the most influential of their universities (it is supported by individuals or congregations, not by any church organization), and Nashville remains home to three of the most influential periodicals aimed at their members, and is the address of a small, private publishing house and bookstore that is unofficially linked to these congregations.

The more ecumenical Disciples would also later split into two fellowships. The conservative wing—Christian Churches and Churches of Christ—is well established in East Tennessee, with its only four-year college (Milligan) and a seminary (Emmanuel) in Carter County. The largest body of historical sources on the total restoration movement is in the Disciples of Christ Historical Society Library in Nashville.[9]

Two of the three largest Pentecostal churches have their headquarters in Tennessee. A modern, organized Pentecostal movement began with ecstatic experience and tongue speaking in Topeka, Kansas, in 1901. It developed within a loose holiness movement, one with roots in Methodism. Independent holiness congregations had joined in several local denominations by 1900, and stressed the Wesleyan doctrine of holiness or perfection, the attainment, in a second conversionlike experience, of a type of sanctification. This second step had gradually lost centrality in the two largest (North and South) Methodist denominations. Such holiness doctrines spread throughout the country, and gained local adherents in several Tennessee cities. In fact, one holiness mission in Nashville became one of the outposts of what, in mergers in 1907 and 1908, became the Pentecostal Church of the Nazarene (after 1919, simply the Church of the Nazarene), the largest noncharismatic holiness denomination today. This led to a growing Nazarene membership in Nashville, and to a very influential college (Trevecca). But the Nazarene denomination would establish its headquarters in Kansas City. Even before 1908, important holiness ministers in Tennessee capitulated to a burgeoning Pentecostal revival, one that first broke out at an Azusa Street mission in Los Angeles in 1906, a revival led by an African American lay preacher, Charles Joseph Seymour. For Seymour, the holiness second step, or sanctification, was intermediary, followed by a baptism of the Holy Spirit, testified to by tongue speaking and fulfilled through several spiritual gifts, with healing the most visible.[10]

The largest Pentecostal denomination today, and one of the ten largest denominations in the United States, the Church of God in Christ, has its headquarters in Memphis. Its founding and first half-century of growth involved perhaps the most influential religious leader in Tennessee history— Charles Harrison Mason. Historians have almost ignored Mason, perhaps because he was black and because he represented a low-status Pentecostal variety of Christianity. In the late nineteenth century, two black holiness ministers—Charles Price Jones and Mason—organized a small holiness denomination in Mississippi—the Church of God in Christ—but soon moved their headquarters to nearby Memphis. Mason first learned about the Azusa revival from visiting white missionaries. He then joined two ministerial colleagues for a 1907 visit to the Azusa Street Mission, and capitulated completely to the doctrines taught in this biracial revival. He returned to Memphis to try to move his denomination to Pentecostalism, but only partly succeeded. Jones was already open to tongue speaking, but would never accept its necessity as testimony of spirit baptism, and thus separated from Mason's followers.

Mason's faction, which retained the denominational name and its episcopal form of organization (borrowed from Methodism), was vitally important in the first decade of an emergent Pentecostal movement. His church already had a state charter, which enabled it to license ministers. At the time, such credentialed ministers alone gained such a valuable prize as free rail passes. Since none of the early Pentecostal movements had a corporate charter, or could legally license or ordain ministers, many white as well as black Pentecostal evangelists came to Memphis to gain a license. Later, almost all these opportunistic ministers separated into white Pentecostal sects (most in Mason's movement eventually joined the Assemblies of God), leaving Mason's denomination as the strongest black Pentecostal church in the world, a church that now claims over five million members in the United States, and a church whose recent growth has been phenomenal.[11]

Mason remained the presiding bishop of the Church of God in Christ until his death in 1961. He seemed to live forever, eventually becoming the often dictatorial patriarch of Pentecostalism. Mason kept his headquarters in Memphis, at what is now the Mason Temple. Here it has most of its several boards, its publishing house, and its periodicals.

The Pentecostal movement proved very appealing in the South, among whites as well as blacks, particularly among small farmers or textile workers. In 1908, the leading Pentecostal leader in the South, Gaston B. Cashwell, who had converted to Pentecostalism at Azusa in the same year as Mason, visited and preached in Cleveland, in Bradley County, at the home church of a dynamic, at times authoritarian, holiness minister, Ambrose J. Tomlinson. In 1903, Tomlinson had become a minister in a sect that began as the Christian Union in the mountains of Tennessee and North Carolina in 1886, and which changed its name to Holiness Church in 1902. As early as 1896, some members of this very emotional denomination spoke in tongues, but as yet no one interpreted this as evidence of spiritual baptism (such priority in tongue speaking allows this denomination to claim to be the first Pentecostal church in America). Cashwell converted Tomlinson to spirit baptism and to the necessity of evidential tongues, and in turn Tomlinson was able to win most of the small but growing denomination to a three-step form of Pentecostalism. Although now predominantly white, this denomination, which took the name Church of God, with doctrines close to those of Mason's Church of God in Christ, and with a similar episcopal organization (overseers or bishops), accepted black members and even at its beginning had some integrated congregations.[12]

The charismatic but authoritarian style of Tomlinson, plus some financial indiscretions, led to later schisms. In 1923, a majority of Church of God congregations overthrew the leadership of Tomlinson, and after a period of litigation the church began listing itself as the Church of God (Cleveland, Tennessee). Today, it is the second-largest predominantly white Pentecostal denomination in America (second to the Assemblies of God), with a membership of over half a million in the United States and an even larger foreign membership. It has its world headquarters, boards, publications, college (Lee), and seminary in Cleveland. The minority in this split remained loyal to Tomlinson until his death in 1943, and usually used the title of Tomlinson Church of God. At Tomlinson's death, it split once again, with one splinter taking the name of Church of God of Prophecy. This small denomination has its headquarters in Cleveland, plus a small publishing house, and is today probably the most successful in biracial cooperation of any American denomination and has led the way in the ordination of women.

This completes an inadequate survey of the ten denominations with special institutional ties to Tennessee. Collectively, these denominations have over thirty-two million members in the United States (they claim even more) and millions more abroad. They make up well over one-third the total Protestant membership in the United States, and half of all black membership. Of course, most members are outside Tennessee, and the elected leaders of most of these denominations come from all over the United States. But because of offices and publications, these Christians have a special tie to Tennessee. For example, Tennessee leads the world in religious publishing. In addition to the large Southern Baptist, United Methodist, and National Baptist publishing houses, Nashville is home to the country's largest publisher of Bibles and devotional books, Thomas Nelson. If one tries to calculate the role of Tennesseans or Tennessee institutions upon American culture as a whole, one has to begin with this religious impact. It is hard to imagine, and hard to overestimate, how much the tons of religious literature, including the enormous number of Sunday school quarterlies, shipped from Tennessee every month help shape the beliefs and values of millions of Americans.

In the area of "high" culture, the contribution of Tennesseans has been meager compared to their role in religious institutions. But to assay the role of Tennessee in high culture raises complicated problems of definition and ownership. The distribution of native talents seems quite democratic. It is likely that as many geniuses, as many people with special talents, have been born in Tennessee, proportionate to its population, as in any other state. And, indeed, it is easy to compile a gallery of native-born Tennesseans who have excelled in almost every area of human creativity. But what does that say about Tennessee? In itself, not much. If these individuals made their mark outside Tennessee, and most did, then possibly the only claim that Tennessee can make is tied to an accident of birth, which is all but meaningless. On the other hand, if Tennessee provided a rich environment for the perfection of talents, if it offered institutional support for the arts and sciences, then it has a special claim even to its sons and daughters who eventually found the best outlet for their creativity elsewhere. Likewise, those individuals born in other states who made creative contributions while in Tennessee, and particularly as part of culturally supportive Tennessee institutions, are rightly claimed by the state in the same sense that it claims Presidents Jackson, Polk, and Johnson. But in each case, the critical issue is one of a supportive environment, not the accident of genes and birthplace.

Even though Tennessee may have contributed its share of talent to the arts and sciences, it has never done its share in the nurturing of such talent. Except in a few special areas, or short intervals of time, it has not been a cultural magnet. That is, it has not had the cultural institutions that attracted people of talent. This is not to argue that it has been a cultural desert, but for most of its history its citizens have been poor and lived in rural areas and its politicians have been exceptionally restrained in raising the taxes needed even for elementary and secondary education. Until very recently, it had no eminent private or public colleges and universities and, in fact, until the end of segregation, no southern universities could recruit the most able faculty, particularly in the humanities. Since the Civil War, the educational achievement of Tennesseans has consistently been in the bottom five or six states in the nation, and it long had one of the highest illiteracy rates in the country, with the burden of illiteracy highest among blacks and poor mountain whites. Such severe cultural constraints contrast vividly with the state's colorful and complex political history, and with the notable contributions of its politicians to the nation as a whole.

Such cultural disabilities are not unique to Tennessee, but shared by most of the South. Thus, to chart the backwardness of Tennessee is to bare all the special problems of the Confederate South, at least from 1865 to World War II, and in many respects, to 1965 and the belated fulfillment of the national commitment to full citizenship rights for blacks. Without the abolition of a legal caste system, the South could not move far in closing the gap that separated it from the rest of the country in income, social services, and cultural achievement. Since 1965, it has closed the income gap to about 12 percent (from 1865 to 1940, southern incomes had only been one-half the national average). It has also closed the gap in the institutions that support creativity and the life of the mind. Finally, the more populous and wealthy southern states have developed state universities that have come ever closer to the quality of those in the Midwest or in California (Texas, North Carolina, Florida, Virginia, and Georgia lead the way). The South now has six large cosmopolitan urban centers (Atlanta, Dallas–Fort Worth, Houston, Miami, New Orleans, and Tampa–St. Petersburg). It does not have a New York City or a San Francisco, but its modern urban culture is also increasingly cosmopolitan, with growing public support for the performing arts, with notable museums, and a growing presence in publishing and broadcasting. Unfortunately, these changes lag a bit in Tennessee. But its growth in population and its consistent improvement in per capita incomes suggest that Tennessee may soon join its wealthier neighbors, such as North Carolina and Georgia. One can even glimpse some serious efforts to turn its state university, heretofore largely distinguished by its football team, into a major graduate and research center. This will take time and money, but one can now conceive of a major state university in Tennessee, while already Vanderbilt University is a solid private university just below the top ten in the nation.

It was through the agency of Vanderbilt University that Tennessee established a leadership role in literature, or in what we now refer to as a southern renaissance. Up until the 1920s, most Americans regarded the South as a literary wasteland. It had celebrated writers before the war, but few afterwards, although the mystique of a lost cause led to a type of romantic fiction about the old South. In humor, it had Joel Chandler Harris, with his Uncle Remus stories, and Tennessee's George Washington Harris, who created the swaggering character of Sut Lovingood. Among local color writers, who gained a large audience by the 1880s, was Mary Noailles Murfree (her pen name was Charles Egbert Craddock), who turned her limited, summertime observations of the people of the Cumberland Plateau into influential short stories and novels about the people of the Tennessee mountains. In the process, although she tried to be realistic, she helped create a mythic image of Appalachia that some mountain folk would take seriously, and even try to imitate, most of all in country music.[13]

Southern literature still rested on such thin achievements when a group of Vanderbilt students, faculty, and townspeople began to gather in Nashville, briefly before World War I, in a sustained seminar afterwards. Infatu-

Mary N. Murfree, c. 1861.
Library Picture Collection,
Tennessee State Library
and Archives.

ated with poetry and letters, they formed a small poetry journal in 1922, and named it *The Fugitive*. It was, in a sense, only another student publication on perhaps the most self-consciously literate campus in the South. But the caliber of poetry, the talents of the young contributors, and the wonderful effect of collaboration, soon established its worldwide reputation. The *Fugitive* poets did not feature the South, or at first even conceive of their little journal as a contribution to any distinctively southern literature. In fact, they most wanted to escape the sentimentality of most writing about the South. But in the decade of the twenties, with all the negative publicity about the South, particularly with the 1925 Scopes trial, they soon were deeply involved with their identity as southerners, and were committed to the cause of better literature in the South.

The *Fugitive* poets, sixteen in all, were about half from Nashville or the surrounding Middle Tennessee. But what is important is not their place of birth, but that they were able to find, or to create, a very sophisticated and demanding literary culture in Nashville. Instead of being a source of able writers, Tennessee briefly became a magnet to attract them, and the Vanderbilt English department, for the next two decades, was second only to Harvard in providing an academic launch for famous writers. Four of the Fugitives—John Crowe Ransom, Donald Davidson, Allen Tate, and Robert Penn Warren—plus one of their students—Andrew Nelson Lytle—subsequently took the lead in organizing an agrarian movement, and in publishing the manifesto *I'll Take My Stand* in 1930. Agrarianism, although influenced by poets and novelists, was not a literary but a political and economic movement, and the notoriety of the book helped further the literary reputation of its contributors.

More critical in American literature, Ransom, Tate, and Warren helped create a new form of criticism (the New Criticism), that in the years after 1935 had a dominant impact on the teaching of courses in literature. In all these ways, these Vanderbilt professors or students were there at the creation of a now distinctive southern literary tradition. None, not even Warren, one of the most versatile poets, novelists, and critics in American literary history, gained quite the fame of William Faulkner, from Mississippi, a state that might well claim, over the past half century, the most unexpected and significant literary output of any state. But Faulkner was simply a part of a renaissance of literature all over the South, one that rivaled the New England renaissance of the middle period, and one that competed with the New York, largely Jewish, renaissance during the same years. In this revival of southern literature, Tennessee would contribute its share of able novelists and poets and critics, but no more than its share. Its distinctive contribution was the role of Vanderbilt in providing an institutional setting for a literary flowering, a special magnet for aspiring writers and critics. In this sense, Tennessee was at the center of the renaissance, and even yet identified with it, much in the same way that it has had a central, originative, institutional role in the history of American religion.[14]

In every known culture, people sing and make music. They also draw or paint, shape wood or stone or cloth to suit their fancy or needs, and mold clay or metal into useful tools or containers. In so doing, they give bent to their own craving for self-expression. Everyone is, to some extent, an artist. Some develop more demanding skills. Some are more talented. Some gain fame for their artistry. It is only convention, or marketing priorities, that supports invidious comparisons among art forms, that leads to artificial distinctions between fine arts and folk arts or crafts. Equally artificial, from any esthetic standpoint, is a distinction between fine arts and merely useful arts, as if an artifact loses esthetic value if one uses it to make a living. Tennesseans have been as creative as other peoples, but very often this creativity has necessarily involved work and play, or the creation of objects that, in a poor society, almost had to have some utilitarian value. In its arts and crafts, Tennessee is not clearly distinctive. The beautiful quilts pieced and arduously quilted by its women are not clearly different from the quilts in other states. The same is true for the work of its potters, wood-carvers, and landscape painters. Even in music, its people have not clearly developed any one distinctive style.

One can classify various forms of singing and music making, but no classifications are worth very much. Tennesseans have been involved with, and made contributions to, every musical form. But Tennessee, until very recently, has not had the cultural resources—in music education or performance outlets—to nourish those skilled in composition or performance in symphonic music or opera. Whether most Tennesseans are proud of, or a bit embarrassed by, the fact—Tennessee is most often associated with what is now called country music, and correctly so. Also, by all impressionistic evidence, such as radio programming, Tennesseans, perhaps in greater proportions than any other state, listen to and appreciate country music. They have endorsed it by their support.

The problem with what people now call country music is one of both boundaries and roots. What is this music, and where did it come from? The problem with the questions is that ever more elusive "it." The label "country" is now a business label, one required by those who publish, record, and broadcast various types of music. Boundaries are very fuzzy, but in general the label identifies often elaborately developed forms of indigenous or grassroots music historically identified with the South and West.

What was this music when first identified and commercially exploited? No one can give a complete or satisfying answer. In a sense, it was almost any form of music widely performed and appreciated by white farmers or ranchers or factory workers in the South and Southwest. All the sources or roots of what became country music went way back. Of least direct influence, but closest to what some would have wanted as a source, and what a few performers, all the way down to the present, have gladly identified with, were the older ballads of English or Scottish origin, which indeed had survived among rural Americans of British ancestry, and perhaps to the greatest degree among some of the more isolated families in the Appalachians.[15]

In the early 1920s, fiddlers, singers, or quartets or other musical groups in the South found a new outlet for their talents in local radio. A few with the greatest local reputations began traveling to New York to cut records as early as 1922. They did what they had been doing all along. Some sang the familiar hymns of their church. Some displayed their local reputation in fiddling or on other instruments, such as the banjo, and, after World War I, the guitar. In effect, three broad musical traditions helped shape the early performers.

Most important were the hymns of evangelical churches. Little of the church music of the South was distinctive to the region, but by the twentieth century an evangelical form of Protestantism was more hegemonic in the South than in any other part of the country. This meant that here, more than in the North, evangelical hymns, particularly those of nineteenth-century origin, and those tied closely to revivals (often now called gospel hymns), had a near monopoly in churches.

In one sense, the South reflected a cultural lag. A warmer and hotter religion still dominated. The population remained more rural. Country churches still relished the older, sentimental hymns, and their choirs competed in local singing conventions. Young men and women formed gospel quartets, and delighted in close, four-part harmony. Until the 1930s, itinerant singing masters still came to rural churches to teach congregations and still used a simplified, shaped note form of instruction. In most of the Upper South, this involved a standard seven-note system, but in isolated areas of the Deep South, and among such sects as the Primitive Baptists, it still included the four-note, or fa-sol-la, system, one used in antebellum hymnals widely popular in the South, many with the title of *Sacred Harp.* This truly old-time church music would have little direct impact on modern country music, although "sacred harp" singing is part of a folk revival in Tennessee. But "gospel" hymns, until recently published for southern audiences with shaped notes, remained more popular in the South than in the North, and nourished a thriving musical publishing business (one of the largest centers was Lawrenceburg, the home of the James D. Vaughan publishing company). Along with the popularity of gospel hymns, southerners, particularly in the mountains and uplands, sang them with a distinctive style, one involving greater nasality or what some saw as a distinctive twang, and one that featured high soprano or tenor parts, a feature that bears some resemblance to the famous Negro spirituals first refined and standardized by the Fisk Jubilee Singers. These similarities led an early student of southern music to label these as white spirituals.[16]

The second major source of what became country music was a very secular tradition, one often at odds with the churches and church music. These were the tunes played at frolics or square dances and later, in taverns or honky-tonks. It was here that the old-time fiddlers performed. This music for dancing often traced back to the eighteenth century, and had both British and African roots, since even in the mountain South blacks were most often accepted and prized for their fiddling or banjo playing. Yet, as commercially developed, this dance music was almost entirely performed by whites for white audiences, despite numerous black influences. Until after World War II, some country performers still appeared in black face, however insulting to African Americans, and southern racial attitudes prevailed in the country music industry. Only belatedly have music historians appreciated the role of a few blacks, such as the great early harmonica player on the Grand Ole Opry, DeFord Bailey. Only in the 1960s did the industry welcome blacks, such as Charlie Pride, but he remains highly visible because he is so exceptional.

In the mountain South, the favored instrumental music usually accompanied local square dances or types of soft-shoe dancing. In the Deep South, it drew more directly from black culture, and often meshed with a musical genre known as the blues. Because so often condemned by evangelical churches, this music always had a slightly disrespectful image and was very much a masculine genre. Later, it easily merged into the music of drifters and rebels, those without a secure home or place. Such music led most early radio programs that emphasized this traditional instrumental music to use the term "barn dance," and from then on forms of dance have had a vital and often neglected role in what is called country music. The difficult question is what, if anything, distinguished local fiddling or dance accompaniment in the South? This question admits of no easy answer. In fact, local regions were variously distinguished by the style of play, by the way individuals held the fiddle, or the fingers used to chord or pick a banjo or guitar. Some of these techniques became identified with the South, and with a genre of music called hillbilly. Note that in rural areas of the South, musicians always used the correct older English term for an instrument that, for some reason, has become more widely known by its Italian name, the violin. The term "fiddle," perhaps more than any other word, symbolized a rustic or anti-elite, but almost never a politically radical, outlook on the part of those who developed commercial forms of country music.

The third source was cowboy music. This paralleled the growing popularity of stories and movies about a mythical West. By the 1930s, such movies and such music were almost a national obsession. "Buffalo Bill" Cody and Will Rogers had already created widely popular roping and Wild West shows. As in the case of mountain ballads, the actual, collected songs of early ranching and cattle drives would have only a marginal impact on the newly popular types of cowboy songs or western swing. But creative performers, such as

W. B. Queen playing fiddle at a Tellico Plains store, 1941. Record Group 82, Tennessee State Library and Archives.

Bob Wills, capitalized on the national popularity of the West, particularly in Texas and Oklahoma (he would perform only once at the Grand Ole Opry, but in 1943, Ernest Tubb brought this southwestern music to the Opry). Local composers and performers leaped at the chance to cash in on this western craze, and succeeded. Out of this came the singing cowboy, with various styles and affectations. The first great star would be Gene Autry. But almost everyone involved in the early, commercial development of barn dance music was influenced by cowboy themes and by such popular cowboy groups as the Sons of the Pioneers. Even in the southern Appalachians, local performers donned boots and cowboy hats or sang about life on the range.

How these varied sources came together in a now very successful musical genre is a fascinating epic, one well told by Bill C. Malone and other historians. But for this essay, the question is how did Tennesseans come to play such a vital role in the development of country music? Once again, as in religion and literature, its role would be largely institutional. It is not clear that Tennesseans have been more talented in this musical genre than performers from other states. That eight native-born Tennessee performers are in the

Grand Ole Opry performance, 1950s. Record Group 82, Tennessee State Library and Archives.

Country Music Hall of Fame (more than any other state, although Texas is close) may reflect a certain regional bias on the part of the Nashville-based Country Music Association. What is much more important is that almost every Hall of Fame performer, and almost all business leaders to gain this elite status, have had some connection to Nashville. Also, perhaps for accidental reasons, East Tennessee was literally there at the creation, very centrally involved in the commercial birth of country music.

The ballad collections of Cecil Sharp, added to local color writers like Murfree, helped create a national interest in a strange, purportedly isolated place called Appalachia. In the eyes of most Americans, this meant, primarily, the southern Appalachians. At least in theory, the various folkways of this largely mythical area were distinctive, although in neither literary depictions nor sociological studies was the focus very clear. But the images, however varied, created an expectation—surely this region had a distinctive folk music, possibly rooted in Anglo-Saxon ballads.

In 1927, Ralph Peer, then a talent scout for Victor Talking Machine Company in New York, came to Bristol (by sheer accident he set up on the Tennessee side of State Street) to audition local musicians, or those who might be likely candidates for record contracts. Peer had, since 1920, traveled widely in the South seeking local talent, and had already recorded both blues, for the "race" market, and several white musicians in what was already a vaguely identified country idiom. By 1927, popular barn dance radio programs existed in at least five cities, including Chicago, Atlanta, and Nashville. Peer would visit other cities even in this trip South. But nonetheless, the Bristol recording became justifiably famous. For example, five subsequent Hall of Fame performers (in three groups) recorded at Bristol. Also, Peer was able to use, for the first time, new electrical recording techniques, thus achieving a new level of fidelity.[17]

Peer wanted to find distinctive, mountain forms of music. It is not clear that he succeeded. But his leading contact at Bristol, and in a sense coconspirator in the recording, Ernest Stoneman, contrived the desired effect. Bristol was a good location, at least for tapping into the best musical talent in a four-state region. Bristol and Johnson City were in the rich valley, but adjacent to the nearby Unakas and Blue Ridge of Tennessee, North Carolina, and Virginia, and also to the dying Alleghenies of southwest Virginia and southeastern Kentucky. It was valley cities, from Bristol to Knoxville, that provided commercial services to the hills, and it would be here that early radio stations developed. These cities were, in a sense, in the mountains but not really of them. They were, in fact, in one of the richest areas of Tennessee. And even the musicians who came into the city to record were not isolated bumpkins, although Stoneman and others gladly played that role. It turned out to be a profitable affectation.

Stoneman, from nearby Galax, Virginia, was already an accomplished performer, with more than fifty records to his credit. His Stoneman Family became an enduring dynasty, particularly after World War II when Ernest and many of his children excelled in the new sounds of bluegrass. Ernest is deservedly in the Hall of Fame as one of the founders of country music. At Bristol, his band, including his wife and several kinsman and neighbors, recorded gospel, fiddling tunes, and even a rather suggestive courting song. In a skit prepared at Peer's request, several of his cronies from country-sounding places talked in a contrived mountain accent, snorted as they pretended to pass around a jug of moonshine, and displayed several types of music supposedly distinctive to the mountains. In this way, they tried to fit themselves to the image that outsiders had of Appalachia, and in so doing gave some artificial content to what Peer wanted from Bristol—a group of recordings that reflected a form of music that he already, in 1925, had labeled "hillbilly." It is notable that this hillbilly music was not so much something discovered as ingeniously contrived with an eye to marketing records, and that a rather sophisticated Stoneman clearly enjoyed the acting and the delightful leg-pulling.[18]

The Bristol sessions, which attracted nineteen groups (they received payment and a record contract), made one local preference clear. The performers and audiences best knew and appreciated gospel music, which made up over half the numbers recorded by Peer. Soloists, a quartet, a Pentecostal group, even a local church choir, all sang sentimental hymns. Of the performing groups, two would become famous. Stoneman had recruited the Carter family from nearby Scott County. Three family members came: Alvin Pleasant Carter, a near middle-aged farmer with what turned out to be sharp skills as a business manager; his wife, Sara; and his sister-in-law, Maybelle Carter, then eighteen and pregnant with her first child. They mainly performed gospel songs. They were serious about their music, and not about to play any assigned hillbilly role. It is not clear that they had any sense of being part of a new genre. But they were original and exceptionally talented. Sara played a simple autoharp. Maybelle introduced a haunting new sound in her guitar accompaniment, one that everyone soon tried to imitate. Peer loved their music, and introduced it to an appreciative audience in the first of what became a flood of Carter family recordings, and for them both fame and a series of family misfortunes. Through Maybelle's daughter, June (the wife of Johnny Cash), and granddaughter, Carlene, the Carter tradition lives on, clearly the greatest family dynasty in country music.

The other star whose recording career began in Bristol did not especially impress Peer. This was a sickly Jimmy Rodgers, who was then living in Asheville for health reasons. He had briefly joined a local Bristol band, the Tennessee Ramblers, and this group had helped schedule his recording sessions. From Mississippi, Rodgers had worked on the railroad, wandered all over the South, and already developed a special yodeling style. His roots were in the blues, not church music (he never sang hymns), and his personal style was flamboyant. He wanted to record contemporary pop music, but Peer finally persuaded him to complete one record only, including a ballad from World War I and a lullaby that featured his yodeling. This record helped increase his already widespread popularity, which boomed in the next six years before his early death in 1933. He soon gained a reputation as the father of country music, made and quickly spent a near fortune from record sales in the early depression era, finally settled in Texas, and incorporated many cowboy songs into his eclectic repertoire. But of all the performers at Bristol, he least reflected the largely evangelical culture of the southern Appalachians.[19]

The Tri-Cities remained a center for country music, but lacked the major radio stations needed to compete with a city like Nashville. In the immediate post–World War II years, it became, briefly, the center of a new, as yet unnamed, bluegrass revival. Bluegrass gained its name from Bill Monroe, from western Kentucky and a longtime Grand Ole Opry performer, who called his band the Blue Grass Boys. After 1945, Monroe rejected innovations such as electrical guitars and engaged some young musicians who introduced new sounds. These shaped an almost indefinable new genre, which in the 1960s became the rage during a folk revival. It never competed well in record sales, but has continued to thrive in regional bluegrass festivals. In a sense, bluegrass was purist and traditional in instrumentation—only acoustic—and improvisational in style, or what some have called the jazz of country music. The most creative innovator was Earl Scruggs from western North Carolina, who perfected a new type of three-finger banjo playing. In bluegrass, the instrumental work is fast and played by ear. Because of its ties to early hillbilly music, in instruments and nasality and high pitch in songs, this developing style was very popular in the four-state area centered on the Tri-Cities. When, in 1948, Scruggs and a talented guitarist and vocalist from the Cumberland Plateau in Tennessee, Lester Flatt, formed a separate band, the Foggy Mountain Boys, they briefly performed on WCYB in Bristol (on the Virginia side), and soon won several other bands over to their style. This made WCYB the mother of bluegrass, in the words of Bill Malone, and for a time many early bluegrass recordings originated in a small studio in Johnson City (Rich-R-Tone). Flatt and Scruggs moved on to the Opry and great national fame, even performing in Carnegie Hall in 1964. Other groups that began their bluegrass careers in the Tri-Cities included Jimmy Martin, the Stanley brothers, and the revived Stonemans. But the smaller radio stations in the Tri-Cities area could not compete with Nashville, and thus this area, like so many others, became a farm club for Nashville. Also, few of the bluegrass stars came from upper East Tennessee. The only performer from Bristol to gain the Hall of Fame would be a suave "Tennessee" Ernie Ford, who helped move country music, not back toward its Bristol roots, but as far as possible toward a slick pop sound.[20]

Knoxville was another incubator of country talent, and into the late 1930s a fully competitive rival of Nashville. Radio stations led the way, but drew upon an older tradition of fiddling and old-time music. The first Knoxville station, WNOX, began broadcasting in the 1920s, and in the 1930s created one of the most popular programs in East Tennessee, the "Mid-Day Merry-Go-Round." Its host, Lowell Blanchard, provided an outlet for a virtual who's who of country music, including two men who would have deserved Hall of Fame status for both their performance and their business and promotional skills, Roy Acuff and Chet Atkins, both from nearby and very impoverished Union County. The comedian Archie Campbell, from Greene County, began on this noon program by impersonating old "Grandpa." Kitty Wells, the first queen of country music, and from Nashville, performed on this midday program. The local grocer and Republican politician Caswell "Cas" Walker built a competing stable of performers on WROL, which for a period was also a host to Roy Acuff and his Crazy Tennesseans.

At the other end of the state, Memphis had a notable influence on forms of country music. West Tennessee would not be as involved in country music as East Tennessee or Nashville. Its one most famous star was Eddy Arnold, who in the immediate postwar years rivaled Hank Williams in fame, and who helped begin the move of country to something closer to pop. But it is important to remember that Memphis was the cultural capital of northern Mississippi, and thus close to the original forms of music that developed among blacks in the Delta. This included blues, a genre much recorded even in the twenties for a black audience, and not clearly separate from other forms of regional southern music. W. C. Handy, from Alabama, came by way of the Delta to Memphis and helped create the fame of Beale Street in blues and rhythm-and-blues. In time, blacks moved on to Chicago and Detroit, and these cities eclipsed Memphis as the commercial home of emerging forms of black music.[21]

Again because of good fortune, as much as location, Memphis was able to preside over the commercially successful merger of the heavily black-influenced blues and white country idioms. This was largely because of Elvis Presley from Tupelo, who moved with his family to Memphis, where he attended high school. There he was "discovered" in the early 1950s by the famous promoter, Sam Phillips, and first recorded on the local Sun label. Presley created a new and unique style, soon called rock 'n' roll. His exact relationship to country music involves definitions, but Presley performed on the Opry and recorded in Nashville. Yet, after 1954, the burgeoning popularity of new rock sounds provided the greatest threat to traditional country music, requiring from its producers both new sounds and some assimilation of rock. In Memphis, Phillips first recorded both Johnny Cash and Jerry Lee Lewis, both of whom combined country and rock in what was soon called "rockabilly."[22]

In spite of East Tennessee's pioneer role in country music, and Memphis's fame in blues and rock, Nashville would eventually dominate the country music industry. It would gain as near a monopoly on publishing, recording, and promoting this music as Detroit ever had in automobiles or Akron in rubber. But this preeminence came slowly, and it was not assured as late as 1950. However defined, the emerging forms of music marketed as country and western were a minor, regionally popular, and in many circles, stigmatized part of the music industry until World War II. Jimmy Rodgers was an exception, both in fame and fortune. Most of the aspiring entertainers, including some who later gained fame, could barely survive in the depression. They had to work hard to earn an income, and this largely from local performances in schools or courthouses in the South. They sought radio time largely to advertise their services, and only with a degree of fame could they gain a recording session. They generally formed small bands of three to six people, selected some hick-sounding name, used familiar terms for their comrades (uncle, brother, cousin, grandpa), and offered up an eclectic mix outfitted to appeal to largely rural audiences. They used radio to advertise their scheduled performances, and needed four or five of these a week to survive. They might travel in an old but well-stenciled station wagon to a small school, their instruments strapped on top, and there perform under the sponsorship of the PTA, collecting twenty dollars for their half of the gate. They adopted some form of distinctive dress, ranging from cowboy motifs to the work clothes of a farmer. Even such famous later stars as Roy Acuff began this way in the hills of East Tennessee. Most such groups failed and disbanded. By the late 1930s, all of them in Tennessee had one goal—to perform on the Grand Ole Opry.[23]

The repertoire of these often impoverished performing groups in the thirties set the enduring agenda for country music, even in its modern upscale format. For part of their audience, and to gain moral legitimacy, they had to feature gospel hymns. They also stressed instrumental music, most from the tradition of local dances or foxhunting, plus love songs or other secular vocal offerings. A few bands featured soft-shoe or clog dancing. Almost all had to have some comic relief, and some of the more popular bands, such as Knoxville-based Homer and Jethro, made this the centerpiece of their performances. The comic aspect was borrowed from vaudeville, and usually involved a stand-up routine, perhaps mixed with music. The clowns, for such they were, assumed their own special dress, often with a hayseed emphasis, and developed a repertoire of jokes, most deliberately corny in nature, or themes later caricatured on the popular television show *Hee Haw*. By far the most famous and beloved of these comics would be "Minnie Pearl," Sarah Ophelia Colley Cannon, the socially prominent, aspiring actress from Centerville, in Hickman County, who happily created the persona that became her alter ego. Minnie entertained at the Grand Ole Opry for fifty years.

In a sense, radio, even more than recording companies, created modern country music. Broadcasts of rustic music began almost as soon as commercial radio, first with a Fort Worth barn dance program, then with the National Barn Dance on WLS, Chicago, in 1923. Large, usually clear-channel radio stations soon developed name programs, and signed contracts with the most popular performers they could recruit. In time, a few of these programs became the incubator of modern country music, most notably stations in Chicago, Wheeling, Shreveport, Dallas, Atlanta, Charlotte, and Cincinnati. Nashville was an early entry, but for over a decade did not rival WLS in influence, although its early barn dance was purer in its commitment to authentic hillbilly, as contrasted to more popular, music.

The commercial background of country music is something of a scandal. One source of income for local musicians had long been medicine shows, those that hawked patent remedies. Nothing much changed with radio, for patent medicines, most of all Crazy Water Crystals, helped ensure the prominence of country music. The Grand Ole Opry did not have a much more distinguished commercial parentage. WSM, a creature of the National Life and Accident Insurance Company, went on the air in 1925, with only a thousand watts. National Life had gained its wealth largely by the sale of industrial insurance or small face policies sold by salesmen largely to poor whites and blacks who agreed to pay small monthly premiums, and these directly to the agents. The policies were very expensive given the coverage, and the worst possible bargain for clients, but lucrative for the company and its fee-based agents. This was just one of many ways of ripping off poor people, but one halfway justified by the fact that this system provided the only means for some poor families to buy insurance. As a whole, in its first fifty years, country music more often than not promoted medicines and other products of questionable value, or such downright harmful ones as tobacco and snuff.

WSM began and long continued with a broad program content. But as part of its early programming, it began its own small, local barn dance. It hired from WLS as its station director George D. Hay, an Indiana native, and before his brief stint with the National Barn Dance a news columnist and radio promoter in Memphis. Hay was committed to authentic forms of old-time music, and in 1925 launched on a Saturday evening the WSM Barn Dance, which involved local musicians performing live in a station studio.

As with almost all early barn dance programs, the primary emphasis was on instrumental music, with fiddling the natural emphasis in Nashville. Its first two stars were Uncle Jimmy Thompson and Uncle Dave Macon, both older and locally famous fiddlers (Macon lived much longer, and became the first star of the Opry and a deserving member of the Hall of Fame, along with Minnie Pearl, Kitty Wells, and Lester Flatt, who were also from Middle Tennessee). In 1927, Hay happily dubbed his barn dance the "Grand Ole Opry," since it followed a segment of grand opera. The title stuck, and in time became legendary. It had more to justify it than most people ever realized, for the storytelling songs on his barn dance bore a close resemblance to the dramatic stories embodied in opera, stories that had broad popular appeal in their European origin. In America, opera was artificial and contrived, a snobbish pretension of the few, and perhaps for this reason usually sung in unfamiliar European languages. Country musicians told stories that were familiar to an audience, which involved the most pressing concerns of their life (home, church, sin, salvation, sex, the open road, loneliness), and in an idiom they understood, thus serving much the same function as opera in its origins and early integrity.[24]

In 1932, in a critical technical coup, WSM won approval from the Federal Communications Commission for a fifty thousand–watt clear-channel station to complement a new and much taller tower. Since it now had the highest allowed wattage (Mexican-based stations were stronger) and was on the long-wave or low-frequency side of the AM band, this tower and wattage gave WSM the largest coverage of any radio station in the United States (at night, most of the country east of the Rockies and parts of Canada). Surprisingly, its live Grand Ole Opry broadcast had become popular with studio audiences, outgrowing its station home and forcing it to move to three different locations before it settled in 1942 in the 3,500-seat Ryman Auditorium, which had begun as a revival tabernacle and still had pews as seats.

In the mid-1930s, the Opry was only one of five or six nationally prominent barn dance radio programs (the closest competitor was in Renfro Valley, Kentucky), but it slowly gained preeminence by the beginning of the war, and has held it ever since. It is now the longest continuously broadcast program in America. New stars helped boost its reputation, beginning with Roy Acuff, who moved from Knoxville in 1938 with his newly renamed Smoky Mountain Boys, and Bill Monroe, who joined in 1939. As these names suggest, the Opry continued to emphasize more traditional rural music, or something closer to Appalachian roots. In a critical breakthrough in 1939, Prince Albert smoking tobacco began sponsoring a thirty-minute weekly Opry program on the NBC radio network. During World War II, Roy Acuff became the second Jimmy Rodgers, with enormous popularity, particularly among American soldiers, who voted him more popular than Frank Sinatra. By the end of the war, the Opry was the most prestigious country music program in America. It had its own large roster of stars, had already begun a performing division, and was able to sponsor very profitable tours of its stars, who gained an audience by the very fact that they were members of the Opry. In fact, by now, even an appearance on the Opry could enhance the appeal of an aspiring musician.

Although everyone wanted to perform on the Opry, until 1942 the country music business had continued to center in New York and Los Angeles. This gradually changed in the years from 1942 to 1957, or the years in which Nashville literally became "Music City" (the title was first used in 1950). In 1942, Fred Rose and Roy Acuff formed Acuff-Rose Publications, the first major entrée of Nashville into the business of music marketing. Acuff provided the money, and Rose the managerial direction, of what became, in the next decade, the second-largest publisher of country music in the United States. Rose was a minor performer, a prolific songwriter, and a skilled manager. He was not southern (he was born in Indiana), and for most of his life not involved with country music. He built a career in pop music, wrote hundreds of songs, and in the thirties was the major songwriter for Gene Autry's movies. When down on his luck in 1933, Rose first joined WSM and moved to Nashville. He began with only an afternoon program, but developed his knowledge of country music and soon helped promote a popular trio, the Vagabonds. Unlike George Hay, Rose never sought any pure country style, but from his first work in Nashville began to blend pop and country, and worked with both types of musicians, composing for either on demand. His tenure in Nashville was intermittent in the thirties, as he often worked in New York and Los Angeles, and in the process built invaluable contacts with almost all the publishing and recording experts in the business. It was this industry savvy that led Acuff to engage Rose for a new publishing company in Nashville.[25]

Publishing may seem a strange entrée for what later made Nashville "Music City." What the new Acuff-Rose company did was help songwriters (who were often also performers) copyright their original songs, and then so promote them as to make money for both writer and publisher. Royalties accrued on the sale of the sheet music, and by various contractual arrangements for records or radio performances. Thus, Acuff-Rose did all it could to procure a recording contract for the songs they managed, helped arrange tours and other promotions for those performers who used their property, and soon began various schemes to influence disc jockeys in order to gain more exposure for their songs. Publishing was a somewhat anarchic business in 1942, with two or three large national firms, and hundreds of small independents, some created by performers to protect their rights to their own songs. Acuff-Rose proved very open and helpful to both writers and performers and helped many secure needed contracts. The company provided a valuable service for young country music performers who came to Nashville because of the soaring reputation of the Opry, even as the work of Acuff-Rose helped increase that reputation.

Acuff-Rose, despite the talents of Rose, might not have made it into the big time except for one happy accident. Except for Acuff, it did not have access to most of the big names in country music. They still worked with New York or Los Angeles publishers, even as they recorded in these two cities. In 1946, a young singer, Hank Williams, who had come to Nashville to be a guest on the Grand Ole Opry, consulted Rose about some songs that he had written. This first contact began a fruitful partnership. Williams—erratic, brilliant, untutored in music—had to have a type of fatherly help. Of course, Rose selected and gained rights to the best of Williams's compositions, and Williams (from Alabama), almost alone, catapulted Acuff-Rose to preeminence in country publishing and promotion because of the intensity, the passion, and the originality of his writing and performing. Within a few years, Williams, with what some called his honky-tonk style, was a hotter star than Eddy Arnold. From 1948 until his almost suicidal death (a heart attack hastened by the abuse of alcohol and drugs) in January 1953, Williams provided over half of the Acuff-Rose songs to make *Billboard*'s top ten hits, although none of his records equaled the sales of "The Tennessee Waltz," which Rose promoted in both the country and pop markets. After Williams's death—to some, his martyrdom because of his recent firing by the Grand Ole Opry— he became the greatest cult figure in the history of country music.

Until the end of World War II, Nashville had no recording companies. Opry stars traveled to New York, Chicago, or elsewhere, to cut records. By 1945, a few companies sent portable equipment to Nashville, or used the recording facilities in Studio B at WSM. At first, Acuff-Rose helped their performers secure contracts from various labels, but in 1947 Rose allied himself to MGM, just then entering the record business, and on the strength of Hank Williams helped push it quickly to the status of a major company. But it had no Nashville studio. It, like other labels, used the only good studio in Nashville, Castle, which originated with a group of WSM technicians, who built their first separate studio in the Tulane Hotel in 1947. All major labels used the Castle facilities until the mid-1950s, when Castle closed. Until 1952, it had the only well-equipped Nashville studio, although Fred Rose accumulated enough of the then rather simple equipment to make records in his own garage. In 1953, Acuff-Rose formed a small recording company, Hickory, to help launch new and untested country performers, but at first it did not have a separate studio. Several independent studios did recordings in Nashville, and one, Bullet, even began pressing records in 1948.

Music Row was still in the future, but by 1952 Nashville was already the recognized capital of country music, and the local chamber of commerce began to exploit this fact. Acuff-Rose was soon joined by other Nashville-based publishers, such as Cedarwood and Tree (Sony-Tree is today the largest in country music). But still, the main recording business was outside Nashville, placing a burden on the increasing number of country music stars who chose to live in the Nashville area, and who made it the base for their tours.

Even this began to change in the mid-1950s. In 1952, Owen Bradley, an orchestra leader at WSM, built a small studio in the basement of a home on residential Sixteenth Avenue, South, or what later became the heart of Music Row. He soon acquired the most recent recording equipment, and built a Quonset hut next to the house, a studio that became a famous Nashville icon. Eventually, it became part of Columbia Records. Even more important was the work of Chet Atkins, who came to the Opry in 1950 as a backup player for Maybelle Carter and her three daughters. He was a master of the guitar, and experimented widely with various types of guitars and playing techniques. Thus, Atkins was in constant demand at recording sessions, the ablest backup musician in Nashville and perhaps in the history of country music. In 1952, he became an assistant to the RCA company in Nashville, helped persuade it to build a new, state-of-the-art studio in 1957 (now a museum called Studio B), and became director of RCA's country division in Nashville. The new studio involved multiple tracks, and allowed dubbing of single tracks and the insertion of background music or choral groups. Atkins, although committed to country music, had personal and entrepreneurial reasons to create records that would sell in the very midst of the commercial crisis created by the popularity of rock 'n' roll. He assembled some of the ablest musicians in Nashville, not only on traditional country instruments but on brass and string instruments plus the piano, or, in effect, background orchestras for recording sessions. The musicians all soon knew each other, were relaxed and innovative, worked out a numbered system for arrangements, and in effect were able, almost on the spot, to fit the backup music to the performer. This recording expertise, plus certain distinctive innovations (background choruses, echo effects, and a rich but relaxed sound) led to the tag "Nashville Sound" and lured musicians to Nashville in order to cut commercially successful records. These new techniques made Nashville recordings accessible to larger audiences, muted the more distinctive and to some more grating country sounds of the past, and brought country and pop much closer, at times virtually eliminating any clear boundaries. One reaction against these innovations was a revival of bluegrass.

This RCA investment in Nashville, and the work of Atkins and soon hundreds of session musicians, created the critical mass. In the next decade, all the major record labels established studios in Nashville. Today, Nashville and the immediately surrounding counties boast over a hundred recording studios, and completely dominate not only in country but increasingly in gospel and other genres.

Along with the recording and publishing industries, Nashville slowly accrued all the institutional supports of a large music industry. Industry executives organized a Country Music Association, basically a trade association, and attracted to Nashville representatives of the two major associations for songwriters. The Country Music Association established in 1961 its Country Music Foundation (archival and historical) and its Hall of Fame (a major tourist attraction after completion of its present building in 1967), which soon helped entice dozens of tourist and souvenir shops to the northern end of Music Row. Meanwhile, the owners of WSM in 1972 built a musical theme park, Opryland, and the first installment of an ever expanding Opryland Hotel (now the largest in the eastern United States) on the Cumberland River northeast of downtown Nashville. In 1974, to the regret of most performers, it moved the Grand Ole Opry to a new auditorium at the theme park. Only in 1994 did the present Oklahoma owners of Opryland restore and reopen the historic Ryman to concerts, by then a part of a larger effort to restore downtown Nashville as a tourist site. Dolly Parton, a certain future member of the Hall of Fame, with an authentic rags-to-riches personal biography (she is from the foothills of the Smokies in Sevier County), built a country music theme park, Dollywood, near her girlhood home at Pigeon Forge, on the road to Gatlinburg and the Great Smoky Mountains. In Memphis, a revived Beale Street, plus the Graceland home of Elvis, also helped establish music as the primary basis of Tennessee's most lucrative industry, tourism.

Today, country music is an almost indefinable and ever shifting blend of several musical styles. It has a national and even a growing international reputation. The number of all-country radio stations has grown from 328 in 1967 to over 2,400 today (second only to rock), and some polls indicate that country music is now the most popular genre in America. It has had a major role in movies and on television (two cable networks are headquartered in Nashville). The performers are from all over the United States, although with a still predominantly white southern or western background (in the mid-1990s, the most successful female and male vocalists, Reba McEntire and Garth Brooks, were from Oklahoma). It is not clear that Tennesseans have any edge in this highly commercialized business, either as writers or performers. But as in religion, Tennessee has an institutional centrality that is all-important. This means that songwriters, stars, backup musicians, and the heads of publishing and recording companies all flock to Nashville or its immediate surroundings. Given the infrastructure and the tourists, it is no wonder that practically every major performer has a home, or at least one home, in the Nashville area, meaning that among the leading attractions are bus tours of the homes of stars, a pattern reminiscent of Hollywood.

To assess the areas in which Tennessee or Tennesseans have had the greatest impact upon a national culture is not to do justice to the total cultural resources of the state. This would mean a very different focus, often upon local beliefs and values that have limited impact beyond Tennessee, or upon unique cultural groups within the state (one thinks of the still somewhat mysterious Melungeons of Hancock County). It would involve a perhaps tedious survey of Tennesseans who have distinguished themselves either in high culture (a Grace Moore in opera or such prize-winning writers as James Agee, Alex Haley, T. S. Stribling, and Peter H. Taylor) or in such areas as journalism (Adolph Ochs, H. Grantland Rice, and Ralph McGill). It might include popular singers (Dinah Shore) or a survey of major and often reasonably successful local efforts to gain viable performances in theater, symphony, opera, and dance. It would include the better museums, and some attention to the Tennessee institutions that have had some important impact on the physical sciences, such as the laboratories at Oak Ridge. It would stress major colleges and universities, and in particular, the special role of Fisk University in cultivating and supporting the work of black intellectuals. It would include those Tennesseans who have distinguished themselves in almost every field of scholarship. But in all of these areas, the contribution of Tennesseans has not been out of line with that of individuals from other states. Only in religion, literature, and country music has Tennessee exerted a major and distinctive influence upon the culture of the nation.

NOTES

1. These definitions and much of the following story draw extensively from my recent book *The Uneasy Center: Reformed Christianity in Antebellum America* (Chapel Hill, N.C., 1995).
2. The most general history of these western revivals is in John Boles, *The Great Revival, 1787–1805* (Lexington, Ky., 1972); for the background on Scottish-style communions, see Leigh Eric Schmidt, *Holy Fairs: Scottish Communions and American Revivals in the Early Modern Period* (Princeton, 1989); I have written on these revivals in both *Cane Ridge: America's Pentecost* (Madison, Wis., 1990) and in an essay, "Caldwell's Boys," *Tennessee Historical Quarterly* 50 (Summer 1991), 71–79.
3. Ben M. Barrus, "A Study of the Factors Involved in the Origins of the Cumberland Presbyterian Church, 1800–1813," Ph.D. diss., Vanderbilt Univ., 1964.
4. Frederick A. Norwood, *The Story of American Methodism: A History of the United Methodists and Their Relations* (Nashville, 1974).
5. Hubert I. Hester, *Southern Baptists and Their History* (Nashville, 1971).
6. See Nancy Tatom Ammerman, *Baptist Battles: Social Change and Religious Conflict in the Southern Baptist Convention* (New Brunswick, N.J., 1990); and Bill Leonard, *God's Last and Only Hope: the Fragmentation of the Southern Baptist Convention* (Grand Rapids, Mich., 1990).
7. Owen D. Pelt and Ralph Lee Smith, *The Story of the National Baptists* (New York, 1960); and Bobby L. Lovett, *A Black Man's Dream: The First Hundred Years—Richard Henry Boyd and the National Baptist Publishing Board* (Jacksonville, Fla., 1993).
8. Katharine L. Dvorak, *An African-American Exodus: The Segregation of the Southern Churches* (Brooklyn, N.Y., 1991).
9. Winfred Ernest Garrison and Alfred T. DeGroot, *The Disciples of Christ, A History* (St. Louis, 1964); and David Edwin Harrell, *Quest for a Christian America: The Disciples of Christ and American Society to 1866* (Nashville, 1966).
10. Charles Edwin Jones, *Perfectionist Persuasion: The Holiness Movement and American Methodism, 1867–1936* (Metuchen, N.J., 1974); James R. Goff, Jr., *Fields White unto Harvest: Charles F. Parham and the Missionary Origins of Pentecostalism* (Fayetteville, Ark., 1988); Donald W. Dayton, *Theological Roots of Pentecostalism* (Metuchen, N.J., 1987); Robert Mapes Anderson, *Vision of the Disinherited: The Making of American Pentecostalism* (New York, 1979).
11. Unfortunately, no scholarly book exists on Mason or the history of the Church of God in Christ. The overall story is in the above books on Pentecostalism.
12. Mickey Crews, *The Church of God: A Social History* (Knoxville, 1990).
13. Richard Cary, *Mary N. Murfree* (New York, 1967).
14. Louise Cowan, *The Fugitive Group: A Literary History* (Baton Rouge, 1959); Louis D. Rubin, Jr., *The Wary Fugitives: Four Poets and the South* (Baton Rouge, 1978); Paul K. Conkin, *The Southern Agrarians* (Knoxville, 1988).
15. Anyone interested in country music has to begin with the almost definitive work of Bill C. Malone, in both his standard survey, *Country Music USA*, rev. ed. (Austin, 1985), and his provocative interpretations in *Singing Cowboys and Musical Mountaineers* (Athens, Ga., 1993).
16. George Pullen Jackson, *White Spirituals in the Southern Uplands* (Chapel Hill, N.C., 1933).

17. Charles K. Wolfe has told the story of these Bristol recordings in his book *Tennessee Strings: The Story of Country Music in Tennessee* (Knoxville, 1977), and in "The Bristol Sessions," an essay issued by the Country Music Association (1987) with its new cassette version of the Bristol Recordings.

18. Most books about country music stars, or ghosted biographies, are thin in content and suspect on details. This is not true for Ivan M. Tribe, *The Stonemans: An Appalachian Family and the Music that Shaped Their Lives* (Urbana, Ill., 1993).

19. Nolan Porterfield, *Jimmy Rodgers: The Life and Times of America's Blue Yodeler* (Urbana, Ill., 1979).

20. See Malone's chapter on bluegrass in *Country Music USA,* 323–67; and Wolfe, *Tennessee Strings,* 82–86.

21. William C. Handy, *Father of the Blues, An Autobiography* (New York, 1941); Lawrence Levine, *Black Culture and Black Consciousness: Afro-American Folk Thought from Slavery to Freedom* (New York, 1977); and William R. Ferris, Jr., *Blues from the Delta* (Garden City, N.J., 1978).

22. Jerry Hopkins, *Elvis: A Biography* (New York, 1972); and *Elvis: The Final Years* (New York, 1980).

23. Much of this description relies on my own personal memory of Roy Acuff and his band, which twice performed at my local elementary school in upper East Tennessee, and on the memories of other family members.

24. Cecelia Tiche, in *High Lonesome: The American Culture of Country Music* (Chapel Hill, N.C., 1994) emphasizes the themes present in country music, relates those to the American literary tradition, and in effect argues that the "country" in the label is fully descriptive—this is, more than any other, the music of the whole country.

25. For this and the following story of Acuff-Rose, I am most indebted to John W. Rumble, "Fred Rose and the Development of the Nashville Music Industry, 1942–1954," (Ph.D. diss., Vanderbilt Univ., 1980). Two more popular treatments of country music in Nashville are Paul Hemphill, *The Nashville Sound: Bright Lights and Country Music* (New York, 1970); and John Lomax III, *Nashville: Music City USA* (New York, 1985).

The Social Memory of the South: Donald Davidson and the Tennessee Past

■   Paul V. Murphy

■

■   *Editor's Note:* Donald Davidson, a longtime professor of English
     at Vanderbilt University, was one of the most important Agrarian
■   writers of the mid-twentieth century. His romantic memories of
     preindustrial rural Tennessee shaped his life and work. In his clas-
■   sic two-volume history of the Tennessee River, Davidson de-
     fended a traditional portrait of Tennessee history and values. He
■   questioned the forces of modernity, such as the Tennessee Valley
     Authority, then reshaping the state's economy and culture.
■   Davidson's Tennessee was strictly a white man's world. Women
     may have a limited role in that story, but he doubted that African
■   Americans were even southerners, much less people who made
     meaningful contributions to Davidson's sense of meaning and
■   identity as a Tennessean.

    While attending prep school, Donald Davidson would sit on a bench
outside a country store, talking for hours with two Confederate veterans.[1]
"The old Confederate soldier was still a familiar figure in my early years,"
Davidson recalled later in life. "I have sat long hours with these old men, in
the country store or by the fireside, and heard their tales."[2] It was his grandmother, though, a young woman who "saw the worst of it all" during the Civil
War, who made the deepest impression on Davidson. "My grandmother on
my mother's side—Rebecca Patton Wells—lived with us for many years, and
practically took charge of me when I was a little boy," Donald Davidson recalled in 1952. "From her I heard many terrible and also stirring tales of her
experiences during the war—all she went through during the Federal occupation of Middle Tennessee."[3]
    Davidson was a native of Tennessee, one of the leaders of the group of social

critics known as the Southern Agrarians, a poet and professor of English at Vanderbilt University for over forty years, and, in the 1950s, the chairman of Tennessee's equivalent of a Citizens' Council. His literary reputation did not match that of his Agrarian colleagues John Crowe Ransom, Allen Tate, or Robert Penn Warren. Nor did he attain their level of influence in American literary circles and intellectual life. But the relative eclipse of Davidson's literary reputation and his postwar record of opposition to the civil rights movement should not obscure his importance in the history of Southern Agrarianism nor his role as a social critic concerned with the function of the past in contemporary life.

In many ways, Davidson's thought and writings reveal most clearly the limitations and possibilities of Agrarianism. Further, Davidson served as a vital link between Agrarianism and the larger world of conservative thought in the United States after World War II. The Agrarians first presented their views in *I'll Take My Stand: The South and the Agrarian Tradition,* published in 1930. The volume was a collection of twelve essays written by twelve individuals; the title page declared the authors to be "Twelve Southerners."[4] Agrarianism revolved around the ambition of Davidson and his colleagues to preserve the small-scale, humanistic society of the South that they believed was endangered by the strictures of modern life. In this sense, it was a very conservative cultural criticism.

Yet, the Agrarians, aside from some limited forays into anti-industrialist coalition building in the early and mid-1930s, did not articulate a comprehensive conservative political economy. Neither did Davidson. However he, like some of the original Agrarians and many of their followers, returned to the issues addressed in *I'll Take My Stand.* He reinterpreted Agrarianism and developed his own regionalist perspective on American culture. In the process, Davidson developed a politics of culture oriented around southern memory and southern identity. It was Davidson's elaboration of a politics of cultural identity that served as the inspiration for later thinkers, most notably the late literary scholar M. E. Bradford, a friend and student of Davidson's, to incorporate the Agrarians into a broader, more comprehensive conservative political tradition.[5] Many postwar conservatives have eagerly included the Agrarians, whom they present as implacable anti-statists and defenders of a traditional moral and social order, in their own intellectual lineage. This is a lineage into which Davidson fits quite well, but which includes many of the original Agrarians most uncomfortably.

An examination of the thought of Donald Davidson and his treatment of the Southern, and the Tennessee, past sheds light on Agrarianism's evolution as a form of cultural conservatism. Davidson was committed to the preservation of the social memory of the South. Indeed, this task was important to him in a highly personal way; the past was a source of identity. Yet he did not have a theoretical politics of memory and traditionalism. Rather, in a more elliptical fashion, Davidson viewed social memory as preliminary to politics. It served as the basis of citizenship. Davidson's sense of citizenship was, then, one of membership in a circle of southern identity. And if Davidson's view of citizenship did not prescribe an explicit politics, the narrowness of its vision, one that excluded African Americans, closely circumscribed what any southern politics could be.

Davidson was born in Campbellsville, Tennessee, near Pulaski, in 1893. His mother was a music elocution teacher, and Davidson, who played piano and composed music as a young man, thought of becoming a professional musician rather than a writer. Davidson's father was a schoolteacher, eventually becoming coprincipal of a southern academy.[6] The elder Davidson was an important intellectual influence on the young boy, not only schooling him in the classics but also imparting a keen interest in American folklore, including songs, stories, and ballads.[7] But it was from his mother's side of the family, in the person of Grandmother Wells, that Davidson imbibed his southern loyalty. Davidson wrote in 1925, "I yield to nobody in my love of the South, and my loyalty to its best traditions. My blood-kin fought at Shiloh and Murfreesboro, and I claim a personal affinity with the soil of Middle Tennessee."[8]

He was educated at home until the age of eight, when he entered the Lynnville Academy in Tennessee and was placed in the fifth grade. When he was twelve he entered a preparatory school, Branham and Hughes, in Spring Hill, Tennessee. Davidson excelled and, by 1909, was thoroughly steeped in a rigorous classical curriculum.[9] From this point until he began graduate work in English, Davidson's education was marked by interruptions and hardships due to financial disability. After a year at Vanderbilt University financed by a family friend, he was forced to withdraw due to lack of funds. He only returned after spending four years teaching school in small Tennessee towns. Eventually, he earned his master's degree and joined the Vanderbilt faculty.[10] Upon returning to Vanderbilt, Davidson and a circle of like-minded friends (including the young professor John Crowe Ransom) began to meet regularly to discuss ideas. For the next twenty years, this loose group of men, with some change over the years, continued to meet; these associations became the center of Davidson's intellectual life in Nashville. Eventually they published a distinguished magazine of poetry, the *Fugitive,* and, in 1930, *I'll Take My Stand.*

Before *I'll Take My Stand,* however, Davidson undertook in his poetry to explore his personal relation to the southern past. Memory shaped Davidson's identity to an extent that was unique among the leading Agrarians. Unlike the modernists Ransom, Tate, and Warren, Davidson's poetic vision was lyrical and romantic. He brought no irony to his sense of southern identity. Indeed, the social memory of the South was a source both of spiritual solace and values for Davidson, replacing the traditional spiritual and ethical function of religion.[11]

Davidson's "emotionalized" understanding of the past was embodied in a minor epic published in 1927, *The Tall Men.* It was, he wrote fellow Agrarian John Gould Fletcher, "in many ways . . . a self-orientation, after which I may go on with a feeling that I know where I am headed."[12] The poem was the quasi-autobiographical representation of one man's ruminations and acts of remembrance as he moved through the routines of daily life in a modern city. Davidson ruefully contrasted the effete modern man, his prosaic and meaningless daily rituals made even more banal by their reliance on homogenized consumer goods, with the "tall men," the red-faced Tennessee pioneers who had hacked a civilization out of the backwoods wilderness. The words of these men were "bullets"; they "Talked with their rifles bluntly and sang to the hills / With a whet of axes."[13]

As the narrator walked the "long street," however—a common figure for the process of recollection in Davidson's poetry—he came to the conclusion that the spirit of the "tall men" lived on in his own blood. The secret vitality of life is present in the seed passed from generation to generation. "Oh, come away death!" the narrator said, "I who have had no ending cannot know / What it is to end."[14] Further, the process of remembering became a source of spiritual renewal that was sacramental in nature. As Michael M. Jordan observed in a recent dissertation on Davidson, Davidson formulated a "declared sacrament of history remembered, a secular memorial of the heroism and valor of the Confederate dead."[15] The ritual of this sacramental remembrance was a visit to the graves of the Confederate dead, men who carried the southern pioneer blood and whose sacrifices Davidson refused to forget. Though the "sod of old battle-fields" had long since been washed clean of blood, Davidson's narrator symbolically partook in the old soldiers' bloody sacrifice, picking a flower from the gravesite.[16] Just as a flower is woven into a chaplet, so he will weave and reweave the memory of past sacrifices, conveyed to him by such as his grandmother and the old veterans outside the country store, into his own life. The re-weaving was both purifying and regenerative. "This is my body," Davidson wrote, in an early emotional climax in the poem. "Broken but never tamed, risen from the bloody sod, / Walking suddenly alive in a new morning."[17] An invocation of a memory-based alternative to the Christian sacrament of communion, the poem conveyed Davidson's deep attachment to the southern past.

The Tall Men also transmitted a conception of tradition. To fail to nurture one's history and fulfill the obligation to those who handed down their lives was to risk the loss of one's claim on the energy and courage of the "tall men" of the past. The losers in Davidson's poem—those who the tall men defeated, namely, the American Indians—have no one to speak for them. Speechless, their sacrifices and particularities lost to history, they are present only in their burial mounds. For Davidson's purposes in *The Tall Men,* they died for nothing, since no one claims their heritage.[18] What was handed down was lost by succeeding generations.

Davidson, with Ransom and Tate, was one of the primary organizers of *I'll Take My Stand.* The authors expressed an anti-modernist distrust with the "business civilization" of the 1920s. Unlike such Left cultural critics as Lewis Mumford, Van Wyck Brooks, and the Young Intellectuals, who were also critical of the crass, materialistic culture of the period, the conservative southerners were not interested in cultural rebellion or the planning of a new type of human community. Rather, the Agrarians reaffirmed the culture and values they believed characterized life in the South, especially in the small towns and country.

Ransom, Tate, and Davidson sought to define a practically effective humanism, one that was defined by a particular socioeconomic structure (they vehemently denounced industrial capitalism) and rooted in southern tradition. The future Agrarians had labored far into the planning of *I'll Take My Stand* without deciding how this southern humanism could be conveyed in a powerful way. The idea of "agrarianism" as an aggressive defense of an agrarian economic system over and against industrial capitalism became the preferred rhetorical device by December 1929.[19] Their definition of "agrarianism" served as a unifying principle that was both a cogent critique of the industrial civilization that they abhorred and an invocation of a mythical southern past. Humanism, Davidson argued, cannot be introduced into society from the top, "by means of a movement which is purely literary and philosophical"; rather, he believed, a "movement of reform must begin at the base of our life—that is, with its economic base."[20]

Ultimately, however, Agrarianism was fated to be remembered as a vivid datum in the stream of American literary history. The Agrarians have been honored as sages and prophets by intellectuals sympathetic to their aims, particularly conservatives like M. E. Bradford, but the practical efficacy of their brand of southern humanism was nil. Despite the fact that in the 1930s, the Agrarians, led by Tate, enthusiastically attempted to link their critique with a wider range of decentralist thinkers, from English distributists to spokesmen for the Catholic land movement to idiosyncratic cooperative and back-to-the-land social planners, the Agrarians lacked an effective politics.[21]

Moreover, the Agrarians themselves split. Almost as soon as the symposium was published, indeed in his own contribution to *I'll Take My Stand,* Tate began to regret the particularist identification of the Agrarians' social critique with the South. Davidson's attachment to southern culture, however, only became deeper. (The same might be said for two of the other original Agrarians, both closely connected with Tennessee's intellectual life in the mid-twentieth century: the novelist Andrew Nelson Lytle and historian Frank L. Owsley.) Davidson looked to the revival of regionalism in the United States as the most effective means to resist the expansive and self-aggrandizing culture of industrialism. Just as Agrarians like Tate moved away from a sharp identification with the South, Davidson stressed ever more strongly the importance of native soil and regional loyalties to American character.

Davidson's celebration of southernness was just one example of a more general trend in American culture in the 1920s and 1930s toward a positive reappraisal of regional folk cultures. This efflorescence of regionalist thinking took many different forms in America: whether in the social planning of Howard Odum and his associates at the University of North Carolina; the collection of folk tales and ballads of the West by anthologists and writers; the fascination with Indian art and culture, which resulted in a renewed interest in native American issues; the attention paid to the folk culture of southern whites, which produced the Appalachian Craft Revival; or the myriad individual inquiries into American folk customs, such as, for example, Constance Rourke's writings about American humor. Regionalism was, as Robert L. Dorman observed in a recent study, "in the air."

Regionalism was a negative response to the modernization of American society. Many regionalists shared the opinion of the midwestern muralist Thomas Hart Benton, who declared that cities "offer nothing but coffins for living and thinking."[22] They believed that genuine culture was rooted in the organic traditions of the folk, the vitality of which derived from a firm sense of place. Many regionalists dismissed the idea of a national culture. Instead, they suggested that America's essence as a nation was the fact that it possessed no single national culture. The folk cultures of America, regionalists argued, possessed great truths, whether economic, religious, or political, even as these cultures were endangered by the inevitable spread of the homogenizing mass culture of the metropolis.[23]

Dorman believed that the regionalist movement—cohesive throughout most of the 1930s—diminished as a major cultural force because the myths and assumptions upon which it was based were not strongly enough rooted in the American consciousness to guarantee success. Further, Franklin Delano Roosevelt's New Deal subsumed many regionalist projects and much of the regionalist worldview. The social engineering of the federal government, best exemplified in a project such as the Tennessee Valley Authority, which was intended to revitalize a region stretching over several southern states, produced a reality of centralized power and decision making that belied the dreams of localist visionaries.[24]

In addition, Dorman argued, regionalists came to see that great differences separated one group from another. Dorman distinguished between backward-looking regionalists intent on creating new myths for a revived civic culture from more forward-looking planners, who insisted that old myths of pioneer unity and virtue were false. Regionalists such as the Agrarians and Donald Davidson, Dorman argued, were defensive, partaking of the same insecurities about their identity as did the second Ku Klux Klan and various 100 percent Americanism and nativist groups in the 1920s.[25] In Dorman's view, pluralist regionalists, in particular proponents of Indian culture and liberal sociologists, moved beyond a narrow sectionalism. This type of regionalism, exemplified by, for example, Dorothea Lange's documentary photography of immiserated migrant workers or John Steinbeck's *Grapes of Wrath*, punctured the rosy myths of folk vitality of the romantic nationalists while still displaying a respect for the strength and integrity of a diverse America.[26] Nevertheless, the overriding goal of the regionalist movement was the reseeding and recultivation of America through attention to the nation's individual cultures and folkways.[27]

Dorman's criticisms of the insularity of Agrarianism are justified, although it is a mistake to see the Agrarians as especially unified in their outlook. Davidson most displayed the narrow defensiveness of which Dorman wrote. Davidson's regionalism embodied a cultural politics of identity. Yet Davidson did not intend to define a politics merely for southerners. His adoption of regionalist arguments was a way of avoiding just that. Davidson wanted to move beyond a sectional viewpoint by celebrating the strength and integrity of all America's regions. In fact, regionalism, like Agrarianism, was a means to sidestep a straightforward politics of southern traditionalism.

Davidson's regionalism took its fullest form in *The Attack on Leviathan: Regionalism and Nationalism in the United States*, a collection of his writings on American culture and southern history published in 1938. Yet a sharp and concise statement of Davidson's thinking had appeared five years previously in "Sectionalism in the United States," a 1933 essay in the *Hound & Horn*.[28] Drawing on many of the currents of regional thought of the day, Davidson portrayed regionalism as, above all, a rejection of the false social identity impressed upon Americans by industrialism. According to Davidson, a "real organic homogeneity which has been remarkably persistent" characterized each section of the country.[29] In Davidson's regionalism, sectional identity tended to be rooted in racial homogeneity. The national, synthetic identity that he decried resulted from an influx of varied ethnic stocks. Davidson professed admiration, for example, for the old New Englander, but this type of person no longer represented that section of the country. Instead, new ethnic stocks, "ignorant of the American past," were becoming dominant. "Their rise to power accelerates the detachment from the thought of other sections into which the urban East is falling," Davidson argued. The America of Waldo Frank's pluralist *Our America,* he added, was not that of Henry Cabot Lodge or Will Rogers.[30]

Nativism, however, was not the sole component of Davidson's regionalism. Although he attributed the loss of sturdy American identities to new immigrants, he also spoke of "native immigrants," by which he meant "careerists who have cut loose from their native soil."[31] An upwardly mobile middle class in which ethnic identity was erased was part of the problem. Despite these tendencies, Davidson became convinced that sectional loyalties—which, for him, in fact amounted to old ethnic loyalties—were resurgent, even if this fact went unnoticed by cosmopolitans. "What reporter of the progress of the Great American Bandwagon has adequately noted our passionate interest in genealogy, the increasing prestige of historical societies and memorial associations, the solicitude to preserve old shrines and landmarks—all the devices that turn Americans toward particularist, sectional attitudes?" Davidson remarked. He saw all these factors as signs of a "new self-consciousness" abroad in America.[32] Sectionalism, he argued, fostered a loyalty that the nation-state, the great Leviathan, never could. The "Republic," he believed, had become too abstract, incapable of inspiring loyalty.[33] Writers such as the Agrarians, Davidson argued, articulated this general

American rejection of the artificiality of the metropolis in favor of a concrete allegiance to place and local tradition. The Agrarians "pointed out a road away from Leviathanism."[34]

Sectionalism, therefore, was a positive, not a destructive, force; the national government and the minority populations within each state could check whatever excesses it might possess.[35] The truest American identity lay in its regional cultures. "Our most characteristic national songs are those that record sectional experience," Davidson observed. "Our literature, architecture, folklore, history, accent dissolve the national complex into sectional entities. Rivers, mountain ranges, deserts, degrees of latitude, differences of soil and climate divide us."[36] To believe in an "American" identity was to believe in something that had no substantial existence—to subscribe to a "characterless and synthetic Americanism." Identity arose from America's regions. "Their national unity consists in the avowal which any section should rejoice for the others to make: that we are Rebels, Yankees, Westerners, New Englanders or what you will, bound by ties more generous than abstract institutions can express, rather than citizens of an Americanized nowhere, without family, kin, or home."[37]

Ultimately, Davidson's regionalism was an assertion of cultural identity. The national government, he argued, had become an impersonal and inhuman juggernaut, a "leviathan." Regionalism, as articulated in *The Attack on Leviathan,* constituted an elaborate program of resistance to the cultural intrusions of northern industrialism and the political intrusions of what Davidson saw as its political equivalent, the federal government.

All the same, Davidson denied that Agrarianism incorporated a political theory as such. In "Agrarianism and Politics," published in 1939, Davidson concluded that the Agrarians did not possess a politics.[38] The Agrarians had affirmed a way of life, Davidson argued, one that recognized biology over mechanism, the spiritual over the material.[39] Industrialism did precisely the opposite, elevating the material over all other aspects of life.[40] The Agrarians, he declared, had been aiming for a "different kind of politics entirely," at least one different from the standard definition of "politics."[41] Undoubtedly responding to the many critics who had derided the Agrarians as hopeless nostalgists desiring to turn back the clock and reverse social progress, Davidson declared that the problem with modern life was not labor-saving machinery or consumer conveniences such as the electric refrigerator, but the role these devices assumed in daily life. The means of the good life, he argued, were being mistaken for the ends.[42] Similarly, the problem with the New Deal was not so much in the reforms it introduced but the way in which these reforms were achieved. The means used—the nationalization of life and the creation of a large state—did not justify the ends.

The task of the Agrarians was to "limit and perhaps finally to transform industrialism," or, as Davidson wished, to make it more human.[43] In a practical sense this left the Agrarians with no set political goals and platforms; rather, their task was to "study the way of life and to work for a slow but certain change."[44] Agrarianism became in Davidson's hands in 1939 a cultural politics, with no definite social or economic agenda. This was a notable retreat from the original Agrarian program. In 1930, the Agrarians had stressed the necessity of resisting the socioeconomic changes wrought by industrial capitalism. To preach cultural values and humanistic goals without challenging the social and economic changes that were undercutting the basis of a humanistic culture would be of no avail. For Davidson, Agrarianism now became merely the resistance of the modernization of social identity. Davidson resisted the nationalization of American culture and the detachment of the individual from the confining strictures of custom and tradition. In this sense, social memory was vital, for it defined one's social identity, and the nature of one's relationship to the polity. It gave body and substance to the very idea of citizenship.

The unhappy consequences that resulted when southerners became "citizens of an Americanized nowhere" were major themes of Davidson's attempt to provide a narrative of the southern past, *The Tennessee*, his two-volume history of the Tennessee River valley, published in 1946 and 1948. *The Tennessee*, begun in 1940 and originally intended to be a single volume, was a part of Farrar and Rinehart's Rivers of America series. The Rivers of America series was itself an example of the cultural nationalism prevalent in the 1930s; each volume reaffirmed the American folk and their common democratic tradition.[45] When approached by John Farrar to do the volume, Davidson eagerly took on the project. Indeed, he had been working with Tennessee historical materials off and on since 1929.[46] In the long history of the river, from its original use by Indians, through the encroaching arrival of white settlers, to its use by Federal naval vessels to help defeat the South in the Civil War, and, finally, to its taming at the hands of the Leviathan federal government in the form of Franklin Delano Roosevelt's New Deal agency, the Tennessee Valley Authority (TVA), with its dams and power plants, Davidson produced a parable for the history of the South as a whole.

The most distinctive aspect of the Tennessee River—which doubles back upon itself and flows across the state of Tennessee twice, dividing it into three sections—was its difficulty of navigation. The whirlpools and rocky shoals of this harsh and inhospitable river were given such names as the Suck, the Narrows, Boiling Pot, Skillet, and Pan. The river's utility as a thoroughfare for traffic in goods and people was always limited, with the upper Tennessee effectively cut off from the lower section of the river by the hazards of the Great Bend, where the river doubled back upon itself. This ungovernability and wildness served as a metaphor for the free-spirited frontiersmen and Indians—the hardy souls who made a culture for themselves in the unsettled Tennessee valley. Their communities, organized into clans, embodied the virtues of a traditional society.

Davidson portrayed the Indians positively (if stereotypically). The Indians and frontiersmen engaged each other in savage warfare, but it was on equal terms and marked by moments of mutual respect. Davidson discussed the great burial mounds, surviving remnants of Indian culture. This was not the first time Davidson used the fate of Tennessee's Indian population in his work. In *The Tall Men*, the Indians existed as memories. They were dead, the victims of white pioneers. Their only remains were the graves, the great burial mounds. With no descendants to remember them, the meaning of the dead Indians' sacrifice was lost. *The Tall Men* ended with an image of a father and son on an overgrown Indian burial mound. The father pointed to the mound and instructed his son to ask what the Indians died for. The answer is "Nothing!"[47] The deaths of the Indians were meaningless because not remembered.

In *The Tennessee,* Davidson discussed the mounds again, this time giving an account of who left them and what function they served. But at least the mounds survived—as some sort of memorial. As a viable community in Tennessee, the Indians did not. They had lost the battle between themselves and with the whites. However, it was not so much the battles with pioneers that destroyed their culture as the corrupting influence of trade and the world of commerce. "It [commerce] brought the Indian tribes into the white man's power," he wrote. "Once they became dependent on guns, axes, and blankets which they must 'buy' and could not make, they lost their self-sufficiency and put themselves at the mercy of an economy and a politics which they could not understand."[48] They agreed to treaties with the whites—and were persuaded to submit to a European crown, listening as a British agent admonished them not to break their solemn vow of loyalty lest they, in the stilted diction thought appropriate when addressing Indians, "would become no People."[49] It was, of course, the whites who broke their solemn commitments;

but it was not they who became "no People." It was the Indians who did, forced to follow a trail of tears to the West, leaving behind only the mounds beneath which lay their dead.

Volume 2 of Davidson's history told of the decline of the sturdy Tennessee communities, as they came under incessant attack from outsiders—namely Yankees—first in the form of Union soldiers, then under the authority of the Roosevelt-era federal government. The Civil War was, in Davidson's partisan account, a savage attack on southern society. In no way was it like the Indian fighting of the colonial era. William Tecumseh Sherman introduced total war into Tennessee, and in Davidson's description one could hear the echoes of Davidson's grandmother as she recounted stories of Yankee atrocities to him as a boy: "Under Sherman's authority, ravage became an official Federal policy. During the later years of the war, therefore, the Federal invasion, especially in the Great Bend, could hardly be distinguished from the inroads of a Genghis Khan or an Attila."[50] Davidson glorified such agents of southern "redemption" as the Ku Klux Klan, whom he portrayed as a noble group organized not to persecute blacks but to fight the agents of commerce, industrialism, and northern domination.

Industrial advance, promoted by southern "New South" boosters and spokesmen, was the most insidious challenge to southern traditions of community. "History was repeating itself," Davidson observed of industrialization in the South, "with an irony that may or may not have been justifiable. They who had invaded the old Indian lands had now in their turn been invaded and worsted."[51] The invasion had not ended but continued into the present. The TVA was its culmination. In his generally even-handed account of the TVA, Davidson did not question the agricultural reforms and navigational improvements resulting from the development of the river (although the man-made reconstruction of the river was an irresistible metaphor for industrialization's defeat of the pioneering spirit) but rather the way in which these gains were made. Davidson was alarmed at the expansive power of the federal government. He referred to the TVA as "King Kilowatt" and suggested that the TVA directors held "powers that kings might have envied."[52] As he explained to a correspondent in 1948, Davidson believed that the states should have had more power in the administration of the TVA and scorned the suggestion that the TVA would be some sort of agent of moral reform for the inhabitants of the Tennessee Valley. The TVA, he argued, "ought to have been set up as an honest river improvement enterprise with clearly defined duties and limits, and not established as a hybrid super-agency devised, as

TVA is, to escape *both* the limits of normal governmental supervision *and* the responsibilities of private enterprise."[53]

Davidson recognized the value of much of what the TVA did, in particular the agricultural reform it fostered. But, in the end, he was deeply troubled by the scope of its activities and the authority with which it was invested— an authority he did not believe was sufficiently accountable to the people the TVA affected. By instituting a system of high dams and locks, the TVA completely changed the nature of the Tennessee River, in particular the upper river, making it, in effect, a series of lakes. The river, Davidson believed, was completely tamed, even lifeless.[54] In the process, thousands of individuals had been displaced and many old farms and small villages and towns had been permanently flooded. The TVA was the "Great Leviathan," pushing the natives off the land just as the Cherokees had been, this time not with soldiers but with marshals and eviction notices.[55] Even old graves were exhumed, the bodies placed in new caskets and taken to new gravesites.[56] Davidson commented elegiacally upon the displacement:

> Old landmarks would vanish; old graveyards would be obliterated; the ancient mounds of the Indians, which had resisted both the plow and the farmer and the pick of the curiosity seeker, would go under water. There would be tears, and gnashing of teeth, and lawsuits. There might even be feud and bloodshed. Yet these harms, inflicted upon a sizable and innocent minority, weighed less in the TVA scales than the benefits that would accrue, in terms of industrial and social engineering, to the nearby or the distant majority who sacrificed only tax money.[57]

The natives of the river valley (and by implication all southerners) were in danger, Davidson warned, of becoming, like the Indians before them, "no People" whose ancestors had died for nothing. They were in danger of losing their history, and in losing this, their identity and their citizenship.

The challenge Davidson's writings pose to modern readers lies in his understanding of citizenship. For Davidson, a strong sense of citizenship was derived from a narrow, particularistic identity. *Citizenship* must imply *membership,* Davidson was saying, with all the limitations, responsibilities, but also privileges that membership entails. For Davidson, this sense of citizenship precluded social equality for African Americans in the South. The social memory to which Davidson responded confirmed white supremacy. Davidson expressed this as early as *The Tall Men* in 1927 when the narrator, addressing the southern blacks, spoke of an age-old and unbridgeable wall between the races. "I cannot / Forget that I was master," the narrator explains, "and you can hardly / Forget that you were a slave."[58] For all practical purposes, race might as well have replaced social memory as the determinant of citizenship in Davidson's thinking. Yet, in his primary justification of segregation, a 1945 article entitled "Preface to Decision," Davidson's use of the concept of history is striking and revealing.

In the article, Davidson contrasted two John Smiths, whom a sociologist would classify as identical except that one was white and the other black. The sociologist, Davidson argued, would ignore the different histories of these two men. But for Davidson, that the ancestors of the white John Smith had once owned the ancestors of the black John Smith, a fact left out by the sociologists, was the "prime cultural fact." History was everything. The black man lost his history in the same way that he had lost his true name (which, Davidson speculated, in Africa might have been "Crocodile-killer" or "Spearmaker"—"a valiant and honorable name"). "It is a tragic business that the Negro John Smith cannot enjoy contemplating his own name in quite the same way the white man does," Davidson wrote, "since there is hiatus or lurking humiliation where there ought to be history."[59] In other words, the fact that the black man was enslaved, brought to America, and denuded of his historical identity may be unjust and tragic, but the fact that he is now an historical nonentity cannot be changed. Davidson saw no possibility of contemporary blacks embodying their heritage, and he saw no black heritage in America. African Americans had become, due to the twists of history and fate, as the Indians had before them, "no people."

The white man, on the other hand, was in a completely different situation, for he "can think back for many centuries without discomfort, or often with pride, if he cares to. His history is with him wherever he goes."[60] History, Davidson held, permeates the institutions of the white South. The white John Smith remembers it the moment the black John Smith in any way challenges the racial status quo. At this moment, Davidson wrote, "the historical element becomes the most powerful element in the whole environment of the two men, indeed in their very being. And white John Smith recalls that his grandfather before him, and his father and he afterwards, never at any time agreed to accept the Negro John Smith as a member of white society, save under such limitations as are symbolized by the separate waiting rooms and other much more intricate but carefully ordered customs."[61] The social memory of the South, the Tennessee and the southern past dictated the exclusion of blacks from the circle of southern identity.

Robert Penn Warren, who publicly opposed segregation in the 1950s, observed at one point that Davidson saw history as "unalterable fate."[62] This is an apt description of the function of memory in delimiting Davidson's sense of the range of politics and the possibilities for change. And yet history did not define any actual political principles, other than Davidson's intransigent opposition to industrialism and the national state. Davidson described himself to John Farrar in 1940 as a "native Tennessean who stands neither with Left nor Right as those terms are commonly understood in the United States."[63] In a 1958 lecture at Bowdoin College entitled "The New South and the Conservative Tradition," which was later published in an abbreviated form in the *National Review,* Davidson expressed reservations about using the term *conservative* to describe the South. The South was pragmatic in its approach to politics, he argued. "The actual South that I know is not enslaved by any theory of the past; but as a somewhat traditional society it retains continuity with its past without being encumbered by it," Davidson declared.[64] The statement is remarkable considering how deeply Davidson's own identity was founded upon the social memory of the past.

A clue to understanding Davidson's meaning is contained in his attitude toward the spokesmen of the New South, who mixed appeals for southern industrialization and progress with paeans to the glories of the Old South. One of the chief aims of the Agrarians, Davidson argued, was to refute mythological views of the South, whether the romantic notions of New South propagandists or the portrait of the contemporary South as a morass of immiseration and social pathologies found in the work of social realist novelists like T. S. Stribling or Erskine Caldwell.[65] Indeed, the Agrarians with whom Davidson felt the most kinship, Andrew Lytle and Frank Owsley, shared his admiration for the "plain folk" of the South. Owsley's influential *Plain Folk of the Old South* (1949) advanced the controversial claim that the yeomanry of the antebellum South lived in peace and equality with the slaveholding elite and shared the social and political beliefs that led the South into war.[66]

The spokesmen of the New South, most notably the newspaperman Henry Grady, excelled at a politics of southern nostalgia, but Davidson saw this use of social memory as illegitimate. It was false, designed simply to disguise the industrial development that he believed antithetical to the humanistic culture of the South. Davidson recalled attending a speech by the popular Democratic governor of Tennessee, Bob Taylor, as a young man. His evocation of the mood of the speech is quite interesting, for it was full of warmth and nostalgia, a warmth and nostalgia in tune with Bob Taylor's rhetorical tributes to the South. The speech, he recalled, was delivered either in the year 1906 or 1907, and Davidson attended—"a little boy in knee pants, long black stockings, and high stiff collar"—while a student at the Branham and Hughes School. Gas lights "feebly illuminated" the lecture hall, but it seemed bright enough to the young Davidson. He recalled the young ladies dressed in their finery and seated in the front rows, an array of young "Gibson Girls," following the fashions of the day.[67]

The speech by Taylor, a famous one known as "The Fiddle and the Bow," carried his audience along on a sweeping emotional tour of southern history and values. Davidson had forgotten the content, but he tried to convey the meaning by appealing to particular images of pioneer life and southern glory that the short, bald-headed orator would have evoked: the old oaken bucket that hung in the well; the pride of America's great expanse stretching from Maine to the southernmost states; the boys "swinging in the grapevine swing," with "cheeks of tan"; the young girl who also occupied the swing and for whom the young boy picked daisies in the dell; the awe-inspiring accomplishments of Tennessee heroes such as John Sevier and Andrew Jackson.[68] "But, we said, how could man die better, Than facing fearful odds, For the Ashes of his fathers, And the temples of his Gods," Davidson wrote, evoking the southern martial spirit.[69] Taylor's rhetoric swept his audience along until they warmly embraced his vision of southern culture. C. Vann Woodward, Davidson observed, mentioned Bob Taylor in his book on the New South as a type of comic agrarian Populist. "That's the trouble with historians," he wrote. "They are never around when things happen, and never understand how people feel."[70]

And, yet, Davidson was well aware that the historical picture Taylor presented was a myth. That is, after all, the problem with politicians: they romanticize and mythologize the past. Davidson knew better than to believe any moonlight-and-magnolias version of southern history; this was the South seen through "rose-tinted spectacles."[71] "The South always knew very well that a plantation is a highly practical enterprise," Davidson wrote. "If any plantation owner thought that it existed merely for his elegant convenience in sipping mint-juleps on a white-columned veranda, he would not very long remain the owner of that plantation."[72]

Upon examination there seems little difference between the cultural politics of social memory that Davidson espoused and the sort of "theory of the past" that he claimed to reject. However, the social memory he trusted came not from politicians but from the old folks at home. Bob Taylor or Henry Grady or any New South orator seeking a closer connection with the industrial North would never have fooled his grandmother, "who in the Sixties had seen her boy-friends captured by marauding Federal soldiers and shot in cold blood on the main street of her home town."[73] Social memory functioned in politics as the emotional core of citizenship, not to vindicate any particular political program. Davidson did not admit the possibility that the memory of the old folks might itself be distorted, for it served as the basis of his values and identity. And while dismissing Bob Taylor's manipulation of the southern past, his "Fiddle and Bow" was, nevertheless, a ritual of southern citizenship, and thus it was a part of Davidson's social memory. But this memory, handed down from generation to generation and sealed in the rituals of southern remembrance, whether outside a country store, at the feet of his grandmother, or in a Confederate cemetery, was not, Davidson insisted, a "theory of the past."

Yet the emotional bonds of Davidson's social memory did define a cultural politics, which entailed, in fact, a "theory of the past," in some sense, and which went beyond the original Agrarian program. As Robert Penn Warren indicated, Davidson believed in only one authentic social memory for southerners, and the definition of citizenship provided by his understanding of the southern past was unalterable and impervious to challenge. The development of Davidson's politics of social memory led to M. E. Bradford's later reinterpretation of Agrarianism as part of a tradition of southern conservatism founded upon a carefully tended sense of southern identity. The social memory of the Tennessee past, however, can be either broad or narrow, it may welcome or discourage social change, and it may be generous or halting in its willingness to expand the circle of southern identity. The reality of the Tennessee past—which includes slavery, segregation, and racism—need not delimit the nature of the Tennessee future. When constructing the social memory of the South, much depends upon the memories to which one chooses to attend.

NOTES

1. Donald Davidson to Louis Rubin, May 10, 1955, folder 47, box 2, Donald Davidson Papers (University Archives and Special Collections, Heard Library, Vanderbilt University, Nashville, Tennessee).
2. Thomas Daniel Young and M. Thomas Inge, *Donald Davidson* (New York, 1971), 19.
3. Donald Davidson to Stark Young, Sept. 29, 1952, folder 33, box 2, Davidson Papers.
4. Twelve Southerners, *I'll Take My Stand: The South and the Agrarian Tradition* (New York, 1930).
5. Bradford argued that the Agrarians were descended from a southern tradition of in-

tellectual conservatism that can be traced to the Old Whig country opponents of the English court party in the seventeenth and eighteenth centuries, the Anti-federalist critics of the American Constitution, and such antebellum southern theorists of states' rights and limited government as John Randolph, John Taylor, and John C. Calhoun. See M. E. Bradford, *A Better Guide Than Reason: Federalists and Anti-Federalists* (New Brunswick, N.J., 1994 [1979]); M. E. Bradford, *Remembering Who We Are: Observations of a Southern Conservative* (Athens, Ga., 1985); and M. E. Bradford, *The Reactionary Imperative: Essays Literary and Political* (Peru, Ill., 1990). Bradford's effort to outline a distinctive southern conservative tradition based on a rejection of finance capitalism and of radical individualism has received the ablest support from a perhaps unlikely source: Eugene D. Genovese, the Marxist historian who has contributed greatly to the history of southern slaves and slaveholders. See Eugene D. Genovese, *The Southern Tradition: The Achievement and Limitations of an American Conservatism* (Cambridge, 1994); and Eugene D. Genovese, *The Southern Front: History and Politics in the Cultural War* (Columbia, S.C., 1995).

6. Young and Inge, *Donald Davidson* 18; Louise Davis, "He Clings to Enduring Values," *Nashville Tennessean Magazine,* Sept. 4, 1949, 6–8. A copy of this article is contained in box 35, folder 11, Davidson Papers.

7. Young and Inge, *Donald Davidson,* 19–20.

8. Donald Davidson, *The Spyglass: Views and Reviews, 1924–1930,* ed. John Tyree Fain (Nashville, 1963), 200.

9. Young and Inge, *Donald Davidson,* 21–22.

10. Young and Inge, *Donald Davidson,* 23; Davis, "He Clings to Enduring Values," 7.

11. See Paul V. Murphy, "The Sacrament of Remembrance: Southern Agrarian Poet Donald Davidson and the Southern Past," *Southern Cultures* 2 (Fall 1995): 83–102.

12. Davidson to John Gould Fletcher, Mar. 21, 1926, folder 8, box 1, Davidson Papers. The poem was to be, he told his publisher, an "emotionalized definition of the modern Southerner." Davidson to R. N. Linscott, Apr. 9, 1927, folder 9, box 1, Davidson Papers.

13. Donald Davidson, *Lee in the Mountains and Other Poems* (Boston, 1938), 65.

14. Davidson, *Lee in the Mountains and Other Poems,* 123.

15. Michael Merritt Jordan, "Donald Davidson's 'Creed of Memory,'" (Ph.D. diss., Univ. of Georgia, Athens, 1989), 304. I am indebted to Jordan's dissertation, particularly chapter 6, "*The Tall Men,* Davidson's Response to the Waste Land Theme," for an understanding of the religious themes in this work. A contrasting reading of the sections of *The Tall Men* on religion is found in Young and Inge, *Donald Davidson,* 81–86.

16. Davidson, *Lee in the Mountains and Other Poems,* 80.

17. Ibid., 81–82.

18. Ibid., 136–37.

19. See John Crowe Ransom to Allen Tate, Jan. 5, 1930, in Thomas Daniel Young and George Core, eds., *Selected Letters of John Crowe Ransom* (Baton Rouge, 1985), 189; and Donald Davidson to Tate, Dec. 29, 1929, in John Tyree Fain and Thomas Daniel Young, eds., *The Literary Correspondence of Donald Davidson and Allen Tate* (Athens, Ga., 1974), 193.

20. *Nashville Tennessean,* Mar. 9, 1930.

21. On the various efforts to form a decentralist intellectual movement in the 1930s, involving the Agrarians and the Distributists, see Michael O'Brien, *The Idea of the American South, 1920–1941* (Baltimore, 1990 [1979]), 156–57; Edward Stanford Shapiro, "The American Distributists and the New Deal" (Ph.D. diss., Harvard Univ., 1968); Edward S. Shapiro, "Decentralist Intellectuals and the New Deal," *Journal of American History* 58 (Mar. 1972): 938–57; Edward S. Shapiro, "American Conservative Intellectuals, the 1930's, and the Crisis of Ideology," *Modern Age* 23 (Fall 1979): 370–80; and Edward S. Shapiro, "Catholic Agrarian Thought and the New Deal," *Catholic Historical Review* 65 (Oct. 1979): 583–99. For the Agrarians' involvement with Herbert Agar in particular, see William E. Leverette, Jr., and David E. Shi, "Herbert Agar and *Free America*: A Jeffersonian Alternative to the New Deal," *Journal of American Studies* 16 (Aug. 1982): 189–206. Some of the Agrarians came to regret their association with Seward Collins, who became notorious later in the decade for voicing profascist sentiments. On Collins, see Robert Kenton Craven, "Seward Collins and the Traditionalists: A Study of the *Bookman* and the *American Review*, 1928–1937" (Ph.D. diss, Univ. of Kansas, 1967); and Albert E. Stone, Jr., "Seward Collins and the *American Review*: Experiment in Pro-Fascism, 1933–1937," *American Quarterly* 12 (Spring 1960): 3–19.
22. Charles C. Alexander, *Here the Country Lies: Nationalism and the Arts in Twentieth-Century America* (Bloomington, Ind., 1980), 179.
23. Robert L. Dorman, *Revolt of the Provinces: The Regionalist Movement in America, 1920–1945* (Chapel Hill, N.C., 1993), 9–24.
24. Ibid., 295–300.
25. Ibid., 107–18, 163–64, 263.
26. Ibid., 219–20.
27. Ibid., 24–25.
28. Donald Davidson, *The Attack on Leviathan: Regionalism and Nationalism in the United States* (Chapel Hill, N.C., 1938); Donald Davidson, "Sectionalism in the United States," *Hound & Horn* 6 (July–Sept. 1933): 561–89.
29. Davidson, "Sectionalism in the United States," 572.
30. Ibid., 570.
31. Ibid.
32. Ibid., 577–78.
33. Ibid., 574.
34. Ibid., 579, 584.
35. Ibid., 588–89.
36. Ibid., 588.
37. Ibid., 589.
38. Donald Davidson, "Agrarianism and Politics," *Review of Politics* 1 (Mar. 1939): 116.
39. Ibid., 115.
40. Ibid., 116.
41. Ibid., 120.
42. Ibid., 115.
43. Ibid., 125.
44. Ibid., 125.
45. Alexander, *Here the Country Lies*, 196.

46. Davidson to John Farrar, Mar. 21, 1940, box 2, folder 1, Davidson Papers; Davidson to Ferris Greenslet, Apr. 28, 1940, ibid.; Davidson to Ransom, July 5, 1929, box 1, folder 12, ibid.; Davidson to Tate, Apr. 14, 1931, box 8, folder 2, Allen Tate Papers (Special Collections, Princeton Univ. Library, Princeton, New Jersey).
47. Davidson, *Lee in the Mountains and Other Poems,* 136–37.
48. Donald Davidson, *The Old River: Frontier to Secession,* vol. 1 of *The Tennessee* (New York, 1946), 80.
49. Ibid., 86.
50. Donald Davidson, *The New River: Civil War to TVA,* vol. 2 of *The Tennessee* (New York, 1948), 112.
51. Ibid., 148.
52. Davidson, *Tennessee,* 2:223. See also ibid., 333.
53. Donald Davidson to Harvey Broome, Apr. 25, 1948, copy, folder 22, box 2, Davidson Papers.
54. Davidson, *Tennessee,* 2:276–77, 282–83, 285.
55. Ibid., 251, 256.
56. Ibid., 259.
57. Ibid., 237–38.
58. Davidson, *Lee in the Mountains and Other Poems,* 91.
59. Donald Davidson, "Preface to Decision," *Sewanee Review* 53 (Summer 1945): 395.
60. Ibid., 395–96.
61. Ibid., 396.
62. Robert Penn Warren to Donald R. Ellegood, Jan. 3, 1956, Robert Penn Warren Papers (Beinecke Rare Book and Manuscript Library, Yale Univ., New Haven, Conn.).
63. Donald Davidson to John Farrar, May 12, 1940, folder 1, box 2, Davidson Papers.
64. Donald Davidson, "The New South and the Conservative Tradition," typescript, p. 29, folder 5, box 22, Davidson Papers.
65. Ibid., 24–25.
66. On Frank L. Owsley's interpretation of the plain folk of the South, see Fred Arthur Bailey, *Class and Tennessee's Confederate Generation* (Chapel Hill, N.C., 1987), 13–17.
67. Davidson, "The New South and the Conservative Tradition," 15–17.
68. Ibid., 17–19.
69. Ibid., 19.
70. Ibid.
71. Ibid., 20.
72. Ibid., 22.
73. Ibid., 21.

TENNESSEE AND TWENTIETH-CENTURY AMERICAN POLITICS

■ DEWEY W. GRANTHAM

■

■ *Editor's Note:* Although no Tennesseans have served as president
since Andrew Johnson in 1869, the state and its residents have
■ maintained a vital role in the national political culture. Throughout the twentieth century, Tennesseans have sought the presi-
■ dency and have held key offices in Congress and different presidential administrations. This wide-ranging synthesis of existing
■ scholarship analyzes the intersection of local, state, regional, and
national political patterns in the twentieth century. "The nation-
■ alization of Tennessee politics and the state's role in southern political affairs," asserts Grantham, "suggest that its modern political
■ experience is instructive . . . for the perspective it provides on regional and national politics." The most important trend was the
■ rise of the Republican party, which always maintained a strong
East Tennessee base, to a position of statewide, and later regional,
■ power.

The political scientist V. O. Key's illuminating book *Southern Poli-
tics in State and Nation* contains a chapter on Tennessee entitled "The Civil
War and Mr. Crump."[1] It is an apt title. In the 1930s and 1940s, Edward
H. Crump of Memphis was perhaps the most powerful urban boss in the
South and the leader of the dominant Democratic faction in Tennessee.
Crump brought his own audacity and organizing ability to bear on the circumstances of his city and state. The effects of the Civil War three-quarters
of a century after Appomattox were still almost as palpable as Mr. Crump's
political influence. The war proved to be a divisive as well as a unifying theme
in Tennessee. Whereas the sectional conflict, southern resort to arms, and
mythology of the Lost Cause and Reconstruction encouraged a strong Demo-

cratic Party in Middle and West Tennessee, the resistance of East Tennesseans to secession and the Confederacy fostered the growth of the Republican Party in that subregion. Geography also helped shape the political patterns of modern Tennessee. It separated the state into three "grand divisions," promoted its economic and social diversity, and made it part of the peripheral South with a kind of border state mentality.

Nevertheless, Tennessee was unmistakably a southern state, strongly marked by its historical experience, sectional self-consciousness, and a pervasive belief among Caucasians in the imperative of white supremacy. It was part of the nation's most clearly defined section and its most notable manifestation of political sectionalism. Most Tennesseans were keenly aware of their place in the southern political universe and of its interaction with other parts of the country. Tennessee also played a role in national politics. Each state's politics was uniquely different from that of other members of the

Carroll County Courthouse, 1992, built in 1930. Photograph by Carroll Van West.

Union, but all of them participated in the national party system, in national elections, and in the national government, especially in Congress.

Tennessee's modern politics grew out of the troubled and uncertain period that lasted from Reconstruction to the agrarian revolt of the 1890s. It was an era of competitive politics, high voter turnout, and political instability. Although the Democrats usually controlled the state's politics, they were divided by personal ambitions and shifting factions. They were challenged on occasion by Democratic insurgents and third parties such as the Greenbackers. The most serious threat came from the Republicans, whose challenge to the Democrats gave Tennessee the most consistently competitive politics of any southern state during the 1880s. Republican strength was concentrated in East Tennessee, but the party also attracted votes from the other two grand divisions, particularly those of urban blacks. African Americans made up almost a quarter of the state's total voting population in 1880. Though the Republican coalition of highland whites and Middle and West Tennessee blacks was a formidable factor in state politics, it was nonetheless an uneasy and somewhat tenuous alliance. The mountain Republican leaders were caught between their desire for black votes and their wish to appeal to white Democrats, an ambivalence revealed in the party's "black-and-tan" and "lily-white" factionalism.[2] Another challenge to Democratic control came from rebellious farmers in the South and West who precipitated a movement calling for economic relief and political reform. In 1890, the Farmers' Alliance was victorious in several southern states, including Tennessee, where it took control of the Democratic Party and won the governorship. But its influence in Tennessee was transitory and its achievements few. The People's Party, the third-party movement organized by the more determined agrarian reformers, was never very strong in Tennessee. Indeed, the agrarian revolt in the Volunteer State was a "reluctant rebellion," one that was "halfhearted in tone and limited in scope."[3]

Democratic leaders managed to regain their dominant position in Tennessee politics, but not without a struggle. They set about unifying their party, made concessions to the reformers, and in the critical campaign of 1896 turned to Robert L. Taylor, a popular ex-governor, to help them retain the governorship. The dominant "Bourbon" faction of the Democratic Party and a rival faction made up of business-oriented "New South" Democrats worked together to overcome their challengers. Fearful of a Populist-Republican coalition, the Democrats invoked the image of Radical Reconstruction, associated Republicans with "Negro rule," and charged Populists with trying to undermine "white supremacy." As one historian has observed, "The state's strong Republican party was a convenient and familiar symbol for convincing voters that political disruption would bring social upheaval and Negro rule."[4] Meanwhile, Democrats in the state legislature had acted, in 1889 and 1890, to restrict the voting of blacks—and illiterate whites—by enacting a harsh registration law, a poll tax requirement for voting, and a secret ballot law.[5]

While the Democrats were reasserting their control in Tennessee and other southern states, the Republicans were sweeping to victory in the Northeast, Midwest, and part of the West.[6] It soon became evident that the elections of 1894 and 1896 had transformed the Republican Party into the nation's majority party, and that the Democratic Party had been relegated to minority status. This dramatic shift in the locus of national political power had striking repercussions for Tennessee and the South as a whole. It largely ended the Republican Party's serious interest in competing with the Democrats below the Potomac and the Ohio, while diminishing the influence of northern Democrats in state and national politics. Thus the party realignment of the 1890s made the Democratic South a majority component of a minority party.

One-party politics soon prevailed in every southern state, buttressed by a drastically reduced electorate and the finality of Democratic ("white") primary elections. For instance, only an estimated 37.6 percent of Tennessee's white male adults voted in the hotly contested Democratic primary of 1908. Only Tennessee and North Carolina had a semblance of interparty competition, and with the exception of several Republican enclaves in the mountains of the upper South, Democratic supremacy in the region could hardly have been greater. To be sure, Tennessee Republicans continued to dominate most of the eastern section, and in a sense Tennessee had "two one-party systems" rather than one.[7] But the Grand Old Party was no longer competitive in middle and western Tennessee, where most white men identified themselves as Democrats and the number of black voters had declined. Yet the presence of Republican East Tennessee influenced the behavior of the fractious Democrats, and when the latter's factionalism became too extreme or their leadership too unpopular, Republicans could become an important factor in statewide politics.[8]

During the first part of the new century, a wave of political and social reform campaigns swept over the United States. The southern states participated in this progressivism, shared in the national reform ethos that characterized the period, and interacted with other regions in developing their own brand of reformism. Embracing the concept of state intervention for the

protection and purification of society, Tennessee progressives closed the saloons, began to establish a modern system of public education, expanded and
strengthened public health facilities, attempted to protect the rights of labor,
and endeavored to make commercial and industrial enterprise more responsive to the public's needs. Reform campaigns in the state's major cities introduced structural innovations such as commission government, tried to regulate public utilities, and expanded public services. Efforts were also made, with
the aid of northern philanthropists, to raise educational standards, provide
more social amenities, and increase the efficiency and productivity of Tennessee farmers, many of whom were landless, itinerant, and illiterate. Meanwhile, black leaders acted, in a time of mounting racial segregation and discrimination, to bring social reform to the African American community.[9]

The most contentious issue of the progressive period in Tennessee was the
struggle over statewide prohibition of alcoholic beverages. Although prohibition was adopted by the legislature in 1909, the problem continued to
dominate the state's politics until the election of 1914. The difficulty of enforcing the prohibition laws and the role of powerful urban leaders like Edward H. Crump of Memphis added fuel to the flames of controversy and
bitterness in the faction-ridden ranks of Tennessee Democrats. In 1910, many
of the prohibitionists, calling themselves independent Democrats, endorsed
Ben W. Hooper, the Republican candidate for governor. This fusionist
movement won the election of 1910, and Hooper was reelected two years
later. Hooper, an East Tennessee lawyer and a vigorous opponent of "the
whiskey evil," was the most prominent progressive to come out of this period of political turmoil in the state. His leadership was a principal reason
for the success of the prohibition cause in Tennessee, which was at the vanguard of the campaign to control alcohol in the South and the subsequent
movement in Washington for the adoption of national prohibition. In the
meantime, the prohibition issue served as a catalyst in creating a bifactional
alignment of Tennessee Democrats.[10]

Reform movements in the southern states, as in other sections, were increasingly affected by national organizations, standards, and solutions. This
tendency was evident in the efforts to regulate railroads and other interstate
corporations, in the prohibition struggle, and in the woman suffrage movement. Southerners took an unaccustomed interest in the presidential election
of 1912, in part because Woodrow Wilson, a native of Virginia, won the
nomination of the Democratic Party.[11] They were quick to claim Wilson as
one of their own.[12] The South, which normally made up the largest and most
dependable constituent of the Democratic Party in national elections, was

in a position to influence the decisions of the national party and to some extent the policies of the federal government. Southern Democrats usually constituted a majority of their party's members in Congress, where their seniority and ranking positions on standing committees enabled them to master the organizational structure and procedures of the House and Senate.[13]

Wilson's election as the nation's twenty-eighth president was followed by a remarkable period of domestic reform, wartime mobilization, and international involvement for the American people. Southern senators and representatives dominated Congress, had a powerful voice in the Democratic caucuses, and headed almost all of the major committees in the two houses. Several Tennesseans—Finis J. Garrett (Insular Affairs), John A. Moon (Post Office and Post Roads), Lemuel P. Padgett (Naval Affairs), and Thetus T. Sims (Interstate and Foreign Commerce)—headed important committees in the House of Representatives for one or more congresses during the Wilson years. Cordell Hull, a member of the Committee on Ways and Means, was instrumental in the adoption of the federal income and inheritance tax provisions of the Underwood-Simmons Tariff Act of 1913. The state's Democratic representatives and senators, like almost all southern congressmen, were strong supporters of President Wilson's New Freedom legislation—such as banking reform, business regulation, and support of farmers and industrial workers—and of his leadership during the First World War. Yet most of them sympathized with southern efforts to apply the principle of racial segregation to the District of Columbia, to deny political appointments to African Americans, and to segregate black and white workers in the federal departments. Along with their fellow southerners in Congress, the Tennesseans welcomed federal benefits for their state and districts but were sometimes uneasy about legislative encroachments on state rights. They were not always consistent. Many southern members stood firmly on the principle of state rights when it came to woman suffrage but overlooked it in supporting national prohibition.[14]

The cause of women's rights did not enlist strong support in Tennessee until the second decade of the twentieth century. As the movement grew, its leaders increased their demands for the ballot, first through state action and then by joining the national movement for a federal amendment. Speaking of suffragist progress in Tennessee, the *Nashville Tennessean* observed in February 1917: "Hostility in 1913, ridicule in 1914, tolerance in 1915, frank approval in 1916."[15] In 1919, the Tennessee reformers won a partial victory by persuading the state legislature to permit women to vote in presidential and municipal elections. By that time, both houses of Congress had approved the Susan B. Anthony Amendment, despite strong opposition from southern members. The Tennessee delegation was split. In the ratification struggle that followed, eight southern states failed to ratify the amendment. After thirty-five states had approved ratification, national attention turned to the Volunteer State, and a large number of supporters and opponents of the measure descended on Nashville in the summer of 1920. The vote was extremely close in the House, but in August 1920, Tennessee became the thirty-sixth (and decisive) state to ratify the Nineteenth Amendment.[16]

The 1920s brought a brief resurgence of Republican strength in Tennessee, the election of a Democratic reform governor, and the emergence of a new factional division in the state's majority party. In 1920, Tennesseans voted to elect Warren G. Harding, the Republican nominee for president, Alfred A. Taylor, the GOP candidate for governor, and five Republican congressmen (along with five Democrats). Republican successes in Tennessee, as Gary W. Reichard has suggested, were largely the result of forces peculiar to that election. Democratic factionalism in gubernatorial politics, strong opposition to a new tax law pushed through the General Assembly in 1919, controversy surrounding the ratification of the woman suffrage amendment in 1920, and a heavy turnout in East Tennessee that included many newly enfranchised women all played a part in the Republican victories, particularly in the campaign for governor. Republican ascendancy in Washington brought federal patronage and recognition to party members in Tennessee. The black-and-tan faction, under the leadership of Representative J. Will Taylor of the second congressional district in East Tennessee, and Robert R. Church, Jr., a black political leader in Memphis, remained dominant among the state's Republicans.[17]

In 1922, Democrats recaptured control of the state government when Austin Peay, a Middle Tennessee leader, defeated Governor Taylor. Peay remained in office until his unexpected death in October 1927. He was an unusually able and successful governor. A "business progressive," he was an advocate of good government, efficiency and modernization, and the expansion of public services, especially roads and schools. He was primarily responsible for the transformation of Tennessee government in the 1920s: the concentration of power at the state level and in the hands of the governor, the administrative reorganization of the state government, success in dealing with pressing fiscal problems through budgetary and revenue reforms, and introduction of state programs that provided Tennessee's rural communities with much-needed public services paid for, in large part, by the state's wealthier urban areas. In spite of the rapid pace of industrialization and urbanization,

Tennessee was still basically an agricultural state. Fifty-four of its ninety-five counties had no urban population at all in the 1920s.[18]

Austin Peay also created, on the basis of the state's shifting factional rivalries and power centers, a potent political coalition that controlled Tennessee politics for almost a decade. Peay had several valuable allies, one of whom was Luke Lea, a former U.S. senator, publisher of the *Nashville Tennessean,* and a rising power broker in Middle Tennessee. The governor enjoyed broad support, including urban backing, in his successful campaign of 1922, but some of his policies alienated many of the urban business and commercial interests, and he found his natural constituency among rural and small-town Tennesseans, who constituted a strong force in state politics and looked with a critical eye on the cultural and political behavior of the burgeoning cities. Peay's organization depended upon the rural counties and towns of Middle and West Tennessee, as well as surprising support from East Tennessee, where Peay won Republican votes in the Democratic primary and the General Assembly as a result of the new public services and certain concessions the chief executive made to the minority party.

Governor Peay's leadership divided Tennessee Democrats into administration and anti-administration factions. This bifactionalism persisted into the 1930s and was characterized by considerable stability. It did not strictly coincide with an urban-rural cleavage, but the leaders of both factions understood the growing importance of the state's cities and the fact that the countryside was overrepresented in the legislature, which had not been reapportioned since 1901. In general, the administration faction sponsored measures that concentrated authority in the state government and the chief executive, while the rival faction worked for local control and the maintenance of decision making in the state legislature.[19]

The anti-administration faction also had strong support, especially in urban areas. One of its spokesmen was Edward B. Stahlman, publisher of the *Nashville Banner* and a bitter enemy of Luke Lea. Stahlman joined with Hilary Howse, the leader of a durable political organization in the capital city, in opposing administration Democrats. Another opposition leader was Edward H. Crump, who had built a powerful political machine in Memphis. Crump had entered politics as a progressive and served as mayor of the Bluff City from 1909 until his ouster in 1916 for failing to enforce the state prohibition laws. His administration worked to improve public services, reduce taxes, and make government more efficient. He created an unbeatable political organization that rewarded its supporters, paid their poll taxes, and made sure that they voted. Crump's machine permitted and even encouraged African

Americans to vote. Memphis, the state's largest city, cast a significant percentage of the vote in statewide elections, and Crump's control of Shelby County made it possible for him to influence local leaders in other parts of the state. Crump was inevitably involved in state politics: in efforts to elect friendly governors, control the appointment of local election commissioners, and make sure that rural legislators did not derail desirable "local bills."[20]

Peay was succeeded by the speaker of the state senate, Henry H. Horton, an inexperienced politician who was soon dominated by Luke Lea. The Nashville publisher quickly became the most powerful individual in the state. He was closely associated with a number of local politicians, particularly in Middle Tennessee, and his acquisition of the *Knoxville Journal* and the *Memphis Commercial Appeal* increased his influence. In addition, Lea was an ally of Rogers Caldwell, who had developed a southern financial empire centered in Nashville. The Horton administration looked to Lea for political support and advice, and the governor reciprocated handsomely by awarding Lea and his associates patronage and state contracts. Lea's ties with Horton also led to the deposit of large amounts of state revenue in Caldwell's banks. The strength and resourcefulness of the administration faction enabled it to remain in control of the state government. Despite determined resistance from the other faction, administration Democrats reelected Governor Horton in 1928 and two years later succeeded in pushing his program through a special session of the legislature and reelected Horton once again. Then, late in 1930, Rogers Caldwell's overextended financial empire collapsed, causing the state of Tennessee to lose millions of dollars and Lea to forfeit his chain of newspapers. A legislative investigation early in 1931 found mismanagement, waste, and fraud in the Horton administration, and while a move to impeach Horton failed, the governor's political influence was destroyed, as was that of Lea, who was forced to serve a prison sentence. In 1932, the anti-administration Democrats elected their candidate, Hill McAlister, to the governorship, and Edward Crump became the dominant political leader in Tennessee.[21]

Meanwhile, several state Democrats remained influential in Congress, including Finis J. Garrett, who served as the party's floor leader in the House for several years. Cordell Hull became chairman of the Democratic National Committee in late 1921, serving for more than two years, and later in the 1920s he was one of the Democratic leaders who worked to restore greater unity to the party. In 1928, Tennessee joined four other ex-Confederate states in casting its electoral votes for Herbert Hoover over the Democratic presidential nominee, Alfred E. Smith of New York. The acrimonious politics of 1928 reflected not only the cultural differences that often divided northern and southern Democrats—Smith was a Catholic "wet" from New York City —but also a struggle along regional lines for control of the national party. Following the election, Representative Hull and other southern leaders were active in efforts to reorient the party and counter the conservative leadership of the national chairman, John J. Raskob, who opposed the nomination of Franklin D. Roosevelt and emphasized national prohibition as an issue. Hull became Roosevelt's chief southern ally, and he was one of the southerners who played an essential role in the New York governor's nomination for president in 1932.[22]

During the Roosevelt years, southerners once again assumed a leading role in Congress. The most prominent congressional leader from Tennessee during the 1930s was Representative Joseph W. Byrns, a Nashvillian who had risen to the chairmanship of the Appropriations Committee. He became Democratic majority leader in 1933 and Speaker of the House of Representatives early in 1935, serving until his death in June 1936. Jere Cooper ascended to the chairmanship of the House Ways and Means Committee by the late 1930s. In the Senate, Kenneth D. McKellar became chairman of the Post Office Committee, a rich source of patronage, and the second-ranking member of the Committee on Appropriations. The Tennessee congressmen, like most other southern members, staunchly supported Roosevelt's legislative program during his first administration.[23] Roosevelt himself made a point of cultivating the southern lawmakers, whose leadership he needed for the enactment of his programs. The president's popularity in Tennessee was reflected in the support he received from both factions of the Democratic Party. Edward H. Crump, for example, was a loyal advocate of the New Deal, in part no doubt because the Roosevelt administration did little to interfere with the distribution of federal relief or political power in the state. "In effect," one historian says of the situation in Memphis, "the New Deal was filtered through the Crump machine."[24] Some Tennesseans became less enthusiastic about the New Deal after 1937, criticizing Roosevelt's court-packing plan and such measures as the Fair Labor Standards bill. Meanwhile, New Deal relief programs, recovery policies, and reform measures brought the national government into the lives of the people in an unprecedented manner.[25]

Several other developments of the Roosevelt era had far-reaching consequences for public affairs in Tennessee, among them Cordell Hull's appointment as secretary of state, the creation of the Tennessee Valley Authority, the political impact of the New Deal, and the enormous influence of the Crump organization in the state's politics. None of Roosevelt's experiments was more riveting to Tennesseans than the emergence of the Tennessee Valley Authority. Its approval in 1933 climaxed a long congressional controversy over the development of the Tennessee River and the benefits that might result in the form of improved navigation and flood control, the manufacture of cheap fertilizer, the conservation of natural resources, and especially publicly produced hydroelectric power. The idea of developing an entire drainage area reaching into seven states, the concept of overall planning, and the multipurpose character of the agency attracted the attention of Tennesseans and many other southerners, who closely followed the authority's early struggles to overcome a series of obstacles and were excited by the transformation that gradually came with TVA dams, lakes, and transmission lines. An aura of reform surrounded the undertaking, particularly in Tennessee, which was located in the heart of the regional enterprise. The project reflected the broader liberalism of the Roosevelt administration, and it stimulated a new vision of progress in the Tennessee Valley. The authority became what one historian has described as "a massive monument of economic growth and development."[26]

Franklin Roosevelt's popularity in Tennessee, the support he received from the state's Democratic politicians, and the backing given his proposals by Tennessee congressmen all testified to the impact the thirty-second president had on the Volunteer State. Yet unlike several other states, in and out of the South, Tennessee could not boast of a "little New Deal." Nor did it have, on the other hand, a strong anti–New Deal Democratic leader such as Governor Eugene Talmadge of Georgia. Although the New Deal did not change the structure of the state's politics, its effects were substantial and its political legacy significant. It forced national issues and standards into state and local politics, stimulated vigorous debate on the fiscal, regulatory, and welfare functions of government, caused many Tennesseans to think in terms of class and economic interests, and made the labels "liberal" and "conservative" more meaningful. Roosevelt's leadership even aroused the political consciousness of the southern "proletariat" of submerged elements like sharecroppers, miners, textile workers, and black domestic workers. In the late 1930s and early 1940s, Roosevelt and Hull contributed to a resurgence of internationalism in Tennessee. Finally, New Deal policies helped transform the South's social and economic structure, and Roosevelt's politics reshaped the national Democratic Party, profoundly changing the place of the South in the Democratic coalition.[27]

Edward Crump's longevity, his dominant role in Memphis politics, and his colorful character made him a familiar personage in the national news.

Crump and his allies exercised a controlling influence in Tennessee politics during this period. Their candidates for governor and other statewide offices were elected with monotonous regularity. Since almost every county in the state supported competing Democratic factions, one of these groups frequently followed the lead of Crump in party primaries. Crump's candidates could usually count on the backing of the state's business interests and more conservative elements. Senator McKellar, a close associate of the Memphis boss, strengthened the organization with his own alliances based on patronage and personal friendships. Perhaps the most important opposition leader was Silliman Evans, publisher of the *Nashville Tennessean,* who year after year subjected the Crump machine to a drumfire of criticism, condemning its alleged election fraud and repression of dissent. Evans and some other anti-Crump Democrats were strong New Dealers, but there was not a consistent ideological division between the Tennessee factions. The opposition to Crump was shifting and amorphous. Writing in 1947, the political scientist Alexander Heard noted that "when the [state] administration is one of repeated successes which have created a myth of invincibility, it is difficult for the opposition forces to obtain campaign money, political respectability, and strong candidates."[28] Heard was describing the effects of Crump's political mastery.

In his comprehensive study of southern politics, V. O. Key called attention to many features that Tennessee shared with other southern states: a low voter turnout (seldom more than one-fourth of voting-age Tennesseans), the dominance of the Democratic Party and its primaries, and the overrepresentation of rural areas in the state legislature.[29] Key also emphasized aspects of Tennessee politics that were uncharacteristic of the South in general: the existence of an organized opposition party, a powerful urban boss, Democratic bifactionalism, and an open system in which Republicans could vote in Democratic primaries. Another distinguishing aspect of Tennessee politics was the participation of the state's black citizens in the electoral process. In 1947, Charles S. Johnson, the president of Fisk University, remarked that the Negro "votes" in East and Middle Tennessee but "is voted" in the western part of the state, a reference to the Crump machine.[30] By the mid-1930s, African Americans in Tennessee were rapidly forsaking their traditional support of the party of Lincoln for the party of Roosevelt. In Shelby County, the Republican Robert Church was no longer needed to persuade black Memphians to cooperate with Crump, and with a Democratic administration in Washington, GOP patronage politics dried up in Tennessee, the

Church-Taylor alliance declined, and the "lily-white" faction grew stronger in the state party.[31]

Even as Key and Heard were probing the intricacies of southern politics, the long life of the Solid South was nearing an end. In the years that followed, the Democratic Party in Tennessee—and the other southern states—assumed a new configuration, the one-party system was disrupted, two-party competition arrived, and the state and region became vitally important in defining the changing character of national politics. These changes resulted from internal pressures as well as developments from the outside, but fundamentally they grew out of external forces like the New Deal, the new Democratic majority coalition, World War II and the prosperity that came in its wake, the reinvigoration of the national Republican Party, and the civil rights movement.

In the 1948 Democratic primary, the Crump faction suffered a major defeat, its first serious setback in many years. The organization's candidate for governor lost to former governor Gordon Browning, and its candidate for the U.S. Senate was defeated by Estes Kefauver, a congressman from Chattanooga. In the presidential election that year, Crump, unwilling to vote for President Harry S. Truman, supported J. Strom Thurmond, who headed the States' Rights Democratic Party. The elderly Crump had become increasingly critical of liberal tendencies he associated with the Roosevelt administration: the rise of the Congress of Industrial Organizations, the campaign to repeal the poll tax in Tennessee, the mounting pressure for change in southern race relations, and the "Red" influences he detected in the national party leadership. Crump disliked Truman and was appalled by his civil rights proposals. Four years later, the Crump organization experienced another reversal when U.S. Representative Albert Gore, Sr., of Carthage defeated Senator McKellar in the Democratic primary. At the same time, Crump contributed to the election as governor of Frank G. Clement, a young lawyer from Middle Tennessee, and to the failure of Browning's bid for reelection.[32]

It was soon apparent that Estes Kefauver, Albert Gore, and Frank Clement represented something new in Tennessee politics. There seemed to be a new spirit abroad in the state, typified by the organization of civic reformers in Memphis and Nashville, the activities of a statewide women's group in helping elect Kefauver, the repeal in 1953 of the poll tax as a voting prerequisite, the increase in black voters, and the decision by a group of returning GIs in McMinn County to overthrow a local machine. New Deal liberalism, with its emphasis on economic interests and issues, was strong in several southern states following World War II. William R. Majors has argued that "the

New Deal coalition emerged in the postwar years as the dominant voting force in the Volunteer State."[33] The death of Edward Crump in 1954 appeared to mark the end of a political era and to encourage party independence. Kefauver and Gore were liberal senators, strongly influenced by the New Deal and the internationalism of the recent war, while Clement pursued his own reform agenda in Nashville.

The two senators and the governor adopted moderate positions in the face of rising southern resistance to federal guarantees of equal rights for African Americans. White Tennesseans, like most residents of the peripheral South, may have "longed to be both southern and American," but segregation as a political issue was not a success in Tennessee.[34] Each of the three leaders campaigned independently and sought to fashion his own coalition and to secure the support of new interest groups: women, organized labor, veterans, urban voters, and blacks. They introduced what one historian describes as "a period of spirited factional competition marked by youth, progressivism, independence, innovative style, and ambition."[35] In 1955, a close observer wrote an article for a national magazine under the title "Too Much Talent in Tennessee?"[36] By that time, it was clear that all three men aspired to higher office in the national arena.

Kefauver was the first to test the water. After attracting national attention as chairman of a special Senate subcommittee created to investigate interstate crime, the Tennessean entered the March 1952 presidential primary in New Hampshire and, to the surprise of many Americans, defeated President Truman, who had not yet announced his future plans. The senator went on to win a series of other primaries before losing the presidential nomination to Illinois governor Adlai E. Stevenson at the Democratic National Convention. Kefauver was the first southerner since Woodrow Wilson to demonstrate a genuinely national appeal in a campaign for the presidency. In 1956, he tried again, without success, and then won the vice presidential nomination, an honor that both Clement and Gore had hoped to receive. Governor Clement had delivered the keynote address at the national convention.[37]

While Frank Clement shared center stage with Estes Kefauver and Albert Gore, the governor created the most enduring faction in Tennessee's Democratic Party during this period. Clement's power resulted from his personal popularity, loose alliances with county leaders, and control of state patronage and the election machinery. He and his ally Buford Ellington held the governorship, in a kind of "leapfrog" fashion, from 1953 until 1971. This administration faction tended to attract conservative Democrats, including remnants of the old Crump-McKellar coalition, but it was a diverse and unstable constituency. Kefauver and Gore, whose supporters overlapped, both appealed to liberals and moderates and to backers of the national Democratic Party. The two senators were rivals, but they shared an apprehension about Clement's national ambitions. Their supporters, encouraged by the anti-Clement arguments of the *Nashville Tennessean* and other critics of the governor, tended to form a broad, undifferentiated grouping in the Tennessee electorate.[38]

Tennessee Democrats seemed to be in firm control of state politics as the decade of the 1960s began. Senators Kefauver and Gore enjoyed strong support within the state and were widely recognized as liberal Democrats and influential senators. The Democratic members in the House of Representatives were less prominent, although for a time in the 1950s three Tennesseans were chairmen of important committees: Jere Cooper (Ways and Means), Thomas J. Murray (Post Office and Civil Service), and J. Percy Priest (Interstate and Foreign Commerce). In 1962, Frank Clement won the governorship for a third time, succeeding Buford Ellington. Two years later, President Lyndon B. Johnson, advocating far-reaching civil rights legislation and a bold program of social reform, won a sweeping victory in the presidential election over the conservative GOP nominee, Barry M. Goldwater, who carried five Deep South states. Then, almost overnight, the political situation in Tennessee changed dramatically.[39]

Leaders of the two major parties in Tennessee had long operated in accordance with an implicit understanding that Democrats would make no serious effort to compete with Republicans in East Tennessee, while the GOP would virtually concede statewide elections to the majority party. Party chieftains, observed V. O. Key in 1949, "look forward to Republican victory nationally, with themselves in charge of the distribution of Federal patronage locally."[40] Men like B. Carroll Reece, who represented Tennessee's first congressional district for twenty-four years and served as chairman of the Republican national committee during the years 1946–48, were not interested in undertaking an aggressive campaign to build a statewide party. Success in such a venture might disrupt their East Tennessee satrapy and threaten their own control. Things began to change after the Second World War. In 1948, Reece, the party's nominee for the U.S. Senate, and the Grand Ole Opry star Roy Acuff, the GOP candidate for governor, made an impressive showing against the Democrats in the general election. By the 1950s, moreover, an increasing number of Democrats had become dissatisfied and even disillusioned with the leadership and policies of the national Democratic Party. The selection of General Dwight D. Eisenhower as the Republican presidential nominee in 1952 brought a breakthrough. Eisenhower won a narrow victory over Adlai E. Stevenson in Tennessee and three other states of the peripheral South. He carried Tennessee again in 1956, and four years later, Richard M. Nixon, the Republican nominee, was also victorious in the Volunteer State. Building on their traditional base in East Tennessee, the Republicans found supporters in Middle and West Tennessee, particularly among the more affluent urban and suburban residents.[41]

In the late 1960s and early 1970s, the Republican Party made extraordinary gains in campaigns that marked the beginning of the contemporary era in Tennessee politics. Encouraged by the rise of new leaders, vigorous organizing activities in such cities as Chattanooga and Memphis, legislative reapportionment resulting from *Baker v. Carr* (1962), a Supreme Court case originating in Tennessee, and the polarizing effects of the civil rights movement, Republicans concentrated on winning a statewide office. In 1966, Howard H. Baker, Jr., son of an East Tennessee congressman and an attractive candidate in his own right, defeated Frank Clement for the Senate seat held by Estes Kefauver until his death in 1963. Democratic factionalism worked to the Republicans' advantage. In the presidential election of 1968, Richard M. Nixon carried Tennessee over the third-party candidacy of Alabama governor George C. Wallace, who appealed to the social conservatism of many Tennesseans, especially in the western part of the state. Vice President Hubert H. Humphrey, the Democratic nominee, came in third. The Republicans also won control of the lower house of the General Assembly in 1968. Two years later, Republican Winfield Dunn of Memphis captured the governorship, and the party defeated Albert Gore to win the other Senate seat. Capitalizing on Gore's liberal reputation, opposition to the war in Vietnam, and apparent remoteness from his constituents, William E. Brock of Chattanooga, the GOP nominee, carried Shelby County and did well in many suburban areas. The Republicans now held all three of the top statewide offices, and in 1972 they won another seat in the House of Representatives, giving the party a five-to-three majority in the state's congressional delegation. At the same time, President Nixon was reelected by a landslide, carrying every southern state (and all nonsouthern states except Massachusetts) and receiving over 70 percent of the popular votes in the ex-Confederate states.[42] Tennessee had become a two-party state.

One source of Democratic strength was the rapid increase in the registration of black southerners, most of whom were loyal supporters of the Democratic Party. In 1970, 240,000 African Americans (76.5 percent of the black voting-age population) were registered in Tennessee, and the Tennessee

Howard Baker, Jr.; Ray Blanton; and James Sasser were prominent politicians during the 1970s who served in the U.S. Congress. Louise L. Davis Papers, Tennessee Historical Society Collection, Tennessee State Library and Archives.

Voters' Council and a variety of local black organizations were active in politics.[43] Seeking to make themselves more competitive, Democratic politicians enjoyed some success in developing black-white coalitions. Temporary alliances of this kind contributed to the election of a group of moderate southern governors in the 1970s. In Tennessee, Ray Blanton, who had represented the seventh congressional district in West Tennessee, reclaimed the governorship for the Democrats in 1974, aided by the Watergate scandal and Democratic success in attracting Wallace supporters back to the party. Meanwhile, the Democrats had recaptured control of the state house of representatives and resumed their dominance of the state's congressional delegation.

The most spectacular manifestation of Democratic recovery, however, was the election of James Earl "Jimmy" Carter, Jr., as president in 1976. Presenting himself as a moderate, New South Democrat, the one-term governor of Georgia turned back George C. Wallace in a series of southern primaries, including Tennessee's, and won eleven nonsouthern primaries on his way to capturing the Democratic nomination. That fall, he carried every southern state except Virginia and Oklahoma and defeated his Republican opponent, President Gerald R. Ford, in a tight race. Black ballots played a vital part in several of the southern victories. Tennessee Democrats also regained one of the U.S. Senate seats in 1976 when James R. Sasser, a young Nashville lawyer, defeated Senator Brock.[44] Millions of southerners felt a sense of regional pride and satisfaction in the election of another president from their own region.

Southern Democrats soon encountered rough weather. In Tennessee, the Blanton administration was incapacitated by cronyism and corruption, and a new Republican leader in the person of Lamar Alexander, a protégé of Howard Baker, emerged to win the governorship for the Republicans in 1978. By that time, the Carter administration was also in trouble, unable to persuade a restless Congress to approve the president's major proposals and plagued by sluggish economic growth and spiraling inflation, as well as mounting hostility from the Soviet Union and a challenge to Carter's renomination by Senator Edward M. Kennedy of Massachusetts. Although Carter turned back Kennedy's challenge, he lost the election of 1980 to former governor Ronald Reagan of California. The Georgian narrowly lost Tennessee—and every other southern state except his home state of Georgia.[45]

The election of Lamar Alexander as governor in 1978 and his reelection four years later demonstrated that, with able and attractive candidates, Tennessee Republicans could win the top state offices as well as presidential contests. The General Assembly was usually the least Democratic of any southern state legislature. In Congress, meanwhile, Howard Baker had become one of his party's outstanding leaders. He won national plaudits in 1973 for his conduct as the ranking Republican member of the Ervin Committee in its investigation of the Watergate affair. Baker became Senate minority leader in 1977 and made an unsuccessful effort to win his party's presidential nomination in 1980. After the Republicans captured control of the Senate in 1980, the Tennessean was chosen majority leader. Alexander and Baker, as moderate Republicans, represented an important feature of the "new Republicanism" in Tennessee.

But there was another aspect of the state's new Republicanism: the heightening of its ideological conservatism. Two-thirds of southern Republicans identified themselves as conservatives in the early 1980s, as compared with only 56 percent in 1972. The symbol of this conservatism was Ronald Reagan, who had made many converts in Tennessee by the time he entered the White House. He was immensely popular in the state and the South as a whole, sweeping to victory in 1980 and 1984 and running stronger in the southern states than in the rest of the nation. In 1988, Vice President George H. W.

Bush, pledging to continue Reagan's policies, was easily elected, carrying every southern state. Reagan, more than any other contemporary leader, changed the image of the Republican Party and brought it into line with the convictions of millions of white southerners. He thereby abetted a process already under way of "southernizing" the GOP.[46]

If the 1980s were triumphant years for the Republican Party in Tennessee, that decade also witnessed a renewal of Democratic strength below the presidential level. Though President Reagan carried the state overwhelmingly in 1984, Albert Gore, Jr., a liberal congressman and son of the former senator, was easily elected to the Senate seat being vacated by Howard Baker. The Democrats now controlled both Senate offices and six of the state's nine seats in the House of Representatives. Two years later, they took over the governorship by electing Ned Ray McWherter of Weakley County, a legislative veteran, and winning majorities in the General Assembly of 61 to 38 and 23 to 10. Senator Sasser was handily reelected in 1982 and 1988, and Senator Gore and Governor McWherter won reelection in 1990. (Between 1976 and 1992, Tennessee Republicans were successful in only three statewide campaigns, not counting presidential races.) While still in his first term in the upper house, Senator Gore sought his party's presidential nomination in a contest eventually won by Governor Michael Dukakis of Massachusetts. Gore was an easy winner in the Tennessee preferential primary, and he also carried Arkansas and North Carolina. But he was second in the region to the black leader Jesse Jackson, who won the delegates of six southern states, and the senator's campaign did not fare well outside the South. In 1992, however, Gore was selected by Governor Bill Clinton of Arkansas, the Democratic presidential nominee, as his running mate. The two southerners led the Democrats to victory in the presidential election that year. There were stereotypical comments in other regions about the "double Bubba" ticket, and one Dixie journalist remarked that Gore's selection brought a slate of two "southern progressives without the baggage of liberal excess."[47] Gore strengthened the Democratic ticket in the South, although he and Clinton managed to carry only Tennessee and four other southern states.[48]

Democratic authority in Washington was quickly disrupted by the Republicans, who, in a nationwide rejection of Democratic congressional candidates—and Clinton's leadership—seized control of both houses of Congress in the midterm elections of 1994. In Tennessee, the Democrats lost both Senate seats and the governorship, while retaining only four of the nine positions in the House of Representatives. They did manage to preserve their control of the General Assembly.[49] The Republican Party's impressive gains in 1994 were not entirely the result of widespread dissatisfaction with Democratic policies in Washington; they also reflected earlier GOP electoral successes, especially in the southern states. Tennessee Republicans won 80 percent of the presidential contests between 1952 and 1988, 50 percent of the senatorial and gubernatorial races between 1966 and 1994, and 39 percent of the legislative elections between 1966 and 1984. Survey data for the South reveal a 22-percentage-point decline (5 points in the rest of the nation) in the number of white Democratic identifiers between 1952 and 1984, while GOP identifiers increased by 18 percentage points (only 3 points outside the South). Meanwhile, straight ticket voting by southern white Democrats dropped from 80 percent of such Democrats before 1962 to 55 percent in 1984.[50] Many white Tennesseans were obviously undergoing a process of realignment, shifting their votes and their partisan attachments from the Democrats to the Republicans. Others were involved in a process political scientists call "dealignment," abandoning their old party ties without developing a psychological attachment to another party.[51]

Tennessee Democrats turned to the Republican Party for many reasons, among them a smoldering resentment among conservatives of the "liberal-labor-minority coalition" they identified with the national Democratic Party. A large number of conservative Democrats were alienated from their traditional party by the civil rights movement and the effects of changing race relations, including the preferential treatment of minorities and the idea of employment quotas. The political consequences of socioeconomic and demographic changes were of fundamental importance; they were largely responsible for the declining influence of the rural areas, the emergence of an urban- and metropolitan-centered politics, and the altered distribution of power in the state. The fast pace of industrialization, economic expansion, and urbanization after 1940 brought unparalleled prosperity to Tennessee, diversified its economy, and created a new social structure dominated by a dynamic middle class. A recent analysis of politics and society in the contemporary South reveals that by 1980 more than half of the region's workers were employed in middle-class jobs. Indeed, the new southern electorate is disproportionately middle class, and in the 1980s, almost two-thirds of its white members identified themselves as conservative or expressed some affinity for the political right. "Democrats," the political scientist Earl Black quipped, "are basically fighting a rearguard action against the creation of an urban middle class."[52]

The prevailing political philosophy of the new middle class is what two close students of southern politics describe as "the entrepreneurial version of the individualistic political culture," which emphasizes low rates of taxation, minimum regulation of business, strong opposition to labor unions, and a dislike of redistributive welfare programs, particularly those emanating from Washington. The fact that the South is the most Protestant part of the country may help explain the importance southerners attach to individual rather than collective responsibility for economic success. A large majority of middle-class white southerners emphasizes individual rather than government responsibility for economic well-being. Recent surveys show that almost half of the region's white working class also stresses individual responsibility as a primary value, as contrasted with 13 percent of black southerners, 72 percent of whom place emphasis on government responsibility for employment and a good standard of living. These ideological differences do not augur well for the success of political alliances between black and white Tennesseans. In addition, the conservative tendencies of white southerners are evident in their support of a strong national defense and in their attitudes on "social issues" such as abortion, prayer in the public schools, gays and lesbians, and capital punishment. Finally, Tennessee's conservative electorate has given its Republicans a decided advantage in the GOP presidential nominating process, in contrast to the Democrats, who employ a process in which new party rules have reduced the power of state leaders, increased the importance of liberal activist groups, and resulted in the nomination of liberal candidates seeking support in the general election from voters who are strongly conservative.[53]

Tennessee has undergone a remarkable political transformation during the long period since Reconstruction. Except for the political upheaval of the 1890s, the bitter divisions associated with the fusion of independent Democrats and Republicans early in the twentieth century, and the turbulent Democratic politics of the 1920s, the state can claim a "politics of peaceful change." For more than half a century, during the era when the Democratic primary was the real election, Tennessee was essentially a one-party state and a part of the Solid South. The New Deal, World War II, and the vast economic and social changes that followed paved the way for the disruption of the Democratic South and the increasing competitiveness of the Republican Party. Two-party competition became a reality in the Volunteer State, and the idea of a genuine party system finally took hold among the voters. New leaders came to the fore, and an enlarged, diverse, and urban-based electorate came into being. Old-fashioned white racism virtually disappeared. Tennessee politics became more accessible and more democratic. Political behavior and ideas in Tennessee steadily converged with those in other regions, and in that sense the state's politics was nationalized as never before in the modern period.[54]

Contemporary Tennessee politics reflects continuity as well as change. The state's geographic divisions, for instance, still influence its politics, although a remarkable shift in partisan attachments has taken place in West Tennessee. The Democratic Party, for all its modifications, remains a powerful force, in control of the state legislature and many local governments and supported by its image as the party of the average person. Over the years the Democrats became more competitive in the eastern division, but their party is still anchored in Middle Tennessee. The party's continued success at the local level owes something to the strength and resourcefulness of Democratic incumbents, to their independent campaigns and emphasis on local issues, and to the prevalence of ticket-splitting in Tennessee. Conservative control of politics has also persisted, though the dominant role of planters, manufacturers, bankers, and the county-seat governing class has largely given way to "corporation-oriented metropolitan elites." The constitution of 1870, an almost unamendable document, has prevented the adoption of a modern and less regressive tax system. The state's fundamental conservatism can be seen as well in the relative absence of organized labor and in the limited part played by women in Tennessee politics, particularly in running for and winning office. The continuing influence of race in politics is suggested by a statistic from the presidential election of 1984: 69 percent of Tennessee's white voters cast their ballots for Ronald Reagan, while 95 percent of the state's black voters supported Walter Mondale.[55]

Tennessee, like each of its sister states, has a unique political history, shaped by internal and external influences. Tennessee became an unusual one-party state, since the Republican Party remained dominant in the eastern section and continued to affect the conduct of the state's politics after the Democrats consolidated their control. While Democratic politicians acted to disfranchise black voters in the late nineteenth century, the state's African Americans (19 percent of the population in 1920 and 16 percent in 1980) continued to vote, and racial demagogues attracted more attention in local politics than in statewide campaigns. Democratic politics was characterized by a recurring bifactionalism, in part because of the Republican presence, and as time passed its leaders included a successful progressive governor, a powerful urban boss, two Senate liberals, and a spellbinder as chief executive. Republicanism in Tennessee had long been stronger than elsewhere in the South, and the Volunteer State led the region, first in becoming a Republican base in presidential politics and then in reaching a truly competitive position in state politics.

Another dimension of Tennessee's politics in the twentieth century is the part it assumed in national affairs, most notably perhaps in Congress during the Wilson and Roosevelt years, when Hull, Garrett, Byrns, McKellar, and later Kefauver, Gore, Baker, and others held sway. Also, Tennessee and the other southern states played a crucial role in the national resurgence of the Republican Party after 1968. No other region contributed more to the nominations of Richard Nixon in 1968, Ronald Reagan in 1980, and George Bush in 1988. In the process, southern Republicans moved their national party to the right and emerged as a major component of the new GOP majority in presidential elections. Earl Black and Merle Black have noted that the contemporary South "is the largest, the most cohesive, and, arguably, the most important region in the United States in terms of establishing the partisan direction of presidential politics."[56] Finally, an unusually large number of Tennesseans set their sights on the ultimate goal, the presidency. Estes Kefauver, Howard H. Baker, Jr., Albert Gore, Jr., and Lamar Alexander, among others, found—and continue to find—inspiration for such lofty ambitions in Tennessee's political milieu and traditions.

Tennessee's modern political experience has had its own distinctive characteristics, which make it a compelling and instructive part of the state's larger history. At the same time, Tennessee's role in southern political affairs and the increasing nationalization of its politics suggest its importance for an understanding of regional and national developments.

NOTES

For critical reading of the manuscript the author is indebted to Professors Hugh Davis Graham, Samuel T. McSeveney, Gary W. Reichard, V. Jacque Voegeli, and Carroll Van West.

1. V. O. Key, Jr., with the assistance of Alexander Heard, *Southern Politics in State and Nation* (New York, 1949), 58–81.
2. Roger L. Hart, *Redeemers, Bourbons, & Populists: Tennessee, 1870–1896* (Baton Rouge, 1975), 1–106; Gordon B. McKinney, *Southern Mountain Republicans, 1865–1900: Politics and the Appalachian Community* (Chapel Hill, N.C., 1978), 21, 23, 28, 31–41, 77–86, 124–25, 133–37, 143–50, 184–86, 197–98, 200; McKinney, "Southern Mountain Republicans and the Negro, 1865–1900," *Journal of Southern History* 41 (Nov. 1975): 493–516; J. Morgan Kousser, *The Shaping of Southern Politics: Suffrage Restriction and the Establishment of the One-Party South, 1880–1910* (New

Haven, 1974), 27, 104–5. Verton M. Queener, "The East Tennessee Republicans in State and Nation, 1870–1900," *Tennessee Historical Quarterly* 2 (June 1943): 99–128; Queener, "The East Tennessee Republicans as a Minority Party, 1870–1896," *East Tennessee Historical Society's (ETHS) Publications* 15 (1943): 49–73.

3. James Tice Moore, "Agrarianism and Populism in Tennessee, 1886–1896: An Interpretative Overview," *Tennessee Historical Quarterly* 42 (Spring 1983): 76–94. For the farmers' movement in Tennessee, also see Hart, *Redeemers, Bourbons, & Populists,* 107–223; Daniel Merritt Robison, *Bob Taylor and the Agrarian Revolt in Tennessee* (Chapel Hill, N.C., 1935), 132–204; and Leonard Schlup, "Conservative Counterattack: Adlai E. Stevenson and the Compromise of 1892 with Tennessee and the South," *Tennessee Historical Quarterly* 53 (Summer 1994): 114–29.

4. Hart, *Redeemers, Bourbons, & Populists,* 223.

5. Joseph H. Cartwright, *The Triumph of Jim Crow: Tennessee Race Relations in the 1880s* (Knoxville, 1976), 199–253; Kousser, *The Shaping of Southern Politics,* 104–23, 241.

6. North Carolina was an exception to this Democratic success in the South. In that state, a fusion of Populists and Republicans took over the state legislature in the election of 1894, and a Republican was elected governor in 1896, even though the Democrats carried the state for William Jennings Bryan. In the West, Bryan carried the Rocky Mountain states and all but one of the Plains states.

7. Kousser, *The Shaping of Southern Politics,* 226–27; Key, *Southern Politics,* 75.

8. William Goodman, *Inherited Domain: Political Parties in Tennessee* (Knoxville, 1954), 31–32; Verton M. Queener, "The East Tennessee Republican Party, 1900–1914," ETHS *Publications* 22 (1950): 94–127.

9. J. M. Shahan, "The Rhetoric of Reform: The 1906 Gubernatorial Race in Tennessee," *Tennessee Historical Quarterly* 35 (Spring 1976): 65–82; Paul E. Isaac, "The Problems of a Republican Governor in a Southern State: Ben Hooper of Tennessee, 1910–1914," *Tennessee Historical Quarterly* 27 (Fall 1968): 229–48; Russell L. Stockard, "The Election and First Administration of Ben W. Hooper as Governor of Tennessee," ETHS *Publications* 26 (1954): 38–59; Joe Michael Shahan, "Reform and Politics in Tennessee: 1906–1914" (Ph.D. diss., Vanderbilt Univ., 1981); William D. Miller, *Memphis During the Progressive Era, 1900–1917* (Memphis, 1957), 64–179; Don H. Doyle, *Nashville in the New South, 1880–1930* (Knoxville, 1985), 131–82; Lester C. Lamon, *Black Tennesseans, 1900–1930* (Knoxville, 1977), 207–30; Dewey W. Grantham, *Southern Progressivism: The Reconciliation of Progress and Tradition* (Knoxville, 1983), 78–82.

10. Paul E. Isaac, *Prohibition and Politics: Turbulent Decades in Tennessee, 1885–1920* (Knoxville, 1965), 81–247; Shahan, "Reform and Politics in Tennessee," 167–328; *The Unwanted Boy: The Autobiography of Governor Ben W. Hooper,* ed. Everett Robert Boyce (Knoxville, 1963), 46–157; James Summerville, *The Carmack-Cooper Shooting: Tennessee Politics Turns Violent, November 9, 1908* (Jefferson, N.C., 1994); Thomas H. Winn, "Liquor, Race and Politics: Clarksville During the Progressive Period," *Tennessee Historical Quarterly* 49 (Winter 1990): 207–17; William R. Majors, *Editorial Wild Oats: Edward Ward Carmack and Tennessee Politics* (Macon, Ga., 1984); Majors, *Change and Continuity: Tennessee Politics Since the Civil War* (Macon, Ga., 1986), 35–49; William D. Miller, *Mr. Crump of Memphis* (Baton Rouge, 1964), 106–16.

11. Arthur S. Link, "Democratic Politics and the Presidential Campaign of 1912 in Tennessee," ETHS *Publications* 18 (1946): 107–30; Paul D. Casdorph, *Republicans, Negroes, and Progressives in the South, 1912–1916* (Tuscaloosa, Ala., 1981), 36–41, 72–73, 85–86, 105–7, 139–41, 150; Richard B. Sherman, *The Republican Party and Black America: From McKinley to Hoover, 1896–1933* (Charlottesville, Va., 1973), 83–112.

12. Tennesseans had a personal claim on Wilson resulting from his family's having lived in Tennessee for several years. His father, the Reverend Joseph R. Wilson, served as professor of theology at Southwestern Presbyterian University in Clarksville from 1885 to 1893. His brother, Joseph R. Wilson, Jr., spent many years as a journalist in Tennessee, working part of that time for the *Nashville Banner.*

13. See David M. Potter, *The South and the Concurrent Majority,* ed. Don E. Fehrenbacher and Carl N. Degler (Baton Rouge, 1972), for a discussion of these congressional tactics.

14. Philip A. Grant, Jr., "Tennesseans in the 63d Congress, 1913–1915," *Tennessee Historical Quarterly* 29 (Fall 1970): 278–86; Richard L. Watson, Jr., "A Testing Time for Southern Congressional Leadership: The War Crisis of 1917–1918," *Journal of Southern History* 44 (Feb. 1978): 3–40; I. A. Newby, "States' Rights and Southern Congressmen During World War I," *Phylon* 24 (Spring 1963): 34–50; Cooper Milner, "The Public Life of Cordell Hull: 1907–1924" (Ph.D. diss., Vanderbilt Univ., 1960), 73–123; Sherman, *The Republican Party and Black America,* 113–44.

15. Quoted in A. Elizabeth Taylor, *The Woman Suffrage Movement in Tennessee* (New York, 1957), 73.

16. Taylor, *The Woman Suffrage Movement in Tennessee,* 34–125; Anastatia Sims, "'Powers that Pray' and 'Powers that Prey': Tennessee and the Fight for Woman Suffrage," *Tennessee Historical Quarterly* 50 (Winter 1991): 203–25; Marjorie Spruill Wheeler, *New Women of the New South: The Leaders of the Woman Suffrage Movement in the Southern States* (New York, 1993), 31–36, 172, 181–82; Watson, "A Testing Time for Southern Congressional Leadership," 26–34; Newby, "States' Rights and Southern Congressmen During World War I," 46–48; James P. Louis, "Sue Shelton White and the Woman Suffrage Movement in Tennessee, 1913–20," *Tennessee Historical Quarterly* 22 (June 1963): 170–90; Marirose Arendale, "Tennessee and Women's Rights," *Tennessee Historical Quarterly* 39 (Spring 1980): 62–78.

17. David D. Lee, *Tennessee in Turmoil: Politics in the Volunteer State, 1920–1932* (Memphis, 1979), 19–23; Paul E. Isaac, "Defeat and Victory: The Republican Party in Tennessee, 1918–1920," ETHS *Publications* 61 (1989): 48–77; Gary W. Reichard, "The Defeat of Governor Roberts," *Tennessee Historical Quarterly* 30 (Spring 1971): 94–109; Reichard, "The Aberration of 1920: An Analysis of Harding's Victory in Tennessee," *Journal of Southern History* 36 (Feb. 1970): 33–49; David M. Tucker, *Lieutenant Lee of Beale Street* (Nashville, 1971), 68–104.

18. Joseph T. Macpherson, "Democratic Progressivism in Tennessee: The Administrations of Governor Austin Peay, 1923–1927," ETHS *Publications* 40 (1968): 50–61; Macpherson, "Democratic Progressivism in Tennessee: The Administrations of Governor Austin Peay, 1923–1927" (Ph.D. diss., Vanderbilt Univ., 1969); Lee, *Tennessee in Turmoil,* 19–75, 159–60; Majors, *Tennessee Politics Since the Civil War,* 56–60; George Brown Tindall, *The Emergence of the New South, 1913–1945* (Baton Rouge, 1967), 224, 228–29.

19. Lee, *Tennessee in Turmoil,* 75. For an assessment of how historians have dealt with the urban-rural theme in the 1920s, see Charles W. Eagles, "Urban-Rural Conflict in the 1920s: A Historiographical Assessment," *Historian* 49 (Nov. 1986): 26–48.

20. Lee, *Tennessee in Turmoil,* 7–23, 26–38, 44–149; David D. Lee, "Rural Democrats, Eastern Republicans, and Trade-offs in Tennessee, 1922–1932," ETHS *Publications* 48 (1976): 104–15; Majors, *Tennessee Politics Since the Civil War,* 54–65; Don H. Doyle, *Nashville Since the 1920s* (Knoxville, 1985), 64; Miller, *Mr. Crump of Memphis,* 117–62; Goodman, *Inherited Domain,* 36; Allen H. Kitchens, "Ouster of Mayor Edward H. Crump, 1915–1916," West Tennessee Historical Society (WTHS) *Papers* 19 (1965): 105–20.

21. In addition to the sources cited in note 20, see Mary Louise Lea Tidwell, *Luke Lea of Tennessee* (Bowling Green, Ohio, 1993), 146–215; John Berry McFerrin, *Caldwell and Company: A Southern Financial Empire* (Chapel Hill, N.C., 1939), 99–115, 189–204; David D. Lee, "The Attempt to Impeach Governor Horton," *Tennessee Historical Quarterly* 34 (Summer 1975): 188–201; Lee, "The Triumph of Boss Crump: The Tennessee Gubernatorial Election of 1932," *Tennessee Historical Quarterly* 35 (Winter 1976): 393–413; Thomas Harrison Baker, *The Commercial Appeal: The History of a Southern Newspaper* (Baton Rouge, 1971), 272–91; and Doyle, *Nashville in the New South,* 199, 223–32.

22. G. Michael McCarthy, "Smith vs. Hoover—The Politics of Race in West Tennessee," *Phylon* 39 (June 1978): 154–68; Key, *Southern Politics,* 322–23; Lee, *Tennessee in Turmoil,* 98–100; Tindall, *The Emergence of the New South,* 245–52; Milner, "The Public Life of Cordell Hull," 375–418; Judith M. Stanley, "Cordell Hull and Democratic Party Unity," *Tennessee Historical Quarterly* 32 (Summer 1973): 169–87; Cordell Hull, *The Memoirs of Cordell Hull* (New York, 1948), 1:140–54; Frank Freidel, *F.D.R. and the South* (Baton Rouge, 1965), 29–33; Dean Pope, "The Senator From Tennessee," WTHS *Papers* 22 (1968): 102–22.

23. Thomas H. Coode, "Tennessee Congressmen and the New Deal, 1933–1938," WTHS *Papers* 31 (1977): 132–58; Coode, "Walter Chandler as Congressman," WTHS *Papers* 29 (1975): 25–37; J. M. Galloway, "Speaker Joseph W. Byrns: Party Leader in the New Deal," *Tennessee Historical Quarterly* 25 (Spring 1966): 63–76; Robert Dean Pope, "Senatorial Baron: The Long Political Career of Kenneth D. McKellar" (Ph.D. diss., Yale Univ., 1976), 225–46, 288–300; Miller, *Mr. Crump of Memphis,* 179–84, 224–41; Tindall, *The Emergence of the New South,* 607–49; Roger Biles, *The South and the New Deal* (Lexington, 1994), 125–52.

24. Roger Biles, *Memphis in the Great Depression* (Knoxville, 1986), 86.

25. For the extent of this federal intervention, see John Dean Minton, *The New Deal in Tennessee, 1932–1938* (New York, 1979). The author of this study concludes that the New Deal "wrought a revolution in Tennessee" (275). For congressional criticism of the New Deal, see James T. Patterson, *Congressional Conservatism and the New Deal: The Growth of the Conservative Coalition in Congress, 1933–1939* (Lexington, 1967). Herron C. Pearson was probably the most conservative Democrat from Tennessee during this period (344, 347–50).

26. Tindall, *The Emergence of the New South,* 446–57 (quotation on 446). See also Paul K. Conkin, "Intellectual and Political Roots," in Erwin C. Hargrove and Paul K. Conkin, eds., *TVA: Fifty Years of Grass-Roots Bureaucracy* (Urbana, Ill., 1983), 3–34;

Richard Lowitt, "The TVA, 1933–45," in Hargrove and Conkin, *TVA,* 35–65; Michael J. McDonald and John Muldowny, *TVA and the Dispossessed: The Resettlement of Population in the Norris Dam Area* (Knoxville, 1982); and Erwin C. Hargrove, *Prisoners of Myth: The Leadership of the Tennessee Valley Authority, 1933–1990* (Princeton, N.J., 1994), 19–64.

27. James A. Hodges, "George Fort Milton and the New Deal," *Tennessee Historical Quarterly* 36 (Fall 1977): 383–409; J. W. Adams, "Governor Gordon Browning, Campaigner Extraordinary—The 1936 Election for Governor," WTHS *Papers* 30 (1976): 5–23; Biles, *The South and the New Deal,* 125–52; Alan Brinkley, "The New Deal and Southern Politics," in James C. Cobb and Michael V. Namorato, eds., *The New Deal and the South* (Jackson, Miss., 1984), 97–115; Numan V. Bartley and Hugh D. Graham, *Southern Politics and the Second Reconstruction* (Baltimore, 1975), 22, 24–25; Majors, *Tennessee Politics Since the Civil War,* 91–92.

28. Alexander Heard, "Comments on Tennessee Politics," Sept. 24, 1947, in Southern Politics Collection, Box 10, Vanderbilt Univ. Library. See also Miller, *Mr. Crump of Memphis,* 185–223, 242–85; Biles, *Memphis in the Great Depression,* 29–47; William R. Majors, "A Re-Examination of V. O. Key's *Southern Politics in State and Nation*: The Case of Tennessee," ETHS *Publications* 49 (1977): 117–35; Majors, *Tennessee Politics Since the Civil War,* 66–73; Goodman, *Inherited Domain,* 32; and Jennings Perry, *Democracy Begins at Home: The Tennessee Fight on the Poll Tax* (Philadelphia and New York, 1944).

29. Key, *Southern Politics,* 58–81.

30. Interview with Alexander Heard, Aug. 21, 1947, Southern Politics Collection, Box 10.

31. Roger Biles, "Robert R. Church, Jr. of Memphis: Black Republican Leader in the Age of Democratic Ascendancy, 1928–1940," *Tennessee Historical Quarterly* 42 (Winter 1983): 362–82; Biles, *Memphis in the Great Depression,* 96–107; Nancy J Weiss, *Farewell to the Party of Lincoln: Black Politics in the Age of FDR* (Princeton, N.J., 1983), 30–31, 206–7, 228, 308; Larry W. Dunn, "Knoxville Negro Voting and the Roosevelt Revolution, 1928–1936," ETHS *Publications* 43 (1971): 71–93.

32. Majors, *Tennessee Politics Since the Civil War,* 78–83; Miller, *Mr. Crump of Memphis,* 323–45; James B. Gardner, "Political Leadership in a Period of Transition: Frank G. Clement, Albert Gore, Estes Kefauver, and Tennessee Politics, 1948–1956" (Ph.D. diss., Vanderbilt Univ., 1978), 62–111, 147–87; Joseph Bruce Gorman, *Kefauver: A Political Biography* (New York, 1971), 35–63; Albert Gore, *Let the Glory Out: My South and Its Politics* (New York, 1972), 65–80; William L. Davis, "Frank Clement: The First Campaign," *Tennessee Historical Quarterly* 35 (Spring 1976): 83–91; Lee Seifert Greene, *Lead Me On: Frank Goad Clement and Tennessee Politics* (Knoxville, 1982), 42–84.

33. Majors, *Tennessee Politics Since the Civil War,* 91; David M. Tucker, *Memphis Since Crump: Bossism, Blacks, and Civic Reformers, 1948–1968* (Knoxville, 1980), 40–99; Doyle, *Nashville Since the 1920s,* 179–221; Robert G. Spinney, "Municipal Government in Nashville, Tennessee, 1938–1951: World War II and the Growth of the Public Sector," *Journal of Southern History* 61 (Feb. 1995): 77–112; J. Morgan Kousser, "Tennessee Politics and the Negro: 1948–1964" (Senior thesis, Princeton Univ., 1965), 3–4, 6–7, 25, 92; M. Jerome Diamond, "The Impact of the Negro

Vote in Contemporary Tennessee Politics," *Tennessee Law Review* 34 (Spring 1967): 435–81; Theodore H. White, "The Battle of Athens, Tennessee," *Harper's Magazine* 194 (Jan. 1947): 54–61; Lones Seiber, "The Battle of Athens," *American Heritage* 36 (Feb.–Mar. 1985): 73–79; Bartley and Graham, *Southern Politics and the Second Reconstruction*, 44–46.

34. Numan V. Bartley, *The Rise of Massive Resistance: Race and Politics in the South During the 1950's* (Baton Rouge, 1969), 137. For Tennessee politics and equal rights for blacks, see ibid., 73, 79–80, 99–100, 141, 143, 275–76, 287; Earl Black, *Southern Governors and Civil Rights: Racial Segregation as a Campaign Issue in the Second Reconstruction* (Cambridge, Mass., 1976), 31–32, 87–90, 118–23, 154–57, 311; and Hugh Davis Graham, *Crisis in Print: Desegregation and the Press in Tennessee* (Nashville, 1967), 62–90, 269–91.

35. Gardner, "Political Leadership in a Period of Transition," 111.

36. Wilma Dykeman, "Too Much Talent in Tennessee?" *Harper's Magazine* 210 (Mar. 1955): 48–53.

37. Gardner, "Political Leadership in a Period of Transition," 281–97, 622–76; Gorman, *Kefauver*, 103–59, 211–65; Charles L. Fontenay, *Estes Kefauver: A Biography* (Knoxville, 1980), 190–229, 244–84; Richard E. McFadyen, "Estes Kefauver and the Tradition of Southern Progressivism," *Tennessee Historical Quarterly* 37 (Winter 1978): 430–43; Gore, *Let the Glory Out*, 89–96; Greene, *Lead Me On*, 221–46; Robert E. Corlew III, "Frank Goad Clement and the Keynote Address of 1956," *Tennessee Historical Quarterly* 36 (Spring 1977): 95–107.

38. Majors, *Tennessee Politics Since the Civil War*, 83–88; Gardner, "Political Leadership in a Period of Transition," 678–707; Norman L. Parks, "Tennessee Politics Since Kefauver and Reece: A 'Generalist' View," *Journal of Politics* 28 (Feb. 1966): 144–68. A constitutional change adopted in 1953 extended the governor's term to four years, without the right of succession. The latter provision may have helped undermine the traditional bifactionalism in the Democratic Party. See Earl Black, "A Theory of Southern Factionalism," *Journal of Politics* 45 (Aug. 1983): 603–4.

39. Majors, *Tennessee Politics Since the Civil War*, 95–97; Lee S. Greene and Jack E. Holmes, "Tennessee: A Politics of Peaceful Change," in William C. Havard, ed., *The Changing Politics of the South* (Baton Rouge, 1972), 176, 180–82; Bartley and Graham, *Southern Politics and the Second Reconstruction*, 104–06; W. Wayne Shannon, "Revolt in Washington: The South in Congress," in Havard, ed., *The Changing Politics of the South*, 645, 648, 658, 666–70; Philip A. Grant, Jr., "Tennessee Congressmen During the Eisenhower Administration," *WTHS Papers* 32 (1978): 103–9.

40. Key, *Southern Politics*, 78.

41. Ibid., 78–81; Majors, *Tennessee Politics Since the Civil War*, 95–96; Alexander Heard, *A Two-Party South?* (Chapel Hill, N.C., 1952), 104, 108, 122, 264; Donald S. Strong, "The Presidential Election in the South, 1952," *Journal of Politics* 17 (Aug. 1955): 368–70, 381–84; Bernard Cosman, "Presidential Republicanism in the South, 1960," *Journal of Politics* 24 (May 1962): 303–22.

42. Earl Black and Merle Black, *Politics and Society in the South* (Cambridge, Mass., 1987), 240, 251, 255; Earl Black and Merle Black, *The Vital South: How Presidents Are Elected* (Cambridge, Mass., 1992), 136; Tucker, *Memphis Since Crump*, 143–51; Wilder Crane, "Tennessee: Inertia and the Courts," in Malcolm E. Jewell, ed., *The Politics*

of Reapportionment (New York, 1962), 314–23; Michael W. Catalano, "*Kidd* v. *McCanless*: The Genesis of Reapportionment Litigation in Tennessee," *Tennessee Historical Quarterly* 44 (Spring 1985): 72–91; Majors, *Tennessee Politics Since the Civil War,* 97–100; Greene and Holmes, "Tennessee: A Politics of Peaceful Change," 183, 188, 190–93, 196, 198–200; Bartley and Graham, *Southern Politics and the Second Reconstruction,* 153–54, 157–59; Jack Bass and Walter DeVries, *The Transformation of Southern Politics: Social Change and Political Consequence Since 1945* (New York, 1976), 292–98; J. Lee Annis, Jr., *Howard Baker: Conciliator in an Age of Crisis* (Lanham, Md., 1994), 23–37.

43. Kousser, "Tennessee Politics and the Negro," 70, 92, 99–100, 103; Diamond, "The Impact of the Negro Vote in Contemporary Tennessee Politics," 436, 453–54, 458–59; William C. Havard, "The South: A Shifting Perspective," in Havard, ed., *The Changing Politics of the South,* 21; Black and Black, *Politics and Society in the South,* 13, 42, 139, 147.

44. Alexander P. Lamis, *The Two-Party South,* 2d expanded ed. (New York, 1990), 169–73; Black and Black, *The Vital South,* 327–43; Majors, *Tennessee Politics Since the Civil War,* 100–101.

45. Black and Black, *The Vital South,* 307–12; Dewey W. Grantham, *The Life & Death of the Solid South: A Political History* (Lexington, Ky., 1988), 184–87.

46. Lamis, *The Two-Party South,* 210–48, 259–60, 290–91, 305–21; Anne H. Hopkins, William Lyons, and Steve Metcalf, "Tennessee," in Robert P. Steed, Laurence W. Moreland, and Tod A. Baker, eds., *The 1984 Presidential Election in the South: Patterns of Southern Party Politics* (New York, 1986), 208–28; David M. Brodsky and Robert Swansbrough, "Tennessee: A House Divided," in Laurence W. Moreland, Robert P. Steed, and Tod A. Baker, eds., *The 1988 Presidential Election in the South: Continuity Amidst Change in Southern Party Politics* (New York, 1991), 201–19; Wayne Greenhaw, *Elephants in the Cottonfields: Ronald Reagan and the New Republican South* (New York, 1982), 202–13; Annis, *Howard Baker,* 65–86, 102–3, 149–94.

47. Cynthia Tucker of the *Atlanta Journal and Constitution,* quoted in Harold W. Stanley, "The South and the 1992 Presidential Election," in Robert P. Steed, Laurence W. Moreland, and Tod A. Baker, eds., *The 1992 Presidential Election in the South: Current Patterns of Southern Party and Electoral Politics* (Westport, Conn., 1994), 200. See also Brodsky and Swansbrough, "Tennessee: A House Divided," 201–19; and Lamis, *The Two-Party South,* 259–60, 290–91.

48. David M. Brodsky and Robert H. Swansbrough, "Tennessee: Favorite Son Brings Home the Bacon," in Steed, Moreland, and Baker, eds., *The 1992 Presidential Election in the South,* 157–68.

49. Rhodes Cook, "Dixie Voters Look Away: South Shifts to the GOP," *Congressional Quarterly Weekly Report* 52 (Nov. 12, 1994): 3230–31; Robert W. Merry, "Voters' Demand for Change Puts Clinton on Defense," *Congressional Quarterly Weekly Report* 52 (Nov. 12, 1994): 3207–9; *New York Times,* Nov. 13, 1994; Hopkins, Lyons, and Metcalf, "Tennessee," 211–13, 221, 226; Robert H. Swansbrough and David M. Brodsky, "Tennessee: Weakening Party Loyalties and Growing Independence," in Swansbrough and Brodsky, eds., *The South's New Politics: Realignment and Dealignment* (Columbia, S.C., 1988), 79–80, 85.

50. One survey of party identification showed that the proportion of Tennesseans identifying themselves as Democrats fell from 42 to 32 percent between 1981 and 1985, while Republican identifiers increased to 29 percent and independents to 39 percent during the same years. See Brodsky and Swansbrough, "Tennessee: A House Divided," 39; Harold W. Stanley, "Southern Partisan Changes: Dealignment, Realignment or both?" *Journal of Politics* 50 (Feb. 1988): 64–66, 78; and Black and Black, *Politics and Society in the South,* 311.

51. In addition to the conversion of Democrats and independents, Republican ranks were augmented by generational replacement and the in-migration of outsiders, mainly northern whites. The number of white residents of Tennessee born outside the South increased from 5 percent of the population in 1960 to 11 percent in 1980, considerably below the average for the peripheral South. See Black and Black, *Politics and Society in the South,* 17.

52. Quoted in Charles S. Bullock, "Contemporary Politics in the American South," *Journal of American and Canadian Studies* 3 (Spring 1989): 111. See also Black and Black, *Politics and Society in the South,* 23–72, 224–30, 259–75.

53. Black and Black, *Politics and Society in the South,* 23–49, 57–72, 189, 192, 213–31, 268, 271, 292–316; Black and Black, *The Vital South,* 241–92; Majors, *Tennessee Politics Since the Civil War,* 103–104, 107.

54. George Brown Tindall, *The Disruption of the Solid South* (Athens, Ga., 1972), 72; Black and Black, *The Vital South,* 14, 132, 136, 147, 213–40, 272, 291–92, 344–66; John R. Petrocik, "Realignment: New Party Coalitions and the Nationalization of the South," *Journal of Politics* 49 (May 1987): 347–75.

55. Stanley, "The 1984 Presidential Election in the South: Race and Realignment," in Steed, Moreland, and Baker, eds., *The 1984 Presidential Election in the South,* 315; Parks, "Tennessee Politics Since Kefauver and Reece," 145–46; Swansbrough and Brodsky, "Tennessee's Weakening Party Loyalties and Growing Independence," 93; Robert Darch, Janet M. Clark, and Charles D. Hadley, "The Changing Role of Women in Southern State Party Politics," in Tod A. Baker, Charles D. Hadley, Robert P. Steed, and Laurence W. Moreland, eds., *Political Parties in the Southern States: Party Activists in Partisan Coalitions* (New York, 1990), 88–102.

56. Black and Black, *The Vital South,* 273, 291–92, 344 (quotation).

Organizing Rural Communities for Change: The Commonwealth Fund Child Health Demonstration in Rutherford County, 1923-1927

■ Mary S. Hoffschwelle

■

■ *Editor's Note:* Rural Tennesseans reacted in varied ways to the reform agendas of early-twentieth-century progressives. They rarely
■ accepted reforms except when adapted to their own circumstances
   and needs. During the mid-1920s, Rutherford Countians were
■ confronted with a progressive-designed model program, supported by the Commonwealth Fund of New York State, to im-
■ prove their children's health. At first the reformers spoke primarily
   to local politicians and elites; local residents showed little interest.
■ But once the progressives initiated grassroots campaigns to enlist
   children and women in the cause of better public health, their ef-
■ forts met with greater success. Officials of the Commonwealth
   Fund learned that rural Tennesseans "could and would organize
■ their own communities for change."

In 1923, the Commonwealth Fund selected Rutherford County,
Tennessee, for an experimental five-year Child Health Demonstration. Child
health masked the demonstration project's more ambitious goal: to convince
a rural county that it should support its own fully staffed public health department. In five years of organizing rural support for public health measures,
the Commonwealth Fund and Rutherford residents developed the nation's
first complete delivery system of rural health care with a publicly funded health
department and a new county hospital, an outright gift to the county from
its benefactor. Yet, as the Commonwealth Fund realized, these institutions
reflected an even greater achievement by the country people who built a net-

work of local organizations committed to improving health conditions in their schools and communities.

The Commonwealth Fund, endowed in 1919 by Anna Richardson (Mrs. Steven V.) Harkness and her son, Edward S. Harkness, supported medical projects with particular emphasis on public health. In 1922, the Fund sponsored a promising community health program in Fargo, North Dakota. Fund officials decided that additional experiments should take place in the South, where the region's distinctive disease environment, social and economic conditions, and lack of medical facilities resulted in unique and pressing public health problems. In 1923, the Commonwealth Fund announced that it would underwrite two five-year child health programs in the South, one in a city of no more than twenty-five thousand people, and one in a rural county of less than thirty thousand people and with no town larger than five thousand. After reviewing applications from local governments, the Fund selected Athens, Georgia, and Rutherford County, Tennessee.[1]

Like other attempts at rural uplift orchestrated by government agencies,

Women and children visiting the Rutherford County Child Health Demonstration, c. 1926. Mustard Collection, Tennessee Historical Society Collection, Tennessee State Library and Archives.

professional reformers, and philanthropic foundations in the early twentieth century, the Commonwealth Fund's Child Health Demonstration employed modern scientific expertise to redeem an allegedly degenerate country life and country people. And like its predecessor in progressive rural public health, the Rockefeller Sanitary Commission for the Eradication of Hookworm Disease, the Commonwealth Fund faced its greatest challenge in convincing rural southerners that changing their standards of living would improve their health.

In Rutherford County, the staff of the Child Health Demonstration (CHD) pursued several strategies for community health improvements. As hoped, programs aimed at children allowed the CHD to reach their parents, and those programs worked best when associated with the local public schools. When reaching out directly to adults, the CHD staff initially courted the local politicians who controlled the county's resources. Politicians' support proved shallow, and so the CHD carefully cultivated grassroots support among groups of rural white women and the African American community. Ever mindful of public opinion, the CHD adapted its programs to prevailing standards of racial segregation and paternalism. Such sensitivity to local sentiment guided the CHD's responses to other troublesome local attitudes, whether expressed by poor white tenant farmers or irate homeowners.

Rutherford seemed a typical rural southern county to Commonwealth Fund administrators. Its white and African American residents exhibited to a moderate degree the problems that officials attributed to their respective races. S. J. Crumbine, director of public health relations for the American Child Health Association, visited Rutherford while reviewing its application. He reported that 31 percent of the adult population was illiterate and attributed this mostly to poor white residents in the hilly eastern part of the county. He noted high rates of typhoid fever and tuberculosis, the latter usually associated with African Americans, and dismissed the reported moderate infant mortality rate as inaccurate and low. Smallpox, diphtheria, and scarlet fever plagued the community; diarrhea and enteritis claimed its young children. Public health measures were practically nonexistent: preventive vaccinations or inoculations were rare, few homes had sanitary facilities, the public water supply was unprotected, and milk control efforts were haphazard. On the American Public Health Association's Rural Appraisal form, Rutherford scored a mere 110 points out of one thousand.[2]

Such conditions might have been typical of the rural South, but what attracted the Commonwealth Fund's interest was that Rutherford also possessed a nucleus of local support for public health measures that seemed ideally positioned within a statewide medical infrastructure. The Commonwealth Fund, following in the tradition of progressive rural reform organizations such as the General Education Board, sought an alliance with state and local government officials, the leaders of educational and medical institutions, and the heads of related voluntary groups. Fund officials believed that these more educated and sophisticated activists provided the essential conduits for transmitting the Commonwealth Fund's message to ignorant locals and organizing them for improvement campaigns.

Thus, Crumbine's initial impressions of Rutherford County focused on its organizations, and his report listed every business, professional, and social group in the county. County court members H. O. Todd and Simeon B. Christy emphasized that the county and the city of Murfreesboro each employed a part-time health officer, that the city supported the work of the Red Cross public health nurse, that local doctors and dentists performed pro bono work, and that the Middle Tennessee State Normal School administration and county school superintendent supported health education. All local women's organizations, including the Women's Club, Business and Professional Women, the Daughters of the American Revolution, and the United Daughters of the Confederacy, promised their support. In a dramatic move, Christy orchestrated the formation of a county Public Health Association during Crumbine's inspection tour; an impressed Crumbine submitted a list of the "representative citizens present at the meeting . . . indicating the high grade character of representation."[3]

State medical and educational agencies also promised their support, seemingly guaranteeing that the CHD would have access to the most modern medical facilities and expertise. Dr. C. B. Crittenden, the state health commissioner, and officers of the state medical and anti-tuberculosis associations, with the medical staffs of Vanderbilt University and Meharry College, had vouched for all Tennessee applicants; Tennessee native Wickliffe Rose at the General Education Board put in a favorable word as well. Governor Austin Peay, Commissioner of Education Perry L. Harned, and the presidents of George Peabody College for Teachers and Fisk University also backed Tennessee applicants. Crittenden and Bruce R. Payne of Peabody gave the nod to Rutherford County. The Commonwealth Fund concurred, impressed by the county's local initiative and the proximity of prestigious institutions. As Crumbine concluded, "The numerous and powerful state agencies so strategically located must be an important factor in the dissemination of useful information and of furnishing an important type of cooperation."[4]

Demonstration director Dr. Harry S. Mustard put his staff to work early in 1924.[5] He supervised a group of six public health nurses (five white and one African American), a health educator, a social worker, a laboratory technician, a statistician, a sanitarian, and two doctors. Funding for the first two years came primarily from the Commonwealth Fund at about $25,000 annually, with $1,500 each from the county and city, $1,720 from the local Red Cross chapter, and $4,000 from the state department of health each year.[6] Initially, services stressed preventive care for infants and young children and school health programs. The maternity service sent public health nurses on home visits for prenatal and neonatal care. Well-child clinics offered vaccinations and examinations to preschool children. School-age children began receiving medical inspections, and then full examinations, with "blue ribbon" health contests providing a competitive incentive for practicing their school health lessons. Meanwhile, the CHD's sanitation service stressed school sanitation and milk control.

The Commonwealth Fund's ultimate objective was that the county would take over the project at the end of the demonstration period, converting it into a rural health department with an annual budget of roughly thirty thousand dollars. That objective could be achieved only by proving the value of public health measures to local residents so that they would shoulder the necessary tax burden for a health department. Harry Mustard acknowledged that school programs "appeared to be a reasonable entering wedge through which to function directly for school children and indirectly as a means of intimately and rapidly coming in contact with many parents throughout the county," with the CHD's message of improved personal and public health standards.[7]

Health education supplemented periodic CHD examinations. White students began using daily health habit record cards in 1925, which teachers summarized on charts depicting the school's health standards and students' report cards. Using individual drinking cups, washing hands before eating, and brushing teeth afterwards became part of routine activities in some schools. Students also learned proper dietary standards and, at the secondary level, studied home hygiene and care of the sick. The Blue Ribbon Contest, initiated in 1926 for white schools, awarded a ribbon bar to each child who could demonstrate satisfactory grades, behavior, and attitude, was "reasonably cooperative" on the subject of health habits, free of any congenital or acquired health problems, and had been immunized. The school with the highest percentage of blue ribbon students won a loving cup. LaVergne Elementary students won the first contest with 36.7 percent. The following year, the first in which black schools participated, African American students at

Salem school won with 40 percent, and white children at Midland school achieved a 95 percent victory.[8]

In promoting school hygiene, the CHD ran up against the harsh reality that few schools were equipped with toilet facilities of any sort, or protected water supplies. Even in Murfreesboro, schools provided wash bowls but not soap or towels; throughout Rutherford teachers resorted to requesting children to bring wrapped sandwiches that they could eat without direct contact with their hands. When the CHD arrived, only five schools boasted sanitary toilets and fifteen had safe water supplies; none of the more than one hundred white and black schools in Rutherford used individual drinking cups. Five years later over half of all schools provided these amenities.[9]

Although school health services clearly provided object lessons for children, additional measures were necessary to ensure that parents integrated classroom instruction into their own personal health practices and then identified their own needs with a publicly funded health agency. Rural people had to be convinced of the value of proper diet, cleanliness, preventive vaccinations, and regular checkups by a doctor; they should further realize that their health also depended on clean water and milk supplies, proper sewage disposal, and ac-

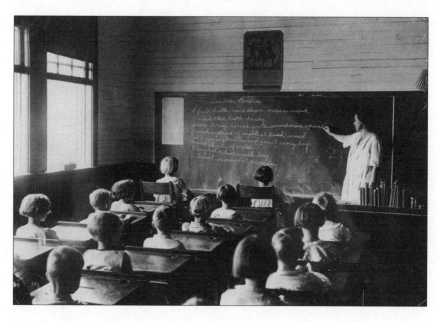

Fourth-grade health lesson, c. 1926. Mustard Collection, Tennessee Historical Society Collection, Tennessee State Library and Archives.

Health lesson at Cemetery School, c. 1926. Mustard Collection, Tennessee Historical Society Collection, Tennessee State Library and Archives.

cess to medical care for all. In Fargo, community health committees bridged the gaps between the demonstration project, local government, and personal health practices. But in rural Rutherford, Mustard postponed organizing local health committees for a year, even though Commonwealth Fund officials deemed them essential to the CHD enterprise.

Mustard blamed his difficulty in even starting local organizations on what he called "the indifference and individualism" of the rural population. His words echoed the perennial complaint of progressive reformers working with rural white southerners.[10] As William A. Link has shown in his study of southern progressivism, rural southerners' stubborn refusal to change their ways stymied many improvement campaigns. Reformers generally attributed this inertia to the apathy and ignorance of poor whites. Harry Mustard aptly described these people's attitudes, even as he condemned them: "Poor for generations, they have gradually come to accept conditions as they find them, and they do not desire any change."[11]

The CHD encountered the greatest levels of suspicion from the poorest of Rutherford's white population, transient white sharecroppers. One Commonwealth Fund official noted that they "seem haunted by the idea that all the world is against them." Any suggestion of a vaccination or medical examination was regarded as a precursor to "other persecutions." After hearing her husband grudgingly agree to send their children to a clinic, one woman anxiously inquired: "Now, tell me the truth—will they take the children away from us, if we bring 'em?" Such worries also plagued poor whites in Murfreesboro's "embrionic" slums. The Pencil Mill District briefly seethed with a rumor that a bathtub had been installed in a house being prepared for a well-child clinic by the Murfreesboro Charity Circle and that all residents were to be forcibly bathed.[12]

CHD staff in Rutherford County found that the ignorance and indifference usually associated with poor whites extended throughout the social order and into local government. "The demonstration is constantly fighting against the colossal smugness of the community. There is a lack of interest, due to the ignorance of existing conditions and a sense of complacency that all is well," lamented the author of one memorandum. Harry Mustard noted that residents equated the CHD with itinerant well-child clinics conducted several years previously by the federal Children's Bureau. Viewing the CHD as yet another temporary government program to collect statistics, they received the demonstration's promise of long-term health improvement with a good deal of skepticism.[13]

Mustard and the CHD also had to navigate the shoals of small-town and rural politics. County court magistrates and school board members were powerful community figures, and thus potential allies or obstacles to the demonstration's work. Rural magistrates suspected any program that might increase county expenditures, and resented any preference given to the county seat, the city of Murfreesboro. Mustard realized that if he moved too quickly in setting up his local networks, he might fall into the trap of tapping more accessible Murfreesboro residents for leadership, and so antagonize country residents. By delaying the organization of local committees, Mustard hoped that he could develop contacts with rural leaders. In the meantime, he refrained from petitioning for increased city or county financial support, and concentrated on rural school services.[14]

Local politics had to be considered in schoolrooms as well. Courtenay Dinwiddie, who conducted the first official review of the Rutherford demonstration's progress in November 1924, found school board chairman B. B. Kerr "indifferent and somewhat evasive on the subject of school sanitation." Kerr and the school board were feuding with school superintendent Jeannette

Moore King, who was conducting an energetic one-person public campaign against tobacco, a controversial stance to the farmers who elected her and the board. Thus the CHD's health education staff members had to distance themselves from King, even as they praised her school sanitation program and accepted her support for school medical examinations.[15]

Mustard's cautious approach toward local committees stemmed from his awareness that he was operating in a county with only a superficial and limited interest in organized reform. S. J. Crumbine's list of local organizations and their representatives meant little in practical terms. The county public health association founded during his 1923 visit had evaporated immediately thereafter. Of the various associations still functioning, all were based in Murfreesboro, and only the Charity Circle and Red Cross engaged in social service work on a regular basis. Rutherford County had just reinstituted a county agricultural extension program in 1925. The new agent had organized twelve local clubs on paper but had not been able to keep them active. No home demonstration agent organized rural women. Parent-teacher associations existed but had not functioned on a regular basis for several years. As Mustard later recalled, the paucity of rural organizational activity meant that the CHD had to take the initiative and yet remain sensitive to local sensibilities. That would require the demonstration staff to operate behind the scenes, guiding local organizations through their local leaders.

Although Commonwealth Fund inspectors sympathized with Harry Mustard and reported their own dismay with local officials, they pressed the Rutherford demonstration director for action. Courtenay Dinwiddie gave the staff high marks for their first year, but deemed the project's greatest weakness to be the lack of local leadership that could implement a long-term public health plan.[16] Mustard dutifully took the first steps toward community organization in 1925, and fell flat on his face.

Mustard stumbled over the hurdle of local leadership. Initially, the CHD staff defined leaders as white men with political power. Courting local politicians, Mustard organized from the top down, appointing committees comprising a county court member, three or four members at large, a doctor, a dentist, and a semiofficial member representing the local school.[17] "Six months experience proved that something was wrong," Mustard recollected. Despite having handpicked members perceived as "important" community citizens, few attended their committee meetings or took responsibility for local health projects. He concluded, "It is now apparent that it was fundamentally wrong to assume that a leader in a given magisterial district was necessarily interested in the health program; and another weakness in the plan was that a county-wide health committee was formed from above downward than from below upward."[18]

CHD staff struggled to find the proper method of organizing local health groups until they started at the community level and tapped the social and organizational talents of white women. Ironically, in many cases this led the CHD back to its starting places in the public schools scattered across the rural landscape. Although the demonstration's primary organizational efforts in 1925 and 1926 focused on local health committees appointed by the staff and led by local politicians, field experience suggested that school-based groups might prove more adept at organization and action. Harry Mustard and health educator Jessie Harris had first expressed their hope of working with "leading women" in revitalizing the county's parent-teacher associations in 1924. As parent-teacher groups labored under a broad mandate for school improvement, the CHD found itself once again directing its efforts at community public health through the rural schools.

The first parent-teacher association (PTA) had been founded in 1922, and operated largely as a social club. As Mustard recalled in his account of the completed demonstration, the staff planted the notion that only united action by parents and teachers would bring about any improvement in rural schoolhouses. This "guidance from the background," as he called it, elicited the desired response, local demand for parent-teacher groups. One formed in 1924, three the following year, and two new associations in each of the next three years, culminating in the formation of a county council of parent-teacher associations in January 1928.[19]

One such group, the Fosterville PTA of sixteen local residents, kicked off an aggressive campaign in 1926 with an ice cream supper. With the fifty-seven dollars thus generated, the PTA purchased lumber for new floors (laid by the principal and two older boys), and paid two carpenters to move windows for proper lighting and install a protected water supply. Proceeds from the next fund-raiser, lunches that local women peddled at a sale of farmland and equipment, purchased materials that their husbands used in constructing sanitary toilets.[20] Fosterville was one of seven parent-teacher associations involved in health measures; three other communities had health committees that also concentrated on school sanitation improvements.

Two years' experience with community organizing simultaneously from the top down and from the local level up led Harry Mustard to abandon his initial organizational plan in 1927. Mustard and the CHD staff, frustrated with the failure of their appointed committees and anxious for increased local involvement along the lines of the parent-teacher associations, tried yet another approach. They gathered together interested neighbors, usually women, into new health committees. The women had been recruited by CHD nurses from their contacts with mothers who brought their children to school health conferences and clinics. The first health committee formed by local women met in the summer of 1926, and within a year, seventeen local committees had been organized or reorganized. Rural organizations now ranged in size from eight members in the community health committees at Blackman and Rocky Fork Seminary to eighty at Walter Hill's parent-teacher association. These female-dominated organizations met during the afternoons and raised funds for their work through such typically female efforts as silver teas and benefit markets of homemade and preserved foods.[21]

Country residents recruited on this basis chose their own organizational structure, which often meant becoming integrated into a broader community group, as at Walter Hill. Smyrna's health committee began as a subgroup of a book club, and three others became subcommittees of agricultural extension clubs. Of nine committees that set themselves up as independent groups, four later expanded into parent-teacher associations with health sub-

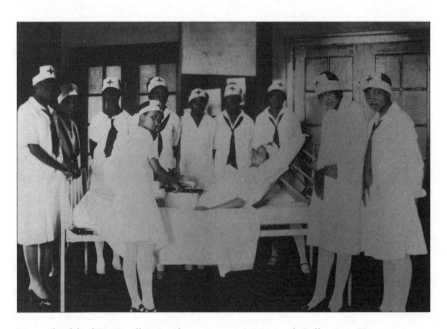

Home health class, Bradley Academy, c. 1926. Mustard Collection, Tennessee Historical Society Collection, Tennessee State Library and Archives.

committees. Each local health committee's chairperson then served on the countywide health committee.

Whatever its organizational structure, a health committee maintained close ties with its local school. The CHD nurse and teachers hung wall charts graphing the results of student examinations after each school visit. At the next health committee meeting, the nurse explained the chart to the local health committee, noting any problem cases requiring further medical attention. Committee members took responsibility for ensuring that those children saw a doctor, regardless of parents' ability to pay. In such meetings, Mustard believed, the CHD nursing staff pioneered a more effective approach to community public health work. Rather than asking for assistance from local residents, the nurse presented children's health problems as a community responsibility, and offered her assistance to them. To Harry Mustard, this obviated potential charges that the CHD wanted residents to do the work for which they had already paid taxes. Just as neatly, the nurse's approach downplayed her authority by representing the nurse as a sympathetic friend offering her help rather than as a professional dispensing instructions.[22]

A separate school subcommittee tackled building improvements, raising money for toilets, drinking fountains, window shades, and landscaping. Still other subcommittees offered communitywide assistance. Subcommittees for social service, supplies, and a loan closet with sickroom linens and infant layettes provided for the indigent. A call committee brought in CHD nurses and social workers when needed. The health center, publicity, and transportation committees informed other residents when the staff would hold clinics in their neighborhood and brought them in for examinations and inoculations.[23]

Mustard credited committee members and their activities as key factors in the demonstration's success and for encouraging their magistrates on the county court to increase appropriations for public health. Actually, the county court took its first step toward a permanent publicly funded health program in the summer of 1926, before the staff abandoned its top-down strategy. Apparently convinced by the CHD's well-child clinics and school examinations, if not by their own involvement, magistrates approved a "health tax" of three cents on every one hundred dollars of property. This increased the county's financial support to seven thousand dollars in 1927, and a rate increase in 1928 brought its contribution up to eleven thousand dollars.[24]

Even as they made contact with receptive and energetic whites, the CHD staff continued to downplay possibilities for community action among Rutherford African Americans. Mustard continually put off local organizational work with black residents, and his Commonwealth Fund superiors found no fault with this.[25] If the school provided the "reasonable entering wedge" to the white community, the CHD moved slowly to apply that model to rural schools for African American children. In November 1926, CHD staff finally introduced black teachers to the daily health records already kept by white children. They had postponed using the records previously "as they [blacks] are hardly situated so they can practice all of the habits outlined consistently." Nevertheless, they found that "the teachers and children are always eager to do the best they can to carry out suggestions offered."[26]

Given the contrast between staff complaints about white intransigence and their continual surprise at African Americans' ready acceptance of health standards, the CHD's slowness in approaching Rutherford's African American communities seems negligent. Perhaps the staff feared that conducting a high-profile campaign among blacks while white committees faltered would upset local racial sensibilities. Certainly that had been the experience of rural school reform groups such as the Southern Education Board, the General Education Board, and the Julius Rosenwald Fund. Their officials had often encountered rural white resistance to improvements for blacks unless white schools received assistance first.

However, the primary reason for the CHD's slowness seems to have been the staff's own racial blinders. CHD staff consistently underestimated African American interest and organizational abilities. Even after recording rural blacks' receptivity to their program, CHD workers could not account for their success. "The responsiveness of the negro, individually and collectively, has been nothing short of marvelous to me. Is part of this eagerness a servility that is anxious to 'do as the white folks say' or just the instinctive imitation to do 'as the white folks do'?" wondered one staff member.[27]

When the staff did work with local committees of black residents, their approach was paternalistic and condescending. African American communities quickly embraced health committees, but the CHD closely supervised their work. Thirty-four local health committees were formed in the first year of work among rural blacks in 1927, almost twice the number of white committees. By the demonstration's end the following year, Mustard recalled, "a number of committees" had built sanitary toilets for their schools and "a few of them undertook and largely completed the installation of a sanitary toilet in each colored home in the community."[28]

White committees worked through grassroots organizations united under a central body, with behind-the-scenes nudges from CHD staff. Black committees, on the other hand, remained under overt CHD control, with no countywide organization. The CHD retained control over black committees

by appointing members "on a basis of previously shown activity and interest" and recommendations from the nursing staff, the CHD sanitarian, and
the county's Jeanes supervising teacher, who monitored industrial education
at black schools. Each committee consisted of four members, usually men,
plus the female teacher, who served as secretary. Women played important
roles in white committees, and black women, like their white sisters, conducted most fund-raisers for schools. Why the CHD focused more exclusively
on male leaders and a decentralized organization for black committees remains
unclear. CHD staff prepared elaborate certificates of appointment for their
committee members. As this formality was never observed with white committee members, CHD staff seem to have been acting on their belief that
African Americans enjoyed pomp and circumstance. With the officious title
"Delegation of Responsibility," these printed commissions ostensibly impressed the committee members with the seriousness of their duty.[29]

Perhaps the most glaring example of white ignorance concerned the sole
black public health nurse, Mary Ellen Vaughn. According to Courtenay
Dinwiddie, she "makes pleasing contacts with her families but is lacking in
initiative and aggressiveness and . . . is more of the type of nurse's helper than
a public health nurse."[30] Dinwiddie apparently did not know (and no staff
member informed him) that Vaughn was a major figure among the county's
black residents. Vaughn had attended Tuskegee Institute and accepted Booker
T. Washington's self-help philosophy. As founder (in 1920) and publisher
of the local black newspaper, the *Murfreesboro Union,* Vaughn promulgated
the self-help principles she had imbibed at Tuskegee and promoted the work
of the CHD.[31] Vaughn's influence within black communities surely is reflected in the rapid pace of local health committee organization. Here a local
leader may well have been the key to rural community organization, yet the
CHD staff never seems to have suspected any connection between Vaughn's
efforts and their organizational success.

The Child Health Demonstration concluded its program in Rutherford
County in 1928, transferring its duties to the new county public health officer, Dr. J. B. Black and the Rutherford Hospital outpatient clinic. A final
public health audit using the American Public Health Association's Rural
Appraisal scale scored Rutherford at 814 points out of one thousand, a 700-
point gain over five years. Harry Mustard pointed out that the demonstration period was simply too short for an accurate assessment of medical
progress, although he could document encouraging decreases in infant mortality. Certainly the construction of a county hospital promised better laboratory, outpatient, and treatment facilities. An entrenched public health de-

partment, which would receive its own building from the Commonwealth Fund in 1931, could be expected to bear fruit.[32]

Success had not come easily to the Rutherford County Child Health Demonstration. Five years of constant interaction with rural southerners taught the Commonwealth Fund new lessons in community organization. The difficult process of trial and error with rural whites proved that successful public health began at the grassroots level and depended on women and schoolchildren.[33] These discoveries almost overshadowed the ease with which the CHD organized Rutherford's African American communities. In Rutherford County, the Commonwealth Fund learned that rural residents could and would organize their own communities for change.

NOTES

The author wishes to thank the Spencer Foundation and the Rockefeller Archives Center for underwriting the research for this work. Portions of this article were previously presented at the 1993 Conference of Tennessee Historians and the 1994 meeting of the Kentucky-Tennessee American Studies Association.

1. Rutherford County had some previous experience with national health programs. The Rockefeller Sanitary Commission for the Eradication of Hookworm Disease had tested residents in 1913. Field agent Dr. T. B. Yancey, Jr., forwarded optimistic reports of his work with the teachers at Middle Tennessee Normal and interested county school officials, yet the county did not cooperate with the Commission on a local dispensary. Perhaps Rutherford's light rate of infection limited support for a treatment facility. The Children's Bureau temporarily resurrected health issues when one of its mobile health units passed through the county. See "Second Child Health Demonstration Under the Commonwealth Fund Program," folder 12, box 1, Commonwealth Fund Archives, Child Health Demonstration Series, Rockefeller Archives Center, North Tarrytown, New York (hereafter cited as CF CHD, RAC), 1–2. Like most other philanthropies, the Commonwealth Fund required financial contributions from state and local governments. See also W. Frank Walker and Carolina R. Randolph, *Influence of a Public Health Program on a Rural Community: Fifteen Years in Rutherford County, Tennessee, 1924–1938* (New York, 1940), 36–43, 61–64, and Robert G. Ransom, *The History of Medicine in Rutherford County, Tennessee,* Part 1 (Murfreesboro, Tenn., 1985), 193–222. On the Commonwealth Fund, see Waldemar A. Neilsen, *The Big Foundations* (New York, 1972), 254–62; A. McGehee Harvey and Susan L. Abrams, *"For the Welfare of Mankind": The Commonwealth Fund and American Medicine* (Baltimore, 1986), 91–107; and Charles R. King, *Children's Health in America: A History* (New York, 1993), 133–34. Walker, Randolph, and Neilsen credit the Rutherford demonstration for highlighting the nationwide need for better prenatal and infant medical care, as well as better hospitals, in rural communities.

2. S. J. Crumbine, "A Study of Rutherford County, Tennessee," folder 13, box 1, CF CHD, RAC, 1, 4–5, and Harry S. Mustard, *Cross-Sections of Rural Health Progress: Report of the Commonwealth Fund Child Health Demonstration in Rutherford County, Tennessee, 1924–1928* (New York, 1930), 7–9, 20.
3. Crumbine, "A Study of Rutherford County," 10.
4. Summaries of Tennessee applications, folder 12; "Report of Dr. Dinwiddie's visit to Rutherford County, Tennessee, August 21–22, 1923," and Crumbine, "Study of Rutherford County," quotation on 11, both in folder 13, both in box 1, CF CHD, RAC. See also S. J. Crumbine to Miss Bertha Tomlinson, July 28, 1923, folder 12 in ibid.
5. Mustard had performed field work for the U.S. Public Health Service in Tennessee and was working in Kingwood, West Virginia, just prior to assuming the directorship of the CHD. Mustard later enjoyed a distinguished career as director of the School of Public Health at Columbia University and author of several textbooks.
6. Mustard, *Cross-Sections,* 17, table 2 on p. 198.
7. Mustard, "Annual Report, Child Health Demonstration, Murfreesboro, Rutherford County, Tennessee, January 1st to September 1st, 1924," folder 34, box 1, CF CHD, RAC (quotation), and Mustard, *Cross-Sections,* 9–10.
8. "Rutherford County Child Care Health Demonstration 1925 Annual Report," folder 35, box 1, CF CHD, RAC, 47; "Annual Report, Child Health Demonstration, Rutherford County, Tennessee, 1926," folder 36, n.p.; and "Annual Report, Child Health Demonstration, Rutherford County, Tennessee, 1927," folder 37, 26–27, 30–31, 32–33, both in box 3, CF CHD, RAC; and "County Wide Interest in Blue Ribbon Contest," and "Midland School Won Blue Ribbon Contest," both in *Murfreesboro News Banner,* Apr. 9, 1927, 1, 4. The standards for African American blue ribbon winners were rather more demanding of parents. In addition to immunizations, each child had to have a sanitary toilet at home, a rare facility among all rural residents, white or black.
9. "Annual Report," 1926; Mustard, *Cross-Sections,* table 17, p. 219; and "Brief Outline of Visit to Rutherford County, Tennessee," Apr. 23, 1925, folder 39, box 3, CF CHD, RAC.
10. "Annual Report," 1927, 3 (quotation); see also "Confidential Report of Mr. Dinwiddie's Visit to the Rutherford County, Tennessee, Child Health Demonstration, November 22–23, 1924," folder 39; and "Annual Report," 1926, all in box 3, CF CHD, RAC, for similar comments.
11. "Annual Report," 1926 (quotation), and William A. Link, *The Paradox of Southern Progressivism, 1880–1930* (Chapel Hill, N.C., 1992). Link discusses the public health work conducted by the Rockefeller Sanitary Commission and the Commonwealth Fund (142–59, 290–21, 215). He notes that medical reformers enjoyed success in arousing public interest but then encountered obstinate local resistance to any proposed changes in their lifestyles. Nevertheless, in the case of Rutherford County, Link quoted the Fund's early frustrations without adding that the CHD grew into a model rural public health system.
12. See minutes of meeting, Mar. 4, 1927, Murfreesboro Charity Circle, Charity Circle Records, microfilm M68, Linebaugh Library, Murfreesboro, Tenn.; "Impressions of

Rutherford County," Apr. 1925, folder 30, 6 (quotations); and "Community Organization, Rutherford County," [1927], folder 38, box 3, CF CHD, RAC, 44.

13. [Courtenay Dinwiddie?], "Memorandum re Visit to Murfreesboro Child Health Demonstration," folder 39, box 3, CF CHD, RAC, 5 (quotation); "Annual Report," 1924.

14. Mustard, "Annual Report," 1924; see also "Memorandum of Mr. Dinwiddie's Visit;" and "Community Organization," 1. In 1925, Mustard reported that while residents in general had developed a more positive attitude toward the CHD and the Murfreesboro City Council was supportive, the county court was not. See "Annual Report," 1925, 4.

15. Dinwiddie also charged that Kerr was "a professional politician . . . not above seeing to it that awards for painting school buildings are made to his own stores. There are eight members of the County Board of Education and no particularly well informed and public spirited citizen stands out among them." King had been a physical education instructor at Peabody College and at Middle Tennessee State Normal School. Another Commonwealth Fund evaluator warned the CHD not to associate too closely with King's superintendency, lest King's "single track mind" and tactlessness undermine their efforts. See summaries of Tennessee applications, 6; "Report of Mr. Dinwiddie's Visit," 2; "Confidential Report of Mr. Dinwiddie's Visit," 5 (first quotation in note), 8 (quotation in text); "Brief Outline of Visit," [1] (second quotation in note); and "Annual Report," 1926.

16. "Confidential Report of Mr. Dinwiddie's Visit," [1].

17. Mustard, "Annual Report," 1925, 4.

18. "Annual Report," 1927, 5–6; "Community Organization," 2–3; and Mustard, *Cross-Sections,* 182 (quotations).

19. Mustard, *Cross-Sections,* 181.

20. "Community Organization," 22–23; see also "Association Meets Buchanan Hi School," and "Parent-Teacher Association Has Made Rapid Growth," *Murfreesboro News Banner,* June 28, 1927. Most health committees reported a school project among their undertakings. In Rockvale, CHD staff slowly encouraged the addition of a public health committee to the local agricultural club, in spite of "religious scruples (old Campbellite church)"; see "Community Organization," 34.

21. *News Banner,* "Blackman Health Committee," May 13, 1927; "Blackman Baby Health Center," and "Market Is Planned For Saturday Next," May 31, 1927; "Health Committee Hold Smyrna Meet," June 23, 1927; "Health Committee," June 28, 1927. Such notices of health committee meetings in the *News Banner,* copies of which are available from 1927 on, listed exclusively female names as chairs of the local group and its subcommittees. These organizations remained active through at least 1931. See such articles in the *News Banner* as "Health Committee Named at Florence," Sept. 30, 1931.

22. Mustard, *Cross-Sections,* 54–55.

23. "Annual Report," 1926. For example, eight Blackman committee members provided transportation for children to their clinic; the District 4 health committee members prepared lists of preschool children in their neighborhoods for the CHD. *News Banner,* May 31 and June 28, 1927.

24. Mustard, *Cross-Sections,* 17–18, 185–87.
25. "Confidential Report of Mr. Dinwiddie's Visit," 3.
26. "Annual Report," 1926.
27. "Impressions of Rutherford County," 8.
28. Mustard, *Cross-Sections,* 187–88 (quotations on 188).
29. Ibid., 93–94, 187–88. The teacher served as secretary by virtue of her sex and literacy—some local chairmen could not read or write.
30. Ibid., 7.
31. Under the masthead "Clinic News," Vaughn ran such articles as "Public Health Nurse and Some of Her Activities," "Keeping the Baby Well," and "Bradley Health Center," *Murfreesboro Union* Oct. 13, 1928; see also *Twenty-Ninth Anniversary Edition of the Murfreesboro Union, 1920–1949,* and *Thirtieth Anniversary Edition of the Murfreesboro Union, 1920–1950.* Louise Houck Wiser, comp., *A History of Rutherford County Schools* (Murfreesboro, Tenn., 1986), 2:84–86, records that Vaughn received her bachelor's degree from Tennessee A & I College, but the *Union*'s commemorative issues depicted her as earning the master's degree. The confusion probably reflects that at this time Tuskegee offered a three-year nursing program. Vaughn operated "Vaughn's Training School" at her home in Murfreesboro from 1933 to 1951. According to Wiser, Vaughn established the school so that blacks could pass the literacy test for voting. For the importance of public health nursing among rural southern African Americans, see Darlene Clark Hine, *Black Women in White: Racial Conflict in the Nursing Profession, 1890–1950* (Bloomington and Indianapolis, 1989), 154–55.
32. A fifteen-year review for the Commonwealth Fund by W. Frank Walker and Carolina R. Randolph found a permanent drop in maternal death rates, stillbirths, and infant deaths that spared an estimated twenty-five lives each year. Typhoid fever was now a rarity. Even though scarlet fever and whooping cough's morbidity and mortality had intensified, and diphtheria remained common, Rutherford County's death rate was 12 percent lower than that in four surrounding counties with no health organizations and at or below state mortality figures. Walker and Randolph, *Influence of a Public Health Program,* 6–8, 13–14. Walker, as associate field director of the American Public Health Association, had evaluated the CHD for the Commonwealth Fund in 1926 and 1927; Randolph had served on the CHD staff.
33. Mustard, *Cross-Sections,* 24, 72.

BUSINESS, LABOR, AND THE BLUE EAGLE: THE HARRIMAN HOSIERY MILLS STRIKE, 1933-1934

■ W. CALVIN DICKINSON AND PATRICK D. REAGAN

■

■ *Editor's Note:* Labor history is one of the most neglected topics in
   Tennessee history. Some attention has been directed at the ten-
■ sion between coal miners and convict labor. More recently, historians have studied the Elizabethton rayon strike of 1929. There
■ the strikers were women; indeed, throughout industrial Tennessee
   during the early twentieth century, textile workers were usually
■ women. In the Harriman strike of 1933–34, women fought for
   their right to organize and engage in collective bargaining. New
■ Deal rhetoric and legislation promising a better day for the American worker, however, proved hollow in this early test of labor rela-
■ tions in the Roosevelt era. The women failed in their efforts to
   unionize the Harriman factory. The strike "ended as a missed op-
■ portunity for enlightened management, better working lives, and
   compassionate government."

   The presidential campaign of 1932 marked one of the most important elections in United States history. Amid the most serious depression in
the nation's existence, most Americans were disillusioned by the inability of
the administration of Herbert Hoover to restore economic health. Most
wanted another administration and a plan; some even advocated an entirely
new relationship between the government and governed. Voters found Democratic candidate Franklin D. Roosevelt's offer of "a new deal for the American people" attractive and politically inviting. In November 1932, by a landslide margin, citizens swept Roosevelt and the New Deal into office.
   Unemployed and discontented working Americans constituted one of the
largest and most important parts of the emerging Democratic national political coalition that would dominate American politics for a generation.[1]
Workers and their unions relished the prospect of finding favor with the

Roosevelt administration after a decade of disdain from the Republican Party. Large segments of the American working class looked to unions as their salvation. Unions could deliver them from tyrannical managers and bosses; unions could deliver them from harsh working conditions and low pay; unions could lead them out of their personal depressions and into a better life.

The textile industry offered little prospect for advancement and prosperity for its workers. Facing intense price competition, declining domestic demand, and tight labor costs, textiles factories often located in economically depressed areas of the South, providing textile workers with low pay and little chance for advancement in a low-skill sector of the economy. If any group of workers needed the protection that unions could provide, textile workers were certainly that group. In 1929 the industry exploded in a national strike that finally ended only through brutal employer repression, federal acquiescence, and a divided textile workforce that in southern mill towns proved resistant to union-organizing drives.[2]

After the failure of the 1929 national strike, most textile workers felt defeated at the prospect of continuing loss of union power. Yet the onset of the New Deal in the spring of 1933 seemed to promise changed relations among business, labor, and the federal government courtesy of Section 7(a) of the National Industrial Recovery Act (NIRA), a law to be administered by the National Recovery Administration (NRA). Section 7(a) represented an expansion of federal labor law that allowed workers the right to organize unions, to select those unions as economic bargaining agents, and to create a system of labor-management relations with the tacit assistance of the national government. In 1933–34, millions of American workers sought to redeem that promise through union organizing or through strike actions on the local level by more than one million ordinary working people.[3]

Textile workers at the women's seamless hosiery mills in Harriman, Tennessee, were among those who tried to seize the opportunity for union power. Yet the Harriman Hosiery Mills strike of 1933–34 showed that the promise of Section 7(a) would remain unfulfilled during the early New Deal. Between July 1, 1933, and July 23, 1934, employer opposition, the institutional weakness of labor unions in the southern textile industry, and the failure of New Dealers to clarify enforcement of Section 7(a) made for a frustrating situation of missed opportunities. The Harriman strike foreshadowed the broad national disillusionment with Section 7(a) that would necessitate even greater changes in labor relations brought about by the Wagner Act of 1935 and the industrial union drives of the CIO in the late 1930s.[4]

Events in Harriman, Tennessee, during the 1933–34 strike provided a local test of early New Deal enforcement of the new labor law represented by Section 7(a). Harriman had been created in 1890 by the sale of 574 lots at an auction conducted by the East Tennessee Land Company. General Clinton D. Fisk, president of the company and 1888 Prohibition Party candidate for president of the United States, stipulated that the property of the town could not be used for "making, storing, or selling intoxicating liquor."[5] Harriman took on the nickname of "Temperance City."

The small East Tennessee town was the site of the new Harriman Hosiery Mills company. Initially capitalized at $100,000 when chartered by the state in 1912, Harriman Hosiery Mills joined an impressive list of manufacturing businesses that had been established in the town.[6] Created in 1890 by the East Tennessee Land Company, the Harriman Manufacturing Company promoted industry in the town. In only a year the company lured nine industries to Harriman: Lookout Rolling Mills, Gibson Agricultural Works, Harriman Hoe and Tool Factory, Harriman Tack Factory, East Tennessee Furniture Factory, Duthie Machine Works and Foundry, Harriman Brick Works, Cumberland Manufacturing Works, and Baily Auger Works.[7]

Several other industries were created at the beginning of the twentieth century, including Harriman Cotton Mills Company, which manufactured high grade cotton yarn and twine. In 1912 Tom Tarwater established a much larger textile factory, Harriman Hosiery Mills. James F. Tarwater, Tarwater's father, had made his fortune in the Roane Iron Company. In 1905 J. F. Tarwater bankrolled the organization of Rockwood Mills, a hosiery firm.[8] T. A. Wright of Rockwood, J. P. Voorhees of New York, and Garnett Andrews of Chattanooga were other major stockholders.[9]

Following construction of a modern factory building on six acres of land, production of ladies' seamless cotton hose began in the spring of 1913. In 1917 new machinery allowed the production of rayon and silk hosiery. A 1927 industrial survey published by the Harriman Board of Trade described the mill's output: "The Harriman Hosiery Mills, making ladies' cotton fibre and mixed silk and fibre hose, has an annual output of 700,000 dozen pairs. The plant does dyeing, bleaching and finishing."[10]

Mostly women toiled at Harriman Hosiery Mills, reflecting a common labor pattern in the textile industry.[11] In Harriman the management specifically sought women workers. One employment advertisement read: "GIRLS WANTED. We want girls 14 years of age and over in our temporary training mill. . . . Steady work, pleasant employment, and good pay while training. Parents are especially invited to inspect our mill at any time. For further particulars, call on or address Harriman Hosiery Mills."[12]

Opening with about a hundred workers, the plant eventually increased its number of employees to about a thousand. In his study of Harriman, Walter Pulliam thought that "Harriman Hosiery Mills was regarded as a model of good management-employee relations," but Pulliam forgot to mention the 1933–34 strike in his book.[13] Like many southern textile mill towns, Harriman prided itself on its friendly, community-oriented way of doing business. But paternalism in labor relations marked most mill towns. In truth, the Tarwater family dominated the town and its economy. The 1930 census revealed that Harriman had a total population of 4,588 people. Among the most influential people in town were mill managers Polk Tarwater, president of the company; Tom T. Tarwater, vice president, general manager, and treasurer of the firm; T. Asbury Wright, Jr., the firm's attorney who had married into the Tarwater family; M. W. Walker, the company's secretary; and J. L. "Jimmy" Tarwater, the plant superintendent.

The Depression hit Harriman hard, forcing layoffs at the mills, which shrank the labor force from 596 in January 1929 to a low of 479 in January 1931. The firm recovered to a level of 873 employees by mid-June 1933. By October 26, 1933, the day the strike began, the firm's workforce had declined further to 746. In mid-November 1933, at the low point in the strike, the workforce had sunk to only 393 employees. In early March 1934, when the strike had been lost, the labor force had still only grown to 542 employees. Clearly, the strike hurt both the mill's productivity and the community's labor force, which had seen only one other labor dispute in the last fifteen years.[14]

Prior to the summer of 1933, employer-employee relations at the Harriman Hosiery Mills had been without major conflict. In the early years workers were satisfied with existing management practices. Management maintained a school for employees on the plant grounds, while employees proved generous in their donations to the Red Cross Fund during World War I: "In about an hour the mill was able to report its subscription as $2,500. Only a very few of the employees were willing to stop at a day's wages—most of them insisted upon giving more."[15] Even during the 1933–34 strike, employees did not officially complain about wages, hours, or working conditions, although speeding up production by assigning more machines to each worker did figure in some of the labor-management discussions early in the strike. The central issues in the strike centered around the reinstatement of workers fired for union activities, the recognition of Local 1757 of the Hosiery Workers union, and the beginning of collective bargaining between the union and HHM management.[16]

By 1933 some of the workers at Harriman Hosiery Mills (HHM) wanted

TABLE **18.1**
HARRIMAN HOSIERY MILLS LABOR FORCE

DATE	NUMBER OF EMPLOYEES
1/12/29	596
1/11/30	556
1/10/31	479
1/9/32	579
1/14/33	756
6/17/33	873
7/1/33	875
7/15/33	871
7/29/33	817
8/12/33	832
9/9/33	768
10/7/33	761
10/26/33	746
11/18/33	393
12/2/33	402
1/13/34	431
3/6/34	542

SOURCE: *Harriman Record,* 7 December 1933, testimony of T. Asbury Wright, Jr., HHM counsel to National Labor Board, January 4, 1934, Folder 1-11, HHM Strike Papers; "Facts in Connection with Harriman Hosiery Mills Labor Dispute, Harriman, Tennessee," March 8, 1934, Folder 2-1, HHM Strike Papers.

a union in accord with Section 7(a) of the National Industrial Recovery Act (NIRA). Part of the bitterness of the ensuing strike stemmed from considerable confusion about the law, management's responsibility in following the law, and Harriman workers' desire to fulfill the promise of Section 7(a). Under 7(a), workers now had the right to organize a union, to select a union as their collective bargaining agent with company management, and to work for a forty-hour week at a minimum hourly wage of 22.5 cents per hour in the South. Passed by Congress on June 16, 1933, the National Industrial Recovery Act went into effect with President Roosevelt's approval of a blanket code of fair competition for the textile industry. Known as the Provisional Hosiery Code, it became effective on August 1, 1933. The permanent textile code received FDR's approval on August 27, 1933, going into effect at HHM on September 4, 1933.[17]

The Harriman strike centered on two key events—organization of the local union on July 1, 1933, and the firing of twenty-three key union activists between July 5 and 14, before either the temporary or permanent textile code went into effect. From HHM management's perspective, they did not have to respond to any complaints over the firing of union members since the new labor policy under Section 7(a) had not yet become law. Union officials and a majority of the HHM workforce felt that their rights under 7(a) had been violated. They tried to engage in voluntary discussions with management to settle the dispute in a cooperative manner, but that did not work. After failing to reach any agreement with management in a series of meetings between late July and mid-October 1933, the Harriman workers went on strike and took their grievances to the Regional Labor Board in Atlanta, and then to the National Labor Board in Washington.

The labor provisions of the recovery act raised the possibility of union organization, recognition, and collective bargaining sponsored by the federal government.[18] Section 7(a) promised that "employees shall have the right to organize and bargain collectively through representatives of their own choosing." Textile workers, in particular, thought that "God had sent [the NIRA] to them," so they hastened to take advantage of the opportunity to form unions. In the year between July 1933 and August 1934, six hundred local chapters of the United Textile Workers (UTW) were chartered, increasing union membership by over 230,000.[19]

Workers at Harriman Hosiery Mills stepped into the front ranks of this enthusiasm. Their struggle to create a chapter of the Hosiery Workers (part of the United Textile Workers of America) represented one of the first responses to President Roosevelt's new labor policy. On July 1, 1933, about 600 workers attended an organizational meeting, and 164 joined as charter members of the union. Within a week of the initial meeting, over 300 more joined, bringing chapter membership to almost 500 out of a total workforce of 870 people.[20] Harriman workers created Local 1757 of the United Textile Workers of America, electing Frank Newcomb chair and Russell Scarbrough secretary/treasurer. Following his election on October 12, 1933, Floyd Johnston replaced Newcomb as the local union president. Roy and Edna Gossage became the union's financial and recording secretaries shortly after the organizational meeting.

City leaders applauded the union. Harriman Mayor J. G. D'Armond "pledged the loyal support of the City of Harriman in our worthy undertaking."[21] In the course of the strike, former three-time Harriman mayor and 1928 Tennessee gubernatorial candidate W. H. Hannah, became the union's attorney. D'Armond and Hannah always supported the union, but other civic leaders and many merchants in the business community remained divided as to which side they supported. On the one hand, the Tarwater family exercised tremendous economic and social influence and the mill was a key employer in the community. On the other hand, the economic impact of employee spending on the local economy and broader resistance to NRA labor provisions by other mill managers could not be ignored.[22] For much of the strike period, a large segment of the community supported the strikers, but that changed as the city's economy was hurt by lost production and jobs.

Management of HHM never welcomed the union. HHM secretary M. W. Walker and Knoxville attorney T. Asbury Wright conducted most of the firm's meetings with union representatives while adhering unswervingly to the Tarwaters' resistance to reinstating the fired workers, recognizing the union, and engaging in substantive collective bargaining.

Plant foremen used a variety of tactics to convince employees not to join the union and to discover what union members discussed in meetings. Plant foreman John Morgan led the anti-union campaign by firing core union activists in a move that led to the strike. Within a week after the union formed, twenty-two workers were fired for union activities or for failing to keep pace with a speedup of production quotas under the NRA hosiery code. By July 18, 1933, sixty-three employees had been discharged.[23] J. L. Tarwater, superintendent of HHM, said that those discharged "had taken to [*sic*] active a part in creating disturbances," and he emphasized that management ran the mill.[24] HHM's managers hoped to destroy the union by punishing union members and rewarding nonunion workers.[25] A local union officer claimed that HHM offered nonunion workers higher salaries and job security.[26]

Between late July and October 26, 1933, representatives of the new union local and HHM met informally to discuss the emerging dispute over the firing of union activists and recognition of the union as both representing the workforce and as collective bargaining agent. None of the meetings produced even a hint of agreement between management and labor. Hoping to build support for their case, union officials collected affidavits from the fired workers and sent them to President William Green of the American Federation of Labor, President Thomas McMahon of the United Textile Workers, and Secretary of Labor Frances Perkins.

Union members proved ready to fight for their right to organize the union and to engage in collective bargaining with HHM officials.[27] On September 30 a small number of union members representing all departments in the factory voted to strike. Twenty-three of the voting members favored the strike;

seven opposed it. Four days later a secret ballot of all union members resulted in a vote of 432 in favor of a strike with 32 opposed.[28]

Looking to Washington, President Roosevelt, and the New Deal apparatus for support, union members indicated that the federal government was to be informed of all actions in the strike.[29] Since mid-July union leaders, on the advice of the district organizer for the United Textile Workers, had kept Secretary of Labor Frances Perkins informed of developments. Before and during the strike, the Harriman workers hoped for assistance from the nation's capital in resolving their dispute. Traditionally nonunion and looking at the federal government with suspicion rather than with hope, southern workers now saw the government as a referee and an ally against oppressive management. Fred Held, an organizer for the American Federation of Hosiery Workers, traveled between Chattanooga and Harriman, serving as an advocate for HHM workers with management and with the federal government. Throughout the strike, Held and organizer R. S. Crawford of the United Textile Workers of America worked with local union officers to bring about resolution of the dispute.

Federal involvement in the strike was complicated by the evolving nature of the labor provisions of the NIRA. Under the original recovery act, the government made concessions to management by suspending anti-trust rules and allowing use of price and inventory information among firms in the same industry in exchange for expanding worker protections such as the right to organize unions, voluntary employer recognition of unions as collective bargaining agents, and minimum wages and maximum hours of work per week. But enforcement of legislative language made for a much more complex situation. NRA administrators Hugh Johnson and his assistant Donald Richberg did not interpret Section 7(a) as meaning that employers must recognize a union as speaking for all employees rather than just those who signed union cards. By the fall of 1933, after hundreds of NRA codes had been developed, Johnson and Richberg confused matters even more by arguing that the unions could speak only for those who had signed union cards, leaving employers to argue that they could bargain with nonunion employees organized in company unions, with both company and independent unions, or with individuals in the guise of "collective bargaining."[30] In the course of the Harriman strike, HHM managers consciously chose to take the latter course, frustrating union officials, union rank and file members, and federal mediators.[31]

In practice, enforcement was left to federal officials working for the Conciliation Service of the Department of Labor, the newly formed National Labor Board, or various divisions of the National Recovery Administration (NRA).

Harriman union officers initially worked with two mediators sent from Washington by Secretary of Labor Frances Perkins. After creation of the National Labor Board (NLB) and a system of regional boards under it, they worked with the Atlanta Regional Labor Board (RLB) headed by Marion Smith, who was assisted by G. W. Ramaker as field officer and secretary. Both Ramaker and Smith would play key roles in attempting to mediate the dispute between HHM management and Local 1757.[32] Later as mediation by the RLB and NLB failed to have any effect, several NRA officials were sent from Washington, further complicating an already confused early New Deal labor policy.

On October 16–17, 1933, HHM management traveled to Atlanta to meet with the regional office of the NLB. The federal government, in the guise of the Regional Labor Board, was interfering on behalf of UTW Local 1757; the New Deal seemed to be prolabor. Organizer Fred Held presented a union contract to HHM officials on behalf of Local 1757 members. The proposal asked for recognition of the union, no discrimination against employees for union activities, seniority rights to qualified workers, reinstatement of those fired, prohibition of strikes and lockouts, arbitration of disputes by a mediator agreed upon by both parties, work hours in accordance with the NRA hosiery code, possible future revision of wages, and automatic contract renewal unless either party gave sixty-day advance notice.[33]

These stipulations were within the guidelines of the NRA textile industry code, yet HHM management officials refused to accept the proffered contract. Although the company ultimately objected to the very existence of the union, its stated objections concentrated on collective bargaining. At every stage of discussion and investigation throughout the strike, management resisted both union recognition and collective bargaining. Local union officers reported to the regional branch of the NLB in Atlanta that "management told our committees that they was not going to bargain collectively with the union unless they was forced to do so."[34] Mill attorney T. Asbury Wright, Jr., asserted managerial power in interpreting the language of Section 7(a) at every step in the process: "It is simply a technical argument over the proper definition of 'collective bargaining.'" He thought that neither "the President nor the Labor Board had no power to make them sign any agreement which they did not want to."[35]

The company's refusal to accept the contract offered in Atlanta initiated the strike that had been voted three weeks earlier. On October 26 a majority of the workers walked out. Estimates of between 400 and 500 of the 746 employees who went on strike showed widespread support for the union's goals. In January 1934 about 400 workers were still out.[36]

Both sides adopted tough attitudes and measures. Management posted notices that all employees who had not returned to work by October 31 would be dismissed and their company insurance canceled. Strikers continued picketing the plant "both day and night in an orderly manner," while union members voted unanimously to continue the strike "until we are given our rights as provided by the law."[37]

On November 17, the union voted to return to work at the request of Marion Smith, chairman of the Regional Labor Board in Atlanta, but HHM management maintained that workers had been dismissed on October 31 and would have to apply individually as new employees.[38] A company official smugly commented, "We are at this time operating very nicely with something over four hundred employees."[39] The company maintained its resistance toward the union, the government, and the law by refusing to recognize the union as a legitimate entity, to engage in collective bargaining, and to recognize the seniority of union members in the factory. Management rejected the contract offered in mid-October and began hiring people from out of town to replace striking employees.[40] The firm's leaders even rejected a proposal by Harriman Mayor D'Armond to turn the dispute over to an arbitration panel of local businessmen and union representatives.[41] Thomas McMahon, president of the UTW, characterized HHM leaders to Senator Robert F. Wagner (D-N.Y.): "There's less democracy and humanitarianism in the heart and soul of these [southern] manufacturers than there is in the coyote dog that wanders about the plains."[42]

After a hearing at the Regional Labor Board in Atlanta on November 23 and 24, government officials began to waver. The RLB report claimed that "management has not sought to evade the code requirements as to hours and pay. . . . We do not find a violation of the code in connection with the lay-offs named." An NRA office memorandum noted that the July firings had occurred before the "effective date" of the temporary hosiery code. The RLB ruled that the company's discrimination against union workers had occurred before collective bargaining became mandatory.[43] New Deal administrators ruled that HHM could not be held liable concerning the charge of dismissing workers because of union membership. In a letter to Senator Robert F. Wagner, Atlanta Regional Labor Board chairman Marion Smith voiced his frustration:

> The investigation [of the Harriman strike] developed perfectly clearly that the fundamental difficulty which prevents peace being restores [*sic*] in this particular controversy is that practically admitted refusal of the

management to give recognition to what we have found to be implied in their obligation to recognize collective bargaining.

We [the RLB] have made the finding and can do no more. On the other hand, if a finding of this kind by our Board is merely nugatory I do not see why anyone should pay any particular attention to us in the future.[44]

Union organizers and members took a different view of the limitations of federal power and the strength of managerial resistance. In late 1933 they took their complaints to the National Labor Board, which held hearings on January 4, 1934. As had happened before the RLB, NLB officials discovered that the union view of the strike was supported by intensive investigation and documentation. Lacking legal authority beyond voluntary suasion, however, neither the RLB nor the NLB could do anything to force management's cooperation. Both times, HHM refused to rehire the fired workers other than as individuals, to recognize Local 1757, or to engage in collective bargaining other than informal talks with individual employees or unilateral suggestions of rules based on managerial power.[45]

Striking workers in Harriman were tired, hungry, and discouraged. As early as December 1933 local union leaders were calling for aid and action. Roy Gossage sent a telegram urging "very necessary some action be taken at once . . . people suffering." Floyd Johnston, president of UTW 1757, gave details in a letter: "Please hasten action as a large number of our people are in destitute condition." In a telegram Johnston asked pleadingly, "Are we to starve waiting for mill to be compelled to obey?" Mrs. W. R. Chambers telegraphed Senator Robert F. Wagner: "Hundreds helpless women and children freezing . . . need coal badly . . . help."[46]

Over the winter of 1933–34 local union activists and Harriman workers grew more and more disillusioned as to the efficacy of federal intervention. By February 1934 union organizer Fred Held thought that the NLB was "giving him the run-around." He thought that the strikers were losing faith in the NLB "due to lack of real action."[47] Ed Stinnett of Lenoir City wrote NRA administrator Hugh Johnson that the agency would lose its credibility throughout the South if Johnson did not do something about the Harriman situation. HHM strikers had been "treated afful [*sic*] bad" by the company.[48] On February 2, 1934, the National Labor Board "strongly condemned" the company's actions against striking workers in a formal statement, but lacking enforcement power the board could take no action against the company.[49]

An injunction granted on December 7, 1933, which prohibited picketing, parading, or congregating on the streets or near the mill, delivered another blow to striking workers' efforts.[50] Union president Floyd Johnston voiced strikers' disillusionment with both HHM management and government officials:

> What we cant [*sic*] understand is how can this Hosiery Mill continue to fly their BLUE EAGLE WHEN THEY ARE FLAGRANTLY, DELIBERATELY, BOASTFULLY, SAYING THAT THEY WONT [*sic*] BARGAIN COLLECTIVELY WITH THEIR EMPLOYEES (FORMER EMPLOYEES NOW). Why the MAYOR OF HARRIMAN, this morning after his efforts at affording a settlement had been turned down, told me that we might as well go back over there and try to get back what we had lost—that there was not a law to make them bargain with us, unless they wished to do so. We are opposed by the entire town almost—it is dominated entirely by the Tarwaters and their relatives. . . . They are determined not to obey that Section 7 of the NIRA. Are they going to get away with it?[51]

A supplement to the injunction, issued in January 1934, further enjoined the strikers from "addressing persons employed or willing to be employed . . . with a view of persuading them to refrain from continuing in or entering such employment."[52] HHM threatened to never consider anyone for employment who violated the injunction.[53]

To strikers, the granting of the two court injunctions, using sheriff's deputies as company guards, and hiring of people from beyond the community to replace strikers introduced anti-union forces from outside their community and aggravated an already tense situation. In January 1934 the Roane County sheriff began to arrest strikers violating the injunction. By the last day of the month, seventy-six men were jammed in a jail with an official capacity of only forty: "There is hardly standing room, conditions are pitiful."[54] Two days later, all had been released on $250 bonds. Wives and families of the jailed strikers took their places on the picket lines.

Sheriff's deputies, guarding HHM, shot tear gas on the strikers. "They treat us as if we were the worst of criminals." A local union member, Edna Gossage, appealed directly to Secretary of Labor Frances Perkins about the sheriff and his deputies, but Perkins gave no direct response.[55] The company requested that Governor Hill McAlister send troops to guard the plant, but he refused. Day-to-day life for the strikers and their families was very difficult. In a moving, sixteen-page letter Mrs. W. R. Chambers, a sixty-five-year-old woman who had been a Republican until voting for Roosevelt, pleaded with the President: "Please do something to make the 7a article *stronger* before it is to [*sic*] late to help a lot of us. Capital an[d] labor are at each other's throat an[d] one or the other is going to start cutting soon if we dont [sic] get this trouble stoped [*sic*]. I dont [*sic*] want a war now after all the other troubles . . . . Please make it so we can get decent wages to live. I still remain your humble servent [*sic*]."[56] Union leaders pointed out to President Roosevelt the importance of this case: "The results of this strike will decide whether or not the South respects the NRA, the Roosevelt administration and the New Deal."[57]

By March 1934, the Harriman strikers had lost considerable support in the broader community. One irate citizen wrote to Senator Kenneth McKellar (D-Tenn.): "Of the eight thousand people in our city . . . I can truthfully say to you that ninety-five percent are with the management of the mill."[58] Mayor D'Armond, however, continued to support the strikers and the New Deal: "I believe in the NRA 100 percent."[59]

A presidential executive order on February 23, 1934, gave the NLB authority to decide whether Section 7(a) of the NIRA had been violated. On March 23 NLB chair Senator Robert F. Wagner (D-N.Y.) turned the Harriman case over to the attorney general and the Compliance Division of the NRA for review.[60] As such, the Tennessee case became one of the first in the nation to come under direct executive and administrative control testing the effectiveness of NRA enforcement in labor disputes.[61] Unfortunately for striking hosiery workers, the review concluded that the Department of Justice did not have sufficient evidence to warrant legal action against the Harriman Hosiery Mills.[62] Without stronger coercive authority, the NRA could not act decisively in the face of strong employer resistance to the new labor policies.

Government sanction meted out to HHM showed the weakness of voluntary NRA actions. Over several months union officials led a campaign to remove the Blue Eagle flag—symbol of business cooperation with the government's NRA policies—from the Harriman plant.[63] NRA, Department of Justice, and NLB officials became embroiled in the debate over removal of the Blue Eagle. After months of wrangling, Attorney General Homer Cummings ruled that the evidence against the company was not strong enough to allow the government to prosecute, but that the company had violated the rules. Hugh Johnson, NRA administrator, could therefore remove the Blue Eagle flag from the plant, using that mild sanction as a warning to HHM management.[64]

Loss of the Blue Eagle symbol had a dramatic effect on the course of the strike. The NRA sent in several investigators to try to resolve the dispute. HHM lost a key hosiery contract with the Pennsylvania Emergency Relief

Board that hurt the company's economic situation. On June 25, 1934, exactly eight months after the strike began, HHM closed the mill in response to the loss of the Blue Eagle and the Pennsylvania contract, with a loss of 653 jobs to the community.[65]

The Blue Eagle campaign proved the last stage in the Harriman strike. HHM sent a strong telegram of protest to Johnson over loss of the flag.[66] The community split along lines of support and opposition to the company and the striking hosiery workers. Sixty-nine businesses and professionals took down their Blue Eagles in protest against the NRA's treatment of the mill managers.[67] Strikers organized a parade through town attempting to garner support: "Show your patriotism by refusing to patronize those who have denounced and withdrawn the Blue Eagle!"[68] Some businesses and professionals backed the strikers and their demands by putting up Blue Eagles they had not previously shown.

On June 25, 1934, HHM locked up its plant. It may have been the first plant to actually close in reaction to an NRA ruling.[69] As originally announced, the closing was intended to be permanent, but this managerial show of force led the NRA to send in another, final investigator. Mayor D'Armond and the city council tried to set up a local reconciliation committee to no avail.[70]

The strike came to an end as a result of intervention by A. R. Glancy, an automobile corporation vice president handpicked by Hugh Johnson to negotiate an end to the dispute. The settlement announced on July 19, 1934, marked complete defeat for the Harriman hosiery strikers. HHM managers and Glancy reached agreement privately without the knowledge or support of the striking workers.[71] The factory reopened, the Blue Eagle flag flew again over HHM, the Justice Department ruled that it lacked evidence to start legal proceedings against the firm, and the striking workers remained unemployed.[72] Local 1757 of the United Textile Workers still technically existed at HHM in that some workers were members of the union, but the company refused to recognize the union or to engage in collective bargaining. Defeated union members did not push the issue.

HHM managers, RLB and NLB officials, NRA administrators, and striking Harriman workers had very different definitions of collective bargaining. Secretary M. W. Walker of HHM said he was "*always* willing to bargain collectively because he'll always talk to employees who have a problem"; however, he would not admit his unwillingness to enter into a collective bargaining agreement with the union. Over the course of the strike HHM management never changed its opposition to union recognition or collective bargaining. The minor concession of a promise to rehire twenty-five of the original strikers was meaningless—many of the strikers had been forced to either find other jobs or move away from the community altogether. The RLB and NLB obviously had a different definition, but they never forced HHM to accept the view that Section 7(a) required collective bargaining and a written contract.[73] Striking hosiery workers thought that collective bargaining meant a good faith effort by management to recognize their union, to negotiate in good faith, and to arrive at a written contract supported by business, labor, and government. The NRA did claim, however, that the HHM case was one of the first to demonstrate that collective bargaining "is something more than mere meeting and discussion, without intention of reaching a collective agreement."[74]

The more expansive definition by Harriman workers proved to be the central issue at stake in the strike of 1933–34, leading NLB chairman Senator Robert F. Wagner to reevaluate NIRA Section 7(a) and attempt to define what it meant. The HHM case was at least a Tennessee contribution to this federal reexamination and later definition of collective bargaining.[75] But in 1933–34, the legal authority of the NLB and the NRA over labor disputes was a matter of considerable debate and dispute among New Deal administrators. HHM refused to submit to the jurisdiction of the NLB. Company officials always maintained that the federal government had no arbitrary authority over a private firm. T. A. Wright defiantly commented, "Without our consent, you [NLB] do not have the power of determining or adjusting this matter."[76] Wright was correct. One Harriman striker, still unemployed months after the strike ended, put the matter bluntly, "We was told to organize and the government would back us. And we organized and had to strike and it has been 13 months. Why cant we get some settlement? T. A. Wright said that they was bigger than the government and it looks that way."[77]

During the early New Deal federal government agencies had not established the authority that they would later apply so effectively in the wake of passage of the Wagner (National Labor Relations) Act of 1935. Without the enforcement teeth provided by the later National Labor Relations Board created by the Wagner Act, early New Deal labor law reform proved halfhearted. As textile labor historian James Hodges has noted, "[C]ertainly, in the beginning, New Deal officials had only the most jumbled and contradictory attitudes towards unions and collective bargaining."[78]

The promise of business-labor compromise, cooperation, and peace through federal intervention via union recognition and collective bargaining ended up as a missed opportunity. Early New Deal labor reform through

Section 7(a) of the NIRA proved to be a promise that could not be fulfilled. Business management at HHM remained stubbornly resistant to any change in labor relations. Government officials in the RLB, the NLB, and the NRA were unwilling and unable to convince HHM managers that the voluntary restraints symbolized by the removal of the Blue Eagle flag were truly punitive. Coercive measures were never tried in large part due to the lack of substantive legal authority. Unemployed textile workers paid a high cost for this missed opportunity. They did not obtain recognition of their union, the start of any collective bargaining, or the tangible economic benefits that a union contract might have provided.

The failure of UTW Local 1757 at HHM to achieve its objectives reflected similar failures in other early New Deal programs. The principles that later made the National Labor Relations Board such a powerful entity were not legally recognized by the U.S. Supreme Court nor administratively enforced by either the NRA or the NLB. Workers at HHM who lost their jobs as a result of the strike paid the heaviest price in the face of weak labor law enforcement and determined employer resistance to unionization and collective bargaining.

As a prelude to the national 1934 general strike in the textile industry, the Harriman strike of 1933–34 in East Tennessee foreshadowed the negative results of the larger altercation that left southern textile workers without much hope until the industrial union drives of the Textile Workers' Organizing Committee in the late 1930s and the Operation Dixie campaign in 1946.[79] More generally, the Harriman Hosiery Mills strike of 1933–34 revealed the overwhelming power of textile managers over their communities, the strength of traditional anti-union sentiment in southern mill towns, and the very real weaknesses in early New Deal labor policy. For Harriman workers, the strike, which had begun in such hope, ended as a missed opportunity for enlightened management, better working lives, and compassionate government. They would have to wait for another chance to bring together more chastened managers, more dramatic changes in labor law, more resolute government officials, and a stronger union.

NOTES

1. Irving Bernstein, *The Lean Years: A History of the American Worker, 1920–1933* (Boston, 1960), 508–13.
2. On the southern textile industry in the 1920s, see Gavin Wright, *Old South, New South: Revolutions in the Southern Economy Since the Civil War* (New York, 1986), 147–55, 207–16. On the 1929 textile strike, see Bernstein, *Lean Years*, 1–43; F. Ray

Marshall, *Labor in the South* (Cambridge, Mass., 1967), 101–20; George B. Tindall, *The Emergence of the New South* (Baton Rouge, 1967), 318–53. For recent histories of textile workers, see Bruce Raynor, "Unionism in the Southern Textile Industry: An Overview," in Gary M. Fink and Merl E. Reed, eds., *Essays in Southern Labor History: Selected Papers, Southern Labor History Conference, 1976* (Westport, Conn., 1977), 80–99; Robert H. Zieger, "Textile Workers and Historians," in *Organized Labor in the Twentieth-Century South,* ed. Robert H. Zieger (Knoxville, 1991), 35– 59; and David L. Carlton, "Paternalism and Southern Textile Labor: A Historio-graphical Review," and Bryant Simon, "Prelude to the New Deal: The Political Re-sponse of South Carolina Textile Workers to the Great Depression, 1929–1933," both in *Race, Class, and Community in Southern Labor History,* eds. Gary M. Fink and Merl E. Reed (Tuscaloosa, Ala., 1994), 17–26, 41–52.

3. On the promise of Section 7(a), see Irving Bernstein, *Turbulent Years: A History of the American Worker, 1933–1941* (Boston, 1971), 27–185; Robert H. Zieger, *American Workers, American Unions, 1920–1985* (Baltimore, 1986), 26–35; Foster Rhea Dulles and Melvyn Dubofsky, *Labor in America: A History,* fifth edition (Arlington Heights, Ill., 1993), 257–64; Tindall, *Emergence of the New South,* 505–12. On the broader significance of changes in federal labor law and federal intervention in labor disputes, see Bernstein, *Turbulent Years,* 635–81; Christopher Tomlins, *The State and the Unions: Labor Relations, Law, and the Organized Labor Movement in America, 1880–1960* (New York, 1985); and Melvyn Dubofsky, *The State and Labor in Modern America* (Chapel Hill, N.C. 1994).

4. Bernstein, *Turbulent Years,* 318–634; David Brody, *Workers in Industrial America: Essays on the Twentieth-Century Struggle,* second edition (New York, 1993), 82–156; James R. Green, *The World of the Workers: Labor in Twentieth-Century America* (New York, 1980), 150–73; Melvyn Dubofsky and Warren Van Tine, *John L. Lewis: A Biography* (New York, 1977), 203–280; and Robert H. Zieger, *The CIO, 1935–1955* (Chapel Hill, N.C., 1995), 1–89.

5. Cited in *WPA Guide to Tennessee* (Knoxville, 1986), 362.

6. Adjacent to Harriman on the south side was Rockwood, a city with an equally im-pressive industrial history. Incorporated in 1890, Rockwood grew around the Roane Iron Company, chartered in 1867 by U.S. Army general John T. Wilder, who had campaigned in Tennessee during the Civil War. The completion of the Cincinnati Southern Railway to Roane County in 1879 enhanced the industrial prospects of the county. William Howard Moore, *Company Town: A History of Rockwood and the Roane Iron Company,* (Kingston, Tenn., n.d.), 14–15. In the twentieth century Rock-wood Hosiery Mills (1905) and Rockwood Stove Works (1916) became major plants employing over seven hundred workers at one time. Tennessee Valley Textile Mills (1930) and Dixie Manufacturing Co. (1914) were two smaller industries in Rock-wood. *Scenes and Information About Rockwood* (n.c., [1930s]).

7. Walter T. Pulliam, *Harriman: The Town That Temperance Built* (Harriman, Tenn., 1978), 495.

8. Moore, *Company Town,* 43.

9. Pulliam, *Harriman,* 499.

10. Pulliam, *Harriman,* 499–500, 511.

11. Exact numbers of women in the mill could not be determined, but union minutes

in Folder 1-1, Record Group 39, Harriman Hosiery Mills Strike Papers, Tennessee Technological University Archives, Cookeville, indicate that women constituted a large part of the Harriman workforce. This collection consists of materials photo-copied from Record Group 25, Atlanta Regional Files, National Labor Board, Records of the National Labor Relations Board, National Archives, Washington, D.C. Here-after cited as HHM Strike Papers. James A. Hodges, "Challenge to the New South: The Great Textile Strike in Elizabethton, Tennessee, 1929," *Tennessee Historical Quarterly* 23 (1964): 345, notes that about 40 percent of the workers in the Eliza-bethton plant were "young girls." Jacquelyn Dowd Hall, "Disorderly Women: Gender and Labor Militancy in the Appalachian South," *Journal of American History* 73 (Sept. 1986): 354–82, discusses women's part in the textile plant in Elizabethton, while Mary E. Frederickson, "Heroines and Girl Strikers: Gender Issues and Organized Labor in the Twentieth-Century American South," in *Organized Labor in the Twentieth-Century South*, 84–112, and Bess Beatty, "Gender Relations in Southern Textiles: A Historiographical Overview," in *Race, Class, and Community in Southern Labor His-tory*, 9–16, deal with the broader images and role of women in the textile industry. Jacquelyn Dowd Hall, James Leloudis, Robert Korstad, Mary Murphy, Lu Ann Jones, Christopher B. Daly, *Like a Family: The Making of a Southern Cotton Mill World* (Chapel Hill, N.C., 1987) is a model social history that emphasizes the role of women in southern mill towns.

12. *Harriman Record*, Nov. 21, 1912.
13. For a classic discussion of southern mill towns, see Tindall, *Emergence of the New South*, 318–90. On Harriman, see Pulliam, *Harriman*, 500. Local union president Floyd Johnston confirmed this at a Regional Labor Board hearing in Atlanta, Nov. 23–24, 1934, Folder 1-9, HHM Strike Papers.
14. "Facts in Connection with Harriman Hosiery Mills Labor Dispute, Harriman, Ten-nessee," Mar. 8, 1934, Folder 2-1, HHM Strike Papers.
15. *Harriman Record*, May 23, 1918.
16. Based on a close reading of hearings before the Regional Labor Board in Atlanta, Nov. 23–24, 1933, and the National Labor Board in Washington, D.C., Jan. 4, 1934, Folders 1-9 and 1-11, HHM Strike Papers.
17. Bellush, *Failure of the NRA*, 30–54, 85–100; and James A. Hodges, *New Deal Labor Policy and the Southern Cotton Textile Industry, 1933–1941* (Knoxville, 1986), 43–59.
18. On the origins of the National Industrial Recovery Act and Section 7(a), see Ellis W. Hawley, *The New Deal and the Problem of Monopoly: A Study in Economic Am-bivalence* (Princeton, 1966), 1–34; Bellush, *Failure of the NRA*, 1–29; Bernstein, *Turbulent Years*, 1–36.
19. Hodges, *New Deal Labor Policy*, 61.
20. Minutes, July 1 and Oct. 12, 1933, Folder 1-1 and "Harriman," Folder 1-3, HHM Strike Papers. J. L. Tarwater, plant superintendent, and Mr. Taylor, assistant super-intendent, were present at the first meeting as noted in Folder 1-9, HHM Strike papers.
21. Minutes, July 8, 1933, Folder 1-1, HHM Strike Papers.
22. R. C. Crawford to Hugh S. Johnson and Frances Perkins, Sept. 28, 1933, and Fred G. Held to W. M. Leiserson, Oct. 26, 1933, Folder 1-3, HHM Strike Papers; *Knox-ville News-Sentinel*, Oct. 26, 1933; G. W. Ramaker, Minutes of meeting with Em-

ployers of Harriman Hosiery Co., Nov. 2, 1933, Folder 1-1, HHM Strike Papers; R. B. Cassell to Hugh S. Johnson, Mar. 31, 1934, Folder 1-4, HHM Strike Papers; *Knoxville News-Sentinel,* Apr. 27, 1934; NRA Release No. 4770, May 2, 1934, Folder 1-7, HHM Strike Papers.

23. Transcripts of hearings before the Regional Labor Board in Atlanta and the National Labor Board in Washington, D.C., Folders 1-9 and 1-11, HHM Strike Papers, contain materials detailing management attitudes and actions about the union. On the firing of union activists, see Minutes, July 8, 1933, and G. W. Ramaker, minutes of meeting with the workers of the Harriman Hosiery Co., Nov. 2, 1933, Folder 1-1, and undated affidavits by fired workers, Folder 1-3, HHM Strike Papers.

24. Earl Chambers, Bill Phillips, Merrill Jenkins, Report of the Boarders Shop Committee, Aug. 14, 1933, Folder 1-3, HHM Strike Papers.

25. Management officials at HHM admitted as much to several employees as seen in Chambers, Phillips, Jenkins, Report; G. W. Ramaker Minutes of Meeting with Workers, Nov. 2, 1933; and Floyd Johnston to Marion Smith, Nov. 6, 1933, Folder 1-1, HHM Strike Papers.

26. R. L. Gossage to Senator Wagner, Jan. 22, 1934, Folder 1-3, HHM Strike Papers.

27. Section 7(a) appeared to guarantee collective bargaining, but the Harriman union wanted to wait until the attorney general had interpreted the document before a union committee presented the idea to management. Minutes, Sept. 9, 1933, Folder 1-1, HHM Strike Papers.

28. Minutes, Sept. 30 and Oct. 3, 1933, Folder 1-1, HHM Strike Papers.

29. The local union notified Secretary of Labor Francis Perkins that workers were fired in July as seen in Minutes, Oct. 3, 1933, Folder 1-1, HHM Strike Papers.

30. Bellush, *Failure of the NRA,* 30–106; and John Kennedy Ohl, *Hugh S. Johnson and the New Deal* (DeKalb, Ill., 1985), 194–217.

31. In hearings before the Regional Labor Board in Atlanta and the National Labor Board in Washington, D.C., as well as in local newspapers, HHM management cited Johnson and Richberg's statements of August 23, 1933, and February 3, 1934, that collective bargaining did not necessarily mean mandatory entry into a specific contract with workers. For examples, see HHM management remarks in RLB hearings in Atlanta, Nov. 23–24, 1934, 9, 11, 137–41, 158–59, Folder 1-9; management remarks at the NLB hearings in Washington, D.C., Jan. 4, 1934, 45–51, 76–78, 152–53, Folder 1-11, HHM Strike Papers; NRA Release No. 3812, Feb. 27, 1934, Folder 1-7, HHM Strike Papers; and *Knoxville News-Sentinel,* Apr. 26, 1934.

32. Ramaker and Smith's roles are covered in detail throughout the material in HHM Strike Papers, which include a variety of reports and findings that they developed in the course of the strike. Correspondence in October–November 1933 reveals the shift from mediation by the Conciliation Service to the Regional Labor Board, while W. M. Leiserson to R. S. Crawford, Oct. 12, 1933, Folder 1-3, HHM Strike Papers details the work of the regional labor board system.

33. George H. Van Fleet to Hugh L. Kerwin, Oct. 18, 1933; Roy L. Gossage to Robert F. Wagner, Oct. 20, 1933; and "Memorandum of Agreement," Folder 1-3, HHM Strike Papers.

34. Floyd Johnston and Roy L. Gossage to Regional Labor Board, Dec. 9, 1933, Folder 1-3, HHM Strike Papers.

35. *Harriman Record,* Dec. 1, 1933 and R. L. Gossage to Senator Robert F. Wagner, Jan. 13, 1934, HHM Strike Papers. Management insisted that collective bargaining could be done with individuals and need not result in a union contract as seen in the firm's response to charges filed by the union with the Regional Labor Board, Folder 2-1, HHM Strike Papers. Following a hearing before the NLB on Jan. 4, 1934, NLB chairman Senator Robert F. Wagner wrote HHM counsel T. A. Wright on Jan. 18, 1934, Folder 1-3, HHM Strike Papers directly contradicting this interpretation.
36. Minutes, Folder 1-1; NRA press release, Folder 2-14; and G. W. Ramaker, Notes on Harriman Situation, Nov. 2, 1933, Folder 1-1, HHM Strike Papers.
37. Minutes, Oct. 28 and Nov. 4, 1933, Folder 1-1, HHM Strike Papers.
38. Telegram from Floyd Johnston to Marion Smith, Nov. 17, 1933; Fred Held to Marion Smith, Nov. 18, 1933; Minutes, Nov. 18, 1933, Folder 1-1, HHM Strike Papers.
39. Minutes, Nov. 17, 1933, and M. W. Walker to Marion Smith, Nov. 21, 1933, Folder 1-1, HHM Strike Papers.
40. Floyd Johnston to Marion Smith, Nov. 29, 1933, Folder 1-3; Johnston telegram to Smith, Dec. 6, 1933, Folder 1-1, Floyd Johnston and Roy L. Gossage to National Labor Board, Dec. 9, 1933, Folder 1-3, HHM Strike Papers.
41. Floyd Johnston and Roy L. Gossage to Regional Labor Board, Dec. 9, 1933, Folder 1-1, HHM Strike Papers and *Knoxville News-Sentinel,* Dec. 10, 1933.
42. McMahon to Wagner, Jan. 24, 1934, Folder 1-3, HHM Strike Papers.
43. *Harriman Record,* Dec. 7, 1933; Paul Herzog memorandum to Dr. Leo Wolman, Jan. 30, 1934, Folder 1-3, HHM Strike Papers; Regional Labor Board to HHM, Dec. 7, 1933; Folder 1-3 and "Facts in Connection with HHM Labor Dispute," Dec. 1933, Folder 2-1, HHM Strike papers. Collective bargaining became mandatory on August 26, 1933, date of approval of the permanent Hosiery Code. Telegram from NLB to G. W. Ramaker, Nov. 23, 1933, Folder 1-3, HHM Strike Papers.
44. [Marion Smith], Chairman, Regional Labor Board to Robert F. Wagner, Dec. 5, 1933, Folder 1-3, HHM Strike Papers.
45. Transcripts of the hearings are in Folders 1-9 and 1-11, while managerial resistance was voiced in T. A. Wright to Floyd Johnston, Jan. 31, 1934, Folder 1-3, HHM Strike Papers; *Harriman Record,* Dec. 7, 1933.
46. Telegram from Roy Gossage to W. M. Leiserson, Dec. 7, 1933; Johnston to Ramaker, Dec. 10, 1933; telegram from Johnston to Hugh Johnson, Dec. 12, 1933; telegram from Mrs. W. R. Chambers to Wagner, Jan. 24, 1934, Folder 1-3, HHM Strike Papers.
47. *Knoxville News-Sentinel,* Feb. 3, 1934; "Labor Board Rebukes Mill," Folder 1-3 and telegram from Held to Robert Wagner, Jan. 18, 1934, Folder 1-3, HHM Strike Papers. Held, Roy Gossage, and Whitson wrote directly to President Roosevelt in March 1934, warning him that they feared strikers might advocate violence rather than waiting for the government to act, Mar. 12, 1934, Folder 1-3, HHM Strike Papers. Yet violence came in the form of the company-requested court injunction that ended with over seventy strikers in jail, sheriff's deputies working for the firm, and the use of strikebreakers hired from outside the community. Toward the end of the strike, a key union organizer was kidnapped. On June 27, five mill employees (including two foremen) who had recently lost their jobs when the plant closed kid-

napped union organizer Fred Held at gunpoint, drove him out of town, and released him with a warning not to come back to Harriman. See coverage in *Knoxville News Sentinel,* June 27 and 28, 1934.

48. Stinnett to Johnson, Mar. 7, 1934, Folder 1-3, HHM Strike Papers.
49. *Knoxville News-Sentinel,* Feb. 3, 1934.
50. *Knoxville News-Sentinel,* Dec. 15 and 16, 1933.
51. Floyd Johnston and Roy L. Gossage to Regional Labor Board, Dec. 9, 1933, Folder 1-3, HHM Strike Papers, emphasis in original document. Union organizer Fred Held mirrored this frustration in Held to Senator Robert F. Wagner, Dec. 7, 1933, Folder 1-3, HHM Strike Papers.
52. Cited in *Harriman Record,* Dec. 7, 1933, copy in Folder 2-1, HHM Strike Papers.
53. HHM to Johnston, R. L. and Edna Gossage, Brewer, Fred Held, William Hannah, Jan. 31, 1934, Folder 1-3, HHM Strike Papers.
54. *Knoxville News-Sentinel,* Jan. 31, 1934; Edna Gossage to Father Francis J. Haas of NLB, Jan. 31, 1934, Folder 1-3, HHM Strike papers; *Rockwood Times,* Jan. 25, 1934.
55. *Knoxville News-Sentinel,* Feb. 7 and 14, 1934, and Edna Gossage to Francis Perkins, Feb. 12, 1934, Folder 1-3, HHM Strike Papers. The local union had first contacted Secretary Perkins about union workers being fired in late July as noted in Minutes, Nov. 2, 1933, Folder 1-1, HHM Strike Papers.
56. Mrs. W. R. Chambers to Franklin D. Roosevelt, Mar. 23, 1934, Folder 1-3, HHM Strike Papers, emphasis in original document.
57. R. L. Gossage, Fred Held and A. E. Whitson to F. D. Roosevelt, Mar. 12, 1934, Folder 1-3, and Fred Bryanton to NLB, Nov. 14, 1934, Folder 1-4, HHM Strike Papers.
58. R. B. Cassell to Senator K. D. McKellar, Mar. 29, 1934, Folder 1-4, HHM Strike Papers. Cassell, a judge, blamed outsiders whom he referred to as "some labor leaders in the East." Another Harriman resident blamed strikers for "profanity" while accusing union activists Held, Gossage, and Hannah of being "agitators," Rowland O. Daughhetee to F. D. Roosevelt, Apr. 18, 1934, Folder 1-4, HHM Strike Papers.
59. D'Armond cited in *Knoxville News-Sentinel,* May 1, 1934.
60. *Knoxville News-Sentinel,* Mar. 4, 1934 and RLB to HHM, Dec. 7, 1933, Robert F. Wagner to Homer S. Cummings, Mar. 13, 1934, Folder 1-3, HHM Strike Papers.
61. NRA Press Release No. 3603, Mar. 3, 1934, Folder 1-7, HHM Strike Papers. President Roosevelt ordered Senator Robert F. Wagner to do something "pronto" about the HHM case as noted in memorandum from M. H. McIntyre to Wagner, Mar. 13, 1934, Folder 1-3, HHM Strike Papers.
62. Ironically, Attorney General Homer Cummings announced the decision the same day, June 25, 1934 (exactly eight months since the start of the strike), that HHM closed the plant in response to union and NRA attempts to use removal of the Blue Eagle symbol from the plant as a final step in resolving the strike. See *Knoxville News-Sentinel,* June 29, 1934.
63. The campaign was closely covered in the *Knoxville News-Sentinel,* while some materials are in Folder 2-11, HHM Strike Papers.
64. Johnson telegram to HHM, Apr. 20, 1934, NRA Release No 4540, Apr. 20, 1934 and No. 6207, July 2, 1934, Folder 1-7, HHM Strike Papers. The Blue Eagle, symbol of the NRA, was awarded to a business that subscribed to the principles and rules of the NRA and adhered to the industrial code provisions for its specific industry.

65. *Knoxville News-Sentinel,* Apr. 28, 29, May 21, and June 23 and 26, 1934.

66. HHM to Hugh Johnson, Apr. 25, 1934, Folder 2-10, HHM Strike Papers.

67. Folder 2-11, HHM Strike Papers. Mayor D'Armond thought that "the people of Harriman are patriotic and will stand by the government." One hundred business-men sent a supportive telegram; thirty-seven citizens sent another. NRA press release No. 4770, May 2, 1934, Folder 1-7, HHM Strike Papers.

68. *Knoxville News-Sentinel,* Apr. 29, 1934.

69. NRA Press Release No. 6207, July 2, 1934, Folder 1-7, and unnamed newspaper article in Folder 2-11, HHM Strike Papers.

70. *Knoxville News-Sentinel,* June 27, 1934.

71. Columnists Drew Pearson and Robert Allen suggested that A. R. Glancy's replacing William Davis as head of the Compliance Division of NLB was one reason for the strike's failure and end. Glancy approached labor disputes from the management viewpoint, and he settled the HHM dispute without consulting the union. *The Daily Washington Merry-Go-Round,* July 26, 1934, Folder 1-8, HHM Strike Papers. NRA press release No. 6618, July 20, 1934, Folder 1-7, HHM Strike Papers admitted this.

72. *Knoxville News-Sentinel,* July 20–22, 1934 and NRA Release No. 6207, July 2, 1934, Folder 1-7, HHM Strike Papers.

73. "Formal Complaints of Employees of HHM vs. HHM," Nov. 22–23, 1933, Folder 1-9; "Facts in Connection with HHM Labor Dispute," Dec. 1933, Folder 2-1; and NRA Release No. 3654, Mar. 6, 1934, Folder 1-7, HHM Strike Papers.

74. Press release No. 3654, Mar. 6, 1934.

75. Memorandum from William Davis to Hugh Johnson, Apr. 20, 1934, and memo-randum from Franklin S. Pollak to William H. Davis, Apr. 17, 1934, Folder 1-4, HHM Strike Papers. For the broader context of these rulings, see James A. Gross, *The Making of the National Labor Relations Board: A Study in Economics, Politics, and the Law,* vol. 1: 1933–1937 (Albany, N.Y., 1974), 51–52.

76. NRA Report of Hearing, Jan. 4, 1934, Folder 1-11, HHM Strike Papers.

77. Fred Bryanton to [National Labor Board], Nov. 15, 1934, Folder 1-4, HHM Strike Papers.

78. Hodges, *New Deal Labor Policy,* 5. Throughout the period, government officials re-mained confused and contradictory about the interpretation of Section 7(a) as seen in the various statements made by NRA administrator Hugh Johnson, his assistant Donald Richberg, NRA Compliance Division officials, and Department of Justice lawyers in William H. Davis to Hugh S. Johnson, April 11 and 20, 1934, Folder 1-5, HHM Strike Papers, and later in Hugh S. Johnson, *The Blue Eagle From Egg to Earth* (Garden City, N.Y., 1935). For the broader context of this labor policy con-fusion, see Bellush, *Failure of the NRA,* passim; Ohl, *Hugh S. Johnson,* 194–217; and Gross, *Making of the National Labor Relations Board.*

79. Hodges, *New Deal Labor Policy*; Barbara Griffith, *The Crisis of American Labor: Operation Dixie and the Defeat of the CIO* (Philadelphia, 1988); and Zieger, *The CIO,* 227–41.

Tennessee in War and Peace: The Impact of World War II on State Economic Trends

■ Patricia Brake Howard

■

■ *Editor's Note:* World War II greatly accelerated the pace of industrial development in twentieth-century Tennessee. It also led to
■ urban expansion in established cities like Nashville, Knoxville,
Kingsport, Chattanooga, and Memphis while creating wholly new
■ cities like Oak Ridge, the secret "city behind a fence." The war
also significantly impacted the people of the Tennessee
■ homefront. More rural people moved to towns and cities. Incomes expanded; women entered the industrial labor force in
■ greater numbers than ever before. African Americans, however,
gained little new economic benefits and they continued their
■ flight north to better opportunities and greater civil rights. World
War II in Tennessee, just as in the nation as a whole, was the
■ watershed event of the twentieth century.

The World War II years marked a watershed period for the United
States. America emerged as the world's preeminent power: it was both victor
and sole possessor of the atomic bomb. On the domestic front, the United
States, as the arsenal of democracy, produced unprecedented quantities of war
supplies and thus quickly reversed the preceding decade's Great Depression.

Perhaps the war's single most significant impact on Tennessee was its ac-
celeration and expansion of the state's industry. During the war, Tennessee
shifted from a predominantly rural, agricultural economy to an industrial-
ized economy. Not only did established industrial centers such as Memphis,
Chattanooga, and Knoxville convert their production almost entirely to war
materials, but the newly established Kingsport mushroomed in growth, as did
the war-spawned Oak Ridge, which almost overnight became Tennessee's

Patriotic poster from
World War II. Tennessee
State Museum.

fifth-largest city. The Tennessee Valley Authority (TVA) also significantly
enlarged its facilities and power output during the war.

As Tennessee's industries expanded during the war years, women throughout the state followed national trends as they sought higher-paying jobs in
war factories. While a significant minority of black Tennesseans entered war
manufacturing jobs, most still remained locked into low-paying, low-status
jobs, particularly in the personal service industry.

After the war, Tennessee veterans, along with their compatriots throughout the nation, seized GI Bill benefits that included school stipends and low
interest rates for housing. Consequently, Tennessee campuses and suburbs
expanded enormously in the immediate postwar years.

Indicative of the industrial growth experienced in Tennessee during the
war was the unprecedented number of new industries in the state. In 1943
alone, twenty-nine new industries were established in Tennessee.[1] By the end
of 1944, plants that had been built since the beginning of the war were val-

ued at $1.5 billion. By November 1944, war supply contracts had also reached $1.5 billion, which was 25 percent of the Southeast region's contracts.[2] Tennessee's wartime employment peaked in the summer of 1944, with a total of 279,000 in manufacturing.[3] Union membership in Tennessee increased 164 percent from 71,000 in 1939 to over 187,000 in 1953.[4]

Following the onset of the war, over seventy Shelby County plants converted to war production, and several new manufacturing firms located in the area. By 1943, nearly one hundred Memphis manufacturing firms held war contracts. The two largest Memphis firms, the Fisher and Ford plants, shifted from the manufacturing of automobile parts to aircraft parts production.[5] Other major war industries in Memphis were McDonnell Aircraft, Firestone Tire and Rubber Company, and Chickasaw Ordnance Works.[6]

The total employment in the Memphis labor market area, which included all of Shelby County, increased from 140,000 in 1940 to a wartime peak of 182,500 in June 1944.[7] During the war, the federal government employed several thousand civilians in the Memphis area at the newly established Kennedy General Hospital, and at several Armed Services installations.[8]

Nashville, the second-largest city in Tennessee with a 1940 Davidson County population of 257,000, experienced a less dramatic transformation in its conversion to war industry. To a large degree, the industrial sector remained virtually unchanged with the major exception of Consolidated Vultee Aircraft corporation, Nashville's "only real 'war baby industry,'" which increased its employment from less than six hundred to over three thousand by May 1945.[9]

Historically, as the state capital, a university center, and county seat, the Nashville labor force had a consistently high proportion of professional and white collar workers. In 1940, nearly 30 percent of those employed in Nashville worked in the professional, clerical, sales or related occupations.[10] That same year only 23 percent were employed in manufacturing, while 47 percent held occupations in the trade and service sectors. Employment in the Nashville Labor Market Area reached a wartime peak in June 1943 at nearly 109,000.[11]

The apparel industry employment more than doubled in the Nashville area during the war, as most of the local apparel manufacturers converted from the production of work clothing to military clothing. The Nashville Bridge Company converted from the building of structural steel for bridges to the production of submarine chasers and mine sweepers, but generally employed fewer than seven hundred workers.[12]

Chattanooga, an important manufacturing area with over two hundred factories before the war, produced ordnance materials, chemical products, steel, iron, and textiles in the defense plants. Many firms in Chattanooga converted to the production of war materials by significant expansion of existing facilities. With the exception of the production of aircraft parts and ordnance supplies, however, Chattanooga manufacturing products remained relatively unchanged during the war; the exception was the Hercules Powder Company, which produced TNT.[13]

The population of Hamilton County grew during the war years from approximately 180,500 to 208,250 for a 15 percent growth rate for the decade of 1940 to 1950. Although significantly less than the 38 percent growth rate that Chattanooga had experienced as a result of industrial growth due to World War I, the 1940s' population growth rate was higher than the rates for both the 1950s and 1960s.[14]

Knoxville, the chief city of the East Tennessee Valley, had a population of 112,000 in 1940. The chief industries there were marble production and textiles, which employed 40 percent of the Knoxville area workers. In nearby Blount County, the Aluminum Company of America (ALCOA) had erected a plant and a town on three thousand acres. ALCOA, which produced aluminum sheeting, employed over four thousand workers in 1939.[15]

Prior to the U.S. involvement in World War II, the Knoxville labor force had been divided equally between agriculture and industry.[16] During the Depression, the employment patterns had changed due to the Works Progress Administration and the location in 1933 of the national headquarters of the Tennessee Valley Authority in Knoxville. The University of Tennessee, Southern Railway Systems, and Fulton Sylphon, which produced temperature and pressure control instruments, also employed large numbers of workers.[17]

By May 1941, Knoxville had already begun to receive large defense contracts totaling over $2.25 million.[18] The contracts proved to be a major boon to the area which was recovering from Depression-related bank failures, factory closings, and high unemployment.[19] Several textile and apparel firms as well as Fulton Sylphon, which had converted to the production of automatic thermostat controls and artillery components during the defense period, obtained important military contracts.[20]

By March 1942, Knoxville manufacturers had procured nearly $8 million in government contracts, exclusive of ALCOA. Of that figure, the textile and garment industries had obtained the most substantial portion of government dollars. In the same year, ALCOA constructed a new North Plant with a federal allocation Certificate of Necessity of $42 million.[21]

In Kingsport, Tennessee Eastman Company became actively involved in the production of explosives for the war effort. Eastman, which had grown from a small hometown plant in the 1920s, employed five thousand workers by 1940 in the production of acetic anhydride, which was used as raw material for safety film and in the early production of plastics.[22]

The National Defense Research Committee (NDRC) approached Eastman to establish a pilot plant for the production of RDX, or Research Development Explosive, whose explosive capacity was 50 percent greater than TNT. Eastman chemists quickly designed a method to produce large quantities of RDX, which previously had been produced only in small batches due to its extremely explosive properties. In addition, Eastman personnel began experimentation with Composition B, which was an amalgamation of RDX and TNT. Composition B was intended for use in projectiles and bombs, and Eastman began producing it in the easily transported shape of chocolate kisses.[23]

Following the success of the pilot projects at Eastman, the federal government granted authorization in June 1942 to Eastman officials to construct Holston Ordnance Works (HOW). Concurrent with ongoing construction, HOW produced and shipped its first 100,000 pounds of Composition B, and by January 1944, HOW became the largest producer of high explosives in the world. Employment at the works peaked at nearly seven thousand and eventually stabilized at five thousand, with women as approximately 40 percent of Eastman's employees.[24] Due to the wartime expansion of industry in Kingsport, the population there increased by approximately ten thousand between 1940 and 1943.[25]

Because of Eastman's achievements in the production of Composition B and RDX, the Manhattan Project contacted Eastman officials to operate the Y-12 plant at Oak Ridge. Eastman's Dr. Fred R. Conklin became the works manager at the Y-12 plant of the Clinton Engineer Works, and several other Eastman employees transferred to Oak Ridge. Eastman oversaw the operations at Clinton Engineer Works from early 1943 to the spring of 1947.[26]

At the time the atomic project was revealed, Clinton Engineer Works and the city of Oak Ridge cost over $1.106 billion, of a total of $1.665 billion spent on the entire Manhattan Project.[27] As work on the Manhattan Project progressed, Oak Ridge grew from rolling farmland and timbered hillsides to Tennessee's fifth-largest city in less than three years, with a peak wartime population of seventy-five thousand. The project employed over ninety thousand workers who produced the uranium isotope, U-235, a major component of the first atomic bomb, which was dropped on the Japanese city of Hiroshima on August 6, 1945.[28]

The East Tennessee source of power supplied by the Tennessee Valley Authority was one of the primary reasons that the Manhattan Project chose Oak Ridge as the site for the construction of an atomic energy plant. Further, the expansion of the ALCOA facilities in Blount County depended on the utilization of TVA-generated power. TVA greatly enlarged its operations during the war. Under emergency authorizations and accelerated schedules, the agency built seven dams and a steam-generating station between 1940 and 1945. TVA expanded its facilities by completing Douglas and Fort Loudoun dams at a total expenditure of $65 million in East Tennessee.[29] These additional installations increased TVA's power capabilities from less than one million kilowatts to over two million kilowatts. Further, the wartime construction of these dams achieved the completion of a 650-mile navigation channel that connected the Tennessee River with six thousand miles of interior waterways in the United States.[30]

Following the atomic bombings of Hiroshima and Nagasaki, and the subsequent rapid conclusion of the war, Tennessee, along with the rest of the nation, looked to postwar reconversion challenges and opportunities. Throughout the South, the postwar years witnessed widespread industrialization. Following the war, consumer industries generally subdivided their manufacturing operations among several firms and located their finishing plants near consumer markets. Due to the impetus of wartime employment, the postwar South enjoyed more disposable income and thus a larger market than it had before the war. Consequently, numerous new industries located in the region following the war.[31]

Postwar industrialization in Tennessee was characterized by two significant trends: decentralization of industry to the nonurban, small-town areas and diversification of industries throughout the state.[32] A significant number of new industrial jobs were created in the outlying counties around Knoxville, Chattanooga, and the Tri-Cities areas during the 1950s.[33] For example, in Chattanooga, new plants and plant expansions provided 8,600 new jobs in the metropolitan area, and 3,100 jobs in its outlying counties; the Tri-Cities area provided 8,000 new jobs in the urban sectors and 3,500 jobs in the outlying counties.[34]

In West Tennessee, Charles Poe, chairman of the Memphis Committee for Economic Development, hoped for the "replacement of war prosperity in Memphis with a peace prosperity." He forecast a 50 to 60 percent increase in postwar employment over 1940 figures.[35]

Poe's predictions for a greatly expanded postwar Memphis economy were realized. According to a study prepared by the economic consultant group of Hammer, Greene, Siler and Associates, economic developments such as installation of military bases and growth of defense industries as a result of World War II created "an almost revolutionary change in the economy of the South, the Memphis Region and Memphis."[36] Between 1948 and 1952, Memphis experienced the location of twice as many manufacturing plants and the expansion of twice as many existing industries as Tennessee's other major urban areas combined.[37]

Thus the war created an emergency-induced catalyst for economic growth that spawned 370 new industrial plants in Memphis between 1946 and 1952. Of that number, 45 percent of the new firms were established in the first two years after the war. Memphis in 1953 boasted over eight hundred plants, compared to approximately four hundred in 1940. Manufacturing employment increased from 23,000 in 1940 to over 45,000 in 1953.[38]

Not surprisingly, the population of Memphis increased substantially during the postwar period, keeping pace with the rapidly expanding economy. The Shelby County population increased by nearly 35 percent between 1940 and 1950, from 358,000 to 482,000.[39]

Because of the relative lack of impact that the war had on Nashville area industries, reconversion problems for the area proved less severe than in other areas of the state. In the spring of 1945, Vultee planned to reconvert to the production of bus bodies. During the latter stages of the war, Nashville Bridge Company planned to change from the wartime construction of cargo barges for the navy to the peacetime construction and repair of civilian barges. Most smaller concerns also planned to continue with prewar types of manufacturing. In 1945, construction began on the Goodyear plant in Tennessee for production of heavy-duty tires. The plant, whose completion was projected by December of the same year, planned to hire over a thousand workers.[40]

Despite the relatively minor wartime industrial expansion in the Nashville area, the population of Davidson County grew from approximately 257,000 in 1940 to 322,000 for a 25 percent increase. During the preceding decade, the population there had increased only 15 percent.[41]

Following the end of the war, Knoxville war plants experienced immediate cutbacks in employment as indicated by substantial decreases in nonagricultural employment in the Knoxville area.[42] Despite the impact that Oak Ridge atomic facilities and the expansion of ALCOA had on the area's economic development, Knoxville's postwar economy did not advance as quickly as many other areas of the South. Between the late 1940s and 1960, nonfarm employment increased by only 5 percent. At the same time, Knoxville's durable goods industry—primarily textiles, clothing, and iron—declined while the service industry expanded. The Knoxville area population patterns paralleled the economic sluggishness of the surrounding area following the war. While 91,000 persons moved into the Knoxville area during the 1940s, due primarily to labor demands at Oak Ridge, only 31,000 persons moved into the Knoxville area the succeeding decade.[43]

By early 1946, Tennessee had achieved virtually all of its postwar reconversion. Memphis alone claimed sixty-four new industries; the industrial projects, however, were spread fairly evenly throughout the grand divisions of the state. Of approximately three thousand manufacturing firms in Tennessee in 1946, the estimated value of manufactured products for the year was $1.3 billion, an 80 percent increase over 1939 figures.[44] In 1946, Tennessee claimed the two largest new industrial projects in the Southeast: DuPont's $20 million nylon yarn plant in Chattanooga and American Enka's $20 million rayon tire yarn firm near Morristown.[45]

Industrial production continued to increase in 1947, with an estimated value of Tennessee manufacturing and products of over $2 billion, which was two times greater than prewar figures.[46] Between the war's end in September 1945 and December 1948, when the immediate postwar period had concluded, seven hundred new industries had been established in Tennessee, with a total investment value of $1.75 million.[47]

The expansion of Tennessee industry during the war also affected the state's migration patterns. Between 1940 and 1950, Tennessee experienced one of the lowest out-migrations since 1870, with the exception of the Depression decade.[48] The state out-migration rate for the war decade was relatively low due to the influx of workers into the major metropolitan areas, which experienced a net 11 percent in-migration rate as compared with a –14.5 percent net out-migration rate in the nonmetropolitan and rural areas.[49]

The rural farm population for 1950 was 1,016,000 as compared to 1,272,000 in 1940 for a loss of 256,000 in farm population for the decade. By 1960, the rural farm population had declined to 587,000. Beginning with the war decade these trends countered the characteristics of the Depression decade, which had shown an increase of 59,000 in the rural farm population in Tennessee.[50]

The war years that signaled an end to the Depression not only affected war factories and migration patterns but also personal income levels as indicated by bank deposits. Total deposits in Tennessee more than tripled between 1940 and 1950, from approximately $650 million to over $2 billion.[51]

Personal income increased from less than $1 billion in 1940 to nearly $3.3 billion in 1950. Per capita personal income nearly tripled from 1940 to 1950, from an annual income of $339 to $994. Despite the statewide increase in personal income, however, Tennessee per capita income still ranked significantly lower than that of the United States, which averaged $595 and $1,496 for the same years.[52]

The increase in personal income reflected the increases in both men's and women's earnings throughout the United States during the war. In 1944, men realized a 52 percent increase in hourly wages over their 1939 earnings and women effected a 57 percent increase for the same period, although at $.745 an hour, their wages were still substantially lower than the men's wage of $1.159 per hour.[53]

As the state's industries expanded during the war to meet the demands of government contracts, the male labor supply was diminishing as all able-bodied men were called to join the armed services. Consequently, the war also provided a large-scale opportunity for women across the state to enter nontraditional occupations in the war industries. Between September 1942 and March 1944, the employment trend of women in several of Tennessee's chief war industries increased by nearly 21,000, or 75 percent, of the expansion in these industries. The increase in women's employment occurred primarily in the ordnance, textile, lumber finished products, paper, chemical, iron and steel, aircraft, aluminum, communications, and government agencies.[54]

Large war plants in Memphis reflected the trend to hire women, particularly during the wartime production peaks. For example, at Firestone Rubber, women comprised 26 percent of the company's employees in 1944; by the end of the war, their percentages had dropped slightly to 25 percent of the total. In 1944, 40 percent of Fisher Memphis Aircraft employees were women, but by the summer of 1945, they comprised only 31 percent of the total employed. Throughout the war, women continued to make up a small percentage of the employment at Ford Motor Company, from a wartime high of 20 percent in May 1944 to 8 percent in July 1945. The ordnance industries also hired large numbers of Memphis women throughout the middle stages of the war.[55]

Nashville in 1940 ranked high among cities in the United States in the employment of women. Thirty-two percent of Nashville women were employed as compared to the national average of 22 percent. In addition to the established blue-collar employment of women in the Nashville textile and apparel industries, a significant portion of women worked in the traditional female sectors of schools and government. Another factor that accounted for the large percentage of employed women in Nashville was that black women, who were employed twice as often as white females there, comprised over 29 percent of the female population in the area.[56]

By May 1945, it was estimated that the employment of women in the Nashville area had increased by 49 percent since 1940. This increase resulted primarily from the high employment of women at Vultee Aircraft plant and in the numerous government installations in the area. Furthermore, local apparel and textile industries expanded significantly to accommodate war contracts. Women also entered the trade and service industries in Nashville during the war to replace men who had either left their jobs for the armed services or for higher-paying war jobs.[57]

Knoxville women paralleled national trends, as they increasingly moved into nontraditional occupations during the war. In 1942, they constituted nearly 37 percent of employment in war industries there. This figure, however, included apparel and textile mills that historically had utilized high numbers of women workers. ALCOA showed the greatest numerical expansion of its female workforce between 1942 and 1943, as the total number of women workers there increased from 320, or 2 percent, of the total to 1,450, or 13 percent, of the total. At the same time, the total employment there decreased by 1,254. More important, ALCOA placed its new women hires in nontraditional jobs.[58] Women moved into "occupations where they have never been used before": electrical engineering and mechanical departments, chemical laboratories, crane operators, and in the rolling mill.[59]

At ALCOA and in other wartime establishments throughout the state, however, women's advancement was inhibited by existing seniority rights and established lines of advancement. For instance, certain jobs open to women were unattainable because they could be reached only through jobs that were unsuitable for women's strength.[60] Thus a woman might fail to reach a supervisory position or a higher-paying job because she had to work up through the ranks by performing jobs for which she was physically ill-suited.

Fulton Sylphon, which had hired women in production areas as early as 1941, greatly augmented their numbers between mid-1942 and 1943. Women at Fulton Sylphon worked in the inspection shop and autostat and instrument departments, as well as in the press, corrugating, machine shops, and assembly departments. Female production workers at Fulton, although somewhat reluctant to join labor unions, generally joined the Machinists' Union and somewhat later became the Steel Workers' Union, although they were not required by law to do so.[61]

Rohm and Haas Company, which was established in Knoxville in 1943 to produce Plexiglas, employed as many women as possible from its initial operations. Although women worked in the production areas from the plant's opening, they primarily found jobs as glass polishers and helpers, and were not employed in supervisory positions.[62] This employment practice was repeated throughout the state and nation.

The long-established textile industry employed nearly twelve thousand persons in April 1943 and constituted the largest manufacturing industry in the Knox-Blount County area. Eighty-seven percent of the textile workers were women who worked for lower wages at ten cents an hour less than prevailing rates for other area industries.[63]

In numerical terms, women's employment in war manufacturing peaked in the Knoxville area in 1943 at over 14,000, or 39 percent of the total manufacturing employment.[64] In all probability, the large-scale employment of women in war industries in Knoxville would have not taken place if the enormous labor demands of the nearby Clinton Engineer Works in Oak Ridge had not skewed the labor picture. In late 1943, Knoxville was reclassified as a Group I Area of Critical Shortage, and none of the war industries was able to meet the labor demands.[65] Despite the increased utilization of women production workers in 1943, Knoxville manufacturers reflected nationwide practices as they hired women as a last resort measure.[66]

TVA followed area trends in hiring women for nontraditional jobs. Women were trained to guard the agency's dams in the East Tennessee area and also to serve as "guardettes" to protect the TVA headquarters in downtown Knoxville. The *Knoxville News Sentinel* apparently found such employment of women amusing, as indicated by articles that praised the night guardettes for not screeching when they saw a mouse.[67]

By 1944, the *News-Sentinel* headlines reported that "'Weaker Sex' Make up 49 Per Cent of Workers in Knoxville War Plants."[68] This was compared to 28 percent in the same industries during "normal times."[69] Temporarily, at least, women had made important inroads into the production lines of area war plants. With the exception of ALCOA and Fulton Sylphon, however, the Knoxville female war employment had already peaked in 1943.[70]

Clinton Engineer Works generated the primary recruitment for women production workers in 1944. Its employment advertisements showed photographs of women production workers, and its classified announcements emphasized that inexperienced women could find work in chemical, electrical, and mechanical operations.[71]

The downward trend of women's employment in the Knoxville area continued from 1943 throughout 1945. By July 1945, women comprised only 38 percent of the labor force.[72] As women's employment was gradually declining at the area's major war plants, the textile industries were gaining women employees whose war industry jobs were being taken by returning veterans.[73]

Although Knoxville manufacturers did not summarily dismiss women when they were no longer needed for the wartime emergency, the adage "Last hired, first fired" certainly proved true for women, particularly at the large war plants such as ALCOA, Fulton Sylphon, and Rohm and Haas. Generally, women's seniority status in the production areas did not surpass that of the men or the returning veterans; consequently, women were the first to be laid off.

In Knoxville, the decrease in women's employment did not occur as rapidly as expected; it declined from 38 percent of the total employment in July 1945 to 36 percent in January 1946. This can be compared with nationwide trends that witnessed a decline in the female labor force from 38 percent to 29 percent.[74] These downward national employment tendencies reversed after 1947 and have continued to increase since then.[75]

The employment of women in Chattanooga increased gradually during the war. In 1943, in fifty surveyed area industries, the ratio of female employees increased from 27 to 35 percent. Women's employment made significant gains in the chemical industries and in aircraft production at Hardwick Stove Company. Their ratio to total employment increased from 14 to 29 percent in chemicals and from 8 to 34 percent at Hardwick during these firms' wartime peak employment of women. In the transportation and communications sector, where women's employment was well established, the female worker ratio climbed from 42 to 50 percent of the total.[76]

Hercules Powder Company in Chattanooga began actively recruiting women for production work in December 1943 because of the "depleted supply of suitable males." Earlier, women had worked there in the clerical, laboratory, and laundry areas and as guards and chauffeurs; however, "admitting them to production jobs is a major concession."[77]

Although the federal government propaganda bombarded women with enticements to work in the war industries, the government, employers, and the public at large were reluctant to accept the concept of working mothers. The War Manpower Commission stated in 1942 that mothers of young children should be employed only after all labor sources had been exhausted. Nonetheless, the WMC initiated strategies to provide access to employment for mothers, particularly in labor shortage areas. Consequently, in 1942, Congress passed the Lanham Act, which provided $6 million for federally funded Works Progress Administration (WPA) child care programs in war-impacted communities.[78] Although the Lanham Act did not limit the utilization of federally funded day care programs to mothers who worked in the war industries, the shortage of funding did.

By 1943, the WPA had established forty-one nursery schools throughout the state of Tennessee, with an enrollment of 1,300.[79] These figures reflected the limited utilization of the federally funded nursery schools, although conceptually, the WPA nurseries served as an important precedent for the acceptance of working mothers.

In Memphis, six segregated Lanham Act–funded nurseries provided facilities for three hundred children. The nurseries, which were operated by the city board of education, served only eighty-two children as late as mid-1943, a peak period for women's employment there. None of Memphis's war plants provided child care services, and women war workers depended primarily on relatives and nursemaids for their child care needs.[80]

The Nashville Department of Education expanded its nursery school program during the war and appeared to meet the local demand. The three nursery schools for white children operated below capacity, while the three black schools operated at capacity.[81]

Knoxville, which was described by the *News-Sentinel* as a "pace setter in Tennessee in the WPA-financed nursery schools for underprivileged children," was the first southern city to apply for Lanham Act assistance for nursery schools.[82] The city obtained Lanham funding to provide facilities to operate ten Children's War Service Center nursery schools.[83] The racially segregated centers were located near war industries or in neighborhoods where a large percentage of mothers worked.[84]

By late 1943, Chattanooga was operating eight nurseries under the federal program. Although enrollment in the federally funded day care centers gradually increased, even during this period when women's employment was near its wartime peak, the participation was only half of the total capacity.[85] The federal government terminated the Lanham funding for the child care centers in 1946.[86]

Throughout the war, Tennessee women proved that they could take on a man's job successfully. As they drove trucks, guarded dams, worked on the production lines of aluminum, chemical, atomic, and ordnance plants, women took advantage of the emergency-induced opportunities for occupational diversity and economic improvement.

Women's wartime employment gains were generally temporary, although the war set the stage for later change regarding women's working patterns. In Tennessee, women's employment increased by nearly 83,000 between

1940 and 1950. During the same period, male employment increased by only 111,000. Although the majority of women's war jobs were terminated following the end of the hostilities, Tennessee women's employment in manufacturing was 23,000 greater in 1950 than it had been in 1940.[87]

Although the war provided opportunities—at least temporarily—for more occupational diversity for Tennessee women, the black population in the state experienced fewer economic gains during the war. Following migration patterns similar to those of World War I, blacks in Tennessee migrated north in large numbers as they sought higher-paying jobs in war production centers.

Between 1940 and 1950, the black population of the state increased from 509,000 to 531,000 due to natural increase rather than in-migration from other areas. During the 1940s, the net migration for black Tennesseans was –44,000.[88]

In fact, the 1940s was the only decade since 1870 in which out-migration of blacks surpassed white out-migration. During the postwar years of the 1950s, the cities of Memphis, Chattanooga, and Nashville became the temporary or permanent relocation centers for many blacks who were moving north from areas farther south. Consequently, during the fifties, the white out-migration again surpassed that of the black patterns.[89]

Perhaps the most significant migration trend in the black population during the decade of the 1940s was its movement away from rural farm areas in Tennessee. Although the percent change in nonwhite, rural farm population migration at –35.5 percent was lower than the United States and South, it was higher than the white relocation from farm areas in Tennessee at –27.2 percent.[90]

The movement of the black population from rural to urban areas was reflected in its population increase in several Tennessee cities. The nonwhite population in Memphis increased from approximately 121,500 in 1940 to over 150,000 in 1950. The Nashville nonwhite population increased by over seven thousand to approximately 59,000. In Knoxville, the population of blacks increased by 3,000 to over 19,000, and Chattanooga realized a similar growth in its nonwhite population with a population of over 39,000 in 1950.[91]

Tennessee's war and postwar employment figures of blacks reflected patterns similar to prewar data as prevailing negative and paternalistic attitudes toward nonwhites remained virtually unchanged by the war. Before the United States entered the war in 1941, Memphis blacks comprised 41 percent of those employed, and 40 percent of those engaged in manufacturing.

Black male employees, however, were employed in the food, textile, logging, and chemical industries, of which the first three were traditionally low-paying industries.[92] Sixty-six percent of the black employed women in Memphis worked as domestic servants.[93] During the war, as indicated during a peak production year, 1943, a survey of forty-five selected war industries in Memphis revealed that black employment did not increase proportionately to total employment. Instead, it remained low at 28 percent of the total employment, as compared to 24 percent in November 1942. Large numbers of blacks continued to find employment during the war in the area textile, rubber, agricultural, and lumber industries, where they comprised 75 percent of the total employment in lumber. Further, black workers constituted 44 percent of Memphis government workers during the war.[94]

The percentage of black males employed in Memphis manufacturing actually decreased from 40 to 37 percent between 1940 and 1950. Nearly 60 percent of black men worked in the personal service industry, as did 84 percent of black women in 1950.[95]

In 1940, of the 11,000 black men employed in Nashville, less than 20 percent worked in manufacturing: they primarily found employment in transportation and domestic service. Of the 42 percent of the black female population who were employed, fewer than 4 percent worked in manufacturing. Over 77 percent of black employed women worked in personal service, primarily as domestics.[96]

In Nashville, where the black population was only 26 percent of the total population, the percentage of blacks employed to the total percentage of the population remained fairly consistent during the war at approximately 7 percent in November 1942 and May 1943. Black proportions in manufacturing remained low also, at 6 percent of the total. In the iron and steel industries, the black proportion of workers actually decreased from 23 to 14 percent during the same time period.[97] Nashville firms, however, increased their utilization of black women workers as truckers, loaders, and bus cleaners in 1943.[98]

By 1950, Nashville blacks had still failed to make significant inroads into the manufacturing sector. Only 15 percent of black employed males and 7 percent of black employed women worked in this area. Black males comprised 50 percent and black females 74 percent of those employed in the personal service industries. On the other hand, however, a significant minority of blacks served as professionals in the Nashville area in 1950, as approximately 30 percent of female and male professionals were black, primarily in the medical and educational fields.[99]

In Knoxville, only 13 percent of black employed men worked in manufacturing in 1940. They found jobs primarily in transportation, trade, and personal services. Nearly 48 percent of the black female population worked there in 1940, of whom 82 percent worked as domestics.[100] As the war progressed, Knoxville housewives complained that they had lost their black maids to the war industries, where black women often earned three times as much as they did as domestics.[101] In 1950, however, black men comprised only 5 percent of male employees in industry and black women comprised only 1 percent of females in industry.[102]

In Chattanooga in 1940, 40 percent of the black male employees worked in manufacturing, primarily in the iron and steel industries. Thirty-nine percent of black women in Chattanooga worked, again primarily as domestic laborers whose ranks claimed 70 percent of those employed.[103] In 1950, black men comprised only 17 percent of males employed in manufacturing. Black males comprised 50 percent of the male workers in the personal service industry, whereas black women comprised 75 percent of the same.[104]

If blacks were fortunate enough to find jobs in war factories, they, as well as the women war workers, faced layoff problems due to lack of seniority, particularly as the Tennessee veterans returned home. In 1944, 95 percent of Tennessee's veterans found employment.[105] Their success at reemployment was as much an indication of Tennessee labor demands as the effectiveness of the state's veterans' assistance programs.

As early as 1944, Tennessee became involved in planning assistance for veterans. The governor of Tennessee, Prentice Cooper, himself a veteran of World War I, appointed a Committee on Postwar Rehabilitation of Veterans to organize a state veterans' program. The same year, the U.S. Congress passed the Servicemen's Readjustment Act of 1944, popularly known as the "GI Bill of Rights," which outlined procedures for the reemployment of veterans as well as educational and low interest rate benefits.[106]

Also in 1944, the Tennessee War Service Advisory Council established local Veterans' Service Committees that assisted veterans in employment procedures. Local chambers of commerce in the larger cities established postwar plans for increasing local employment through industrial development.[107]

During the 1945 session, the Tennessee General Assembly created the Department of Veterans Affairs, which supplanted the Ex-Service Men's Bureau and coordinated federal, state, and local laws and services pertaining to the returning servicemen and women. The state legislature also created the War Records Bureau.[108]

In addition, the assembly granted veterans' privileges to "women who have served as nurses or in any auxiliary to one of the armed services." The General Assembly also mandated Tennessee counties and cities to establish service offices for assisting veterans in their transition to civilian life.[109]

The returning veterans, anxious to participate in the GI Bill's educational benefits, greatly expanded the state's universities and colleges, which during the war had experienced a dearth of male students. The University of Tennessee in Knoxville had an enrollment of nearly 6,000 students in 1939. But with the U.S. entry into the war, increasing numbers of male students left the university to join the Armed Services. After the graduation of ROTC students in 1943, whose deferments had been granted so that they could finish their degrees, and the call up of the Enlisted Reserve Corps, the campus was nearly void of males except for those registered 4-F and the older faculty members.[110]

In 1944, veterans began to return to the University of Tennessee under the GI Bill. Their numbers increased exponentially during the late 1940s, and UT could not find adequate housing for all of them. Many of the vets were married and brought wives and children with them. The university provided temporary housing in the form of trailer camps near Ayres Hall on "the Hill" and on the agriculture campus. A former University of Tennessee coed remembered attending classes on the hill in the autumn of 1946: "Scores of trailers dotted the hill behind Ayres Hall and along Cumberland Avenue, and scores of gray-haired veterans filled the classrooms."[111] In 1947, enrollment at UT increased to 8,700 students, including over 5,000 veterans.[112]

This increase in enrollment and the subsequent crowded conditions of the university engendered a massive expansion of the university. Acting president Cloide Everett Brehm proposed sizable construction and operating budgets to the Tennessee General Assembly. As a result of a 2 percent sales tax, Brehm received $6 million for construction and nearly $2.7 million for maintenance and operating costs for the school.[113]

Vanderbilt University civilian student enrollment dropped significantly during the war as young men were called to service; military contracts with the university, however, kept the enrollment up to prewar levels as military units such as the Army Air Force Reserve Corps, the Army Specialized Training Division, and the Navy Reserve utilized the campus facilities.[114]

Following the war's end, Vanderbilt experienced an onslaught of returning veterans anxious to utilize their GI benefits. As at UT, housing was the most critical problem, and Vanderbilt built temporary prefabricated houses and permanent concrete-block apartment buildings. The immediate postwar years at Vanderbilt witnessed expansion and addition of new departments and the reopening of the law school, which had closed during the war.[115]

Other Tennessee colleges experienced similar wartime and postwar enrollment patterns. East Tennessee State College in Johnson City had a 1941 enrollment of 253 men and 409 women; in 1943, the enrollment there had dropped to 43 men and 233 women. By 1946, ETSC's enrollment climbed back to prewar figures with a student population of 645. Memphis State College witnessed a sharp decline in enrollment from over 1,000 men and women in 1941 to 216 in 1943, even though there were several armed services groups on campus. Enrollment increased to 767 in 1946. Tennessee Agricultural and Industrial State College dropped from approximately 1,000 students in 1941 to less than 700 in 1943; by 1946, the black college expanded to 924 students.[116]

The returning veterans also reshaped the appearance of the landscape in Tennessee towns as their demand for housing greatly accelerated postwar suburbanization. In December 1945, Congress amended Title V of the Lanham Act, which authorized nearly $4 million in federal funding to provide reusable war housing. In 1946, Congress enacted legislation that established the Veterans Emergency Housing Program. This program provided assistance by offering mortgage insurance for privately built houses and encouraged the production of building materials and prefab-type houses.[117]

To implement the strategies of the VEHP, cities throughout the United States established local Mayors' Emergency Housing Committees. In 1946 and 1947, Memphis estimated that it needed 8,500 family dwellings, while Chattanooga and Knoxville requested nearly 8,000 dwellings and Nashville requested 3,600.[118]

To offset the housing demand, local governments and public funds provided temporary housing such as Quonset huts, barracks, trailers, and demountable dwelling units. While local construction firms were building houses in unprecedented numbers throughout Tennessee, communities converted war housing to civilian use. In Memphis, the housing authority described the housing shortage: "From box cars to finished apartment in ten weeks."[119]

Housing authorities predicted that approximately 80 percent of the new housing projects in 1947 would demand the utilization of undeveloped land. They also projected that a significant portion of the new veterans' housing would be assumed by large-scale developers.[120] Their predictions proved true as developers began dotting the raw landscape outside the major cities with subdivisions during the late 1940s and 1950s.

As evidenced by the immediate postwar years, Tennessee industry as well as its cities, suburbs, and universities experienced rapid growth explosions. As veterans returned home, they created an immense market for housing and educational services. Underlying potential race and gender problems would not surface until the late fifties and early sixties. Ecstatic that the war was over, most Tennesseans in the late 1940s were grateful that their home front had once again become home.

NOTES

1. George I. Whitlatch, "Industrial Tennessee During 1943," *The Tennessee Planner* 4 (Feb. 1944): 86.
2. George I. Whitlatch, "Industrial Tennessee in 1944," *The Tennessee Planner* 5 (Feb. 1945): 86, 87.
3. George I. Whitlatch, ed., "Tennessee Industrial Planning Newsletter," Industrial Development Division, Tennessee State Planning Commission, Feb. 1, 1946, 2, 3.
4. Leo Troy, "Distribution of Union Membership among the States 1939 and 1953," Occasional Paper 56, National Bureau of Economic Research, Inc. (1957): 4.
5. Labor Market Developments Report, Memphis Area, Tennessee, June 15, 1943, U.S. Employment Service, Record Group 183, National Archives, 33.
6. Labor Market Developments Report, Memphis, Tennessee, Dec. 1945, U.S. Employment Service, Record Group 183, National Archives, 6.
7. Memphis Report, June 15, 1943, 34; Memphis Report, Dec. 1945, 1.
8. Memphis Report, June 15, 1943, 33.
9. Area Employment Summary, Davidson County, Tennessee, May 1945, War Manpower Commission, Record Group 211, National Archives, Atlanta Regional Branch, 2, 3, 8.
10. Ibid., 3.
11. This figure included Rutherford and Davidson counties, ibid., 3, 6.
12. Ibid., 8, 9.
13. Labor Market Developments Report, Chattanooga Area, Tennessee, Dec. 15, 1943, War Manpower Commission, Record Group 211, National Archives, Atlanta Regional Branch, 29.
14. Larry Smith and Company, Inc., "An Economic Analysis of Chattanooga, Book II, Basic Economic Trends," Dec. 10, 1968, table 1.
15. Tennessee Unemployment Compensation Division, Survey of the Employment Situation in the Knoxville Area, Tennessee, May 9, 1941, Bureau of Employment Security, Record Group 183, National Archives, Part 1:1 ,3, 4.
16. Ibid., Part 7:1.
17. Ibid., Part 8:2.
18. Ibid., Part 1: 1.

19. Michael J. McDonald and William Bruce Wheeler, *Knoxville Tennessee: Continuity and Change in an Appalachian City* (Knoxville, 1983), 61–62.

20. Tennessee Unemployment Compensation, Survey, Part 1:5.

21. Office of Defense, Health, and Welfare Service, Region VII, Atlanta, Georgia, and Tennessee Valley Authority, Knoxville, Tennessee, Report on Knoxville-Alcoa, Tennessee Defense Area, Nov. 16, 1942, War Manpower Commission, Record Group 211. National Archives, Atlanta Regional Branch, 10, 11.

22. Margaret Ripley Wolfe, *Kingsport, Tennessee: A Planned American City* (Lexington, Ky., 1987), 140.

23. Ibid., 139–42.

24. Ibid., 143–45.

25. Labor Market Developments Report, Kingsport Area, Tennessee, Oct. 15, 1943, War Manpower Commission, Record Group 211, National Archives, Atlanta Regional Branch, 28.

26. Wolfe, *Kingsport,* 146, 147.

27. George I. Whitlatch, "Industrial Tennessee in 1945," *The Tennessee Planner* 9 (Feb. 1946): 110, 111.

28. Charles W. Johnson and Charles O. Jackson, *City Behind a Fence* (Knoxville, 1981), xviii–xx, 169. The Oak Ridge site also included a pilot plant that manufactured small amounts of plutonium, although it was primarily produced at Hanford, Washington.

29. *Tennessee Planner,* Feb. 1944, 86.

30. George F. Gant, Annual Report of the Tennessee Valley Authority, Dec. 16, 1946, 2, 3.

31. Hammer and Company Associates, "The Economy of Metropolitan Knoxville," prepared for the Metropolitan Planning Commission of Knoxville and Knox County, Nov. 1962, 78.

32. George I. Whitlatch, ed., "Tennessee Industrial Planning Newsletter," Industrial Development Division, Tennessee State Planning Commission, Oct. 1, 1946, 1, 7.

33. Hammer, "Knoxville," 83, 84.

34. Ibid., 84.

35. "There Won't Be Any Letdown in Memphis When It's Over," A Series of Articles Describing the Actual Plans of Memphis Industries, *Memphis Press-Scimitar,* n.d., circa 1943, War Manpower Commission, Record Group 211, National Archives, Atlanta Regional Branch, introduction.

36. Hammer, Greene, Siler and Associates, Economic Consultants, Washington-Atlanta, "The Economy of Metropolitan Memphis," prepared for Memphis and Shelby County Planning Commission, Sept. 1965.

37. Harland Bartholomew and Associates, "A Report Upon the Comprehensive Plan, Memphis, Tennessee," prepared for the Board of Commissioners, Dec. 1955, 2.

38. Bartholomew, "Memphis," 2–4.

39. Memphis and Shelby County Planning Commission, "Population Study," Mar. 1965, 19.

40. Area Employment Summary, Davidson County, May 1945, 15–18.

41. Bureau of the Census, *Census of Population: 1950,* Vol. 2, Pt. 42, Tennessee (Washington, 1952), 42–10.
42. Labor Market Development Reports, Knoxville Labor Market Area, Jan. 1947, Record Group 183, Bureau of Employment Security, 1.
43. Hammer, "Knoxville," i–iii.
44. George I. Whitlatch, "Industrial Tennessee in 1946," *Tennessee Planner* 7 (Feb. 1947): 111, 112.
45. Ibid., 113.
46. Industrial Development Staff, Tennessee State Planning Commission, "Industrial Tennessee in 1947," *Tennessee Planner* 8 (Feb. 1948): 108.
47. Industrial Development Division, "Industrial Tennessee in 1948," *Tennessee Planner 9* (Feb. 1948): 72.
48. Robert S. Hutchison, "Migration and Industrial Development in Tennessee," a Report to the Industrial Development and Migration Subcommittee of the Tennessee Legislative Council, Oct. 1, 1958, 8, 40.
49. Ibid., 40, 41.
50. Mary G. Currence, ed., *Tennessee Statistical Abstract 1971* Center for Business and Economic Research, Univ. of Tennessee, Knoxville, 5.
51. Ibid., 71.
52. Ibid., 385, 386.
53. U.S. Dept. of Labor, Women's Bureau, "Women's Wages in Wartime," Nov. 1944, War Manpower Commission, Record Group 211, National Archives, Washington, 2.
54. Research and Statistics Section, War Manpower Commission, United States employment Service, "Employment Trend of Women in Identical ES-270 Establishments in Tennessee During the Period September 1942–March 1944," Oct. 27, 1943, War Manpower Commission, Record Group 211, National Archives, Atlanta Regional Branch, 1.
55. Report, Memphis, July 1945, 9, 10.
56. Davidson County, May 1945, 4.
57. Ibid.
58. Labor Market Developments Report for Knoxville Area Tennessee, Aug. 15, 1943, Bureau of Employment Security, Record Group 183, National Archives, 18.
59. *Knoxville News-Sentinel,* Aug. 19, 1945.
60. Labor Market Developments Report for Knoxville Area Tennessee, Apr. 15, 1943, Bureau of Employment Security, Record Group 183, National Archives, 4.
61. Seniority Roster, Robertshaw Controls (Fulton Sylphon), 1944, made available to the author by the personnel department; George Ogdin interview with author, Knoxville, Oct. 21, 1987.
62. Manning Table-Certificate of Acceptance, Rohm and Haas Company, Apr. 21, 1943, War Manpower Commission, Record Group 211, National Archives, passim.
63. Labor Market Report, Knoxville, Apr. 15, 1943, 23.
64. Demand-Supply Supplement for Knoxville Labor Market Area, Sept. 1944, Bureau of Employment Security, Record Group 183 National Archives, 10.

65. Labor Market Developments Report for Knoxville Area Tennessee, Dec. 15, 1943, Bureau of Employment Security Record Group 183, National Archives, 1.
66. Ibid., 4.
67. *News-Sentinel*, May 19, 1943.
68. *News-Sentinel*, June 25, 1944, sec. A.
69. Ibid.
70. Demand-Supply Supplement, Knoxville Labor Market Area, Sept. 1944, Bureau of Employment Security, Record Group 183 National Archives, 10.
71. *News-Sentinel*, Sept. 20 and Oct. 15, 1944.
72. Demand-Supply Supplement, Knoxville Labor Market Area, Mar. 1945, Bureau of Employment Security, Record Group 183 National Archives, 11.
73. Labor Market Developments Report, Knoxville Labor Market Area, Sept. 1945, Bureau of Employment Security, Record Group 183, National Archives, 1.
74. Labor Market Survey Reports, n.d., Bureau of Employment Security, Record Group 183, National Archives, 2.
75. National Manpower Council, *Womanpower* (New York, 1957), 161.
76. Labor Market Report, Chattanooga Area, Dec. 15, 1943, 17, 19.
77. Ibid., 17, 18.
78. Karen Anderson, *Wartime Women: Sex Role, Family Relations, and the Status of Women During World War II* (Westport Conn., 1981), 123; Conference on Day Care of Children of Working Mothers Called by WPA in Washington, July 1, 1942, Women's Bureau, Record Group 86, National Archives 1, 2.
79. Tennessee State Dept. of Education, General Outline of Proposed State Program for Services to Children of Working Mothers, Office of Community War Services, Record Group 215, National Archives, 1.
80. Labor Market Report, Memphis, June 15, 1943, 29.
81. Labor Market Report, Nashville, Dec. 15, 1943, 23.
82. *News-Sentinel*, June 27, 1943, sec. C.
83. Knoxville City Schools Dept. of Child Care Facilities, Operating Child Care Units, Office of Community War Services, Record Group 215, National Archives.
84. *News-Sentinel*, May 15, 1943.
85. Labor Report, Chattanooga, Dec. 15, 1943, 24.
86. Anderson, *Wartime Women*, 146.
87. Census, 1950, 42–282.
88. Hutchison, "Migration" 9.
89. Ibid., 22.
90. Ibid., 15.
91. Bureau of the Census, *Characteristics of the Population, Tennessee, 1940* (Washington 1940), 608, 707, 716, 725; Census, 1950, Tennessee, 42–62, 42–63.
92. Census, 1940, 714, 716.
93. Ibid., 716.
94. Labor Report, Memphis, June 15, 1943, 24, 25. Fisher Memphis Aircraft Division, which employed approximately 7,000 workers, removed all race records from their files subsequent to November 1942.
95. Census, 1940, 716; Census, 1950, 42–294.
96. Census, 1940, 725.

97. Labor Market Report, Nashville, June 15, 1943, 19.
98. Labor Market Report, Nashville, Dec. 15, 1943, 18.
99. Census, 1950, 42–295.
100. Census, 1940, 707.
101. *News-Sentinel,* May 14, 1943.
102. Census, 1950, 42–293.
103. Census, 1940, 698.
104. Census, 1950, 42–292.
105. Jean Noland, "Tennessee Program for Veterans' Assistance," *Tennessee Planner,* 5 (Oct. 1944): 15.
106. Ibid.
107. Ibid., 16–19.
108. "A Summary of Selected 1945 Legislation in Tennessee," *Tennessee Planner* (Apr. 1945): 113, 114.
109. Ibid., 113.
110. James Riley Montgomery, Stanley J. Folmsbee, and Lee Seifert Greene, *To Foster Knowledge: A History of The University of Tennessee. 1794–1970* (Knoxville, 1984), 202.
111. Marie S. Brake, interview with author, July 6, 1991.
112. Montgomery, *To Foster Knowledge,* 212.
113. Ibid., 216, 217.
114. Paul K. Conkin, *Gone with the Ivy: A Biography of Vanderbilt University* (Knoxville, 1985), 417–20.
115. Ibid., 436–38.
116. Tennessee State Committee on Postwar Education of the Southern Association of Colleges and Secondary Schools, "Postwar Higher Education in Tennessee," Sept. 1944, 10, 18, 38; "Public Education in Tennessee: A Study of Tennessee's Program of Public Education and Suggestions for Continuing its Development," 1945, 430.
117. E. Bruce Wedge, "Veterans Housing and Community Planning," *Tennessee Planner* 7 (Feb. 1947): 104, 106.
118. Ibid., 104,105.
119. Ibid., 106, 107.
120. Ibid., 108.

"WE SHALL OVERCOME": TENNESSEE AND THE CIVIL RIGHTS MOVEMENT

■ CYNTHIA G. FLEMING

■

■ *Editor's Note:* Fleming chronicles the nationally important role
played by Tennesseans, both famous and those more anonymous,
in the struggle for civil and political rights during the twentieth
■ century. Tennessee was an important battleground in this battle
for equality. Through institutions like the Highlander School and
■ leaders from the Nashville student movement, such as Diane
Nash and John Lewis, the state "made invaluable contributions to
■ the civil rights movement of the 1960s." Tennesseans of both
races responded in a "unique," moderate fashion to the movement
■ and this response, according to Fleming, was "rooted in the state's
unusual history of slavery and race relations."

    During the decade of the 1960s, African Americans all over the South
challenged the system of segregation that had oppressed them since the end
of the previous century. This system had disfranchised them politically, enslaved them economically, and circumscribed their educational aspirations.
Conversely, white political power and economic prosperity in the region had
been built on this relentless restriction of black lives. There had been sporadic attempts throughout the early twentieth century by African Americans
who were determined to change this system. But black challenges to segregation in the 1960s were different from these earlier attempts because of the
sheer numbers of people challenging the system, and because the federal government had finally begun to support black rights. Black and white southerners reacted to this challenge in a variety of ways.

    Tennessee's response to the civil rights movement and the forces it un-
leashed is unique among the states of the old Confederacy. While residents'
responses varied widely from one community to the next, the unique nature

of these responses is rooted in the state's unusual history of slavery and race relations. In the first half of the nineteenth century, many East Tennesseans expressed their opposition to the institution of slavery. Long before the advent of militant abolitionism, East Tennessee had been a hotbed of anti-slavery sentiment. Through the decade of the 1820s, one-fifth of all anti-slavery societies were located in East Tennessee, while the number of residents who belonged to these societies constituted almost one-sixth of the total membership of anti-slavery societies throughout the country.[1] At the same time, many white East Tennesseans who did own slaves still had serious reservations about the institution. Consequently, as the Civil War approached, the majority of East Tennessee slaveholders placed their loyalty to the Union first. On the other hand, slaveholders in the middle and western regions of the state were sympathetic to the Confederacy. Thus, the state's white residents were plagued with irreconcilable interests on the eve of the Civil War. This wide chasm that separated white Tennesseans set the stage for the state's unique Civil War and Reconstruction experience.

In this highly charged atmosphere, divided white residents and concerned black ones looked on with mixed emotions as the Tennessee General Assembly passed an ordinance declaring the state's independence and dissolving the federal relations between the state of Tennessee and the United States of America.[2] The issuance of this proclamation ostensibly committed the state to an anti-Union position. Yet, white East Tennesseans were prepared to defy the ordinance of secession and the force of the Confederate Army that supported it; they remained absolutely loyal to the Union. White easterners refused to be persuaded, cajoled, or even forced into supporting a slavocracy that they had long viewed with suspicion and dislike.

Because of the widespread and tenacious opposition to secession that existed within her borders, Tennessee was the only Confederate state that could muster enough loyal voters before the end of the war to inaugurate a new state government. Accordingly, in January 1865, Tennessee's loyal white citizens convened to establish a new state government. But the establishment of this new state government was accomplished in an atmosphere of intense hostility and animosity. The state's black residents were caught in the middle of this hostility that was so pronounced that it reached the attention of the United States government. In 1866, the Thirty-ninth Congress appointed the Joint Committee on Reconstruction to investigate conditions in the former Confederate states. General Clinton B. Fisk, commissioner of the Freedmen's Bureau for Kentucky and Tennessee, reported: "Tennessee is peculiar. In no other state do you find the same sort of opposition [to the freedmen] as in Tennessee."[3] In this atmosphere of intense antagonism and suspicion, Tennessee's black residents evinced great concern about their new status as free people. As early as 1865, a group of African Americans met in the African Methodist Episcopal Church in Nashville to protest the General Assembly's denial of their rights: "The government has asked the colored man to fight for its preservation and gladly has he done it. It can afford to trust him with a vote as safely as it trusted him with a bayonet. Will you declare in your revised constitution that a pardoned traitor may appear in court and his testimony be heard, but that no colored loyalist shall be believed even upon oath? If this should be so, then will our last state be worse than our first, and we can look for no relief on this side of the grave."[4]

The right to vote was granted to black Tennesseans in 1867 only after they had engaged in additional vigorous agitation, culminating in a second state convention of colored citizens and the organization of the State Equal Rights League.[5] William G. "Parson" Brownlow, Tennessee's newly elected Reconstruction governor, lent his support to black demands in an address before the state legislature in November 1866. Brownlow reasoned that "the time has come when it is proper and right to confer the ballot upon the colored man."[6] The demands of black Tennesseans for the franchise were strengthened not only by Governor Brownlow's support, but by important changes in Washington as well. In the same year that black Tennesseans received the right to vote, a Republican Congress passed the First Reconstruction Act over the veto of President Andrew Johnson. Tennessee legislators who wanted to ensure the unconditional readmission of their state to the Union were undoubtedly sensitive to this change in federal policy. Tennessee thus became only the second state outside of New England to extend the franchise to African Americans.

The effectiveness of black bids for political power in postwar Tennessee depended to a considerable extent upon black numerical strength. An assessment of this strength reveals the lack of a statewide numerical majority. In 1860, Tennessee's 283,019 black residents constituted only 25.5 percent of the state's total population of 1,109,801.[7] Ten years later, 322,331 black Tennesseans comprised 25.6 percent of the state's total population of 1,258,520.[8] Clearly, the black population did not constitute a statewide numerical majority, but black residents did comprise a large block of the electorate in several western counties. This demographic reality reflected the concentration of slavery in West Tennessee prior to the Civil War. Of a total of ninety-six Tennessee counties, twenty were over 25 percent black. Of those twenty, ten were over 40 percent black, and of those ten, black citizens held a clear majority in two counties, Fayette and Haywood. Almost one hundred years later, Fayette County would be the scene of one of the first mass voter registration campaigns among black southerners that would instigate violent white repression.

Some Tennessee communities tolerated black political activity. But in other areas black efforts to participate in the political process aroused white anger. Into that atmosphere of intolerance the Ku Klux Klan was born in 1865 in Pulaski, in Giles County. The invisible empire spread like wildfire among discontented native white Tennesseans. Members of the Klan perpetrated all manner of fiendish cruelties against black Tennesseans who attempted to exercise their right to vote or any of their other new prerogatives as free people. The Klansmen were active in all areas of the state, but they were particularly active in those counties with a large concentration of black inhabitants.

This statewide reign of terror was a matter of concern to the Tennessee General Assembly. In an extra session of the legislature in 1868, the Joint Military Committee reported that several witnesses testified about the existence of an organization of armed men who wore disguises. The committee concluded that this organization devoted itself to persecuting black Tennesseans by stealing their firearms, and hanging, whipping, and shooting them. Such incidents reportedly occurred throughout Middle and West Tennessee, and in some portions of East Tennessee. Black residents of Maury, Lincoln, Giles, Marshall, Obion, Hardeman, Fayette, and Gibson counties were plagued by an excessive amount of this Klan violence.[9] The committee report provided further insight into the nature of Klan activities: "Your committee also find[s] that there has been a determined effort, and still is a determined purpose, all over Middle and West Tennessee, to keep colored men [from] the Polls."[10]

Thus, it seemed that serious disagreements over slavery in antebellum Tennessee led to the application of very uneven policies governing the freedmen in postbellum Tennessee. This postwar pattern of racist brutality continued and even accelerated as the nineteenth century drew to a close. In response, African American leaders across the country publicly condemned the barbaric and frequent lynchings of their people. One of the strongest voices of condemnation was that of Ida B. Wells. Wells, a black Memphis resident, activist, and newspaper editor, became well known during the late nineteenth century for her vigorous anti-lynching crusade. Yet, even as many white officials and citizens regularly committed acts of repression designed to frighten and subordinate the state's black residents after the Civil War, others continued to sympathize with the plight of black Tennesseans through the end of the nineteenth and on into the twentieth century. The existence of such sympathy facilitated sporadic attempts at interracial cooperation through the first part of the twentieth century. One of those attempts resulted in the establishment of the Highlander Folk School, which came to have an enormous impact on the establishment and direction of the black civil rights struggle both inside and outside the state's borders. Founded by Myles Horton in Grundy County in 1932, the school originally championed the cause of organized labor.[11]

Horton tried to attract African American workers to the school with very limited success before 1944. But finally in that year, the school organized a workshop for the United Auto Workers that included both black and white employees. Horton recognized the workshop's significance when he commented, "This session was historic because, for the first time, Negro and White delegates studied, worked and played together at a southern school."[12] Horton had been concerned about the racial injustice he witnessed in his region for some time. As more black workers came to Highlander for training sessions, Horton's focus increasingly shifted to the issue of race. Because

Ida B. Wells portrait by Larry Walker, 1994. Tennessee Historical Society Collection, Tennessee State Museum, Photograph by June Dorman.

of this shift, the school decided to host a conference in the early 1950s to explore the potential problems that would arise should the Supreme Court rule to end segregation. From then on, the school would hold numerous workshops for civil rights activists. Some of the most famous people in the civil rights struggle, like Martin Luther King, Jr., Rosa Parks, Bernard Lafayette, Jr., Marion Barry, James Bevel, John Lewis, Diane Nash, and Julian Bond, participated in Highlander training sessions at one time or another.

In fact, the movement's anthem "We Shall Overcome" had its roots in the Baptist church and the labor movement. Over the years, the song had become a standard that was sung by participants in Highlander's workshops for labor organizers.[13] But "We Shall Overcome" really came to be more closely identified with the civil rights movement after Guy Carawan, a musician of the protest tradition who was closely associated with the school, began to teach it at Highlander workshops and civil rights rallies.[14] The song inspired many, especially the student activists, who would begin singing it during their demonstrations and rallies. "We Shall Overcome" became synonymous with the civil rights struggle. While Highlander exerted a profound influence on the national civil rights movement, its interracial activities aroused hostility among local residents and limited its impact within Tennessee.

Other efforts at interracial cooperation in the state were more successful in creating a sympathetic atmosphere. President Fayette McKenzie of Fisk University in Nashville founded the Triangle of Peace in 1918. This group was designed to facilitate dialogue between African Americans and white Tennesseans who were concerned about improving race relations in their community. Later, Fisk University founded a Race Relations Institute to carry on the Triangle's work. Well-known sociologist Charles S. Johnson, who was a member of the Fisk faculty, started the institute in 1944.[15] Ironically, one of the speakers who addressed the Institute's members was a young Nashville politician named Ben West. West, who would later serve as Nashville's mayor during the sit-ins, advised "Negroes to take a more active part in their government through political action, and help elect the officials that will be good." He listed as local improvements the equalization of teacher pay, employment of black police, and the election of election officials by wards.[16]

Another effort to foster interracial cooperation was born on the Knoxville College campus. Mrs. Frankie Adams, who graduated from Knoxville College in 1925, recalls the circumstances that produced this interracial effort: "There was one little organization which . . . grew out of this YMCA thing [on the Knoxville College campus] called the Interracial Commission which the YW and YMCA organized between Maryville College up at Maryville,

Tennessee, and the University of Tennessee at Knoxville, and Knoxville College. And so we all got together as a group every so often. . . . Professor Carey [of Knoxville College] was more or less the counselor or supervisor of that little nucleus group on race relations."[17] The existence of urban efforts like these to facilitate interracial dialogue and foster interracial cooperation helped to lay the foundation for compromise and acceptance later.

On May 17, 1954, the United States Supreme Court ruled in *Brown v. Board of Education of Topeka, Kansas* that segregated schools were unconstitutional. The court's decree sent shock waves across the South. Many southern politicians reacted quickly and declared that they would never allow desegregated schools in their community. They urged fellow white southerners to defy the court's decree. On March 12, 1956, southern congressmen introduced a "Declaration of Constitutional Principles" into both houses of Congress that pledged open defiance of the *Brown* decision. Some 101 southern congressmen signed the document, including 8 of Tennessee's 11 congressmen. However, the 3 who refused to sign were very influential indeed. Those three holdouts included both of the state's U.S. Senators, Albert Gore, Sr., and Estes Kefauver, and the House Democratic Whip, J. Percy Priest.[18]

Throughout Tennessee, many public officials advised their constituents to obey *Brown* because it was the law of the land, but they rarely recommended enthusiastic acquiescence. The stoic acceptance of Mayor Ben West is typical of the attitude displayed by many. As his city faced the very real possibility of school integration, segregationists challenged West to defy the Supreme Court's decree. West refused. He "told a group of segregationists they would have to take their protests against Nashville's integration to Congress. He said he was 'sworn to uphold the law of the land.'"[19]

Tennessee's governor also refused to condemn the *Brown* decision. Even though Governor Frank Clement was facing a reelection campaign, he refused to use defiance to *Brown* as a campaign issue. On the contrary, he urged moderation: "I must point out it is a decision handed down by a judicial body which we, the American people, under our Constitution and law recognize as supreme in matters of interpreting the law of the land." But, while Clement counseled his constituents to respect the decision, he reassured them by explaining: "Inasmuch as no final decree had been entered, and in view of the fact that the court has invited participation by the states in further deliberation, no change is anticipated in our school system in the near future."[20]

Clement's plea for respect of the court's decision was faintly echoed by the state adjutant general, Major General Joe W. Henry, Jr. Henry was much more critical than the governor of the court's decision. In his estimation, the

Brown decision "thrust sin upon the South." He further charged that the Supreme Court's decree "has done more to retard race relations" than any other official act in this nation's history. But, despite these feelings, Henry still insisted that he would rather "have my two boys go to an integrated school than to have the belief forced upon them that law and order can be supplanted by mob rule."[21]

The resolve of state officials to uphold the law regardless of their personal beliefs would soon be put to a very severe test in a most unlikely place. As early as 1951, three years before the *Brown* decision, five black high school students had petitioned the federal district court in their region to allow them to attend their neighborhood high school in Clinton, Tennessee, a small town of just under four thousand residents in Anderson County. For many years, the few black high school students in Clinton had been bused eighteen miles to Knoxville to attend Austin High School, the lone black high school in Knox County. Federal judge Robert Taylor originally denied the students' petition based on the segregation provision in the Tennessee state constitution. After the U.S. Supreme Court ruled in the *Brown* case, however, the United States Circuit Court of Appeals sent the case back to Taylor. Taylor eventually ruled that Clinton High School should be desegregated.[22] During the summer of 1956, as Clinton began to prepare for the inevitable, segregationists began to rally their supporters. At the same time, an itinerant segregationist, John Kasper, came to town and sought to organize local dissent. Although Kasper was arrested just before school opened, some of his supporters were on hand to protest when the first black students registered for classes. In the meantime, the local weekly newspaper appealed for calm. *Clinton Courier-News* editor Horace V. Wells advised his readers: "We have never heard anyone in Clinton say he wanted integration of students in the schools, but we have heard a great many of the people say: "'We believe in the law. We will obey the ruling of the court. We have no other lawful choice.'"[23]

The first few days of class were uneventful. Things took a dramatic turn for the worse during the long Labor Day weekend when Asa Carter, president of the North Alabama White Citizens' Council, came to town to rally support among local segregationists. Carter gave a defiant speech denouncing school integration to a large and enthusiastic crowd on the courthouse square. Although Carter left town immediately after his speech, the audience did not disperse and quickly became an unruly mob. Soon, the mob began to attack black passersby. Clinton's mayor, the board of aldermen, and the sheriff feared that the situation was out of control, and they appealed to Governor Clement for assistance. Clement immediately sent one hundred state troopers to Clinton, and followed this action by sending the National Guard. The governor's quick action averted a crisis and restored order. The rest of the 1956–57 school year passed without incident. Clement's action in this crisis is in stark contrast to the actions of Governor Orval Faubus in neighboring Arkansas during Little Rock's Central High School crisis. Yet, even though it seemed that the Clinton community was adjusting to school integration, extremists bombed Clinton High School the next year in 1958.

Nashville also suffered its share of unrest as it sought to integrate its schools. For some time after the *Brown* decision, city officials had been studying the question of school desegregation in their community. But the action of Nashville African Americans forced officials to stop studying and start planning for school desegregation. In September 1955, Alfred Z. Kelley, a Nashville barber and father of high school student Robert Kelley, filed a class action suit, *Robert W. Kelley, et. al. v. Board of Education of Nashville,* demanding open admission to Nashville's schools, irrespective of race.[24] When the court ruled in favor of the plaintiffs and ordered the city to formulate a desegregation plan, the board of education responded by proposing what became known as the "Nashville Plan." According to its terms, only one grade a year would be desegregated, starting with the first grade in 1957. Another provision of this plan provided those opposed to integration with a very large loophole. This provision stipulated that any student could transfer out of a school if parents submitted a written request and the student attended a school where a different race predominated.[25] The plan's emphasis on gradualism disturbed many black parents.

As the beginning of the 1957 fall semester approached, Nashville held its collective breath as everyone wondered what the children would face. Some 115 black first-graders were eligible to enter Nashville's white schools that fall. Because the parents of many of these black children were harassed and threatened, ninety-six families took advantage of the transfer provision in the Nashville plan. That left only nineteen black first-graders to begin integrating Nashville's public schools.[26] As school began, segregationists stepped up their attempts to intimidate all of those involved in the integration process. There were "threats to principals and other officials of the integrated schools." Parents were also threatened "if they send their children to school." Mass meetings were held by "an almost uncontrollable mob of robbed [*sic*] Ku Klux Klansmen on school grounds."[27] Even after school began, black parents and children were still harassed. "At least three of the parents were warned by anonymous callers yesterday that they and their children would be harmed unless the youngsters were withdrawn from the white schools." These black Nashvillians refused to be dissuaded. They "vowed today they would keep their youngsters enrolled despite telephoned threats of physical violence."[28] During the first few days of the semester, as black students began to attend previously all-white schools, they were often met with small but vocal white mobs shouting racial epithets. Mayor Ben West instructed the city's police force to keep the peace and protect the right of these black students to attend class.

On the evening of September 9, 1957, the tenuous calm exploded when one of the newly integrated elementary schools, Hattie Cotton, was rocked by a bomb blast that completely demolished one wing of the school.[29] Many Nashvillians were horrified. They never thought anything like this could possibly happen in their community. The bombing particularly distressed students at Hattie Cotton. Ten-year-old Carrie Wofford exclaimed, "It's awful. . . . I wish I was back in school."[30] One of Carrie's classmates, Jimmy Travis, agreed with her, saying, "I'm sorry, I wish I was back in school."[31] Still another Hattie Cotton student, Patricia Baker, was just adjusting to having a black girl in her class. That adjustment was difficult enough without having to cope with the bombing of her school. After thinking about both of these important events, Patricia concluded: "It wasn't the colored girl's fault."[32]

After the explosion, Mayor West and city officials worked hard to restore calm in their community and public confidence in the schools. Eventually, calm was restored, but critics charged that the slow implementation of school integration in Nashville was a failure. Over a decade after Nashville's first attempts to integrate its public schools, one contemporary observer commented, "On paper, Nashville now has less racial isolation in its schools than all but a handful of American cities. But, in fact, it is victimized by a desegregation plan that is less comprehensive and less equitable than it should have been, by a school hierarchy that has become resigned to a mechanical shifting of bodies but not to the much larger task of changing attitudes."[33]

The Nashville Plan generated a great deal of black dissatisfaction. Accordingly, Z. Alexander Looby and Avon Williams, two prominent black Nashville attorneys, filed suit in federal court. The Sixth Circuit Court of Appeals ruled in favor of the Nashville Plan, and when Looby and Williams tried to appeal the case, the U.S. Supreme Court refused to hear it. Many other communities across the state and across the South adopted the plan, even though it had only limited success in Nashville.[34] The plan generated little open defiance and little overt trouble, but also little commitment to real substantive change.

As school systems across the state wrestled with desegregation plans, the state's major tax-supported university, the University of Tennessee at Knoxville, was soon confronted with its own desegregation challenge. Some years previously, in 1952, the university had quietly desegregated its graduate school when Gene Mitchell Gray had been admitted. A few years later, a number of southeastern states, including Tennessee, faced legal challenges by black undergraduates seeking admission to tax-supported, but segregated, universities. One of the first universities to face that challenge is located in Alabama just south of Tennessee. February 3, 1956, was the first day of class for black undergraduate Autherine Lucy, who became the first black student ever to enroll at the University of Alabama. Lucy soon found that she was in for a very rough time. While she sat in class, an angry mob gathered on campus. She could hear the mob outside yelling, "Let's kill her, let's kill her."[35] Lucy was convinced that the mob meant business, and she clearly remembered her thoughts at the time:

> I was very much afraid at this time. I sat there and tried to compose myself, and naturally the next thing that I thought of doing was saying a prayer. . . . I can remember in this prayer that I asked to be able to see the time when I would be able to complete my work on the campus, but that if it was not the will of God that I do this, that he give me the courage to accept the fact that I would lose my life there, and to help me accept it, because this was a time when I felt then that I might not get out of it really alive. Of course, I wanted to, but I wanted the courage to accept death at that point if it had to be that way.[36]

Shortly after this, Autherine Lucy was expelled—permanently.

A few years later, in 1963, two black students, Vivian Malone and James Hood, again attempted to integrate the University of Alabama. By this time things were a little better. But Vivian Malone remembered that she was subjected to harassment. As she put it, "I would walk across the campus to the Commerce Department, and some of the students would say: 'Here comes our nigger,' and they'd laugh. But I was never physically hurt." Malone continued, "Of course, I did have twenty-four-hour protection."[37] Hamilton Holmes and Charlayne Hunter were the first black students to attend the University of Georgia. Holmes and Hunter also suffered their share of harassment. Ironically, they started school at Georgia on the same day that

Theotis Robinson became the first black undergraduate to attend the University of Tennessee.

Robinson, a native Knoxvillian, vividly remembers the circumstances surrounding his attempts to register at the University of Tennessee. He graduated from Austin High School in the spring of 1960, just as some students in the community were beginning sit-ins to desegregate downtown lunch counters. Theotis became involved in these sit-ins, which were conducted by a community organization called the Associated Council for Full Citizenship. While the sit-ins continued, the council decided to place an ad in the *Knoxville News-Sentinel* detailing the grievances of local African Americans. The list of grievances included discrimination in public facilities, employment discrimination, and the University of Tennessee's refusal to admit black undergraduates.[38] Robinson remembers that when he read the ad he immediately got an idea. "That Sunday evening as I sat there reading this list of items and I came down to this one (UT's discrimination). [I] said, 'Well here's one I can deal with.'"[39] Robinson wanted to major in political science. He had already received a scholarship to attend Knoxville College, a private black college, but the school did not offer a major in political science.

Prompted by the ad in the *News-Sentinel,* Theotis Robinson decided that he would apply to the University of Tennessee. He recalls, "I sat there at our dinner table and wrote a letter to the university requesting that I be admitted as an incoming freshman to U.T. in September." Robinson was particularly careful not to mention his race in this letter of interest. As he put it, "I did not mention race, I did not mention which high school I had graduated from. The neighborhood in which I lived was in transition, so that there were black families and white families living within the immediate blocks surrounding where I lived."[40] Regardless of Robinson's efforts, the university quickly became aware of his race. Within ten days, he received a reply that unequivocally refused to consider him as a candidate for admission because "the university did not admit Negroes to the undergraduate school."[41] Robinson speculates that the university had probably begun screening applicants on the basis of race since so many southern universities were beginning to receive inquiries from black students.

Robinson's letter assured him that the university would be willing to answer any questions that he might have about the school's admissions policy. He immediately called and requested a meeting with school officials. Accordingly, two university admissions officers met with Robinson and his parents. These school officials assured the Robinson family that they were powerless to change school policy, but they could arrange a meeting with Andrew Holt, the university president, if the Robinsons wanted to pursue the matter. Robinson and his parents agreed, but in their meeting with Holt, he merely echoed the sentiments expressed by his admissions officers. He explained that only the board of trustees could change the school's admissions policies. The Robinsons urged Holt to consult the board. Theotis clearly remembers Holt's response: "He explained to us that he could not guarantee what the outcome would be because he could not speak for the board. We told him we understood that but that he and the board should understand that if they did not act on my request in an affirmative manner that they could expect that a law suit would be filed against the University of Tennessee to force the desegregation of U.T."[42]

In November, the university board changed its policy, and Theotis, along with two other black students, became the first black undergraduates to attend the University of Tennessee. Robinson remembers that when he and the others first started attending classes in January 1961, the campus remained quite calm. There were "no problems." Although Robinson never saw any evidence of efforts made by school officials to provide protection for him and the others, he remarks, "In hindsight I can imagine that there had been long and extensive discussions beginning with security. . . . I never saw any sign of security, but, then, that's when security is at its best." Theotis remembers never having any real trouble on campus. As he put it, "It was an easy transition for me."[43] Theotis Robinson did not board on campus, but lived at home. He is convinced that had he lived in a dormitory, he would have encountered some real unpleasantness.

Avon Rollins was another early black undergraduate at the University of Tennessee. He began classes in September 1961. Rollins remembers experiencing a few unpleasant racial incidents, but he never sensed any serious danger. According to Rollins, one of the most serious annoyances he faced was the existence of segregated restaurants and coffee shops around campus. The only place black students could eat was at Rafters, a restaurant in the University Center. In response to this situation, an integrated group of students formed an organization called Students for Equal Treatment (SET). SET conducted sit-ins at various businesses surrounding the campus. In a short time, campus-area eating establishments desegregated their facilities.[44]

Clearly, desegregation at the University of Tennessee was accomplished much more easily than at the major tax-supported universities of some neighboring states like Alabama, Georgia, and Mississippi. Once again, it seemed that, regardless of their own private convictions, the state's public officials refused to defy Supreme Court mandated school integration on any level.

School integration was a key goal of the early civil rights movement in Tennessee and throughout the South. Two other movement goals that were equally important, though, were the desegregation of public facilities and the registration of black voters. Ever since the latter part of the nineteenth century, black voters all over the South had been routinely and regularly disfranchised. Grandfather clauses, poll taxes, literacy tests, and understanding clauses were just some of the methods used by white southerners who were determined to keep black citizens from the polls. And, if all else failed, there was always the threat of physical violence and economic intimidation.

Yet, there were exceptions to this general southern hostility to black voting, and a number of those exceptions were found in Tennessee. Indeed, voting privileges were quite liberal in the state's larger cities. In Knoxville, for example, African Americans were never prohibited from voting. Of course, it is important to add that the city's black residents constituted only 7.5 percent of Knoxville's total population in 1960.[45] Furthermore, the gerrymandering by city officials effectively neutralized the voting strength of this small group of black residents. In Memphis and Nashville, black voting rights had been restricted. But by the 1940s and 1950s, African Americans in these communities had begun to organize voter registration drives. In some cases, white public officials actually took steps to facilitate these drives. Davidson County officials, for example, discontinued the poll tax as early as 1941.[46] The state officially repealed the poll tax in 1953, well in advance of federal civil rights legislation, including the voting rights act of 1965 and the adoption of the Twenty-fourth Amendment.[47] Because of this tolerant atmosphere on the eve of the civil rights movement, Tennessee had the distinction of granting the right to vote to more of its black citizens than any other southern state. By 1958, some 62.7 percent of all eligible black voters were registered in the state of Tennessee.[48]

However, two glaring exceptions existed to this generally sanguine picture: Haywood and Fayette Counties. Both had large black populations and troubled racial histories. The Justice Department under the Eisenhower administration singled out these counties and took legal action forcing them to grant black access to the franchise.[49] Emboldened by federal support, scores of black residents, many of whom were sharecroppers, attempted to register to vote.[50] Local officials reacted swiftly and ruthlessly. People were threatened with economic and physical reprisals. Local merchants refused to extend credit, and bankers mysteriously started calling in loans. In short, the local chapter of the White Citizens' Council declared war on black residents attempting to register to vote. From June 1959, when the first black residents attempted to register, until well into 1960, some seven hundred sharecropping families in Fayette and Haywood Counties were evicted from the land they had farmed for many years when they attempted to register to vote.[51]

Many of these homeless and desperate sharecroppers ended up living in what came to be known as Tent City. Tent City was composed of tents, donated by the Congress of Racial Equality, that were erected on land donated by local resident Shepard Towles.[52] Conditions in Tent City were miserable because the tents often did not provide adequate protection from the elements. Food was often in short supply and residents were particularly uncomfortable in the winter. In fact, things became so bad that several residents died. One Tent City resident, Georgia Mae Turner, explained how difficult it was to live there: "It worries me so that I don't have a home. Sometimes I get off and look back at the tents, I can't help but cry. But I thank the Lord to have one for shelter. You know, it's better than nothing. I love the tents sometimes, and I hate them sometimes! I'm just going to get out of here one of these days."[53] Regardless of how difficult and uncomfortable their circumstances became, however, Tent City residents remained determined to register and vote. Georgia Mae Turner eloquently explained the reasoning of many: "They say if you register, you going to have a hard time. Well, I had a hard time before I registered. Hard times, you could have named me that—Georgia Mae Hard Times. The reason I registered, because I want to be a citizen. Mr. Ferdie Franklin told me I had as much right to register and vote as anybody else. This here is a free country, that's what he told me. I registered so that my children could get their freedom. . . . I registered for my children so they won't have to stand around at the back door."[54]

Clearly, Tent City residents saw their struggle in very personal terms. Yet others who were connected with the struggle saw its wider significance. James Forman, a native of Chicago who would later become the executive secretary of the Student Nonviolent Coordinating Committee (SNCC), was one of those who recognized this wider significance. Because these counties adjoined the Mississippi state line, many white southerners were afraid that black voting in Fayette and Haywood could mean the end of white political control across the border in Mississippi. Forman reasoned that opponents of black voting in Fayette and Haywood counties were really much more concerned about maintaining white supremacy in the state of Mississippi. As he put it, "It was only a matter of time before ferment and change would come to that state too. At stake was political power as well as the maintenance of a feudal economic structure which included sharecropping. The situation presented a crucial test of strength."[55]

All across the country, many Americans were moved by the struggle of the poor sharecroppers in Fayette and Haywood counties. Consequently, a number of out-of-state groups pledged their aid. The Chicago chapter of the United Packinghouse Workers sent shipments of food and supplies to the sharecroppers. The AFL-CIO Industrial Union Council of Cook County (Chicago) voted to support Fayette and Haywood residents.[56] SNCC even dedicated an entire issue of its newspaper, the *Student Voice*, to the Fayette-Haywood struggle, and called on its supporters to send contributions to Tent City: "We urge you to act immediately in support of this campaign already endorsed and launched by so many groups."[57]

As black residents in Haywood and Fayette struggled for the right to vote, student sit-ins to desegregate public facilities began to break out across the state and across the South. On February 1, 1960, four black freshmen from North Carolina Agricultural and Technical College sat-in at Woolworth's lunch counter in downtown Greensboro. Within a few short weeks, a number of Tennessee cities began to experience sit-ins. In Knoxville, Knoxville College students met on February 15, 1960, to plan sit-ins for their community.[58] Adult community leaders moved swiftly to dissuade the students from demonstrating downtown. At that point, the city's mayor, John Duncan, took the unprecedented step of confronting chain store executives in New York City. The mayor decided on this unusual course of action after managers of downtown chain stores insisted that they could not desegregate their lunch counters without approval from their home offices. Consequently, Duncan invited two Knoxville College students and two members of the city's chamber of commerce to accompany him to New York to confront chain store executives. Student leader Robert Booker vividly remembers the response of chain store executives to the Knoxville delegates: "The committee was told by the national representatives that they would not sit in a meeting with students because they would thus open themselves up to having to meet with student groups from all over the country."[59]

Sit-ins also began in Memphis during the spring of 1960. Interestingly enough, however, black students from LeMoyne College in Memphis did not sit-in at lunch counters initially. Rather, their first targets were the public libraries.[60] Later, the same spring, demonstrators began to sit-in at local lunch counters. By early summer, Memphis libraries and lunch counters were desegregated.

Nashville had the most active student movement of any in the state. Furthermore, many of the leaders of the national student movement, SNCC, came directly out of a group founded by Nashville college students. As in other Tennessee cities, Nashville's black college students began their sit-ins on February 20, shortly after sit-ins began in Greensboro. Very early the Nashville movement exerted a profound influence on the national civil rights struggle. One of the reasons for that influence was the participation of James Lawson, a black divinity student at Vanderbilt University. Lawson was much more than just a sit-in participant. On the contrary, he conducted a series of workshops that taught nonviolent techniques to student demonstrators.[61] Student activists from all over the South participated in Lawson's workshops. As the sit-ins continued, scores of student demonstrators were arrested, but the students refused to back down. On the steps of Nashville's city hall, April 19, 1960, student resolve ran up against official white intransigence and an extraordinary moment resulted. Student leader Diane Nash of Fisk University asked Nashville's Mayor Ben West in full glare of television cameras about "his feelings . . . as a man, as a person [about segregation]. . . . I have a lot of respect for the way he responded. . . . He said that he felt it was wrong for citizens of Nashville to be discriminated against at the lunch counters solely on the basis of the color of their skin. That was a turning point."[62]

From this remarkable incident, Diane Nash went on to become a major force in the Student Nonviolent Coordinating Committee. She inaugurated SNCC's "Jail No Bail" policy in Rock Hill, South Carolina, in February 1961. In May 1961, she recruited a number of student volunteers to continue the Freedom Rides that had been started by the Congress of Racial Equality. The rides, which were designed to test compliance with a Supreme Court ruling that desegregated interstate bus transportation, would have been suspended had Nash not intervened. One of the participants in the Freedom Rides was John Lewis, another member of the Nashville student movement. Lewis went on to participate in many other important civil rights campaigns throughout the South. He eventually became chairman of SNCC and was one of the featured speakers at the March on Washington in August 1963.

Thus, Tennessee made invaluable contributions to the civil rights movement of the 1960s. The importance of an institution like Highlander was profound. At the same time, some of the movement's most influential leaders and policy makers had roots in this state. Yet, despite the importance of these contributions, many think of Tennessee as the place of the civil rights movement's untimely death. On April 4, 1968, Dr. Martin Luther King, Jr., the movement's spiritual leader, was assassinated in Memphis. The shock and the horror of King's death often overshadows the reason why he was there. In fact, Dr. King had come to Memphis to support a group of striking sanitation workers. His interest in this strike clearly signaled a profound change in the movement's direction. By this time, King and other civil rights activists had moved far beyond issues of racial discrimination to issues of economic equality. Thus, the purpose of King's visit to Memphis signaled the beginning of a new direction for the civil rights movement. As Tennessee's citizens reflect on the impact of the civil rights movement on their state, a curious mix of viewpoints and conclusions emerges. Many Tennesseans of all races proudly assert that segregation in Tennessee was never as restrictive as it was in the rest of the South. They are particularly proud of the state's record on black voter registration. More black people were able to register to vote here than in any other southern state. Many Tennessee citizens are equally quick to point out that many of the state's public officials were moderates who clearly demonstrated respect for law and order during this volatile period. That is why, these Tennesseans argue, far fewer violent confrontations took place in their state during the civil rights era.

Many African American Tennesseans have a very different perspective. Most agree that the majority of white state public officials chose the path of moderation during the movement. As the Reverend Harold Middlebrook put it, "The mentality of a lot of [white] folks from Tennessee was 'we ain't never had this problem, so we ain't going to have it now.'" Such moderation helped the state avoid the worst violence during the civil rights era, but Middlebrook and others are convinced that progress in race relations suffered as a result. Middlebrook reasons that "the states where you had the real difficulty, [that's where] you see blacks rising to control." He goes on to point out that few black Tennesseans hold positions of political power and influence today as compared with neighboring southeastern states. Regardless of their criticism, however, most black Tennesseans agree that their state has changed since the era of the civil rights movement, but they question how substantive those changes are. As Reverend Middlebrook succinctly concluded, "Things change, and yet they remain the same."[63]

NOTES

1. Asa Earl Martin, "The Anti-Slavery Societies of Tennessee," *Tennessee Historical Magazine* 2 (Dec. 1915): 278.
2. William R. Garrett and Albert V. Goodpasture, *History of Tennessee* (Nashville, 1903), 136.

3. U.S. Congress, *Report of the Joint Committee on Reconstruction,* Thirty-ninth Congress, 1866, 112.

4. Alrutheus A. Taylor, *The Negro in Tennessee 1865–1880* (Washington, D.C., 1941), 2.

5. Joseph Cartwright, *The Triumph of Jim Crow* (Knoxville, 1976), 11.

6. Ibid., 11.

7. U.S. Dept. of Commerce, Bureau of the Census, *Ninth Census of the U.S.,* 8.

8. Ibid.

9. Tennessee General Assembly, Senate, *Senate Journal of the Extra Session of the Thirty-Fifth General Assembly,* 1868, 131.

10. Ibid.

11. Frank Adams with Myles Horton, *Unearthing Seeds of Fire: The Idea of Highlander* (Winston-Salem, N.C., 1975), 27.

12. Ibid., 100.

13. Ibid., 89.

14. Ibid., 146.

15. Don H. Doyle, *Nashville Since the 1920s* (Knoxville, 1985), 224.

16. *The Tennessean,* July 6, 1949.

17. Frankie Adams, interview with author, Atlanta, Ga., Oct. 25, 1978.

18. Hugh Davis Graham, *Crisis in Print—Desegregation and the Press in Tennessee* (Nashville, 1967), 87.

19. *Knoxville News-Sentinel,* Aug. 29, 1957.

20. Graham, *Crisis in Print,* 63.

21. *Knoxville News-Sentinel,* Sept. 12, 1957.

22. Graham, *Crisis in Print,* 74–76.

23. Ibid., 95.

24. Doyle, *Nashville Since the 1920's,* 235.

25. Ibid.

26. Ibid., 235–37.

27. *Knoxville News-Sentinel,* Sept. 13, 1957.

28. Ibid., Aug. 29, 1957.

29. Doyle, *Nashville Since the 1920s,* 239.

30. *Knoxville News-Sentinel,* Sept. 12, 1957.

31. Ibid.

32. Ibid.

33. John Egerton, "Robert Card on Southern School Desegregation," *Saturday Review,* Apr. 1, 1972.

34. Doyle, *Nashville Since the 1920s,* 243.

35. Howell Raines, *My Soul Is Rested—The Story of the Civil Rights Movement in the Deep South* (New York, 1987), 326.

36. Ibid.

37. Ibid., 333.

38. Theotis Robinson, interview with author, Knoxville, Tenn., Feb. 28, 1995.

39. Ibid.

40. Ibid.

41. Ibid.

42. Ibid.
43. Ibid.
44. Avon Rollins, interview with author, Knoxville, Tenn., Feb. 8, 1995.
45. J. Harvey Kerns, *Social and Economic Conditions in Knoxville, Tennessee, As They Affect the Negro* (National Urban League, 1967), 5.
46. Doyle, *Nashville Since the 1920s,* 225.
47. Ibid.
48. Graham, *Crisis in Print,* 190.
49. Ibid., 190–91.
50. Ibid., 191.
51. James Forman, *The Making of Black Revolutionaries* (Washington, D.C., 1985), 126.
52. *Student Voice,* Jan. 1961, vol. 2, no. 1.
53. Forman, *The Making of Black Revolutionaries,* 125.
54. Ibid., 126.
55. Ibid., 126–27.
56. Ibid., 132–33.
57. *The Student Voice,* Jan. 1961.
58. Knoxville Area Human Relations Council, *A Chronology of Negotiations* (Knoxville, 1960), 1.
59. Ibid.
60. Reverend Harold Middlebrook, interview with author, Knoxville, Tenn., Mar. 27, 1995.
61. Woodrow Geier, "Sit-ins Prod A Community," *The Christian Century,* Mar. 30, 1960.
62. Henry Hampton and Steve Fayer, *Voices of Freedom—An Oral History of the Civil Rights Movement From the 1950s Through the 1980s* (New York, 1990), 66.
63. Middlebrook interview.

CONTRIBUTORS

■

■

■

ELIZABETH FORTSON ARROYO is Assistant Professor of History at the University of North Carolina, Charlotte.

JONATHAN M. ATKINS is Associate Professor of History at Berry College, Rome, Georgia.

FRED ARTHUR BAILEY is Chair and Professor of History at Abilene Christian University, Abilene, Texas.

PAUL K. CONKIN is Distinguished Professor of History at Vanderbilt University.

WAYNE CUTLER is Research Professor of History at the University of Tennessee, Knoxville, and Editor of the Correspondence of James Polk.

W. CALVIN DICKINSON is Professor of History at Tennessee Technological University, Cookeville.

JOHN R. FINGER is Professor of History at the University of Tennessee, Knoxville.

CYNTHIA G. FLEMING is Director of the Center for African and African American Studies at the University of Tennessee, Knoxville.

KENNETH W. GOINGS is Associate Professor of History at the University of Memphis.

DEWEY W. GRANTHAM is Holland N. McTyeire Professor of History Emeritus at Vanderbilt University.

CANETA SKELLEY HANKINS is Projects Coordinator at the Center for Historic Preservation of Middle Tennessee State University.

PAUL HARVEY is Assistant Professor of History at the University of Colorado, Colorado Springs.

MARY S. HOFFSCHWELLE is Assistant Professor of History at Middle Tennessee State University.

PATRICIA BRAKE HOWARD is a Member of the History Department at the Webb School, Knoxville.

CONNIE L. LESTER is Associate Editor, Tennessee Encyclopedia of History project, Tennessee Historical Society, Nashville.

JAMES L. McDONOUGH is Professor of History at Auburn University.

ROBERT TRACY McKENZIE is Associate Professor of History at the University of Washington.

PAUL V. MURPHY is Visiting Professor of History at Truman State University, Kirksville, Missouri.

PATRICK D. REAGAN is Professor of History at Tennessee Technological University, Cookeville.

GERALD L. SMITH is Associate Professor of History at the University of Kentucky.

CARROLL VAN WEST is Senior Editor of the *Tennessee Historical Quarterly* and a member of the Center for Historic Preservation at Middle Tennessee State University.

MARGARET RIPLEY WOLFE is Professor of History and Senior Research Fellow at East Tennessee State University, Johnson City.

KATHLEEN R. ZEBLEY is a Doctoral Candidate in History at the University of Tennessee, Knoxville.

INDEX

■

■

■

Tennessee History: The Land, the People, and the Culture was designed and typeset on a Macintosh computer system using PageMaker software. The text is set in Adobe Garamond; chapter titles are set in Decoratura. This book was designed by Todd Duren, composed by Angela Stanton, and was printed and bound by Thomson-Shore, Inc. The recycled paper used in this book is designed for an effective life of at least three hundred years.